J. M. TURNER
1986.

RELIGION AND VOLUNTARY
ORGANISATIONS IN CRISIS

CROOM HELM SOCIAL HISTORY SERIES
General Editors:
Professor J.F.C. Harrison and Stephen Yeo
University of Sussex

CLASS AND RELIGION IN THE LATE VICTORIAN CITY
Hugh McLeod

THE INDUSTRIAL MUSE
Martha Vicinus

CHRISTIAN SOCIALISM AND CO-OPERATION IN VICTORIAN ENGLAND
Philip N. Backstrom

CONQUEST OF MIND
David de Giustino

THE ORIGINS OF BRITISH INDUSTRIAL RELATIONS
Keith Burgess

Religion and Voluntary Organisations in Crisis

STEPHEN YEO

CROOM HELM LONDON

First published 1976
© 1976 by Stephen Yeo

Croom Helm Ltd., 2-10 St. John's Road, London SW11

ISBN 0-85664-017-4

Printed in Great Britain
by Biddles Ltd., Guildford, Surrey

CONTENTS

FOR EILEEN

PREFACE

This book has grown or, more accurately, shrunk from a doctoral thesis submitted to the University of Sussex in 1971. The thesis ('Religion in Society: a view from a provincial town in the late nineteenth and early twentieth centuries') may still be useful for those who wish to do related projects as well as read results. It contains lists of sources of statistical and other local information, openings 'down the passage which we did not take' and some local material omitted here. The list of local organisational records in Reading [Bibliography D, pp. iii-xxiii] might be useful to those interested in other towns.

History is always made to look tidier for the reader than it appears to the writer before he boils it down into paragraphs. This may be a good thing. But concealment of the experience of research may also serve to keep others unnecessarily off the grass. Somehow it is made to seem that precisely the correct sources, methods and tools were available to the author — exactly designed to answer the questions he had always wanted to ask. Reading some sociology conveys the impression that society was created ready-packed for the sociologist to take home and dissect. A certain amount of model-building, a quantum of sophisticated methodological preparation has to be done, for sure, but after that diagnosis and prescription can be swift and valid!

Any neatness of approach which has been achieved in this book is not meant to contribute to this lie. Behind the argument lurked the usual painful and insufficiently articulated experiences of research students before they have learned the short cuts. The feeling that generalisation would be dishonest before a mountain of evidence has been accumulated (a feeling which some historians learn later on to control all too well); the hunger for the ever-retreating horizon of completeness — for a time when *no* stones will have been left unturned; the hope that in the end the sources would themselves do the work, immaculately conceiving arguments and structures ... all these illusions were powerfully present during the course of research.

In this case they were perhaps stronger than usual, owing to the subject chosen for study and the sources and methods selected. The lens of the historian's camera was kept open and moving for an unusually long time before processing, because there were no readily available guides to the precise angle necessary to get a good snapshot. It was impossible to know beforehand what sources would exist in a local case such as this, let alone the nature of the evidence they would present. To a considerable extent the student of religion in society at the local level does have to let himself be impelled by his sources rather than by his concepts, before the creative quarrel between the two can start.

To get these sources local co-operation and generosity were essential. Scores of people in Reading gave their time and records most helpfully. Among the demands of local inhabitants in search of a recipe for cooking, an address, or the temperature of the place in which they were going on holiday, my own enquiries were dealt with by a patient and overworked staff in the local collection of the public library. Local guide books, some organisational records, annual reports, plus one or two chance extras such as cuttings-books or unpublished memories, provided the best way into Reading. Only after these did the continuous reading of the local press make any sense. The hunt for records outside libraries was exciting. To discover records as full as those of some chapels presented its own problems, but they were the right sort of problems. The hunt was also frustrating. To get to Elm Park football ground with high hopes only to be told that most of the Reading Football Club records had been bombed in the war was disappointing. But bombs (or fires such as the one which destroyed Reading Trades Council records) have not been the most destructive agents. The speed of commercial exploitation of mid-town public sites in the last fifteen years means that a study such as this will not be possible in the next generation. Unless local librarians are given the time to collect them, there will soon be no local organisational records. In his *Religion and Society in England 1790-1850* (1972), W.R. Ward recently warned of the same danger at the denominational and seminary level.

Newspapers in Reading were the single most important source. Although the work was not done in this logical order, in retrospect it is clear that the next step after the local collection, for research of this kind, should be concentrated on the fullest local newspaper available over a sustained period. In this way annual reports of organisations, important events in the life of the town whether annual or occasional and leading town voices can be picked up. There are obvious problems about what is *not* reported in the local press, and perspectives which do not break through into it. These problems are less acute in the late nineteenth- and early twentieth-century local press. At that time there was a far greater proportion of straight, often verbatim, reporting of sermons, speeches, the proceedings of annual meetings, 'annual courts' of hospitals and the like. There were correspondingly less over-written, slanted 'news' items. The opinions expressed in speeches and editorials had more often to do with the locality in a more than simply illustrative sense than they do today.

These features were subject to change during the twenty-five year period (1890-1914) of detailed study for this project. The changes in sources were part of the total change of context being studied. The *Berkshire Chronicle,* for example, became a much less useful local source in the early years of the twentieth century. In this and other papers much which had been in the main body of the paper was relegated to a column or two of 'local news', before being jettisoned. Speeches got less full treatment, the statistics in annual reports disappeared as advertisements broke out of single columns into half or whole page splashes. But for the most part what *was* there in the papers in this period can be taken directly by the historian without worrying about the middle-man: reporters were reporters not aspirant Alistair Cookes. minute books which record much else besides the bare decisions taken between 1890 and 1914. It gets rarer as the period progresses to find Minute Books which record much else besides the bare decisions taken and who was there to take them. The gradual disappearance of the beautifully uniform copper-plate clerical handwriting in huge leather bound volumes of minutes, and its replacement by the typewriter, led to thinner and more hasty records rather than to the fuller accounts which became technologically possible. The elaborately printed annual report, which even a single chapel or an athletic club had been able to afford, was less a feature of 1913 than of 1890. But where records do exist, especially in the case of churches and chapels, it is surprising how much they contain rather than how little.

In the creative quarrel with these sources through several drafts I owe a lot to many people. Professor Asa Briggs was patient, stimulating and receptive as a supervisor. J.F.C. Harrison, David Martin, Daniel Jenkins, Tom Bottomore, Raphael Samuel, Brian Harrison, Arno Mayer and Jim Obelkevich all read the whole, or substantial parts, of earlier drafts. Their reactions were various but helpful — even the reader who told me, 'you have bitten off more than you (or any other single historian in twice the time you have taken on this) can chew ... You could perhaps tackle the subject you have chosen, in the way you have tackled it, after about another ten years' research'. I hope that the final version, which none of them have seen, is interesting enough to justify their work. The text will make it obvious how much I owe to previous writers on Reading, particularly W.M. Childs, T.A.B. Corley, and

Anne Cook.

The project could never have been undertaken without the support of my mother, Mrs Joan Yeo-Marsh, who lives near Reading. She provided frequent hospitality and help of all kinds. More important, she was interested in the results.

The project could never have been finished without the constant help of my wife, Eileen. Special thanks are due to her: she believed in the value of the work at times when I no longer did: she read it, talked about it, and worked on it at all stages, particularly at the final stage, in an invaluable and creative way: she understood what it was about and wanted it done: she helped me over all kinds of moods.

1 INTRODUCTION

This book aims to be helpful to religious organisations, and to all
voluntary organisations which aspire to some active, critical dialogue
with society rather than to comfortable co-existence in its interstices.
What follows is aimed at clarifying choices by locating them in a
system, place and period.

The book is informed by one simple idea: that there may be a
common situation or context for voluntary and other organisations in
different phases of capitalist development, rather than a series of
discrete situations for different subject-areas for organisation such as
religion, production, sport, education, welfare or politics. By
emphasising the context of which religious organisations were themselves
a part and in which they had to work, the intention is to grope towards
an equivalent for the late nineteenth and early twentieth centuries
of 'the Rise of Capitalism' part of R.H. Tawney's great work on
religion in the sixteenth and seventeenth centuries. 'Religion and
...what?' is the question. An answer would be enormously helpful,
indeed essential, for any organisations which aspire to a prophetic
rather than a merely diverting role. The main elements towards an
answer which this book arrives at are as follows: religion and the
consequences of what religious organisations chose, or were
constrained, to be; religion and absolute and relative deprivation for
most people; religion and changing patterns of local middle-class and
working-class presence; religion and changing modes of capitalist
organisation, in production, distribution and leisure; and religion and
the altering presence of the State and centre in relation to the life of
a locality.

This book covers a wide territory, from Congregational chapels to
the Social Democratic Federation, from Hospital Sunday Parades to
Literary and Scientific Societies, from the Reading Football Club to
Huntley and Palmers' biscuit factory. The study is located in Reading,
a town which is taken by modern market-researchers and psephologists
as an average town, but which, like every town, has its own peculiar
history. It may therefore help to nail down immediately some assertions
which inform what is to follow. At this stage bones will be presented
without flesh.

1

1. 'Religion' is never coterminous with religious organisations; but *c.* 1890 in Reading, religion was dominated by continuous organisations such as churches and chapels. The religious space occupied by such organisations was probably greater than it had been eighty years before, or was to become eighty years later.

2. Many religious organisations *circa* 1890 in Reading were, alongside many other voluntary organisations, trying to attract numbers unlimited into their doors. By a variety of provisions *for* people, they were trying to render themselves *of* unlimited numbers of people to the deepest extent possible.[1] They wanted active participation by large numbers of people in a wide range of continuous organisations.

3. Religious organisations, alongside many other voluntary organisations, were not entirely happy with their performance in this regard. But they gave explanations for their discontents which historians can try to improve upon.

4. Such religion, trying to do such things, becomes more understandable in terms of a whole society's ideal view of itself, and to some extent a whole society's actual organisation which had been waxing in Reading since *c.* 1850, and which has been waning in Reading and elsewhere since *c.* 1890.

5. Some religious organisations actively shared this ideal view of society and worked to realise it. Others did not, but were still affected by it, as part of the context in which they had to work.

6. The circumstances in which religious organisations were working in late nineteenth- and early twentieth-century Reading were not of their own choosing. But religious organisations could have identified, modified or challenged them in a more deliberate way than they did.

7. Some of the contradictions in the context, as they impinged upon religious organisations, so far from being confronted, were made worse by what religious organisations did.

8. The circumstances in which religious and other voluntary organisations were working were changing during the period 1890 to 1914, in ways fundamental to understanding the current situation of religion and many other activities.

9. To understand their situation, religious organisations and any organisations which are not entirely satisfied with their situation, need to understand the social context.

10. The society they have needed to understand for the past three hundred years or so in Britain, has been a capitalist society.

11. A capitalist society is one in which a class of persons privately

Sounds like an old
fashioned 3 Marxist
textbook

owns the means of production and has at its disposal the surplus
value created by the labour power of another class of persons who
get only wages: it is thus based on a fundamental, structural
inequality. A capitalist society produces commodities for exchange
in a market, the organisation of which changes greatly in different
periods.

12. Capitalist society in Britain has generated, and has to some
extent been generated by, noble aspirations, *viz.* those towards a
self-governing community of fully-participating citizens in voluntary
associations. These aspirations have been taken up with varying
degrees of seriousness at various times, by sections of the middle and
of the working class.

13. Capitalist society is unable to universalise these noble
aspirations without being transformed into another kind of society
in the process. Pressures towards such a transformation have to
be contained by the system in the interests of its survival as a set
of property relations. Such an inability to realise the best of itself
may be called one of the contradictions of capitalism.

14. Capitalist society has ways of preventing, or making difficult,
or encouraging evasions of an understanding of itself and its
contradictions by religious and other organisations.

15. These smokescreens have unfortunate consequences for
religious and other organisations, encouraging them to adapt in ways
which can make their situation worse.

16. 'Religion' is not necessarily, by its very nature, one of the
ways of encouraging evasions. Whether it functions as such depends
upon the forms and actions it takes (and can choose not to take)
at particular times.

17. Society, capitalist or otherwise, does not exist independently
of what it contains (for example, religious organisations) any more
than what it contains exists independently of society. It is thus not
a question of religion *and* society, but of religion *in* society.[2]

18. One of the principal ways of understanding society is
through the experience of the elements which compose it, in
relation to each other — for example the experience of organisations
engaged in economic production alongside the experience of
religious and other organisations. By means of this juxtaposition, a
social context of dominant ideologies and organisational
styles can be established and the relative weight of the
various elements in shaping or unmaking a context can be
assessed.

19. To understand the social context in a manner helpful to
religious and other organisations, means understanding social change —
social change not as a continuum, but taking place in qualitatively
different epochs (feudalism, capitalism) and in qualitatively different
periods within epochs. There is a period-specific, as well as an epoch-
or system-specific situation for religious and other organisations. It
is on the level of a period or phase in the development of capitalism
in a particular place, rather than on the level of the system itself, that
this book will operate.

Such propositions are, of course, an end rather than a beginning. They
are placed here in order to help as map-references on the way to the
end. The beginning of this book lay in personal concern and experience
of a kind not easily contained in such statements. So many committed
activists across a variety of subject-areas for voluntary action, like
religion, politics and sport, seemed to share a common unease about
their organisational styles and the possibility of achieving their
aspirations in the face of problematic social factors, impinging on them
all and beyond their immediate control. Shortage of money, the
implications of putting on sideshows in order to attract customers only
to find the sideshows taking over the central activities, 'apathy', the
tyranny of bricks and mortar. . .all these seemed to be common
problems. It appeared urgent to try to use such experience in order
to articulate the nature of the social context in such a way as to make
the constraints and the room for manoeuvre more clear.

My focus was originally on trying to understand the situation of
'religion', and hence the situation of forms of religion characteristic
of modern Britain — churches and chapels. There was comfort in the
fact that such a focus seemed commonly shared during the course of
the research. From ecclesiastical sources there was continual evidence
of an obsessive, but potentially creative, introspection on 'the future
of the church'. In the case of Anglicanism, in the decade of the Paul
Report on *The Deployment and Payment of the Clergy* (1964), this
introspection reached massive proportions. Each effort at understanding
from the inside, from E.R. Wickham's *Church and People in an
Industrial City* (1957) to David Edwards' *Religion and Change* (1971),
as well as the work of sociologist outsiders like Bryan Wilson, found
its way on to the desks of concerned clergymen and other activists.
This is not a turn of phrase: I kept seeing such books as I went around
Reading looking for less elevated material like Parish Magazines. The
press added its own 'in-depth surveys' of the crisis in religious

organisations and the stories of those who were trying to face up to them. No matter if the colour-magazine coverage of the responses, and the responses themselves, seemed to be part of the problem rather than part of the solution, the concern was there. As was said in 1916, 'of all the distinctions that place ministers and clergymen apart from the members of other trades and professions, their humble criticism of themselves and their work is the most remarkable'.[3]

The work of research in the local press, in the records of scattered local organisations and in the local reference library was not pleasant. But there were happy times, when relevant structures began to emerge from plain information, or when meeting activists in a church, a Friendly Society, a Recreation Club, or a political grouping who wanted to do more than reminisce. Blank incomprehension sometimes greeted my requests for records. Some Ministers or Honorary Secretaries said at first that they had none, when it later turned out that they had, simply because they could not conceive of any possible relation to contemporary concerns that the records might have. But others seemed to understand quickly what the research was about, and to feel that it might be relevant to them in their daily work.

While doing the early research I was involved in constituency politics as a candidate in two general elections. This was a relevant, if distracting, experience. It involved doing what many of the people or organisations studied in subsequent chapters were doing. The surrounding circumstances had, of course, altered. The degree of national intervention in the conduct of a mid-twentieth-century political party, even though in this case strenuously resisted by an unusually alive local Labour party in North London (Hornsey), was qualitatively different. But the same effort was being made to project, 'sell', provide *for* a public an organisation which would involve the maximum number of that public in the greatest degree of commitment. Hopefully, the organisation would become genuinely *of* that public. Political activists in Reading in the late nineteenth and early twentieth centuries would have recognised an activity similar to their own, even though some of them would have despised many of the modern manifestations. So would ministers of religion, Pleasant Sunday Afternoon propagandists, Reading Working Men's Regatta enthusiasts, and the founders of the first branch of the Association for the Promotion of the Higher Education of the Working Classes (later the WEA). The feelings of a canvasser in London suburban streets — the massiveness of the mountain which had to be moved — the shared experience of the effort, traps and difficulties involved in sustaining

effective voluntary organisation, political or otherwise, were
encouraging to have had because they gave a direction and urgency to
the research, and clarified its central subject matter.[4]

Before starting the work I also had some experience of Reading.
Familiarity with its appearance and geography made the continuous
reading of the local press less deadening, and was one of the reasons
for selecting Reading in the first instance. Having been brought up in a
village eight miles away, Reading was a place visited not for
entertainment but out of occasional necessity — for opticians, dentists
and department stores. Crowded on shopping days and with few
'places of interest' immediately obvious to the outsider, it had little to
recommend it. Then, later on, came an Easter march in the Campaign
for Nuclear Disarmament, when Reading was a stopping place on the
Aldermaston-London route. At this time, the contradictory experiences
of such a campaign were fully felt — euphoria sometimes at the degree
of public acceptance in the streets, depression at other times at the
enormity of the task of persuasion in such a large, rambling area of
bricks and mortar — so many homes, with people so firmly shut inside.
Such experiences would have been familiar to many of the people and
organisations studied in subsequent chapters.

Early in the research, I felt the necessity of moving beyond the
walls of churches and chapels into a wider range of organisations, and
into society more generally. So much so that a reader of an earlier
draft felt that 'for a book about religious organisations in context,
religion does not get its fair share of the wordage or the limelight'.
Some preliminary description of the directions of the move may
clarify the reasons for this imbalance.

The move outwards was not made in order to hang churches and
chapels cleanly, as variables dependent upon 'basic' factors like the
occupational structure of the town, population movements or
economic fluctuations. Such a death might be useful for sociologists,
and historians of religion interested in comparative anatomy; but it
would not be the most useful outcome for organisations themselves.
Nor was the move made in order to locate religious organisations
neatly in the cultures of different class or status groups.[5] Nor was the
purpose to isolate and define 'religion', so that 'its' special role and
function could be identified, for example as a cause or consequence of
social and economic change or as a stimulant or sedative to political
activism.[6] Nor did the move aim to get at the view from below. Any
social history of popular religion which breaks out of an institutional
framework will need patient collation of material on a national, or at

least a regional scale. The sources used here do not permit writing about the majority of Reading's inhabitants from the inside. So much of the material about the majority was refracted through the lens of a particular minority. It is none the less interesting for that, but 'the difficult problem' remains a problem: 'to discover some method for observing and recording what the French call the *état d'âme*, i.e. the thoughts and emotions, the habit of mind and life of persons in their interior and intimate relations with one another and with surroundings ...How can we decipher and record people's ideals, their characteristic ideas and culture, and the images and symbols which habitually occupy their minds?'[7]

On one level the move into as many subject-areas for organisation as possible was dictated by the simple fact that religious organisations in the late nineteenth century were already organised in those areas, or had ambitions to be, or felt themselves being superseded by other organisations which were. More importantly, it was to explore the notion of an ecology, or common and changing context for organisations, rather than discrete situations for different subject-areas for organisation or different types of organisation (church, sect, party, union, etc.).[8] This book is only a first stab at such an idea: in this case the academic cliché is appropriate, much more work remains to be done. The idea to be explored is that during any single phase in the development of capitalism there are hegemonic types of organisation and dominant directions of change for organisations. These types and directions are different in and between different periods. In other words, the question of what happens to an organisation unless deliberate steps are taken is different in different periods. Prevalent types of organisation, and characteristic directions in which they are being pushed in any one period may be resisted, modified, or reversed through the work of organisations. But only if they are first mapped.

One of the best ways of mapping the contours of a social context and prevailing directions of change is to chart the changing experience of organisations in relation to each other. By placing the experience of organisations engaged in economic production alongside the experience of religious and other organisations, it may become possible to get a sense of dominant aspirations and organisational styles in a particular context. It may also be possible to avoid flattening out the tensions involved in trying to realise the dominant aspirations or to resist hegemonic styles. The major forces making for contextual change, dissolving the cement of an earlier configuration and laying the foundations of the new, may become more visible as they impinge on a range of organisations. Again, the growing strains and contradictions experienced at a time of transition can be fully exposed.

For organisations concerned with change as well as understanding, an honest articulation of their changing experience is a necessary first step. The view from within the organisation will be more helpful than the vista from any social scientific Olympus. Context and organisation cannot be separated, since what organisations do becomes part of the setting which affects them. The very best way to map the common context would amount to starting to change it at the same time. If organisations would systematically chart their own experience in relation to their aspirations, and if, in order to do so, they would juxtapose such autobiography with that of other organisations, the freedom which derives from the knowledge of relevant constraints would be on the way to being achieved. Meanwhile, collective biography from the outside may be a small step towards collective autobiography from the inside.[9]

There are to hand a variety of less helpful ways of understanding the situation of religious and other organisations. Some of them are located in disciplines such as the sociology of religion: others originate with organisations themselves. Some of the most important of these less helpful ways were peculiarly strong or originated during the late nineteenth century. It will therefore be worth examining four of them at some length, before attempting to supplement them. They existed, and still exist, as temptations — particularly in the path of religious organisations — tempting them to inaction, despair, or to purposeful adaptations with unintended and undesired consequences.

The first temptation has been to wrench religion apart from the society or period in which it is set. Such a separation has led in three quite different directions. First, it has led to discrete examination of religious organisations. Secondly, it has led to emphasis on the history and difficulties of contacts *between* religious organisations and society. Thirdly, it has led to explanation of religious organisations wholly in terms of the society which includes them. Each of these directions needs brief examination in relation to what follows in this book.

Discrete examination of religious organisations as a particular *genus* has meant explaining them in terms of the behaviour of species such as sects, denominations or churches. The best work has been done on sects.[10] Lack of evidence was the initial reason for not following up such work in Reading. Except in rare cases where chance records survive, studies of sects in a local context will be better done in a contemporary setting, especially since they now flourish greatly in a place like Reading. A choice was also made to concentrate upon local sources rather than on national denominational sources with occasional local bearings. This implied an under-playing of the denominational variable, which can only partly be justified by the increasing tendency for denominations to resemble each other in the late nineteenth and twentieth centuries.[11]

In this project, however, objection to explanations based upon organisational type was not only practical. Analysis of the mechanics of, for example, sect behaviour, on the level of the organisations themselves — recruitment, leadership, worship, generational problems and so on — while of interest, does not reveal all that is discoverable about sectarianism. Full understanding even of the mechanics, needs work on how the particular place, period, and social system — as opposed to other places, periods, and systems — discouraged or encouraged the mode of operation of the sect: what else was going on at the time in that place (even where sect members did not participate in anything else): what was happening in the wider society at that time compared to other times. Abstracting an organisational type from system, place and time can lead to deadeningly misplaced sociological determinism, of the kind pioneered by Michels in his *Political Parties* (1911). In what follows, aids to the understanding of the situation of religion will be looked for in the two wings of the YMCA in Reading, even in the Reading Athletic Club, as well as in churches, denominations, or sects. More important, 'sectarian' or other directions of organisational development will be looked for in these and other non-religious organisations as well as in churches and chapels. If such directions of development can be identified, and if some of the pressures towards such directions can be articulated in a more plastic way than in terms of 'iron laws' of organisation, the range of freedom of manoeuvre for churches and chapels or other organisations should become clearer.

Examination of the history and difficulties of contacts *between* religious organisations and society has been one of the main thrusts of work in this field, particularly among Christians. The motivation has often been to reverse the moral and social attenuation of religion described in R.H. Tawney's *Religion and the Rise of Capitalism* (1922). The method commonly chosen has been to describe 'the relations of the church to the problems of the industrial population in terms of individual contacts and efforts'.[12] Such descriptions have, incidentally, suffered from insufficient use of classifications of religious organisations, rather than the over-reliance complained of in the previous paragraph.[13] Some broadly progressive process in society has commonly been assumed — say 'social reform', the rise of the welfare state or the growth of a conscious labour movement. The felt unsatisfactoriness of the situation of religion has then been ascribed to lack of identification with this assumed process. Because what was happening to society is adopted as a constant in this line of argument, rather than inspected critically through the experience of organisations, elements in the social process which bear upon many other activities as well as religion have been ignored. So far from being a determinist way of pulling apart religion and society this way suffers from an opposite but equally debilitating defect. It ascribes total freedom to religious organisations, and can therefore pin total blame upon them. The dialogue between the nature of 'individual contacts and efforts' and the organisations, places, periods and systems in which they are made is not articulated. Individual contacts and efforts could therefore, it seems, have taken an infinite variety of forms. At the same time there were giant, benevolent historical processes at work, making religion seem pigmy. The depth of frustration and internalised blame which can result from such assumptions can be readily understood. It is registered in the depression of many ministers and activists.

The third direction in which pulling religion apart from society has led, ignores the particularities of religion rather than the particularities of society. Explanation of religious organisations wholly in terms of the society which includes them, involves a separation of religion from society in the sense that a society *without* religion is anticipated, desired or considered to exist already.[14] Religion in industrial society can then be seen as an extra, on the way to redundancy, or as a disease on the way to cure. Religious organisations can be 'placed', seen as 'transitional', or understood as mere agencies of social control. Such an overview is intellectually exciting and plausible. Some evidence for it will be found in succeeding chapters. But it is not a helpful perspective for activists in religious organisations — a feeling of absolute powerlessness corrupts as much as absolute power. While that does not make it untrue, it is certainly over-simple. Given the context, the question should be 'why this response rather than that response?' rather than given the context, *therefore* this or that response. Even the language of context and response is a distortion. In the ecology of organisations the response continually becomes part of the context, as will emerge in considering churches and chapels later. And the context for one subject-area for organisation (say religion) is made up of responses in many other subject-areas for organisation rather than of blind historical forces. Such historical forces can be recognised, and thus be faced and engaged, through the experience of fighting them or submitting to them in as many different subject-areas for organisation as possible.

The next three temptations have to some extent been anticipated in the first. They will be labelled the secularisation temptation, the band wagon temptation and the apathy temptation. As ways of understanding the changing situation of religious organisations in society, the last two were particularly powerful in the late nineteenth and early twentieth centuries and have remained so since. All three have strengths. One of the concerns of this book will be to find out in what sense they are true. Uncritical acceptance of any of them can have devastating consequences for those involved with religion and its organisations. Religious organisation informed by the view that for a long time things have been getting more secular, that for a long time one progressive subject-area for organisation after another has been taking over from religion, and that for a long time people have been getting more apathetic — whatever such terms mean — has problems. 'If you can't beat them join them' would be only the most obvious among many unfortunate adaptations in the face of such problems.

The argument in this book will be that the three labels, in their commonest forms, are only labels. They are not the contents in the bottle. Indeed like many labels they can be misleading about the contents of the bottle, in the interests of suppliers rather than consumers. Secularisation, the band wagon, and apathy refer to crucial problem-areas. But the problem of problems is to get at the system behind them in such a way as to focus attention on its specific mediations, rather than on tempting evasions. In the case of religious organisations, this means turning attention outwards on to helpfully articulated directions of social change, rather than inwards on to their own anatomy, or sideways on to seemingly attractive competitors, or upwards on to timeless and irreversible processes, or downwards into 'human nature'.

Secularisation is an evasion upwards. It may or may not be a good label for the changes which have happened since the various base lines commonly taken for it — the foundation of Christianity itself, the Reformation, the Enlightenment, the French and Industrial Revolutions, etc.[15] Whether it is a good label for social changes in nineteenth- and twentieth-century Reading, the interested reader can decide for himself. This book will not enter into the general debate on secularisation, except to say that the blanket perspective of religious decline as applied to this period is not a particularly helpful one. In discussions of religious decline base lines referring to some supposed previous state of affairs have become blurred; periodisation has been loose; and intellectual developments with huge but unspecified social consequences have been asserted.[16] Above all, the specific mediations of the changes to which the label 'secularisation' refers get lost in such a way as to make the process look as independent of human will and social structure as the weather. Beliefs and organisations also get confused, and analysis of what was happening to one slips into assertions about what was happening to the other. Thus going to church or, at a further remove, the Membership Population Ratio of denominations becomes an index of the supposed decline of religion, and the major preoccupation of some students.

This book will offer some information on such indices. During the course of research statistical data on the performance of religious organisations and other activities were collected.[17] It will be analysed elsewhere. There are two broad preliminary conclusions from such data. First, that sub-agencies of churches and chapels were doing worse between 1890 and 1914 than the services for worship and membership indices: secondly, that membership and attendance in core organisations was not declining catastrophically in absolute terms in Reading, yet was not quite keeping pace with population increase. This book aims to cast light on why such indices should be regarded as so central in the first place. Before the 'decline of religion' became elided into the performance of particular organisations, the hegemony of organisations which defined religion in terms of specific types of act — like organisational participation for everybody — had to be achieved. Once that had been achieved, given the forms it took and the economic and social conditions in which it was achieved, anxiety about the performance of those organisations was inevitable. Such anxiety reveals more about patterns of supply from above than about patterns of demand from below.

The band wagon is an evasion sideways. It is a convenient label for a view of the changing situation of religion in society which was influential before 1914 and has remained so ever since. It has taken three main forms, the labour band wagon, the welfare band wagon, and the leisure band wagon. The term band wagon is appropriate because religious reformers, along with many others, looked sideways to a wagon they thought was rolling and felt they would neglect to jump on it at their peril. The suggestion has been that an idea, or a set of organisations, or a whole historical process, has taken over from religion or religious organisations. Exactly when this happened has not always been specified. Either a labour movement rooted in the historical development of the working class, expressing the aspirations of the class, involving it increasingly in a whole way of life, providing it with a complete 'secular' ideology and reaching some kind of a climax in the late nineteenth and early twentieth centuries; or a steady progress towards a completed welfare state, with admitted 'gaps' remaining for religion to work in; or a similar progress towards more and more 'freedom' made possible by the leisure opportunities afforded by affluence and a beneficent technology (e.g. the car) — one or all of these band wagons rolling through twentieth-century history have been seen as taking over from religion and leaving behind religion's organisations, its thinkers, its followers and, in latter days, its 'image'.

This perspective has encouraged organisations like churches and chapels to blame the success of other organisations for their own felt sense of failure. A specific subject-area for organisations — say progressive politics, old-age pensions, or football — has been seen as taking over from the declining subject-area of religion. The perspective is fed by the common feeling in voluntary organisations in unfavourable times for such organisations — a feeling which will be familiar to anyone with direct experience of such organisations — that someone else, even everyone else, is doing better than one's own group. The perspective in turn feeds the common feeling in religious organisations that it is urgently necessary to adapt, often in some drastic way, in order to catch up. For example, if it was true, as Bishop Gore thought in 1906, that 'the churches if they are ever destined to become a living reality and an energising force in the life of the nation, need to be intimately associated with some movement which in the life of the nation can claim reality and energising force', and if it was also true that the labour movement was 'the one creative force in the life of the nation', then the labour band wagon was more than just interesting to watch as it passed by. In his *Labour and the Churches* (1912) R.A. Bray thought that 'unorganised labour is. . .labour in the process of absorption; unorganised religion is religion in the process of dissipation'. The idea that politics has in some sense replaced religion has also grown up, not specifically tied to the labour movement. 'That part of the Englishman's nature which has found gratification in religion is now drifting into political life', wrote Beatrice Webb. Or, as an historian has put it, 'alternative outlet(s) for social energy' came into being after the mid-nineteenth century, allowing for 'a transfer of social energy from religion to politics'.[18]

The labour band wagon was postulated by social theoreticians of great stature. Some even considered that it had already rolled successfully by, leaving only litter such as religion in its wake. Max Weber thought that as the proletariat developed, religion would be supplanted:

> In so far as the modern proletariat has a distinctive religious position it is characterised by indifference to or rejection of religions common to large groups of the modern bourgeoisie. For the modern proletariat, the sense of dependence on one's own achievement is supplanted by a consciousness of dependence on purely societal factors, economic conjunctures, and power relationships guaranteed by law. Any thought of dependence upon the course of natural or meteorological processes, or upon anything that might be regarded as subject to the influence of magic or providence has been completely eliminated, as Sombart has already demonstrated in fine fashion. Therefore the rationalism of the proletariat, like that of the bourgeoisie of developed capitalism when it has come into full possession of economic power, of which indeed the proletariat's rationalism is a complementary phenomenon, cannot in the nature of the case easily possess a religious character and certainly cannot easily generate a religion. Hence in the sphere of proletarian rationalism, religion is generally supplanted by other ideological surrogates.[19]

Engels in 1844 expected that 'hard necessity will force the workers to give up their religious beliefs. They will come more and more to realise that these beliefs serve only to weaken the proletariat and to keep them obedient and faithful to the capitalist vampires'.[20] E.J. Hobsbawm, in *The Age of Revolution,* considered that in the large towns by the end of the nineteenth century the transfer had actually taken place — 'the established churches. . .neglected these new communities and classes, thus leaving them, especially in Catholic and Lutheran countries almost entirely to the secular faith of the new labour movements which were eventually, towards the end of the nineteenth century, to capture them'.[21]

The welfare band wagon has been of more retrospective significance than of contemporary significance during the period of this study. But particularly during the years of Liberal welfare legislation from 1908-12, it did seem to be rolling fast. Each act of progressive legislation was endowed with a significance greater than that normally claimed in the rhetoric of politics. Acts put together were seen as creating an altogether new social order and new social attitudes. A whole teleological interpretation of twentieth-century social history, constituting a welfare interpretation to replace the old Whig interpretation, has grown up, seeing each step as part of an ineluctable process moving towards a finished structure – the 'welfare state'.[22] Religious organisations have been seen, by themselves as much as by others, as victims of this process. Old tasks performed by them have become new tasks performed elsewhere. The 'institutional church' movement in the early twentieth century may be seen partly as a desperate effort to reverse or to catch up with this and with the leisure band wagon. As subject areas for organisation moved away from church or chapel one by one, a last effort to pull them all back at once was made in order to provide 'something for all and a place for everyone' at the level of the individual church.[23]

The leisure band wagon was the most noted of the three at the time but has been, until recently, the least investigated by social scientists and historians. At the time, as the story of the Reading Football Club will show, the way of organising leisure was subject to great change and to heated controversy. A decrease in hours worked, larger concentrations of population in cities, technological innovation and rises in real wages for some strata of workers were among the national factors increasing opportunities for leisure consumption during the late nineteenth century. At the same time, such developments constituted a threat for older providers of leisure activities like churches and chapels. There was a danger, observed by a Reading minister in 1910, of 'regarding the social and recreative features (of life). . .as something apart from the distinctively religious'.[24] Each innovation in the means of communication from the railway to the telephone, to the gramophone, to the cheap national daily press, to the bicycle, to the cinema, to the motor car has been seen as a threat to older social habits, particularly to religious attendance. Not only did they constitute alternatives, but they also encouraged passive styles of entertainment rather than active styles of self- and mutual improvement. 'Games, with all their spiritual and moral benefits, were to be played, not watched.' When to spectator sport was added the reproduction of spectator sport on film, a bad message was compounded by a worse medium.[25] 'Most attacks', as the movie magazine the *Bioscope* reported in 1909, 'come from the clergy who condemn any form of amusement which they are unable to control'.[26] Recent students of religious decline have concentrated upon the bicycle as the destructive agent. [27] It seemed at the time and has seemed since as though a series of take-over bids was being made from many directions. They were compounded by being made, or at least gathering pace, in a concentrated period of time during the late nineteenth and early twentieth centuries. 'The connexion between tennis rackets, the bicycle, the half-penny newspaper and the statistics of church attendance is inescapable.'[28] Interestingly enough Max Weber's interests in 1908 included athletic leagues as well as religious sects and political parties.[29] The question, however, remains: how best to pursue these inescapable connections?

The band wagon perspective focuses on competition between organisations, and on a chronology of subject-area for organisation succeeding subject-area. In each of its variants it is a perspective informed by an idea of progress towards some better state, against which religion can be evaluated and found wanting. In its leisure variant it can also be a perspective informed by an idea of a competitive market, in which demand is seen as sovereign. Changes in consumer taste and in demand from below were responsible, so the argument runs, for new types and subject-areas for organisation succeeding older ones. Supply from above benevolently followed, enabling consumers to express what they had really always wanted, or to reveal what they had really always been like. Thereby attention gets diverted away from the possibility of changes in the structure of supply from above, across subject-areas, acting to alter the context for demand, and thereby to contain demand or to change the possibilities available for its expression. Attention gets diverted away from the possibility of regress or uneven development, in this case the possibility that aspirations in capitalist society may get taken up by different classes, and may inform organisations for a time, only to be contained or destroyed in the interests of the system's efficient survival as a set of property relations. Such containment or destruction would present a problem for religious organisations different from the band wagon, demanding resistance rather than pursuit. Attention could then be turned towards analysis of a common context for organisations, in which the centre of gravity of the relationship between supply from above, and demand from below might change, altering the context for demand in many subject-areas besides religion.

Before seizing, for example, on bicycling as a band wagon rolling away from religion on a Sunday afternoon, it might be as well to ask: what was happening to bicycling at the same time as bicycling was supposed to be what was happening to religion? During the early 1890s activists connected with bicycling were as exercised about questions like spectator-sport compared with participatory club bicycling, the effect of professionalisation, the dominance of business and competitive modes, as were activists worrying about parallel developments in religious organisation.[30] No more than a start will be made in this book in subsuming bicycling clubs, the Social Democratic Federation, the WEA, the Football Club, the Dispensary, and churches and chapels under general directions of change, and in identifying those general directions through the experience of such organisations. But that will be the aim. The theoretical gains to be derived from studying organisations across all subject-areas in a manageable place over a manageable period of time are greater than the actual gains made during the course of this book. Organisations ideally studied should reveal as much about those outside them as about those inside.[31] Recent interest in non-organisational aspects of the sociology of religion, and the growing concern in social history with society seen from below, will be fruitful if they lead not to avoiding organisations, but to more contextual ways of studying them. If these can be developed, notions like the inter-organisational leapfrog of blame which will be described later, can be superseded. The dialogue between possibility and constraint on what C. Wright Mills called 'the knife-edge of the present' can then be articulated. To this tall order can then be added, in the ideal study, the relationship of religious and other organisations to the knife-edge in different periods.

Back to the third temptation – that of apathy. There is no doubt that behaviour for which apathy is a possible label has existed for some time in English society.[32] The complaints about apathy during the late nineteenth and early twentieth centuries, which recur in different chapters in this book, were not delirious – not even that of the Reading Co-operative Society which, in 1903, 'regretted the torpor and apathy of the workers' and 'a sleeping sickness'. 'There appeared to be the same lack of enthusiasm not only with regard to politics, but also religion and everything else'.[33] Many of the people in modern Reading who helped with this research were depressed by 'apathy'. Its supposed increase has become a major way in which the changing situation of religious and many other organisations are now understood. The question is: how best to understand such complaints in order to get nearer to the reality for which apathy is no more precise a label than 'the mixture' on a medicine bottle?

There is a complicated interaction between description and

prescription in judgments on this topic. Diagnoses are made which
become true because they have been acted on. Seventy years after the
complaint of sleeping sickness made by the Reading Co-operative
Society, the 'Members Relations Committee' of another Co-op. in the
South of England put out an advertisement. After declaring that 'The
Co-op. is your biggest store and you can become a shareholder or a
director', the advertisement continued with the bland assertion that
'most people don't actually want to run a business worth millions of
pounds but they like to make suggestions and to see improvements'.[34]
There is a lot of specific Co-operative history between this
advertisement and the complaints of the Reading Co-op. in 1903 which
cannot be explored here. The point at this stage is that an organisation
which frequently complains about apathy, and which offers a mere
'making suggestions and seeing improvements' relationship to its
members, is ratifying that apathy by announcing what 'most people
don't actually want' without producing any evidence. An organisational
structure which used to have more ambitious goals, and which
discourages or prevents less apathetic control from below, is being
ratified in terms of what 'most people' are like, disregarding its own
effects, and those of similar organisations upon those people.[35]

   This is a central element in the uses of 'apathy' as a label for the
changing situation of religious and other organisations. It turns
attention away from supply on to demand. It displaces blame away
from structures, towards the supposed characteristics of aggregates of
human beings, often called 'masses'. Sometimes the presumption is even
that 'human nature' is essentially apathetic — once the affluence, civil
liberties and, until recently, the political stability of post-war Western
democracies graciously allow that nature to reveal itself.[36] This
amounts, in fact, to a moral interpretation of alienation from
organisations analogous to the better-known moral interpretation of
poverty.

   Such an interpretation is dangerously attractive to religious
organisations because it ratifies particular versions of adaptation which
can make the situation, in their terms, even worse. It also conceals
structural obstacles to commitment and participation, like poverty,
lack of time, lack of cultural resources such as education, or the
hegemony of organisational types which encourage and depend upon
apathy or passive consumption. An illustration of one characteristic
twentieth-century adaptation favoured by religious organisation — that
of amalgamation — may be taken from a Methodist magazine defending
ecumenicalism in 1919. Merger was being promoted in Methodism in

order to counter sluggish performance. But it was meeting with
unapathetic resistance from below. It is not difficult to imagine such
resistance leading to sullen non-co-operation or even to a walk-out
(which could then be called apathy) in the face of attitudes and
language like the following:

> Don't be anxious as to the 'reception' the proposals for Union may
> have among the 'people'. . .It is said among our own congregations,
> 'the people are not much interested or concerned'. This was
> unimportant. For the generality there is in most high and spiritual
> movements little that stirs, or even touches the imagination. . .Why
> are 'leaders' desirable save that they are necessary as an offset
> against the torpor of the average. . .They ought to be interested, and
> it is our business to compel their interest.[37]

Those who seek to compel interest, and who have a view of 'the
generality' like this should not be surprised if they meet a mass of deaf
ears. When they abuse the deaf ears with words like 'apathy' or 'the
torpor of the average', they say more about themselves than about the
generality.

Another characteristic twentieth-century adaptation, similarly
informed by the *a priori* assumption of apathy, is that of diluting the
product, changing its package, surrounding it with loss-leaders to make
it more 'attractive'. Such an adaptation may be fine for retail stores
interested in speed of turnover per inch of shelfspace, but presents
problems for religious organisations. For them the right hand has a
habit of being affected by what the left hand does. The message cannot
be kept hygienically separate from the medium. This type of adaptation
will be encountered in later chapters: it can be observed better at a
local level than can mergers which necessarily involve 'head office'
history. Its classic ratification is to be found in Michels' *Political
Parties* (1911). Writing 'from personal experience in three typical great
cities, Paris, Frankfurt and Turin', Michels observed how:

> Within the large towns there goes on a process of spontaneous
> selection, in virtue of which there is separated from the organised
> mass a certain number of members who participate more diligently
> than the others in the work of the organisation. This inner group is
> composed, like that of the pious frequenters of the churches, of two
> very distinct categories: the category of those who are animated by
> a fine sense of duty, and the category of those whose attendance is

merely a matter of habit. In all countries the number of this inner
circle is comparatively small. The majority are as indifferent to the
organisation as the majority of electors are to Parliament.

'Indifference' and 'slackness' prevailed, he thought. He then described
how,

The great majority of the members will not attend meetings unless
some noted orator is to speak, or unless some extremely striking
war-cry is sounded for their attraction. . .A good meeting can also
be held when there is a cinema-show, or a popular scientific lecture
illustrated by lantern slides. In a word, the ordinary members have
a weakness for everything which appeals to their eyes and for such
spectacles as will always attract a gaping crowd.

There is something more than a description of 'iron laws' of social or
psychological behaviour here. If the word 'crowd' suggests to the
activist the word 'gaping', if he operates with a fixed conception of
'ordinary' members and others, if it is his belief that 'the great struggles
which go on among leaders. . .are not merely beyond the understanding
of the rank and file, but leave them altogether cold',[38] then any
movement or organisation − religious or otherwise − which that
activist creates, or adapts or in which he is influential, will be liable to
reflect that set of attitudes. This in turn will be liable to induce genuine,
and justified indifference, which may then be labelled 'spontaneous
selection'.

There will be evidence in this study for the kind of changes which
Michels considered to be built-in to organisational dynamics, or human
psychology. Centralisation, growth in size and elaboration of
organisation were quite evident in late nineteenth- and early
twentieth-century Reading. For example, it will be shown that Hosier
Street Congregational Methodist Chapel and Caversham Free Church
were atypical in their relative independence from external links with a
national or regional denominational structure. Even denominations
with powerful inherited resistance to centralisation were submitting to
it at a galloping pace during the late nineteenth century.[39] Broad Street
Pleasant Sunday Afternoon movement suspected any Brotherhood
structure beyond the walls of the Broad Street Congregational chapel.
Yet they became involved in just such a structure. Activities initiated
by small local groupings, like the Trinity Alphabetical Society and the
Redlands Literary and Scientific Society, will be watched as they

transformed themselves, through 'success', into pan-town organisations, with a correspondingly larger formal organisation, and sometimes the burden of a building. The comparative history of the original local Church of England YMCA and its national successor will be traced. Organisational elaboration will be observed, via the law of the accumulation of bricks and mortar.

But the aim here is not to provide illustrative specimens for the sociological law-shop. Particular types of organisation obviously affect behaviour in particular ways, for example, by encouraging apathy. However, they then ratify themselves by deploying the idea that those particular types of organisation exist because of an innate preference or tendency in masses of men to be apathetic. So far as apathy is concerned, this book aims to cast light on the context, presence and experience of organisations which perceived behaviour as apathetic rather than on the quantity or quality of the 'apathy' itself. The point is to see whether, by juxtaposing developments in religion with developments in other subject-areas for organisation, a changing relationship between organisational forms and the possibilities of committed participation from below can be traced, and some causes of the change identified. Is it possible to think in terms of a whole social change from one period to another, rather than in terms of organisational dynamics abstracted from time? If so, much more accurate responses by dissatisfied organisations could be anticipated. Those responses would look outwards from their own experience, juxtaposed to that of others, to the contours of a whole system at specific stages of its development, rather than upwards to impersonal processes (secularisation), sideways to competitors (the band wagon) or downwards into organisational or psychological dynamics (apathy).

Even if it is accepted that there is an intrinsic connection between, say, the size of structure and apathy, the connection cannot be effectively illustrated without examining the whole range of organisations in a place over a period of time. Otherwise one organisation's apathy may be another organisation's commitment. Moreover, the relationship between organisational forms and apathy can only be established by examining the total possibilities of participation from below, in specific places at specific times. Otherwise what is not there or is not supported, may be a function of the pattern of supply and the varying possibilities of altering that pattern, rather than a function of demand. Extreme caution has to be exercised before accepting the supportive ideology central to capitalism, namely that what is present (in voluntary organisation or any other product) is present because 'most people' want it and that what is absent is absent because most people do not want it. The location of the activity and the organisation, both in relation to other organisations and in relation to a power structure more generally, is necessary before any meaningful connections can be made between that organisation and apathy. Such is the perspective which this study aims to develop in a preliminary way. There is a tempting and functional tendency for organisations in capitalist society to see what happens to them and to society more generally as progressive and desired by most people, even if not intrinsically desirable. Such a tendency should at least be examined carefully, particularly by religious and political organisations.

R.H. Tawney's *Religion and the Rise of Capitalism* (1922) is important for this study both because Tawney was dealing with religion and what seemed an easily identifiable period of wider socio-economic change, and because his approach to that period was part of his reaction to the less easily identifiable period with which this book is concerned. He was reaching back to find the origins of an unsatisfactory relationship between religion and society which he spent much spirit trying to help change in his own time. He wanted to address himself directly to the conditions of his time, and did so elsewhere. But in this work, directly concerned with religious ideology, he felt unqualified to do so,[40] although he was quite confident about articulating the fundamental changes of an earlier period. 'The rise of capitalism' was both relevant and, broadly speaking, agreed as a backcloth. Against it he could measure 'the most fundamental movement of the seventeenth century', 'the growth, triumph and transformation of the Puritan spirit'. *Religion and the Rise of Capitalism* turned out to be a study of what capitalism did to religious ideology, and a rebuke to churches for not playing a more aware, prophetic and resisting role. Tawney had a clear definition of the process he was studying; he could see the closeness of the connection between what happened and Puritanism; and he could see that too close a dependence upon ideological evidence would not disentangle the relationship he was studying, even though that was the evidence on which he concentrated.[41]

For the study of what a later stage of capitalism does to religion, unless it is resisted, the context is not so easily defined. Steps towards definition will be taken as the experience of organisations in different subject-areas is explored.[42] It might help to clarify such steps if at this stage a leap forward is taken and a tentative sketch of the contemporary ecology of religious and other organisations is attempted. Such a sketch will be tendentious but might provoke activists to articulate their own. No full picture of the modern common context for organisations will be attempted in this study. The concern here will be for the route out of an earlier phase, and for the strains to which that route subjected a whole range of organisations during the twenty-five years before 1914. It would be naive to presume unilinear development of any tendencies over the long gap between 1914 and 1976. But a longer perspective may put in bolder relief some features of the period 1890 to 1914. 'Epochal pivotal events', 'determining events and positive dates' in social history do not always stand out in the short term.[43] This is particularly so when, as will be argued below, they are such seemingly trivial events in the period 1890-1914 as the decision of the Reading Literary and Scientific Society to meet in Reading University, or the decision of the Hospital Sunday Parades of the Reading and District Trades and Friendly Societies to institute house-to-house collections rather than relying on the parade itself, or the decision of W.H. Palmer not to come to the meetings of the Reading Athletic Club. Even the more obvious milestones, such as the transition of the 'Partnership Era' at Huntley and Palmers into a limited liability company, or the professionalisation of the Reading Football Club, may get neglected by not being juxtaposed and by not being seen from further along the road.

Two features stand out in the contemporary ecology. First, and most distressing from the activists' point of view, most people are not actively involved in any organisation at all. A home-centred culture has replaced a work-centred culture or one involving organised voluntary activity. There is plenty of instrumental membership, of trade unions for getting a job and a wage, of the Church of England for being buried, and so on. Services once provided by voluntary organisations for their members have in many cases ceased to depend upon membership.[44] Occasional adherence survives, in Easter communions, membership in a chapel for old times' sake, or voting in a club, a local, or a general election. But active joining and full-scale participation in the life of a voluntary organisation – political, religious, educational, etc. – is the pursuit of a minority of a minority. Whether words like apathy adequately describe such a situation, or whether non-participation amounts to shrewd assessment of the modes of participation on offer, is another question. In the total spectrum of social activity, less space is occupied by continuous, participatory, ambitious voluntary organisations than was the case during the second half of the nineteenth century in England.[45] Correspondingly more space is occupied by intermittent, often very intense, *ad hoc,* informal association which comes and goes unpredictably — whether it be rank-and-file trade union activity, religious revival campaigns, attendance at football matches or community agitations. There is a dichotomy between 'apathy' as regards a whole range of formal organisations whether they are photographic clubs, Congregational chapels, political parties, football supporters' associations or the State itself, and close commitment elsewhere. Such a dichotomy worries those interested in social control and order, as well as those trying, from a different point of view, to man formal organisations interested in change.

Secondly, in the total spectrum of voluntary organisations a large space is occupied by three distinct types. Each of the types spreads across different subject-areas for organisation. There is, first, the centrally directed, amalgamated, large, consumer-conscious organisation. Such organisations often started out very differently from what they have become. For example, rather than seeing themselves as embryos of a new and developing social order, they have come to see themselves as providers of a specialised product for the leisure or satisfaction of a particular group in the existing order, whose fixed contours they take for granted. Recently many such organisations, from sects to churches to clubs and so on, have come to operate, and even to see themselves, as businesses. They have been preoccupied with management techniques, public relations, modernisation and rationalisation.[46] Trying to be in a shallow sense *for* everyone, they have ended up as being in a deep sense *of* no one. They have been tempted to sacrifice quality, or their original goals, for intended quantity, or for what immediately seems capable of arresting decline or generating growth. The opposite effect has often been achieved. Merger, and increased attention to advertisement or packaging, have become common. The modernisation of the Boy Scouts in the last ten years, at the cost of dropping foundation texts like *Scouting for Boys,* is only one example of a process which has affected organisations as different as the Church of England, the Womens' Institutes, the Rugby League, the Salvation Army, the Labour Party, the Co-op., and the Working Men's Club and Institute Union.

The tendency to become like a business and thereby to displace goals in the interest of turnover is a tendency which can be, and has been, resisted. But it is a tendency which would have to be a major theme in any contextual juxtaposition of the experience of voluntary organisations with a later focus than this one. That it is a theme which applies to religious organisations, and that it was developing before 1914 may be illustrated by an example from outside Reading. As the best book on Methodist ecumenicalism puts it:

> Some held that Methodism was a *business*, dealing in evangelism,
> supplying salvation, manufacturing saints: an especially attractive
> notion when the persuasive idea of rationalisation was in the air.
> 'We are told', said the Rev. Joseph Kirsop in 1901, 'that things in
> the twentieth century have to be done on a great scale. Small
> businesses, small churches. . .will be an anachronism in the age on
> which we have entered'. Nineteen years later French told the
> Wesleyan Conference that 'He did not believe that a small church
> could live today, any more than a small business or a small Army'.
> Even opponents of union adopted this terminology. 'This business',
> complained Mr T. Bolam of Willington Quay, 'savours too much of
> company promoting and watered stock, with the interest of the
> small shareholder at a discount'.[47]

The second predominant type is the sect. In the twentieth century it
has not been entirely distinct from the first type. The sect as a business
has been common since the Salvation Army, to the occasional scandal
of observers. Tight, rigorous, 'better fewer but better' organisations
pursuing a well-defined and internally deeply shared set of goals have
been flourishing recently in religion, politics and other subject-areas
for organisation. Sociologists predicted that this would be likely to
happen in circumstances which have already been sketched. Loose,
minority 'belonging', combined with the predominance of centralised,
bureaucratised and diluted organisations, create, as their necessary
opposite, tight sectarian organisations. Majority spectating creates a
need for minority playing. 'Audiences' displace 'publics' from the
centre of society but create many smaller circles on its periphery.
Anomie in a wider setting necessitates belonging in a smaller one.[48]
Whatever the truth of these general observations, it is certainly true that
as organisations develop in the direction described in the previous
paragraph they risk generating, whether through secession or
independently, tighter and more fundamentalist versions of themselves.
This is not only true in the familiar territory of sectarian religion, with
regard to the consequences of denominationalisation and ecumenicalism,
but is also true in other subject-areas for organisation as well. The
typology of sects is complex but relatively clear: the chronology of
types, as opposed to that of individual examples, is relatively
unexplored. Which type of sect flourishes in which period or type of
society is hardly known except in third world situations. But *a*

predominant type of sect in contemporary Britain, if not *the*
predominant type, is undoubtedly one which tends towards withdrawal
from central questions of power in society, at least in their day-to-day
manifestation. A new social order may be on the agenda of many
modern religious and political sectarian organisations from the Jehovah's
Witnesses to Socialist groupings. But it has been put there, they think,
by God or by History or by some external agency rather than through
the agency of members.

The third predominant type of organisation in the modern ecology
is the pressure-group. Again, the chronology of types of pressure group
has been less explored than the history of single examples, or the
politics of pressure groups as a whole category. But it is clear that the
characteristic type of pressure group in modern Britain is not, for
example, the characteristic type of the first half of the nineteenth
century. The mass 'moral reform crusades' of that period have given
way (*pace* the Campaign for Nuclear Disarmament) to groups more
closely tied to government, local or central. The distinction between a
government agency and a pressure group has frequently become
blurred. Experts with their mouths close to telephones and their heads
full of reasoned papers have tended to replace crowds with their feet
close to main squares and their heads full of movement-material as the
predominant mode of operation of pressure groups. Single-issue
campaigns regarding their single issue as sufficient unto itself have
tended to replace campaigns which were 'reaching out for a juster social
order' and which, even where they were single-issue, regarded that issue
as a key to total social change. Central, metropolitan organisations have
tended to replace organisations where the initiative flowed from the
provinces and from base to apex. Such developments amount to a
diminishing of ambition in the organisations concerned.

These three types of voluntary organisation (alongside the political
party which has elements of all three) exercise a certain hegemony in
the modern ecology. They are poles of development which, unless
deliberately resisted, tend to pull organisations in many different
subject-areas towards them. To test this proposition adequately would
require analysis of the experience of many different organisations over
a more recent time-span than that covered by this book. Individual
organisations may get pulled in all three directions or they may resist
the pull altogether. The dissipation of the classic or bourgeois political
party into business/leisure, sectarian, and pressure-group modes or into
no organised modes at all on the local level, has recently become
visible to the naked eye. The implications of such a common context

for other major subject-areas for voluntary organisation in the mid-twentieth century such as religion or trade unionism are not so obvious. The point here, however, is not to follow these through into the contemporary situation, but rather to use such a sketch of the contemporary ecology of voluntary organisations as a backdrop to what follows. Whether or not the sketch is totally accurate matters less than the fact that it can be used to highlight a time when it was totally inaccurate. Reading in the second half of the nineteenth century was not a place to which such a sketch applies. But there were clear signs between 1890 and 1914 that Reading might come to be a place which the sketch more accurately represents. Was it important for religion that the common aspirational and organisational context *c.* 1890 in Reading was different from this sketch? Was that context changing between 1890 and 1914? If so, how and why? It is these questions that the situation and experience of religious and other organisations in the late nineteenth and early twentieth centuries may be used to explore. Reading, and the period 1890 to 1914, were initially chosen for personal and more or less arbitrary reasons. As it turned out, the distinctive nature of Reading during the second half of the nineteenth century, and the critical changes taking place in Britain between 1890 and 1914, meant that the period and the place were peculiarly appropriate for working towards a contextual view of the situation and experience of religious and other organisations.

Modern Reading has become a favourite town for market researchers. 'Typical' in its employment patterns, physical presence, and degree of affluence, it has fewer inconvenient quirks than other places.[1] Near to the village of Bray, it has tended to copy the notorious vicar of that place by changing sides with the appropriate marginal majority at each Parliamentary election.

Studying the place, such typicality was one of the problems. Walking round the town, looking at its buildings, reading its records, talking to its people, it was difficult to step back and see anything as strange or accidental. Everything about it seemed so normal as to be inevitable and not worthy of special observation. It was a common experience during the research to go home after a day's work, on what later proved to be illuminating records, thinking that nothing had been collected of any possible interest to the study of religion in society. The fact that so much social scientific writing on religion had been about extraordinary phenomena did not help either. Reading's streets and their religious buildings seemed so quintessentially ordinary.

And yet precisely that sense of strangeness, of particularity, the feeling that things need not or might not have been as they were, the sense of one way of life or culture as opposed to another way of life, which is relatively easy for the anthropologist or historian of earlier periods to cultivate as part of his equipment, proved necessary for the understanding and analysis of the period studied here. It is doubly important not to take anything for granted, and to step back and to try to periodise, since this study is concerned with social change. Definitions can get blurred and changes be missed because parts, especially religious parts, of our most important starting point, Reading society *c.*1890, survive now. Buildings survived, at least until redevelopment schemes of the 1960s. A few chapel notice-boards in 1970 looked like many chapel notice-boards in 1870. One of the distinctive features of religious organisations is their longevity. Four Anglican churches in use in 1890, and two Nonconformist congregations still in existence at that date, were founded before 1650. No other organisations were so old, unless the Poor Law is included. Continuities can get in the way of more significant breaks in social history if sufficient detachment of view is not achieved. Reading in the second

half of the nineteenth century was a very different kind of society from
Reading in the second half of the twentieth century. In the differences
may lie clues to the changing situation and experience of religious and
other voluntary organisations.

One aid to an over-view is to realise the relative novelty of a
phenomenon like Reading, as it was by the early twentieth century. The
Edwardian journalist and Liberal politician C.F.G. Masterman used the
phrase 'unique in world history' to describe 'the city type' in the late
nineteenth century.[2] With a population of 88,603 in 1911, Reading
was one of a type of place of which there had been only twenty in the
world in 1789.[3] It had almost reached the category of 'metropolitan
town' which students of urbanism have blinked at and tried to define
as a novel social fact of twentieth-century life.[4] Such is human
adaptability that it may appear to people on a Saturday morning in
crowded Broad Street in Reading in the 1970s that nothing could be
more normal: but in fact in world historical terms nothing could be
more abnormal than the society of which they are a part.[5]

This was more frequently noted in the late nineteenth and
early twentieth centuries when the 'newness and staring redness' of the
town were novel, and when the fact that 'today everything is modern
about Reading' was an object for surprised satisfaction rather than for
metropolitan disdain.[6] In fact, the speed and recentness of
discontinuous change was one of the basic elements in the context
within which religious and other organisations had to work in our
period. Smith's *Directories* owed their existence to what the 1892
Reading volume called 'the extensive and numerous changes' which
took place every year. So extensive and numerous were they that after
1875 they 'rendered the annual production of the Directory a
necessity'. In that year the first volume consisted of 150 pages. Fifteen
years later the 1890 volume, which drew attention to the 'vast numbers
of changes and removals in Reading', contained 500 pages. An
Australian revisiting Reading after fifty years in about 1900 'felt quite
shocked that little Reading had improved more in proportion than big
Sydney'. A local historian pointed out that 'the wanderer' in Reading in
1905 will see 'street after street. . .lined with houses every one of
which has been built in the lifetime of a boy or girl of 12 years of age'.
And late in the nineteenth century, Alderman White of Birmingham, a
distinguished émigré from Reading, took his audience in the Reading
Literary and Scientific Society on an imaginary walk around the
Reading of 1830. Touching on that delightful before-and-after nerve
which produces such a fascinating sensation in times of drastic change,

he recalled how, past Greyfriars church, they were 'at once among the beautiful elms and park-like grounds', and how 'the site of the biscuit factory was a solitary meadow with a broad ditch seeping into Watlington Lane. Here the haymakers were busy in summer, and in the winter on the frozen flood waters he first put on his skates'.[7]

In the period from the mid-nineteenth century to 1914, Reading exploded from a population of 21,456 (1851) to a population of 88,603 (1911). Allowing for borough extension (1888 and 1911), the largest percentage rate of growth of population over a twenty-year period (1871-91) coincided with the growth of the dominant economic organisation of the town – Huntley and Palmer's biscuit factory. Employing 920 people in 1867, the factory was employing 4,053 in 1889. By 1905 the figure was 6,000. 'What Reading would have been without the immense works which comprise the biscuit factory none can imagine.'[8] Few single factories in any industry have ever been the size of Huntley and Palmers at its numerical peak. In 1912 it employed between a quarter and one-fifth of the working population of the borough. The imperatives of twentieth-century capitalism later meant that far fewer workers were needed for vastly increased output. In 1905 Huntley and Palmers was thirty-eighth in order of capital size in British manufacturing companies, only just behind Lever Brothers, 'the wonder firm of the age'.[9]

Long before becoming 'biscuitopolis', Reading had had some economic importance in the sixteenth century as a clothing town.[10] A gravel terrace, with gravel on both sides of the Kennet at this point, made it the most convenient place for a route like the London-Bath route to cross the river. It was not accidental that two overwhelmingly important organisations in the history of the town – Reading Abbey (until its dissolution and the hanging of its Abbot in 1539) and the biscuit factory – were adjacent to each other on one end of this terrace. After the decline of cloth in Berkshire, Reading 'reposed in undisturbed tranquility while ages of improvement rolled by'.[11] The population was almost the same in 1800 as it had been in 1700. Mary Russell Mitford described the end of that period for Reading in her *Belford Regis* (1835), a series of delicate, unhurried, alkaline vignettes of small-town life.[12] Developments in the infrastructure took place – in canals, roads and pavements. By 1840 W. Fletcher, in his *A Tour Round Reading,* observed signs of quickening. 'Like individuals, cities now seem to be emulating cities and towns rivalling towns, as well in their deeds of charity as by their advance in science and the arts. A change has come over this town and it depends upon its men of

Halifax NR quite analagous for textiles always employed more than say Mackintosh's.

property and commerce and public spirit whether this change shall be snail-like and imperceptible. . .or like the seed sown in a fertile soil, soon to spring into life, vigour and beauty.'

The engineering genius of the biscuit firm, George Palmer (1818-97), arrived in Reading in 1841. His public life, like his manufacturing life, did not take long to germinate. By 1850 he was on the town council. In 1857 he became Mayor. In 1878 he was Liberal MP for the town. His brother William Isaac (1824-93) came back to Reading, after an initial spell in Liverpool, in 1851: in 1857 he joined the partnership, the first partner, Thomas Huntley, having died. Thereafter the Palmers of the first generation, and to some extent of the second, were omnipresent, whether in the British School, the Mechanics' Institute, on the Council, in the movement to build the town hall, in temperance, the provision of parks, sport, or the building of churches and chapels of different denominations. By 1898 the reign of the first generation of three brothers was formally over. Samuel (1820-1903), who had been based in London looking after export and finance, retired from partnership. A limited liability company was created. George William, Howard, Walter, Alfred, Albert, Ernest and Charles Palmer were in charge – with W.B. Williams and William Lea at their sides.[13] The *Daily Mail*, no friend of the Palmers, suggested in 1897 that a local era was at an end: 'what will change now that the founders and heads of the old firm are gone and there is every possibility that it will develop into a huge joint-stock company cannot be foreseen.'[14]

Other crucial dates in local development also clustered in the decades after 1840. This was not only true for businesses like brewing, tin-making (for biscuits) and seeds, but also for municipal and social events. The Great Western Railway arrived in 1841. The Reading Athenaeum was founded in the same year. A Local Board of Health was formed in 1850. The Forbury Gardens were laid out between 1855 and 1860. The amalgamated Reading Gas Company started in 1862, the Waterworks were taken over in 1867. Reading Philharmonic Society was founded in 1863, Reading School in 1870, Reading Football Club in 1871. Manor Farm was purchased for sewage in 1873. The first Medical Officer of Health was appointed in the same year, and King's Meadow public recreation ground was acquired in 1875. Reading became a County Borough in 1888.

Rather than characterising the town between 1840 and 1890 in the manner of an economic historian interested in indices of growth, or in the manner of a local historian interested in civic milestones, the aim here will be to sketch the type of society flourishing at this time. Reading society will be described immediately before it was greatly affected by 'the imperialist phase of the historical evolution of the bourgeois class', when 'industrial power has become separated from the factory and is concentrated in a trust, in a monopoly, in a bank, or in the State bureaucracy'. Our period in Reading saw 'the liberal phase of the historical evolution of the bourgeois class', when 'the proprietor was also the entrepreneur and the industrialist. Industrial power and its source was in the factory'.[15]

But before going into the quality of that phase one further preliminary is necessary. The distinction should be made between ideology and organisation, between aspiration and practice, between what the society wished to be believed about itself and what existed on the ground. Even within aspiration, there is a distinction between what might be called rhetoric (bogus aspiration cloaking self-interest in noble phrases) and language (genuine aspiration committedly followed through into practice). In Reading the extent to which the ideology described had an organisational base in practice – the extent to which it was a language spoken because it was meant rather than a rhetoric deployed because it was convenient – was probably greater than in many other places in nineteenth-century capitalism. Explicit statements by middle-class persons, like the Palmers and other business-men, will be used to indicate the type of society they believed in or said that they believed in. No assumption will be made that that type of society actually came into complete being, although the extent to which it did in Reading may well be more interesting than the extent to which it did not. The perspective and experience of workers in the biscuit factory between the mid-century and 1890, or of inhabitants of the notorious slums around Silver Street or the brick works, was utterly different from that of the speakers, writers and editorialisers who appear for the historian in the local press, and in most annual reports and organisational records. The historian, at least in this type of study, does tend to listen to those who talk loudest and from the highest places (if, for example, the annual reports of the Reading Athletic Club or Parish Magazines can be called high places). But if it would be stupid to extrapolate carelessly from ideology to organisation and from aspiration to social reality, it would be equally stupid to deny that ideology and aspiration are part of social reality. Their content, their quantity, their tone, indications as to their acceptability and sharedness, all have to be taken seriously as important social facts. They were part of the type of society existing in Reading, and cannot be dismissed simply as guilty rationalisations of an exploitative capitalism, or as mere hypocrisy.

The ideas that follow were to varying degrees central to capitalism itself, which, like other systems, generates aspirations and modes of organisation whose full development it cannot contain without either itself being transformed or without those aspirations and modes of organisation being channelled into more convenient forms, transforming themselves in the process. Capitalism does not develop in straight lines. It cannot universalise the best of itself: had Reading society embodied the ideal notions of itself waxing from *c*.1850 onwards, but under increasing strain from *c*.1890 onwards, and to some extent realised in organisations and movements during that time, it, and the surrounding society outside Reading, would have been very different from what they have turned out to be in the twentieth century. At the macro level, capitalism, the contradictions between ideology and organisation, were always sharper in the second half of the nineteenth century than they were on the micro level of a town like Reading although the intensifying of contradictions was a visible part of Reading's history between 1890 and 1914.

Thus, while some of the things which will be said below about Reading were true about mid-nineteenth-century capitalism generally, and while all of the things which will be said about it need locating in a wider understanding of late nineteenth-century society, what will be said was quintessentially true about Reading. This was because of its take-off into industrial importance after 1850, rather than earlier or later, its domination by a single industry, the domination of that single industry by a single (Quaker) family, the purity of its middle-classness as a town ('in no way under any territorial or lordly influence', as W.I. Palmer put it in 1891) and the possibilities inherent in its size — big but still not too big in 1900. William Isaac later reflected that when his brother George had arrived in Reading the town was meet for his kind of economic activity and social ideas, 'probably there was no town in which there were so many independent holders of property, and where the great mass of the people felt that they had a direct interest in the well-being. . .of the town'.[16] For a long time the lack of concentrated, pre-industrial-capitalist ownership and wealth had been remarked on by observers, so that 'here the influence of love can do much, the influence of power or property little'.[17] But to some extent this is not the point. Whether or not the ideology/aspiration became organisation/practice in a sense does not matter for the student of religion in society. That the aspiration was there at all mattered for

religious organisations, as part of the context which shaped their
expectations of themselves, part of the total situation which made
them what they were. The history of the context-sensitive expectations
religious organisations had of themselves is just as important as, and
essential for understanding, the history of what they were, what they
were doing, and what they were undergoing.

Anyone who has been to a British public school, particularly to one
like this writer's founded in the 1870s, has the advantage of direct
experience of some of the ruling ideas informing the life of a town like
Reading in the second half of the nineteenth century. The local press,
like the school notice-board, was divided on important occasions (such
as the last week of the year, or a town breakfast with the Mayor
presiding — as it were at a speech-day) into sections: 'commercial',
'philanthropic', 'religious', 'municipal', and 'athletic'. Reports were
given on the progress of these areas of 'activity', sometimes explicitly
linking them into a common moral framework. Each was important; to
be involved personally in more than one besides work was highly
desirable; to be committed to at least one in a dedicated and continuous
way was an essential attribute of the good citizen, who was part of the
good man. While the local Liberal press was not unlike the school
magazine, it also served the function for the whole town which more
detailed records of particular organisations served for them —
amounting, at its best, to a kind of civic minute-book. The town was
seen as the encompassing organisation, with constituent sections, and
as the locus of a healthy community. The speech-day exhibition took
the form of 'Industrial Exhibitions' of local people's work, employers
as well as artisans.[18]

Everybody should either be participating actively in one area of
town life or else should be on the way to being involved. This included
the working classes; indeed that it included the working classes was
stressed as a defining feature of the age compared with any other age.
At a proud event such as the opening of new buildings for the Reading
YMCA in 1897 persons of 'nearly all shades of opinion and all classes'
were said to be present. At the very moment in the life of the
organisation when the acquisition of a grand new building meant that
it was bound to be *of* only a limited stratum of people (even if it had
facilities *for* others), the audience was told how:

> there was a time, and that not so far distant, when no men except
> of the higher classes were privileged to take such pleasures as can be
> found in similar social and intellectual gatherings. What one hundred

years ago was there in Reading, for example, in the shape of an association of men of different classes congregated for their mutual benefit? Amongst other improvements in the nineteenth century we have learned to band ourselves together for good. . .who can contemplate the effect in every considerable town of such societies?

The presentation of a testimonial to William Isaac Palmer in 1885 was put off until the evening to allow working-class subscribers to attend. More than 3,000 attended 'of every class and every shade of religious and political opinion'.[19] Help should be given to those unable or not yet able to participate, but help which stimulated an active response, not demeaning, pauperising help. Such help, as in matters of welfare, should be given by local social leaders or by neighbours in the Samaritan sense, not by experts, professionals or except in the last resort, by public entities beyond the town such as the State.

For Canon Payne, at the Mayor's breakfast in 1890, 'it was a matter of great gratification to see how many lines were opened up in which the benevolent feelings and tendencies of our townsmen might find some scope for exercise'.[20] None of these 'lines', including the religious, were in a different moral league from the others. All were equally meritorious, but none had merit on its own. The important thing was to relate to at least one thoroughly, and to discern its links with the others. Overdevelopment of one 'line' by an individual, a class, or a town to the extent that it involved neglect or suppression of the others was almost as culpable as ignoring them all. Hence the concern that Reading might become a mere suburb of London — involving the segregation of work from home on a more fundamental scale than was already happening inside the town itself. 'It is no more to be desired', wrote W.M. Childs, 'that Reading should become a suburban monstrosity than that it should become an industrial anthill'.[21] Hence the concern, as the contradictions grew between 1890 and 1914, that sport or 'amusement' pursued for its own sake or, even worse, pursued for the sake of profit, was on the increase. Sport had wider ends and connections, but these were part of an interlocking system of duties which, vigorously pursued, would generate a healthy community. George Palmer told members of the Cricket Club at their 'annual tea and social gathering' in 1891 that they 'should not forget that there were other duties besides cricket. He referred to the Schools of Science and Art, which he would very much like to see appreciated to the full by all young men'.[22] Hence, too, the concern that sport could cease to mean participation, for to participate regularly and seriously, not in periodic fiestas as in earlier periods, but in continuous well-structured associations, was vital.[23]

What impressed those in Reading with a sense of before-and-after in relation to 'the great change' between early and mid- to late nineteenth-century Reading was the violence, disorderliness, and intermittency of pre-1840 Reading culture. Events were the focus of activity rather than associations, May Day Fairs rather than Temperance Festivals.[24] Public hangings or the whipping of a man to death through the streets in 1816 were recalled, amid the stench of the blood of unmunicipalised slaughterhouses running on to the roads. There was a sense that 'it wouldn't happen now'. In Octogenarian's account of his youth in Reading (written in 1884) the air was thick with cruelty, and what he regarded as primitive occasions like bull-baiting, stocks, pillorying, and prize fighting. The Stranger's account of 'Readingensionis' (1810) 'whose sensibilities do not appear to be of the finer sort' reeks of blood and dung. In this atmosphere, a different kind of communality was recalled – involving, for example, whole areas of the town dining in the streets together. 'We cannot imagine,' wrote Childs in 1905, 'all Reading people dining together in the streets nowadays, or even wanting to do so'.[25] After the 1910 elections the Rev. P.H. Ditchfield revealed some research he had done on the election in Reading in 1827. It was, for him, unbelievably extraordinary. There had been a public procession:

> first came a herald on a grey horse, dressed in orange uniform with a horseman on each side carrying banners. Then came a long line of horsemen, followed by a band carriage drawn by four horses, followed by a large number of others belonging to the county people, four trumpeters lent by the Lord Mayor of London dressed in velvet, adorned with much gold lace, a Knight of the Forest in superb brass armour with helmet and plumes, riding a fine grey charger, accompanied by three mounted standard bearers. Then came a cavalcade of the committee and a full military band, a Knight of Malta in sheet armour on a grey Arabian steed, a long line of friends of the new member with Union Jacks, and another band and then five gentlemen of the bodyguard and at last appeared the new member, Fyshe Palmer MP in a Roman triumphal car drawn by six horses richly caparisoned with postillions in orange sachels.

Ditchfield was a man of his own time rather than an empathetic social historian equipped for understanding the earlier time. The difference between these two times was beautifully conveyed by his comment on this scene — 'the people must have wondered whether a circus had lost its way'.[26] On the contrary, they must have realised that an election was on.

From the mid-nineteenth century, community was largely defined as the civic nexus of continuous local organisations. Desirable participation meant activity within such groupings. The fact of participation was at least as important as the formal goals of the organisation participated in. Welfare associations for example, whether Friendly Societies, the Reading Philanthropic Institution, the Reading Soup Kitchen, the Temperance and General Philanthropic Institution or the Charity Organisation Society, had to meet as well as perform their external functions. To be too particular about the formal goals would be to diminish the notions of unity within an overall system, of which each separate activity was a part. It should not be assumed that separate organisations had strictly specialised functions. So important was the idea of interconnection within the local system, that organisations tended to create a balance within themselves, by operating in fields aside from their formal goals. Whether the biscuit factory or institutional churches, they came to resemble overlapping smaller totalities, but retained a sense of place, in the larger whole of the civic polity.

C.F.G. Masterman found 'a large disorder' in Britain's 'submerged cities'. Looking at metropolitan conurbations larger than Reading in 1904, he was distressed that there was 'no evident system or mutual dependence, or effort towards an organic whole; here are a thousand worlds, each pursuing its separate functions'.[27] Even though this book will not trace the kind of overlaps in personnel which led modern students of South Wales to write of 'a local system of associations',[28] Masterman's feeling was not one which Reading in the second half of the nineteenth century inspires in the historian. Nor was it a feeling expressed by contemporary commentators on the town. The impression is strong that a *system* existed, even if more definite in the minds of social leaders than in the facts of social life. The separate parts of social life were interconnected and related to one another self-consciously in a manner less true of the periods immediately before or since.

From all sides the contemporary activist was bombarded with assertions about the connections between the different parts of this assumed system. Whether it was the moral and social implications of the manufacture of biscuits (for instance their effect upon the crime rate), or the 'unity of thought' which the naming of the courts and alleys in the town revealed, or the fact that 'the external appearance of the town', was 'in perfect harmony with the social tone of the inhabitants' (something that was explicitly denied later on), or the stress on the vital equipoise between the industrial, the commercial, the residential and the educational, or the view in a survey that compulsory national and voluntary local charity for the relief of poverty were in balance, the weight of opinion of this type was formidable.[29]

Illustration of the degree to which such ideology found organisational expression will be found in later chapters. Local association was certainly sizeable, even if not as total as the aspirations. There was exaggeration when William Isaac Palmer at his last Reading Temperance Society annual meeting in 1892 claimed that 'one quarter of the total population of Reading was total abstainers', or when the Reading Dispensary claimed to serve 'a fourth of the population of the borough, and this without in any way interfering with the prosperous working men's clubs which were doing such a great deal of good work in the town'.[30] But that such estimates could be made at all brings this phase of Reading's social history into sharp relief. In the total array of events or organisations attracting large numbers of participants or spectators, locally organised, continuous, voluntary and socially ambitious organisations were probably more prominent during the second half of the nineteenth century than at any other time. These of course included religious organisations. Indeed a local Baptist magazine asked aggressively, after a successful visit of Gipsy Smith to Reading in 1897-8 which filled the town hall at every service, 'what other subject or interest could have filled it so?'[31]

The Reading Pleasant Sunday Afternoon Societies rallied a 'mass meeting' of 3,000 members as part of the celebrations of the Jubilee in June 1897.[32] No such deliberately local agencies of churches and chapels could have drawn such numbers in the mid-twentieth century, although agencies dominated by efficient national structures such as the Boy Scouts, or internationally organised revival campaigns, continued to be able to do so. Comparing what could attract crowds during the late nineteenth century with what could attract crowds in the 1970s highlights the distinctiveness of the earlier period. The changing experience of an annual event organised by the Friendly and Trade Societies of Reading — Hospital Sunday — will be traced later. Until it began to have difficulties, it attracted thousands into the streets of the town for purposes other than the modern one of 'spending' time in shopping. After the funeral of a physician at the Royal Berkshire Hospital in 1885, 10,000 people were alleged to have visited the cemetery: Dr Wells had lived in Reading for fifty years, and had been a Councillor and a 'friend of the poor'.[33] Similar events arising from the local factory also attracted great crowds. So did one of the most popular annual events in the town in the second half of the nineteenth century, the Temperance Festival in Coley, and later Prospect Park. In 1894 it was reported that the 'members of various societies' who participated 'numbered about 4,000 and the total number of visitors about 14,000. . .showing a falling-off compared with the last few years'.[34] Events with a similar amount of proudly local organisational preparation which could attract crowds of that order during the second half of the nineteenth century included Reading Athletic Club meetings and Reading Working Men's Regattas. Large attendances were claimed also by continuous series of 'popular lectures' mounted by the University Extension Movement before it was absorbed completely into the University which succeeded it. In 1898 it was claimed that the average attendance over the previous five years for such lectures had been 1,000 to 1,400, 'the largest university extension audience in the kingdom'.[35]

No occasion has been found when the 1,125 members which the Reading Help-Myself Society claimed in 1895, turned out at the same time. But as a local meeting-oriented society, and a sub-agency of the Reading Temperance Society particularly dear to the heart of W.I. Palmer, its membership was interestingly large compared, for example, to Friendly Societies. Specifically local Friendly Societies were under increasing strain throughout the late nineteenth century.[36] Of the lodges of local societies sending in returns to the Chief Registrar in, for example, 1892, the Reading Friendly Society (founded 1848) had 78 members and the Reading Benefit Institution (founded 1848) had 119.[37] The Help-Myself Society was even impressive compared to individual lodges of the national machines which the giant Foresters and Oddfellows had by then become. In 1892 the average lodge membership of the Ancient Order of Foresters in Reading and a wide surrounding District was 229, with 5,940 members in 26 Courts.[38]

Before the full meaning of such figures can become apparent, some definition is necessary of the activity for which membership was being sought. An insurance agency is not the same as a Saturday Evening Temperance Meeting, any more than going to church or committing larceny in 1800 was the same as going to church or committing larceny in 1900 — although such indices are sometimes misleadingly put on the same line. Thus, the relative smallness of gates at the Reading Football

Club compared to what they later sometimes became – the first game of the 1896 season attracted 2,500 spectators – needs interpretation in terms of the meaning and organisation of football at that time compared to later. This will be attempted later. And the approximate continuity in size of political crowds may conceal important differences in the quality of the occasions involved.[39] Less local initiative, less participatory control from below, a nationalisation or commercialisation of control may maintain or increase numbers but change the experience. It can certainly be said, from a 1970s perspective, that any contemporary 'success' achieved by organisations in the town such as the football club or political parties looks distinctly fragile. In football, for example, it would be no more surprising in the 1970s if fourth division RFC went out of business than if the giant company, of which Huntley and Palmers is now a part, decided in the interests of 'modernisation and rationalisation' to close down the factory upon which so many nineteenth-century events and organisations in Reading depended.

There were of course moral certainties and structural constraints within which participation in voluntary organisations was thought to be desirable by middle-class leaders in Reading during the first phase of Huntley and Palmers' existence. It was not a question of participation in order to achieve freedom of the do-your-own-thing kind. Freedom was to be understood in the context of perfect service, and subordination to one's betters. Those betters had, however, become 'betters' under one's eyes, rather than being born betters behind the hedges of some remote estate. Any equality in the eyes of God, which was seldom mentioned in church, did not mean social equality of the kind which might require the immediate transformation of social institutions by political means or a suddenly transformed total society. The view was that such transformations had occurred, were occurring and should go on occurring without discontinuous leaps, through the extension of associational life. To revert to the school analogy, while prefects were promoted from the ranks, and while everyone in the ranks had, in theory, the possibility of becoming a master sometime after being a prefect, this did not mean that the role of master or prefect would become redundant at any future date.

Unlike the ideal of associational life generated by working-class movements, and embodied in organisations like the Reading Co-op, there was little stress on the importance of democratic control accompanying participation. At best, if a patron was closely involved with the life of an organisation, there was a kind of tactful paternalism, morally directive in a discreet way. Thus, from 1872 onwards, W.I. Palmer was continually present at (as well as paying for) the Saturday Evening Meetings of the Reading Temperance Society. He described the recipe for success as 'letting the parties amuse themselves as they think best, or are able, slightly controlling and directing them into a higher and better way'.[40] Not all 'vice-presidents' were so personally committed to their organisations and no doubt the absence of any close 'surveillance' could permit the emergence of a more democratic mode of operation. Certainly a striking presence in Reading organisational life during the late nineteenth and early twentieth centuries was a vision, and to some extent an embodiment in organisations, of a working-class, democratic version of voluntarism. Organisations like the Reading Industrial Cooperative Society, or the Broad Street Pleasant Sunday Afternoon movement will be described later. A working-class conception of voluntary life was being articulated in some subject-areas for organisation for the first time, related to middle-class language about associative control of social life and local self-government, but extending it to its ultimate extreme, in such a way as, in the end, to be in contradiction with it. Both versions of voluntary action, the 'Vice-Presidential' and the democratic, were to take a severe battering in the changing context of the early twentieth century.

However incompatible paternal and democratic versions of voluntarism may have been, they were both quite distinct from later twentieth-century versions of 'democracy'. The idea of a competitively selected élite, whose 'necessary' role was buttressed by occasional elections, a functional general apathy and a highly developed capitalist leisure industry, was completely foreign to Reading between 1850 and 1890. The social changes which were to provide the background to the development of such an idea were key parts of the social history of the years 1890 to 1914. For Reading's middle-class leaders, the freedom of perfect service, mass moral self-control and common commitment to dominant moral ideas was to be achieved by active participation in continuous organisations in which voting, for example, played only a trivial part. The way to mute dissonant tendencies, like personal satisfaction at the expense of the social family, sectional aspirations at the expense of the community or ideologies stressing conflict rather than co-operation, was continually to extend areas and constituencies for active consent rather than to enlarge areas, like entertainment, for passive consumption.[41]

Voluntary commitment, both of time and money, was essential.

Going to town meetings, initiating even the most public projects (such as a town hall), supporting organisations other than your own (such as denominations to which you did not belong), attending pan-town events (such as the funeral of a biscuit factory almoner, the opening of the new YMCA buildings or the annual event of the Reading Working Men's Regatta), should all be done voluntarily. Almsgiving, the decline of which Beatrice Webb reckoned to be the most striking of all the changes in her lifetime,[42] meant time as much as money. Indeed there was something wrong with vicarious generosity involving no follow-through, just as there was something wrong with easy acceptance of the gift with no consequent *quid pro quo*.

Interconnections, and the unity between the different foci of voluntary commitment were stressed. It was easier to stress them in a town of Reading's size where single individuals could stretch like octopuses over a large area of town life. Thomas Rogers came to Reading in 1841. In 1847 he got on to the Council. In 1852 he became Clerk to the Local Board of Health. From 1841 to 1848 Tory politics had dominated Reading. In 1847 Rogers entered active Liberal politics and helped to break Tory control. In 1852 he acted as Liberal agent. From then until his death he was 'the recognised head and leader of the Liberal party. . .Under his guidance Liberal representation prevailed for upwards of 30 years'. In 1866 he became Town Clerk. Born a Nonconformist, he worshiped in Reading at St Mary's and All Saints Anglican churches. He was actively connected with street widening, Reading School, church developments in St Mary's parish, the settlement of the public lighting question between the Board of Health and the Gas Company (1862), the acquisition of the waterworks, the giving of the site for the Primitive Methodist chapel at Emmer Green, sewage, the Town Hall movement, the formation of the Redland Estate Company. . .and so on. His 'indefatigable energy and public spirit. . .touched more or less nearly every effort for the welfare of the town'. The involvement of such men was not of the vicarious 'sponsorship' or the sleeping-committee-member type. It was personal, multiform, active and locally focussed.[43]

When we read in the *Reading Observer* in 1879 that a speaker at the beginning of the Town Hall saw it as 'a picture and a type of the best form of present civilisation' and that another said that 'every humble townsman can feel it belongs to himself',[44] we can either look at the buildings now (they are shortly to be pulled down) through the lens of present attitudes to town halls, and laugh patronisingly; or else we should be alerted to take what was going on, and how it was seen, as

serious guides to an unfamiliar phase of Reading society. In 1864 the
Reading Philharmonic Society had given an organ to the town. In the
Municipal Address to the Society, Councillors were proud of being
representatives, but pointed out that they were 'yet members of the
general community', allied with associations like the RPS. 'Municipal
Councils have become social rather than commercial or political
institutions.'[45]

On the same site (itself significant) in the fourth quarter of the
nineteenth century were built the Town Hall, the Schools of Science
and Art, the Free Library, the Museum, and the Art Gallery. As was the
case with churches and chapels during this period of Reading's history,
the private initiative and cash of small numbers of donors were
essential to the operation. Voluntary effort, in the form of a gift of a
collection of shells from Mr Blandy which then had to be housed,
three large donations totalling £20,000 plus some smaller ones (which
still left £10,000 to be found by a reluctant corporation), and the
convening of a meeting on 1st May 1877 to set the movement afoot,
started and sustained the first stage in the operation — the Town Hall
itself. Without voluntary effort, as the Mayor conceded, the Building
Committee could not have functioned.

The laying of the memorial stone in 1879 was an elaborate local
occasion, with Freemasons taking the lead in the procession: 'the
emblems, vessels and insignia of the order were of magnificent
appearance. The procession formed a spectacle such as is rarely
witnessed.'[46] After the outdoor ceremony, the hymn 'All people that
on earth do dwell' was sung: then a luncheon was held, with elaborate
speeches. Two things became clear: first that this was, in aspiration,
not just an occasion for the owners of the means of production and
possessors of formal civic power. 'The people' or 'the working classes'
were a continual refrain in the speeches. It was not the mere beginning
of a town hall to house a municipal bureaucracy and to collect rent and
rates, but an 'undertaking having for (its) object the social and moral
good of the people'. Secondly, that the other proposed buildings on the
site were an integral part of what was being done. So were many other
recent events in Reading's history. Achievements such as an adequate
sewage system, organisations such as the defunct Mechanics' Institute,
institutions such as the British and National Schools were all seen as
part of that system of which the Town Hall and the other buildings
were 'the crowning work'. 'Before it aspired to the magnificent and
splendid edifice which is about to crown its labours, these labours
commenced with the far more important duty of constructing the

necessary underground works for its improvement.' The connection
with the school system in the town and with the Free Library was made
by a visiting dignitary. Then George Palmer got up 'in response to loud
and persistent request' to put him right on a couple of points. The
visitor had suggested that a Free Library in the new complex would be
a novelty for Reading. On the contrary, said George Palmer in the few
words to which he always limited himself, there had been a library in
the late-lamented Mechanics' Institute, and there still was one in the
premises of the Temperance Society in West Street. 'This was a public
library in every sense of the word, which will I believe be the nucleus
for the new library. . .and was also the starting point and the incentive
which led to the larger library about to be provided.' In 1864 the
Reading Mercury had backed the suggestion of the local Elocution
Society, which gave public 'readings', that its surplus funds should go
towards a free public library.[47]

William Isaac Palmer's speech was received by 'immense cheering'
and applause. Typically, he chose to stress his hopes for the
workmanship in the construction of the building as part of its moral
presence: 'the perfection of it all round will be a worthy memorial of
the rectitude and the honesty as well as the skill of English
manufacturers, tradesmen, and workpeople.'[48] His view was set out in a
fascinating speech which he, unusually for Palmers, wrote out six years
later when 3,125 subscribers gave him a presentation portrait, album
and plate from 'the people of Reading', for 'one whose daily life is
lived amongst us' in recognition of his work in the town hall movement.
At this meeting the Mayor thought that he could refer to 'the town of
Reading' meeting, since 'never at any one meeting' before had the town
'been more fully represented. . .by the presence of members of every
class, every creed and persons of the most opposite views on nearly
every subject'. The buildings were explicitly connected to the work of
the Temperance Society in West Street and 'details of the work of
which this hall forms so important a part' were remembered. William
Isaac Palmer admitted that 'in carrying out what I have felt to be my
duty I have not entirely gone with the stream, and I have been thought
by some persons to be rather extreme in certain directions, but I have
not been conscious of intentionally hurting the feelings of others'.

His belief that 'the establishment of these institutions will be even
more valued in the future than at this moment' was over-optimistic.[49]
1885 was a climax for the meanings he gave to these events, not a
beginning. In the same way the excitement of the *Reading Observer* in
November 1891 looks forlorn to modern eyes. The *Observer* had

reported another local occasion – the procession for the opening of
Palmer Park. It had taken an hour to pass a given point, and had been
manned by a cornucopia of local organisations. It had been 'the most
remarkable and striking manifestation of public sentiment the town
has witnessed'. It had not been for a national event, but 'purely for
one of their own citizens' who had helped in the giving of the Park. It
constituted a 'remarkable illustration. . .of the power of the people for
self-government'. Only a very different national and local history of the
half-century after 1891 could have allowed such a phrase to resonate,
or could have vindicated the *Observer's* belief that 'the fourth of
November 1891 will ever remain memorable in the history of our
town'.[50] It has, of course, been totally forgotten.

Not all the organisations which participated in the Palmer Park
procession explicitly saw themselves, as did the Reading Philanthropic
Institution, as 'epitome(s) of a free community'[51] and as
representatives of the best notions of organisation and conduct which
should be extended to become hegemonic within the whole society.
But neither did they see themselves in the modern way simply as
providers of entertaining ways to consume Tuesday evenings. Allied to
other organisations they were, they thought, much more than
manufacturers of leisure products: the pressure to become just that was
a major theme in the experience of many voluntary organisations
between 1890 and 1914.[52] The notion of 'hobbies' safely insulated in
a 'leisure' vacuum away from work, away from the business of shaping
one's own future, having nothing to do with the way in which a whole
society should and could be run was, in aspiration, as foreign as the
notion of work which had nothing to do with the rest of life, simply an
activity which the worker 'sells to another person in order to secure the
necessary means of subsistence'.[53] So even the biscuit factory was
frequently compared to a town within a town because of its events
alongside work, its ceremonials, its mutual improvement activities, its
welfare and athletic clubs and funds. The dream was to mould social
fate through the nexus of associational life in the locality.

To a considerable extent, even if riven with contradictions not yet
fully apparent, the second half of the nineteenth century in Reading
was a local phase. It can too easily be assumed that during the last two
hundred years localities have been becoming steadily less effective units
for loyalty and influence in the face of an ever more powerful
metropolitan culture.[54] The overall process of nationalisation is
undeniable, but was not a unilinear one.

Reading's economy prior to 1840 was already nationalised via coaches and canals.[55] Disease, the weather, prices in distant markets, levels of demand for products like cheese at the large annual cheese fair in the town, and harvests, were all critically important in the life of Reading in the eighteenth and early nineteenth centuries. And yet they did not even seem to be patient of local control, or even of much human influence.[56] Whereas the key economic organisation of the later period – the biscuit factory – had grown under the very eyes and management of visible local people, from nothing to a vast enterprise. It had not 'arrived' in the town, like many later economic organisations, as a result of a decision made in a remote board room or government department. Universities are now regarded as components in a national 'system'. For the main-spring of Reading University in its early days, W.M. Childs, it was, by contrast, a natural complement to the Reading Literary and Scientific Society, not a rival to it.[57] After all, in 1872 there were about 1,000 members of local voluntary organisations where books could be read or borrowed – reading rooms, mutual improvement societies and the like – before the State intervened.[58] A major medium of communication makes the point sharply – newspapers. The high point for a local press in Reading was the forty-five years following 1855. About fifteen different newspapers existed at some time during these years. Then conditions began to change in this area, as elsewhere. Of the papers founded then only two were still going by 1900. 'The possibility of another great burst of newspaper activity in Berkshire such as the one which followed 1855 had passed by the beginning of the twentieth century.'[59]

Nationalising agencies such as technology and government activity were of course visible well before 1890. But in the specific forms they took at that time, they serviced the locality in the short term before weakening it in the long term. The penny post (leading to an immediate increase in the monthly average of letters posted in Reading in 1841 from 3,800 to 10,000), trams (six cars with 14,000 passengers per week in 1879) and telephones (225 subscribers in Reading in 1892) were all less nationalising in their impact than cars, cinemas or broadcasting in the twentieth century.[60] Even a major outside invasion like railways had local mediations at this time. Whether the Great Western Railway came to Reading at all depended to some extent on the opinions and actions of interest groups which the possibility of its arrival provoked in the town. Local opposition during the critical time of March 1834 when petitions and counter-petitions were being presented to Parliament could theoretically have resulted in leaving Reading, like Abingdon, off the track. Railways in Reading were also

related more in this period to a local chain of command than they
have been since. Local businessmen were on the board of the GWR.
The construction and demand for reconstruction of the Station (not
achieved till 1898-9) was an issue for local politics and some local
finance. And a huge user of the line like the biscuit factory had its
own sheds, its own tracks and coaches. In the long term it came to
look as if what E.J. Hobsbawm has called 'the notion of a gigantic,
nation-wide, complex and exact interlocking routine symbolised by
the railway time-table' made things happen almost as independently of
local initiative as the weather. But in the short term an exhilarating
addition to local freedom and autonomous rationality appeared to have
been made.[61]

Similar but more sustained and influential local initiatives were a
necessary part of the developments in public health, even though,
again, in the long term social reform was a nationalising agency. Public
health legislation tended to be permissive not compulsory: who got
on to the council, how the fight between economists and 'civic patriots'
(a phrase of 1908) went, how much of their money, time and talent
the local business élite was prepared to devote to municipal matters —
all this radically altered the chronology of the sanitary history of
nineteenth-century cities. 'It is not every town that had achieved by
1872 a good water supply under municipal control, efficient lighting,
solid all-round improvement: very few towns had their municipal
abattoirs or had instigated any clearance of slum property, provided
parks or recreation grounds, or streets with trees.'[62] That Reading had
taken steps like this owed something to legislation certainly, but was
also owing to local action by people whose horizons were to a
significant extent contained within their own town. A municipal
interest had to be staked out, separate from private interests. Not just
businessmen either, but professional groupings, particularly doctors,
played a key role at the local level in making things happen when they
did and in the form they did.[63] Moreover, mid-nineteenth-century issues
related much more to the *place* than did the later issues of State social
policy like children, unemployment, or old people.

'Men conscious of a power to help their fellows,' said George Palmer,
'should be willing to take their share in municipal and other government'.
'Other government' included philanthropy, which was part of the ideal
of local self-government. Indeed municipal and national government
were only a small part, and a lesser part, of what 'government' properly
meant.[64] The human will was seen as being immensely powerful; and
conscious individual choice, rational and responsible, was the only basis

upon which a proper politics could grow. Spending money, hours, mental energy in an organisation often divided into many branches, yet seeing its relationship to other agencies; relying upon that type of agency rather than upon the 'change society first' option (and not necessarily thereby merely reformist); stressing individual moral commitment as the most powerful agency for alteration of social circumstances, but expressed through continuously existing local associations, which did not see themselves mainly as pressure groups acting upon the central government; opening these organisations theoretically to everybody, or at least providing them for everybody rather than leaving them as the exclusive property of a special constituency – all this was highly characteristic of Reading society's dignified view of itself by 1890.

3 RELIGION (I)

In a society where the aspirations just described were central, it is not difficult to anticipate that religion in the form of churches and chapels could have an important place. Indeed it is easy to see that religion, at that point in time and in that kind of place, would be likely to take the form of organised churches and chapels.

Since we are still living with some results of that point in time and that kind of place it is tempting to see religion and churches and chapels as synonymous. But 'religion is prior to the church, both analytically and chronologically: religion at certain times and places creates churches'.[1] The sense that Reading churches need not have been as they were is again necessary to cultivate. People who doubt this should read themselves, for example, into a feeling for the eighteenth- and early nineteenth-century 'old religion' evoked by George Eliot in her novels. The 'maiden days of the Dodson sisters' were quite different from what will be described in late nineteenth-century Reading – 'if their Bibles opened more easily at some parts than others, it was because of dried tulip-petals, which had been distributed quite impartially, without preference for the historical, devotional or doctrinal. Their religion was of a simple, semi-pagan kind, but there was no heresy in it – if heresy properly means choice – for they didn't know there was any other religion, except that of chapel goers, which appeared to run in families, like asthma'.[2] 'Religion' could have been many other things besides this 'variety of Protestantism unknown to Bossuet': it could have been personal and privatised as in the mid-twentieth century; or it could have been conversionist, based upon regular mass revivals from below with the boundaries between members and adherents ill-defined and shifting as in the first half of the nineteenth century; or it could have been preoccupied with doctrine, carried by groups of schismatics who moved in and out of particular buildings with relative ease, following the dictates of conscience, again as in the early nineteenth century.

It is easy to see that religion could take the forms which will be described here, because such forms were natural components of the effort to create continuously existing, local, voluntary organisations *for* a public, but designed eventually to become fully *of* them, and designed to operate within dominant moral certainties about conduct

51

and organisation. Churches and chapels were the most local, universally available and accessible voluntary organisations in the society described in Chapter Two. If commercial organisations are included in the range of non-domestic buildings into which 'the man in the street' might go, only the corner shop and the pub were more universally and more locally available on most streets in the late nineteenth and early twentieth centuries. And both corner shop and pub were either already undergoing, or were later to undergo, strains similar to those which will by faith or by works this was by any standards important, more so than religious organisations. In the longer term they were both to decrease in numbers, suffer from merger and control from above, and lose some of their varied participatory functions less directly concerned with the distribution of commodities.

The context of aspiration and organisation in Reading by *c*.1890, while vital for understanding, does not fully explain religious organisation in late nineteenth-century Reading. For explanation, the actions and choices of religious organisations, and the peculiarities of religious compared to other organisations are relevant. Religious organisations were not only the most local and widely disseminated amongst voluntary organisations. They also made different claims upon potential customers for which a greater degree of institutional elaboration could easily come to be seen as essential. Their central business, when they remembered it, was worship and salvation. Whether by faith or by works this was by any standards important, more so than most versions of playing football, going to an adult education class, a political meeting or a Hospital Sunday Parade. 'Most versions' because there were groups engaged in such activities in Reading which made just such ultimate claims on customers, like the WEA in its early days or the Social Democratic Federation. A depth or totality of commitment, or at least a priority of commitment, ideally differentiates religious organisations from many others. In its ideal version, after all, a church claims to 'give men a power in its work that no other society can wield, and it has to make a demand on men which no other society has a right to make. And it is a demand which the church has no right to make on society merely as a rival society, but only as the prophet of the Word of God in Christ'.[3] For the demand to be put to a public, however, it seemed at the time as if the Word needed incarnation in priests and buildings and an immense range of sub-organisations. The particular forms that religion took in late nineteenth-century Reading will be outlined in this chapter. In Chapters Five and Six some contradictions involved in maintaining these forms in a changing context will be explored.

How then can religious organisation be better understood in the light of the outline description of Reading society by *c.* 1890 already given? An exercise which helps is to imagine the society without its churches and chapels. What would be missing from the ecology?

The first answer must be, quantitatively, a lot. Indeed the very size of the presence of organisations like churches and chapels in society at that time helps to define the type of society that it was. No longer were the pub and the chapel the 'only social centres available to the majority of the inhabitants', as Davies suggests was the case in South Wales earlier in the century.[4] But as active, local and many-faceted voluntary organisations, churches and chapels were certainly large on the leisure landscape of Reading during the second half of the nineteenth century. 'It is astonishing,' said the Rev. W.B. Bantry to the St. Lawrence Church Institute in 1884, 'how many churches and chapels there are and how many efforts there have been made for the welfare of everyone. . .Yes, Reading is a very busy place: all who work prosper, and the number of meetings for religious, charitable, literary and social purposes is immense'. Religious organisations were major suppliers of such meetings, amongst a whole range of other local voluntary organisations supplying similar products. At the Mayor's Breakfast in 1890 the Bishop was asked to speak on 'the religious life of Reading'. He was 'quite satisfied that there was no town with which he was acquainted that so well met the religious needs of its inhabitants as Reading. If it is not a religious town it was not for the want of a good supply of the means of grace'. 'Well ordered activity and zeal pervading all denominations', wrote a guide book in 1904, 'and strenuous efforts for the good of souls characterising all who are willing to promote the spiritual interests of the town'. A parish priest was convinced that 'the universal growth and expansion of the church of God. . .is the leading characteristic of the most glorious and beneficent reign in the history of England'.[5]

If 'the church of God' meant bricks and mortar it was indeed visible. The size of the presence of churches and chapels in the urban landscape in Britain generally, and in Reading in particular will be familiar to anyone who has seen the roof-tops from a train. Standing on the pavement in some neighbourhoods in Reading (particularly near St. Mary's-in-the-Butts) the buildings can be seen in all directions. Competitors stare at each other from behind their columns or gravestones across narrow streets. The means of grace were more visible than the means of production, and even more so a hundred years ago, before many of the means of grace had been turned into means of distribution in the form of furniture shops or warehouses.

On the only day for which general figures are available — Sunday 30th March 1851 — religious attendance in Reading was high. On that day total attendances at all Reading places of worship (not allowing for those who went more than once) were 68.5% of the population. This was higher than the national average for all types of location on the same day (61%), and considerably higher than the average for towns of more than 10,000 inhabitants (49.7%). Only five towns of more than 10,000 inhabitants (Colchester, Exeter, Bath, Ipswich, and Wakefield) exceeded Reading's 'index of attendance'.[6] About one in three of Reading's inhabitants (Colchester, Exeter, Bath, Ipswich and Wakefield) exceeded (6,198 instead of 7,068) in the evening. Of these attenders four out of every seven went to Anglican churches, the rest to 'all others', including 55 to the Latter Day Saints or Mormons.

In 1851 the proportion of sittings available which were occupied at the best-attended service on census Sunday was high.[7] Later information is on sittings rather than on attendance, but it would not be legitimate to extrapolate attendance from such information. Nor can a meaningful Membership Population Ratio, of the kind that Currie has used nationally for Methodist denominations, be calculated for religious organisations as a whole in Reading. Methodists revised their membership lists quarterly: other denominations were laxer than that.[8] If number of sittings per head of population are an index of religious growth or decline, then some decline took place in Reading between 1851 and 1894.[9] The one to three ratio of 1894 had been almost one to two in 1851. Equally, whereas there had been a separate 'church' for each 1,000 inhabitants in 1851, by 1894 there was one for each 1,300 inhabitants. The denominations which had grown most over this period, measured by seats, were the Anglicans and the Primitive Methodists. But other denominations, especially the Wesleyan Methodists, were to become active builders in the early years of the twentieth century.

In 1891 there were some 60,000 people in Reading. The nearest corresponding religious statistics were those for 1894.[10] At that date there were 11,500 seats available in Anglican churches, divided among 18 buildings, most of them churches dedicated to saints, three of them 'iron rooms' or 'missions'. There were 14,150 seats in Nonconformist chapels, making a combined total of 25,650 seats in the town. The Nonconformist seats were divided among 28 buildings, four Baptist chapels, one Baptist mission room, two Particular Baptist chapels, three

Congregational chapels, one 'Congregational Methodist', one Friends
Meeting House, one Presbyterian, five Primitive Methodist, three
Wesleyan, two Plymouth Brethren, one Unitarian, three Salvation Army
Halls or Citadels and, included on this list, two Roman Catholic
churches. 'Congregational religion' as Max Weber observed, 'is a
phenomenon of diverse manifestations and great fluidity'.[11]

The next convenient date at which a comparable set of figures
exists is 1902.[12] By then, 800 more Nonconformist seats had been
provided (more seats at Grovelands Baptist Chapel, a new Coley Hall, a
new Presbyterian church at Caversham, a new Roman Catholic church,
and more Salvation Army seats). And 200 new Anglican seats were
available (one new church in Elgar Road). The proportion of seats to
population had not significantly altered: the ratio remained one seat
per three inhabitants. A fair number of these seats were privately
appropriated. But when babyhood, disease, Sunday working, poverty
and senility are taken into account, it was not as though, as the Bishop
recognised, there was any crying shortage of this particular means of
grace. Expressions of distress at shortage of churches or chapels, and
resulting energetic building programmes, came out of
interdenominational rivalry as well as from felt overall lack of
worshipping facilities. In 1903 the Wesleyans became anxious because
'instead of providing for the religious needs of 10% of the population –
the generally accepted ratio for Wesleyan Methodism – our people
found that their churches would seat 3%. . .Methodist hearts were
touched, Methodist heads were put together and the result was a
scheme'.[13] Whatever particular denominations felt about their
performance in relation to competitors, the proportion of the
population for which there were seats was much more remarkable than
the proportion for which there were not. By this unsatisfactory but
frequently employed criterion, Reading was possibly an example of a
locality as 'religious' as any locality of the same size in any society at
any time in world history. Precisely for this reason – because of
expectations and their location in buildings – religious activists
sometimes saw Reading as profoundly irreligious. The many people
who could not be involved in religious organisations were sometimes
viewed as components of a problem of irreligion or religious decline
even though non-involvement had more to do with the constraints of
the social system, like poverty, and with the choices made or not made
by religious entrepreneurs and activists in that context.

At this point, however, the sheer size of involvement in some
religious organisations in Reading needs emphasis. Even if always

inadequate in the eyes of the most committed members, there were great heights from which to fall. Churches had gone a long way towards becoming harried 'elderly multiples'.[14] 5,525 members of the Reading Sunday School Union in 1893, or 5,222 members of the Band of Hope Union, were large figures indeed. In 1900-01 the total strength of an intentionally 'better fewer but better' agency like the Christian Endeavour Societies in the Reading and District Union was 1,438. A single branch of the Church of England Temperance Society (St. John's) reached 686 members in 1900. The St. Giles parish annual meeting and Conversazione in the town hall in 1904 attracted more than 500 people: the Oxford Road Wesleyan Pleasant Sunday Afternoon had an average *attendance* in March 1906 of 700. There was a Church of England Men's Society meeting in the town hall in September 1906 with 2,000 present: the Salvation Army in August 1914 had an adult membership of about 450. All this when expressed as Membership Population Ratios may not appear 'significant'. But that depends upon your expectations. Such figures must certainly have felt significant to the activists involved as impresarios for such numbers, to the 216 different men employed as priests by the Church of England in Reading between 1890 and 1914, or to the 158 men employed by other churches during the same period.[15] In a world of finite resources of energy, time and money, the work involved must certainly have appeared significant to other areas of activity, like education, in which the same churches and chapels were also heavily committed.

In trying to get beyond the scale to the nature of the presence of religious organisations at this time awkward questions of interpretation are involved. There is a danger of anachronistic and indiscriminate judgments. In the interests of clarity, however, qualifications will be made after some wider judgments.

Basic to the life and work of religious organisations were Sunday services at various times of day and of varying degrees of sacramental significance, week-night services either for the whole congregation or for sub-sections of it and prayer meetings preparatory or supplemental to services. Or at least worship was the face they chose to present to potential consumers in local Directories and Guides — as they still do. But occupying as much or more time, commitment and money were huge arrays of sub-organisations. Institutes, guilds, recreational and sporting clubs, meetings and movements for reacting to the poor, schools, libraries, brotherhoods, men's societies, women's owns, youth sections, temperance societies, missionary guilds, halls, coffee taverns ...clustered around churches and chapels in astonishing profusion.

'The present is preeminently an age of societies', explained a cutting filed in the records of St. John's church, 'and when some future historian takes pen in hand to narrate the characteristic features of the latter half of the nineteenth century, one of his chief duties will be to trace the rise and progress of the associated movements which have so largely developed in our midst during the past 50 years'.[16] Many such movements from football to the Boy Scouts latched on to the propensity of churches to accumulate what they thought would be agencies serving their main purpose. Only the public house was as fertile a host as churches for ways of using leisure time during the nineteenth century.[17]

Some subject-areas for organisation were more favoured by religious organisations than others. 'Welfare' was an area in which churches and chapels were especially interested. Such interest was regarded by many members of churches or chapels as automatically accompanying their religion, as an especially Christian province. Forms and ideologies of concern varied across the whole spectrum, but total unconcern would have been unthinkable to many religious activists at this time.[18] There would have been wide assent to Athos's last remarks after his tour of local churches for the *Reading Observer* in 1906-7: 'Friends of every denomination have made their special pleadings for this tenet and that tenet, but putting every disturbing factor out of sight it seems to me that the only relevant question is, "are you trying to make the world better, and, if so, are you trying to do it upon the right lines?"'[19]

If one could imagine Reading without its ministers or churches and chapels at this time, there would be greater differences in other organisations and in town debates and discussion on welfare and poverty than in any other subject-area, including education. Town institutions like the Royal Berkshire Hospital depended to a considerable extent on clergymen to man their committees and speak at their 'Annual Court' meetings. Town movements like the Reading Guild of Help (founded in 1909) would have been hard-pressed to man ward committees, or to staff the central committee without such workers as the Revs. R.W. Carew Hunt, Guy Rogers, C. Lewes, F.J. Kernan, A. Swift and others.[20] When official bodies such as the Prince of Wales Relief Fund of 1914 were set up, it was natural that the chairman of the Relief Committee for Church and Katesgrove wards should be the vicar of St. Giles.[21] As men with opinions, skills and time, ministers were an integral part of the machinery of relief and welfare provision. So were their organisations. At times the church apparatus played a semi-official role at the town level. When it was decided to give the 'Aged Poor' a dinner during the Coronation of 1902, the District Visitor apparatus was unhesitatingly used by the town committee as the agency of administration.[22] The Royal Berkshire Hospital relied on church and chapel collections for part of its income (1881 – £1,036; 1896 – £1,107), although this, as we shall see, was changing.

Concern was evidenced through sub-organisations attached to the main body. Sometimes the concern was missionary rather than welfare-oriented, as in the case of the 'earnest vangelistic *(sic)* effort' of Hosier Street Congregational Methodist chapel, with its visitation of the courts and alleys surrounding the chapel, its Bible Classes, its reclamation of fallen women, its paid workers among the poor. But most often the help was seen as an end in itself rather than as a means to conversion. It was a necessary part of church or chapel life, and an integral part of the religion of those who provided it. The effect of the poor on the religion and attitudes of those just out of or above the 'abyss' was more profound than vice-versa. The agencies included: Poor Funds in most chapels, Ladies Visiting Associations (at Elm Park Methodist Hall the LVA paid for a full-time Sick Visitor in 1905), Sunshine Funds attached mostly to Christian Endeavour groups (Kings Road Baptists and Trinity), Dorcas societies (at Greyfriars this group's activity amounted to Sweating in the form of relief, with garments sent out to be made up by 'needy widows' and then sold at cost price), Soup Kitchens (Tilehurst Anglicans charged 1*d.* a ticket in 1891), Mothers' Meetings to work on behalf of the Poor, Provident Clubs, Coal and Clothing Clubs, Loan Blanket societies, Infants, Friends Societies, Penny Banks, Poor Stewards (in Methodist chapels), Maternity groups ...and much else besides. Helping the poor became part of winter programmes, one item among other items requiring attendance at regular meetings – just like Shakespeare recitals or lectures on electricity. Any large church or chapel would have most of the above agencies. The sheer accumulation of groupings only reinforces their unattractiveness to the modern observer, and perhaps to many citizens at the time. Their limitations do not need pointing out. What is chiefly remarkable is the way in which such agencies clustered like fungus on the trunks of groupings like the Church of England Men's Society or the Pleasant Sunday Afternoon movement, which in many respects were opposed to their ideology and atmosphere. Pressures to do something immediate in response to the plight of the poor were intense. Churches and chapels responded in remarkably uniform ways. Each agency, whether Sunday School, PSA, or Christian Endeavour, and each Mission Hall mirrored the main church or chapel of which it was a part, by the way in which it created its own cluster of sub-agencies for dealing with the poor.

Educational agencies were also an inevitable part of the cluster. Sometimes the preoccupation of the agency was with assisting upward social mobility. So at Christ Church Institute in 1890 a member could take part in shorthand and writing classes as well as recreational activities. The 'Rising Sun' coffee tavern in Silver Street, attached to St. Giles, offered technical classes for youths every evening at 7.30. The Lady Worker paid for by Greyfriars church spent part of her time in 1906 'educating girls from all parts of Reading for domestic service'. Sister Caroline of St. Giles was praised in December 1902 for the way in which during the previous ten years 'she had transplanted nearly 100 girls from Silver Street to safer and happier surroundings'.

The most highly organised educational agency was the Broad Street Congregational Chapel Working Men's College, started in 1895. In March 1897 it had classes in Arithmetic, Shorthand, Book-keeping, Composition, Geography, and 'the Science of Common Things'. It worked closely with the Industrial Committee of Reading University Extension College. Trinity Congregational Chapel had an Adult School between 1905 and 1910 where 'sympathy and brotherhood' were 'fostered and encouraged'. Papers were read on 'matters affecting the well-being of the people'. Lecturettes were given. 'The reverent and thoughtful study of the Bible is however the important feature of the Adult School movement;' 'the Fatherhood of God and the Brotherhood of man form the basis of belief and the object is to seek the truth whatever it will be and to follow it wherever it leads.' There were at least five such schools in Reading and, in 1909, twenty-nine in the region.

More fundamental than these were the Anglican and Nonconformist denominational schools. Each church or chapel of any size supported often quite large schools, as well as the inevitable Sunday School — with consequences which will be spelled out later. Running a Mutual Improvement Society (as at Hosier Street) was a qualitatively different operation from running a voluntary school: that local organisations such as churches and chapels should expect and be expected to do the latter, itself contributes to the definition of society in the second half of the nineteenth century already attempted, even though national denominational machinery was essential to the operation as well as local effort.

Recreation was also a favoured field. Entertainments (as at

St. Saviour's or Grovelands Baptist), Gordon Boys' Clubs 'to provide
recreation for boys who have left school but are not old enough to join
the Caversham Reading Room' (as at Caversham Anglican churches),
Social and Musical Unions (as at the Unitarian chapel), Social and
Debating Clubs (as at Broad Street PSA), Men's Clubs to provide
'healthy recreation for the men of our parish during the long winter
evenings' (as at St. Giles). . .such groups played a part in the social life
of the town, and a larger part in the activity of churches and chapels.
In a suburb of Reading, Caversham, a large slice of the social and
sporting life of the place was carried on in at least formal connection
with the Anglican parish. The Caversham Cricket Club, the Caversham
Choral Society, the Caversham Horticultural Society, the Caversham
Football Club — all founded in the late nineteenth century — were
made to appear in the pages of the Parish Magazine as if they were part
of the life of the Church of England. This probably represented an *idea*
of church work and an ideal conception of the parish as much as actual
links, but the idea was still there in 1900.[23] Sport was an increasingly
favoured branch of activity. Such groups as the Athletic Union at
Wycliffe Baptist chapel or the Gymnasium classes (St. Luke's, Christ
Church and Grovelands Baptist) proliferated. Sometimes the church or
chapel initiated the group, more rarely it took an existing group under
its aegis and carried it on as a branch of church work.[24]

Politics was more problematical as a subject-area for church
organisation. Whatever might be said, there was no question about the
intimate involvement of churches and chapels as political interest
groups at each stage of the development of a State school system after
1870. There was party political involvement too. The Liberal
Association was intimately involved with the Nonconformist side and
the Conservatives with the Church side. There was also 'politics' of the
worst kind, with pacts between leaders designed to exclude democratic
contests by carving up the spoils.

Involvement was especially intense in relation to the Education Act
of 1902. It seemed critically important to keep the children of the
chapel away from State-supported Anglican instruction, and to preserve
the right to teach proper Biblical doctrine. Not only was government
policy to be carefully watched; the Reading School Board was to be
captured and held by election. Divisions on the Board were between
'church' or 'moderate' party representatives and Nonconformists, until
a member of the Social Democratic Federation got a seat in 1892.
Voting was by plumping. All the votes of one elector could go to one
candidate or be distributed in any way he fancied. This put a premium

on effective electoral organisation. In Reading the church or moderate
party held control throughout the life of the Board, until 1902.[25] When
the Board merged into the town council, new life was injected into
council elections owing to 'a desperate effort' by Nonconformists and
Radicals to capture the new education authority.[26] On both sides the
battle was intense and quite explicitly political both in idea and in
tactic. In 1903-4 there were about 110 'passive resisters' in Reading,
refusing to pay rates and being arrested for it, resisting the
implementation of the Education Act of 1902.[27] To them Balfour was
outrageous. Gladstone and Lord Salisbury had been men of honour,
thought the Rev. H.H. Snell, secretary of the Reading passive resisters
in May 1905, but 'the decline from their high standard of rectitude and
honour which is now so painfully apparent in their successor has
outraged the religious sentiment of the country and will doubtless
bring its due recognition when the country has the opportunity of
recording a verdict'.[28] United action against Conservative rule brought
its benefits to the chapels: a common enemy generated zeal.[29]
   Similarly on the Anglican side, when a threat was felt from the
Liberal Education Bill in May 1906, resolutions, demonstrations and
petitions were actively encouraged.[30] It had been clear from the tone
of parish magazine pronouncements for two years before this that, from
the perspective of many parish priests, almost any action would be
justified in the face of such serious dangers:

> The question of the maintenance of the Christianity of the nation is
> of far more importance than any other to the interests of the
> country and such influence as we can bring to bear upon candidates
> for municipal or parliamentary honours should mainly be directed
> towards obtaining in our schools perfect liberty of conscience, so
> that the children of the church may be taught the definite truth
> 'once for all delivered to the saints'.[31]

When, for both sides, 'the definite truth' was so inextricably linked
with particular organisations and modes of instruction the recipe for
active politics was to hand.
   Churches took party sides, but the *idea* of taking party sides, even
the notion of there being party sides and government depending upon
them was, for many within churches, repugnant. There were, it seemed,
moral issues. Politics sometimes coincided with those issues and
expressed them. More usually, and increasingly in the late nineteenth
century, it seemed to the churches not to do so. Politics was not a

natural part of the church/chapel penumbra, in the way that football was or philanthropy. A Literary and Debating Society, a Social Union, the Philanthropic Institution, had no difficulty in borrowing a church hall in which to meet in Reading. Chapels like Hosier Street were willing hosts to Liberal Party ward meetings (1903). But the SDF, and campaigners for women's suffrage even before the violence of the WSPU, were refused space to meet at Hosier Street (1896) and elsewhere. The local political arena was being enlarged from the 1890s and the new working-class presence, whether the secularist SDF or the Reading Trades and Labour Council, washed its hands of the denominational dogfight and called for secular education in state schools.

There were sometimes interesting tensions between the rank-and-file of a chapel and its leadership. Cumberland Road Primitive Methodist chapel, near the biscuit factory, was the place of worship of a number of socialist activists for part of their lives. One of them, J.W. Burness, an SDF member, was elected to the School Board in 1892, breaking an electoral pact which would have given the church side seven seats and the chapel six, and angering them for 'entailing expense and introducing into the School Board elements of difference'. A letter of support for him appeared in the local press signed by 'Primitive Methodist local preacher', saying that he had 'received a very hearty and general support from us as a body'. This led to swift denials by the minister of the chapel, expressed quite viciously, and revelations that Burness had been specifically asked *not* to stand by a deputation of circuit ministers and 'a number of leading officials of our church'. The minister (the Rev. A. Beavan) wrote,

> as a people we do not recognise Mr Burness in any sense representing us on the Board. The truth is we were well satisfied with the work of the Board and had not the remotest wish to occasion a contest. . .had the matter rested with us, Mr Burness, instead of being placed at the head of the poll, would have found himself in the position exactly the reverse. . .with regard to the deputation. . .though not official in the sense of being appointed by an official meeting it may be well to state that it consisted of circuit ministers and the visit was paid at the request of a number of the leading officials of our church.[32]

Such tensions between ordinary members and officials of the chapels were the source of strength of other chapel agencies, particularly the Pleasant Sunday Afternoon movement, which, in some chapels at least, belonged to the rank-and-file, or at least to the Deacons rather than to the Minister. There were some people in religious organisations who welcomed the demand for working-class power in the community and religious agencies under effective democratic control.

The universality of some directions of work among religious bodies of very different beliefs and organisation is itself interesting. Hosier Street Congregational Methodist Chapel, for instance, prided itself on its temperance work, under an organisation called the Cadets of Temperance. The chapel had played an important initiating role in the history of temperance in Reading. Its Band of Hope, founded in 1854, was second only to that of the Primitive Methodists founded in 1853.[33] It placed great emphasis on this branch of work.[34]

But so, in the third quarter of the nineteenth century, did practically every other church. 'Since the Church of England clergy have so heartily taken up the Temperance movement' (they came relatively late into the field) 'the adherents of the cause have rapidly increased in numbers, and the temperance platform now forms a common ground upon which all parties and members of all religious communities can unite'.[35] After Sunday Schools, temperance was the most important inspiration of church/chapel penumbras from the mid-nineteenth century onwards. The Primitive Methodists took most readily to it. The Reading Temperance Society said in their *Annual Report* for 1881, 'the chapels of that persuasion have been opened to us with greater readiness than that of any other section of the Christian church and it is amongst them that the most flourishing societies are to be found. They have shown an aptitude for laying hold of the movement, and utilising it as part and parcel of the work carried on in their sanctuaries for the promotion of the spiritual and common welfare of the people which others would do well to emulate'. Bands of Hope and Temperance Societies for all age groups mushroomed, sometimes with individual memberships of 500 and more.

There was no religious organisation in Reading which attacked or failed to encourage this area of work after the mid-nineteenth century. This universal embrace is of some significance. Bands of Hope confirm what will be suggested later about the fragmentation of age-groups, the affinity of religious organisations for hierarchical disciplining movements, and the felt need to capture youth as it moved beyond the tentacles of Sunday School. But the temperance movement went interestingly against a trend which will also be highlighted in Chapter Six. Whereas in other activities it was the pattern that churches and chapels lost some of the impulse behind what they were doing to pan-town agencies (e.g. in sport, literary and educational work, or YMCAs), as far as temperance was concerned the Reading Temperance Society felt itself to be losing out to dynamic local groupings attached to churches and chapels.[36] They latched on to this work with unusual alacrity and vigour.

What kind of movement was it? Temperance work was of great contemporary social concern. Politicians and moralists talked about it.[37] It was held to be relevant to urgent facts about the wider social and economic scene. And yet it was interpreted and received into the penumbra of churches and chapels in Reading as a particular type of activity. Temperance was a moral question, a matter for individual decision and self-discipline supported by participatory groupings with regular meetings and social activities. It was not a matter of political concern, in the full sense of the word political. The politics of the question was a matter of responding to and anticipating government intentions on Licensing legislation. The work, as interpreted in Reading, was not that of a pressure group primarily anxious to change political and social structure. It was a variegated cluster of organisations anxious to change individuals through collective association. 'By all the evidences appealing to human understanding this cause stands declared synonymous with the laws ordained of Heaven whereby God deigns to bless mankind.'[38] And yet 'we have never put the advocacy of Temperance legislation in the front rank of our activities', for 'the great function of the society is Moral Suasion'. They sought 'to avoid wherever possible the arena of politics'. From the 1870s onwards they accumulated (and published) 'satisfactory evidence of a religious and saving change having passed upon' many working men in the town. Redemption happened to some without joining the Society. But this was only second best, for the change was not complete until they showed others the way, through the Society: 'for we contend that the principles of self-preservation and of charity should never be separated, indeed they form the main pillars of the great cause in which we are engaged'. They were interested in 'that charity which teaches others how to help themselves'. And they had William Isaac Palmer as their 'almost model man'. For him systematic connections were obvious, for temperance was:

> like building an expensive sewer in a town at the expense of the
> inhabitants. It is of the greatest benefit to the town but all
> underground and not seen. . .but those engaged in it can see that
> happy homes are being made by the gradual spread of the practice

of temperance, which will ultimately bring about a condition of
things when many social evils, only abolished by reaching the homes
of the people, will be finally got rid of. . .If only we can do that I
care not much about the laws and regulations which may be
arranged by those who wish to reform by legislation.

A man who died rather than take medically recommended alcohol
became an early hero of the society — another model man. That was the
proper way to die, an inspiration to the movement, combined with a
maintenance of complete personal moral integrity. More of that type of
behaviour and the true society, or as near as you could get to it on
earth, would be brought closer.[39] Missions, consecrations, meetings,
outings, prayers — in these ways could it be said that 'temperance,
religion and purity were handmaidens and walked hand in hand' — not
in others.[40] It was on those terms that religious organisations allied
themselves with the temperance movement.

There was a curious tendency, as if by some natural law of growth,
for sub-organisations, if they were successful and grew to a certain size,
to acquire their own 'penumbra' (a phrase of Charles Booth's) of
sub-sub-organisations. So an Adult School, like the one in Sidmouth
Street (started May, 1905), in its first two years acquired a Savings
Bank, a Slate Club, a Benevolent Club, and other siblings where
'sympathy and brotherhood is fostered and encouraged'. Originally it
had been an agency of Trinity Chapel. The same chapel's Young
People's Institute (re-founded 1909) for 'providing wholesome
amusement and instruction for young people over the age of fifteen',
at the point where it had two hundred members, also had a Bible
School, a devotional section, a missionary and social services section, a
Guild section, and a recreation section. Such size implied building.
£250 had to be found for special rooms for the cluster of meetings.[41]
Quite other activities than the one originally pursued were taken up,
initially in order to further the original pursuit, but acquiring, in a
world of finite resources of energy, time and money, their own sapping
momentum. The process had a logic of its own. When at a meeting of
the Silver Street Fireside Club and Mission (founded 1884) a member
suggested that they should have a Rifle Range as one of their activities,
A.W. Sutton, their chief patron and activist, had to agree, 'of course
they must have one, or the men would go somewhere else for one'.
Thus easily could shooting become part of a mission.[42]

Growth was rapid. Attached to King's Road, the main Baptist chapel
in Reading, were at least forty sub-organisations. In March 1906 the

Vicar of St. Giles boasted of forty funds in his parish — all of which, except for the Clergy Fund, were at that date solvent. In one week in 1902-3 in the largest Primitive Methodist chapel in town, there were seventeen meetings to which a member/attender might go, or of which he or she might be a card-carrying member. Expectations came to be shaped by these meetings and associated forms of 'well-ordered activity'. Visiting, sewing, discussing, listening, teaching, abstaining, selling, reading, collecting, singing. . .these and much else besides, became expected parts of church or chapel life. A total and interlocking system of participatory organisations, all of which ideally involved forms of *joining* or continuous *attending* had become part of the self-definition of religion in the town. Active, committed, sustained participation in a range of organisations, some specialist and some inclusive, came to be a large and visible part of what religion was trying to generate in Reading during the second half of the nineteenth century.

There was even a common ambition towards comprehensiveness. 'The church', pleaded the pastor of Kings Road Baptist chapel in 1898, 'to fulfill its true aim should be able to take up each child in youth, manhood, business, family, old age, all through its career, and the church should have, in its life, work for and scope for men, women, children and families of all grades of life'.[43] On occasions the ideal appeared to have been met, as at St. Giles in the early twentieth century:

> the parish was working as a unit, with the church at the centre, well-staffed with priests and sisters, with the day and Sunday schools functioning well and followed up by the apprenticing of any child who showed ability, with Junior and Senior Guilds, where those who joined were taught to think for themselves and to speak for themselves, with full mission churches feeding the mother church and providing an outlet for the good works of those with means and charitable intentions, with organised interests in many directions, ranging from temperance to the mission field, there was something for all and a place for everyone, whether at St. Giles or at one of its mission centres.[44]

It was ambitious in the extreme, designed to relate to the outward-moving concentric circles of man, the home, the business, the town, the nation and, as if that was not enough, the world.[45] It was not so much, in intention, a question of what W.T. Stead called 'institutional sideshows'[46] but an effort to relate to and include man's whole life in society. And this at a time when obstacles to success in an effort of this kind were annually growing more formidable, not just for religious organisations, but for many other voluntary organisations which aimed to be rooted in the life of a locality.

Two levels of work were involved. On the one hand, work within the confines of the church or chapel was felt to need co-ordination. Some centre had to be provided, sometimes expensive bricks and mortar, sometimes an organisation from which all other siblings radiated, sometimes a magazine, sometimes the reiteration of the idea of coordination by a spokesman like the minister. The most usual name for the centre was the Institute. Where it took the form of a Hall, as in many Anglican churches, its sale, decay, or take-over by a commercial concern or branch of state welfare activity has provided the second half of the twentieth century with visual evidence of what has been happening to this aspect of society in the longer term. Over the years 1890-1914 great hopes and much commitment went into these projects, and in Reading they were almost universal for churches and chapels with an annual balance sheet above c. £250.[47] At St. Giles from 1904 onwards, the records were full of the need for a bigger building than St. Giles' Hall. For the vicar, such a project was 'an absolute necessity'; 'we cannot develop the social side of our work without it'; 'they could not effectively work the organisation of an enormous parish like St. Giles without some rallying point, some centre'.[48]

It was towards the level of the immediate urban environment, beyond the religious organisations themselves, that some of this unifying work for a total approach was directed. 'Something for all and a place for everyone' meant in aspiration precisely that: not just within the parish machine but for those outside as well. 'In the past', explained Sewell in the first number of the Broad Street *Magazine*,[49] 'the church was secret and concealed and for its own adherents'. Now 'external claims are recognised more and more at home and abroad. . .the claims of the thousands of our fellow citizens standing aloof from religious attachments of every kind. . .in these directions will be found the key to every one of our church activities, public services, Sunday School, Band of Hope, Christian Endeavour Society, Bible Classes, Pleasant Sunday Afternoon, and Pleasant Weekday Evening – all aim at the rallying of ourselves and others round the living Christ'. Chapels as well as churches strove to set up parochial visiting structures, expressing an obligation felt to the whole locality for the first time, in many cases. The danger of allowing any aspect of social life to be pursued away

from the umbrella of the local chapel appeared sharply to some
ministers, at precisely the time when much larger social changes beyond
the level of religious organisations made any such local aspiration a
desperate last throw. There was a danger, observed by the Rev. Albert
Swift, of 'regarding the social and recreative features (of life). . .as
something apart from the distinctively religious'.[50] For the Committee
of the Park Institute and Chapel in 1909,

> the principle has it that in such an organisation the church occupies
> a central place and no longer confines its attention to religious life
> alone but mother-like fosters all that is good and true in existence
> and becomes as a focus to which gathers all the mental, social and
> spiritual forces of a district.[51]

It was as if 'institutional churches' were attempting to become
microcosmic totalities, thus bravely harking back to a whole set of
aspirations and organisations in the wider society just at the time when
those aspirations were receiving a severe battering from larger social
forces. This outward-facing type of re-organisation was marginally less
common than the systematisation of internal church and chapel work
in Institutes, Guilds and Halls.

What religious organisations were trying to do did not, of course,
always coincide with what they were in fact doing. In any social system
purposeful actions have unintended consequences specific to a period
and shaped partly by contradictions in the system. Intentions are not
the same as functions, in relation to the particularities of Reading
society by *c.* 1890 or in relation to any other society. There may also
be a particular set of relationships between intention and function
which are special to religious organisations as opposed to any other
kind of organisation, rather than special to a system or to phases in the
development of a system.

But before opening such questions, caveats anticipated earlier must
be considered. What proportion of religious organisations in Reading
resembled the picture given above? Out of the eighty-three places of
worship available for use by the inhabitants of Reading at some time
during the period 1890 to 1914, I was only able to find records for
about forty.[52] Some of these were slight, supplemented by occasional
references in the press. Some were full to overflowing. But there is a
bias inherent in the sources. A small, detached sect without a penumbra,
without any professional mouthpiece and clerk − in the shape of a

priest – without any of the characteristics of religious organisation which are being stressed here, would be unlikely to leave a good trail for the social historian. The only reason, for example, for knowing of the existence of a group such as the Reading Agapemonites was that they were sufficiently freakish to attract press coverage, and because John Betjeman likes curious buildings.[53] Equally, a church which followed-through, theologically and organisationally, the assertion made at the laying of the foundation stone for a new Catholic church in Reading in 1905 – that 'the church was for God primarily and for the people only secondarily' – would not be so easy to cover as, say, the burst of activity following the Wesleyan Twentieth-Century Fund in the town. This book has probably compounded such intrinsic bias by concentrating upon local church/chapel rather than national, denominational 'headquarter' sources.

'Balloon-views' of the religious scene as a whole have dangers. To lump all seats and buildings together, then to express them as proportions of the total population, and to conclude that the groups with a high proportion were doing well and those with miniscule followings were doing badly, would be to misunderstand the very nature of some religious groups. An organisation which is small is not always doing worse than one which is big. Nor is a small organisation always intending to become a larger one, although the contextual pressures in some periods may be in that direction. Indeed a small organisation would frequently be failing in its own terms, to the extent that it grew in size beyond a certain point.[54] It was not because they were less 'successful' that the Particular Baptists, the Congregational Methodists, the Friends, the Plymouth Brethren and others, had seats for a smaller proportion of Reading's population than did, say, the Anglicans. It was because they were a different type of organisation. Clearly, the Synagogue in Reading did not expect the whole town to be converted to its beliefs or to attend Sabbath services. It was a building *of* a specified number of families in the town rather than *for* the entire population. Nor did the Psychical Society when it started its Sunday services and its evening discussions in April 1906 expect, even in the long term, that the whole town would or should become adherents.[55] The Zoar Street Particular Baptists could not have remained the kind of body their minutes show them trying to be – self-governing, exercising control over the conduct and beliefs of members, watchful of permanent priesthoods – had they grown much larger. They were as concerned to exclude as to include. By contrast, when the Salvation Army started their campaign in a railway shed, then founded Corps in temporary buildings at the West and East ends of town, and finally acquired a main-street Citadel early in the twentieth century, their ambition probably was to convert and involve all who were not already deeply committed to a parallel path.

Attempts to measure religion by a common yardstick like numbers of adherents or seats to total population arise from an attitude to religion in society which has become common, perhaps even predominant, later in the twentieth century. It is a 'supplier's' attitude, based on the organisation of religious provision *for* the maximum number from a centre at the lowest common denominator of commitment. To the extent that it predominates, it eventually creates the need for its opposite, in the form of sects. Its nearest parallel is that of the species of multiple retailer which was starting to become important from the 1880s onwards in Britain. Speed of turnover per inch of shelf-space was the preoccupation, rather than range of choice, quality of goods, or the quality of the experience of shopping, or the type of community encouraged. The impact of such developments on Huntley and Palmers will be discussed later. Such retailing developments also eventually create the need for their opposite, the health food shop, the delicatessen, and boutique sects. The question is: how relevant is this syndrome to pre-1914 Reading?

By no means every church or chapel aspired to the machinery described above. On the other hand, there were, for example, no Anglican churches which rejected diverse institutional apparatus on principle. There was a common ministerial attitude that, 'the steady plodding work of our great historic church is that which will tell in the long run, as it has done all through the centuries of its existence. Although there may be less novelty in its methods than in some modern movements, there is no stagnation and although there may be less excitement, there is more genuine growth'.[56] Some district or mission churches were seen as an agency rather than a full church, and had a limited range of groups attached to them. Some churches (like Holy Trinity or St. Mary's Episcopal) did not have parochial responsibilities, and did not feel obliged to have their territory completely covered by District Visitors.

Churches with a less full range of organisations around them did seem in this period to be on the way to acquiring a fuller one, rather than deliberately forswearing such work. For example, early in the life of St. Luke's in the late 1870s, they only had services, a Sunday School, a Children's Service, a school for religious instruction on Saturday mornings, a Choir and Mission support groups. Activity was still closely clustered around the worshipping life of the church. But they were aware that 'the district is still increasing and there is abundant scope for more organised church work'. By 1910 there was a Church of England Temperance Society, a Church of England Men's Society, a St. Luke's Men's Club, a series of Saturday concerts, a Church Lads' Brigade, a Choral Society, a Girls' Friendly Society, Missionary services and a Hall. Among Baptist and Congregational chapels were to be found the most developed organisations of all. In one chapel of the Wesleyan circuit and one of the Primitive, fully fledged organisational life was present. It is not clear, especially in the case of the two inner-urban (Cumberland Road and Oxford Road) Primitive Methodist chapels whether absence of much surrounding apparatus was because they were too poor to sustain such work, or because they were the type of organisation not to want it. The latter was the case with the Strict Baptist chapels, and probably with the Brethren. A denomination such as the Primitives which had not been surrounded by 'more organised church work' before, came to be so in the second half of the nineteenth century.[57] A denomination which was quintessentially so – the Salvation Army – with its bands and myriad groupings for different age-groups, was the product of the period. In terms of the kind of agencies they had, the chapels of the major denominations were increasingly coming to resemble one another. Deliberate decision was necessary to avoid this tendency. A week's programme in a major chapel of one, looked very much the same in another. Increasingly the actual organisations were the same, being branches of organisations with their headquarters beyond the confines of a single church or even (as with Christian Endeavour) beyond the bounds of a single nation. The scale varied with the geographical and socio-economic location of the church and with its age, but the scatter was remarkably similar across denominations.[58] Similarly, in matters such as architectural style and size of buildings there was more variation within than between denominations. It was not contrary to the nature of late nineteenth-century Baptism, Congregationalism, Presbyterianism, Primitive Methodism, Wesleyanism, or Roman Catholicism in Reading to have buildings like those of the larger Anglican churches – even if only one in each case.[59]

The historian is warned by local sources from time to time that 'there may be a success which figures do not represent, a spiritual harvest of which the Church Book can give no account', or that 'we have never liked statistics as a test of religious progress'.[60] But in spite of these warnings, and in spite of the tantalising intermittency of

surviving statistical records, and their intractability as far as easy
conclusions are concerned, what was noticeable in late nineteenth-
century Reading was the readiness, even eagerness, of churches and
chapels to evaluate their progress in terms of figures. This was a more
central characteristic of religion in Reading at the time than
commitment to any 'spiritual harvest of which the Church Book can
give no account'. It was a characteristic which grew upon itself. As
agencies were started to reinforce or recruit for more central activities,
so those central activities themselves came more to resemble the
agencies. As a Methodist from outside Reading put it in 1900, referring
to the 'higher place' and 'responsible duty' discharged by statistics,
'they are the criteria of our corporate strength, and our spiritual
condition. We allow them to exercise considerable dominion over us,
and are elated or depressed according as they are favourable or
otherwise'.[61]

When the Rev. Sewell of Broad Street Congregational chapel
emphasised 'external claims' and 'the claims of the thousands of our
fellow citizens standing aloof from religious attachments of every kind'
as 'the key to every one of our church activities' in 1893, he may have
been right for his own dynamic chapel. But to say that it was only 'in
the past' that the church was 'for its own adherents' was exaggerated as
a blanket judgment of religious organisations in late nineteenth-century
Reading. Even though religious organisations collected the wide
penumbra of joinable, participatory agencies described above they did
not always want 'members unlimited' in the worshipping part of the
chapel of one looked very much the same in another. Increasingly the
have been to fend off social groups who were, consciously or
unconsciously, not wanted too near the centre of the sun.

A curate in St. Mary's parish recalled his time there thus:

> I preached at All Saints, very wrongly and presumptuously as
> curates sometimes do, advocating the free sitting. I was very properly
> directed to the vicar by a kind old gentleman, a friend of mine, who
> heard the sermon and the vicar very properly took me to task over
> it. It made a little stir among the congregation at the time, and not
> in my favour. A sententious remark of the verger upon the matter
> was merely 'You can't mix oil and water!' It is curious that such
> bitterness of feeling can be aroused over the monopoly of a sitting in
> church; it seems in this case to be the better the place the worse the
> feeling.[62]

'You can't mix oil and water!' might have been a 'sententious remark' for a verger to have made in such a deferential parish organisation, but it is one whose bearing on the meaning of membership of churches and chapels merits exploration.

The opinion of the verger would have been shared for instance by members and officials of the Reading Athenaeum, a Literary Institution turned social club to be discussed later. They would not have expected or wanted the whole town, or varying social strata, or indeed many more of the social stratum for whom the club existed, to have joined. A few more members of the existing type would have helped to pay the bills and fill out the rooms, but that was all. The social historian would waste his time asking why the working classes, or why the inhabitants of Tilehurst, or why a 'significant' proportion of the inter-censal percentage increase of population in the town, were not joining the Athenaeum. 'You can't mix oil and water', any more than you would be well advised to follow those whom Gulliver met trying to turn sunbeams into cucumbers. How far was this also true of churches and chapels?

One clear difference between dominant types of religious organisation and, say, the Reading Athenaeum in this period was that, whereas nobody in the Athenaeum was *advocating* the addition of water to oil (at least after the Athenaeum had become a social club[63]) somebody was at St. Mary's. The presumptuous curate was, after all, as much flesh and blood as the verger. There was not the tension between a wider 'public' and 'the congregation' in the Athenaeum minute books, which characterised religious records and activities of the period.

Religious organisations at minimum felt that they *ought* to be concerned with numbers unlimited at this time. At local and denominational levels there was a remarkable degree of self-criticism and active argument about directions of development. They were not, for the most part, *merely* places where status could be comfortably and discreetly enjoyed, in a way which simplistic functional interpretation might suggest. Nor were they, for that matter, places where a distinctive way of life (that of Christ) was practised or a distinctive creed deepened and disseminated, disregarding market-appeal as Christ did. Nor were individual churches or chapels which aggressively wished to convert the whole world to their own particular message or organisation characteristic of the religious landscape of Reading during this period.

There was a concern with means, to an end which was primarily defined in terms of attracting a wider and larger circle towards

participation in organisational life. There were contradictions stemming
from the pursuit of such an end in the surrounding social circumstances,
and flowing from the particular means favoured. There was a tendency
for the means to displace deeper ends. There was also a tendency to
anticipate or to adopt means, like 'attractive' packaging, or breaking up
consumers into endless class-specific, sex-specific or age-specific targets,
which might be appropriate for organisations in other subject-areas, but
which posed problems for religious organisations.

A wholesale switch to organisational modes more characteristic of
the twentieth century had not, however, been made before 1914.
There were signs of pressures in this direction, but also of resistance to
them. Balloon-views of the religious scene as a whole rather than as
seen from below, from the perspective of a single sect or church;
alteration or dilution of the product to achieve mass sales;
rationalisation of organisation into merged super-denominations
expressing centrally the lowest common denominator of their
constituent local units; allowing the medium to determine, as well as to
convey the message. . . ,such modes were beginning to be used as
yardsticks for judging 'success', but they were not yet predominant. In
many ways the Salvation Army anticipated such modes, although
particular focus upon this organisation nationally would modify such a
judgment with resistances and counter-tendencies. Other denominations
with a particular tilt towards the working class were aware of pressures
to make quantity an enemy of quality, and knew how the conditions of
the contemporary market might contradict what they wanted to
provide.[64]

Characteristic forms of religious organisation in Reading during this
period carried with them our rash curate's sensitivity about 'monopoly',
and his hesitant grope towards openness. They worked in a competitive,
but federal framework. Evidence from Anderson Baptist church in
Earley and from Caversham Free church to be used in Chapter Five,
will suggest that whenever a direct choice was posed, such chapels gave
precedence to, and saw the interests of Christianity in a neighbourhood
in terms of their own particular organisation and its advancement.
Inter-denominational rivalry was a spur to church building, in the same
way that inter-unit competition within the biscuit factory was a spur to
production during the second half of the nineteenth century. Yet there
were moves through the Free Church Council (founded in 1897), not
towards merger and rationalisation in the twentieth-century business or
super-denominational sense, but towards assignment of territory to
different denominations. The Federation was more of a treaty for

reasons of local and national group interest than a preparation for amalgamation. There was the ambition to fit into an informally federated set of religious and other voluntary organisations, each of which had their own distinctive commitments but which, together, represented a federal ambition towards universal participation. In this perspective, different denominations, different buildings, different ministers, different beliefs and practices, different constituencies, different voluntary organisations, had their own roles to play, but none should seek to colonise or ultimately to absorb the others.

There were many ways in which federal competitiveness, which was characteristic of business as well as religious organisation during this period, expressed itself.[65] Thus, ministers from the whole range of denominations frequently appeared on common platforms at pan-town events. In spite of his feeling 'shut out', George Palmer appeared at Anglican consecrations and gave land for St. Bartholomew's; William Isaac contributed towards building the synagogue; Walter Palmer went to Primitive Methodist occasions, and so on. It was not within the terms of reference of the Reading Athenaeum to absorb or make redundant the Reading YMCA; nor did Huntley and Palmers rush to take over biscuit factories in the town, or to 'cut up' the trade nationally; nor did chapels wish to drive each other out of existence, any more than Heelas, the new local retail-revolution department store, expected *all* the shopping in town to gravitate towards it − although part of the novelty of this type of late nineteenth-century business enterprise lay precisely in its proximity to this aim.

In Reading, no final answers can be given on the chronology of this difficult area of openness or exclusivity, but suggestions arise from the evidence of the period. At this point discussion will be confined to matters directly bearing upon the worshipping life of the churches, such as membership and pew rents, rather than on sub-agencies. There was a wide range of meanings attached to membership of churches and chapels, varying from the extreme exclusiveness of the Agapemonites to the extreme inclusiveness of some Anglican churches. At one end of the spectrum, the Agapemonites were attacked for 'advocating' the separation of husband and wife, at the other end, St. Giles Church Board could find no firmer qualification for membership in 1866 than that 'all churchmen belonging to the Congregations of St. Giles and St. Stephens be members'.[66] In some chapels, like the Unitarian, the formulation of unifying principles clearly implied limitation to a certain type of person with a degree of experience in other religious groups which could not be very widely shared amongst the inhabitants at large.[67] In others, such formulations were explicitly designed to be minimal, to define the lowest common denominator rather than the highest common factor.

The nature and degree of commitment differed widely even within the chapels of a single denomination. When Park Institute Congregational church came together in 1906 their language was instrumental, showing that they had clearly in mind a public whom they were going to 'serve'. Every member entered into a covenant to work 'to the utmost of my power for the benefit of our fellow men' and signified assent to minimal theological propositions: 'I agree that the common ground of our belief is the Headship of Christ as the spiritual foundation of our whole life, and the value of the Bible as a record of the Grace of God.' Even such an Institute, when it opened in 1907, was said to be specifically for 'shop assistants, elementary school teachers, clerks, living-in clerks'. It was left to Ambrose Shepherd, who had earlier described his own congregation at Trinity Congregational chapel as consisting of 'a large number of those who are usually denominated the upper middle class', and who had been invited back for the opening of the Institute, to speak complainingly at the opening ceremony. He 'trusted also that it was meant for the working class'.[68] By contrast, Caversham Hill Congregational Church came into existence in 1855 to serve the needs of an existing body of worshippers. They agreed a number of resolutions which amounted to a full profession of theological faith, proclaiming the sinfulness of man, the gift of God's grace, the role of Christ as intercessor and their own 'duty and privilege to present to Him our bodies, souls and spirits a living sacrifice...devoutly praying for grace and wisdom to love one another, bear one another's burdens, maintain a consistent profession, honour the Lord Christ, and serve our generation according to His will, to whom be glory now and ever, Amen'.[69]

Elements other than theological were obviously at work, making it apparent to outsiders how far they were allowed on the grass of particular churches. As late in his career as 1891, George Palmer could tell a meeting of twenty Nonconformist congregations that he felt 'shut out from the Church of England by its extraordinary creed and rules. The people of that persuasion were careful to let him feel he was not one of themselves. He did not find that among Nonconformists'.[70] At the very least it can be said that what came through to some potential consumers of some churches and chapels was an emphasis that everyman and his wife were *not* in membership, rather than an aspiration to the reverse.

After all, the 'Hebraic' life of a church or chapel had considerable compensations for those inside it. The 'Hellenistic' perspectives of outside observers like Matthew Arnold, with his acid passages of irony in *Culture and Anarchy* (1869) on the 'Dorcas Societies and Tea Meetings' of Nonconformity; the anguish of observers like Mark Rutherford in his *Autobiography* (1881), with his failure to find social as well as theological meaning amongst Congregationalists and Unitarians; and the humour of fictional accounts by writers like H.G. Wells or R. Tressell, have surrounded this culture with a certain disdain, snobbery and metropolitan patronisation of provincial life. But exclusiveness and localness carried with it a comfortable sense of being included and belonging. Many organising jobs to be done carried with them a sense of responsibility. A round of meetings and activities in a tight sub-community could bolster a sense of security, respectability, social place and improvement in an economically and socially shifting world.[71] Later the contradictions involved in this kind of religious organisation in that kind of society will be emphasised. At this point it should be said that they were contradictions only from a certain point of view. If one purpose was to give comfort, first aid and buttresses to those already involved, then such satisfactions must have been achieved for many members.

One of the most elaborately documented of churches, St. John's, warned the listener to the *Annual Address* of 1891, and hence the historian, how 'much work is going on which cannot be classified under any of those things which are here recorded'. Organisations, funds, workers and services were not all they wished to be judged by. There are many warnings in the records against judging the 'real' work by the 'machinery' – a word being used to describe religious, as much as it was coming to be used to describe political, organisations in the second half of the nineteenth century. After all, even the most elaborate machinery was remembered occasionally as being preparative to 'the Lord's coming'. 'Our membership has now reached 142', recorded the St. John's Church of England Temperance Society in 1904, 'but we long to have many more joining us, so that at the Lord's coming a people may be found prepared for Him in Godliness, Righteousness, and Soberness'.[72] Beneath the main organisational matter of this chapter, oddly moving moments in the life of a chapel occasionally surface, and should be taken as representative of much about the quality of personal experience of religious life which will not be chronicled here.

For example, a fifteen-year-old Sunday School boy belonging to the

Wesleyan Church, Lower Caversham, died in 1890:

> The School and Society here has just sustained a loss through the
> removal by death of one of the most promising lads in the school
> ...William Day was fifteen years of age, and one of a large family
> whose parents are Godly people...two years ago...during some
> special divine services, he, with several other lads in the school got
> soundly converted to God. He has since that time been a good,
> devoted, and promising young Christian. His teacher reports that he
> had a very marked influence for good over the other lads in the
> class. He frequently prayed in the Teachers' Prayer meetings (to
> which older scholars are always invited) also in the Society prayer
> meetings, and always prayed for his classmates. During a fortnight's
> illness he suffered greatly. And when told of his critical condition he
> said he was not afraid to die, as he was going to Jesus. His last
> utterances were the first line of hymn 310 (Scholars' Book) 'Lead
> me to Jesus', and 'Mother they are coming they are coming' and
> then he passed sweetly away. He worked in a factory among many
> ungodly lads who persecuted him very much at times. They however
> sent a wreath to be placed on the coffin, and have several of them
> since been to William's parents, expressing sorrow for their
> treatment, saying they never knew him to return anything but kind
> words. On Wednesday last the remains were taken to the chapel,
> born by members of the Junior Society class, prior to interment in
> the cemetery, where a very impressive short service was conducted
> by the Rev. W. Hirst...Many friends and scholars were present and
> were moved to tears during the address. At the grave the hymn 'Lead
> me to Jesus' was sung by request...[73]

Or again, a church worker called Miss Gay retired from full-time work
for Hosier Street Congregational Methodists in January 1901. She
wrote a letter to the chapel saying:

> I do appreciate reference made to any service I have been permitted
> to render, and sacrifice I have been able to make in connexion with
> the church at Hosier Street. It has been a joy, I may say the joy of
> my life, not unmixed with deep sorrow. That the work has been
> clumsily and stupidly done and has I fear often been trying to my
> friends I am fully aware...But such as I could give I have given
> heartily as would the Lord, and I earnestly pray that the future of
> the church may be altogether better than the past.[74]

Pew rents meant that, while attendance in some part of the buildings
was possible for the non-paying public on most occasions, the feeling
of full participation in many churches and chapels was difficult of
access. At St. Lawrence's Anglican church in 1894-5, 'persons requiring
sittings in the church are requested to apply by letter to the church
wardens'. At Wycliffe Baptist church in May 1898, 'it is getting difficult
to find unallotted sittings for friends wishing to become regular
attendants'. At the Synagogue the *Rules* stated that 'each member shall
be allotted seats. . .for himself and his wife according to the amount of
his contributions provided that the said member shall have paid not
less than four monthly contributions'.[75] Even where seats were not
rented they could be 'appropriated' for money to a specific person or
family, as at Christ Church Whitley in 1903, or even at the working-class
mission church of St. Stephen's until 1909. A new creation of the
period such as Caversham Heights Methodist church had seat rents from
its inception. There is no sign in the records of any debate about the
matter at all. The first five seats from the pulpit cost two shillings per
sitting, the rest three shillings. A reduction could be made to families
taking four or more sittings. 'Stewards may put strangers into any pew
after 10.55 in the morning and after 6.25 in the evening'.[76] Another
new creation, the Baptist chapel at Earley, had seat rents in August
1910, but when 'the somewhat delicate question of sittings was. . .dealt
with by the pastor' that year, the Stewards were exhorted to exercise
'a little gumption, judgment and good taste in not excluding people by
ownership of seats'.[77] At least the issue was not taken for granted in
that chapel.

Even where rents had been abolished, other forms of payment had
to be substituted. Either a mother church had to subsidise its offspring
in a poorer quarter of town, albeit complainingly, or a regular envelope
system of 'free-will offerings' had to be instituted, or fund-raising by
bazaar had to become a necessary part of church activity, or central
denominational or diocesan funds had to be tapped in order to rescue
congregations from hopeless debt. In 1914 St. Mary's church was freed,
but the vicar wrote that 'we should like it to be clearly understood that
all those who have already had seats appropriated will be undisturbed in
their possession'. In that parish half the seats in the richer churches
(St. Mary's and All Saints) but none of the seats in the poorer two
(St. Saviour's and St. Mark's) were appropriated. St. Bartholomew's in
January 1899 aimed at paying for church expenses out of collections.
Amongst Nonconformist chapels, the 'envelope system' was the most
common alternative to rents. At Grovelands Baptist chapel the

allocation of seats even under the envelope system, which they introduced when they formed themselves into a church in October 1899, was according to seniority of membership in the Chapel. Only at specially designated services, such as the Peoples' Services started in August 1903, was the allocation of seats for specific individuals lifted. It is interesting that amongst the Primitive Methodists, it was not only the large London Street headquarters which had seat rents – so did Oxford Road, a small and poor chapel.

This raises a fundamental aspect of the contextual situation of religious and other organisations in the period. Unless they were to be clients of a richer 'Vice-Presidential' stratum, which was becoming increasingly difficult between 1890 and 1914, or unless they could make a profit or become an agency of the State, organisations which wished to be *of* the working class and have control of their operations 'from below' had a limited range of options. Seat rents were more, not less, necessary for them than they were for religious organisations with a richer clientele. The only alternative was total reliance on a national denominational machine, unless the bold decision was taken to axe all high-cost items (buildings, priests, schools, a penumbra of agencies). Seat rents (which were hard to afford) were the equivalent for religious organisations of the gate money that football clubs needed to survive as organisations *of* the working class in any sense. Thus London Street Primitive Methodists relied on seat rents for £83 out of a total income of £171 in 1901-2, £79 out of £177 in 1902-3, and £78 out of £167 in 1903-4. At this stage they were running at an annual deficit of about £50 p.a. In 1900-01 they were proud that they had raised £500, since 'in considering the church and all its various agencies it must be borne in mind that its membership is made up of the working classes. . .There are no wealthy members associated with it'. No rich Reading outsiders helped by then, as they had done thirty years before.

The situation was clearly spelled out in an article on 'Chapel Affairs and the Conference of 1890' in the Primitive Methodist national denominational magazine. In this article Thomas Mitchell not only clarified the problem but anticipated many of the contradictions and ways out which will be examined in Reading in subsequent chapters.

Seat rents were, he observed, declining, even where congregations were not. Competitors were getting rid of them altogether, and 'it can hardly be doubted that the tendency of modern ecclesiastical methods is against rather than in favour of the perpetuation of seat-rents'. Primitives would have to face the fact that 'although the time has not yet come', it would come – the time when all seats would be free even in their denomination. Debts were also increasing. At the end of each of the last few decades the burdens had frighteningly increased. 'This increase was caused by an enormous outlay in new erections, and erections of a much larger and more costly type than we had built formerly. . .many of our most pressing trust difficulties of today are traceable to the excessive, and not always wise, building activity of that period' (1871-1880). Moreover, individual chapels were suffering from the death or removal of wealthier supporters.

So what was to be done? Aggressive spiritual work was suffering, since 'our energies were absorbed and our attention to spiritual work diverted, by burdens of debt'. One way out was to start a Connexional Chapel Fund, for making grants to local Trusts in difficulty. This could be raised by individual donations, profits from the Book-room and Insurance Company of the denomination, and by richer areas helping poorer. But something else was needed in a situation where debts 'often deter people from attending our services and joining our Communion'.

The Conference accepted a 'bold and comprehensive' business way out. A Chapel Aid Association 'warranted an immediate commencement of business'. This was to be a company, for investment like any other. The company would make loans to local Trusts, although 'it cannot lend to trustees who are unable to pay their way'. A Liverpool businessman (W.P. Hartley) was to help the company. Smaller shareholders were to be encouraged by the fact that 'the interest allowed — 3% up to £20, and 3½% above £20 — is more than is given at the Post Office Savings Bank, or at any ordinary bank; so that whilst surrendering no part of their remuneration from such investments, indeed, while increasing it, our own people may help forward a worthy Connexional enterprise'.[78]

No clear overall direction of change was discernible in the matter of how many seats in churches and chapels were marked and owned by particular individuals and families in Reading between 1890 and 1914. Opposite moves were made. New chapels with pew rents (in the case of Grovelands Baptists a change to rents after other systems had been tried in 1910) as well as moves to liberate churches and chapels entirely from appropriation, were evident. Perhaps the tendency to free seats was marginally stronger than the uncritical adoption of this mode: but not overwhelmingly so. No statistics as to the relative number of free seats in 1890 and 1914 are available. But even if the facts of change were ambiguous, the *idea* of religious organisations as being ideally 'free and open' was gaining ground. The idea that they *should* become the kind of organisations which were not firmly *of* a set of people who had paid, but also belonged to a public, and were in the business of attracting that public, was frequently expressed in our period. After debate at St. Mary's in 1914 'we have all agreed that our ideal should be a free and open church'.[79] It was thought right that at least some services should be open in many chapels – like the People's Services at Grovelands. 'As a matter of principle', in St. John's parish, 'where the majority of seats in the parish church are lettable no one can deny that it is only right that the District church should be absolutely free, so that the poorest shall have an equal chance with the richest of the best seats'. So the mission church of St. Stephen's was freed in 1900. Even Zoar, the tightest sect in Reading for which any first-hand evidence has been found, took a decision for the first time in October 1896 to allow empty seats to be given to the public when the service began. Such a change demanded a discussion and a self-conscious decision; it was not self-evident that even part of your ecclesiastical activity should be open in this way. A conscious decision had to be taken to become that type of organisation, and for Zoar to take it implied some wider cultural pressures.

As with pew rents, so with the quality and degree of commitment involved in membership of churches and chapels it is difficult to be confident about any overall direction of change in the late nineteenth century. There were certainly efforts at tightening and deepening the implications of belonging. Visitation was a device frequently discussed, and efforts were made by many chapels to improve its quality and regularity. Even in a chapel like Carey, trying to be as open as possible within Baptism, prospective members were to be visited by two members and had to write or relate their experiences of God to the church before being accepted. The same was true of Kings Road in 1905. At Park Chapel (Congregationalist) joining involved visitation by one member, and then election by the chapel. At Trinity Congregational church the process was slightly more elaborate: you had to communicate personally or by letter with the minister. The minister then told the deacons, and interviewed the applicant himself. You were then nominated at a church meeting and elected or not elected. At Hosier Street there were two grades of membership – full membership and 'communicant' status. Before the latter, visitation was made by two members, and only after a year could the progression to membership be made. As with Methodist chapels and their Covenant meetings, so too at Hosier Street, a strengthening device was the periodic reading of the Trust Deed of 1872 setting out the beliefs and

Articles of Faith of the congregation.

Methodist preoccupation with the Class Meeting — 'perhaps the most precious as it is certainly the most distinctive inheritance of Methodism' — is a good index of changing meanings of membership. Little evidence — itself significant — has been found in Reading for the existence, let alone the dynamism, of the Class system. But national preoccupation in the denominational press was intense.

It was estimated in 1900 that at least one-third of Wesleyan members did not attend Classes, which were the basic disciplinary and devotional means of the church. In some Societies within Primitive Methodism there were no Classes at all. People were not being removed from registers for non-attendance, and Class membership as a qualification had in practice been abandoned. The ratio of attenders to members in Wesleyan chapels was increasing greatly (the spectator as opposed to the participatory mode). 'It is useless to say that this is due to the fact that our conditions of church membership are more rigorous and exigent, because as a matter of fact, whatever the theory, they are not'.

Conflicting imperatives were expressed. On the one hand the situation was a scandal. There was a need for 'better fewer but better' emphases, over against dilution and the penetration of secular modes. If the Class system was not used 'some other means would have had to be devised for testing. . .the continued desire and fitness for membership of the church, unless all church discipline was to be frankly abandoned'. On the other hand there were pressures towards openness if ever the church was to be fully *of* the working class. Yet even laxity acted in favour of the privileged. 'Men who have influence in the Church and are sought out for office are much more easily retained in Church membership although they do not attend a Class meeting, than is the labourer or the poor woman who, burdened with the cares of her family, can seldom attend either a week-night or a Sunday service'. There was also Christian feeling against exclusiveness, which could easily degenerate into wet liberality,

The conditions of Church membership are laid down for all time and for all Churches in the New Testament. No man may add to them or take away from them. If a man conform to these conditions, not even the Wesleyan Conference. . .is entitled to exact any other condition from him in order that he may enter upon the rights and duties of church membership. The most unjust and cruel thing is to tell such a man that if he will not conform to the practice of Methodism he had better go somewhere else.[80]

The Friends, of all groups in Reading, were the most continually concerned with actions and discussions and organisations to deepen the quality of commitment and degree of common subscription to the attitudes and beliefs of the group.[81] There was continual attention paid to the instruction of the young in specifically Quaker beliefs and attitudes. The Library at the Meeting House figured more prominently in the life of the denomination than did similar collections of books attached to other churches and chapels (e.g. the minister's library in the vestry of Trinity Congregational). Investigations of potential members were minute and careful, membership being seen as a privilege demanding a corresponding obligation. Common subscription to certain principles of business and social conduct, and common assent to resolutions about world and national affairs were held to be important. Only Hosier Street Congregational Methodists and Zoar showed concern for a similar type of solidarity amongst the membership. In August 1894 a monthly meeting for religious instruction in the principles of the Friends was inaugurated; in November 1897 a preparative meeting for those not in membership but in regular attendance began. In 1905 the core of vocal members suggested that they themselves should have extra meetings for fellowship and prayer.

Changes in practice in this area and continual attention to it, like sermons on usury in the period studied by R.H. Tawney, may be taken as evidence either way. They could mean a trend towards closer solidarity, 'better fewer but better', or they could mean a trend in the opposite direction which continually had to be resisted, only to reassert itself as each effort to resist was exhausted. In only two chapels do the records include a definite statement as to long-term direction. The minister of Broad Street (J. Wilding) in the early 1960s was of the opinion that membership had ceased to mean very much in a disciplinary and common doctrinal sense after the early 1870s.[82] It is rare to find instances of actual expulsion, or the definition of the position of a congregation over against single members of it or applicants to it, in any denomination at this time.[83]

The meaning of membership was a live issue, at the top of the consciousness of many ministers and activists, especially in Baptist chapels. In some cases, this involved a deliberate and self-conscious opening up of membership which previously had been regarded as more exclusive. At Grovelands in 1887, 'it was determined. . .that the only condition of membership should be conversion to God evidenced by a godly character and life'. Early in the life of the chapel, Carey Baptists decided by a majority of twenty-nine to seven that 'the Lord's

Table should be open to all Christians'.[84] At Caversham Free Church
they were conscious of a certain slackness which might be involved, but
chose deliberately not to make any conditions like the writing of letters,
the declaration of faith, or the visitation.[85] The rationale for chairs in
the place of pews in Elm Park Methodist Hall was to give the appearance
of greater accessibility. At Zoar there was intermittent argument in the
Minutes for less exclusivity, both in theology and in social relations. At
Anderson after a long debate in 1910 they decided to become more
open, the pastor, W.C. King, arguing both that the test of Baptism was
unscriptural, and that they could do better work if they were to 'throw
our arms around these friends admitting them as members without
immersion'. The *idea* of openness in order to attract the maximum
number who were within range was certainly gaining ground, even if
alongside actual moves towards such a posture there were some
opposite moves (which will be examined later) towards a tighter, more
cohesive, more inturned and more exclusive type of religious belonging.

It would be foolish to miss the fact that one of the things organised
religion was doing, as part of its embeddedness in late nineteenth-century
Reading society, was simply being there, as part of the furniture. This
was remarked upon endlessly by observers, in relation to the variety and
presence of religious buildings. 'Churches and chapels often rank(ed)
amongst the principal objects of interest in a town', for Guide Books,
local newspapers and Directories.[86] Smith's *Directory* for 1896 described
the growing suburb of Caversham thus,

> a new church has recently been erected at Lower Caversham,
> dedicated to St. John the Baptist. It is built of bathstone and faced
> flint, in the modern style, with red tiled roof. . .The parish also
> possesses several charities, a fine Congregational and Baptist chapel
> (called the Free Church) built in 1872, and also a small Wesleyan
> chapel. A police station and sessions house have been erected. The
> district is under the supervision of its own Urban District Council.
> The cemetery, laid out in 1885, is near Hemdean Road and is under
> the control of the UDC.

What more could a place want?
   The furniture melted into the building itself. Religious organisations
and their spokesmen were to be found blessing, legitimising, propping
up or running along behind, most of the organisations and events in the
culture. Whether at the opening of the new Town Hall, or the beginning

of a Council meeting inside the Town Hall, or at the celebrations in honour of the sixty years of Queen Victoria's reign, the civic chaplaincy role was willingly accepted both by Nonconformists and by Anglicans.[87] It was quite in keeping that before the Jubilee 'in accordance with a resolution adopted by the council the Mayor has issued an exhortation to all persons resident in the borough to attend some place of worship on this day (Sunday June 20th) to offer thanksgiving to Almighty God for national blessings during Her Majesty's reign'. The day would have been incomplete without such an exhortation. The role was not only accepted, it was eagerly competed for. It was an event of great importance, or rather it was treated as such, when the Mayor, Owen Ridley, visited Trinity chapel in his full mace and regalia in 1894.[88] The last time a Mayor had so dignified a Nonconformist chapel was 1869. The privilege of having a chaplain of your faith in attendance at the workhouse was vigorously sought after. Anglicans were also in attendance at the extremely harsh Prison and at the Hospital, in an official capacity. Being 'in attendance' at whatever went on, but not using that opportunity for any fundamental or even mildly critical challenge in the name of your beliefs, was a part of what religious spokesmen were seen to be doing at this time.

There is some evidence that when the building shook, churches were filled more than usual. For example the death of Queen Victoria packed St. Lawrence's, St. Giles, and St. Mary's in February 1901. The Primitive Methodist chapels were also reported as having been unusually full. At St. Stephen's, 'in the evening the church was crowded, almost the whole congregation being attired in mourning, although largely composed of the working classes'.[89] Edward VII's illness and death was reported as having had a similar effect. So did the sinking of the Titanic — 'did they not notice that it was easier to worship on the Sunday following the Titanic disaster which drew all people towards religion'.[90]

Ministers and religious buildings also had more concrete relations with the aspirations and organisations of Reading society. Religious plant, in the shape of halls and meeting rooms, played an essential role in such a society. Churches and chapels were larger suppliers, and more local suppliers, of such premises than all other suppliers put together, with the possible exception of pubs. Large businesses, or for example Suttons' Abbey Institute (1880), or the Biscuit Factory Recreation Club rooms, the municipality, political clubs, the Ancient Order of Foresters, the Coop., the Temperance Society and pubs all had places available for groups to congregate. The business mode of supplying halls had been tried in 1876 with the establishment of the Victoria Hall

Company (capital £3,000) to provide a lecture hall, club room and meeting place for the population at the Eastern end of the town.[91] But such provisions would not have been sufficient by themselves. Anyone who has tried in the recent past to book rooms at the ward or parish level of British cities will know how, as other suppliers refuse, change their character or cease to exist, churches still remain important in this physical sense — although they too are selling up (or out) fast.

Ministers were even more omnipresent than buildings in voluntary life. Although the absolute increase in numbers of ministers between 1890 and 1914 barely kept pace with population or with numbers of separate congregations, it did not matter in this context.[92] Precisely because their jobs beyond a certain area were undefined, clergy had time to create a presence in a town out of proportion to their numbers and not dependent upon any particular ratio per church or per head of population. Ministers were well-educated, often energetic, zealous and only partly contained by the chapels or denominations which paid them. A tithe, at least, of their time was uncommitted. When A.J. Davies left Carey chapel in 1908 after seven years' work in Reading it was said that, 'he has so established himself not only in the affections of his church, but also in the warmest regard of all sorts and conditions of people in the town that the rumour of his approaching departure is causing widespread regret...among...political and social movements...and any cause which would tend to the betterment of the people'.[93] The least that can be said is that had ministers and paid officials of churches and chapels *not* been there, a wide range of voluntary organisations would have had to look much harder for activists and committee members.[94] In groups, ministers attempted to exert collective influence. The most obvious example of this was the Free Church Federation. But less formal groupings were also significant. When Fidler offered Prospect Park to the Corporation for sale, their first impulse was to refuse to buy it. There then came into being an 'Open Spaces Society' to change their mind. On the Executive Committee sat at least three reverends and at a town's meeting which they organised, seven more sat on the platform. One of them, Canon Ducat, was busy at the same time pressing for Municipal Tramways and for a Corporation Infectious Diseases Hospital.[95] Clergy were natural leaders for deputations to the council, such as the one which the vicar of St. Giles led in 1904 presenting a petition on the unsatisfactory condition of Silver Street.[96] A lone clergyman, still more a small grouping such as the Christian Social Union, had a presence in the town disproportionate to their formal following. That this possibility was under-exploited should not be taken to mean that it was not exploited at all. Indeed the role of clergymen as prime movers in organisations, even where they later withdrew or were overtaken, is a theme worthy of wider exploration in nineteenth-century social history.[97]

4 PRODUCTION

This chapter will concentrate on Huntley and Palmers' biscuit factory, and consequent conditions in Reading in the late nineteenth and early twentieth centuries.[1] In relation to the emphases so far given and to what will follow, the factory was of strategic importance — not only because of its dominating position in the local economy. Understanding the particular nature of Huntley and Palmers will help, first, to give further flesh to the bones of Reading society *c.*1890 — in other words to the context in which religious aspiration and organisation had to operate. Religious organisations have to be understood partly in terms of the surrounding social context, and the nature of Reading society has to be understood partly through the large presence and specific quality of its churches and chapels.

In the case of the biscuit factory, there is something of this double optic also. But in its heyday it was an organisation more determining than determined by its local context. During the 1890s the factory's experience was increasingly shaped by forces outside the town, beyond its immediate control; forces which were of importance in the experience of many other organisations in the town not directly involved with production. Through the biscuit factory it may also be possible to identify contradictions in Reading society, taken as an example of an industrial capitalist seat of production. Such contradictions shaped the experience of churches and chapels — what they could or could not be or do, what would result from what they did — as much as did the dignified aspirations of Reading society outlined in Chapter Two.

Unique as an institution. . .by far the largest of its kind in the world. Order, precision, exactitude pervade its various departments and ramifications. The visitor is at a loss what to admire most — the mechanical and structural appliances of the factory, or the arrangements everywhere visible for the comfort and good order of the work people. The firm evidently look upon their employees not as mere human machines capable of so much work but as men and women, endowed with moral and spiritual natures and capabilities. Ample provision is made for their intellectual and religious instruction and in every aspect the firm of Huntley and Palmers is a

89

model one in which the antagonism too prevalent between capital
and labour appears to be quite unknown.[2]

One can hardly imagine an industry more happily placed than the
biscuit factory at Reading. Both are more or less like each other. The
town has a pleasant healthful atmosphere. It is clean and looks
prosperous. The Thames and the adjacent meadows give it an air of
holiday. . .The biscuit factory is a town within a town. It is a series
of buildings, connected with each other by bridge and passageways.
The river Kennet flows through it and helps to make it picturesque.
You enter the works from the King's Road. Within the portals you
realise at once that you are in the presence of a well-disciplined
establishment. Nothing that you see is likely to discount in your
estimation the popularity of the biscuit. . .Touching that same
atmosphere of Biscuit Town, it is never oppressive, and it is always
clean. . .All the time our path is over iron-sheeted ways, lined with
shining rails, along which small trucks are being propelled by
cheery-looking labourers who are conveying stores to the mixers.
We also encounter similarly engaged white-aproned men with shining
buckets of milk, in which yokes of eggs are floating, giving the
mixture a most rich appearance.[3]

Such quotations, of which there are innumerable examples, present a
pretty picture. They also present a problem. The idea the biscuit
factory had of itself, the ways it struck contemporary observers, and.
some unfamiliar features of its actual organisation, have to be taken
seriously. And yet a delicate path has to be trodden between
understanding the factory during the 'Partnership Era' (1841-98) on
its own terms, and remembering what T.A.B. Corley has tactfully
called the 'less than complete generosity over wages', the long hours,
and the intermittently ruthless and always paternal industrial relations
which also characterised it. As statements and actions by Palmers are
used to convey what they believed, and as such statements and actions
are not dismissed as rhetorical gestures masking sinister intentions, the
enormous profits accumulated by the partners out of the labour of
their underpaid 'hands' should be borne in mind. On a turnover of
£1,486,800 in 1910-11 the company made a net profit of £242,100.
That was the largest net profit in any single year before 1914 but profit
figures as a proportion of turnover were, to say the least, personally
satisfactory for pre-1914 partners or shareholders.[4] They make
shocking reading set beside the statistics of A.L. Bowley on Reading

conditions which will be set out later. During the nineteenth century the main ingredient for biscuits, flour, accounted for over a third of total costs. Wages accounted for less than ten per cent.

But the realities of exploitation in what almost amounted to a sweated industry should not obscure the very particular character the factory had from the 1850s to the mid-1890s and to a diminishing extent thereafter. The continuity of capitalist social relations and their capacity to survive should not obscure real changes in their forms, and hence in the experience of living through them, over relatively short periods of time. Admiring observers romanticised the cleanliness, order and cheerfulness of the factory: low wages, long and monotonous work were forgotten.[5] Nevertheless, whatever the whole experience of being a worker in the Reading biscuit factory was during the second half of the nineteenth century, part of that experience was membership of a now unfamiliar version of industrial community. The factory in the Partnership Era (under the first Palmer generation until 1874, and then gradually admitting the second who were in sole command by the early 1890s) had six major characteristics of importance to the argument here. The more recent the point of comparison, the more distinct each of these characteristics becomes. The factory was unlike modern companies and unlike what it is now. But in many ways it echoed other organisations, including institutional churches, and resembled the town of Reading itself in this phase of its history.

First, Huntley and Palmers was departmentalised in a special sense. The firm was a whole, 'a town within a town'.[6] Overall, there was a powerful sense of purpose expressed, at this time, in terms of the product and the morality of the organisation rather than in terms of profitability. But the firm consisted of a federation of departments which were themselves like smaller totalities. Departments were distinct, as were the different factories — the North Factory, the South Factory, etc. — of which the complex was composed. Members of one department were not allowed to go into any other, anymore than boys of a single House in some Public Schools are allowed into another. Whole processes were not allowed to go into any other, any more than boys of a single House in some public schools are allowed into another. Whole processes units, along with departments for many other trades which nowadays would not be on the same site or on the same pay roll.[7] Division of labour between different units had not proceeded as far as it would later, any more than division of labour between organisations in subject-areas other than production (entertainment, religion, education, etc). Smaller interlocking totalities were as yet commoner than larger, specialised, single-subject organisations. The 'long range of offices and counting houses belonging to the export department' were part of 'a business kept entirely distinct in every way from the executive offices on the ground floor at the entrance of the factory'.[8] Continental export was separate from export to the rest of the world: even packing and invoicing for the Continent and the world were kept apart. Departments were fiefs controlled by individual partners and managers: the family Directors took the chair at Board level in random order, until attempts at rationalisation were made after 1904. Departmental loyalties within an overall family unity stretched beyond work. They were expressed in annual events of the Reading Working Mens' Regatta when, for example, the Sugar Wafer Factory would row against the Engineering Department. The analogy with the public school, used earlier with reference to the whole town, again suggests itself. Such occasions, with rivalry reinforcing unity, resembled the annual ritual of House matches.

Integration was real partly because the whole enterprise was concentrated in a single place. This local focus was a second major distinguishing characteristic of the factory. It was manifested in a variety of ways. George Palmer lived locally and walked to work. The factory invented, made and maintained much of its own equipment, from desks to ovens. It owned its railway locomotives; even the fire-fighting apparatus was made within the factory.[9] National centres of decision-making, whether in trade union offices, State bureaucracies, or merged company headquarters were resisted. Local producers of raw materials from honey to flour were deliberately helped, even though the firm rapidly came to need more than the contiguous area could supply. The Victorian notion of the virtue accruing from business eggs being in a single basket was expressed in the fact that the Partners resisted outside financial and business commitments, except in the case of a single Directorship of the Great Western Railway Company. Unlimited liability led to unlimited local commitment spilling over far beyond manufacture. It also delayed the later contraction in the number of separate foci for concentrated commitment of business and other loyalties. The factory was only the largest among a whole cluster of organisations in this period, from chapels to the Reading Philanthropic Society, to the Temperance Society and to other businesses, which aspired to be a nexus for a whole range of commitments beyond their own formal goals. The dream was of a set of overlapping local totalities, each voluntarily linked to others. It was not until 1918, for example, that Huntley, Boorne and Stevens, the exclusive tin suppliers for the factory, lost their independence and passed into Huntley and Palmers' ownership. H.O. Serpells co-existed peacefully in Reading as an independent biscuit firm from 1851 until closure in 1959. The economic penalties of such a federalist local focus were later to become severe in the context of twentieth-century competition. As with other partnership strengths, this one had its corresponding later weakness.

Thirdly, there were senses in which Huntley and Palmers was a family firm beyond the obvious one that it was owned and controlled by Palmers. From a late nineteenth-century perspective the firm had literally grown within living memory. This applied not only to the locally visible life-times of Palmers, but also to the life-times of lesser breeds within the firm. Fathers and sons were common at many levels of responsibility. A major family event in any family, the funeral, was paid for by the company. Workers went to Palmer funerals; Palmers went to selected workers' funerals. Rites of passage in the life of the Palmer family and in the life of the firm were celebrated collectively in ways which would become unthinkable well before the mid-twentieth century.

G.W. Palmer's (1851-1913) twenty-first birthday provided the factory with a typical occasion for a celebration, which took place at The Acacias – the home of his father, George Palmer. Two to three thousand men were invited to tea; 'Kiss in the Ring' and 'many other rustic sports were indulged in', and 'dancing was kept up with much spirit', out of doors. Then a manager, himself the son of a manager, Mr Charles Brown, made a presentation to the young heir 'earnestly hoping' that he would be a worthy successor 'not only as a man of business but also in the personal worth of character which has distinguished each of them'. George Palmer made co-operation the theme of his speech, beginning 'Ladies and Gentlemen and fellow cooperatives in the Reading biscuit factory'. Mr Brown had referred in his speech to a previous party in the factory twenty-two years before when George Palmer had himself brought home a wife. George mentioned that day too, and estimated that one in ten of those present had been there twenty years before. Long continuity of service was indeed continually stressed at the factory in the nineteenth century. In 1881 it was estimated that one in twelve had served in the factory for more than twenty years. In 1898 it was one in ten and in 1913, according to a letter in the *Daily Mail*, it was as high as one in three. Co-operation had been, for George, the key to success, 'a co-operation with as little which jars upon our social nature as will be found in any establishment existing'. He thought of himself, he said, as just one among all the co-operatives in the factory. His brother Samuel then spoke saying that 'while our workmen as a body serve us well, it is our wish to meet their wishes in every respect; and I only hope that in any point that possibly may arise in a large concern like this, that they will at once agree upon what their grievance is and the remedy, and lay it plainly before us, and I am sure that there will be every readiness on our part to meet their wishes'. For long after, the firm continued to resist trade union modes of 'grievance procedure'.

Typically, William Isaac was more personal and anguished in his speech, feeling heavily 'the great many responsibilities' of the work. 'There is a fear that either our example or our conduct in some way should be the means of placing others in a false position. I felt that more strongly perhaps this evening when I saw our people streaming in here for more than one hour. I felt that to be connected with an establishment of such magnitude involved a large amount of responsibility which will make us all the more anxious to do all we can to secure the happiness, success and prosperity of those by whom we are surrounded.' He 'looked forward to meetings like this bringing us all together and making us feel one together in our efforts to create success in our weekly and daily business'.[10]

William Isaac's personal anxieties and commitments always came through more strongly than did those of other Palmers on the many occasions like this in the life of the mid- to late nineteenth-century factory. There was also a detectably greater bond between him and other ranks in the factory and town. Another similar event was the betrothal in February 1881 of one of Samuel Palmer's four sons. Even though Samuel worked in the London office a great factory meeting was held. Samuel marvelled at 'how entirely we curve in and dovetail one interest with the other'. George William, Alfred (1852-1936), Walter (1858-1910) and Charles (1860-1937) also spoke, but none of them in response to 'deafening calls and plaudits again and again renewed' as there were for William Isaac,

I feel that the choice he has made will be another addition to the happiness of our family and that you will share in that enjoyment when the future Mrs Palmer comes down on occasions similar to these, joining with you in any entertainment you may have. We have, as you all know, one great difficulty occasioned by the large numbers of hands which we employ. And so, if we cannot always do all we should like to do you must bear this in mind. . .And remember we are all passing along in life in one wide family, some richer and some poorer — and after all, the rich have their troubles as well as the poor — and as we pass along we may all do something to make life a little easier and happier for others. Then when our time comes we may find we have lived for some good purpose. . .although there may at times be little differences amongst us we can agree to help each other forward.. .[11]

It was not for long in the history of production in Reading that occasions like this would happen in anything other than a transparently perfunctory sense, nor was it for long that such a language survived even in a debased rhetorical form. While it did, it figured in the local press not as something extraordinary, but as representative of much else in the culture besides the biscuit factory. However inadequate he was in the face of total social conditions, it was a specific type of factory which turned a worker (John Holder), who joined the works before 1850, first into 'a kind of unofficial almoner' and then an official sick visitor and temperance missionary (1871-83). He was 'a genius in practical philanthropy'.[12] At his death 10,000 people were at the cemetery, plus three carriages of Palmers and twenty heads of departments and foremen at the factory.[13] 'The constant occupation of visiting the poor, the intemperate, the sick. . .had made him familiar with the great mass of the poorer inhabitants.' Another early worker in the factory, J.R. Moore, who joined the firm in 1847, ended up before he died in 1896 as head of the North manufacturing department. He was a Baptist, on the executive of the Reading Liberal Association, an active member of the Biscuit Factory Cricket Club. Between four and five thousand people turned out for his funeral, part of the factory was closed, and 500 workers preceded the corpse in procession to the cemetery. Four Palmers came, two sent apologies. The sermon by the Kings Road Baptist minister both described what Moore represented, and showed how that could no longer be taken for granted by the year 1896:

His one life gathered up in itself the business history and human memory of 50 years growth of a great industry. . .(how great his power was). . .for the creation of that good feeling between worker and manager and between worker and master which makes all the difference between content and discontent and between good work and bad.. . .the spirit of the worker must always influence his work and therefore that manager who wins the esteem of his masters in his own way and in the place where the great Taskmaster has set him, helps to advance that true Kingdom of God and of man which are

ever more one Kingdom. And in these days when the necessary
trend of business is to the massing of capital and therefore of labour
in one place the need is the greater for just such men as Mr Moore
has been, who shall keep alive as far as possible those more human
feelings between servant and master without which work is apt to
feel like slavery and masterhood like tyranny. Such men prevent
money being the only nexus between worker and his master; they
make us feel that even yet in business 'a man may be more precious
than gold'.[14]

A fourth characteristic of the factory, in that phase of the 'fifty years'
growth of a great industry', was that it was not a discreet commercial
operation separated from the rest of personal and local life. This can be
illustrated through the Palmer family, through further events in the life
of the factory and through organisations in or stemming from the
factory.

William Isaac Palmer (1824-93), for example, was important in the
explosive economic growth of the factory. But he did not define himself
primarily as a business man. The product was more important to him
than productivity or than the rate of return on capital invested. Indeed
the first Wages and Tonnages book, which would have allowed such
calculations to shape decisions about, for example, how many varieties
of biscuits should be made, was not introduced until mid-1903, some
years after the first Palmer generation had handed over. William Isaac
was proud that the Palmers had 'left the producing industry'
(agriculture), only because they had done so 'to take up the
manufacturing of a useful and beneficent article for the great mass of
the people'.[15] His concern for the 'great mass' was not expressed mainly
in mass terms. When he was at home there would be 15 to 20 people
outside his house every day at 9 a.m. 'all wanting advice, money, or aid
of some kind'.[16] Besides his work in the town hall movement (1879-82),
he was President of the Temperance Society, active in the Mechanics'
Institute, prime mover behind West Street Hall (1862), President of the
Extension College, Chairman of the Free Library, President of the
Sunday School Union, an active Liberal and Home Ruler, founder of
the Help Myself Society, founder of the Reading Working Lads'
Association, Chairman of the Reading and District Gardening
Association. . .and so on. These commitments were not honorific: they
involved attending meetings on a regular weekly basis, meetings for
which Palmer prepared by praying as well as by filling his wallet.[17]
When he died his assets were valued at the relatively small sum of

£123,000. His benefactions and promises for the future were found to exceed this figure, so the rest of the family had to honour them. William Isaac was being unduly modest when he told a Pleasant Sunday Afternoon meeting in 1892 that 'he felt it was always the duty of those who·had the pleasure of being in any shape leaders of the people among whom they lived to obtain some knowledge of the public work that was being done for the good of their fellows in their own towns'. He had an active obsession with such work. At the Temperance Society meeting after his funeral in 1893 (another pan-town event, at which 'thousands were visibly affected') a friend told how 'self-repression was the keynote of Mr Palmer's life. . .he sympathised with suffering wherever he found it, but at times, when he was depressed, almost wished he was a poor man in order to escape the responsibility of the wealth that bore him down'.[18]

Events in the life of the factory were intended to be as improving as William Isaac wanted his life to be. Thus, when new buildings were opened in November 1873 there was 'a monster tea and entertainment' in the factory to which four thousand workers and their families were invited. The entertainments were organised by the Royal Polytechnic Institute, and resembled the Reithian conception of the BBC. There were eight different shows in different departments of the factory, ranging from Light Programme dances and variety, to Home Service drama, to Third Programme lectures and scientific demonstrations.[19] Participation was more immediate in the absence of radio – although there was a hint of the future when an electric signal conveyed simultaneously to every room brought the celebrations to an end at 10pm. On a more regular basis, leisure, welfare and educational needs were partially met through annual excursions, organisations such as the factory Mutual Improvement Society (1854-), the Recreation Club (1898-), the Sick Fund (1849-1911), the Penny Bank (1868-1903), the Temperance Band and the Reading Working Men's Regatta. There was even a school-master in the factory during the 1860s, paid £40 per annum. To the Sick Fund, 'all hands are required to contribute according to the amount of their wages. This is disbursed to any who need it on the recommendation of the medical attendant who is elected by the men themselves'. At the end of the year the surplus was divided amongst all. 'The amount actually contributed is but trifling whilst the system avoids the injury to the men's spirit of independence.'[20] Non-contributory pensions were paid to employees after fifty years service. Features of the factory such as *Rules* which went beyond regulating conduct directly relevant to productive work, and days such as the summer morning in 1914 when 7,000 people left Reading station for the seaside, recall a society as foreign to the modern factory and town as the 400-plus varieties of biscuits which were being manufactured in 1900.[21]

The final two characteristics were closely related. First, there was a heavy emphasis upon durability, expressed not only in long-service figures for labour, but also in fixed capital. Alfred Palmer's (1852-1936) loving attitude towards his machinery in the Engineering Department was expressed in his naming of the three generating machines he installed in 1882, 1899 and 1908, 'Alice', 'Phyllis' and 'Betty', after his wife, daughter and granddaughter. No wonder the firm of valuers which reported on the firm early in the twentieth century complained that too much effort went into maintaining and retaining old machinery. Ovens installed in 1873 were still in use in 1905, in spite of considerable technological improvements being made by specialist suppliers outside Reading. A hand roller for stamping the names on biscuits used when there were eight employees in the factory was still in regular use in 1931. The biscuits themselves were also built to last. The reception room, where I worked on the company records, displayed a biscuit from the days of the Crimea. Biscuits were wholesaled, for some time after cheap packets had come into vogue, in large lined boxes or tins. These were technically excellent but commercially inconvenient in twentieth-century retailing contexts. The coloured Christmas tins which were a speciality of the firm, and which may now be bought in antique shops, were not 'packaging' in the modern sense. The package itself was designed to last and be useful in its own right, rather than to draw the hand to the supermarket shelf only to be thrown away soon after.

This emphasis upon durability went with a long-sustained commitment to manufacturing an exceptionally wide range and high quality of biscuits. Criteria like relative cost of production and relative rate of sale were subordinated to an obvious pride in what the firm could make. There were other commitments to think of too. Not for long after 1884, for example, would the pressure of a man like the Rev. V.H. Moyle be responded to, and yet the response was characteristic of the firm at that time. Moyle came from nearby Burghfield, and was Honorary Secretary of the Berkshire Beekeepers' Association. He wanted to foster the cottage industry of beekeeping; so the firm introduced a complicated novelty called Honey Drops, with a proportion of honey guaranteed in each one. 'These biscuits have been made to meet the views of benevolent persons who are anxious to create markets for honey produced in cottage gardens.'[22] At this period

in the history of the firm, advertising was not regarded as being
desirable on any scale. The most acceptable form of advertising was the
product itself; a sample of biscuits was given to first-class rail passengers
leaving Paddington station. The priority was to express 'moral rectitude'
rather than economic rationality, to 'play fair and not cut up the trade'.[23]
Cheapness in the interests of a larger turnover was, to a fault, ignored.
Neither did they reap the full cash benefits of their attitudes. Through
the nineteenth century the firm 'adjusted prices almost entirely
according to changes in ingredients'. They passed on savings in costs to
the customer even at times when they need not have done so, 'since
demand remained almost embarrassingly buoyant'.[24]

Huntley and Palmers was a Victorian success story. Like other such
Reading success stories, it was portrayed at the time as a model or
pattern.[25] But it is not difficult for the modern reader to guess that its
very first-generation success contained germs of later difficulties.

Even in its partnership days, the firm exemplified a fundamental
contradiction relevant to the situation of many other quite different
organisations in the town, including churches and chapels. It is in the
nature of business organisations to tend to go for numbers unlimited,
unless profits can be increased in other ways. Such a tendency is not so
marked a feature of voluntary organisations in subject-areas such as
religion, although in particular periods, as we have seen in Reading,
organisations in these areas may come to resemble business
organisations in this respect. They may even try to get numbers
unlimited by imitating or anticipating business modes.[26] In partnership
days, however, Huntley and Palmers had reasons other than profit for
going for numbers unlimited. These reasons were akin to those of
churches and chapels. The factory was, after all, producing something
good. The product was often defended in moral terms. Biscuits were 'a
useful and beneficient article'; they were being manufactured in
wholesome ways, in a wholesome organisation which itself expressed
many of the best aspirations of the society. For William Isaac Palmer it
was essential that the whole enterprise should be as expressive of moral
worth as the workmanship on the Town Hall. So he was pleased with
what he was making, 'for the great mass of the people'.[27]

The contradiction was, of course, that 'the great mass of the people'
could not possibly consume the products of the factory. The biscuits
were indeed a quality product, which was the justification for producing
them. But they were being produced in a system (of which Huntley and
Palmers was not just a reflection but a leading element) in which quality

(like voting) was out of the reach of the largest quantity of people. Real wages went up during the phase of maximum growth of the factory, perhaps doubling between 1857 and 1899. During most of the 'Great Depression' Reading did relatively well.[28] But for long after this, quality biscuits were not 'articles of general consumption'. They did not become so through free business development either. It was the State which made them generally available through war-time subsidies and rationing.[29] Huntley and Palmers did not help the situation in their own locality, since they paid particularly low wages. Workers in the factory consumed their product only by gift. They took home one pound of broken biscuits each per week. These were also the terms upon which the generality could consume the predominant forms of religious organisation in the same period. Moreover, in the same way that religious organisations worsened their situation by what they did, what the company did towards the end of the nineteenth century — by persisting with some of the older features of the factory — served to make the contradiction sharper. Relative costs went up, meaning that the product became still less accessible as real wages stopped rising in the early twentieth century.

Elsewhere in the biscuit industry, competitors reacted to new working-class purchasing power in the late nineteenth century, by operating in ways radically opposed to Huntley and Palmers. Even before a cheap biscuit industry had developed very far, quality manufacturers like Peak Freans had begun to outstrip Huntley and Palmers.[30] In a changed context, it was no more possible for the biscuit factory to grow in the forms it had assumed than it was possible for churches and chapels, the Royal Berkshire Hospital, Football Clubs, and many other organisations to flourish on older terms during the twentieth century. Some of the principal pressures on voluntary organisations in the new context can be identified through the experience of Huntley and Palmers which was a cause as well as an index of the changing context.

The Co-operative Wholesale Society's works at Crumpsall (Manchester) were pioneers in the cheap biscuit trade from 1873 onwards.[31] The conditions for success in this trade were as follows: fewer and cheaper varieties, manufactured in rationalised plants in long runs on the most automated machines available, regardless of where they were made; a poorer quality of product, in terms of ingredients, packaging, durability and quality control; intense advertising in focussed campaigns, not sample or goodwill advertising; guaranteed outlets in multiple retail stores tied to manufacturers; willingness to cut prices in order to 'cut up the trade'; and willingness to manufacture in more than one place, wherever the cheapest labour was available. Firms which met such conditions began to reach a large consuming public during the twentieth century, but on new terms.

As the terms changed, Huntley and Palmers was bound to undergo strain. In one year alone (1927), thirty-four family grocers who had between them bought almost £9,000 worth of Reading biscuits were absorbed by chains which switched almost all of their trade to other manufacturers. When a top executive at Huntley and Palmers recommended that the firm buy automatic plants made by Vicars, like those used by cheaper competitors, the response of the Executive Committee was that the machines 'will not make Huntley and Palmers biscuits; only the rubbish turned out by the cheap people'. So a great part of the twentieth-century story is of how the firm 'stood aloof from these far-reaching developments in the industry it had done so much to create'.[32]

What alternatives had they? To explore alternatives leads into speculation about what did not happen, but may also serve to clarify types of choice which faced many other organisations in the same changing context. The firm could, first, have stripped assets, gone out of business, sold out to other companies, or used their capital to do something else somewhere else. Companies in other industries were doing this in the late nineteenth century. The Reading firm had offers, including two from the United States. Urban churches in the mid-twentieth century have of course been doing precisely this on a large scale. They could, secondly, have taken what might be called a sectarian line. They could, in theory, have gone on making the kinds of product they wanted to make in the kind of organisation they wanted to run, not worrying self-consciously about a market. If viable at all in twentieth-century conditions, this would have led eventually to contraction into the delicatessen sects. Or they could, finally, have adapted completely and speedily to the new context.

This last alternative would have been to deny much of what the firm in the partnership era stood for. It would have been to sell out, for example, to new forms of retailing and thus to change the relationship between the factory, the product and the consumer. The family grocer on whom Huntley and Palmers relied in the partnership days, like so many of the organisations flourishing in the same period, aspired to provide a wide variety of goods under a single, local umbrella of service and quality. Depth of satisfaction (necessarily but not intentionally for the few) was aimed at, with consequent customer loyalty.[33] Shopping was a slower experience in which consumer and owner actively participated. The multiples — Sainsburys, Greigs, Liptons, the Home and Colonial, the Maypole Dairy — were centralised organisations, vertically integrated (some with their own biscuit factories) rather than integrated into a single locality.[34] They were interested in cheaper goods, in speed of turnover per inch of shelf space. They wanted fewer, quicker-selling varieties. The number of shoppers was more important than the degree or range of satisfactions achieved by any single shopper.

To adapt would also have meant taking the radical advice of the valuers who visited the factory in 1905 in order to remove what the official historian has called 'unmistakable signs of inefficiency' around that date.[35] Machinery would have had to be tended less, discarded sooner and be replaced from outside. Lines would have had to be reduced. Departmentalism and consequent bureaucratic accretion would have had to be axed. Amalgamation would have had to be welcomed earlier, instead of being resisted.[36] Marketing methods would have had to be changed through advertising, and so on.

What actually happened after incorporation as a limited liability company in 1898 was slow adaptation through the exigencies of circumstance. Such a course was partly determined by the very commitment to and investment in earlier forms, but also by the impossibility of continuing with them in changing economic and social circumstances. The contradictions imposed by the adaptation were symbolised in the fact that, in order to supply at least some of the cheap market, Huntley and Palmers deliberately used to break up good stock and sell it as broken biscuits. The family withdrew from total, as opposed to cash, commitments to the factory and locality. The culture of the factory changed, in terms of events and organisations. Francis Hackett, a clerk who joined the works in 1859, remembered the internal life of the factory as being quite different in his younger days from what it had become by 1919. He attributed the change to technology, especially in the means of communication.[37] An event as important as the centenary of the firm, wrongly celebrated four years late in 1926, was utterly different from G.W. Palmer's birthday party, or earlier celebrations of factory extensions.[38] The main event was not held in the factory, or at a Palmer home; fewer workers came; speeches were nothing like earlier direct conversations between the family and their 'co-operatives'. Long before this a few machines had begun to be imported, for example, for making chocolate biscuits. Management was slowly routinised and centralised. Packaging was hesitantly adapted, and advertising expenditure increased.[39]

One of the most important agencies of change in the longer term was the State. Its impact is important to trace since it was a key contextual factor in the experience of many other organisations in Reading. So far as the biscuit factory was concerned, the impact of the State was mediated later in the twentieth century through war. World war offered an entirely novel role for a business of this kind. During both wars the company became, in part, a direct manufacturing agency for the State. In the 1914-18 War they made shell-cases as well as biscuits on contract. For a time in August 1914 the wives of three Executive Committee members even turned part of the factory into a kind of Dorcas Society, to make clothes for employees who had gone to war or for their dependents. Full-time work soon returned, however, and world war proved to be quite a favourable economic experience for the firm. Through the enforced planning and Food Control of both wars, the factory was brought into active alliance, and eventually merger, with other biscuit companies which it had previously resisted. Individual Palmers became 'industrial statesmen', rather than local entrepreneurs and activists. They became intimately involved with government as well as with the industry generally. Industrial relations were also slowly nationalised, although, even after trade unions were embraced by management (c. 1915), continued efforts were made to keep negotiations inside the factory as much as possible. In the end, it was the 1939-45 War which rationalised production, by cutting down the number of lines and the number of workers.

Before 1914 the role of the State as a variable shaping the experience and nature of the factory was also evident. When bakehouses were to be brought within the scope of factory legislation through the Factories and Workshops Bill in 1877, Huntley and Palmers were willing for once to act in conjunction with six other firms to press amendments on the Home Secretary. National Insurance legislation ended the factory-based Sick Fund and its Committee in 1911. Its replacement, a committee of eight members to advise management on welfare questions, was an important link in the chain which was to lead to bases for independent bargaining by workers in national organisations in the middle of World War I. The threat of intervention through the Trade Boards Act of 1909 was a factor in proposed improvements of wages and hours in 1914. Increased taxation, especially the estate duty of 1894, was a major impelling factor behind the decision of Huntley and Palmers, like many other such companies, to change to limited liability in 1898.[40]

By the 1960s, the firm was in almost every respect different from what it had been in the partnership days. A transformation had

occurred as complete as that of any other organisation, voluntary or
otherwise, in Reading, even if the continuity of the name, location and
products of the factory made the transformation less evident to citizens
at large than were changes in other subject-areas for organisation.
Tonnage of production was up, but the varieties of biscuits produced
drastically down (40 in 1968, compared to the old 400). Six varieties of
biscuit accounted for half the home turnover in 1968. The labour force
was one-fifth of what it had been at its largest. Huntley and Palmers
had become a fully-owned subsidiary of The Associated Biscuit
Manufacturers Ltd. (1958). Internal and external (beyond Reading)
rationalisation of production and centralisation of executive control
had proceeded a long way. Overseas links had been forged, to create a
set of international companies. Marketing methods had been transformed
through advertising and retailing concentration — in 1968 over twelve
per cent of home trade was going to four multiple retailers. Machinery
was being supplied by international specialist companies. All the
paraphernalia of industrial consultancy, market research, business-school
executives and mass production were fully present. Palmers still worked
in the company at the highest levels, but they no longer controlled it.
Old attitudes of paternalism, local patriotism, departmentalism, factory
and product loyalties were explicitly attacked. The companies in the
combine were to be seen as 'tools, or fixed capital investments which
were required to produce so much profit for shareholders'. Language
which William Isaac Palmer would have deplored, had he understood it,
had become the new 'laws by which the business game should be
played'.[41]

The twentieth-century form of capitalist economy in Britain was no
more to be a multiplication of Huntley and Palmers in their partnership
form peacefully embracing a mass market, than the twentieth-century
form of society in Britain was to be the aspirations and organisations
described in Chapter Two (including churches), fully realised and with the
working class included. Powerful agencies were at work, detectable in many
subject-areas for organisation, ensuring that such a direction could not
be taken. These agencies included the altering presence of the State,
new forms of business organisation (as in the cheap biscuit industry)
and the penetration of business modes into new areas such as leisure
and communications. The experience of the biscuit factory, or religious
organisations, football clubs, the Hospital, the Worker's Educational
Association and many other organisations in Reading cannot be
understood without these central facts.

At the beginning of the chapter mention was made of a double optic in relation to the biscuit factory. Contextual change has to be analysed through the factory as well as the factory through changes in the context. So far the factory has been used mainly as a possible analogy for understanding the nature and experience of organisations in other subject-areas. It has been seen as a register, or means of getting at the types of organisation and the agencies of change affecting its own experience as well as that of very different organisations.

There were at least two respects, however, in which the biscuit factory and its owners had decisive effects on voluntary organisations elsewhere. The first of these was that, from approximately the 1890s onwards, the relationship of the family to the factory and, above all, to the locality began to change. The change can be taken as a paradigm of a wider change in the relationship of the 'Vice-Presidential' stratum of the local bourgeoisie to the locality and local organisations. The Palmers were only the largest and richest of a cluster of middle-class men in Reading who taxed their time as well as their incomes in the interest of the voluntarist ideology and organisations, including churches and chapels, already described. When they, or their successors, no longer did so, their withdrawal was felt in detailed as well as in general ways. Thus it mattered to Mr Preston's Bible Class at the Reading YMCA, a class which lasted for more than thirty years, when Martin Hope Sutton (1815-1901) of the seed firm was no longer so available after 1890.[42] It mattered to the meetings of the Help Myself Society when they lost their 'mainstay and prop' in William Isaac Palmer. It is clear from the local press, particularly from obituaries, that the passing of a generation meant the passing of a whole local style of life.[43]

When the first generation of Palmers took time off from the factory, from the late 1850s onwards, they spent their time on political, temperance, educational, religious and other voluntary organisations in Reading. After all, 'leisure hours can best be disposed of by devoting them to public duties'. George Palmer became Liberal MP for Reading. He had strong localist feelings; 'in the year 1849 he with some kindred spirits resisted the attempt of Liberal leaders in London to impose a candidate on the constituency. . .no attempt has been made since that date (to 1897) to force a candidate on the constituency'. He did not hold the seat for all that time, but could say by the end of his life that 'for nearly forty years I have taken a more or less active part in every political contest which has occurred in Reading'. It was typical of the style of his concern that even an event like the annual meeting of the scholars of the British School took place at his home, and his wife regularly attended school outings. When opening Palmer Park in 1891, he made typical connections between what he was doing there and his other concerns for Reading society as a whole: 'well conducted playgrounds are a fitting sequel to the training of our public elementary schools. Play in the right proportions is as much a moral duty as work.' While George Palmer was still alive, a statue by a local sculptor was 'uncovered in his presence on the occasion of a popular demonstration in his honour'.[44] It remained in the middle of Broad Street until, with symbolic appropriateness, the needs of the motor car forced it out of the centre of town in 1928. When his son George William died in 1913, he was seen as having carried on Palmer traditions. He had been elected to the Town Council in 1882, and to the Mayoralty in 1888. In the presence of his father, G.W. said that 'he considered it to be their duty to do all they could to maintain municipal life, believing that the strength and progress of our nation rested. . .on the interest people took in the public life of the town and districts in which they lived'.[45] He too became Liberal MP for Reading, in 1892. But on a day such as the one in December 1902 when G.W. Palmer and the second generation Sutton of the seed firm unveiled a statue of Edward VII and received the freedom of the borough, there was nostalgia in the references to those who had gone before. M.J. Sutton was correct, as well as modest, when he said that he 'felt sure that it was not so much to him and for his career that they were bestowing the honour, as that of his father they wished to recognise'.[46]

After a £2,000 gift to the Hospital Improvement Fund in the same year a local paper wrote that 'members of the great Reading firm are scarcely less in touch with the necessities of the town now that in so many cases they reside far beyond its borders'.[47] That depended upon what was meant by 'in touch'. When the second generation took time off from the factory (only two directors were required to be in at any one time) they tended not to be in Reading.[48] There were huge Palmer donations to Reading University, particularly by Alfred (1852-1936), and commitments to individual organisations by individual Palmers such as that of Howard Palmer (1865-1923) to the Reading Athletic Club.[49] But centres of gravity were changing. Both William Isaac and George Palmer had bought land, but they were not country gentlemen in the sense that their successors became. There was a switch in the second generation from Quakerism to Anglicanism, from commercial education to public schools, from Liberalism to Conservatism (except for G.W.P.), from modest 'provincial' town life, to extravagant metropolitan or country life, from refusing State honours to accepting them.[50] Signs of

change smaller than the strategic one of the formation of a limited
liability company in 1898 were plentiful in the local press during the
1890s. 1891 was the last year of George Palmer's active Reading life. In
1892, an economistic town council defeated an improvement scheme,
based largely on voluntary financing, put forward by William Isaac. In
1893, William Isaac died. In the same year, Harry Quelch of the Social
Democratic Federation spoke to a crowded meeting of the
newly-formed Berkshire Agricultural and General Workers' Union in the
Reading Town Hall about how 'all personal relations between
manufacturers and the employed had ceased, they were simply "hands"
to make profits'. In 1894, G.W. Palmer came under strong attack for
the first time at a local election meeting in Redlands ward. In 1895 he
lost a general election to a Unionist. In 1896 he finally left his Reading
home for his country seat. In 1897 it was noted in the *Reading Observer*
that W.H. Palmer was absent for the first time from Reading station, to
see off the fifth annual train excursion of the biscuit factory in the
early morning. In 1898, he told the Athletic Club that he was resigning
from active participation because 'he did feel that the gentleman who
held the position of Captain, Hon. Treasurer and Chairman of the club
should live in Reading. . .since he left Reading he found it difficult to
attend all the meetings'. It was not until a few years later, in April 1905,
that Alfred Palmer's resignation marked the severance of the Palmer
connection with the Society of Friends in Reading. But links had been
weakening for some time before.

Parallel with the withdrawal of middle-class leaders from the local
scene, there was a decline in working-class deference or an increasing
articulation of working-class interests which will be traced more fully in
Chapter Ten. Labour relations in the factory began to take a more
antagonistic form than previously. One early sign of change was that
the Social Democratic Federation increased its recruitment in 1894 and
1895 when Huntley and Palmers fired two SDF members – one,
F.S. Barnes, for taking time off to serve on the Board of Guardians. A
period of unease culminated in the first-ever strike at the biscuit factory
in 1912 over sackings at Christmas time. The decreasing middle-class
presence in other organisations also created space for an open
assertion of egalitarian versions of voluntary action. Even if it was a
minority who expressed such views, they were bringing to the surface
an undercurrent of resistance to acceptance of the deferential version
of moral purpose offered in some organisations. They were also showing
the possibility of another direction of development which, although it
was later blocked, was not thereby hopelessly pursued at the time. It is

difficult to be confident about the extent of support for this alternative direction because there was a much more visible obstacle to participation; large numbers of the working class were simply too poor to join any voluntary organisation.

The second decisive effect of the biscuit factory on the context for organisations in Reading was that it was responsible for a considerable degree of absolute economic deprivation in the town. The importance of this poverty for the situation in which religious and other organisations had to work was compounded by the fact that it was at its worst in the first decade of the twentieth century — just at the time when the effects of the withdrawal of the active 'Vice-Presidential' stratum, and just before a major increase in the State's presence as an alternative patron were being felt (through Liberal legislation and war). The withdrawal diminished a crucial source of time and money 'from above', at a time when spare resources 'from below' were also drastically diminished.[51] It thereby restricted the freedom of manoeuvre of voluntary organisations needing resources of time and money; they had either to pull in their horns (the 'sectarian' alternative), or to appeal upwards towards national (denominational, etc.) structures, or sideways towards other localities (see the WEA in Chapter Nine), or to adapt in such a way as to raise smaller intermittent sums from larger numbers of consumers (see the Football Club in Chapter Seven), or to adapt by becoming agents of some other patron (e.g. the State).

Relative, as opposed to absolute, deprivation was, of course, an inherent feature of the context in which organisations worked, rather than a feature of any particular years. Structural inequality of power and wealth was a permanent feature of capitalism which voluntary organisations were bound in some measure to reflect, but which they could fight, reinforce, be indifferent to, or pretend not to notice. Such structural inequalities determined what the consequences of particular organisational styles would be, although not the organisational styles themselves. Thus, if a voluntary organisation, such as a chapel with a £2,000 annual balance sheet was to be sustained, it had to be paid for. Even if the organisation desperately wanted to become *of* the working class, there was a limited range of options as regard sources of finance, just as there was a limited range of options for a firm wanting to compete in the mass market for biscuits in the twentieth century. During the partnership era at the biscuit factory (1841-98), the main option for voluntary organisations was to be supported by local people with spare resources, i.e. the middle class, such as the Palmers. There were reasons at that time why this situation did not appear to run contrary to the notion of universalising quality, or to the possibility of making the best of capitalism generally shared. One of the fancy Christmas tins used by Huntley and Palmers was designed to look like eight books bound together. One of these was Samuel Smiles' *Self-Help* (1859). Smiles' central maxim, 'what some men are, all without difficulty might be'[52] had a certain plausibility during the partnership era. The Palmers had visibly grown from small origins in a single life-time; there was a certain amount of similar mobility even within the factory; controls still seemed, and to an extent were, local; people like the Palmers felt so strongly that the ideas outlined in Chapter Two were capable of dynamic development that they were badly placed to compete economically when the rules of the game later changed; William Isaac poured himself into one of his favourite projects — the Help Myself Society; and real wages were rising.

The reality was different even in the partnership era. To the extent that the Palmers grew, it was that much more difficult for anyone else locally to do so. But the reality became manifestly different in the early twentieth century.

The Palmers had always been 'less than generous' over wages. They paid as little as the market would bear.[53] As the major employer in Reading they had a powerful influence over the whole local wage level. 'Reading as a Commercial Centre' became attractive:

> An almost unlimited supply of unskilled labour can be obtained at reasonable terms, and the skilled labour rates compare favourably with those obtaining in other places. . .there is no large undertaking (mining for instance) in the neighbourhood to drain the labour of the town by offering high wages for arduous work. Girl labour is abundant, and there is a full supply for any factory that might be started in Reading.[54]

In evaluating the possibilities open to any section of the late nineteenth-century urban working class, one document from outside Reading, but from another town dominated by Quaker employers, is worth citing in full. In his quantified study of poverty in York, a city not thought to be exceptionally poor, in 1899, a year known to have been better than many, Seebohm Rowntree included a qualitative description of the life of the 43.4% of the wage-earning class or 27.84% of the total population, living around or below the 'physical efficiency' level:

A family living upon the scale allowed for in this estimate must never spend a penny on railway fare or omnibus. They must never go into the country unless they walk. They must never purchase a half-penny newspaper or spend a penny to buy a ticket for a popular concert. They must write no letters to absent children, for they cannot afford to pay the postage. They must never contribute anything to their church or chapel, or give any help to a neighbour which costs them money. They cannot save, nor can they join a sick club or Trade Union, because they cannot pay the necessary subscriptions. The children must have no pocket money for dolls, marbles or sweets. The father must smoke no tobacco and must drink no beer. The mother must never buy any pretty clothes for herself or for her children, the character of the family wardrobe, as for the family diet, being governed by the regulation 'nothing must be bought but that which is absolutely necessary for the maintenance of physical health, and what is bought must be of the plainest and most economical description'. Should a child fall ill, it must be attended by the parish doctor; should it die it must be buried by the parish. Finally, the wage earner must never be absent for a single day...[55]

Severe constraints indeed; without understanding them in a Reading context more than 'background' would have been omitted. At a Town's Meeting to form an association of working men to help finance the Royal Berkshire Hospital in 1902, the Social Democratic Federation speaker, J.F. Hodgson, explained how he 'did not believe in charitable efforts in the direction of house to house collections and processions' for 1*d.* a week or 4/4*d.* a year was a great deal for working men 'in view of the almost universal poverty in the town'.[56] It is important to understand that he was not taking up an ideological position here, but making a statement of fact.

Fortunately, this major constraint of poverty can be documented both quantitatively and qualitatively for the boom town of Reading in this period. Where repeated applications were made to the Reading Distress Committee, it is even possible to glimpse the struggles of a single family over time, even if applications were *per se* atypical, and several re-applications might indicate exceptional hardship or unusual willingness to use relief machinery.

George Baker applied for help on 15th December 1905.[57] Like many other Reading workers, he had first been a farm labourer. In 1894 he had come to live in Reading at No. 8 Bosier Square where he

stayed for eleven years. Before his application to the Distress
Committee, his previous two jobs had been 'labouring' — first for three
years 'fairly regular' then for eight months. In November 1905 he was
discharged. He was 47 and had seven children from 16 to 1 year old.
The two oldest boys (16 and 14) earned 14/- per week between them,
one as a baker (possibly in Huntley and Palmers), the other in Huntley,
Boorne and Stevens' tin factory. The family paid 5/3d. a week for four
rooms. George Baker had earned 12/- in the week before applying.
They had lived at 2, Spring Grove, Mount Pleasant, for the previous
three months. On 20th December 1905, he 'found regular employment'
and disappeared from the books of the Distress Committee for that
year. On 14th September 1906, he applied again. He now had eight
children. The eldest three were working, as a factory operative, a
packer and a labourer respectively, probably in Huntley and Palmers.
The total family income in September was £1.1.6d. per week, although
George Baker's previous labouring job for nine months with a building
firm had earned him £1.3.0d. per week, when in full work. The family
had something coming in from a Slate Club. The visitor from the
Distress Committee (a body manned and partly financed from voluntary
sources) observed that the 13 year old daughter was epileptic, deaf and
dumb, and had been chargeable to the Guardians since 1902. The
home was poor and 'not very clean'. The visitor also remarked on the
Record Paper that the applicant was 'a good man to work', was generally
in employment but 'I am informed could do better with his earnings'.
In November 1907 he applied again. At the previous application he had
lived at 5 Katesgrove Lane, he had then moved to 11, Church Street. In
1907 he was living at 9 Katesgrove Lane and paying 5/6d. a week for
six rooms. There were nine children. His previous job had been for six
weeks as a builder's labourer with a Croydon firm at an average wage of
13/- per week. There was a daughter earning 7/6d. as a factory
operative and a son earning 9/- as a labourer. The applicant had been ill
for several weeks of 1907 and had had outdoor relief from the
Guardians during June. Many of the children now had opthalmia, the
home was 'squalid', and the imbecile daughter now in the workhouse.
The comment was made by the visitor who went to verify this
information that 'the applicant is a decent worker when employed, but
could have done more with his earnings when he was in health'. Baker
applied to the Distress Committee again in July 1908, September 1909,
December 1910 and February 1914. In that time the family had moved
house a further three times. George Baker had had three or four jobs
before settling down to irregular employment with W. McIlroy. The

children in the home went down from a maximum of nine to four by 1914. Meanwhile their work experience had been as chequered as that of their father. At various times a daughter had worked at Serpell and Sons at 8/- a week, a son aged 19 had worked at H. & G. Simmonds at 10/- a week, other children had had jobs at 12/- a week and part-time work at 5/- and 2/6*d.* a week. Twice (1908 and 1910) a boy was reported as unemployed at the time of the applications. Usually the rent was paid up. A visit by a member of the Distress Committee on 4th October 1909 revealed that 'the applicant works well when employed and is pretty steady, but is inclined to talk too much and is not very choice in his language'. Later another visitor in March 1914 expressed the view that 'he is a good worker but has rather an obstinate disposition. In other respects his character is satisfactory'.

The level of wages revealed in this family biography over the period 1905-14 is not the only, or perhaps the most important item of significance. Irregularity of work when obtained, uncertainty of finding a job once one was lost, frequency of moving house — sometimes within one street, sometimes from one part of town to another — and the kind of contact with bodies like the Guardians and the Distress Committee, 'them' from outside the home with their ideologies clearly expressed on the Record Papers, which this situation involved, did not make George Baker or his family likely potential candidates for the kind of participation which churches, chapels, regattas or Friendly Societies wanted to offer them.

The experience of any single family was of course a changing one, as Rowntree observed in York. A still photograph of urban society in the early twentieth century would capture that 'mass of labour which is half in and half out of industry, a class which is found in good times and bad times alike, which does not earn a living wage and yet does not starve'.[58] It would show what another observer of Britain during the years of George Baker's applications to the Reading Distress Committee argued was 'an integral part of industry. . .a body of men constantly passing into and out of employment. . .a reserve as well as a regular army of labour'.[59] It might even reveal the clear cases of starvation leading to death that were to be found in Reading.[60]

What such a photograph would not express was the sense of impending disaster, the expectation of future want which in so many cases must have been fulfilled. It was this which led a 'loyal labourer' to write to the *Berkshire Chronicle* in 1893 pleading that although he had 'the greatest possible repugnance against republican and revolutionary views', places of business must not be closed on the

wedding day of the Duke and Duchess of York, for the loss of three or
four shillings to 'a very large number of labourers' in the town would
be catastrophic.[61] It was this which led a Co-op. journalist to remark in
1905 that 'the outlook for labour at the outset of the New Year is
indeed dark and dismal. The despair of the unemployed as debt and
starvation stares them in the face is piteous and pathetic. . .'[62] When a
still photograph is used, related to the possibility of generating
continuous mass voluntarism, related to more in social history than a
mere analysis of economic conditions, it should not be forgotten 'how
terribly near the margin of disaster the man, even the thrifty man,
walks who has in ordinary normal conditions, but just enough to keep
himself on. The spectre of illness and disability is always confronting
the working-man; the possibility of being from one day to the other
plunged into actual want, is always confronting his family'.[63]

A.L. Bowley took such a still photograph of Reading in 1912.[64]
Based on sample visits to 1 in 21.5 households, it gave an invaluable
view of the conditions and therefore the opportunities of George
Baker's neighbours. Material was collected about rents and housing, the
composition of working-class families and earnings and poverty; the
findings were later incorporated, with work on three other localities, to
produce the comparative study, *Livelihood and Poverty* (1915).
Although Reading had the highest rents investigated (67% at more than
6/-), conditions as measured by overcrowding were comparatively
good.[65] But the median rent paid by families in different income groups
was a high proportion of income. It ranged for different income groups
from 59% to 10%, with the lower groups having the higher percentages.
For the 20/- to 25/- a week group, median rent formed 25% of income.
Questions on the composition of working-class households in relation
to their earning power showed that while 15% of wives and widows
were at work, 41% of male heads of families were assisted by wife or
children earning alongside them. But wages were 'abnormally low'.
Twenty-five per cent of the households investigated included wage
earners with 30/- or more a week (in Stanley, a mining town, the
figure was 75%). In Reading the proportion of workers on less than
20/- a week (15%) was higher than it had been in York in 1899 (10%).
The average wage for a full week's work by a man over 20 in Reading
in 1912 was 24/6*d*. In York in 1899 it was 26/6*d*. Between the two
surveys (1899-1912) wages had risen nationally by about 10%. 50.5%
of workers in Reading in 1912 were on less than 24/- a week (York,
1899, 36%).

Using a 'New Standard' of poverty, [66] as well as Rowntree's old one,

Bowley concluded that the results of these housing and earning figures were that just over 1/5 of working-class families in Reading were living below the two standards (1/17 in Stanley, 1/12 in Northampton, 1/8 in Warrington). More than 1 person in every 4 of the working class was living in the autumn of 1912 in a state of primary poverty. Of the total population this was 19%. A number of refinements were made in this analysis which it is not necessary to investigate – but one more subdivision is useful. Of the school children in Reading not earning, 47% were living in poverty (25% Warrington, 16% Northampton, 12% Stanley).

The causes of this situation had to do with wages, and to a considerable extent with the wages of Huntley and Palmers, which employed between 1/4 and 1/5 of the working class of the town at that date. The labour force was overwhelmingly used for unskilled labour; the highest rate for work at the biscuit factory in 1912 was 'generally stated' to be 23/- a week. Besides the biscuit factory, there were 'a large number of co-existent and independent trades', but there was 'no considerable group of highly paid workers'. It was stressed in the survey that the conditions described were not due to short time, or to unemployment, or to national economic fluctuations, or to the weather. They were 'not intermittent but permanent, not accidental or due to exceptional misfortune, but a regular feature of the industries of the town concerned'.[67] The tone of the survey was less emotive even than Rowntree's. None the less to the authors the results were not only surprising but 'shocking'.[68] About 17,000 people in Reading were living in primary poverty. All these would have found it impossible to relate to most of the organisations to be described later in anything other than a client capacity. It was to some 'a mystery how they manage to exist'.[69]

The statistics in the 1911 census were conveniently arranged in such a way as to help to give flesh to the bones of the Bowley survey. The category in the census which included workers at the biscuit factory (Food, Tobacco, Drink and Lodging) together accounted for 29% of the jobs held by males aged ten years and upwards. Biscuit factory wages, as already observed in the Bowley survey, were low. So too were building wages, where employment was irregular and seasonal.[70]

Beyond this major slice of one in three male workers, there were others who fell into a very low paid category. These, at the least, amounted to a further 12% of earning males.[71] The remainder fell into three categories. The 'retired' or 'unoccupied' (16%); those in a clerical or managerial job (11%);[72] those in skilled or possibly better-paid jobs

(24%).[73] All these categories, especially the last, included many men who would have found simple economic constraints overwhelmingly powerful in preventing them from being continuous members of organised social groupings. While, normally speaking, the 2.5% in the printing trades, for example, should be included within the 'aristocracy of labour', and they therefore have been put into the better paid category, in fact Reading printing wages were low because Reading was outside the London wages area.[74]

A breakdown of the 31% of females aged ten and upwards who were 'engaged in occupations' in the same census revealed a mere 6% in possibly better-paid jobs (teaching, food dealers, general shopkeepers, dealers, drapers, linen drapers, mercers, dealers in dress, board, lodging, and dealers in spiritous drinks; commercial, bank, and insurance clerks, law clerks). The remainder were working at low paid jobs. So measured just by a narrowly defined version of economic conditions, leaving out such matters as formal hours of work (at the biscuit factory 58½ until 1877 and then 54 until 1918) and working conditions, a high proportion of those over ten in Reading, together with their dependents, were in no position to figure as active members in the type of organisations being studied here whether 'Vice-Presidential' or democratic. Anything provided would be likely to remain *for* them rather than become *of* them. Equally, the more that was provided, the more working people would be seen in distorted ways, refracted through the disappointed expectations of the providers.

5 RELIGION (II)

By returning to religion immediately after examining the biscuit factory and social conditions in Reading, it is not intended to imply that religion and its organisations were mere epiphenomena 'reflecting' a material base.

Indeed, partly because of the sheer variety of religious organisations and partly because they employed so many professionals without specifying precisely what they should do, there was evidence of quarrelsome personal interaction between so-called superstructure and base. An Anglican clergyman, the Rev. R.H. Hart Davis, played a leading role on behalf of the workers in the dispute at Huntley and Palmers in 1912. The vicar of St. John's and St. Stephen's had Palmer money withdrawn from his over-stretched ecclesiastical machine for following through the assertion that 'men in my parish were trying to bring up their families on 18/- a week'.[1] The Rev. Gilbert Laws of Carey Street Baptist Chapel was more circumspect, but his meaning was clear when he welcomed the idea of a CWS jam factory in Reading in 1912, 'for it is a recognised fact that the society pays wages which are. . .to say the least at a subsistence level. This alone will mean a lot for our town for I am sorry to find that this does not exist in certain industries in the town'.[2] The Rev. H. Bassett seconded the main resolution at the meeting of the Berkshire Agricultural and General Workers' Union in the Town Hall in 1893.[3] Members of the Salvation Army backed a Workers' Electoral League Candidate for the Council in 1903. Two ministers were closely involved in the Independent Labour candidature of H. Watts for the town council in 1907, and so on.

Plucking examples at random like this does not carry analysis far; and there were many counter-examples.[4] All it serves to do is to blur lines which can be drawn too sharply. The point here will not be to re-draw such lines, but rather to set religious organisation into a context in which the biscuit factory was indeed a determining organisation. But religious organisations were mediators of their own fate and, by their actions, functioned to compound or diminish the contextual constraints surrounding their work. This chapter will stress unintended consequences rather than aims. As organisations in a specific society, churches and chapels operated within constraints. Some of these were inherent in a system (capitalism); some were

inherent in a particular phase or period in the development of that
system, as it changed its mode of operation; some were inherent in
particular local circumstance; and some were perhaps inherent in the
nature of religious organisations, as opposed to other subject-areas or
types of organisation. The assumption that religious groups worked in
an a-social vacuum of total freedom was, and still is, a source of
agonising feelings of failure among activists. But it is a false one. Right
hands have an awkward habit of being affected by what left hands are
doing. The constraints involved some necessary or objective, and some
unnecessary or self-imposed contradictions between aspiration and
actuality. By necessary contradictions are meant those, like poverty
and the shapes of town expansion, over which religious organisations
had no direct control – which is not to say that they had no
responsibility to resist or to fight to remove such contradictions. They
could have taken a critical stance only by first becoming more aware
that such contradictions existed.[5] By unnecessary contradictions are
meant those for which religious organisations were more directly
responsible – even though such contradictions were also powerfully
shaped by changing contextual pressures. Necessary and unnecessary
contradictions will be considered in turn. When dealing with
unnecessary contradictions, this chapter will focus on the tendency to
accumulate bricks and mortar and the increasing tensions between
commitment to large items of expenditure and achievement of other
facets of religious aspiration.

   The single most important fact about early twentieth-century
Reading, in the experience of the largest number of people who lived
there, was poverty. Observers from outside the abyss were not always
conscious of poverty: indeed there were many voices speaking loudly
to deny it.[6] But the relative and absolute deprivation of large numbers
of inhabitants – deprivation of spare resources of time, money and
education – cries out to the historian, even if A.L. Bowley did not
have the vividness of voice of R. Tressell of Mugsborough (Hastings)
in his *Ragged Trousered Philanthropists* (1914).

   Poverty had formidable implications for the prevailing type of
religious organisation in Reading. Theoretically religious organisations
might have been less affected, if they had been of a different type. But
given what they became, there was bound to be a contradiction
between what they aspired to be, or what they thought they should
aspire to be, and what, in the circumstances, they could be. To the
extent that they wished to appeal to numbers unlimited, and to the
extent that they tried to involve the working class in particular versions

of continuous participation, their task was impossible. In the language of *Lux Mundi* in 1889, 'in consequence of the structure of social life there are always large classes of the community who, while just provided with the bare necessities of life, have not sufficient means to enable them to sustain the expense of the organs of the higher life in any form'.[7] How many people had the spare resources of time and education to go through the preliminaries of membership described in Chapter Three?

Being a part in any continuous sense of a church or chapel also involved money, even if only pennies. This was probably more fundamental than the 'respectability' barrier stressed by recent historians. As a Labour Church 'Pioneer' outside Reading wrote in 1893, 'I hate collecting cards. Every church or chapel makes them their tax collector & in most households the District Visitor is but another name for beggar, and the whole system is generally spoken of with contempt by working men'.[8] The embarrassment principle was effective precisely because it was embarrassing — hence the open plate rather than the bag at a chapel like Broad Street Congregational in 1905: 'will friends kindly note, and let their contributions be in silver as it takes a lot of copper to raise a sovereign'.[9] There were doubtless opportunities for getting pennies, or for learning skills which would earn more pennies through attendance at churches and their agencies. But you could not pass 'Go' until you were on the Monopoly board.[10] And even when you were on, there were those who told you sternly to spend. St. Stephen's Anglican church was designed to be specially 'adapted to meet the requirements of the working classes who reside in the vicinity. The church is substantially built after Ruskin-like ideas'. But, scolded the preacher, 'it is nothing less than a disgrace to any congregation that the expenses are not met weekly by the offertories'. 'It is surely not too much to ask from a congregation worshipping in a chapel where all the seats are free that they shall provide sufficient money to meet the cost of warming, lighting and cleaning the church and all the other necessary expenses of conducting divine worship'.[11] Hosier Street Congregational Methodist chapel, conscious of its location in an extremely poor inner-urban area, was unusual in not taking collections at services 'so that the poor might not be discouraged from attending'. Even so, to join its most cherished agency — the Hosier Street Temperance Society — a minimum of 2d per annum was needed.[12] To relate in one way often meant relating in another — for example sending your children to Sunday School. That too could involve expense. It was not merely seat rents, although those were probably as much a part of the scene in 1914 as they had been in 1890. The whole experience of being part of a large organisation, with all the pressures and opportunities which that imposed, meant expenditure of money as well as time. At a meeting to discuss why the men of the working-class Coley area did not go to St. Saviour's Hall, a Labour councillor, S.G. Jones, won wide assent when he said that it was due 'in the main to social conditions which rendered attendance almost impossible'.[13]

In view of this, the quantity of comment by people within religious organisations suggesting some success in reaching and involving sections of the working class was interesting in Reading. Religious organisations may not have been very successful in appealing across class lines; they may, however, have been more successful than other organisations, and more successful than circumstances would lead one to expect. There was plenty of comment on failure. This has become familiar in studies of post-industrial revolution religion, boosted by reactions to the 1851 census and continuing into the worried introspection of generations since then. But it was balanced by other comment. For example, in the Anglican parish of Greyfriars with its population of 6,000 'factory workers, labourers and compositors', Evangelical services were consistently well attended. In 1906 they reported that 'men's work had succeeded beyond our most sanguine expectations'; in the same year it was said that 'it is indeed a wonderful sight to see two to three hundred people of whom a large proportion are men in their working clothes on a weeknight to hear a simple Gospel message'.[14]

It is difficult to discover precisely which churches and chapels successfully involved the working class in worship; a few social profiles of congregations shed only fragmentary light on the question. A Congregational chapel wrote of itself in 1905:

> Broad Street chapel is filled, floor and balconies alike with men for the most part of the respectable mechanic and labouring class of earnest and intelligent bearing. . .all activated by a desire to get good for themselves and to aid their fellow men to get good for themselves.[15]

Occasionally lists of the trustees of chapels were accompanied by their occupations. It is not surprising that these did not generally include 'labourers'.[16]

The best consistent evidence in Reading on social composition of members or adherents in this period comes from three Primitive Methodist baptism registers. They recorded 1109 baptisms between

1837 and 1914. They included information on family occupation.[17] In Table I the occupations given have been classified into six groupings A-F, and baptisms in each of those groupings have been expressed as percentages of total baptisms in different ten-year periods. It is impossible to be sure that these registers are comprehensive, but it is interesting that as many as thirty-nine per cent of the 1109 recorded were labourers in category C. In the years 1850-60, 1881-90, and 1891-1900, the percentages of labourers were 49, 47 and 52 respectively. The next biggest category was that of artisans such as blacksmiths, french polishers and the like, with twenty-eight per cent of total baptisms over the whole period. This percentage did not vary much from decade to decade except for the pre-factory period of Reading's social history when the figure (between 1837 and 1859) was fifty-one per cent. If categories A, B and C are added together (Table II) — that is to say servant-type employments, artisans and labourers — then eighty-three per cent of all baptisms recorded throughout the period fall into this category. And when the percentage of A-C was lowest (between 1901 and 1914 — seventy-three per cent) the proportion of those who were labourers was still as high as forty-eight per cent. These figures obviously say more about Primitive Methodism than about religious organisations generally, and more about rites of passage than about worship or penumbras; but at least one denomination, as measured by one index, was involving the working class with some success.[18] Such involvement, in the conditions of the day, carried with it the problems already quoted from the *Primitive Methodist Magazine* for 1890.

More permanent obstacles to working-class religion than absolute deprivation were posited at the time, and have been reiterated since. But many of these in the end come back to poverty. 'Urbanism' or 'the city race' have been treated as essentially irreligious, but in language which evades the particularities of system, time, place and religion. W. Rauschenbusch's *Christianity and the Social Crisis* (1907) was the best contemporary contextual view of religious organisation — noticing such elementary and neglected influences on the possibility of religious organisation as land prices. His voice was the voice of many worried supporters of organised religion since the industrial revolution,

> I am sure that there is no great city in which modern industrialism has set up its smoking and flaring altars of mammon in which religion is not struggling for life like a flower growing among the cobble stones of the street. The larger our cities grow the less hold

Table I   Primitive Methodist Baptisms by Occupation

Occupation Date	A	B	C	Percentage of Baptisms D	E	F	Number of Baptised	Percentage of total for all years
1837-49	20	51	15	7	0	6	80	7
1850-60	9	29	49	8	0	5	76	7
1861-70	20	28	33	14	1	4	163	15
1871-80	20	27	39	4	1	9	233	21
1881-90	14	24	47	3	3	7	117	10
1891-1900	7	30	52	6	2	2	161	14
1901-14	16	22	35	12	6	5	279	25
All years	16	28	39	8	2	6	1109	100

A = Servants or Servant type employments (groom, gardener, etc.)
B = Artisans, skilled workers (Blacksmiths, french polishers, etc.)
C = Labourers, undesignated or specifically listed as biscuit, brewing, railway or brick workers.
D = Shopworkers or retail sellers (travellers, etc.)
E = Clerical
F = Others (includes soldiers)

Table II Primitive Methodist Baptisms by Occupation

Date	Column I	Column II	Column III	Column IV
	Percentage of all Baptisms in occupational categories	Percentage of Baptisms in Col. I which were in occupational category:		
	A + B + C	A	B	C
1837-49	86	23	59	18
1850-60	87	11	33	56
1861-70	81	24	34	42
1871-80	86	23	32	45
1881-90	85	17	28	55
1891-1900	89	8	33	59
1901-14	73	22	30	48
All years	83	19	34	47

a comparison with say Congregationalism would be interesting does religion seem to have over the multitude of men and the general life. The church is inquiring for the cause with compunctions of conscience and anguish of heart. It has sought to improve its organisation, to try new methods, to elicit more funds. It has blamed the tired workers for their lack of success. But it still looks like a losing race.

And he tentatively connected such a cry to a context,

Is it not perhaps true that as the social life of the people grows more sordid, as the home and family life are contracted and crushed, and as the future looms up in dreary uncertainty and helplessness, the religious sense of the people is choked, the natural basis for religious life dwindles?[19]

With the substitution of 'altered' for 'choked', 'spare resources' for 'natural basis' and 'religious organisation' for 'religious life', such a diagnosis makes more sense than others in the same genre.[20] It makes much more sense than those which seek to posit some absolute opposition between either the situation of the proletariat in capitalism and *any* religion,[21] or between working-class culture and any joining or membership-type activity, including religious. It may or may not have been true of the poor in late nineteenth-century cities that 'present and immediate facts filled their whole field of contemplation',[22] but such a judgment generalised to the working class *per se* becomes ideology — and ideology which has an important function in ratifying the supply of particular debased cultural products. The equivalent in another subject-area would be to say that the working class in the twentieth century preferred cheap biscuits; instead of saying that that is all they could afford. It may have been true in twentieth-century working-class Leeds that there was a sense of 'the personal, the concrete, the local', that 'group life started from the home and worked outwards in response to the common needs and amusements of a densely packed neighbourhood', and that people 'react(ed) instinctively against consciously planned group activities'.[23] But Hoggart also pointed out the financial barriers between the working class and 'consciously planned group activities'. To make any more general opposition between working-class culture and organised membership or 'joining' activities would be to fly in the face of huge creations such as Friendly Societies, Trade Unions, Coops., not to mention the considerable twentieth-century working-class adherence to religious sects. At any one time there are systematic constraints upon such working-class organisations, and a context which fingers the interplay between supply and demand for them. But that is not to say they cannot exist and, for a time, express genuine demand from below.

There were, however, ways other than poverty in which religious organisations in Reading were faced by a context carrying impositions over which they had no direct control. Being organisations in society means being organisations in a certain kind of society, whose arrangements are neither inevitable, permanent, ordained by God nor common to all societies. In this particular case it meant being organisations in a society in which people, like George Baker, moved home a great deal. Population growth was one thing (1881-91, 22.3%; 1891-1901, 20.3%; 1901-1911, 8.4%). As important was the fact that it involved considerable migration inside, and from outside the town. Of the 12,613 persons added to the population between 1891 and 1901, for example, excess of births over deaths accounted for two-thirds and gains by migration for as much as one-third. Two-thirds of both sexes in the census of 1891 had been born in other regions. Of each 1000 of each sex enumerated in Reading in the 1911 census, only 511 males and 478 females had been born in the town. Internal movement was also considerable, and the changing contours of the town illustrated 'the tendency of English towns since 1851. . .to spread over wider areas than before'.[24]

It is easy to write, as does Phelps Brown, that 'the effect of this (population) movement on the life of the British people must have been profound' — less easy to specify in what ways. Movement was constantly regretted by religious activists. But there was little that could be done about it at least at the level of the single chapel, or at the level of the single town. No sooner had a successful grouping of youth within a chapel been achieved — for instance a Christian Endeavour group — than its leading members left the neighbourhood, perhaps partly as a result of the impact of the group upon their lives. Churches which felt that they needed long lists of parochial staff like District Visitors had to replace a sizeable proportion each year owing to migration. It was this loss as much as 'apathy' which caused demoralisation in religious organisations, as much as in political parties. In one year (1899) St. Bartholomew's Church lost 50 communicants out of 450 — mostly by 'removal'.[25] Midtown churches were especially affected — St. Mary's Castle Street finding in 1905 that 'the character of the congregations has changed completely, the wealthy members having died or migrated to other parts of town'.[26] Where success in recruitment was expected, as in the case of St. Andrew's Caversham, in a rapidly growing suburban district 'so largely composed of better-to-do people', with a new minister after 1910, it did not always happen. Disillusion resulted.[27] At Kings Road Baptist chapel in 1896 it was noted that 34 out of the 45 members added and 21 out of the 40 members lost were due to transfers in and out of the neighbourhood. It was difficult for any organisation to keep pace with such change.

Observations made at the opening of Grovelands Baptist church were made somewhere in the records of most chapels in Reading. The mood behind them is an inseparable part of the social history of nineteenth-century religion,

> the extraordinary growth during recent years of the western-most end of Reading has probably hardly been realised by many people. As soon as one has passed under the Great Western arch which spans the Oxford Road. . .one enters practically a new town. On the South side especially the builder has been hard at work for some few years past, and street after street lined with houses mostly packed pretty closely together gives striking evidence of the rapid increase of population. . .When they remembered something of the circumstances of this locality — carrying their minds back to a few years ago — many must recollect how the town of Reading then stopped at its western end at the railway bridge in the Oxford Road. The town had now developed in all directions but in no part so much as westerly.[28]

Bewilderment and fright at the implications of such population growth and movement was frequently expressed. G.P. Crawford thought that growth in St. Mark's district was 'the sort of development which makes a vicar wonder how on earth he is going to cope with men and money for such an increase of work in his parish'.[29] At the same time growth was seen as providing opportunities for bodies like the Reading Town Mission or the YMCA which were not necessarily confined to a single locality or a single building — if only enough pan-town resources could be found.[30]

Population movement and growth forced a religion of bricks and mortar on to the agenda of religious organisations in Reading — even though the building option did not have to catch the chairman's eye as relentlessly as it did. At the same time, the agency of such movement highlights a feature in capitalism of considerable contextual importance for religious organisations, and more permanent than absolute poverty

– namely, inequality. And the results of such movement highlight other fixed furniture in late nineteenth-century capitalism of considerable contextual importance for religious organisations – namely types of urban sub-society such as the suburb.

Religious organisations could neither choose where, if they wanted to be widely available, they would have to extend, nor in what type of district they would have to operate once they had extended. They could, of course, have identified who or what was responsible for where they would have to extend. They could also have identified some relevant features of resulting sub-societies. Powerful external constraints, so far from negating, necessitate the prophetic mode, in modern urban society as much as in ancient captivity. Grovelands Baptists saw how on the other side of 'the Great Western arch which spans the Oxford Road. . .the builder has been hard at work'. It was indeed the builder who shaped, within limits, the directions and type of expansion of Reading 'over wider areas than before'.

Before its take-off into industrial importance Reading was, in an 1840 classification, one of the 'inland towns not the seat of any particular manufacture'. Of that type it avoided two common fates – that of death through failure to replace stage-coach by railway station in the mid-nineteenth century, and that of resurrection only as a residential satellite of a large city in the mid-twentieth century. Instead it grew, and of the two principal types which grew – consumption towns with an element of forethought and planning in their construction and production towns without – it fell into the latter category. 'It was the private builders, operating piecemeal and without regulation in whatever areas had an immediate demand, who built (these) towns.'[31] As Reading spilled out of its ancient triangle between two rivers, up the slopes Southwards beyond George Palmer's house to Christ Church Road, and Northwards to Caversham, along the valley East and West around the five main arteries leaving the town, it was the speculative builder rather than the municipal planner or social idealist who was the agent of the extensions.[32] Self-interest and technology aided the process via, for instance, the tram. The leading advocate of a municipal system of tramways, the Mayor and retailer A.H. Bull, was quite honest when he celebrated the municipalisation of the tramways in November 1901. 'He hoped that these tramways would decrease any expenditure that might be necessary by the corporation on "artisans' dwellings" by taking them further afield.'[33]

Once established, sub-districts of cities may on occasion be able to influence or divert powerful external agencies of change. Until then, however, the decisions which affect their essence are not their own. The implications of such a weighted distribution of power for religious organisations need articulating theologically in ways which will not be attempted here. More elementary implications can, however, be extracted, and consequences sketched. If they were to meet other than in dwelling-houses or fields, and in some situations even then, religious organisations needed sites. Building sites became expensive and were owned or wanted in such areas, by builders. They therefore required the raising of large sums, or the charity of wealthy individuals, including builders, with all that charity meant to the stance of the organisation which received or sought to receive it.

More important than the cost and ownership of building-sites was the resulting nature of whole areas of town, and the consequent nature of the town itself. In her brilliant book on *Charitable Effort in Liverpool in the Nineteenth Century* (1951), Margaret Simey referred to 'the spontaneous sorting out of the population on a basis of social status', and speculated about the connections between geography and changing attitudes towards social welfare. Although the process was not spontaneous, it undoubtedly took place, and forced religious and other organisations into the roles of victims as much as villains.[34] The process catapulted religious organisations, and indeed the dignified ideology of Reading society, into contradictions in the late nineteenth century. The society described in Chapter Two aspired towards a version of community, in which physical propinquity of classes supported mutual responsibility. It was a society in which George Palmer walked to work, lived amongst 'his people', and in which the kind of interconnections between different aspects of life — work, leisure, mutual improvement and service — were expressed in physical lay-out as well as ideology. At the very least, such interconnections were not severed by distance. The big religious diffusion centres, the most dynamic extenders and institution-builders, were all within, or on the edge of, an inner-urban area where different classes and different activities were not wide apart. It was possible to walk in ten minutes through the doors of the Reading Temperance Society, the Reading Dispensary, St. Mary's Anglican Church, Broad Street Congregational Church, St. Mary's Episcopal Church, Hosier Street Congregational Methodist chapel, and the citadel of the Salvation Army. In so doing one would be in the middle of an area where shopping, living, working and recreation all took place. This is not to say that a social embodiment of the ideas presented in Chapter Two existed in microcosm in such a space, only that it was not out of the question that it should.

The characteristic strains to which inner-urban areas were subject, once the initial growth of industrial Reading had fostered them, were outwards. Unplanned decentralisation took place, involving segregation of one activity from another and one class from another. Growth outwards took at least three forms. Earliest in time were the 'carriage' districts. These involved the spread of substantial residences along the London or Bath Road and on Castle Hill. These were not complete districts in themselves, for important aspects of life (work, entertainment, worship, shopping) were carried on in the inner-urban area, in the same area as the inner-urban workers. Next in time, although overlapping, was another primarily middle-class decentralisation. This led to the building up of complete suburban areas. Initially these were quite near to the inner area (viz. the Redlands Estate), and then further afield, as in Caversham. Here a definite type of society began to be created in which work was further removed from the 'home' area. Worship, entertainment and shopping could be local as well as in the centre of town.[35]

A vast range of fascinating observations have been made on the effects of suburbs on social life and organisations. All that will be done here is to point out that agonised characterisations of 'the suburbans' as a species, which were first made in this period by writers like H.G. Wells or C.F.G. Masterman, and later characterisations of 'suburban religion', can displace attention from the meaning and structure of the suburb itself. 'The attempt to separate material needs and the ways in which they are to be met, from human purposes and the development of being and relationship, is the suburban separation of "work" and "life" which has been the most common response of all to the difficulties of industrialism.'[36] It was not surprising that there were voices denying that Reading was yet a suburb, and decrying suburban tendencies, since those tendencies were in efficient contradiction with the dignified ideology of interconnection already described. When religious organisations showed a bias towards discrete activities, towards concentration upon individuals within an ongoing, rendered-unto-Caesar social order, and towards pure leisure consumption without a wider framework of collective intention, they were to some extent acting as their locations determined, or at least made tempting. When they persisted in trying to make the institutional church a microcosmic community, they were bravely working against increasingly adverse circumstances.

Parallel in time with middle-class suburbanisation came a larger working-class suburban shift along the Oxford Road. From the 1870s onwards new streets sprang up in Tilehurst, off the Wokingham Road, in parts of lower-lying Caversham and in Elm Park — in fact, forming a belt around the entire inner-urban area. These were single-class areas. Because of the tram, they could be further removed from work. They were bisected by arterial exits from the town. The exits became the sites for shops and self-consciously planned church extension, such as the burst of Wesleyan Methodist building at the turn of the century. The uniform red-brick houses closely packed together, with the name and date of the row placed prominently on one house, and with small shops and pubs built into the rows on corner-sites, remain a striking but hidden feature of Reading, as of so many other towns, to this day.[37]

These were problem-areas for church extension because they could not themselves, in spite of complaints like those made of St. Stephen's by St. John's, initiate or maintain elaborate plant. If 'religion' was to take forms similar to those in other parts of town, and if a local cadre of monied support was not available to help it do so, it would have to arrive via the agency of national denominational structures like that of the Wesleyans, providing religion *for* such areas. There were indeed problems about religion of this type ever becoming *of* such districts. Pan-town commercial organisations like the Reading Football Club could be located in the middle of one such area, Elm Park, and could in a limited sense be *of* the working class. But they would have to feed off the pennies of all such areas put together, just as the WEA had to appeal, as we shall see, to branches in other towns. Payment was made possible only by extensions of space or time. The Coop., a working-class organisation in Reading which had branches as well as a main shop, instituted a Club in December 1903 whereby members could 'obtain by weekly payments, drapery, clothing, boots and coal — goods which are a periodical requirement in every household and run away with large sums at times'. Otherwise the only organisations which existed in many areas and which were also *of* working-class areas were corner-shops (which often gave credit) and pubs. In the longer term these too were to be tied to central 'denominational' machines such as chain-stores and brewers. In this period they could still take a distinctive form in working-class neighbourhoods, even an increasingly distinctive form,[38] (while pressures of brewers and chain-stores allowed it) because they could make a profit by distributing commodities. Churches did not have a product which they could break up, sell intermittently, or in small units, like small bags of coal. There could have been more 'corner-churches' — analogous to American store-front churches — in such areas, as adapted to local needs and as distinct from other churches as corner-shops were distinct from other shops. Indeed there probably were more such units than the historian can now detect.[39] The story of the coming into being of more conventional churches and chapels will show how it was the hegemony of conventional forms in the religious imagination which on some occasions destroyed house-meetings, missionary groups and similar religious activity. From a later perspective, this kind of 'corner-church' activity looked much livelier to activists than its replacement by elaborate plant. But, to an extent insufficiently realised at the time, it was districts themselves which were important determinants of what could or could not go on inside them. It was the locality and its place in the weighted dynamics of a wider system that churches and chapels needed to understand, and if necessary to fight, if they were to be more than victims of changing contexts.

The origins and early days of those individual churches and chapels who were self-conscious enough to record them provide a convenient link between necessary and unnecessary constraints and contradictions as they impinged upon religious organisations. Individual examples of such origins show a fascinating interplay between intention and constraint, between resistance to paths made attractive by surrounding social forces and eager abetting of such forces.

The best qualitative examples come from the early pages of Baptist minute books. They were unusually concerned to articulate their organisational autobiographies, even if only to illustrate 'the truth that it is not in man that walketh to direct his steps'. Only the WEA minute books in Reading during this period provided equivalent qualitative material. Multiplication and juxtaposition of such evidence in different places and periods could unravel much about the history of the relationship between what men need or want or create from *below* and what exists or flourishes or is supplied from *above* in capitalist society, and thereby much about the history of the changing situation of religion. In this case it will be worth going into particularities before attempting overall conclusions derived from more scattered evidence. The detail of factors at work in individual cases over time will at least serve to show the range of freedoms which are available to specific organisations *in time.* Static and tidy enumeration of macro 'causes' across the board tends to obscure the fact that, within limits, things need not have been as they were. There was some room for freedom of manoeuvre, even if it was diminished rather than enlarged by what churches and chapels decided to be.

Both the freedom and the limits, as they bore specifically on religious organisations, are important to understand. From the point of view of a member of a typical congregation in Reading, say between 1890 and 1914, much about his experience of worship and activity in his church — where the building was, what type of building it was, how much time had to be spent raising money for it (given the distribution of resources in society at that time), how it related to denominational structures within or beyond the town, what type of person dominated it — needed the detail of recent history to be understood.

The way in which the structures of one generation, or in the case of churches often of one man, define the operations of the next, and the burdens of inheritance in a rapidly changing society, bear especially heavily on religious organisations. Fulfilled needs at one time can become albatrosses at another, particularly where elaborate plant (in chapels as in biscuit factories) is involved. And there did seem to be a law of accumulation of bricks and mortar at work in the life of religious organisations from the mid-nineteenth century onwards in Reading, regardless of the differing original impulses behind the organisation concerned.

For example the Primitive Methodists in early nineteenth-century Reading, from the start of the Berkshire mission in 1829, were an aggressive conversionist sect struggling against persecution to win souls, without benefit of permanent buildings. Even Class meetings were held in the open air for many months. Everything was subordinate to conversion. In 1837 they were preaching at fifty-seven different places in the town, had twenty-four scattered Societies and eight 'cottage and other stations'. 'Camp-meetings, revival meetings, protracted meetings, and open-air preachings were among the most successful of the methods employed.' Early in 1841 'a wonderful work of conversion broke out' in a revival which lasted for several weeks and netted more than sixty souls. 'Because of the many marvellous conversions which took place great excitement was created in the town, and many strange reports were put in circulation.' The original impulse towards permanent plant came only because of the impossibility of continuing this kind of work with a borrowed building. They were given notice to quit from their 'sanctuary' in London Street Chapel in 1837 'because of their early, late and noisy meetings'. No other place could be found. So 'Mr Ride saw the owner and requested a renewal of the tenancy. This was obtained only on the condition that they began at 6 instead of 5 in the morning and continued not later than 8.15 in the evening; and they were not allowed more than three nights a week.'

Such limitations were as cramp to the young body. 'One Sunday evening just before closing time a wonderful work of conversion broke out, but they were obliged to close the meeting.' So when a Mr T. Baker (a local Independent) offered financial help, Salem Chapel in Minster Street was bought as their first owner-occupied home in October 1839. The peak of work in this phase of Primitive Methodism was reached soon after, with 290 members in 1844. Then there was stagnation and loss until the mid-1860s. The next period of expansion followed through the logic of having Salem, with consequences which were later regretted. When Salem chapel was felt to be inadequate, a chapel 'situated in the heart of the town, and constituting a most desirable centre for Christian activities' was acquired in 1866. In the next dozen years three buildings were put up until, by 1887, there was a debt of £2,000 on an estimated value of chapels, schools and ministers' houses of £12,000.[40]

Such a tendency presented special problems for religious organisations — greater problems than equivalent tendencies in the experience of other organisations. This was because the enduring ends of religious organisations — salvation, the worship of God and a consequent way of life — are more vulnerable to changing means than, say, a goal like making a profit or entertaining. Clothes cannot easily be put on and taken off by religious organisations without affecting the body itself. It matters to them more than most that, as R.H. Tawney put it, 'institutions which have died as creeds sometimes continue nevertheless to survive as habits'.[41]

Rarely was the creation of a chapel in Reading before the early twentieth century an entirely rational, planned event, though sometimes, as in the case of Wycliffe Baptist Chapel, it was presented as such in later records. The *Jubilee Brief History, 1881-1931* (a typical celebratory pamphlet) presented Wycliffe as a copy-book case, entirely controlled by felt needs and thought-out stratagems. A dynamic pastor (William Anderson) at Kings Road from 1872 onwards, sought outlets for the energy of his congregation, and wanted to extend the number of Baptist chapels. At first village work seemed most appropriate but, after careful investigations in which chapel capacity in relation to population was tabulated, they decided in favour of inner-Reading extension. The 'rapidly growing East End' seemed a good target, 'ordnance maps were procured and with the assistance of a young helper the new houses and roads were plotted. . .the increasing population calculated or allowed for'. A derelict plot was chosen and the decision made to erect a chapel costing £3,700. In 1881 it was opened entirely free of debt. Eighty of the Kings Road congregation were transferred to start the new church. 'The whole movement was carried out in a true spirit of Christian concord and love. . .Wycliffe church started on its divine mission born, not of dissension, disagreement or secession, but of a strong faith, goodwill and lively hope.' By 1895, 'it is getting difficult to find unallotted sittings for friends wishing to become regular attendants'.

Nothing could be more 'successful'. Walking round a mid-twentieth-century town looking at churches, this is perhaps the way many observers, used to this style of operation, would assume that most of the plant had arrived. In fact, accident and social circumstances played a larger role even in this case than the *Brief History* allowed. Before they turned to the idea of village work, they had tried to extend in the town and failed. Only after that did they do a survey of ten miles around Reading, before the Wycliffe site unexpectedly became available at a price (£404) which they could afford. So they then switched back to inner-Reading expansion. Availability and price of land was the crucial variable, not at all subject to their control.[42] Nonetheless the role of such variables was relatively small in this case. Wycliffe preceded its congregation or 'church', and came into being as a building provided *for* a growing area of town rather than as an expression *of* the beliefs of a group who could not go on worshipping where they had been before.

The harmony which prevailed in this case was not universal. Another Baptist cause — the Anderson chapel in an outlying area of Reading — came into being with more tension. The first steps came from a Bible Class within Wycliffe, run by a layman.[43] They felt the need, in the same way that Kings Road had felt the need, for an active field of service for their Christianity. In 1892 they were invited to help in Earley by a married couple in the area, and the minister agreed to let them go. 'All of us were working people. . .we had no money', wrote one of them later. Service rather than chapel building was the explicit goal. They raised funds among themselves for the old, held open-air services calling for conversions, and instituted cottage meetings. Long before a formal 'congregation' was formed or a church built, active religious work was generated, arising out of the impulses of a Bible Class but trying to involve the people of Earley and provide help for them.

Success in the work created the ambition for something more permanent, 'the manifest blessings of God upon their labours was such'. By themselves, however, they could only raise £9 to carry the work forward. Wycliffe would not help, and 'here commenced an evident lack of understanding and sympathy on the part of the officials of the church with the aims and ideals of the young people to whom that work was a vital force in Christian life, and not to be treated lightly'.

Early in 1893 they started Lads and Girls Classes for those 'loitering about our dark streets', using private houses. These were a success, 'eagerly attended by many of the rougher element'. As a result, they were committed to their first expense for church furniture — two 'forms' at 13/4*d*. each. Opposition from 'the parent church to the forward movement involving the erection of a building for public worship as distinct from purely cottage or open-air meetings was not easily understood by the mission workers and was a source of real grief'. Later, the building of the chapel (opened in 1910) led to a longing for the cohesion, commitment, success with 'the rougher elements' and real involvement with the problems of Earley which the mission band had achieved without it.

It was not unusual for the energetic founders and builders of churches, who had been with a congregation or mission group before they started accumulating bricks and mortar, to look back nostalgically to early days. For instance, the Anglican parish of Earley was carved out of Sonning in 1842. In 1877, the parish of St. Bartholomew's was in turn carved out of Earley. As in the case of Anderson, the neighbourhood was poor. What became the church of St. Bartholomew's 'was literally born in a stable, with benches sinking into straw in Mr Oliver Dixon's meadow'. In 1877 they got a mission room and started on the thirty-year process which was to lead to a large church, vicarage and hall. The first vicar was able to look across the whole period. Before the church, 'we were a funny lot and supremely interesting. We did not fare at all badly, although gentlemenly folk at Whiteknights Park looked askance. . .When we became somewhat respectable under cover of the mission house, and then of the church, and then when the vicar got into his palace of a vicarage, there set in signs of the commonplace. I believe we all longed for the stables again; and I know some of us cried when we left the mission house'.[44]

In the case of Anderson, the £1,000 chapel pushed for by the missioners led to a debt still present in 1913, which was almost as great as the cost of the chapel. This debt was the result of the interaction between the dynamism of the founders and land prices, Earley people's financial resources and Wycliffe's mixture of antagonism and fear of schism.

In 1893 they almost bought a cottage in order to knock down the internal walls (to cost only £150) and use it as a chapel. Had they done this and kept to that scale, the relationship between their future work and its surroundings might have remained more in the spirit of the original enterprise. It would have been less institutionalised and less set in the ways that a conventional chapel building in a society characterised by poverty and inequality entails. But they could only raise £35 and 'how to raise the remainder?' was the big question.

A public meeting was called. Twenty people came and 9/2d. a week was promised – 'little enough, but sufficient to test the zeal and earnestness of the band, some of whom failed at the test and left the work.' By then it should have been apparent that while activity was possible, any elaborate building could not be *of* the people of Earley or *of* the original workers, but would have to be provided *for* them from outside. This was not a situation unique to the subject-area of religion. To the social historian it is clear that this was the critical moment when decisive choices were available determining the nature of Baptist work in Earley for years afterwards. In spite of finances, the decision was made to go for a building.

Two plots were bought for £42 in Amherst Road – to be paid by instalments. A building committee was formed. At this point the Primitive Methodists in Earley asked if they could co-operate. The request was as interesting as the fact that it was turned down. Autonomy was seen as more important than alliances to achieve quicker results. When Wycliffe were faced with an ultimatum – 'either the church must move in this matter or we should proceed in our plans without their assistance' – they decided to help. A joint committee reversed the previous decision on the cottage; one was bought in December 1893 and the inner walls knocked down.

Even having a modest building, however, triggered the beginnings of a penumbra of sub-agencies. The penumbra then became a new variable pushing independently towards larger premises and a full chapel apparatus. A Sunday School and a Band of Hope were founded for the children of the district, 'many of whom apparently run wild'. When the Sunday School outgrew the cottage, tensions between the Wycliffe deacons and the men in the field again surfaced. The deacons were prepared to think of an iron room, the workers wanted something more chapel-like.

The deacons were pressed in 1894 to buy another plot in Amherst Road, on a corner site adjoining one of their present plots, so that a school church and a mission room could be built for the existing work and then, when justified, a full church facing the main Earley thoroughfare in St. Peter's Road. This was another moment of critical decision for the future. There is a considerable difference between a main-street church among other main-street organisations and a residential-street church among houses. The former might appear to be the deserved reward and ratification of missionary enterprise and service. Once built, it would shape who went there, what they had to spend their time doing, and what people who did not go there thought of it, in ways which would not help the continuation of the original impulses behind the mission. The suggestion went unheeded by the deacons and a main-street site was avoided.

Instead the joint committee decided to build a hall on a plot already owned in Amherst Road. The cost was not to exceed £300. Throughout 1895 work towards this went on, 'busy as were the friends endeavouring to raise funds, the spiritual work was kept to the front'. So a distinction between these two things was consciously maintained. £100 was borrowed at 4% and building proceeded. 'Who can describe (in August 1895) the joy of the workers at the consummation of their hopes and plans, as with prayers of gratitude and renewed vows of consecration they dedicated simply, without rite of ceremony, this building to the glory of God and the saving of souls.' Deliberate efforts were made to keep the 'spiritual' side of the work going, in spite of institution-building, and to relate to the original mission band. At the first service, two laymen of the band preached. But at this stage their liabilities were still £225.

Congregations increased 'to bright evangelistic services'. It was the infant class of the Sunday School which first outgrew the new hall. Pressure was generated for further building. In June 1903 it was decided that the mission should become 'a separate cause'. Thirty-seven members were dismissed from Wycliffe to become the nucleus of the new church. The deacons of Wycliffe wrote: 'we trust that this new step may prove for the furtherance of the Gospel and that those united may dwell together in the unity of the Spirit and that we all may be finally united as part of the general assembly and church of the first-born, whose names are written in heaven.' With this step, another decisive moment shaping the nature of the presence of Baptism in Earley passed. The mission now had more financial and administrative responsibility and therefore, in a world of finite resources, less money and time for other types of activity: it also now set about *excluding*, and drew up a constitution which outlined who should and should not be members of the cause. The Constitution (July 1903) committed them to having a Pastor, and to 'baptism by immersion on profession of faith', as conditions of full membership. The *Rules* (August) regulated the terms upon which unbaptised persons might be accepted into church services and church administrative affairs, and set procedures for the visiting of members who applied, or who seemed to have lapsed, in order to test their seriousness. It was as a separate congregation that the final step was taken to erect their debt-laden £1,000 chapel, opened in September 1910.

It is at this level of detail that the particular forces at work creating religious organisations become apparent. Such organisations were deeply embedded in the society surrounding them, dependent upon building costs, land prices, and the distribution of wealth and extent of poverty. They expressed those social facts, as well as the needs *of* schismatic or missionary groups, or the wish to provide *for* new areas of population felt by religious organisers, permanent officials, and members of churches and chapels. What was possible or impossible, what would happen or not happen if certain things were done, had to do with society as much as with people's enthusiasm or lack of enthusiasm for religion. As Rauschenbusch argued in 1907 in his *Christianity and the Social Crisis*, 'the causal influences running back and forth between the civil and the ecclesiastical organisation of the people are far more powerful than is generally understood'.

Sometimes an end-product resulted which none of the initiators had desired — indeed, in the case of Caversham Baptist Free Church, one they explicitly had not wanted. In the middle of Caversham there stands a hugh brick chapel seating six hundred people, erected in 1877-8 at a cost of £5,000. For almost one hundred years it has been maintained as a building and centre, no doubt for 'good and useful work', but at great cost in commitment and cash by a few people. When it was erected, its narrative was put forward as 'an illustration of the truth that it is not in man that walketh to direct his steps, for nothing was further from the thoughts of those who began the work than the establishment of a separate and independent society'.[45] How then did it happen?

Dissenters in Caversham in the 1860s mostly went the short distance to Reading to worship. A Mr Goldston, a follower of Spurgeon, held services at his home in the village/suburb, but that was about all. This caused concern to a dynamic minister (Aldis) at Kings Road Baptist chapel in Reading — a keen extender. When a private individual offered a site for a church, action was catalysed.

A meeting of interested people was held to consider the offer. E. West, a rich Baptist, was the prime mover, and since most of those who came to the meeting were Baptists, it was a Baptist cause of some kind that was considered. Two leading Caversham citizens (West and Talbot) were anxious to have anything that was promoted 'open', not

exclusive, open to non-baptised people not just for the receipt of
communion but for full membership and as deacons and elders.
Mr Goldston stood for more exclusivity. Even though 'it was felt highly
desirable that, if possible, united action should be secured', there was
disagreement, and the cause went on — but without Goldston, the only
man who already had a visible congregation, without heavy overheads,
meeting in his house. West was against having anything to do with a
denomination at all. 'It was felt most undesirable to set up a separate
interest.' But pressures, especially financial, were felt to be
overwhelming in a denominational direction: 'as human nature is
constituted and in the present condition of the Christian world it was
impossible altogether to ignore "denomination".' They intended to be
merely a preaching station, with a £1,650 building, for 'our wish is not
to weaken any existing church, whilst undertaking purely evangelistic
labours here', but even for that the support of a denomination was
considered necessary. The station could not come out of the efforts of
Caversham alone, even with West as a backer.

The first building was completed in 1866. West paid for two-thirds
of it.[46] Three years later the minister of Kings Road was pressing for
moves towards a more fully-equipped church — with a minister, regular
services, administration of the ordinances, clubs and the rest — i.e.
precisely what had initially been avoided. Aldis of Kings Road said that
he knew the dangers of multiplying separate chapels, but thought
alternatives impossible. He had wanted open membership shared with
Kings Road under a double pastorate in order to prevent the
duplication of chapel superstructure, but in the end he rejected the idea
as impractical. In a letter to West, one of the imperatives in Aldis's mind
was shown to be the competitive desire to start something new, in
order to pre-empt the more exclusive Baptist cause which might
threaten to build in Caversham. The locals agreed, a minister at £150 p.a.
was hired, and the Lord's Supper celebrated for the first time in the
building in July 1869.

The final push towards the formation of a separate church with its
own rules, and its own massive 1877 building, was provided by the
unpredictable resignation of Aldis's successor at Kings Road after a
quarrel with his deacons and congregation. Although some of the
members of the Caversham cause wanted to join with other chapels in
the area, this minister came over to Caversham and started trying to
organise an entirely independent chapel. He took the Lord's Supper for
the first time for them in 1871, and 'suggested for their consideration
the propriety of forming themselves into a Christian Church, that by

such closer union the edification of the individual members might be promoted and their influence for good on others around might be increased'. 'The way thus being hedged up, our choice lay between prolonging the somewhat anomalous condition. . .and the formation of an entirely separate church.'

In 1872 they formed such a church. 'We hereby agree to form ourselves into a Christian Church, which shall have as its essential condition of membership a sincere profession of repentance towards God and of faith in our Lord Jesus Christ, to be evidenced by a consistent holy life: and that relying on Divine Aid we now convenant with each other to faithfully fulfil all the duties of Church members as we shall discover them by a reverend and prayerful study of the Word of God.' The massive building followed, in spite of the fact that, at the time of construction, membership was one hundred, and seating accommodation in the existing building was three hundred. The major part of the £5,000 cost came from large donations – a mere £51 from local collecting cards.

The balance between local, widely-spread effort and donations of individual businessmen, the relationship between the formation of the church as a building and the church as a congregation, the degree of planning in relation to supposed need, as opposed to the expression of the imperatives of groups and individuals wanting active spiritual outlets, the role of ministers, all varied greatly even amongst this small sample of chapels in Reading. Whatever the mix between them, the inheritance passing down to later activists seemed overwhelmingly to be a more or less elaborate building. Bricks and mortar seemed to be magnetic in their attractive power, regardless of consequence.

In many cases beyond the examples so far cited, the mix needs no special narrative. Two important Anglican churches (St. John's and Holy Trinity) were, quite simply, 'temple(s) built at the individual expense of a munificent clergyman'. They were built in 1836 and 1826 respectively. St. John's was later rebuilt in 1872 at a cost of £12,000. Holy Trinity had a pre-history. Before the Rev. Hulme weighed in with £6,000 in 1826, church extenders at St. Mary's had been considering a 'share-holders' church', in which those who invested would have the right to profit from the seat rents; but discussion was cut short by Hulme's 'munificence'. The way in which such building came to be seen as improvement of the urban furniture was shown in a biography of Hulme's successor, a man who built schools, a vicarage and two houses to go with Holy Trinity: 'church, schools, dwellings, formed indeed a group harmonious in style and one no less creditable to his

taste than beneficial to the principal edifice, while it was welcomed by
the public as an improvement of a suburb of Reading where an
important road, leading from Oxford, entered the town, not to speak
of the increased efficiency which it contributed to the Master's
ministry. . .'⁴⁷

Elsewhere it was not so simple. For proper understanding of how,
for example, St. Luke's came into being on the Redlands estate, a
blow-by-blow account, too long for this chapter, would be necessary,
of which money would form only one part. At several points between
1878 and 1883 it almost did not happen; some did not want it to
happen, realising what would later be involved. That it finally did get
built was again to a significant extent due to one man – Mayor Blandy.
Although the role of the locality was stressed in the accounts of the
forming of St. Luke's, in fact it was secondary at each stage. At the
lunch to celebrate the consecration service in 1883, the vicar was proud
of the fact that 'one lady had collected £6 in pennies, one other had
collected £72 in shillings and almost the first subscription towards a
special appeal for £500 had come from a factory girl'. Although
showing the aspiration towards making the church an organic product
of the Redlands area, these collections were small beer compared to
free gifts of the land by G. May, and very large sums from
Mr and Mrs Blandy. George Palmer attended the consecration having
already subscribed large sums to the fund. At it he spoke of the 'true
spiritual unity' of the different denominations, while also rebuking the
Church of England for not doing enough in fields like temperance,
education, and social reform. Once the building process started, it
seemed difficult to stop. Halls were seen as equal in importance to
churches in the late nineteenth and early twentieth centuries. St. Luke's
spent many years in the early twentieth century trying to raise one-sixth
of the cost of the church for a £1,600 Hall. They had great difficulty in
doing so.

There was one other very different type of foundation which should
be looked at before general questions about origins can have meaning.
In 1898 St. Mary's Episcopal Chapel Castle Street celebrated its
centenary. It had been part of a chain of a certain type of churches and
chapels which started in order to serve the immediate worshipping needs
of specific groups of schismatics. Groups moved in and out of buildings
as needs dictated. Later some of these churches developed the need to
work at the creation of other churches for outlying areas. But initially
it was doctrine, liturgy, or the charisma of a minister which was the
impulse. However, they often spawned large permanent structures.

At St. Giles the vicar until 1774 was a successful evangelical minister.[48] His successor (until 1797) started anti-evangelical, but was changed by his congregation and became as ardent as his predecessor, and drew large crowds.[49] The next minister did not change the anti-evangelical views with which he started; as a result of a sermon on 'the probable causes and consequences of Enthusiasm' a great part of his congregation withdrew and resolved to worship more after their own fashion. The schismatics wrote to each of the three vicars in Reading for permission to erect an episcopal chapel in the parishes, with their own appointees as ministers. They were refused permission, so they went ahead. They opened their own St. Mary's Chapel, not five hundred yards from the parish church of St. Mary's, and only a little further from St. Giles. Preaching was basic to the life and success of the parent church and the new chapel. But once they got a permanent minister in 1807, St. Mary's Chapel itself began an active programme of rural church extension involving six churches. The services remained the main thing, 'every sitting in the spacious chapel, said to hold 1,200 persons, was soon let; and for years the aisles were filled at almost every service, 'This surprised no one more than myself' (wrote James Sherman, the minister from 1807 to 1821). 'The ministry was neither original, nor learned, nor intellectual, nor mythical, nor comic. The doctrines were those usually styled moderate Calvinist.'[50]

A chain reaction was set off by this secession which led to some of the most important nineteenth-century religious furniture in Reading. On the then edges of the town, members of Sherman's congregation met and held services in the kitchen of a Caversham farm. A landowner in the neighbourhood, a friend of Rowland Hill, wanted to erect a church. She asked Sherman if she could build near the Caversham farm. It was agreed; in 1827 the congregation worshipping in the farmer's kitchen 'was transferred to the more convenient sanctuary' of Caversham Hill Chapel. For how long would it really be 'more convenient'? An inadequate endowment was left by the landowner, and the whole process of hiring ministers, building up chapel machinery and forming a separate congregation with its own rules started. The chapel was formed into a congregation in 1855 administered from Castle Street Congregational Chapel, until a break towards independence was made in May 1902.[51]

Long before this there had been a secession from St. Mary's Chapel in 1808 leading some of the congregation to move to Salem Chapel, a disused Presbyterian church in Minster Street. Like a number of other buildings in Reading (such as St. Giles Hall, and Victoria Hall in

Fatherson Road), Salem served as an adaptable staging-post for congregations to move in and out of as needs drove them. It was useful in nineteenth-century cities to have such buildings free from the burdens of continuity. The 1808 secession united the refugees from St. Mary's with others from Broad Street Congregational and from the Baptists in Hosier Street. They did not last long; in 1820 they moved to London Street. A High Calvinist congregation succeeded them, and then, until 1900, Salem was used by Primitive Methodists. Thereafter, it was absorbed into the local department store — Heelas, in the mid-twentieth century itself absorbed into the John Lewis partnership. Touching the history of congregations of this type at one point leads into many others, for such was the dynamic of this type of religious growth. If we follow the 1820 move into London Street we find them in a building opened by Unitarians in 1814; the Unitarians had failed to sustain a congregation; so did the Rev. J.S. Watson, the leader of the 1820 move. In 1826 he moved on and in 1827 the congregation dispersed.

Moving back to our starting place in St. Mary's Chapel, a further secession took place in 1836, after Sherman had left and the Trustees had decided to license the chapel as 'a place of worship according to the usages of the Church of England'. Two hundred members of the congregation met at Broad Street and decided to build a large new place of worship, Castle Street Congregational Chapel, immediately opposite St. Mary's, facing it across a narrow street. This chapel, now a retail showroom, lasted longer than most of the ten- to twenty-year congregations described above. It died in 1905, having been host to a migrating congregation from St. Augustine's Congregational Chapel in Friar Street in 1886, which itself had been built in 1877 as the result of a secession from Broad Street in 1869. This dense religious undergrowth spreading without artificial fertilisers was an utterly different phenomenon from the slow, painful, time-consuming, anxious creation of new churches and chapels which went on alongside it, and which succeeded it. It was not a question of 'if a church be not speedily provided for these people they may entirely lose the habit of church going' as on the Elm Lodge estate, or of 'a vicar wonder(ing) how on earth he is going to cope with men and money for such an increase of work in his parish' as at St. Mark's, but of people providing for their own immediately felt religious needs. These needs, however, also led to structures which burdened and shaped the religious activity of later generations.[52] The undergrowth could not easily be cleared every season; it grew into large trees whose shade then began to weaken the undergrowth itself.

Reviewing the social history of particular congregations and churches as individual cases gives some sense of the materials out of which wider assertions have to be attempted. The first general area of enquiry will be chronological. Which churches and chapels were the products of which periods of Reading's social history?

A remarkable feature of Anglicanism was that six large churches (including Caversham and Tilehurst) standing in 1890 survived from pre-sixteenth-century Reading. Four of these were fertile mothers of new churches later, and all of them were strategic churches in their neighbourhoods.[53] Equally strategic were two survivors from the earliest phase in Nonconformity – Kings Road Baptists (1640) and Broad Street Congregationalists (1662-89).[54] Precisely what differences such longevity made to the performance and experience of these churches in our period could only be explored comparatively – via a town or suburb whose entire religious plant had to be created from scratch.

For the Church of England the period between the sixteenth and the mid-nineteenth centuries was relatively unimportant.[55] Elsewhere it mattered more; new denominations and new chapels owed their beginnings to this time. The Congregational Methodists, the Wesleyans, the Primitives, the Baptist schismatics at Providence (1802) and at Zoar (1819), all started their life in Reading during this period.[56] The Unitarians and the Presbyterians established a foothold in Reading at this time, but it was not maintained and they had to re-start later on.[57] Three Congregationalist churches – Castle Street, Tilehurst and Caversham Hill – were added to their stock before 1840, alongside much village extension work.

Activists in the period 1890-1914 in Reading lived in a religious house mostly built and furnished in the fifty years following 1840. The Church of England in those years was working almost entirely with organisations either created or remodelled during this time.[58] The Primitive Methodists were working with organisations created between 1866 and 1896. The Congregationalists did some building between 1890 and 1914, but mostly outside the town – they too lived in these years with the results of the period 1840-1890. Most Baptist chapels came from a burst of expansion late in the same period. The Strict Baptists, the Jews, the Brethren, and the Unitarians all inherited their churches from this time. As was said in 1882, 'in the last twenty years a spirit of religious enthusiasm has awakened both parties to their duty to provide for the spiritual requirements of the rapidly increasing population. . .church and chapel accommodation has more than doubled in that time'.[59] But if 1890 to 1914 creations are separated artificially from those before, only the Salvation Army, the Wesleyans, and the Railway Mission (1905) — all highly centralised operations — used worshipping plant mainly created between 1890 and 1914.[60] Other denominations added a great deal of subsidiary plant during these twenty-five years.

In asking questions about origins and development, proportions quantitatively expressed based upon the inclusive figure of eighty-three places of worship available for use at some time between 1890 and 1914, or any sub-group such as the twenty-nine Anglican places of worship, would be impossible and even where possible, misleading. There is an absence of documentation in many cases. Hard conclusions would also be misleading because of the many different types of building involved — mission halls, rooms used for worship, full chapels, etc. A small proportion may be more significant than its size, owing to the churches and chapels it includes; a large proportion may not mean what it suggests, for instance if it includes a large number of halls.

Carefully constructed generalisation informed by numbers may, however, be helpful. Questions as to the chronology of growth by schism, the periodisation of types and sources of money, the length of time involved between conception and realisation of churches and chapels in bricks and mortar, the order of precedence between a 'church' or formally defined congregation in the sense used in the Baptist examples described above, and an actual building, can be tentatively answered. The role of independent growth 'from below' as opposed to provided growth 'from above' — the relationship between religion *of* and religion *for* — can be explored chronologically up to a point.

A further case which epitomises what is meant here by schismatic growth as opposed to other types of growth is that of Zoar Strict Baptist chapel in South Street. 'A brief account of the rise and progress of the church of Christ meeting at Zoar Chapel, South Street, Reading' was entered in the *Minute Book* of the chapel in December, 1882. 'About the middle of the year 1858, four or five believers who could not, from conscientious motives, join any church then existing in Reading, having become acquainted with each other and feeling united together through spiritual conversation agreed to take a small room at 76, Oxford Street for the purpose of holding prayer meetings, and occasionally to hear a Minister who might be passing through the town.'

They continued in this way until August 1860. Then several members of Providence Baptist chapel resigned, and with the 'few friends' already meeting agreed to take a room at New Hall, London Street (the old Mechanics' Institute, then (1866) the headquarters of Primitive Methodism in Reading, then editorial offices of the *Reading Standard* until, with the arrival of the newspaper magnate Lord Thomson in the 1960s, the building was put up for sale). 'Here the Lord was pleased to increase their numbers and establish them in truth as it is in Christ Jesus.' Then another group joined – a meeting was held with those who had been members of 'a gospel church' in December 1862, 'to consider the propriety of being formed into a church.' 'After some consideration' they agreed to develop in this way. So six years after the original meeting three Deacons were appointed, and the Lord's Supper was celebrated for the first time in 1863. They 'adopted Mr Goldsby's article of faith'. They thus had a room, three merged groups of believers, a 'church' with deacons, communion, and articles of faith, adopted in that order. What next? 'The inconveniences' of meeting in London Street Hall were felt, and in October 1864 they decided to build for themselves. In March 1866, still not having built, they moved to the Black Horse room in Queens Road. At the end of that year a site was obtained. In 1869 a plan was agreed upon. On 29th October 1869 a building was erected at a cost of £615. Within six years the debt had been cleared 'so that we believe the Lord's approbation rests on our endeavours'.[61]

Not all cases of 'schismatic' growth were as clear as that. Judgment has to be exercised on fine distinctions between chapels like Anderson Baptist or Caversham Methodist Church[62] where it was the missionary imperatives of groups within an existing church, but sometimes not encouraged by it, which led to new chapels, and pure schismatic groups who deliberately broke away from the parent body because they found its practices inadequate or unacceptable. Closely related to the latter were congregations which formed without the patronage or parentage of existing organisations – 'believers', like the first of the three groups who coalesced into Zoar 'who could not, from conscientious motives, join any church then existing in Reading'. These for our purposes will be included amongst 'schismatics'. Dividing up schisms as opposed to other types of origin by denomination is not useful, since, for example, by definition once a schism occurs within an Anglican church (e.g. St. Mary's Episcopal Chapel) that church ceases to fall (for a time at least) under the heading 'Anglican', and conversely Strict Baptist chapels were in part breakaways from parent, usually Baptist bodies.

It is better to try an overall assessment, across denominational boundaries.[63]

A minimum of ten places of worship existing between 1890 and 1914 had been the product of schism. While not perhaps an impressive proportion of the eighty-three, they included important organisations – such as Trinity Congregational Chapel and Hosier Street Congregational Methodist Chapel, with strategic importance amongst the total array of halls and churches. Of these ten, five belong to the period before 1840, five to the period after that date. This means that as a mode of initiating new religious organisations, schism was relatively more typical earlier than later, even though absolute numbers were more later. This is confirmed when organisations initiated earlier which did not survive into the period 1890-1914 are added to those which did.[64] Schism was becoming less typical as a way of starting religious organisations in Reading through the nineteenth century. Between 1890 and 1914, with the qualified exception of Anderson, no single example has been discovered. Supply *for* was becoming a more significant generator of churches and chapels than demand *of.*

A related conclusion emerges from the methods of finance in the building up of the stock of churches and chapels available for use in the late nineteenth and early twentieth centuries.

The constraints imposed on organisations by economic and social circumstances in nineteenth-century capitalism were formidable even in this boom town. The availability of local funds to meet the needs of the Baptists was depressingly small in 1892-3 in Earley. Their difficulties were not exceptional.

At various dates Primitive Methodists, Wesleyans, and Baptists all issued debenture shares as an alternative to raising a mortgage at high interest rates. Holy Trinity, as has been seen, was to have been a 'shareholders church' before a large donor rescued it. Anderson Baptists self-consciously copied the Primitives in April 1910 by issuing £1 debentures 'upon the deeds of the bank, offering 4 or 4½%...which was an inducement to anyone with capital which was at present only realising 2½%'. By this means their ambition was to raise £500 of the estimated cost of the £1,000 chapel before its opening. Such a resort to stock exchange techniques failed. By opening day, the cost of the church had risen to £1,300 and the amount already raised was a mere £259.

Oxford Road and Beecham Road Primitive Methodist Chapel resorted to direct borrowing. The chapel cost £990; £200 came from a donation from another circuit, £50 from George Palmer, and £500 had

148   *Religion and Voluntary Organisations in Crisis*

to be borrowed at 5%. Small donations added up to a total of £7.17.6*d*.
Some indication of the social strata involved here can be gained from
an 1896 *List of the Trustees* of the chapel. They consisted of a butcher,
three labourers, a stableman, a baker, two brick and tile makers, a
foreman, a clerk, a tailor, a grocer and a carpenter. The situation of a
Methodist chapel – Caversham Heights – in a much more affluent
neighbourhood and with more affluent trustees was also difficult. Soon
after opening in 1909, £246 of the £2,295 which the chapel had cost
remained to be paid. This position had been achieved only by
borrowing, initially £700 at 4%, then another £1,000. When in July
1912 the £1,000 creditor asked for an instalment to be paid back, they
were in serious difficulties and had to ask the Extension Committee of
the Reading circuit for emergency help. In September 1913 another
creditor asked for £250. He was asked to wait for a year. They could
just keep their current account going each year, with slight deficits.
Their capital account could only be serviced by continual new loans
making their long-term situation ever more difficult. Such a situation
explains the necessity for national efforts like the Twentieth-Century
Fund.

There was some self-consciousness amongst religious organisations
about ways of raising money. There were aspirations towards local
self-dependence, scattered resistance to forms of money-making
activity like bazaars, which were felt to be undesirable, and realisation
of what it meant to rely on a few rich men. But it was a common
situation that, as the vicar of Caversham wrote in 1890 after the freeing
of one of his churches from debt, 'liabilities of this kind too often hang
like millstones upon the neck of the incumbents, with their straitened
incomes and fetter their free action for years'. Anderson Baptists
rationalised their story, already told, by suggesting at the opening
ceremony that 'the committee had endeavoured to provide a building
simple in structure and well ventilated, in the very midst of the people
for whom they had laboured so long, and at a price proportionate to
the means of those whom they hoped would worship there. . .they had
done so rather than migrate to an expensive site. . .to spend many
thousands upon a building, and land the church with an enormous
burden of debt'. So they could have been in a worse position than they
were. Christ Church Whiteley allowed the vicar to pay his own salary,
but even so he had to complain of the reliance of the church on four
rich men. At St. Bartholomew's and at St. Giles there was a hierarchy
of means and ends in relation to raising money, 'we have always
contended that sales, concerts, etc. are secondary and inferior channels

of charity, but for a secondary object, like the repair of the Iron Church. . .a sale would be appropriate'.[65] Both St. Stephen's and St. Mark's were chided by their parent churches for not being able to pay for themselves.

Within these constraints, some areas of the town, and entire economic and occupational groupings, could not possibly provide the dominant types of building, and then man and maintain them, for themselves. Resort to capitalist modes of finance was a possible way out, and a viable one in the case of other organisations in the town in the late nineteenth century, like the Football Club. But religion did not seem to be able to adopt completely this characteristic twentieth-century mode, although business modes of organisation were tried, and the distribution of commodities in bazaars and sales of work was a resort frequently favoured. Not only was religion an activity inherently unlike football (as some purists were forced to argue against those who seemed to be disagreeing) but also there was resistance to such modes even within denominations (such as Wesleyan Methodism) which were busily trying to adopt them.[66] There were, however, other ways of finance, which can tentatively be arranged over time.

The contributions of large local donors were of fundamental importance during the second half of the nineteenth century. They became less available between 1890 and 1914, meaning that denominational machinery would have to become more important if building was to go on. Elaborate churches and chapels in Reading were, in significant numbers of cases, the expression of the impulse and donations of local wealthy men, and could not have been built without them. These churches and chapels then acted as diffusion-centres for the provision of further buildings later on. Such buildings tended to be of a different type – more purpose-built, with the needs of the neighbourhood taken more self-consciously into account, and using national denominational funds rather than local individual gifts.

The contrast, at its best, was, for instance, between the work of a man like Alfred Sutton within the evangelical wing of the Anglican church in the mid-nineteenth century, and the work of Wesleyan extension in the town after 1903. Sutton (1818-97), 'an Evangelical churchman of the type which seems to be less common than it was',[67] was a partner in the seed firm during its maximum expansion period. He lived in the town, was on the School Board for fifteen years, was superintendent of St. Lawrence's Sunday School until 1855, became a church warden and Bible Class leader at St. John's, built a coffee house called 'The British Workman', and was personally responsible for the building of three mission rooms or churches 'in populous parts of the town', as well as St. John's Reading Room in Princes Street. The phrase 'at its best' is appropriate in his case, since the funds he provided for church building were accompanied by much personal commitment of time and energy.[68]

By contrast to this type of church provision, the most successful operation between 1890 and 1914 was the £25,000 burst which led to the building of four Wesleyan Mission Halls or chapels in Reading, between 1903 and 1910.[69] This led Methodism to boast of being 'the greatest Free Church in Reading'. The scheme was provoked by the national Million Guineas Fund, from which an initial £1,000 was promised at the first meeting in May 1903. The spur was also the realisation that instead of ten per cent — 'the generally accepted ratio for Wesleyan Methodism' — local Methodist buildings could only seat three per cent of the population.

The scheme followed a lot of earlier building. As with the Primitives, early revivalism, open-air and temporary- and rented-building modes were succeeded by the gradual acquisition of elaborate plant. The first big step (1817) was a mistake. 'A gentleman' promised £3,000, to encourage them to enlarge a building. But he reneged, leading to a debt of £2,500 hanging round them until a three-day bazaar, national denominational donations, and local subscriptions wiped it out at the building Jubilee in 1867. 'Freed from this load the circuit took a new lease of life', and spent £25,000 on trust property even before the 1903 scheme.[70]

The big scheme aimed to get away from the 'family Methodism' of the earlier chapels, towards provision designed for the working class. Two of the buildings were to be large Halls, having 'all the features and excellences of our great central city halls'. Rather than being primarily regarded as temples in God's honour, or centres of worship in set services, these were self-consciously designed for community purposes. They were also designed as an adjustment to the spectator — as opposed to the membership mode of relating to religious organisation. 'They must find some way of recognising in connection with their church life the millions connected with Methodism who were not tabulated in their figures.' In one case the hall section of the building was its main part, with the chapel pushed upstairs. It was a centralised market-research type operation — an attempt to supply what was thought to be needed from the outside, rather than the immediate result of the impulse of a pious Reading citizen of means, or of the imperatives of groups of Reading worshippers who could find no satisfaction elsewhere.[71]

Outside money and subscriptions were necessarily important. But, led by one Thomas May who had become a local preacher in the Reading circuit in 1882 and who was a wizard at raising money, there was much aspiration towards local finance. There was 'a constant series of exploits for years', principally exchanging commodities in elaborate bazaars and sales of work. 'The Ladies' were essential; 'sales of work are regular and many, being an unfailing source of income to all the financial schemes'. In October 1908 a £1,000 bazaar, with the theme of 'Old Abbeys and Castles', was planned to last a week. No less than six bazaars were arranged to celebrate the centenary of the circuit in 1911, when it was estimated that £4,000 was needed 'so as to allow of the circuit income meeting expenditure'.[72] The story takes on a nightmare quality when one reads the further pleas for money made at the Oxford District level, of which the Reading circuit was a part, in November 1912. Reading was relatively strong, but:

> at present our people in town and village are crushed beneath intolerable financial burdens. The energies of poor, but loyal and devoted circuits have been exhausted in raising thousands of pounds solely for the purpose of paying interest on loans, which has prevented them engaging in any aggressive enterprise...this is well-nigh breaking the hearts of some of our best workers...We could write stories that would be read with incredulity by many, that would be full of horror were it not for the sadness and pathos of the circumstances.

They needed a further £28,000.[73]

Other aspects of the coming into being of churches and chapels about which it is possible to attempt more than the citing of individual examples, are the questions of timing, and of the order in which things happened. Consideration of the latter extends the point already made. On the question of the precedence of a spiritual or a physical church, denominational but not chronological observations can be made. Within some denominations it was common, but not universal, for a 'church' in the sense of a congregation of believers to precede bricks and mortar; in other cases, such a church either did not exist, or existed in doctrine but not in regulations or practices which made much difference to the day-to-day conduct of attenders and their organisations. There might be signs or sacraments denoting degrees of commitment – baptism, confirmation, etc. – but these denoted commitment to 'the church' at large, the body of Christ on earth, rather than to a particular group or community of believers in a particular building in a particular street in Reading, such as those at Zoar in South Street. At St. George's Anglican Church in Tilehurst it was hoped that, 'as we see the House that is being built for His honour in our midst, growing step by step to its completion, so may He help us, His living stones, gradually to grow into a spiritual temple, acceptable to Him through Jesus Christ'.[74] The evidence does not allow a statement as to whether communities of believers defining themselves as a church preceding buildings were less common between 1890 and 1914 compared to any other time in the social history of the town. Such evidence would assist in sorting out the relationship between 'from-below' and 'from-above' elements in religious organisation over time.

A common procedure within Anglicanism, especially from the late nineteenth century onwards, was for a main church to be preceded by an iron church provided by the mother (St. Giles or St. Mary's) church. After some branch or activity had outgrown the iron church it would then be replaced by a more permanent structure. Frequently the branch or activity would be part of the penumbra of surrounding agencies such as the Sunday School, rather than of the worshipping, Sunday or mid-week service part of church life. Thus at St. Michael's Elgar Road a Sunday School chapel developed into the church. A third stage, very frequent in the twenty-five years following 1890, would be the construction of a Hall. Sub-organisations such as Class meetings within Wesleyan Methodism, to the extent that they continued to be a part of church life (there were intermittent complaints as to their absence in the town), aimed at being instruments for the ordering, controlling, and deepening of the commitment of existing groups of believers with existing buildings, rather than the seeds from which societies and chapels would grow.[75] In two Methodist cases in Reading there was evidence of groups of believers preceding buildings: one at Spring Gardens where a 'society' preceded Whitley Hall; the other cottage prayer meetings out of which Lower Caversham started. Salvation Army 'Corps' certainly existed for a long time without purpose-built citadels. Indeed, that was a central characteristic of the Army in Reading, including the Central Corps until Fidler's building (see n.71) intervened. Within Congregationalism it was equally common for 'churches' to precede buildings (Park Institute) and to follow them (Caversham Hill built 1827, church formed 1855). Both also occurred within Baptism (preceding — Carey, Grovelands, Caversham Free, before the final building; following — Anderson). The Strict Baptists at Zoar formed a 'church' seven years before they built one, the

Congregational Methodists also existed before they took over Hosier Street. The Jews formed a society – the Reading Hebrew Burial Society – in 1886, fourteen years before the synagogue. The Unitarians called themselves a church before the building. Eleven years after they had built a church there were some signs in a minister's farewell address in 1888 that it may have made them appear less distinct as a group:

> This little church (the Unitarian chapel of 1877) is a monument of self-sacrificing zeal. You have realised that God and duty belong to the present; God to us is only here; to us the New Jerusalem is not in the clouds, it covers the world. Its limit is our furthest horizon. You embarked on an arduous enterprise. Universal Truths are at the first only held by a few. You resolved to bear witness to the truth, to remind all our dear and honoured friends around us that universal religion embraces all of them. At first they resented the erection of this Church. I am not surprised; they supposed we were going to cast scorn on the traditions they loved. They found it was not so. . .

A common feature of the process of bringing chapels into being between 1890 and 1914 was that halls often deliberately preceded, and took precedence over, formal chapels. This was not only the case with the Twentieth Century Wesleyan Fund but with other late nineteenth-century Wesleyan foundations and with energetic chapels in other denominations. It was as if diagnosis of neighbourhood needs, for a place of meeting for clubs and societies, for a centre for entertainment and recreation, for a common base for all the organisations specific to particular age-groups and classes, took priority in the suppliers' minds and pockets over holy places set apart for worship and prayer in the traditional architectural styles. A Hall in Oxford Road (1892) preceded the permanent Wesleyan chapel there (1893). The first permanent Methodist structure in Caversham was the School Hall opened in October 1891. Whitley Hall and Elm Park Hall were within the Twentieth Century Fund scheme, 'erected to meet the needs of the population in our Western and Southern suburbs'. 'They were living in a new age, when conditions were altered, and the Wesleyan church must meet the conditions. . .(the Hall) stood for a form of social religion. Large numbers of people turned to these places as some others turned to their homes. . .in the ethical side of religion they stood for all-round application of the truth of Christ in daily life.' Other important examples were Anderson Baptist Church and a very deliberate and self-conscious 'Institutional church' – Park Institute

Congregational Church. The latter prided itself on being adapted to the needs of a new age and being a 'modern' type of foundation. Its chronology was: 1892, preliminary discussion; 1900, land acquired; 1907, Institute built; 1923, final chapel built.[76] From the time of initial conception to the time of actual realisation it generally took longer to bring into being a church or chapel in the period 1890 to 1914 than had been the case during the preceding fifty years. But if a building was to be the final goal, the longer the delay the more the religion of the man in the pew would have had to do with bricks and mortar — preparing for the supposed climax.

Whatever the motivation, the consequences of the vast voluntary outcrop of religious building in Reading, and the accumulation of bricks and mortar which commanded so much religious space, were to exaggerate the impact upon religious organisations of constraints imposed by the wider society. A change would no doubt have taken place in Primitive Methodism after the mid-century anyway, but the weight of external constraints upon the organisation (described in the 1890 *Primitive Methodist Magazine* article already quoted) was made heavier by their own 'erections', particularly given the fact that their constituency was a working-class one. It is difficult to separate cause and effect here; we are dealing with consequences of consequences. But it was in no sense inevitably determined that buildings should have accumulated in such a way as to define, as they evidently did for the Wycliffe pioneers in Earley, missionary success. Indeed, implications of such a weight of building were quite apparent to those activists at the time who had experienced before-and-after in the life of a single church. The change from zeal to routine, from confident aggression to worried organisational concern which was experienced by Primitive Methodists through the nineteenth century was quite explicitly connected to building and accompanying apparatus.[77]

Highly successful Christian groups, such as the Amish in Pennsylvania, have long forsworn separate church buildings altogether.[78] There is no intrinsic connection between Christianity and ecclesiastical architecture, any more than there is between Christianity and twentieth-century denominational structures. But it *was* necessary, in the society of that time, that if buildings were to accumulate, religion would in some measure have to be client to local sources of money, or, when they became less available, to commercial, denominational, or State sources. That this constituted a barrier to religion becoming fully *of* numbers unlimited was realised by a perceptive contemporary religious

entrepreneur like General William Booth, who took deliberate steps to
keep the financing of local Corps of the Salvation Army as 'from
below' as could be. The more elaborate the plant, even though
designed precisely to avoid restriction, the less it could be the property,
in the fullest sense, of anyone other than that class of persons who
could afford it. He who pays the piper does not always call the tune,
but he does influence the whole manner, setting and audience in which
the piper plays. How much the piper costs is also important; and that
can be influenced by people other than the paymaster, through
decisions on what kind of piper is wanted and what he is required to
play.

Churches and chapels were present not only as buildings of varying
sizes, but also as employers, or joint employers with supra-town
denominational structures, of full-time ministers. Such ministers had
their own interests in organisational matters, leading them sometimes
to take an active or even a determining role, for example in building.
Denominations such as the Wesleyans, the Primitives and the Salvation
Army recognised the potential danger to other commitments of
long-term local interests by insisting upon quick rotation of ministries.[79]

Ministers have to be added to buildings, and to church commitment
to educational plant, before the full weight of in-turning organisational
pressure can be grasped. The general point is simple; large organisation
must compete for finite energies and resources with other imperatives
such as, in religious terms, doctrine or way of life. The extent and
distribution of those finite energies and resources depends upon the
particular period and system. Put crudely, it depends upon who owns
what. In some circumstances, organisation can so eat up other
imperatives as to become a primary imperative in itself.[80] This can be
watched as it happened in Primitive Methodism in Reading through the
nineteenth and early twentieth centuries. In the period 1838 to 1914
there were thirty-five lay-people in Reading who merited obituaries in
the national *Primitive Methodist Magazine.* Analysis of these obituaries
shows the changing qualities esteemed in the lives of activists, no
matter whether these qualities were in fact exhibited. Drawing a line
before and after 1860 (and counting in both halves those with twenty
years of activism either side of this line) it is clear that qualities such as
experience of conversion, manner of meeting death, strength under
persecution or aggression in evangelism, gave way to qualities such as
contribution to building works, work in the penumbra of chapel
organisations, worldly success and gentle virtues like geniality or
kindness, as the most prized assets of a Methodist life. The same

change can be watched as chapel anniversaries, and events associated
with the life of schools attached to chapels took over from revivalist
occasions as the standard local matter in the national denominational
press.[81] The main point here, however, is to show the scale of
organisation involved and thereby its nature as an unnecessary or
exaggerated constraint, and also to show that it did indeed lead to an
in-turning, and was felt at the time to be so doing.

The importance of a full-time professional ministry varied from
congregation to congregation, and denomination to denomination. In
Anglican parishes, having an adequate staff was seen as parallel in
importance to the church fabric, and to schools. This meant, for
example, eight curates in St. Mary's parish in 1890 where, in 1832,
there had been one clergyman alone. St. Luke's parish became worried
when it looked as though their staff would have to be cut: 'it is quite
clear that a district as large as St. Luke's cannot be efficiently ministered
to by less than two priests, and it would be disastrous if the failure of
the parishioners to recognise their duty in regard to the maintenance of
the clergy should lead to the withdrawal of one of the priests.' In a year
when the total expenditure of St. Peter's church in Caversham was
£1,147, £355 went on Assistant Clergy, £250 on Church Expenses, and
£153 on Educational Purposes.

The quality of individual men of course made a difference to the
life of the congregation and to the life of the town, even though an
exceptional minister may have been transferring members and attenders
from one place of worship to another rather than increasing absolute
numbers.[82] A change of minister did often produce improved individual
congregational statistics.[83] But having fewer ministers, or having no
settled minister, or having no minister at all did not inhibit dynamic
performance. Broad Street Congregational Chapel, where there was
never more than one minister between 1890 and 1914, was no less
'successful' by the most commonly-used criteria, than St. Mary's Parish
Church, a short walk away, where there were never less than six
full-time staff. During a gap in ministry at Kings Road Baptist Chapel
in 1894 the chapel minutes recorded that 'our Lord's Day congregations
have not suffered as we feared they might, if anything they have slightly
improved'.[84] The Unitarians noticed in 1901-3 how 'the absence of a
settled minister, instead of depressing the congregation has stimulated
them to increased activity'. After W.G. Hailstone had been forced by
the deacons to leave Wycliffe Baptist Chapel in 1896, the members did
not look for a regular pastor for a time. They preferred to be without.

During this period schools were felt to be even more essential to

many churches than professional staff. The commitment of Anglican
churches was on a scale sufficient to colour the whole operation of the
church, and to affect what it could or would do elsewhere. For example,
in St. Mary's parish, £7,500 out of the £33,000 spent on buildings
between 1875 and 1894 was spent on schools. They were constantly in
deficit, but (1898-9) 'we simply cannot let them go'. It was only after
the State, through the 1902 Education Act, had limited their
responsibilities to the fabric of their schools, that they were able to go
ahead with the building of the new church of St. Mark's. Until then it
was the School Fund which prevented them from starting. Greyfriars
were forced to give up their commitments in 1914, after spending a
sizeable slice of their annual budget on schools (in 1911 £140,
compared to £240 for church expenses).[85] The tone of complaint was
continual at St. Giles. They had spent £10,773 on schools between
1870 and 1906, 'all this had been done by churchmen for the sake of
their faith and because they desired to give to the children of their
poorer brethren the benefit of a religious education'.[86] As compulsory
standards rose after 1902 they tried desperately to keep up. A reader of
the Parish Magazine over the next ten years could be forgiven for
thinking that raising money for St. Giles' schools *was* Christianity.
Especially when they read, as in 1906, that any other option faced them
with 'the appalling abyss of mere secularism'. At each step there was
complaint at inadequate local support and inequitable government
policies, and much distress that control was being lost to His Majesty's
Inspectors.[87]

Not only were schools another variable pushing churches and chapels
into spending time on raising money from available sources, they also
forced religious bodies into intense political competition for the ear
and purse of the State. The fight was, however, over a contracting
territory. The local authority and the State were moving into an area
where voluntary efforts had had an exclusive empire. In 1871 in
Reading the only public elementary schools were the fourteen
voluntary ones. A government grant was indirectly received by the
3,495 children within them. Thirty years later in 1901, thirteen of
these schools were still open. But alongside them were ten Board
Schools. Of the 13,511 children at that date in receipt of indirect
government grants, 8,252 were in the Board schools.[88] In 1901, after
almost eighty years of independence, the Nonconformist Reading
British School was subsumed under the School Board. Such massive
change in the relationship between State and locality, and between
State and voluntary organisation, is one which will be echoed later in

other subject-areas for organisation. It was part of the whole changing
context for voluntary activity in the late nineteenth and early twentieth
centuries. Partly because of the depth of organisational commitment in
parishes like St. Giles, such a change was not articulated by those
experiencing it in this wider context. Rather it was seen as necessitating
a desperate effort to generate more of the same. A competitive fight
between Anglican and Nonconformist interest groups took place to
obtain the benefits, or to avoid the penalties of the new band wagon.

Running an organisation such as the typical large church or chapel
in Reading between 1890 and 1914, with an annual budget of
£2,000-plus, inevitably implied that much of what the organisation
was doing was raising money to service itself. Anything spent outside
the chapel (including the time of its leading activists who in such an
organisation were forced to choose between chapel and outside
commitments) was a luxury – like the small fraction of the budget
which went to the poor. Park Institute could only give to the Hospital
Sunday Fund in 1913 after it had taken 'church expenses' out of the
collections for that day, yet the Institute had been created especially
to look outwards and to be less ecclesiastical. Even where special
priority was given to foreign missions, as with the Baptist chapels in
Reading (in 1905 Kings Road raised £338 out of a total budget of
£1,698 for such Missions) the work entailed for activists was similar in
type to the work required in keeping the chapel apparatus going.[89]
Even a small-budget new organisation such as St. Mark's Mission Room
(after 1905 a church on its own) with receipts of £75 in a typical year,
spent as high a proportion as £66 on entirely internal objects.

Given the economic conditions in Reading and the view that
'welfare' was a particularly Christian province, the amount religious
organisations spent on the poor was a critical index of the
contradictions produced by introversion. For instance, Trinity
Congregational Chapel raised a total of £2,442 for all purposes in 1890.
On their own poor, as opposed to the poor outside the chapel on whom
they spent less, they spent £26. The expenditure of the Society of
Friends on all objects in 1890 was £374 – £59 of this went to 'Poor
Friends'. Grovelands Baptist Chapel in July 1902 needed between £4
and £5 a week to meet necessary organisational expenses. Collections
at the time amounted to £2.15/- a week. This left little margin for
community expenditure. Of £859 raised by Wycliffe Baptists in 1894,
£18 went into the Poor Fund. Smaller bodies spent proportionately
more. Zoar Strict Baptists recorded in their Minutes for the last
quarter of 1911 an Income of £10 and expenditure of £13, of which

£2.5/- went to the Poor. In the case of a poor congregation such as the
Oxford Road Primitive Methodists, where members' needs and the
needs of the immediate locality were apparent, the main item on the
Expenditure Account for 1897-8 was £60, for repaying a loan. Gas,
coke and repair bills absorbed most of the rest, with the only detectable
welfare expenditure being 5/- for the 'Widows and Orphans Fund'.
There was, of course, concealed expenditure and care which records do
not reveal in most churches and chapels. But the emphasis of this
paragraph would probably be correct even were that remaining
expenditure known. It was simple, as a church worker in the poor
district around St. Saviour's Coley saw it in 1904; there were people
starving 'for want of fuel and bread', if less were spent on church
machinery and over-organisation, the church would have more to
spend on the poor.[90]

Such critical perspectives found their echo in contemporary efforts
by particular churches and chapels to turn outwards, and to break
away from their apparatus into positive connection with the forces
bearing upon the economic and social life of Reading. The Caversham
Baptist Free Church formed a Christian Effort Committee in May 1893,
joining the Sunday School, the Working Men's Society, the Young
Men's Society and the Choir into an alliance to discuss directions for
work in the community outside the chapel. The St. John's CETS in
1909 formed a special committee to consider in what ways the branch
could 'bring its influence in matters affecting Temperance work to bear
upon the forces which control the life of the town'.[91] The Friends
Preparative Meeting in 1909 formed a study circle on Social Service
which was more than a rescue agency, or a moralising source of
charitable funds. They were to discuss unemployment, housing and
the Licensing Bill and to relate to 'the work of the Social Service Union
and the Anti-Gambling League formed largely by the enthusiasm of
Friends now undertaken by the Reading Citizens Association, whose
aim is to purify life in many directions'.[92]

Sometimes, however, the effort to break out was less significant
than what happened to that effort in relation to more introverted
chapel work. This was the case after the re-organisation of Trinity
Congregational Chapel in 1907 following Albert Swift's arrival. One of
the divisions of chapel work he insisted upon was a Social Service
Committee alongside a Benevolent Committee. The former was to
include 'all such matters as pertain to the promotion of social
redemption. It shall focus the activities of the members of the church
and congregation who are engaged in civic and philanthropic work in

the community, reporting the same to the church, with a view to promoting greater interest in all that pertains to social well-being'. Two years after its foundation it was reported that this branch had 'hardly come into its own yet, probably due to the fact that we have been so busy in other departments of church work'. In 1910 there were only five members on the Committee. In 1911 there was no trace of it. It was the first of his elaborately conceived branches of institutional church work to fold.

In the case of one chapel — the Anderson Memorial Baptist Chapel at Earley — the parallel processes of institutionalisation and introversion can be observed as they were actually happening. In the days when they were the Earley Rise Mission Band, springing from the efforts at extension made by members of Wycliffe Chapel and fighting for their existence with cottage meetings, open-air services and the like, they reported their work thus:

> the meeting had already brought to our notice several poor old people and other sick and needy ones and the desire to assist such quickly followed. A fund was started to which members of the Mission Band contributed not less than 1*d* per week. Gifts usually to the value of 2/6*d* were made in money or kind. . .this piece of service, although humble in its way added not a little to the future success of the work.[93]

Before there was a chapel, with a minister and an organised congregation, there was active concern for the poor of Earley in ways which involved sacrifice for the 'missionaries'. Such 'service' was seen as integral to what they were doing. Ironically it was one of the factors leading to 'success', or in other words to a situation of a growing chapel in which such work was less possible. Later records of the chapel make it clear that, once formed, it became an enclosed organisation. There were no references to the outside world except for two allusions to the 'indifferent' world of Earley Rise. 'Indifference' was a function of the new organisation as much as of basic attitudes in Earley. No policy resolutions were passed. Their special 'Visitation Committee' of November 1905 was started for sick and absent members — no one else. There was a Poor Fund, in 1904-5 at least. If that year was typical, the proportions were of the order already outlined — of £219, received for 'all branches of church work' about £5 was given out to the Poor Fund. They were fully aware that this was not enough, but this was what, in their established situation, they gave.[94]

It was the exception, 'a singular denomination' – Hosier Street Congregational Methodist Church – which proved the rule.[95] 'Congregational in its method of government and services, Methodist in its doctrine', in other words deliberate and thoughtful about its structure in relation to its beliefs, it was a fascinating case. The chapel had left the Wesleyan Reform Union, in the second schism in its history in 1864. At several points it demonstrated its impulse to be different – deliberately to resist tendencies it observed elsewhere. When there was a question of replacing the building which had been inherited with a larger, more elaborate structure the chapel took the rare decision to resist going up that expensive and energy-consuming path. They were a proudly self-sufficient group. They leased their chapel (a rare arrangement in itself) from 1854 until 1870, when they bought it for £975. In 1860 J. Milsom, a member, paid outright for their school room. In 1867 they debated a £3,000 new chapel scheme but deliberately decided against it in view of the constraints it would impose. They confined themselves fourteen years later, in 1881, to re-building and alterations costing £1,000.

In a *Memorandum* of 1871, they chided the Baptists, from whom they had taken over the building, for moving out to 'a more respectable locality'. 'The neighbourhood of Hosier Street is densely populated and has long been characterised by irreligion and gross immorality. The greater part of the inhabitants are of the poorer class and need the most earnest evangelistic effort.' They saw themselves as having a definite responsibility for that neighbourhood, and relating to it was more important than providing themselves with fine buildings. They operated on a small financial scale, with balance sheets fluctuating around £50 p.a. They confined themselves to a limited range of surrounding agencies – a Sunday School, a Band of Hope, a Mutual Improvement Class (started 1894), and a Christian Endeavour Society (started 1894). And yet they were involved in their locality, employing a full-time mission worker – in effect a social worker – for 'fallen women' and others in distress.

They were also deeply involved in outside affairs both at the level of the town and the wider society outside. One of their main officials – D. Clark – was active on the town council as a Progressive from 1903-4 onwards. Measured by local press coverage, they had a presence in the town disproportionate to their size and wealth. Politically they were active in the Liberal interest, allowing Liberal Association ward meetings to be held in their chapel (1903) while (1896) refusing to allow the Social Democratic Federation to use the premises.[96] Their attention was continually focussed on large public issues rather than bazaars.[97] And as a congregation without a formal professional leadership they did not lack at least some of the benefits of such spokesmen. D. Clark's tenure of the office of chairman throughout the period 1890 to 1914 was a vigorous and public type of organisational and spiritual leadership, both in the congregation and in the town. But Hosier Street was the only chapel of its denomination in Reading.

6 RELIGION (III)

Occasionally the activist's eye view of church and chapel life can be caught by the historian. A deputation of members went from Wycliffe Baptist Chapel to Burnley early in 1907 to report on a potential pastor. When they got back, 'they remarked that the buildings were not so large as Wycliffe, but the church membership was greater, all the institutions seemed to be in a flourishing condition and the church seemed to be greatly attached to their pastor'. Buildings first, then membership statistics, then the penumbra of sub-organisations, then congregational relations with the minister.[1]

This chapter will turn to the third of their priorities – the penumbra. An idea of its scale, wide distribution and matrix in a society where there was a general stress upon participation in ambitious and continuous voluntary associations has already been given. Here, as in the last chapter, implications and unintended consequences will be looked for, necessary and unnecessary contradictions explored. The interest will not lie in deducing the array and experience of religious organisations from a social context, but in exploring, within that social context, the implications of what religious organisations did or were for what else they could do or be. The aim will be to get some way further towards examining the difference between intention and function for churches and chapels.

One result of the quantity of machinery around churches and chapels was frequent overheating. 'We may be paying too high a price for our modern highly organised church life.'[2] In the case of at least two ministers in our period the price was nervous exhaustion, needing total withdrawal from action for a time.

> The tendency of parochial work [wrote a departing vicar of St. John's] was to increase and multiply in every direction. Each class and sometimes each section, and sometimes each profession wanted something specially done for themselves. They wanted their guilds for girls and also for boys, their Bible classes for factory girls, for servants and for shop assistants, and in addition to that there was the ordinary routine of a parish and no-one who had not worked in a parish could have any idea of the amount of work, strength and time required in simply keeping things going.[3]

163

'The tendency for some years', wrote Albert Swift of Trinity in 1910, 'has been to form a new and independent society for every fresh bit of work needing to be done. This has gone so far that many chapels are all but buried beneath their accumulated societies'. The cries of anguish were frequent.

In no case, however, did commensurate action to cut down the work take place. In St. Bartholomew's *Parish Magazine* in March 1909, it was found 'astonishing how increasingly large our undertakings have become'. But 'we must not grudge the money needful to produce the good results of these manifold organisations'. At St. Mary's in 1904 there was 'the almost herculean task of keeping our parochial home in order'. 'I confess that I am overwhelmed by the many difficulties which I did not anticipate when I accepted the onerous position of vicar of St. Giles', said the vicar in 1912. 'Every day the Treasurer and myself experience sensations which in the commercial world are the prelude to an appearance in the bankruptcy court', said the vicar of Christ Church in 1914. 'I think the greatest personal anxiety which I have in the parish is that of filling gaps, and finding new workers for carrying on our continually increasing work'. 'The strain of finding new workers for carrying on our large organisations has been considerable', complained the vicar of St. John's in 1910 and 1913.

On a more disturbing level, there was a felt conflict between organisational and spiritual success. The machinery which had been created to serve its master could become the master and displace the goals which, occasionally, churches and chapels remembered to be theirs. W. Rauschenbusch, in *Christianity and the Social Crisis* (1907) expressed the position with his customary lucidity: 'the tendency of organisations and institutions to aggrandise themselves at the expense of the ends for which they were called into existence is one of the most important phenomena in moral life. There is no permanent institution but has succumbed to this temptation. The organisation of the church is simply one sinner among many, and not the worst by any means.'[4] It was not only that doing one thing, like running schools or paying ministers or erecting buildings or manning organisations, meant less resources for doing another thing. It was that some activities vigorously stirred turned the mixture sour. 'In older times', observed an active Reading Baptist who later turned Quaker because of this, 'the church and the world were in antagonism, today they are merely in competition. So far the church has come off second best. She has not provided so full a choice of amusements; but she is gradually widening her selection and at the present rate of progress should soon overtake her rival'.[5] This type of success meant, and felt like, failure. There was something being forgotten or weakened. 'What is the work in its essentials? It is not the church machinery which has been set going. It is not the church's organisation, complex as it is and many sided. It is not the numbers in the congregation. These things have no doubt bulked the largest to the eye of the onlooker. But the work itself is different. It is the power of the Christ life in you, in each one of you...' It was that power about which R.H. Sewell had doubts as he looked back at one of the most active ministerial careers in late nineteenth-century Reading.[6] He was not alone in his doubt. In his *Annual Address* for 1897 the vicar of St. John's was disturbed about 'those deeper things which are of infinitely greater value than matters of finance and organisation', 'we have a splendid organisation...why should we not have more power?' 'Here is an edifice', wrote a local Baptist magazine in December 1898, 'standing on a main thoroughfare, imposing, grand and stately. The visitor is struck with its beauty of architecture, whilst the resident regards it with no small pride as an ornament to the town; the musical parts of its services are chaste and beautiful; and the pulpit ministrations brilliant and refined; its pews and aisles are thronged with eager listeners. "Prosperous", you say, "very". But is it?'

Within individual agencies the tension between goals and performance was visible. It was all very well having thirty-eight societies affiliated to the Band of Hope Union in Reading and District with a combined membership of 3,664, but, they wanted to know at their annual meeting in 1901, 'what about the results of all that work?'[7] It was estimated in the Christian Endeavour movement that of a total membership of the YPSCE Union for Reading and district in 1900-1 of 1,438, only 163 became church members. Only fifteen of the forty-four boys on the roll of St. Mary's Castle Street Boys' Brigade attended any church, school or other religious meeting in 1913; whereas forty-seven out of the seventy members of St. Giles CEMS in December 1906 were 'engaged in some definite parish work'.

Commitment to organisation and size had other logics of its own. At Whitley Hall (Methodist) they had taken the rare decision deliberately to forgo one 'successful' agency – the Boys' Brigade – because of a felt conflict between its (State) goals and their own deeper (spiritual) ones. 'This meeting recognising the military spirit which the Boys' Brigade fosters, refuses to sanction such a brigade believing as they do that militarism is against the principles of Christ's teaching.' Three years later, following the relative failure of their own alternative – the

Boys' Life Brigade — they set a Boys' Brigade in motion in their chapel. It was evidently more important to keep going than to worry about where you were going.[8] Elm Park Methodists had similar anxieties about the Boys' Brigade. They decided in 1911, when 'letters were read of a private nature asking the church. . .if they approved or otherwise of accepting aid from the military authorities', after careful discussion, not to approve the scheme. Park Institute (Congregational) was doubtful about the Brigade, and tried to keep some distance between 'chapel effort' and such State work. But it started there in 1908 with the reservation that 'it might ultimately be considered as part of the chapel effort'. In the event, it folded in December 1908. The problem was continually present, since the State seemed increasingly ready to provide ways of financing church penumbras.[9]

'Nothing more is heard of them', complained the Friends in 1904-5 about the almost 100% wastage of members of their 'successful' Band of Hope after they became too old for it. Although the Adult School movement was a going concern, the *Triennial Report* of the Friends for 1897 bewailed the fact that few accessions to the Quaker church were ever made as a result of its work. A Wesleyan outside Reading even attributed the *decrease* of Wesleyan membership in 1895-6 to 'Endeavour Societies, Wesley Guilds. . .and the like'.[10]

No doubt such organisations were, in part, their own justification. They were a 'service' the church/chapel intended to provide for those in or outside membership, regardless of ulterior purpose. Having a family with thriving siblings, constituting an almost autonomous culture and providing responsibilities, self-respect and recreation for those who took part in it, did not necessarily need to be measured by other criteria. But the quantity of unease in Reading, of the kinds being quoted here, confirms that there were indeed other standards of measurement.

We do not let down our Sunday services but they are insufficient. Just as the British learned in South Africa that the frontal attack was no use, so the church must change front, and get at the people by a sort of flank movement. . . .There are sewing classes, boys brigades, gymnasiums, cooking classes, basket-weaving classes, millinery classes and many other classes and societies which in the aggregate bring a great number of people under the influence of the Gospel.[11]

Commitment to the centre of church/chapel life was intended as more

than an incidental by-product. It was the ultimate rationale for the
whole array. Seen as such, the means seemed recalcitrant. They seemed
to acquire too vigorous a life of their own. Some of them had been
made available by entrepreneurs in the wider society with ends other
than the prosperity of local churches and chapels. They carried with
them contradictions and penalties from the point of view of local
religious organisations. Even if the sensation had not been of drowning
before, clutching at too many such straws made it feel so afterwards.

 Endless age-specific groups were adopted, tailor-made for the
difficult cohorts of post-Sunday School youth. These adapted
themselves to elements in the culture thought to be of special appeal
to their age-groups. Within such organisations, devices for maintaining
discipline, exciting mutual emulation, or creating a hierarchy which
looked attractive to climb, were deliberately employed. This response
was extremely common, resulting in a rash of similar groupings
scattered widely among many denominations.[12] 'The advancement of
Christ's Kingdom amongst lads of all classes' could best be secured by
'the promotion of reverence, discipline and self-respect, and all that
tends towards true Christian manliness'.[13] Hence the Church Lads'
Brigade (1891), confined to Anglicans, or the Boy's Brigade (1883) for
other ranks, or Boy Scouts (1907).[14] When the boy from the Sunday
School went out to work, it was explained at Broad Street, 'he is
spoiled before the church institutions could throw their meshes around
him'. In case of doubt, 'it cannot be too emphatically said that the
Boys' Brigade is a religious movement'. The Company Bible Class, and
the Address at the Weekly Drills ensured that. It was not, they argued
defensively, a war-like movement. 'It simply enjoys military organisation,
drill and discipline as the most stimulating and interesting means of
securing the attention of a volatile class, and of promoting self-respect,
chivalry, courtesy, esprit de corps and a host of kindred virtues'. There
was a schismatic Scout movement called the British Boy Scouts which
established a Troop in Reading in 1911, and which attacked the State
militarism of the Baden-Powell Scouts as 'quite incompatible with
avowed principles of fraternity'.[15] Badges, tests, certificates, ceremonies,
uniforms multiplied from the Sunday School upwards. The
paraphernalia may now be bought in junk markets along with
gold-embossed Sunday School prize books but at the time it was
eagerly competed for. Following the new rules adopted in 1890 at
St. George's Tilehurst Sunday School, twelve marks a week (six
morning and six evening) constituted a full score for punctual
attendance, good conduct and lessons. At least fifteen attendances were

necessary for a treat, two bad conduct marks meant no treat — 160 marks in a year meant a prize. The youth temperance movement — the Band of Hope — was similarly geared to tests and exams hierarchically arranged to generate maximum discipline. It was the most universal of all the pre-1914 agencies of church/chapel work in Reading.

Such organisations did not achieve the results expected of them by their sponsors at the level of religious organisation. And it is hard to evaluate their other consequences. But they may well have had a significant impact on the lives of some of the two and a quarter million men — 'the greatest volunteer force ever raised in any country' (A.J.P. Taylor) — who volunteered for war before March 1916. A certain romanticism may have become associated with militarism for new strata of the population. Such a function was not in all cases in the minds of the pre-war sponsors. But it has not been very noticeably regretted or apologised for since by those who made homes for such organisations. And when war came, there were some who proudly identified with it, encouraged by the letters from the Archbishop of York and the Bishop of Oxford sent to Reading branches of the Church of England Men's Society in October 1914: 'we should be anxious to help in any way in which the authorities make a claim upon us willingly and gladly. . .To make each branch a keen and effective unit in the supreme effort which church and nation are now called to make for the safety and honour of the empire.' When the *Berkshire Chronicle* in September 1914 noticed 'the amazing change which has come over the whole face of our political and national life during the past few weeks . . .(which) was illustrated in a striking manner at Reading on Monday when representatives of every phase of thought and opinion in the borough assembled. . .to take part in a patriotic meeting on behalf of Lord Kitchener's appeal', and when enthusiastic recruiting meetings were held at the factory, many of the audiences had been well-prepared for the sentiments expressed and the values extolled by their contact with ecclesiastical machinery during the previous decade.[16] Whether anxiety 'to help in any way in which the authorities make a claim upon us willingly and gladly' was quite what Christ, or St. Paul, or organisers of religious activity in Reading, intended to be the relationship between religious organisations and the State is open to argument. What is less questionable is that such was the tendency of some of their nationalising organisations.

Regardless of ideology, a nationalising tendency was at work. In one flourishing local branch of a national organisation — the Broad Street Congregational Chapel Pleasant Sunday Afternoon or Brotherhood —

there was a deliberate effort to resist connection with any wider groupings, in order not to dilute strong internal solidarities. None the less, such a movement was a national one with centrally issued books and speakers, whose commitment was to the movement rather than to the chapel. In some cases, such as the Band of Hope, the main supra-chapel organisation was on a regional level; in others, such as Christian Endeavour, the District was based upon the town. Whichever it was, gathering pace with the youth movements of the late nineteenth century, there was a massive addition to churches and chapels of a whole apparatus of non-locally based organisations. It was evidently becoming easier to invent or to sustain an agency if it was not dependent on purely local initiatives, infra-structure and money, in just the same way as central denominations had to be tapped for building programmes where small donations or local businessmen's gifts failed. Once such a process started it became more difficult for any single church or even denomination to resist it. The Salvation Army resisted the Boy Scouts. They substituted their own equivalent — the Life Saving Scouts — because they suspected organisations with external ties and disliked Boy Scout ideology. Indeed the Salvation Army — in the persons of General William Booth and G.S. Railton, two sharp instinctive sociologists — was doubtful about the whole process of penumbra-acquisition.[17] But even their own organisation went the other way, and such resistance as was offered stemmed from the denominational rather than the local level.

There was also a lower-level shift in the centre of gravity of activities away from churches and chapels into the town. This was another way in which a sense of failure could accompany success. An activity which had been well carried on at the level of the individual church or chapel or which had been initiated there, changed in scale and became part of the activity of a different organisation. The church could be proud that it had been an inventor or a predecessor but none the less as an organisation it was weaker, and felt weaker, if something which it had previously done was now done somewhere else. So University Extension Lectures were the cause of the changeover of the Trinity Young Men's Society (started 1891) to the Literary and Social Union, and of the decline of the Broad Street Working Men's Evening College (started October 1895). Neither could compete with an incipient university movement in the town.[18] An interesting case was the Trinity Alphabetical Society, started in January 1874.[19] As a grouping it is one of an important genre in nineteenth-century provincial urban history. The names on its roll read like a list of the business and to some extent the political elite in the town of the next twenty years. As Ridley wrote, 'the usefulness of the society was increased by the helpfulness of many who have since made a name and place in the public and business life of the town'. The grouping of business and political élites in embryo around chapels and this type of agency, and their subsequent separation and change in loyalties and style of life was an important part of the whole change in context for religious organisations in the late nineteenth and early twentieth centuries. The Alphabetical's members at the start were 'chiefly the rising young men of the congregation'. They had weekly meetings at the chapel. 'Our aim is both intellectual and religious, we wish to think religiously and be religious thoughtfully. . .we want those who desire to use their knowledge for the good of man and the glory of God.' Because of the success of the organisation, activity quickly moved beyond the walls of the chapel — in October 1875 to the Athenaeum Club. Two years later a member expressed another quintessential nineteenth-century local aspiration when he wrote to the chairman, 'I believe if a well sustained effort were made to elevate the Alphabetical into an association equal in aim to the Literary and Philosophical Societies of other towns you would ultimately secure the active cooperation of all the cultured men of all forms of political and religious thought in the town. . .' Such local collegiate aspiration was very different from its twentieth-century version in Rotary Clubs. For the chapel the change was a double loss, a dynamic agency had gone, but to the extent that it became even more dynamic at the level of the whole town, to that extent it would occupy the commitment of leading chapel members, who were already preoccupied with 'the responsibilities of family life and the cares and anxieties of increased business engagements'. Moving beyond the level of the individual chapel did not signify the 'decline' of this particular activity, although that too was to happen before long; too often at the time and since, this trend in social history has been confused even with the 'decline' of religion.

A local publication, *The Occasional Magazine,* mocked in 1900: 'when we were told to see to it that the Gospel should be preached to the whole world, it was intended (though not so mentioned) that the money should be raised by a bazaar.' An elision between means and ends had indeed taken place. Churches were evidently needed to support bazaars, not vice-versa. In St. John's parish, in the whole of the year 1900 'the great event of the year was undoubtedly the Bazaar. . .a splendid success. Not only was a large sum of money raised, but a vast amount of voluntary work was called forth, and the whole parish was united more closely together as the result of this combined effort'.[20] Bazaars were a minor part of the confusion. As we have seen, whole chapels were created deliberately as Institutes or Halls.

And yet, as throughout this chapter, the movement can be detected partly because it was not all one way. There were resistances, and efforts to reassert different priorities. Much of the early work of Park Institute (Congregational) in Wokingham Road — a deliberate Institutional Church — went into getting the Institute under chapel control, rather than the opposite situation which was originally intended. It took about four years of internal struggle before the Chapel Committee assumed control. Along the way much of interest had been written, including an extraordinary inversion of 'institutional church' perspectives in 1909: 'it is difficult to offer any explanation of the slowness of our growth, but it is perhaps only a natural consequence of an utter lack of public nucleus at the start, and *the absence of any appearance of being a place of public worship*' (my italics). A form and an appearance adopted in order to get over more ecclesiastical images was blamed for precisely what those images had been blamed for in the first place. The Park Institute Club, as it then became, was quite successful, but only on terms which the chapel found less than ideal. So in 1910 the pressure was felt to 'draw closer the ties between the religious work of the Church and the more general aims of the Institute'. The 'amusement' side of club work was to be underplayed — but at the cost of losing members. The pressure built up for beginning the process, via building funds and the like, which was to lead to the creation of a normal Congregational chapel. In September 1910 church members protested to the Institute about the use of the Hall for Whist Drives — it was felt to be degrading to use the place for such purposes when worship took place there on Sundays. After a ministerial change in March 1911 the new situation was formalised. He ceased being called a 'superintendent' and became a 'minister' and the agency/chapel precedence was reversed.[21] An experiment in elision was over.

Dilution and confusion were fitfully challenged by important new agencies in the penumbra of many churches and chapels. The Christian Endeavour movement, for example, took root in Reading at Carey Baptist Chapel in 1892. In 1893 it had a Reading membership, there and in other Nonconformist chapels, of 350 (national membership in that year was 1,577,040). 'To promote an earnest Christian life among its members, to increase their mutual acquaintance, and to make them

more useful to the service of God,' it was deliberately devotional rather
than for entertainment, and was determined not to sacrifice ends for
means.[22] It was enthusiastically adopted by many chapels, with high
hopes 'to arouse and strengthen one another in their spiritual life, and
to draw out their activities, each one being found something to do for
the Master'. Broad Street Christian Endeavour asserted at its inception
that 'while we have nothing to say against the gathering up under the
auspices of the church of influences which appeal to every aspect of
our many sided nature. . .music, sociality, athletics, recreation. . .it
remains true that the central business of the Church and its various
ministries is character building'. A counterpart, but not precisely
similar, was the Church of England Men's Society.[23] Again, devotional
rather than recreational aspects were stressed, and a depth of individual
commitment to specific spiritual work was aimed at. The first secretary
of St. Giles' branch (C. Gill, later a Labour activist in his ward politics)
had to stress in 1906 that 'there is still some misunderstanding as to
what the society really is and what it aims at. It is not merely a
debating society, our Sunday afternoons with their helpful discussions
are not an end in themselves, but only a means to an end. The
existence of the CEMS is a real attempt by men to regain for the church
those men who she has lost or who have never been within her
influence'.[24] By 1907 there were eight Reading branches. The majority
of sizeable churches and chapels possessed either a CE or a CEMS early
in the twentieth century in Reading. Besides them there were further
instruments for deepening commitment, for a 'better fewer but better'
emphasis.[25]

Their passage was not easy. 'For not a few of them', said the
President of the Reading Christian Endeavour Union in May 1899 at
their annual conference:

Christian Endeavourism had passed beyond the stage of an
experiment and had established itself in their confidence as one of
the permanent parts of their church organisation, fulfilling a
specific and highly important function. They said that in spite of
what might appear to be adverse signs. They had heard even in their
own Union of a CE society dying a natural (or an unnatural) death,
and in connection with the movement as a whole in this locality
there was probably not the same exuberant enthusiasm, not the
same strut and swing that they witnessed a few years back.

'How often', lamented St. Pancras Guild at St. Bartholomew's, in 1908,

'have those who have had the true welfare of the guild at heart grieved
at seeing the want of enthusiasm among the members, at the apparent
lack of interest in the guild'. 'It is to be regretted...that but few of
our members make an effort to attend the meetings of the branch' —
the branch being St. Bartholomew's Church of England Men's Society,
first formed in November 1906 and complaining in those terms in
January 1912. Quite quickly after enthusiastic starts such laments were
heard in church and chapel circles.

It must have been one of the most depressing features of the life of
anyone connected with the agencies surrounding churches and chapels
to watch them die. Even agencies in which great hopes were invested,
like the CE societies or the CEMS, flourished briefly only to wilt well
before 1914.[26] There was a constant restarting of bodies with similar
aims to their predecessors. Clubs for men connected to St. Agnes
Church succeeded each other in rapid succession, as did Guilds, Book
Clubs and Alphabetical Societies at Trinity Congregational Chapel. If
this had always been happening it could be written off as having no
bearings on wider social change beyond the level of the religious
organisations, and as being the inevitable results of age-groups within
each chapel growing up. But during the early years of the twentieth
century there was more of a pattern of failure than that would imply.
The volume of evidence is important here, and the way in which failure
was experienced by previously highly successful groups. For example,
the Book Club at Trinity (started 1872) was a dining-cum-literary society
which was powerful in deciding chapel affairs as well as transmitting
outside 'culture' to leading members of the chapel via discussions of
such controversial texts as General Booth's *In Darkest England and the
Way Out* (1890) or Mrs Humphrey Ward's *Robert Elsemere* (1888).
'Not only has it provided for the circulation of high-class literature in
the form of books and magazines which have aided us all in our general
culture, but it has afforded us opportunities for discussing movements
and works which have thrown light on many subjects and aided general
progress.' But between 1906 and 1908 it folded.[27] Or take the Monthly
Meeting Institute (founded in 1890) of the Quakers in Church Street.
This was a type of grouping which was repeated in many places in this
period. With its *tableaux vivants*, Shakespeare evenings, impromptu
speeches, debates, it provided a typical late nineteenth-century menu.
Yet in its records there was a continual refrain of concern about lack
of interest and attendance. In 1903 'there are many friends who are
rarely if ever seen at our meetings'; in 1910 other meetings were blamed,
'the increasing number of meetings and organisations in which Friends

are interested does undoubtedly affect the attendance at our meetings';
by 1912-13 'the question of the future work of your Institute is a
matter for full consideration'. Meetings were cut down and lectures,
previously the basis of the work of the Institute, were dispensed with.
Years before, in 1903, the Cycling Club had already folded for lack of
attendance.[28] The St. John's Church of England Temperance Society
was the third largest branch in the UK. But once more the refrain of
poor attendances was present — only 50 out of 685 members were
reported as attending meetings in 1901. The peaks of success of the
branch were reached before 1905.[29] These were three of the most
dynamic groups; the pattern was repeated with lesser organisations.[30]
There were some signs in Reading in the five years before the war of a
deliberate turning away from large national organisations by churches
and chapels, back to their own separate Guilds and Institutes.[31] There
were closely attached agencies, such as the Trinity Guild in 1906,
where deliberate effort achieved approximate parity between average
attendance and membership. But agencies in general seemed to be
undergoing more strains than worship. Statistical evidence on this is
fragmentary, but the relationship between congregation and
membership in chapels between 1890 and 1914 was of the order of
two to one. Twice as many attended as were members, in main chapel
services. Whereas the ratio of attenders to members or numbers on the
books of auxiliary agencies was of the order of two to one the other
way. Half the members came.[32]

The YMCA saw itself as 'an organisation managed by Christian men on
a Christian basis and as an adjunct to the churches. . .its aim was to
rescue, to protect, to educate, and to redeem young men. It called into
active operation every legitimate means for the accomplishment of this
high purpose. . .It was a centre for the development of strong, healthy
religious tone, where cant was held at a discount and where an honest
confession to have any weight must be backed by honest living.'[33]
Here, in the YMCA — The Society for Improving the Spiritual
Condition of Young Men Engaged in Trade as it was originally called —
the means/ends separation was frank, the view of adjuncts to the
churches clear. 'It called into active operation every legitimate means
for the accomplishment of (its) high purpose.' Having an extensive
penumbra at all to some extent implied a similarly self-conscious use
of means among churches and chapels. 'Symbolic methods of thought'
had, through the nineteenth century, been weakening amongst religious
organisations, which were increasingly 'viewed in instrumental terms as

devices for producing particular results'. Long before 1890, 'the Kingdom of God seemed delivered over to instrumental and associational principles, and disorderly organisations were created, quite impatient of symbolic understanding'.[34] But the penumbras of churches and chapels were faced in the late nineteenth century by particular signs of the times, demanding interpretation by their parent organisations in terms of their own specific goals. Such signs were, on the whole, not interpreted prophetically in Reading; their impact upon religious organisations was either exaggerated by, or simply mediated through the sub-agencies.

A major tendency in the wider society, of which the whole notion of sub-agencies was to some extent a reflection, was a felt pressure towards 'brightness', towards making the church or the agency more 'attractive', towards advertising it more widely and in better ways, towards adding to it something aside from its main purposes which would attract the public. The loss leader, or temptation, was not something confined to the burgeoning techniques of the concurrent retailing revolution. At the same time as such techniques were being applied to selling goods, they were also being applied to selling voluntary organisations and to selling religion. At the same time as Huntley and Palmers became concerned with packaging in a serious way, so too did churches. The trouble so far as religious organisations were concerned, of course, was that such changes were not guaranteed to increase turnover and they were bound to affect the goods sold. Means are not neutral unless, as with making a profit, they are also the end.

On one level, changes for churches and chapels seemed like common sense and obvious progress, in the same way as did the re-presentation of professional football by clubs like Coventry City in the 1960s. In 1907-8 the usual place of meeting of the St. John's Church of England Temperance Society was changed from the Queens Road Schools to St. John's Hall, because 'as a rule the meetings were not well attended, but now with a well ventilated hall, free of draughts, good fires, excellent lighting and comfortable seats for all who attend, there will be no excuse left for staying away from meetings and giving that personal support which is so essential in this work'. But too distant travel along such a path, with all the misattribution of cause it implied, could lead far off the main track. A pervasive view was that 'by making a few alterations in the method of conducting our services we shall make them as attractive as ever', or that, by a new type of service, we should 'continue to reach a class of people hitherto untouched by ordinary methods. . .(for) many who for years have attended no place of worship have been attracted by these methods', or that by adopting, for example, Sankey's hymns, a string band and a stronger choir (as at Grovelands Baptists in 1903) 'as a means of inducing many of the people who do not attend any other place of worship' greater success would be achieved.[35] A stepping back from the potential consumer in order to weigh him up; a stepping back from the worshipping life of a church in order to weigh it up, not with regard to the felt needs of participants spontaneously met, but with regard to the supposed needs of other groups; a making of each part of church life into a method — these were central features of the times, across denominational boundaries. In late nineteenth-century Methodism they even led to the abandonment of defining features such as the Class meeting, and the transmuting of, for example, the sermon into 'an enjoyment, an entertainment'.

Once again pressures can be identified partly through resistances. Baptists at Kings Road were pleased in 1893 that 'our Sunday congregations have been fully maintained without resorting to exceptional methods which may be held to be out of harmony with Christian work'. The Young Men's Institute at Broad Street Congregational Chapel was pleased in 1900 that 'in these days of devotion to sport and pastime. . .it is pleasant to notice that the favourite hour of the Broad Street Young Men is that devoted to Bible study'. Particularly against motiveless 'amusement', Nonconformist resistance was strong. 'There is in these days a tendency to waste time in vacuous amusements', it was said when a new Alphabetical Society was founded at Trinity Congregational Chapel in 1900 specifically to counter the trend (by 1901 it had been 'suspended for the present'). The Christian Endeavour, and Church of England Men's Societies were part of the resistance. At Cumberland Road the Primitive Methodists, when providing an Institute for the 'amusement' of young people in the Sunday Schools, refused to allow card games. They insisted on papers being read twice a month on some 'serious' subject. Where adaptations once allowed were checked it sometimes proved disastrous. Thus, when the Rev. W.R. Neville tried to tighten the rules and tests of membership of the St. Mary's Church Institute, it folded completely in its original form, after twenty-five years' existence; so too Park Institute lost members after similar efforts. Overwhelmingly, however, adaptation took place and agencies were adapted or multiplied, in case by meeting some other need, they could serve their main purposes better. The records of the Broad Street Pleasant Sunday Afternoon, for example, show continual complaints about the 'Brief Bright and Brotherly' aspects of the movement coming to predominate over the

'real Brotherhood spirit'. It seemed as though large social change was
occurring, beyond but including religious organisations, pressing upon
them to develop in particular ways. In twentieth-century Methodism,
'while chapel celebrations began to display a surprising if bewildered
worldliness, and entertainment criteria were introduced into chapel life
alongside new entertainment technologies, acts of worship were
themselves increasingly interpreted as entertainments'.[36]

Another sign of the times which was either exaggerated by, or
simply mediated through the penumbra of religious organisations, was
a tendency towards division of organisations and activity into separate
age groups, occupational groups or class groups. Whether 'each class
and sometimes each section, and sometimes each profession wanted
something specially done for themselves', that was certainly what many
churches and chapels gave them at this time. Again, large social changes
were occurring in the wider society in this area. New age groups were
being invented. They were then elaborated upon, given meanings, and
exploited by other agencies – business and otherwise, including
churches. Thus, the category 'adolescent' was coming into prominence
in the second half of the nineteenth century both in structural and in
commercial ways.[37] Marketing and sales strategies and leisure
entrepreneurs defined new 'targets' to which they appealed in new
ways. There was thus bound to be some preoccupation in, for example,
ministers' minds with 'the youth problem', and with what to do with
the post-Sunday School age group.[38] 'We have the children, but they
slip out of our grasp as they grow up.' This left the feeling that 'the
church is largely left behind in the rush of our manifold life. New
methods are adopted on every hand'. A dominant response was to
jump on the band wagon of those 'methods'. 'Is it not possible to make
a study of the methods that succeed among various classes of the
community? We have the data. A careful study of the "methods that
answer" worked up into a text book would be of great service.'[39]
Existing occupational, social, age and sex differences were not only
observed and catered for, but were even exaggerated by the
subdivisions into which the life of many churches and chapels fell.
The national denominational periodical from which the above
quotation came had, in the same year, a 'Housewives' Column', a
'Children's Column' and a feature 'From the Woman's Standpoint'.
Such developments were not seen as posing any special problems about
the kind of organisations Christian organisations should be, or the kind
of community they should be trying to represent; it was a set of social
processes which were either passively reflected, or positively aided and

abetted by churches and chapels. On the national level a few prophets saw what was happening and tried to resist it in the name of Arnoldian (and therefore elitist) ideas of 'community' and a common culture.[40] On a local level there was little evidence of such awareness or resistance.

Even modes of worship were frequently not expressions of an implicit idea of common humanity, or the occasion for bringing varying strata of the population into common, shared activity, but were held to be appropriate in one form for one section and another form for another section. When the Vicar of St. Giles wanted to introduce incense in 1917 he had to walk warily. He got the sanction of his leading congregational activists provided that he was 'discriminating'. He undertook not to use it on Sunday evenings since 'the vicar recognises as was expressed by more than one speaker that there is a difference in the congregations who are present at the High Celebrations and those who come to Sunday evensong'.[41] The same parish mounted special services for the tramwaymen whose depot was in their territory, although what was peculiar about the religious needs of tramwaymen was never articulated. At St. Bartholomew's in 1895 'all masters and mistresses are desired to make it convenient for. . .the servants of their respective households to receive the Holy Communion on Christmas Day at 6.30 or 8 o'clock'.[42] It is to be hoped that 'masters and mistresses' after their later celebrations found a good breakfast and the fires burning when they returned home to begin their observation of Christ's birthday. One level of operation, frequently in the Anglican case one building, was reserved primarily for 'our poorer brethren', who needed specially 'attractive' worship. For example, Greyfriars 'Mission Hall' which (1906), 'is beginning to respond to the original purpose for which it was founded many years ago. It now meets the need of the working people in Greyfriars to whom the full prayer book service is difficult'. Or Caversham, where the type of churchmanship in the daughter churches like St. Andrew's Caversham Heights was quite different from that obtaining in the mother church, even though they were very much part of the same parochial machine.[43] The function of a mission church or a Hall was to prevent those of a different class who might have been tempted to worship with the social groups dominant in the main church from doing so — to segregate rather than to unite.[44] The function of the myriad youth movements was to reinforce generational and even smaller age gaps rather than to promote mutual acquaintance, participation, and obligation across those gaps.

Age gaps were compounded by class — so that for instance in 1892 Ambrose Shepherd of Trinity Chapel complained that even though the

Sunday School there had 400 or 500 members and was therefore a
'success', yet church members had nothing to do with Sunday School
members both because of their age and lower-class origins. Late in 1914
the Friends discussed the Report of a committee they had set up to
review the state of the Monthly Meeting. The report was critical of the
way in which 'our religious life moves in the quiet routine of our own
circle'. But more than this, there was 'too little sense of a Quaker
movement'. Common purpose had been subordinated to institutional
goals, so that, for example, 'adult school work brings many men and
women under Quaker influence, but largely through difference of
education and social standing very few of these are drawn into closer
fellowship with the society. This may be due to our own exclusiveness
and to a lack of ministry which would appeal to them, or it may be
that our method of worship does not appeal to them'.[45] The social
historian could add that it may be also that the mere existence of
Adult School work for the less educated, and its 'success', was partly
responsible for what the main meeting was like and its admitted
'failure' at that date, in just the same way as the devotion of much
effort to week-night 'people's services' at Kings Road Baptists, or at
Caversham Free Church after 1907, would come to affect the nature
and social composition of the Sunday services – even if the intention
had been to strengthen the latter. When Anglicans in Caversham decided
to promote lectures on nursing in February 1891, it excited no
comment that 'it is proposed to have one afternoon lecture for Ladies
and one in the evenings for the working classes each week'. It was rare
when some awareness of the tendency broke through – as at St. Giles
in 1905. 'The special danger of our own parish lies in the fact that all
social classes are represented in it, and that each class has little or no
knowledge of the rest. . .we want a centre of union.'

Notions of what it was right for churches and chapels to promote,
theological or social perspectives on the nature of man in his social
relationships, ideas as to the virtue of 'union' as opposed to separation,
or about the vigorous outward-looking presence which Christians ought
to represent in the society – such aspirations, which were no doubt
shared by many activists – were contradicted at many points by what
religious organisations had become, and by what they had decided to
provide. Unless firm decisions about aims were self-consciously taken
and unless continual efforts were made to relate organisation to those
aims, and so avoid a variety of traps, reports like that of the Friends on
the 'quiet routine of their own circle' in 1914 were inevitable.
Unintended consequences do follow purposeful social action unless

enormous care is taken.

Religious organisations have special problems in this regard. They have a distinctive agenda, differentiating them from other voluntary organisations. Salvation is not the same as recreation, education or social reform, although each of these may be involved in it. Religious organisations had a subject-area for organisation which, during the second half of the nineteenth century in Reading, had come to be accompanied by the feeling that it should involve everybody and every activity. Such an ambition is not built-in to Christian organisations. It is encouraged by the ideologies and organisations of particular periods. The scale of the ambition was shared in late nineteenth-century Reading by a revolutionary socialist organisation such as the Social Democratic Federation. But it was not shared by other subject-areas for organisation such as football, although they too were ambitious on a wider social/ moral front than they later became. Unlike the SDF, however, the ambitions of religious organisations are ultimately extra-social and permanent, even though all kinds of social and period-specific goals may also be involved. This means that religious organisations tend to survive. They tend to continue from epoch to epoch, and period to period — different, even transformed, but with elements of continuity.

It is the very scope and continuity of their ambition which, however, involves religious organisations, to an even greater degree than other voluntary organisations, in the changing period-specific contexts for all organisations. Their nature as religious organisations makes them especially vulnerable to contexts as they change. In the second half of the nineteenth century in Reading they became the most universal, ambitious, available and therefore local, voluntary organisations. At the same time they had a built-in tendency to be the organisations with the highest capital costs (in buildings) and running expenses (in priests, schools, penumbras, etc.). But, in the second half of the nineteenth century in Reading they also saddled themselves with a great width of provision, stretching across many activities, as well as a localness and a volume of provision. Expensive items such as buildings or priests had more than a temporary place in their frame of reference. They could not easily have been jettisoned, any more than they could easily be supported except in the ways and with the consequences society made possible at that time. Other voluntary organisations may also be tempted towards elaborate buildings and professional staff, but without the same symbolic and sacramental thrusts as religious organisations. But the constraints imposed by scarce resources and by the particular patterns of distribution of those resources in late nineteenth-century Reading could at least have been modified by decisions about degree. More deliberate adjustment of means to ends could have been made. The penumbra or machinery attached to churches and chapels made the contextual constraints more formidable and they could have been made subordinate or dropped.

Continuity implied that to the extent that religious organisations clothed their ambitions successfully in the dress of one period or type of society, they would have special problems of adaptation if they were to survive and flourish in the next. The more 'successful' they were at any one time, the more vulnerable they became to changes in the props of that success at a later time. Such changes were not specific to religious organisations, still less to 'religion'. Partly because of their nature, and partly because of the particular forms they chose to adopt, religious organisations were, nevertheless, peculiarly vulnerable to such changes. Their ambition also made them peculiarly distressed by circumstance. It was doubly important for religious organisations to try to articulate what changes in the props of success were, and to see their own experience in the context of wider social changes as experienced by other organisations. Only in this way could they have made sense of what was happening to them in such a manner as both to understand their experience and, where it was an unhappy one, put themselves in a position from which to attempt to change it.

That such an understanding was necessary cries out from the documents. Caversham Methodist Sunday School desperately needed help from *somewhere* when the statistical returns for 1903 were read, showing a decrease of twenty-four scholars on the books. 'A discussion took place as to how this unsatisfactory state of affairs could be remedied, but as no plan could be arrived at the chairman suggested that the following resolution should be put to the meeting, "that the teachers and scholars present, deploring the decrease of scholars pledge themselves to more earnest and devoted service during the year".'[46] Some sharper prophecy was needed than the vicar of St. Giles managed in his monthly letter in the Parish Magazine for January 1911. He detected in that year 'an atmosphere of restlessness and change'. They had, he thought, to remember the text 'Seek ye unchanging things', but at the same time to realise that 'change for us here is a necessary condition of growth and progress, though indeed all changes are not fraught with blessing'.[47]

St. Giles Church Lads Brigade felt it necessary in the 1890s to run a band, a football club and a cricket club in order to keep the lads together. They considered it important for the kind of organisation

they wanted to create to be self-supporting, and in other respects they
were. Yet in this case they lamented the fact that in 1895 'we must ask
our friends to assist us if we are to have (those facilities)'.[48] They were
in a trap, common to many organisations and yet it was experienced as
accidental. If they were to rely on themselves for their expenses, the
subscriptions would have to be high enough to price the kind of people
they wanted to reach out of the group altogether. If they did not, if
they relied on non-participating donors, they would be moving their
organisation nearer the *for* than the *of* end of the spectrum. They
would be relying upon a particular type of society, and would
themselves become a particular type of dependent organisation. There
were no alternatives, other than not having the facilities concerned, or
folding up altogether (as did the Caversham Football Club temporarily
in 1897) or adapting away from the church into being a frankly
commercial organisation (as did the Caversham Coffee House Company).

Similar constraints operated on, for example, the Reading Industrial
Co-operative Society. In February 1902 a member proposed a Co-op.
Choir as 'a means of forming another nucleus for activity and thought
in our movement'. The Editor of the *Reading Co-operative Record* liked
the idea, as a singer himself. But he argued against it because 'a
choirmaster or conductor would have to be found, and paid for his
services; a hall would have to be hired for practice and paid for. Music
would have to be provided and paid for; likewise at least a piano. A
lady or gentleman of musical tastes and abilities would have to come
forward and volunteer to do a lot of thankless "hack" work as
honorary secretary'. Such an operation would strain the Educational
Sub-Committee of the Co-op. too much: it would therefore be better,
thought Esrom, to rely on self-produced, unpaid entertainment and
propaganda singing.[49]

A key contextual factor in this situation has already emerged more
than once; there were many signs that the type of society which made
it easy to attract local 'friends to assist us' was passing, or was at least
under severe strain before 1914.[50] This was true financially, and also
personally. The East Reading Adult School, for example, started in
1905. It was financed initially by contributions from leading Quakers,
both local and national. But it was dependent upon the commitment
of one man, C.E. Stansfield. By 1910 the first note of difficulty
entered into its records. 'East Reading have suffered from the frequent
absence of C.E. Stansfield and it is very necessary that more Friends
should feel responsibility for this meeting and pay it occasional visits.'
By February 1912 it was worse: 'East Reading has not born out the

hopes with which it started: the attendance diminished rapidly and about 1911 the position became very serious.'[51]

Some extra factors were at work in the difficulties being experienced by, for example, St. Mary's Provident Society early in the twentieth century. The annual *Reports of the Parochial Charities and Associations* of St. Mary's parish after about 1902 make it clear that this Society was in crisis. Among the causes of their problem in 1906 they listed 'insufficient advertisement of the Society'. But the trouble went deeper. In 1908 the Society disappeared altogether from the *Reports.* In this case there was as much need for articulation of a wider context as in the case of St. Giles Church Lads Brigade, but even less consciousness of that context. St. Mary's, like other churches and chapels, had inherited from earlier periods a whole range of responses to poverty and welfare, made permanent in 'funds' and societies. These included Alms Houses, a Penny Bank, St. Mary's Needlework Society, a Sick and Poor Fund, and 'The Society for the Relief of the Aged Poor in the parishes of St. Mary and Holy Trinity', for relieving poor women when 'they are drawing near to that time when their strength is but labour and sorrow' (1828).[52] Much work went into keeping these organisations going. But decrease in the financial support of subscribers, a slower but perceptible decrease in demand from potential recipients, difficulty in finding 'helpers' or activists, together with the changing role of the State in areas such as savings or pensions, meant that supporting this inherited apparatus was becoming more and more of a problem for St. Mary's between 1890 and 1914. Putting together factors such as the changing presence of the State, a decrease in local sources of middle-class commitment and money, the constraints of poverty and unequal distribution of power and wealth, a growing working-class reluctance to accept deferential relationships, and adding to them other contextual factors such as changes in the economy, particularly as regards the ideology and organisation of leisure, may enable us to make a map of the changing situation of voluntary organisations as a whole in the late nineteenth and early twentieth centuries. It is a map which religious organisations, whether they liked it or not, were on, but which cannot be charted without the experience of organisations in other subject-areas.

There are two main problems: for us now to try to understand what was going on, and for us now to try to understand why contemporary activists on the whole did not seem to articulate what was going on. For the second problem the nature and scale of contemporary religious organisation is essential. It was realised to be so by the insistent voices in the denominational press calling for an end to the domination of the 'organiser' and a reassertion of the prophetic role.[53] For the first problem the prophet would indeed have helped. But the historian half a century later has at least the advantage of hindsight, and the opportunity of surveying the experience of other organisations in the same changing context, in order to discover its contours.

7 LEISURE

Leisure was an important focus of late nineteenth- and early twentieth-century social development. A number of social changes, including increased real wages for some groups in the population, the aggregation of population into large cities, changes in hours worked, changes in goods made and in methods of selling those goods, made leisure, its uses and abuses, a central subject for national discussion. For consumers of leisure, and for producers or organisers, critical developments took place within this period, shaping much of modern British culture.[1] Key features of working-class social life, not just in politics but in football, food and entertainment assumed their modern pattern in the late nineteenth century.[2] Profit-oriented, market-dominated leisure suppliers whether in newspapers or in holidays, in music halls or in sport made great strides in the last quarter of the nineteenth century.[3]

For understanding religions in society the subject is of special interest. A major, or the major, thing churches and chapels were doing in Reading was providing a varying but remarkably uniform range of ways of using or 'improving' hours not worked. Partly this was deliberate — the starting of literary societies, football clubs and the like. Outside Reading one of the most exaggerated forms of such provision was the People's Drawing Room movement.[4] But partly the social history of leisure is the setting within which the most central activity of churches and chapels (services and worship) must also be examined. Going to a service was one way among many other ways of spending Sunday morning or, increasingly between 1890 and 1914, a weekday evening; always assuming that these times were free from work.[5]

As often happens, a minority of the people whose organisations and whose town are the subject of study were aware, at least for a fraction of their time, of the changes that now interest the historian. R.H. Sewell, the minister of Broad Street Congregational Chapel, was responsible for annual 'Industrial Exhibitions' which displayed items made at work and at home, and which were major pan-town events, attended by the Mayor and other dignitaries. He defended them, with their mixture of 'work' and 'leisure' products in a thoughtful way in 1897:

The object they had in view in these exhibitions was to aid in the

185

turning of leisure time to a judicious account, in the first place working days and then holidays. Perhaps it might be considered somewhat inconsistent to couple work and leisure, but happily it was becoming less so as civilisation proceeded and deepened its hold on the people. He ventured to think that the increase of leisure increased the responsibility of leisure.[6]

Frequently the matter became one of public controversy. Ambrose Shepherd of Trinity Congregational Chapel lectured in the same year on 'a subject of great importance' — 'Athleticism'. He warned of the dangers of too much physical and not enough mental recreation, 'it is essential that what leisure exists should be turned to the best account ...play we must, and to do us justice play we do. The only question at issue is whether, playing, we play wisely'. The local press took the matter up and gave it prominence.[7] What was happening was not just the expression of the anxiety of puritan consciences which could not keep up with the passing of morally dominative leisure styles, but basic change which would not run in the channels Sewell and Shepherd desired.

'Reading is a town whose social activities and amenities are of greater range and almost at the highest power possible for a town of its size and population.' So thought a guide-book writer in 1911. Religious bodies provided only a fraction of these amenities. A survey confined to sport alone goes some way to justify the enthusiasm of the guide-book. Major organisations included the Reading Football Club (1871, claiming just before it went professional to be the third oldest amateur club in the country), the Reading Amateur Football Club, the Reading Cycling Club (1899), the Reading Wheelers Cycling Club, the Reading Rovers Cycling Club, the Reading United Quoit Club (1892), the Reading Amateur Regatta, the Reading Working Men's Regatta (1877), the Reading Rowing Club (1867), the Reading Rifle Club (1901), the Reading Swimming Club, the Reading Cricket Club, the Reading Biscuit Factory Recreation Club, the Reading Athletic Club (1882) and the Reading Angling Association (1877). These were only the most prominent formal organisations. 'The question seems to be not so much what there is as what there is not.' G.W. Palmer, in a speech for the Reading Biscuit Factory Recreation Club in 1899, was staggered by the facilities available at that date compared to those of his youth when there was only 'a certain amount of recreation associated with the every-day business of life'.[8] A large slice of the leisure activity of Reading citizens revolved around events and activities sponsored by these voluntary bodies.

They, and their counterparts in other activities such as Temperance or 'Literary and Social' Clubs or the YMCA, were obviously not churches and chapels. Nevertheless, it is worth setting them within the moral and social categories within which they set themselves. The Reading Athletic Club in its heyday was an exaggerated but not unique case. The people surrounding it saw it as having functions quite beyond athletic ones:

> Athletics form so integral a part of our national life that no historian can leave it out of his purview. A pursuit so universal, so stamped with authoritative approval cannot fail to leave its mark on the national character. It is a common topic of conversation between most self-respecting citizens, a topic nearly as staple as that of the weather. . .It does seem therefore most important for us to gauge this force, whose influence on society and the individual is so immense. . .[it breaks down] those curious bulwarks of caste which are not merely out of date, but which are real dangers to the social well-being. . .[it produces a feeling of] Christian brotherhood.[9]

Such sentiments permeated the Reports of the RAC and were shared in one form by Esrom the Co-operator, whom we shall meet elsewhere, and who was for a time in the early 1890s the main scribe of the Club.[10] During the 1890s, and to a diminishing extent in the years preceding 1914, they were common. The Rev. R.H. Hart Davis in 1900 was,

> delighted to see that so many of our representative athletes had gone out to the war. At intervals during the war English sports had not been forgotten even during a temperature of 116° in the sun. At Mafeking, Sunday was the only day on which sports could be indulged in, to the shame of the few voices in England which had been raised against it but who had not found many followers. . . There was too a religious side to games, and as a minister of the Gospel he expressed his great gratitude to the athletes for the good they were doing.[11]

With football the tone was milder and less overtly Christian, but even here there were frequent justifications for the Reading Football Club which went beyond the game itself.

It is not only a healthy and an exhilarating pastime, but it affords
a little recreation on a Saturday afternoon to those people who
give themselves up solely to business during the week, while it
undoubtedly does much to create a broader and a better feeling
amongst all sections of the community.[12]

At the annual 'Smoker' of the Reading Football Club in 1898 the
Tory candidate for Reading, who had made it his business to be seen
to be connected with football, called the club 'the most popular
institution in Reading'.[13] The Chief Librarian would have contested
this claim — 'the Town Library of Reading is without doubt the most
popular institution in the Borough' — and with statistics on his side.[14]
Nevertheless the Football Club was sufficiently important in Reading
society to be worth examination on its own. A look at what was
happening to it in the late nineteenth century will pull together in one
place a number of social changes, before they are separated out in
relation to lesser organisations, both sporting and otherwise.

In 1890 there were a variety of different football clubs in the town
of which the RFC was the largest. It had been able to resist, and was to
profit from the centralising tendency which was to change the scale of
leisure activities during this period. The Minster Club (church based)
and the South Reading FC were already co-operating, and when the
Kendrick Club became interested in amalgamation in 1886 the RFC
because of its size was able to 'decline to take part in the proposed
amalgamation of the clubs of Reading'.[15] The centralising tendency,
however, was strong for in 1894 a District Football Association
appeared in the local Directory for the first time with fifty clubs
affiliated to it.

The RFC was, in structure, like the other clubs. It had a President,
a long list of Vice-Presidents and a 'Club Room' at the Queen's Hotel.
Both the football and the club were doing well, if on a small scale.
They won the Berks and Bucks Cup in 1892 'before the largest
attendance of people ever seen at a match in the county', and at a
presentation to the retiring Honorary Secretary in 1893, at which
Walter Howard Palmer of the biscuit factory and most of the 'leading'
Vice-Presidents were present, the mood was self-congratulatory. The
task of 'awakening the enthusiasm of the people of Reading towards
football' had gone on apace.[16]

In 1894 there were signs of change. Problems and opportunities
which had been there since at least 1885 presented themselves.[17] They
were the basic problems attaching to any organised activity which

aspired to be *of* the working class on any scale. More particularly they attached to any activity in which *quality* was important, and which needed specialist personnel (in this case players) and elaborate plant (in this case a football ground). In the case of football there was a new problem to add to the old one of providing teams and playing facilities. It was becoming a spectator (but not necessarily thereby a passive and powerless) activity. A whole new set of working-class demands was being expressed, making large-scale, regular working-class football (playing and spectating) a possibility for the first time. But shortage of money and shortage of players made it difficult to find teams and to enable people to watch them play and relate actively to them. It had been all very well when the Captain had been in sole charge and subscriptions had been up to 7/6d., but success and size were precipitating a new situation. The Club had ceased to be for those who could afford, or were physically able, *to play* football alone, and for those who could afford to pay high, honorary member-type subscriptions. Over the next few years it was to be a fascinatingly open question what form new developments would take; the directions in which the question was closed in the twentieth century were to be influential in the whole ecology of voluntary organisations, and were to reveal some of the major contextual factors surrounding twentieth-century organisation in any subject-area.

In September 1894 a special meeting of members was called to discuss the question of professionalism.[18] It drew a large attendance and excited heated argument. The Committee of the Club recommended that professionalism should be brought in, but only to a limited extent. The policy should be 'not to pay big wages but simply to pay men for loss of time'. The consensus of the meeting was against such a change. They regarded it as a major shift, not as an inevitable development of demand, or as part of 'progress'. It was seen as a deep issue of policy, even as a moral decision. Even as an amateur club gate money had been economically essential (in 1894-5 forming £737 out of £936 total receipts, with members' subscriptions at £47 and other subscriptions and donations at £19).[19] So it was not only the pay-at-the-gate as opposed to the Vice-Presidential mode of finance which was at stake. The case for professionalism was, first, that of necessity; 'the club could not go through the season without the aid of professionals'. Secondly, they would be able to get better players if they paid them, and more people would want to watch quality football. 'What had lost them the games they had lost? Simply the continual alterations in the team.' Working-class life (as Lenin and the Webbs saw in a political context) made successful part-time activity a problem. 'If they could get a team together the members of which were accustomed to one another's play, they would be higher up in the Southern League.' Thirdly, what was wrong with paying someone? Contrary to the high-minded, middle-class, pure sport position, 'it was nothing derogatory for a man to be paid for his services'. Indeed, 'many of their players were not in an independent position from a monetary point of view, and it was hardly fair that they should ask working men to sacrifice time and strength for their gratification. To ask them to sacrifice nearly two days, as had many of their players this season, was wrong'.

The case against professionalism was a layered one. There was, at the top, a morally-dominative, 'Vice-Presidential' case backed by leading local businessmen like James Simonds. To mix sport with money was quite simply wrong, and would lead to worse evils and disorders. Alongside this case, overlapping but distinct, were other working-class worries. First, given the constraints of working-class life there was no guarantee that professionalism would work financially. Other Clubs which had gone professional were in severe financial straits. They might untie from one mooring, and not be able to get through the currents to another. This applied not just to subscribers' money, but also to players. 'There were gentlemen connected with the club who had played for them hitherto, and had been the main support of the club. Were they prepared, should professionalism be adopted, still to play for the club, or should they find some of their best men leaving them altogether and thus landing them in a worse mess than before?' Secondly, an amateur club would aim to produce their *own* players, 'so that they would not have to go away for men'.[20] Thus would *local* football be encouraged as a self-produced activity. Thirdly, professionalism would lead to loss of local control and identification. Esrom thought that 'where professionalism had been brought in, it had ruined sport, it had made it a purely commercial speculation. Professional teams would come and play for what they could get, and they would as soon sell their services when they get the chance of being better paid for it as not. If they kept to amateurism people went there for sport and it would be healthy and pure, but if they went in for professionalism they would be only encouraging betting men and it would eventually ruin the Club'. Mr H. Wright feared that 'when they paid professional clubs to play them, what did they care whether they won or lost, but if they got a good local team they played for the love of the thing, and they felt there was no chance of being "sold"'.

Esrom and other supporters had their own position which was
articulated through the *Reading Co-operative Record*. As a quintessential
working-class activist, in the Co-op. and its penumbra (see Chapter Ten
below), in the Reading Athletic Club, Ye Ancient Cogers and so on,
Esrom stood for a whole style of leisure organisation which was under
threat. When the Co-op. thought of a 'Hobbies and Pastimes Exhibition'
in 1905, it was not in order to pass the time: 'the object would be the
encouragement of art and industry at home amongst the members, as
most people are better off for having some inclination to art and
industry for their own sakes, rather than for mere monetary reward.'
Democracy, participation, self-production were all important. That is
why he objected to the manner in which the professional idea was
being introduced as well as to the substance. There should, he thought,
be 'a special general meeting of members called expressly for the
purpose', if a constitutional change in the Club was to be on the
agenda. He liked football, he even liked watching it, but he did not
like a 'Spectatorate'. He did not like 'the Mania that has of late years
surrounded football'. It led people only to read football papers, to
spend all their 'spare coppers. . .in "coupons" for guessing results of
games', to hero-worship 'pro's' who are then 'sometimes spoilt by the
too free attentions of the football fool both in play and reputation', to
fight with other fans in a state of over-excitement, and to 'bully, abuse
and assault officials who have given decisions contrary to their. . .
desires'. It was also degrading the game and making it brutal. 'I suppose
it is a sort of hysteria, possibly caused in a measure by the "fast" lives
we have to lead in these days.'[21]

At the first meeting in September 1894 resistance was successful.
The decision was shelved. Fortunately the Honorary Secretary was
able to announce at the meeting that older patterns of support for the
Club would continue, provided that they did not change the nature of
the RFC: 'two gentlemen had very generously stated that whenever
they wanted men they would always be pleased to send a man or so or
more and they could rely on their being really good men; but if the
club ran as a professional team, they could not give the assistance in
any way.'

By June of 1895 another meeting was called to re-open the
question.[22] Splits repeated themselves. The President (James Simonds,
one of the largest businessmen in the town) was against the change.
But professionalism was carried by vote. At this date prospects looked
good. During the previous season they had sometimes had what were
regarded as 'enormous gates'. Even membership had increased from

180 before the change, to 300 by August.[23] It seemed as though a new pattern for the Club, relying more on the money of consumers through the gate and less on men like Walter Howard Palmer or James Simonds, would take off into quick success. It also seemed as if membership modes as well as passive consumer modes might survive.

Arguments at the meeting were not resolved, for soon afterwards another meeting was called to start Reading Amateur Football Club by the minority.[24] About forty people came, including some ministers. Much was said against sport being seen as a business for profit. A week later James Simonds and Esrom were prominent at another meeting at which the ex-Honorary Secretary of the RFC was elected Honorary Secretary of the new Club.[25] A trap similar to one already described in relation to the agencies of churches and chapels was set for this body, for membership subscriptions were set at the exclusive figure of five shillings. Vice-Presidents were to pay one guinea. Who, of the people they wanted to appeal to in the name of 'pure sport' and participation and localism, could afford that?

A small, participatory (for a few), morally dominative activity supported in the usual manner by Vice-Presidents and Honorary Subscribers, but with gate money too, was on its way to becoming a large, spectator-oriented, morally neutral RFC run as a business (even if not successfully), financed by gate money and transfer fees. The change was not instantaneous; at each stage the survival of old ideas and old patterns was as noticeable as their impending demise.

Acquisition of a new ground in a more suitable place was an important step. Elm Park, the eventual home of the RFC was, like the new St. Mark's Church or Elm Park Methodist Hall nearby, in the middle of a growing working-class area out along the Oxford Road, full of slightly less than 'mean' streets. If a ground could be had there, the club would become a very different organisation from the one which played on Caversham Cricket ground, and then at Coley Park (1888-9 season). Coley Park was the home of W.B. Monck — a local squire who had stopped allowing his park to be used for football because of 'rowdyism' by 'the rougher elements'. But how to get the new ground? At a meeting in 1896 expense was the problem.[26] J.C. Fidler had guaranteed £20 on the condition that 'no liquors were to be sold on the ground'. That condition having been granted, it was thought that 'it had secured for them the support of that large class of society which they wanted to bring into their net'. But only £175 had resulted. 'That large class of society' was not so available and not so interested as once it had been. In the end older patterns came to the rescue.[27] Elm Park was acquired in the only way possible, by a large donation and by financial guarantees from rich supporters.

At the first game at Elm Park a gate of 2,500 meant takings of £44, which was more than membership subscriptions for the entire year. But money was still short. There had been pressure in April 1896 towards taking a step as important and as hotly contested as the professionalisation of the club — turning it into a limited liability company. As with professionalisation the step was initially resisted and on similar grounds. There was an additional fear here, beyond the dislike of sport for profit. Members would lose total control of the club to shareholders and their board of directors. Crowded meetings of members, up to five hundred attending, were held.[28] Frame, a leading member of the Board of Guardians, was among the speakers passionately against the proposed change because 'moneyed gentlemen would control the Club. . .they would run it for profit alone'. But in May 1897 the step was taken.[29] At the first meeting of shareholders, discussion was purely financial; none of the earlier language of the type already quoted was used.[30] It was clear at this meeting that the ways of relating to the Club available to people were beginning to separate out on the basis of money. There had been attempts to issue shares. Directors were to be elected from shareholders. One of the Directors was surprised that more people had not bought shares. He suggested, oddly in view of the active opposition to Reading Football Club Limited, that 'the Reading public was not a body that was apt to be too enthusiastic at first sight about anything'. He confused supply with demand, or 'anything' with his particular chosen mode. At the meeting there were two preoccupations. One was to introduce turnstiles so as to stop two spectators getting in for the price of one. The other was whether shareholders should have special entry terms. 'Many could not reach the ground until five or ten minutes before the game started, and then found the stand fully occupied.' The chairman promised shareholders (not members) seats in the pavilion. The long process of shifting control away from Vice-Presidents or members, into the hands of shareholders and directors, and later into the hands of dictatorial managers, had begun. The possibilities of player and/or spectator control were being by-passed.

Those attached to the club were still sensitive to attack. When Frederick Hunt, the Secretary of the Reading YMCA, remarked in November 1897 that the Club was a team of professionals 'whose sole object is the making of money' two directors sprang to their own defence (J.C. Fidler and A.H. Bull).[31] They claimed the dividend was only five per cent maximum, that it was usually less than that for clubs in the Football Association (formed 1863), and that they were on the Board explicitly in order to stop the club allowing drinks or betting to grow up around it. In 1895 they resolved 'should their finances be satisfactory' to make donations to the philanthropic and medical societies of Reading. But J.C. Fidler's tone, in spite of these defences, was morally rather more relaxed than had been the case in the early days of the club, or was still the case with other sports,

> personally, I have never been able to attend a football match, but I am none the less interested, for apart from the reasons I have given, I cannot ignore the fact that there are thousands of persons of the working classes that need catering for in some way. They toil on week by week from Monday till Saturday afternoon, work hard and get little or no recreation whatever. If therefore it is possible to establish some such innocent amusement as I am sure our RFC affords, to induce many hundreds of these persons to spend a couple of hours in the fresh air, I do not think our efforts will be altogether useless. . .the YMCA is doing a splendid work in its way, but it does not cater for one of the most important bodies in our town – the working man.

It was a matter of 'catering *for*' the working man, even though the working man was paying for the bulk of what he got;[32] but there were less moral by-products in a phrase like 'innocent amusement'. There were none at all in the language of the chairman of the shareholders two years later. J.B. Messer said at a Bazaar in 1899, 'their football gave pleasure to many thousands of people unable to get pleasure in any other way, if those who condemned professional football would inquire into matters they would support the game.'[33] In 1902, at a meeting to raise money for the club, the then Mayor of Reading (A.H. Bull, the retailer) put the matter in a fascinatingly inverted way, signalling much of the change which had overtaken the RFC since the early days, 'if the working man rallied around the club in sufficient numbers he was quite certain that the gentry and the business people of the town would follow the lead'.[34]

A transition central to the social history of leisure in this period had been made. A working-class organisation, in some senses, had been created, but made possible by being within a specifically business mould. Neither its 'working-class' nature nor its organisational type had been typical of mid-nineteenth-century Reading leisure provision; both

were to be hegemonic in mid-twentieth-century Reading, and wider
society. But the RFC as a case for this chapter cannot be left at this
point. Its experience and difficulties *as* a new type of club also relate closely
to problems already raised in connection with churches and chapels.
They also confirm that demand for models other than the passive
'spectatorate' one remained.

Things were not easy for the RFC in the early twentieth century.
Most seasons it was in deficit – in 1906 for instance, the club made a
loss on the season of £300.[35] Some seasons it was in crisis. Early in
1900 there was talk of winding up the Club altogether.[36] The language
used about the situation might have been used by a minister talking
about an Institute, a Christian Endeavour Society, a Bible Class or
church attendance. The chairman of the directors spoke of the 'apathy'
of the working classes.[37] 'The public of Reading', declared Mr Cox,
'ought not to expect half a dozen gentlemen out of their own pockets
to find sport for them. If they did not get the support they had better
close the show at the end of the season. . .he hoped the public would
take the matter to heart.' The perspective from which to look at
religious organisations is not that of large dynamic organisations in
other subject areas 'taking over' from declining churches and chapels,
nor that of things like sport which represented 'the future' and things
like churches and chapels which represented 'the past', but rather that
of a changing context within which both religious organisations and,
for example, sporting ones were operating.

In response to difficulties at the Football Club a number of things
were tried. The Reading Theatre was approached to give special shows,
as it was by religious missions as well. Bazaars were held. In March
1899 a Reading Football, Athletic and Social Club was started as a
kind of supporters' association. This body was in one of the traps
described earlier on. Half the committee of the club were directors of
the RFC. When in 1900 they tried to raise the subscription from
1/6*d.* to 2/6*d.* a year, they had to rule a man out of order who, 'on
behalf of the working men', protested against this move, before they
could get it through.[38] Attendance was a continual problem.

Four years later, in 1904, there was another crisis.[39] A scheme was
announced in the local press for 'Helping the Reading Football Club'.
It was sub-headed 'How Everyone May Participate'. A return to an
older pattern had been suggested, with one guinea subscriptions from
gentlemen. But J. Rabson, a friend of Esrom's, an active member of
Broad Street Pleasant Sunday Afternoon movement, later to become
the first Labour Mayor of Reading, had other ideas.[40] He wanted a

model of organisation which working-class advocates were to try to follow through in subject areas other than football, with the aim of localising grass-roots participation and stimulating an active relationship between supporter and club. His model was not confined to asking people to buy shares. He knew the financial straits which supporters and the Club were in, and had earlier suggested allowing working men to pay for their football over the summer months as well as in the winter.

Rabson proposed that an active Committee should be set up. It came to be known as the Special Effort Committee. Although he was soon disappointed with the results, and although his was not the direction in which twentieth-century football clubs were to go, within seven weeks he had managed to get some five hundred people working on behalf of the Committee.[41] 'They suggested, as time went on, a division of the town into convenient districts and further sub-divisions, and so create an organisation by which the supporters of the club would keep in close touch.' An early proposal for raising funds was 'a really comprehensive exhibition for the town and district, combining industrial, agricultural and trading exhibits'. There was to be a Card Collection in each of the large industrial establishments in Reading. 'Mr Stock offered to arrange that collections be made during the summer months in the hotels where Buffaloes Lodges met.' There was a suggestion for a 'Football Saturday' in Reading, with the Reading Temperance Band parading the streets along the lines of the Friendly Societies' Hospital Parades, and later on for an August Bank Holiday Fete, and a Smoking Concert. At the Smoking Concert, Esrom felt sufficiently in sympathy with the aims of the scheme to perform, as he did at Co-op. propaganda and other town meetings. After all, as Rabson pointed out, 'the games at Elm Park provided healthy outdoor sport for their working classes − it was ridiculous to talk to 98% of their middle-aged men about taking an active part in the game'. The Club had not yet moved as far from non-playing versions of taking an active part, as it and other professional clubs were to do in the twentieth century.[42]

None of the other 'social activities and amenities' whose range the guide-book writer found so impressive in Reading in 1911 merit treatment at the level of detail given in the case of the Football Club. But to illustrate and extend the outlines of social change in the leisure area in the late nineteenth and early twentieth century, it will be helpful to isolate problems and to pursue them into other sporting and leisure organisations. 'Literary and Social', Temperance, and YMCA activities will be among those used, as well as further sporting groups.

The problem of money was a constant preoccupation of all groupings, as it was with churches and chapels. There is no point in documenting the problem as experienced by each grouping in turn. The interest of the experience of financial shortage in each case is the way in which it signals key social changes and key features of the context within which both religious and other organisations had to function.

'Anyone who studies sport', said the Reading Athletic Club in their *Annual Report* for 1899-1900, 'knows very well that a large amateur society cannot be successfully carried on without the. . .contributions of influential supporters'. The trouble was that those supporters were disappearing. Between 1900 and 1908-9 the RAC lost twenty Vice-Presidents and 'it was difficult to fill their places'. From about 1900 onwards trouble was continual, and before that losses on the season were frequent. 'We must cease to exist', they said in 1904-5, 'if we go on as we are going'. In the case of this particular club it was not just financial difficulties which signalled this change. W.H. Palmer of the biscuit factory had, in the early 1890s, been personally very involved with the Club as an athlete, member and 'captain'. By 1911 he was just 'patron'; this was not just a factor of his ageing, for he no longer even came to watch the sports. The year 1898 was the first time he had not been there for twelve years. 'To be or not to be that is the question', wrote Esrom in the Report for 1907-8. It was a mystery to enthusiasts around the Club, for the virtues of the sport were, to them, enormous. Both private capital and the State should recognise those virtues. 'Athletic qualities are getting to command premiums among employers who are worth working for', for they inspired initiative, hard work and self-government. According to a visiting MP, 'if there had been an athletic club half so successful and so prosperous as the RAC in every town in the land, there would have been no need for the public discussion on the state of physique and public feeding of elementary school children which had taken place in politics that year'.[43] These were the terms on which the YMCA also appealed to its supporters, but it was hard going for them as well. They were going to have to change during the twentieth century in a direction comparable to that of the Football Club. They were going to have to cease being a membership- and meeting-oriented society, and become a semi-commercial hotel-like organisation, providing a 'service' for passive consumers. Enjoying the benefits of the YMCA was going to

depend no more on activity at its core than in the case of the
twentieth-century trade union, Co-op., or Workers' Educational
Association.

The Reading Temperance Society was another victim of this
situation. Ordinary members' money had always played a small part in
the total financing of the society; other sources in our period were
drying up, 'as year by year old subscribers are removed by death it
becomes an increasing anxiety to the committee how the work can be
maintained in efficiency'.[44] William Isaac Palmer had been the main
prop, and very personal inspirer of many of the Society's activities. His
death produced both a financial and a leadership crisis. The former
could not be resolved until, in 1911, six of his nephews liquidated the
mortgage on the £4,700 building which the Society had constructed.
Even self-consciously and intentionally independent organisations like
the Reading Working Men's Regatta, which saw itself as being very
different from the gentlemanly Reading Amateur Regatta, were forced
to rely on special appeals and their subscribers' lists rather than on
self-generated members' or attenders' money. Palmer money was vital
even in a year of record attendance.[45] It was very difficult to run an
organisation which cost anything at all without Vice-Presidential help;
it was increasingly difficult to get that help, and unless the scale of the
operation was large enough to seem potentially profitable and therefore
to adapt to capitalist business modes of organisation like football, no
other help was available.

These were the terms of 'success', and thus the recipe for 'failure',
for any large social organisation in the leisure field in Reading before
1914. Even the directly subsidised and factory-based Reading Biscuit
Factory Recreation Club, which could not have existed without the
Directors' backing, was in a financial trap.[46] It is clear from their
records that the members wanted to achieve a measure of independence,
and to be in control of the Club as much as possible. Yet to do this
subscription had gone steadily up from 1/- in 1878, to 1/6d. in 1880,
minimum of two shillings per year to play cricket, an impossible fee
for many. An organisation like the Reading Literary and Scientific
Society was clearly for a clientele with more spare resources of time
and money than the Biscuit Factory Recreation Club. But they too
were anxious about membership: 'the subscription is a nominal one
and has been kept low in order that no one in sympathy with the
objects of the society may be deterred from joining'[47]: yet that
subscription had gone steadily up from 1/- in 1878, to 1/6d. in 1880,
to 2/- in 1884, to 3/- in 1895.[48] While wanting a wide membership,

they fixed subscriptions at a level which precluded one. The Reading Athenaeum was a club for a still more affluent clientele, with town members paying £2.12.0*d.* a year in 1905-6. But it was in acute financial difficulties from about 1910 onwards and would not have survived without special appeals and large donations from non-members.

Financial problems were closely related to another problem which has already been touched on at the level of churches and chapels and their agencies, that of survival. It was not just the agencies attached to churches and chapels which were experiencing a pattern of difficulty in keeping going between 1890 and 1914. There is evidence from Reading to suggest that the 1914-18 War was not the villain, or at least not the only villain, which interrupted and impeded a whole range of voluntary organisations. There was a more general crisis in the early twentieth century for social activists of many different types and ideologies.

To some extent the Biscuit Factory Recreation Club was insulated from wider social circumstances by being within, and heavily dependent upon, the factory and its owners. But from 1901-2 onwards their Reports were full of the difficulty of getting members and attendance both at older styles of recreation, and at the new styles which they had adopted because of lack of success. In 1903-4 the Committee were 'at a complete loss to account for the serious falling off in members, as the programme of sport and entertainment provided for the members reached the usual high standard of excellence. . .considering the low rate of subscription the committee had every reason to expect an increase of membership'. They did not suggest changes in spending power as a reason. A low point was reached in 1910-11. Cycling was another interesting case. Throughout the 1890s clubs were having special difficulty in attracting support for their most participatory social activity – 'Club Runs'. They were seen as important items in Cycling Club activities since they brought members together. Thus A.T. Heelas, a department-store retailer, complained at the annual dinner of the Wheelers' Cycling Club in 1899 that 'from the social point of view the runs had been a failure and he was not surprised at this. He did not know a club for a long way whose runs had been a success. He had gradually seen a decay of the Club Run, and now they were practically a thing of the past'.[49] The larger United Cycling Club was experiencing very bad attendance, and this 'considering the size of the Club and its being practically the cycling club of the district is certainly not a good sign of interest taken in it by individual members'. Gates at the Reading Athletic Club decreased as sharply as subscribers and led, as we shall see, to a change in the nature of the Club.[50]

Patterns of difficulty in the Reading Athenaeum and the Reading Literary and Scientific Society can be described later when the problem of adaptation is considered. The first major crisis of the Literary and Scientific Society came in 1901-4. Thereafter vigorous missionary efforts plus acceptance of a smaller role in changed circumstances were the routes chosen for survival. In the case of the Reading YMCA, local financial difficulties caused partly by an ambitious new building (as in the case of the Temperance Society, the Athenaeum, and many churches and chapels) preceded local and national membership difficulties which came to a head in about 1910.[51] Because membership was decreasing fast, the two secretaries were asked to draw up a report on the organisation and its future. After considering documents from national headquarters in May 1909, the Executive Committee 'after a careful and frank discussion which was begun in prayer and continued in a spirit of Christian brotherhood. . .were obliged to admit that so far as evidenced by the apathy of our Full Members, the National Council Report was fully justified'.

The shifting of the centre of gravity of leisure activity away from the agency of the chapel or church on to a pan-Reading level was also part of the pattern affecting many other organisations. The small Athletic Society of 1874 became the Reading Abbey Athletic Club of 1882 which became the Reading Athletic Club of 1883. The Reading Wheelers' Cycling Club and the Reading Cycling Club amalgamated into the Reading United Cycling Club of 1899. The Reading Literary and Scientific Society was the product of an evolution similar to the one already described in the case of the Trinity Alphabetical Society. In their case the species evolved was more hardy. A grouping attached to the Unitarian Free Church in 1878 became, in about 1879, the Redlands Literary and Scientific Society for 'the promotion of Literary and Scientific Culture by meetings for the reading and discussions of papers and by such means as may appear desirable'. In 1887 the Redlands society in turn became the Reading Literary and Scientific Society. Small changes were enormously important in later perspective. For instance, that the Reading Literary and Scientific Society found it difficult to find anywhere suitable to meet between 1878 and 1912 might not seem significant (they met in six different places – Unitarian Chapel 1878, Lodge Hotel 1883, Suttons' Abbey Hall 1891, YMCA Hall 1904, Duke Street 1907, Denmark Hall 1911). Finally in 1912, 'the prospect which the Committee had to face was almost as gloomy as in 1902'. They approached the Council of University College

Reading, and obtained the use of the history room there. This was in reality a strategic date in the social history of the town. That the dense nineteenth-century history of Literary and Philosophical Societies and Mechanics' Institutes in Reading should finally be centralised into the University orbit indicated a new phase in the social history of adult learning and intellectual enterprise, one in which the State was in the end to predominate.

The most interesting problem in relation to Reading leisure-providers was that of adaptation. Here again what was happening to religious organisations can be shown to have been happening to utterly different organisations.

Difficulties about finance and other types of support and interest have already been mentioned. They were the preoccupation of many of the *Annual Reports* of the Reading Athletic Club between *c.*1895 and 1914, although the Club was as successful as any in England, and operating on an impressive scale. The *Report* for 1898 counted 3,000 people at the Sports meeting. It said of this figure that, 'the attendance was fair. . .but some disappointment was expressed that the sixpenny- and shilling-enclosures were not better filled'. *The Sporting Life* was quoted in the same Report as saying that at least what crowd there was showed enthusiasm, compared to the 'apathy' of metropolitan meetings. In spite of such favourable comparison there was no doubt about the continual crisis of the Club. In 1908-9 Walter Howard Palmer was quoted as saying, 'the only question that perplexed his mind was that if the club. . .should become defunct what would become of the rising generation? If it were not for that problem he should strongly urge the officials to continue for one more year and then dissolve the club'.

Adaptation of the product of the RAC took two main forms. The first was the familiar response of changing methods and styles to 'attract' the public. Concentration on advertising methods was suggested (1899-1900). Diversification into new events was pursued, although this involved the trap of supplying items which were not central to the main aims of the RAC in order to help it to survive, and then having those things themselves cause difficulties. In 1903-4 the RAC had to remind themselves that although 'it had been suggested that they should include some special race in their programme to make it more entertaining for the general public. . .catering for the public meant the expenditure of money and they must always remember that the Club was formed not so much to amuse the public as to give everyone in the neighbourhood the opportunity of going in for athletics'. Again in the following season, it was reported how 'the general public have of late evinced a tendency to give us more support if we provide them with "side shows" and "light entertainment", unfortunately however this sort of thing entails extra and heavy expenses for us'. The standard of comfort offered to the public, as with the St. John's CETS, was blamed for lack of support. So such items as Whist Drives and Wrestling were introduced to get the public in. But they were seen as being a far cry from the language which clustered around the Club in the early 1890s.

Adaptation in this direction, towards 'brightness' — as it were towards cheaper biscuits, towards a more market-conscious, less morally-dominative style, towards a greater self-consciousness about means leading to a sacrifice of ends — went so far in the case of the RAC that in 1897 they even cut out local events in the sports altogether. Like Honey Drops they had become 'irrational'. 'This proceeding', not unnaturally, 'aroused much opposition'. So in the latter half of our period the adaptation to the changing context went in a different, indeed an opposite way. The Club turned in on itself and decided to try to do well, regardless of 'the public' which it was there for. 'To save the club from collapse', wrote Esrom in 1907-8, 'we must abandon music and costly prizes and cater for our local athletes alone'. In 1914, before the War, it was decided to discontinue the general Sports meeting altogether and to concentrate on small members' meetings and races. The terms on which the club *could* survive after about 1908, and the terms on which they came to *want* to survive, were as a small group of athletes who liked meeting together to race and to train, not as a type of organisation of interest either to Vice-Presidents or Boards of Directors.[52] Such a response may usefully be labelled a 'sectarian' one at this point.

A similar response was made by the Reading Literary and Scientific Society. Faced by the fact that 'in recent years there had been a somewhat rapid decline in membership',[53] they adapted only very slightly in the direction of diversification, and much more strongly in the direction of decisive pursuit of their central purposes regardless of a wide public. They added excursions to their activities (1887-8) but resisted (1889-90) 'practical work' like photography, for which there had been some demand. They continually appealed to members to play a more active role, but had unusual resistance to easy ways out: 'it is felt that no greater error of policy could be made than to "play to the gallery" for a mere addition of numbers. Their motto will rather be *alta petens* and their purpose to band together, be they many or be they few, those who have a real desire for mental culture in literature and science.'

The Athenaeum, originally a similar body to the Reading Literary and Scientific Society, went a different way. It took over from a 'Literary Institution'. From a *Rule Book* of 1853 it is clear that, for a time, its aims remained the same — 'the promotion of Literature and Science in the neighbourhood'. But there were signs of strain early on. A Committee in 1854 recommended either a dissolution or a remodelling of the organisation. In 1884 there was talk of the need to 'improve' the Reading Room and add a card room and a smoking room to it. By 1885 the Athenaeum had become just a reading room with a few garnishings. By the forty-fourth Annual General Meeting (1885) 'the institution was in a condition which gave rise to serious doubts as to the possibility of continuing its existence'. A member therefore undertook to prepare plans for turning it into 'a social club upon a more popular footing'. A furniture fund was started, despite the resistance of some who said that it was undesirable to change the aims of the Athenaeum in this way. By March 1885 altered and improved premises were open, much money having been subscribed, some of it by Palmers. From then on it was a Club in the West End sense, with billiards, cards, etc., run on more or less commercial lines. It ceased to be the Reading Athenaeum and became the Athenaeum Club (24 August 1888). By 1902-3 it is clear that the conditions upon which some of the money for the 1885 transformation had been given — namely Temperance — were no longer being observed. In November 1905, at a time when membership was falling, a Social Committee was appointed: 'with a view to bringing the club more prominently before the public, the Committee are shortly issuing a booklet setting forth the advantages to be derived from membership.' The New Rules (10 January 1898), and the whole way in which the Club presented itself and its relationship with the public, were a complete transformation of its original *alta petens* self of the mid-nineteenth century. Then it had been more interested in what it stood for, than in how to attract the public.[54]

Two further cases of organisations experiencing and adapting to the pressures being described here are worth outlining — the Reading YMCA, and a sub-agency of the Reading Temperance Society, the weekly entertainments. Both provide evidence of fascinating awareness of what was happening to them; both after much anxiety went with the tide, in the case of the YMCA, locally and nationally, with a considerable degree of 'success' through the twentieth century.

The YMCA as a national movement (as opposed to its world

dimension) has adapted at least twice in order to survive.[55] Such
adaptation has been a necessary condition for continued 'success' in
more than a century of rapid social change – over which it has exerted
no control. The first adaptation was from a strictly evangelical
Christian origin – consisting of meetings of members – towards a more
recreational orientation, although defended in evangelical terms; the
second was towards the hostel work – involving gate money rather
than membership money, as in the RFC – by which the YMCA is
known now.[56] It is the first of these adaptations and the anxiety it
generated which is of interest at the level of the Reading Association.

The Reading YMCA proper dated back to 1882. It benefited from
the centralisation process already described, absorbing or out-growing
the three other YMCAs which existed in Reading up to 1891 and the
one other, the Church of England YMCA, which lasted until 1903. The
Reading Church of England YMCA was the brain-child of Martin Hope
Sutton the seed manufacturer, and in its origin preceded, or at least ran
parallel to, George Williams' work in London. Its first formal meeting
was held on 18th December 1846, but it had existed before that. It
retained its evangelical strictness and anti-amusement orientation until
it ceased in 1903.[57] The aims of the main YMCA were made clear in its
Rules in 1900. Rule II stated 'that the object of the Association be the
improvement of the spiritual, social, mental and physical condition of
young men'. Rule III stated 'that the agency employed for the attainment
of this object be that of the members of the association in the sphere of
their daily calling, devotional meetings, classes of Biblical instruction, and
for Literary improvement, a Library for reference and other means in
accordance with the Holy Scriptures'.[58]

It was around the 'other means' and their relationship to the stated
means and object of the main Association that tension was to grow.
There were certainly an enormous number of them. At least twenty-five
sub-agencies of activity had clustered around the main body by the
summer of 1899.[59] But at the opening of the new YMCA building in
Friar Street in 1897, at which Sir George Williams and many of the
leading townsmen of Reading were present, it was clear that at least
formally, and in the eyes of those who financed and spoke for it, the
YMCA was still primarily an evangelical religious agency. The
embellishments were secondary means to an agreed end. Lord Kinnaird
made an aggressive speech at the opening ceremony:

They wanted to make this world more like heaven, and if, instead
of singing so many psalms about it they would put their shoulders

to the wheel, determined that they would bring heaven into Reading, into their counting houses and into their different offices, so that a young man should be able to go safely into his counting house or workshop and they should be no more training places for the devil. . .[60]

They were clear that 'in proportion as (it) is definitely Christian in its tone will the object in view be achieved'.[61]

Controversy grew about the terms upon which the YMCA could flourish in the years 1890 to 1914, in relation to its exalted ideals. It first broke out into the open in 1895. At the South Midland Union of YMCAs, Mr Souttar had attacked the idea of having any games at all attached to the local Association. The local Liberal press, while admitting that the YMCA had 'extended in a manner Mr George Williams little dreamt of', editorialised against such a purist response to changing demands for leisure provision. 'Recreation' in its right context was defensible, 'there are other attractions which appeal to youths and especially to those who are engaged in sedentary occupations or have to do work in badly ventilated rooms or offices or at unhealthy trades. In order to fit such young men for the severe battle of life they must not only have a sound mind but a sound body, and to obtain the latter they must indulge in recreation'.[62]

Two years later tensions again surfaced.[63] At a conference in Reading it was recognised that the 'physical section' of the work was attracting people. Yet it was in danger of submerging its other more important sides, like the Library, Bible Classes and prayers. 'Certain it was that by providing for the means for wholesome recreation and amusement they attracted a number of young men who would not otherwise be brought under the influence of the devotional side of the Association', yet 'attracting' these young men weakened the impact the Association wanted to have on them. They were in the familiar trap. The Secretary, Frederic Hunt, who has already been observed attacking the Reading Football Club, was worried about non-participatory recreation growing at the expense of action. 'He was heartily in sympathy with all physical exercises but he hoped the members of the Association Football Clubs would not scratch their matches on purpose to see a *performance* by the Reading Club – a team of professionals.' A climax of discussion was reached in 1909-10 at the time of acute local and national membership problems.[64] A Special Committee was set up, on which the Reading secretary sat, to investigate why the main aims of the YMCA were being subordinated to subsidiary activities, and why even those subsidiaries were not prospering as they should. In the Report of the Committee a leapfrog of blame was brought into play. Lack of success was partly, they thought, owing to church and chapel Institutes, which themselves were blaming pan-Reading agencies like the YMCA. 'The measure in which the institute and social agencies are allowed to obscure or displace the definitely religious agencies' was found to be a national not just a Reading phenomenon.

Efforts were made to correct the trend. Stricter tests for Members, concentration on the cultivation of Members rather than Associates, reinforcement of 'the inner life of the Association' were all tried between 1909 and 1914. But the real trend was clearly the other way. There was a distinctly new tone in the early twentieth-century records of the Association. In the same year as the Secretary had been asked to recommend changes in order to counter the tendencies reported by the national enquiry, significant items appeared in the Executive Committee Minutes. In October 1909,

> the question of arranging for the better use of the Lecture Hall which was now used as a games room was fully discussed and it was resolved that the Hall be converted into a lounge, reading and writing room, and the present Reading Room be used as a Bagatelle and Ping-Pong room and other suitable games.[65]

To attract people to Social Hours, it was decided to get an orchestra to play. It was by then necessary to plead that such a central activity as Members' meetings should occasionally be included in the programme.[66] A little later questions of advertising more effectively, printing more attractive cards, and allowing smoking on the premises were raised and approved. 'Congenial surroundings' were becoming more of a preoccupation than 'the principles of the movement'. By then the Reading Church of England YMCA, which had remained separate and stood against these developments in the movement, and through its main protagonist (M.H. Sutton) had spoken against such things, had collapsed, leaving a worried and remodelled Association to try to react to social change.

One of the many agencies attached to the Reading Temperance Society was a long-standing series of 'Saturday Evening meetings' or 'Entertainments'. William Isaac Palmer started them in 1872. He was personally involved with them for the rest of his life. 'We make no pretence that these are religious meetings', he wrote when giving advice to other towns on how to use this agency of emperance work, 'although we do not exclude religion and temperance. Both subjects are brought out and they come naturally without any arrangement on our part'. According to W.I. Palmer, twenty working men who had been reclaimed from excessive drinking and wanted something to do on Saturday nights, started the meetings. 'The principle element of success for these meetings is to begin with a small number, letting the parties amuse themselves as they think best or are able, slightly controlling and directing them into a higher and better way.'[67] Such meetings mushroomed in Reading through the 1880s. By 1890 there were Saturday nights started the meetings. 'The principle element of success nights. Expenses, of course, were met by men like Palmer.[68] By 1890 the meetings had 'passed through several phases since their commencement. For years the stated lecture formed the staple commodity provided from the platform, but the ever changing exigencies of progress have been felt in this department of labour. . .the present demands are short speeches and a measure of entertainment'. The familiar contradictions were there, 'whilst seeking to comply with the popular demand your committee are ever solicitous to keep in full view the great object for which they are banded together, that is to teach and promote the practice of teetotalism among their fellows'.[69]

Nine years before, the same contradictions had been felt. The Reading Temperance Society in its Annual Report (1881) said, 'your committee have felt that they are not justified in simply providing meetings for entertainment, however popular they might be, but that every meeting should be distinctly leavened with sound temperance teaching, in order that the hearers might be edified'. The contradictions had been met by insisting upon 'the great object'. After about 1902 external social pressures were such, and the attitudes of the Reading Temperance Society (now without William Isaac Palmer) were such, that the contradictions were met by adapting the product. Pure entertainments without lectures, but with musical and other attractions, were now provided. They were defended on different grounds; 'a real want is being met in providing entertainments for the many hundreds who throng the streets'.[70] In 1904 meetings were moved to the town hall for a while to have a wider attraction.[71] They were therefore very different occasions to the ones over which W.I. Palmer had presided and much less easy to connect with the central aims of the Reading Temperance Society.[72]

Some of the individuals involved with the organisations discussed in this chapter knew well some of the constraints within which they were

working. The one most regularly singled out was the economic
constraint – the constant lack of spending power, indeed the primary
poverty of a large segment of the Reading population, making it
difficult to say that what happened was entirely the result of demand
from below. This was chronic, but worse early in the twentieth century.
Even the Committee of the Athenaeum Club referred to 'the great
depression which is here so keenly felt. . .which has considerably
affected clubs and similar institutions'.[73] Esrom of the Athletic Club
was fully aware of the constrictions of poverty.[74] So was J. Rabson
with the Football Club.

But both, as we have seen, had wider and more interesting things to
say in their diagnoses. Poverty meant that activities involving the
intermittent expenditure of small sums were more possible for the
working class (but not thereby more desired) than regular membership
activities. To state that, for example, the shift towards cheap,
intermittent entertainment in the menu of voluntary organisations
reflected the nature and capacities of the working-class 'public' would
be equivalent to saying that the class *preferred* broken biscuits (which
is what they got) to Honey Drops. What the shift registers is one
possible route forward (in some subject-areas) for organisations in a
changing context. 'The public' were, perhaps, prepared to consume
·entertainment from Vice-Presidential sources from whom they were
no longer prepared to buy ideology. This was particularly the case if
the entertainment was cheap. But to extrapolate from this that the
public or, as they were increasingly called, 'the masses' did not *want*
participatory membership-type activity, only wanted entertainment,
and were not interested in alternative ideology (ideology which was, in
fact, closer to that of W.I. Palmer than it was to twentieth-century
entertainment entrepreneurs), would be wholly unwarranted. This will
become even more apparent in the next three chapters. Another
possible route forward was the *alta petens,* 'better fewer but better',
low overheads, low capital expenditure, 'sectarian' route.

The changing limits to the freedom of operation of voluntary
organisations as leisure providers were not simply economic. The social
change to which they were subject had other dimensions, and in the
perspective of later twentieth-century history, more long-lasting
dimensions. About these, contemporaries were, perhaps necessarily,
less clear. Bewilderment characterised much speculation on the 'success'
or 'failure' of particular activities in non-religious groups as much as in
religious. We have seen the Committee of the Biscuit Factory Recreation
Club in 1904 'at a complete loss to account for the serious falling off in

members'. The Athletic Club both blamed the tendency towards professionalisation and delocalisation in their own sports for lack of attendance and interest, and the same tendency elsewhere for attracting people away from their own sports to other meetings (1902). More usually, a leapfrog of blame occurred, with church institutes and political clubs blaming pan-Reading organisations like the YMCA for their failures and vice-versa.[75] Such phrases as 'the depressed spiritual conditions which have prevailed throughout the country generally in recent years' were resorted to. W.H. Palmer observed in 1910 'how other societies in Reading seemed to be in a weak financial state, but he could get no satisfactory reason for that. One thing he had been told was that it was on account of the many cinematograph shows in the town, but surely people did not go there on hot June afternoons'.[76] The decline of aspects of cycling was a mystery: 'why it has done so is not an easy matter to determine, but nevertheless the fact remains. It is not difficult to recall the early days of the pneumatic safety when most towns had their one, at least, clubs. . .can that be said at the present day?'[77] 'Where are the Reading sporting public?' asked the *Berkshire Chronicle* in an editorial in August 1904. Churches and chapels were not alone in introspection and concern.

8 WELFARE

At a joint meeting of the Reading Fabian Society and the Independent Labour Party in the Town Hall in 1912 Philip Snowden referred to 'the almost complete revolution of mental attitude which had taken place' towards welfare and poverty. 'All political parties in the country today recognised the existence of what they termed the social problem. It was not always so.'[1] It was not merely in attitudes, and not only in political parties that drastic changes were happening in the area of 'welfare' in the late nineteenth and early twentieth centuries. It is widely recognised that the fifteen years before 1914 were critical in the history of 'the welfare state', and that the thirty-five years before 1914 were critical in the development of attitudes towards the poor.

It is not the main purpose of this chapter to add to knowledge of the social history of welfare and poverty at the national level. There are a number of points at which the story needs correcting, and it is being corrected by a concentration of recent historical research in this field.[2] Simple ideas as to the replacement of an age of 'individualism' by an age of 'collectivism', or as to the deliberate, inevitable, piece-by-piece construction of a firmly structured and liberal 'welfare state' can no longer by used. As a by-product of this chapter ideas will be generated which may add to the national picture, still far from fixed. But the main purpose is to continue analysis of the wider context in which religious organisations were set, through the experience of other voluntary organisations. Pre-1914 social investigators, such as Charles Booth, A.L. Bowley or Seebohm Rowntree, did not neglect the role of churches and chapels and their charities, but agreed on their limitations in the face of 'the social problem'. 'Broadly speaking the recipients of charity are the poor, i.e. those who from causes "primary" or "secondary" are below the poverty line; and the number of the poor who are lifted above it by charity must be small.'[3] It is through other, sometimes much larger, organisations that what was happening to the society in which religion was set must be understood.

In the last chapter a single organisation – the Reading Football Club – was used to pull together a number of lines of analysis. The same can be done here with another pan-Reading organisation – the Royal Berkshire Hospital. To the Reading branch of the Social Democratic Federation the Hospital was odious. It was run by the exploiting class for themselves. They only used the workers' bodies to experiment on; such organisations would be 'next to useless if they were living under a proper system of society'.[4] But elsewhere in the town it was widely considered that 'no institution is the centre of greater usefulness'. The Reading Co-op. had growing reservations about it, but 'we all had a very kindly feeling towards an old institution'.[5] What was happening to it?

The Hospital had been founded in 1839, initially through the commitment of a lone clergyman who had propagated the idea and collected early funds. Landed benevolence helped it on its way — the land being given by Lord and Lady Sidmouth and £4,000 by the owner of a local stately residence, Richard Benyon de Beauvoir. In the opinion of the Rev. W.A. Findlay it was 'a monument to the influence of Christianity'.[6]

The first important fact about the Hospital in the late nineteenth and early twentieth centuries is that it was in a chronic financial crisis. The deficiency in ordinary income compared to ordinary expenditure was £1305 in 1897, £1692 in 1898. In the ten years between 1888 and 1898 receipts had increased by about £500, expenditure by about £1500.[7] The annual loss was running at about £2000 by the turn of the century, and getting worse.[8] Special appeals, which could not by their very nature be regular, and legacies, masked a situation which otherwise would have been insupportable between 1890 and 1914. A special committee appointed to enquire into the financial and general condition of the Hospital reported in 1899 that the only possible way out of a desperate plight was to decrease the number of beds.[9] Such a paring down was more difficult for Hospitals than for organisations with less essential products, like biscuit factories or football clubs.

This situation is, by itself, of little interest. Before any significance can be given to the condition of the Royal Berkshire Hospital we must know in more detail what it was, and from which directions it was suffering the strains reflected in the balance sheets.

To an extent difficult for the modern observer to grasp, the Hospital in the mid-nineteenth century was rooted in the locality. Not so much a branch of a national 'service', or a place where scientific advances in treatment automatically arrived from outside, or a place whose financial situation was, within limits, secured by state policy and taxation — it was rather the centre for local social action, a focus for the local medical profession with its Pathological Society (1841) and Museum, in some respects a local social movement. The 'Annual Courts' of the Royal Berkshire Hospital were major town and county events. Leading members of the business, professional and land-owning élites, together with other types of interested person, came to them. Their proceedings were reported in two or three full columns of the local press, with verbatim accounts of the major speeches and some of the subsequent discussion. Local sources of voluntary finance were the Hospital's economic base. Donations, legacies and subscriptions were the most important. Increasingly from the third quarter of the nineteenth century onwards, other means became significant — church collections, the Hospital Saturday Fund (started in Reading in 1886) and the Hospital Sunday movement. The latter involved a pan-town event which depended on the interest and active commitment of large numbers of members of Friendly Societies, together with other members of the public, to take part in processions, meetings and contribute to collections.[10]

So that it mattered when it was said, in 1895, that 'the town of Reading does not support the Hospital as well as it ought to do'.[11] From a number of directions strain was being experienced.[12]

Hospital Saturday suffered first. In 1897 it was taking £100 less than at its peak in 1892. The first talk of ending it reached the local press in 1899. It finished in 1900.[13] Hospital Sunday went through more vicissitudes. A typical Hospital Sunday took place in 1891.[14] Three processions of the Friendly and Trade Societies went round the town collecting money. Services were held at the main churches and chapels of the principal denominations. The official preacher that year was the Rev. R.H. Hart Davis who preached at St. Lawrence's, the municipal church. He gave perfect expression to the nature and ideology of the occasion. He was on the one hand determined to make voluntarism work, and to point to the consequences, for rich and poor, of it not working.

What would be the position of ratepayers in the town if the whole burden of expenditure necessary to maintain in sickness the husbands, wives and children of the working classes were placed upon their shoulders. . .what would be the distress, the opening of the heart of every compassionate citizen whose occupation brought him into touch with the family life of working men, if there were nothing but the mere pittance granted under the Poor Law?

At the same time he was, to an extent, in favour of welfare legislation. He wanted a national system of insurance for sickness and unemployment and a national system of pensions — but always within a voluntaristic framework. He was a passionate Friendly Society supporter, for 'he saw no manliness in a false spirit of humility'. It was through them and other local organisations that any national system of benefits must be administered. Local voluntary organisations must not be by-passed, even in such obvious and expensive necessities as Pensions.[15] Hospital Sunday was not just one way, among other ways, of raising money for the Royal Berkshire Hospital, to be judged solely by its efficiency at doing that job. It represented a particular relationship between the Hospital and the locality, a particular way of relating to welfare and social needs. In 1892 Hart Davis preached on the text 'You have the poor with you always, and whensoever you may do them good'. He asserted his own position strongly; 'some believe that only a considerable number of human evils may be materially mitigated, others, more buoyant, have convinced themselves that with time and patience and intelligent exertion every evil not essential to a finite existence may be got rid of, and the gulf between the actual and the ideal at last bridged over. This faith is my own and I am convinced that it is shared by the vast majority of the working class.'[16] Hospital Sunday was a typical part of this 'intelligent exertion'.

In 1896, after some deliberation, a significant change in the form of the day took place. As well as collecting in the streets, as well as the participatory parades, a house-to-house collection was started. In the same way that the decision to base meetings of the Reading Literary and Scientific Society in the University was a significant date in the social history of the town, so too the switch in emphasis from 1891-type parades and services to house-to-house collecting in 1896 was a change resonant of far wider changes in society. The concentration of social life on, the confinement of leisure time to, the orientation of attitudes and consumption around, *the home* is a strand of twentieth-century social history as important as the centralisation already touched on. It was to affect pubs, through the growth of off-licences, as much as it was to affect churches, hospital parades and other voluntary organisations.[17] The change away from parades was also a sign of the times in relation to the history of processions in Reading. Before 1850 there had been carnival events like election processions, fairs or political celebrations, of events such as the ending of the Napoleonic wars. From 1850 through to the 1890s was the heyday of processions generated by local organisations or voluntary associations such as biscuit factory funerals, hospital days, Palmer Park openings. Thereafter such processions were to be less common, until, by the mid-twentieth century, processions dominated by advertising for private companies and state agencies (e.g. the army), modelled on Lord Mayor's day, held the field.[18]

Hospital Sunday in 1901 was, financially, a good day. A record
£176 was raised – of which no less than £117 came from the
house-to-house rather than from older activities connected with the
day.[19] Among these older activities there had also been signs of change.
In 1894 crowds had not been as large as usual. Mass meetings were
tried instead of the usual services. The local press blamed the lack of
interest (and money) on this change, there was 'an impression abroad
that the management had got into the hands of Radicals. . .the service
partook of the nature of a public meeting with a political colour about
it'.[20] In 1895 the experiment was abandoned in favour of 'a reversion
to primitive methods', but with the change the traditional three
processions were reduced to one.[21] In 1901 further surgery was
necessary, 'owing to the poor attendances at the services in recent
years at St. Luke's and the town hall in connection with the parade
these services were discontinued this year, the members of the Friendly
and Trade Societies who followed the procession were not very
numerous. . .it certainly seems a pity that members do not support
their lodges and courts better'.[22]

Changes in Hospital Sunday were part of a more general crisis for
the Hospital. The cost of treatment, or the cost per bed, was escalating
rapidly.[23] This meant that, in the system of each donor organisation
getting a ration of admission tickets corresponding to its contributions,
by 1895 the Hospital was having to issue tickets at a loss. The only
alternative was the drying up of this important source of funds.[24]
Similarly in 1899, against much opposition, the Hospital found it
necessary to stop allowing Club and Friendly Society out-patients to
get free treatment. Such a system was as out of date as allowing
concessions to YMCA members in University Extension classes was to
become in twentieth-century 'state' universities. They were being forced,
in terms of the older ways of supporting themselves, to cut off their
nose to spite their face.[25] Nor was this the only centre of controversy
indicating an altered social role for the town in relation to the Hospital.
At the Annual Court in 1896 a major debate took place over the
question, which had been discussed for some time and was to be a
continuing theme, of professionalising the Board of Management. The
town had half the composition of the Board at its disposal. It was felt
by the doctors that they, as professionals and experts, should control
the Board. No such radical step was taken that year, but after heated
argument it was agreed by an extremely slim majority at the Annual
Court that some more doctors should be allowed to participate in the

management.[26] The process was to go further before 1914. With each of these developments, the relationship between the Hospital and local society and its voluntary organisations was visibly altering. Previous modes of government, finance, and administration of treatment were rapidly becoming impossible to sustain.

The situation was fascinatingly poised. Landed or manufacturing philanthropy was insufficient. The State had not yet moved in. Professionals were not yet in complete control. There was thus space for other paths to be taken, including ones which quickly petered out or were blocked, but which at the time seemed possible carriers of working-class ideas and organisation. Working-class organisations like Friendly Societies or the Co-op. were prepared to work for the Hospital but only if it was to be governed in a representative way. They also pressed for adequate rewards, in terms of treatment of working-class patients. By 1902 the Co-op. had decided to decrease its financial support for the Hospital because of lack of democratic control in its management. Esrom was in a cleft stick. He disliked the SDF logic behind this decision, which, he thought, would lead straight to municipal or State control. But he agreed that the Hospital would have to develop in a different direction from the one it seemed to be taking if voluntary modes were to be viable or desirable.[27]

In the same year a new direction was taken. F.C. Barnett founded the Reading Workpeople's Hospital Fund Association. Money was to be collected by the workmen of Reading under the aegis of a Committee run by them. Three members of the committee were to be allowed to sit on the Board of Management of the Hospital. Organisation was to cover the whole of the town and to be based upon individual workshops and factories. Tickets in proportion to the amount collected were to be distributed via elected representatives of each place or department of work. In a letter to the *Berkshire Chronicle* in April, F.C. Barnett appealed to 'the Men' to give a penny a week. He stressed 'certain conditions which are necessary to success and permanence. One is that the effort must be perfectly voluntary'. Another was that it be 'really and truly a workingman's scheme', in other words that it be democratic. 'Let the men in a shop select one of their number to represent them. He will look after the money, and receive the tickets for the use of the men. He will form one of a large central committee of his fellow delegates, who will, through their own officers, and through a small executive committee, administer and regulate the collection of this most important fund.' Any other terms than these, he felt, would not be acceptable.[28]

Correct interpretation of this development has some importance for the understanding of what was happening in our period. In the face of the crisis of an organisation, a way of rescuing it in changed social circumstances was being attempted which involved revitalising old models rather than adaptation to new ones. This attempt should be compared with J. Rabson's proposals for the Reading Football Club at almost exactly the same time. New working-class strata were to be added to old forms of social action and organisation. 'Workmen' were to be asked to contribute money, active organisation, and self-government, in a direct way to the Hospital — in the same way that higher strata had been doing for many years.

A working-class and democratic version of the ideology and organisation described in Chapter Two was trying to break through. It failed. But while it was there it even extended to ways of running such things as soup kitchens. The Royal Antediluvian Order of Buffaloes ran one early in the twentieth century which by 1905 was called the Reading Soup Kitchen. Rabson was one of its main activists. The Co-op. begged members for money, 'send it along to our Brother Buffs to help forward their labour of love among our poorer brethren'. Esrom agreed that changing the system was essential. But 'in the meantime we have to face the semi-starvation only too prevalent in many (so called) homes'. 'We should be *all* doing' the work of alleviating poverty, by filling up collecting cards with twelve 1*d.* spaces on them. 'If charity does not, the wolf comes in at the door.' Support was urged on the basis of the democratic nature of the Committee. In 1906 it was supported by the Co-op., Ye Ancient Cogers, the Reading Amateur Football Club, the PSAs and others. Alderman A.H. Bull, the department-store retailer, thought that it should become a municipal undertaking, supported in the Vice-Presidential mode, by subscribers who would have the right to nominate recipients of relief. Rabson disagreed. His reaction was the same as his reaction to the financial problems of the Football Club. They did not need the Council; they should divide the town into small districts, involve as many people in it as they could and run it themselves, without subscribers.[29]

Limited success was achieved through such modes. In the plight of the Royal Berkshire Hospital the sums of money contributed by the Reading Workpeople's Hospital Fund Association were welcome indeed.[30] But in terms of the total budget, growing as it was, such sums were not, and could not be, long-term solutions to the problem of the RBH. That was not to be the way in which Hospitals were to be run in the twentieth century, any more than Rabson's proposals for the

Football Club were to be its long-term basis of support. Quite other
and larger forces were at work, and some people knew it. In the case of
Reading Workpeople's Hospital Fund Association, for example, not
only was the SDF against such tinkering but so too was the trade union,
labour representation, voluntarist 'labourist' left in the town. The
Association only got started after considerable organised working-class
opposition which was pressing for municipalisation and centralisation
of Hospital funds.[31] Small victories were achieved by the Association
in terms of alterations of Hospital rules for the benefit of 'workmen'.
Alongside these victories was pressure from the same quarter to
democratise the hospital internally by allowing house medical and
surgical staff on to the Board of Management as well as consultants. The
staff were to be elected by their colleagues. A model of internal and
local associational democracy was being pressed for, as different from
the conduct of a twentieth-century hospital as Rabson's ideas were from
the conduct of a twentieth-century professional football club.[32] The
interest of the Association here is not only that it existed, but that it
was not to be allowed to work in the long term as a way of relating the
people of Reading to their Hospital.

Apart from official, mostly elected, bodies such as the Board of
Guardians, the Town Council, and the School Board, Reading pullulated
with voluntary agencies designed to relate to welfare or poverty. The
official bodies were clearly significant. Debates and decisions were
taking place on them, mostly in response to national debates and
decisions, which greatly affected the lot of, for instance, ill-fed and
ill-shod schoolchildren, people with tuberculosis or a small proportion
of the unemployed. Something will be said of the significance of such
developments later.

But it was of the voluntary philanthropic organisations that many
mouthpieces of the town were most proud. Such organisations as the
Reading Dispensary (1803), the Queen Victoria Institute for Nursing
the Sick Poor (1897), the Blind Aid Society, the Temperance and
General Philanthropic Society (1879), the Philanthropic Institution
(1882) were much praised. The Mayor (W. Ferguson) boasted in 1897,
'if any further proof were needed of their municipal prosperity and
progress, he would remind them of the number of institutions of all
kinds which had sprung up and were flourishing in their midst. . .and
especially that they had within their own borders important benevolent
and educational institutions, such as the Royal Berkshire Hospital, the
Reading Dispensary, Free Library and Museum. . .amidst all this

prosperity they could not forget that poverty and misfortune still fell
to the lot of many – far too many. . .they ought to bear this fact in
mind'.[33] There were in fact fifty-seven agencies distributing some form
of relief in the town in 1898.[34] It is these that will now be examined.

As with the Royal Berkshire Hospital, the social history of these
organisations depends for its meaning on a proper understanding of
their nature and surrounding ideology. The attempt to look at a large
number of different organisations together, rather than following them
through into the intricacies of each of their stories, will necessarily
involve some idealisation. Not all the ideas which will be extracted
were held by any one of the organisations surveyed, nor did practice
ever measure up to theory. But what, at least in idea, and sometimes in
a town the size of Reading in practice, was at stake in the social history
of voluntary welfare organisations?

A continual effort at co-ordination of *all* welfare action at the town
level was one vital strand. It was felt that if only comprehensive
controls over what already existed, together with ordered innovation,
could be organised, something which might almost be called a Reading
welfare state, might be brought into being. This would have all the
advantages of effective concern for poverty, without any of the
disadvantages of passive receipt of doles by the poor. The Reading
Guild of Help, which grew out of the Poverty committee of the Reading
Citizens Association in 1909, was the final important effort of this
kind. Its Central Board of Management in 1913 had representatives
from forty-five groups on it, from the WEA to parishes, to the Reading
Insurance Committee, to the NSPCC, to the Friendly Societies Council,
to the PSA Federation. The idea was 'mutual service carried out on a
perfectly organised plan'. At the town's meeting called to promote the
Guild, at which socialists moved a successful amendment against it, a
supporter of the idea emphasised 'the enormous possibilities that lay
with civic work, if they could but link it up with the charitable and
religious work of the town'.[35] Before the Guild, there had been other
attempts usually sponsored by the Mayor of the day and only slightly
less ambitious.[36] Each time the attempt failed to grow after two or
three years, but it was regularly renewed.

The organisation most commonly associated with work of this kind,
at least in London, was the Charity Organisation Society. C.S. Loch's
vision of 'the church of charity' in 1903 was perhaps the most noble
expression of the aspiration.[37] That the COS in Reading was *not*
central (it had been in the town since 1874), that it was regarded with
suspicion and could not grow except on terms which worried it, reveals

a lot about local impulses behind co-ordination and voluntary organisation. The COS locally was always in difficulties, 'however eloquently it may be defended it will probably never be possible to wholly remove the popular prejudice with which the COS is regarded'.[38] It complained of its fate in the town continually, sometimes shrilly, sometimes stoically. As a speaker at a meeting in 1896 to found a 'Registration of Relief Society' said: 'there was very great prejudice for some reason or other against the COS; perhaps the word "charity" in the title prejudiced the poor against it. They had been accustomed to think of charity as a personal and spontaneous thing, not made after inquiry by a paid officer,' and he was glad 'that the Mayor had not adopted the word charity in the title of the new society but "relief"'.[39] Within the Society, and from activists outside, the COS was attacked. It protested that it gave relief and did not just pry. But its methods were thought to be inquisitorial and piecemeal, and its machinery slow and ill-financed.[40]

Evidently there was felt to be something lacking in the COS. It was felt to be abusing charity, as someone outside Reading put it, 'of recent years there has grown up a strange and unlovely thing termed "organised charity" [it] ended by claiming to be a complete substitute for personal charity. . .this advocacy of reasoned callousness in the face of unmerited suffering'.[41] In Reading some clergymen (notably the Rev. H. Last) attacked all forms of rationalised giving, in the name of immediate, spontaneous neighbourliness. It was not necessary to go that far in order to see voluntary action and philanthropic organisations in a different light from that cast by the COS.

A vital assumption underlying voluntary action, and upon which plans for social reform were based, was that personal action — often called 'service' when done by the rich, and 'initiative' or 'independence' when taken by the poor — was a *sine qua non* of acceptable advance. Individual commitment, family determination and collective effort, were or should be, the motors of progress. Anything done by impersonal agency — whether municipal, State, professional (in the sense of paid), or expert — was second-best compared to private or associational exertion. It was the 'sacred responsibility' of different groups or classes to bear one another's burdens, often in a sacrificial manner.

Different classes should act as if they were in a community, for that was what citizenship meant. If they did, something more nearly resembling a community than the existing social order, widely recognised as defective, could be brought into being. Participation in welfare-oriented organisations was essential. Such organisations had a life quite apart from their function as givers of first aid, and quite as important. They had to meet as well as to do. Such ideas and the work they generated did not depend upon the notion that environment played no part in generating social conditions. A dichotomy between 'collectivists' who believed in environmental causes and 'individualists' who believed in 'moral' causes of social conditions is to a great extent a false view of late nineteenth- and early twentieth-century debates. 'Individualists' certainly believed in personally generated *solutions* to social problems, and parallel to this certainly believed in the local level of control as opposed to the central or national level. But they cannot easily be pushed into a category of those who believed in the ultimate insolubility or unimportance of the social problem. They did not think that 'pie in the sky' was the answer, or that the only gains possible were marginal adjustive reforms which left intact society as it was. Their modes of action and strategy however eccentric to us (in our very different society), were thought by them to be capable of delivering great — sometimes total — change.

Such assertions about organisations in the welfare area need backing with evidence. Before going on to analyse the severe battering being experienced by these organisations between 1890 and 1914 we must go slightly further to find out, qualitatively, what they were. To do this a meeting, two organisations, and 'a leading townsman' will be used.

The meeting was called by Mayor W.M. Colebrook to co-ordinate town action on 'Distress' in 1907.[42] As well as G.W. Palmer of the biscuit factory, most important Corporation members were there, plus many officials of such bodies as the Guardians and the Education committee, and activists from different religious and political organisations. The Mayor had 'for the past fortnight, he might almost say, dwelt within the tents of distress'; he was of the opinion that 'where the law stopped their love could start, for charity was, or should be, only another name for love of their brother man, and for the women and little children who were suffering'. The priorities of any Fund must be to save homes and find work, whilst discouraging 'the lazy skulker'. Help should come early, before men's strength had been sapped,

> Here was the golden opportunity for sympathy, that golden link
> which overrides all class-interests, that enriches all who come within
> its blessed influence; to the man who gave tenfold was given in the
> joy of first, having done his duty, and second, in the feeling that his
> own comforts, his food, and his home were made more enjoyable

by having shared his means with a brother man who for the moment had lost hope and heart and almost home.

The Mayor was moved by the prospect of bad conditions in the town getting worse during the winter. His speech was enthusiastically received. The Rev. R.W. Carew Hunt, vicar of St. Giles, moved a motion of approval for his proposals to open a Fund and to try to get money from the government for providing work for the unemployed, 'it would be infinitely preferable to have a fund which was spontaneous and voluntary, and came out of the free-will offering of men who wanted to do something for their poorer brothers, than have to depend upon the necessarily mechanical, unloving operation of the Poor Law'. In his speech he also faced two arguments which might be used against their action. He knew that what they were doing was 'reformist', and had to be part of a wider, more radical approach: he also fully recognised the causal role of environment as opposed to character,

It would be said that they were only dealing with the mere fringe of a great social evil, that that was only a piece of tinkering which was likely to do more harm than good. The prevailing distress, it would be alleged, was simply the normal and natural outcome of industrial conditions, the foundations of which were rotten. Therefore what was wanted was not to deal with the superficial side, but to deal with the cause of unemployment. That was a criticism which would be made, and which was worthy of consideration. For his own part he felt convinced that there were many matters in the social and economic life of their time which demanded readjustment and alterations. There was no question at all about that. He was certain from what he had read and seen that the tendency in the industrial world at the present time was, to a far greater extent than before, to create unskilled labour, with the result that they got those considerable periods of unemployment. He would go further than that, and say that, in dealing with the flotsam and jetsam of their population, not the unemployed but the unemployable, it was unjust to say that such cases were due to the men's own vices; they were much more due to the social environment in which they had been trained and brought up. (Hear, Hear.). . .He felt sure that great changes would come, but changes in the social life of the country, if they were to be in any degree permanent, must come very slowly. The question before them was how to deal with circumstances which lay at their very door at that moment, and therefore they had to take refuge in a palliative. A second criticism brought against the scheme would be that granted some relief must be given, why did they not appeal to the rates, why have the distress fund carried out by voluntary agencies? He held with unrelenting tenacity the truth they must keep before themselves, in dealing with a matter like this was that they must do nothing which, in any way, would weaken the springs of self-reliance and independence. (Hear, Hear). . .

Two organisations which may further understanding of what was at stake in this subject-area are the Reading Philanthropic Institution (1822) and the Reading Dispensary (1803). The RPI, a remarkably long-lived grouping which still (1973), just, survives, is difficult (precisely because it belongs to a different type of society) to classify. Partly a Friendly Society, partly a Masonic-type group, partly a charity, partly a sect — its members met regularly together, helped others, entertained and 'improved' themselves. Its annual dinners were, until the 1890s, major pan-town events, on a smaller scale than the Annual Courts of the Royal Berkshire Hospital.

By a 'pan-town event' is meant a type of meeting which was often repeated in a town of Reading's size. At Annual Courts of the Hospital, or town's meetings on distress, or discussions on the professionalisation of the Reading Football Club, or meetings to discuss working-class adult education, the list of attenders and speakers given in the local press was often similar. When it was said that 'a largely attended and influential meeting took place' it is possible to predict the core of people who would be there. This became less true in the early twentieth century as part of the social changes being mapped through the experience of organisations in these chapters.

Always called 'the Phil' in the town, the RPI carefully helped as many families as members' subscriptions allowed. It was an active, participatory, meeting-oriented society, organised on democratic principles. The chairman of the weekly meeting and 'Harmony' changed every third meeting. Esrom, the Co-operator, wrote an evocative piece about it in 1917.[43] He liked the Phil 'because I find there among the members friendship, fellowship and fraternity'. 'I like the Phil because it brings back memories of the good old days before the coming of the picture palace craze. . .the days when the tradesmen and the toilers fraternised in comradeship and conviviality, and warbled and whiffed the weed. . .they do not desire the limelight, preferring to work in privacy for the alleviation of local distress, giving their services willingly and cheerfully.' There was a Phil song. 'The objects of the Institution', stated in 1843, were 'the relief of *real* distress in whatever shape it may present itself, and the promotion of social union, order and harmony'. 'The scattered beams of benevolence which, separately, having scarcely the power to cheer for a moment the gloom that envelopes (*sic*) the unfortunate, when brought together to a focus, may shine with comfortable light and renovating warmth, may dissipate the chilling mist of want, anguish and anxiety and their whole horizon round may again be invested with bright rays.'[44]

It was a fascinating organisation, critical of surrounding society, but anxious to develop it without conflict at its most hopeful points. It regarded itself as 'an epitome of a free community', not just a pastime. It explained itself in 1843 thus:

> Some associations are founded on the principle of reciprocal aid in poverty, sickness or old age — a principle not only lawful but commendable. The RPI, however, takes a wider range and more enlarged views. The members of this society are no further interested immediately in the pursuit of its objects, than man is interested by feelings of benevolence and sympathy in the welfare of his fellow creatures, in social concord, decent hilarity, and in procuring for himself, to a degree that his circumstances and station in life will afford 'the luxury of doing good'. The union of individuals for the attainment of good ends, by lawful means, is found to conduce as much to the improvement of human nature, as union for bad purposes does to its degradation. But independently of this it is observable that religious sects, political parties, and competitors in business, by crossing of their views, the collision of their tenets, worldly interest, and importance are often ruffled into animosities, in which charity and candour appear to be entirely lost sight of. Now a society erected on the broad basis of certain all approved maxims of conduct, and framed for the pursuit of general objects of benevolence has a tendency to allay these animosities, and smooth all those asperities, by affording a new point of union and cooperation, by embracing in its wider circle many individuals of opposite persuasions, opinions and parties, and surrounding them, as it were with a medium through which they see one another in a more favourable light than they had done before. . .An institution of this kind may be regarded as an epitome of a free community.

More organised than the Phil, was the Reading Dispensary.[45] It had become a Provident, rather than merely a charitable source of medical treatment in 1870. From about that time, until killed by the National Insurance Act of 1911 (although it had an afterlife), it was a key organisation in Reading society.

To benefit fully a potential patient had to become a member and pay regularly. His payments would be supplemented by the subscriptions and donations of Governors, Trustees, and other interested persons. Government was not by medical men. The President, Vice-Presidents and a Board of Governors were in formal control. Voluntary help, as well as money, was important to the functioning of the Dispensary. It had ambitions to provide what might be called a Reading Health Service, but confined to those whose incomes were less than 30/- a week. Those on less than 15/- were eligible for free treatment.[46] A wide range of specialised treatment was available, together with branch dispensaries in the East end of Reading (1892) and in the West (1903). Special departments for diseases of the skin and eye were opened in 1899, a fully equipped dental department in 1903 and a women's diseases department in 1905. Departures from normal rules were made to meet special expenses in ways which anticipate the attacks of post-1948 politicians on the principle of the National Health Service. To meet the cost of the East end dispensary, each person getting medicines there was charged 1*d.* until the deficit was removed; at the Dental surgery 'stoppings and dentures will be procurable at fees within the reach of the members of the Dispensary'.

The importance of this organisation lies not only in its nature but in its size and success when at its peak. The secretary claimed in 1892 that 'there cannot. . .be a doubt but that it is a matter for sincere congratulations that so large a proportion of the working classes as one quarter of the entire population of the borough have by their own payments. . .secured for themselves medical attendance and medicines in time of sickness'. For a significant slice of the population something local, voluntary, and leaning heavily on middle-class patronage provided the amenity of medical treatment outside hospital.

The 'leading townsman' to be used as an example is William Isaac Palmer, who was active both personally and financially in many organisations. He was as much a philanthropist as a biscuit manufacturer, choosing Temperance as his main platform, but also supporting such organisations as the RPI and the Reading Dispensary. He was in a sense a classic 'individualist', but once what he thought is examined, an extension of stereotypes of 'individualism' becomes necessary.

In a dispute in 1878 on low wages and drink he protested against

one correspondent that he was not an employer 'who thinks that
people have no business to have any money for fear they should spend
it in drink'. 'Let every man be well paid for his work, let him spend his
wages *as he likes* (his italics), but do not be offended with me for
thinking that the happiness and prosperity of himself and his family
depends on what that liking is.' He was convinced that while high wages
did not always lead to improvidence, they often did, and that
intemperance was the largest cause of poverty. 'I shall take every
proper opportunity of stating plainly what I think is the greatest cause
of poverty and misery amongst the people. . .that cause to my mind is
intoxicating drink' (his italics).[47] At the same time, he told a conference
in London in 1885, that there were other causes of wretchedness: 'it
will probably be found that the causes may be classed under two heads,
internal and external, and each of them capable of a number of
divisions.'[48]

'External' causes were conceded. But there was a reason for
concentrating at that stage on the 'internal': 'it need scarcely be said
that there is wisdom in considering first of all those causes of prosperity
or misfortune which are dependent on ourselves, because it is probable
we should find we have them under our control.' He believed in the
possibility of eliminating present poverty, not in adjusting sufferers to
their mortal lot, even if the means chosen were, to us now, eccentric.
Other means then being proffered were, to him, at best irrelevant:

> I believe that the misery and wretchedness around us might to a
> great extent be got rid of. We have had a sensational pamphlet about
> the 'Bitter Cry' and since then we have had a Royal Commission,
> but the outcome of the Royal Commission might be written by the
> word 'naught'. The people of London are as badly off as if no
> pamphlet had ever been written, and as if no Royal Commission had
> ever sat. We do think that here we have a simple and practical remedy
> for much of the evil we see around us.

Reacting to poverty was a matter of personal determination exercised
through voluntary organisation, such as the Working Men's Clubs to
whom he was talking in 1885. Human will, not central enactment or
sensational journalism, was the place to start in order to generate
change; through that will, changes of more than just a marginal kind
could be brought about involving other, less personal, levels of change.

What was happening to this dimension of Reading aspiration clustering

round many organisations and expressed by many committed
individuals?

It was experiencing great strains from different directions, of a kind
which can be anticipated from the analysis of what was happening to
the Royal Berkshire Hospital. Such strains that, although it is dangerous
to try to compress too much subsequent social change into the period
before 1914, already by the end of this period the kind of society
which could make efforts at total co-ordination seem hopeful, the
Reading Dispensary seem successful, or William Isaac Palmer
understandable, had gone.

Each of the directions in which strain was being experienced could
be described via any of the fifty-seven agencies existing in 1898, where
records survive. In each case representative agencies will have to stand
for others.

First, there was a progressive contraction in the availability of a
certain type of funds. This was more than the constant and growing
constraint imposed by economic circumstance. It was a question of
decrease in 'honorary subscribers', for the whole range of welfare
organisations which relied on the money of those who did not benefit
directly from them. This was the case with older organisations, and
with one started within the period. So with the Temperance and General
Philanthropic Society (founded 1879 and much supported by William
Isaac Palmer), by 1904 'our income had been going down for the past
few years'.[49] And with the Guild of Help there was already a crisis of
finance by March 1910. In June 1912 a special sub-committee was set
up to find ways round the annual deficit.

Secondly, there was a progressive contraction in the availability of a
certain type of commitment. Attendance at meetings and action in the
town were becoming agonisingly more difficult to stimulate. Many
organisations depended for effective working not just on cash but also
on 'nomination' of a potential recipient of help by a member. This was
the case with part or all of the activity of the Reading Philanthropic
Institution, the Dispensary, the Temperance and General Philanthropic
Society, and even the Hospital. Such nomination in turn depended on
direct face-to-face contact, or at least on recommendation based upon
such contact. If, as the COS was recommending in 1892, and the
Guild of Help was trying to implement sixteen years later, 'Reading
should be mapped out and a tabulated list of the poor made so that
each district might be properly looked after',[50] this would have involved
much personal contact and activity. For the Guild of Help 'it is the
helper who is the keystone on which all in most cases depends', and

yet helpers were always being appealed to for more work.[51]

In the argument with socialists at the Town's Meeting in 1909 it was this version of personally initiated social change towards building 'a new Jerusalem below' which was being stressed by Guild spokesmen. As J.R. Brooke said: 'he was afraid that Socialists were inclined to underestimate the great importance of turning out in this generation efficient citizens. They were thinking of great social and political changes, but they were forgetting that every one of these changes had got to be made by men...'[52] By no means all socialists in the town would have disagreed. But for them, as for organisers of voluntary welfare organisations, such a version of social change was becoming increasingly difficult to staff. It does not seem to matter where one looks, if the aim was (as with the Guild of Help in January 1913) 'not to call upon others to do things but to find out and to declare how much the individual can do' through organisations, the going was difficult. Even a local learned society, like the Reading Pathological Society (founded 1841), which relied on the participation of a definite and interested group, was not finding things easy. In the 1886 session average attendance was low. In 1897-8 efforts at publication of the society's proceedings halted. There were fascinating similarities in response to this situation of decline, between organisations described in this chapter and those described in the last. For example, the Reading Philanthropic Institution attempted to adapt to changing circumstances by becoming more 'attractive'. They tried to cut down the business side of the Lodge meetings and to have Whist Drives, entertainments and the like. These started in the ten years preceding 1914. They were also thought to be part of that leapfrog of blame described earlier. Their decline was pinned at one time on to the increase of 'recreational and athletic societies'.[53] Esrom, as we have seen, connected the decline to cinemas.

Next, there were twin pressures towards specialisation and towards professionalisation. Moves similar to those at the Hospital to get doctors on to the Committee of Management had taken place in the Dispensary by 1896. The sharp distinction between 'Governors' and 'Medical Staff', and the subordinate role of the latter (there were no doctors on the committee in 1890) were being upset, with some resistance. The trend towards self-conscious diagnosis and treatment of 'cases' in 'social work' was noticeable in the Reading COS, the Philanthropic Institution, and the Guild of Help.[54] This was a threat to the idea of comprehensively-planned pan-Reading neighbourliness and sympathy as being the only proper approach to social ills. There was a noticeable divergence growing up in the thinking of the Guild of Help between 'case work' and 'joint activity on broader grounds', with the former coming to predominate.

The history of this divergence reveals much about the direction of social change. The Guild had been started precisely in order to assert that no such dichotomy did, or should, exist. They ran a magazine (*'The Citizen Magazine'*, circulation 600-700) to assert the connections.[55] But the ideal was always over the horizon, impossible to reach. It was always being projected on to another, newer organisation which, it was hoped, would do the job. So at the Annual Conference of the National Association of Guilds of Help in Halifax in 1913 the Reading Guild was, in its own Minutes, very impressed with a speaker who defined Guilds as essentially case-work organisations. 'Problems of a wider nature' should be dealt with by Councils of Social Welfare which would be able to take 'concerted action of all the represented societies' and so 'strike at the root of the evil in question'. The Reading committee agreed, 'since our efforts. . .to deal with wider issues have only been partially successful'.[56] Councils of Social Welfare went the way of Guilds of Help, the hopes pinned on them too were illusory.[57] The truth was that the nature of these 'wider problems', the nature of the State within which they existed and were defined, the relationship between the localities and the State, and social changes within those localities, were together making the responses outlined in this chapter less and less possible and appropriate.

A massive qualitative change, which can be understood at the level of specific developments outside Reading, was being experienced in the early twentieth century in the town. That change had mostly to do with altered diagnoses of particular evils, and above all, with legislation.[58] Levels of taxation may also have been an important variable. The connections between 'individualism' and localness of social control in the ideology of Reading dignitaries have already been stressed. The Guild of Help in its earliest days in Reading was militantly local. Its Central Board only grew up after a number of District Committees were working. The Reading Guild was very reluctant to affiliate in 1910 to a proposed National Association of Guilds of Help.[59] The connections between individualism and localism were infinitely more important than any supposed link between individualism and such ideas as personal rather than societal causes of poverty, or the ultimate insolubility of disastrous social conditions. It was precisely that localness of social control which was disappearing at a greatly accelerated rate in the early twentieth century. The change cannot be

encapsulated neatly within a short period of time. It had been
proceeding for at least seventy years before 1900, and never reached
(certainly not before 1914) a definite completion point. None the less
an important phase of the process happened between 1906 and 1912,
nationally and, through legislation, locally. Already in 1904 the newly
elected Mayor said that there was no hope of an uneventful term of
office since 'the work of that, as of other Councils, was continually
growing, and no sooner did they get used to administering one Act of
Parliament than another was passed, and it required all their care and
ability to keep pace with the fresh Acts which they had to administer'.[60]

The main vehicles of the process in Reading were three issues —
unemployment, National Insurance and Old Age Pensions. Each
involved local discussion, local interest groups, the creation of new
types of town or area organisations, and, slowly, an alteration of the
relationship between individuals, organisations, the locality and
'welfare'.

In the case of unemployment, all the pressures were towards
moving the controls in theory and in organisation where they had long
been in fact — away from the individual and away from the town. The
most advanced available diagnosis was in terms of calling for more hard
information, and in terms of the proposition that 'to make more work
we have only to spend rather more and save rather less' — i.e. to create
work by public policy. Central funds were needed to set up a Labour
Bureau, and high wages should be paid by manufacturers so that
'circulation will begin to be restored in all the healthy parts of the
social body'.[61] Such policies could only make remedies like those of
William Isaac Palmer, with his advocacy of temperance, seem at best
marginal. They were not of course acted upon. But significant changes
did occur. The Reading Distress Committee (a body brought into being
in 1905 by central enactment, even though mainly voluntary in nature)
was one of the few such committees to establish a Register of the
Unemployed with separate staff.[62] A Board of Trade Labour Exchange
was opened in the town in 1910.[63] All the significant agitation (by the
Social Democratic Federation and others) was away from a local,
individual approach, towards establishing the responsibility of the
Town Council and of the central government for investigating the facts
of unemployment and taking appropriate long-term and short-term
action.[64] It was no wonder that it was found to be unemployment
'that sets real problems to a District Committee' of the Guild of Help
in 1913. By its very nature the problem never had been, and
increasingly was being recognised as not being, amenable to their kind

of approach.[65] It needed professional investigation, 'expert' theory, and national, increasingly international, political action before anything other than immediate first-aid could be applied.

Rufus Isaacs, the Liberal MP for Reading, called the National Insurance Act 'one of the greatest measures of social reform ever passed'.[66] Liberals naturally made the most of the benefits of an Act few of them had advocated for long. Benefits were in fact delayed (until 1913), greatly exaggerated, and confined to a minority of the working population. Much of the writing about it was deliberately contrived political propaganda.[67] None the less the Act was of fundamental importance. The propaganda connected with it was itself a new factor in the situation, altering the relationship between the citizen and the State. Never had there been such a government educational apparatus attached to a piece of legislation, with organised newspaper series, lectures and other devices all explaining the intricacies of the Act and expounding the 'benefits' the individual was being given by a benevolent reforming government.[68]

The Act was in fact 'a very complicated piece of legislation'. Administrative expertise, and much technical information was needed, if it was to be fought or amended on anything other than the level of basic principle. Once the Act was there, even if a small dedicated organisation had principled objections to it, these had to be worked out in terms set by the Act. It had a perceptible effect on the way in which 'welfare' and the social problem was discussed in Reading, and on who amongst discussants and pressure groups would be listened to. The debate in the Reading Insurance Committee in January 1914 on whether the upper income limit should be £160, how the income for the limit should be calculated, or whether there should be no limit at all, while passionate, was not the same type of debate as late nineteenth-century debates leading to simple demands for comprehensive insurance or cures for unemployment.[69] A new type of expert-reformer-cum-social scientist, of whom Sidney Webb was the quintessence, was bound to dominate voluntarists such as Friendly Society members in any discussion of avenues of social advance.[70] Once there, the Act led radicals to ask for completion and development in the directions in which it pointed. So the Reading Trades Council demanded a national medical service in December 1912.[71] Moreover the Act created new organisations in which these new discussions took place, and in which radicals and socialists had to work if they were to have any influence. A Provisional Committee, and then the Reading Insurance Committee were set up through which men like J. Rabson

had to channel their demands.[72] These were centrally initiated bodies
designed to administer an Act, and to work out the details of its local
application. Their meetings would not in the smallest way resemble a
meeting of the Reading Philanthropic Institution, the Temperance and
General Philanthropic Society, or even the Reading Dispensary.

The latter organisations were bound to suffer as a result of the
operation of the Act. The year 1912 was 'a momentous one in the
history of Reading Dispensary'. What happened to it is a fascinating
case in the effect of state intervention in its field, and in the resulting
take-over by professionals. They had the option of becoming an
Approved Society under the Act, for the administration of medical
benefit. A scheme was evolved for doing this. It was approved by the
governors in July 1912. In August the entire medical staff of the
Dispensary showed the dedication to the public interest for which
doctors have become notorious in the twentieth century. They resigned,
'in view of the attempted provision under the National Insurance Act of
medical benefits on terms which the BMA did not approve'. The
Committee of the Dispensary therefore decided not to proceed with
becoming an Approved Society. They also resolved to cease receiving
members' subscriptions for the Dispensary after January 1913. In
October 1912 they received a letter from the Reading District
Committee of the Reading division of the BMA enclosing a copy of
rules 'for the Public Medical Service' proposed by the BMA and
suggesting a conference with the Dispensary on those rules. After 'long
and anxious consideration' the committee decided to let the Dispensary
buildings to the 'Local Medical Service' as its Headquarters. The service
was to be known, appropriately enough, as 'the Borough of Reading
Medical Society Limited'. The doctors, professional and business-like,
had won. The Dispensary in the form in which it had existed since it
went provident in 1870 was finished.[73]

Elsewhere a brave face was put on large changes. For the directors
of the biscuit factory the Act was in a sense convenient. They could
suspend their Sick Fund. Another step in the alteration of the position
of the factory as a self-contained organisation in the town was taken.[74]
For the Friendly Societies which had 'a strong hold. . .upon the
populace' in Reading, the change in the long term was to be serious.
They were already not making progress in 1905 when, like the Free
Churches earlier, they formed a Friendly Societies Council in the town
to protect their interests.[75] Both Pensions and National Insurance
drastically altered their role. Brother Wightman of the Sons of
Temperance Friendly Society was shrewd, but at the same time sadly

over-sanguine, when, in February 1912, after saying how 'it appeared that voluntary effort had reached its climax', he welcomed the Act as an opportunity for Friendly Societies, 'if they could permeate all England with the brotherly feeling already existing among Friendly Society members that would be worth more than the monetary benefits under the Act'. Assimilation of the Act by talking in terms of a 'National Friendly Society' was, in a twentieth-century perspective, wishful thinking.[76] A change in direction was involved, and recognised by the Friendly Societies Council.[77]

Old Age Pensions provide a precisely parallel case. These were small in amount (five shillings) and confined to the very old (seventy plus), but Rufus Isaacs was correct to herald a qualitative change when he referred to the State at last giving something 'not as charity but as something which (it) willingly gave'.[78] The first Pension Day in the town was a day of more obvious importance in the social chronology of Reading than the days already selected – the day of the moving of the Literary and Scientific Society into the University and the day of a change to house-to-house collection on Hospital Sunday – and was seen as such at the time.[79] In the same manner as National Insurance, it generated its own organisations – the Pension Committee of twenty-six members including initially one each from the Friendly Societies and the Trades Council, whose job it was to investigate claims, and administer the Act generally.[80]

It also visibly affected both Friendly Societies and the nature of the biscuit factory as an organisation in relation to its workers.[81] In 1897 it had already been utopian for a speaker to the Reading Printers' Relief and Provident Association to state that 'he should not be surprised if with the assistance of the Honorary Members they were able to solve the question of Old Age Pensions and that they would be able to provide medical aid free to all their members'.[82] Some years before, Canon Blackley had been in the town advocating his limited scheme of State intervention in pensions and had made little impact.[83] But it is appropriate for the argument of this chapter to note that by 1908 the Reverend R.H. Hart Davis who, as we have already seen, liked best a world where the Printers would have been able to 'solve the question of Old Age Pensions', had adapted to changed times. He wrote to *The Spectator* twice in that year. Once he argued that the working classes should not have to contribute for their pensions, the State ought to do the job. The second time, as a champion of the Friendly Societies, he demonstrated that these were not adequate to cope with the problems of old age. Ironically he was quoted in the

House of Commons by Lloyd George who referred to 'that remarkable letter'.[84] Remarkable it was for Hart Davis, and only intelligible in terms of strains experienced over the preceding period by Friendly Societies and other organisations in this subject-area.

9 EDUCATION

In May 1907 there was a dispute over a threat to one of the parish schools in St. Giles parish from a possible merger with a Board school — George Palmer Senior School. The vicar of St. Giles told the chairman of Reading Education Committee that 'these senior schools can never be of real service to the community so long as there is no compulsory continued education in England as in Germany'. By this he meant post-school education, while at work. It is from the experience of an effort to provide such education voluntarily *for* and *of* the working class by 'The Association for the Promotion of Higher Education of the Working Classes' (ultimately the Reading WEA) that much can be learned in the subject-area of education about the changing society in which churches and chapels were set. Both what the Association was, and what happened to it, provide fascinating analogies with earlier organisations studied and important leads into the changing constraints and possibilities surrounding all voluntary action during the late nineteenth and early twentieth centuries.

As it happens, Reading branch was the first to exist in the WEA. It was proud of its status as 'the pioneer branch'.[1] It came into being as the result of a conference promoted by the Reading Industrial Co-operative Society in the Palmer Memorial (Temperance) Hall in West Street on 1st October 1904. Albert Mansbridge was there (he had started the movement in August 1903), and so was W.M. Childs, the new principal of Reading University College. The meeting was also 'thoroughly representative of both the working men and the educational machinery now existing in the town'. As with other working-class efforts at voluntary organisation, its experience can be traced through the *Reading Co-operative Record.*[2] The Association was widely agreed to be 'one of the most promising and valuable movements which have been started in Reading for a long time'.[3]

Different versions of the possibilities of the movement were raised from the start. Mansbridge's ideas focussed on the universities, and on preparing the working classes for making their legitimate claims upon them. A Co-operator in December 1904 thought 'they were going to be what they might call a "Help Ourselves Society"'. J.F. Hodgson of the Social Democratic Federation was in favour of pressing the State through the Association to raise the school leaving age to sixteen, as the priority target: 'when they considered the lives and homes of the working men. . .they could hardly be hasty in condemning them for not taking advantage of the educational facilities that were provided.' Others wanted it to be merely supplemental to School Board evening classes or to the University.

It was W.M. Childs who had the most general and exalted ideals for the movement.[4] Working-class education, for him, could be divided into 'bread' studies and 'liberal' studies. It was the latter that were desperately needed. It was not good enough that 'he had seen a larger crowd assemble to hear a football match result than one of the battles in the Boer War'. That indicated woeful lack of liberal, public spirited, interest. He had put on lectures for the working classes some years before in the town. They had not worked because of the lack of three vital qualities which the new Association would have to cultivate — enthusiasm, organisation and experience. 'There must be something with a spirit of brotherhood if the movement was to be permanent, and if they had to break down the apathy, especially of the younger men in the town.' He asked, 'would the working classes come and back up that movement which was led and manned by their own representatives?' They had to be careful that they did not go the way of the old Mechanics' Institute. It was not simply by going to meetings and listening that they would make the Association a success, 'they must believe in it, make an effort for it, sacrifice for it'.[5]

As a movement whose explicit purpose was to awaken the enthusiasm of the workers of Reading for a voluntary purpose, involving commitment of time, energy and money, the Association clearly has significance for our themes. It was trying to organise from below. The first mention of Higher Education in the *Reading Co-operative Record* in September 1903 asserted that 'the one thing lacking in the curriculum of working-class schools is the treatment of History from a purely working-class point of view'. They were aiming at what Esrom called the 'Workmen's University'. In order to achieve this they stressed the necessity of *joining* the Association, either individually or through organisational affiliation. It was to be local, self-managed and active. 'The spirit of the Association is one of social brotherhood and good will.' 'It needs a great deal more of the working men than mere reading of a newspaper if they wish to fit themselves to obtain deliverance from the present state of things, materially, politically and co-operatively.'[6]

We have already seen the difficulties faced by working-class organisations, unless they could become a capitalist limited liability company run in the interests of profit, watched but in no real sense controlled by their members, or an agency of the State. Nationally the WEA was to adopt the spectator mode after 1924. Until then students had to be members; by 1939 only forty-three per cent of WEA students were members. 'The Association for the Advancement of the Higher Education of the Working Class in Reading' (its second name, adopted in November 1904) was unusually aware of contextual constraints. Some of its activists were determined not to get caught by such constraints. There had been a previous history in the town of educational efforts for the workers which were 'in every way more suitable for the middle class'.[7] Like other provincial towns Reading had a rich history of local cultural and educational groupings through the nineteenth century.[8] This organisation knew that it might go the same way as earlier associations unless the initiatives in the WEA came from the members rather than outsiders. J.F. Hodgson considered 'that they ought not to be dependent even in a small degree on honorary members who belonged to a different class'.[9] At a council meeting of the Association in 1912, F. Critchley, like Hodgson a socialist, 'hoped the Association would live up to its reputation and note that when wealthy people gave their money to pay the piper they expect to call the tune'.[10] In 1905, two years before the tutorial class idea got into the WEA nationally, it was being proposed in Reading that, alongside weekly lectures on subjects of general interest, they should have sets of small classes of between four and six workers on subjects of serious concern to working men.[11] Small, sect-like, face-to-face groupings of this kind seemed to be culturally attractive and economically possible for the working class during the nineteenth century, from the Methodist Class Meeting onwards. In WEA terms such groups were intended to generate a deeper type of commitment than lectures. Such sharp perceptions of constraints and possibilities were rare elsewhere in the town.

And there is no doubt that the Association *was* overwhelmingly a working-class body. This is apparent from the list of those who came together to form it,[12] and from an occupational breakdown of two of the earliest tutorial classes.[13] The 1907 Committee was a typical one. The President was an SDF man, the ordinary members consisted of: two from the Co-op., one from the Trades and Labour Council, one from the Bricklayers trade union, one from Christ Church Institute, five from Broad Street Pleasant Sunday Afternoon movement, one from the National Union of Shop Assistants, one from the National Union of Teachers, two from the Typographical Association, two from the Association of Carpenters and Joiners, one from the ILP, two from

the Lithographic Printers, one from the Stonemasons. Elections to this
and other bodies connected to the Association were hotly contested.
Internal democracy worked well. It is interesting to note how such
organisations as the PSA, the Adult Schools, and the church Institutes
were, at this stage, natural components of such a body as the WEA in
the same way that trade unions were. The PSA in particular needs
moving from the slightly comic fringe where it has normally been
placed (when noticed by historians at all) into the centre of
working-class activism.

There is no doubt either that the Association, in some way,
'succeeded'. It is, after all, still there. In the years from 1911 onwards
it grew well, both in individual membership and in the number of
affiliated societies; individual members numbered in: 1911-12 — 276,
1912-13 — 420, 1913-14 — 504; affiliated societies 1911-12 — 27,
1912-13 — 30, 1913-14 — 40. The important thing to discover is in
what ways it succeeded and through what experiences.

Inevitably the starting point has to be finance. Articulate members
knew what it meant to be dependent on outside monies. In the
conditions of the capitalism of the day they could not exist without
being thus dependent. No organisation which planned any elaborate
activities or wanted any large-scale plant, whether a chapel, an athletic
club or an association for education, could work by itself. Deficits
were continual from July 1905 onwards; March 1911 was the first
report of a year's working which had broken even. Sometimes the
situation was acute. In January 1911 they had a debt of £45. Normally
members had to pay 6*d*. p.a., affiliated organisations 2/6*d*. and there was
also a category of Honorary Members who were asked to pay 10/6*d*. p.a.
Rather than appealing vertically to donors to rescue the 1911 crisis,
they agreed to act horizontally. They sent a circular to secretaries of all
other branches of the WEA, asking them to levy a 1*d*. tax on members
to save 'the Reading pioneer branch', in order that 'the deficit be
wiped out and the General Secretary be enabled to devote himself to
the work of organisation instead of that of professional beggar'.[14]
Working-class organisations which wished to remain *of* the class had to
rely on small irregular sums from large numbers of individuals. In a
subject-area like education, unlike football, this meant widening the
catchment area across the nation.

In spite of the Association's preference for other modes, 'gentlemen'
from time to time did help. After Hodgson was elected President he
announced that he hoped to make the Association independent by
cutting down on such things as publicity costs, but 'if that could not

be done he was prepared to go to the people who would help them'.[15]
The Reading Education Committee helped in a small way, giving £10 in
1908 and £25 in 1912. But this source presented difficulty too. In
order to get better treatment they realised that they should seek
representation on the committee, and they pressed to get it. But this
was a compromise of principle 'in view of the present constitution of
the Education Committee'. They were against co-option,

> we are of the opinion that no better system could be devised for
> excluding the workers from participation in the control of the
> education of their children. We therefore urge the government in
> any future Education Bill to abolish the system of election by
> co-option and to substitute election on the lines of the old School
> Board, thereby replacing autocratic rule by democratic.[16]

The business of keeping solvent involved them in much work, and in
types of appeal which they did not relish.

The base was intended to be the interest of Reading workers in the
aims of the Association. It was stressed how one of their purposes was
to arouse such latent demand rather than just catering for something
already expressed — 'there is quite as much to do in creating a demand
for knowledge as in supplying it'.[17] 'Apathy' had always seemed a
problem in previous efforts in this direction — it continued to be so.
1909 was a particularly difficult year owing to 'lack of a sufficiently
keen and extended interest in (the) work'. Hodgson (of the SDF) even
resigned his Presidency in that year in case any political flavour which
his leadership of the Association might have given it was keeping
people away.[18] Missionary efforts were frequently made, with special
committees set up to arouse interest in workshops and to improve
attendance at the lectures. Responses to difficulty took forms with
which we are by now familiar and which were indications of a common
context for organisations in Reading in the early twentieth century.
One direction was towards relying on presenting the product better
'by means of improved posters, handbills, the syllabus, and
advertisements in the newspapers' (1909). Another direction was
towards the grass roots, to try to build up a ward structure with ward
secretaries in each district of the town, 'to disseminate news of
rambles, lectures, etc. and to foster a demand for future classes of all
kinds for adults' (1912). The idea was to have many local committees
feeding into the central Reading movement, as with Rabson's schemes
for football, the soup kitchen, or the Hospital Association.

This direction of development was, however, contrary to the main drift of WEA work. More and more it was moving in the early twentieth century into a position of dependence on the University. For one thing, as with the Reading Literary and Scientific Society, it was difficult to find a cheap hall outside the University which gave the facility free. The original committee meeting had been in Childs' room at the University. It had set out one of the main aims of the Association as the encouragement and support of Evening Classes at the University. These, as Childs conceded, fell mainly in the 'bread' category, rather than the 'liberal' one which he considered ought to be the Association's main work.[19] Eight out of seventeen 'fixtures' of the season 1905-6 were paid for out of University funds. Once tutorial classes started as a major accent of Association work (in 1910 in Reading; R.H. Tawney had initiated the experiment in 1908 in Rochdale) they were run by a joint committee, half from the Association, half from the University. A major facet of the Association by 1914 was its function as a link between socially interested lecturers acting in their professional capacity and the town of Reading. The lectures, either short courses or sets of widely various talks, remained aside, directly under the aegis of the Association as an independent organisation. But they were less typical of its presence in the town than they had been earlier on. They became incidental.

The tendency was away from 'recreative' work towards more directly 'educational' activity. Initially, popular lectures such as those in January 1905 on 'the United States of America' and 'Socrates', together with debates, such as one in the same month on 'Arbitration', and outings and musical evenings, were typical of the diet offered. The Association resembled many other Literary and Social Unions or Institutes in the town. Recreative activities like rambles remained popular. But it was not primarily on those terms that the Association fixed its identity, or had its identity fixed in our period. The pressure was more towards University work, and towards working-class 'interest group' activity. This took a variety of forms.

Educationally it was self-consciously and deliberately geared to subjects of importance to the class, rather than to the individual. In March 1914 there was a long debate on the merits of sending individual members to University. It cost £200 to send one man. That was equivalent to the cost of two or three tutorial classes. So the dilemma arose — individual self-help or class collective help? Whereas there was a section within the Association which asserted that 'a working man did not cease to be a working man because he went to college. They

must have the acorn before the oak', the majority disagreed by vote.
Mr Critchley, for example, said that 'his experience was that a person
sent from the working classes to the Universities left his own class,
attached himself to a class above his station in life, and forsook the
class from which he sprang'. Another speaker thought that sending
individuals to the University was like 'making a splendid pauper, or
gilding the working class'. The Reading delegate to the national WEA
conference on this subject was mandated to express that opinion —
to press the government 'to include adequate provision in their
Education Bill of next year to provide a highway for the worker from
the elementary school to the University'. The State should open the
highway for the class as a whole, rather than the Association opening
the highway for the fortunate few. 'They did not beg for philanthropy,
but for justice.'[20]

Classes were arranged in directly useful subjects. So much so that
by 1913 complaints were heard. A speaker at the annual meeting felt
that:

> there had been an undue preponderance of Industrial and Economic
> lectures, certainly ten out of seventeen. . .though fully recognising
> the importance of such questions, burning questions, on the life of
> the worker — yet. . .the great aim of the WEA was to afford to
> those who crave for knowledge a broad base of general information,
> upon which each might specialise as he felt disposed.

Such views were evidently expressed quite often. C.H. Davies
remembered in *The Reading Citizen* in September 1950 how
'discussions often developed into ding-dong arguments between those
who wanted "pure" education and those who urged the lecture room
as a platform for educating the workers in the economics of their own
misery'. Not everyone approved of the terms on which the Association
was trying to flourish. From being the type of movement Childs had
visualised at the start it had become three main things — a means of
access to University instruction, a source of economic and industrial
knowledge useful to trade union and working-class betterment, and,
parallel with this, a pressure group acting on a wide front on
working-class issues in the town. In this last capacity it became
increasingly active. Early in 1914, for example, the issues it chose to
articulate were: the use of students as blacklegs in strikes, slum
clearance, and the urgency of increasing the library rate since 'there is
a steadily growing desire on the part of the wage-earners for good

literature'.[21] These were typical of its concerns, alongside a frequent
interest in industrial law. They had realised that 'industrial conditions
are much less favourable than in many other towns'[22] to a movement
of the original kind. Conditions in Reading were not making it easy for
independent, self-financed, 'liberal' studies to be pursued via
self-generated small groups and well-attended general lecture series.
What the WEA became was shaped by what it was possible to be in that
kind of society.

Both W.M. Childs as an individual and what ultimately became Reading
University as an institution played a major role in the social history
of Reading WEA. They also played a major role in the social history of
Reading. They can serve as witnesses of a uniquely articulate kind to
competing versions of social action characteristic of this period. The
University Extension College, as it was in 1897, was proud of itself.

> what other institution in the United Kingdom can within two
> months hold an Art Exhibition with 1,050 visitors, draw 1,000
> people to a University Extension Lecture, organise a special class in
> Dairying, carry off two awards to Oxford — and at the same time
> keep all its many lectures and classes going, elementary and
> advanced?. . .The College has been compared to a Polytechnic, but
> it is more than a Polytechnic. . .the union of literary, technical,
> scientific, and artistic studies in an institution rapidly acquiring the
> *esprit de corps* of a great college, the whole having reference to the
> needs of the people of Reading and the surrounding district — this
> is the aim which its best friends have from the first steadily urged
> upon the college.[23]

It came a long way fast, using routes important to trace. At the same
time Childs, who arrived as a lecturer in 1894 and became Principal in
1903, had well-thought-out ideas as to what it should be. One of the
many occasions on which he expressed these was when the Literary and
Scientific Society moved into the college,

> Personally he had for a long time wished that the society could
> meet under the friendly roof of the college, but he had always been
> afraid to say it, because, as some of them might know, there was an
> idea in some people's minds that the college was ambitious and
> continually trying to annex things. . .If they considered carefully
> what were the objects of the Society and those of the College

they must conclude that, if not identical in their aims, they had a
great deal in common, and in their main purpose they were in
sympathy with each other. . .He gathered that the object of a
Literary and Scientific Society was in the main to gather together
the more thoughtful men in the town for the purpose of exchanging
ideas and collectively promoting their intellectual welfare. So a
University College which had the audacity of wishing one day to
be a University, had no more vital function than that of persistently
striving to be a rallying point, not merely for the professional
students who went there for the purpose of taking a degree but of
all thinking people who were within the radius of its influence.[24]

The identification of a University with a town Literary and Scientific
Society, self-consciousness about its 'annexing' role in the town, the
relationship between 'the professional students who went there for the
purpose of taking a degree' and other functions of the University in
the town, the strategy through which the audacious ambition was
fulfilled, and the nature of the end-product are all fascinating leads
into Reading society in the late nineteenth and early twentieth
centuries.

Before pursuing any of them it would be well to get clear what,
in a simple narrative sense, happened.[25] Extension work began in
Reading in 1885, led by the Rev. W. Butler. It failed at first, but
restarted in 1887. At that date it was made into an Association. In
1892 the 'University Extension College in conjunction with the Schools
of Science and Art' replaced the Association, via an initiative taken by
Christ Church College Oxford and Halford Mackinder. Christ Church
desired to 'establish a connection between [the College] and one of the
University Extension centres, with a view to giving system and
completeness to the educational work'.[26] In 1896 the College was
incorporated by the State under the Board of Trade, leading to a
Treasury grant of £1,000 p.a. from 1902 onwards. Its Council, partly
elected from public bodies in Reading, was replaced by a Court of
Governors, a Council and an Academic Board.[27] 1892 to 1898 were
years of 'fortifying and extending' the position won in 1892. At every
stage the language and ideas surrounding the University movement are
of critical interest. The change made in 1896 cannot be left without
quoting Halford Mackinder's reaction to it — 'he, indeed, ventured to
dream that they might be a little nucleus which gradually should aim
at converting Reading into some sort of local Florence, a place devoted
to industrial development and also to the cultivation of art and

learning'.[28] In 1898 the Prince of Wales opened new buildings for the Extension College now called 'Reading College'. These remained its home until a move to a site in London Road adjacent to George Palmer's home 'The Acacias' took place in 1905-6. This was the centre of the University until the national, post-Robbins burst of State expansion in the 1960s moved it to the suburban outskirt of Whiteknights Park. By 1906 a local guide book could refer to the College as 'beyond question the most important and far-reaching of modern local establishments'.

Such is the skeleton; flesh can now be added in such a way as to extend the argument of these chapters. The starting point, as it was the starting point for the movement which generated the University, must be the prominent part the locality played from a number of different points of view in the *idea* of the movement and the Extension College, and to some extent also in actuality.

Local initiative was a *sine qua non* of the development of higher education in the town, in spite of the obvious supporting role of outside bodies such as Christ Church Oxford. Childs acknowledged not just the likeness in conception but also the College's debt in personnel to the Literary and Scientific Society.[29] The Schools of Science and Art were one of the streams which fed directly into the vital amalgamation of 1892. These were formally directed from South Kensington, but there is no doubt that in flavour, government and leadership they were more importantly a Reading organisation than they were the off-shoot of a government department.[30]

One of the quintessential types of event in Reading during the second half of the nineteenth century in all subject-areas, not just in education, were the 'conversazioni' held to mark episodes in the life of local organisations. They are redolent of an utterly different society from our own — as evocative (and of the same thing) as the clocktowers in the streets and parks of provincial cities. One of these, in 1890, was typical of the Schools of Science and Art. The Literary and Scientific Society combined with the Schools, with the Berkshire Archaeological Society, the Microscopical Society, the Natural History Society, and the Photographical Society in arranging for a conversazione in the town hall where the prizes for the Science and Art classes were distributed.[31] Another, held in October 1891, hosted by Walter Palmer in the Town Hall where the prizes for the Science and Art classes were distributed.[31] Another, held in October 1891, hosted by Walter Palmer in the Town Hall, marked the first real foray of Halford Mackinder into when the Guild of Help was mooted, or the Jubilee discussed, or the

Football Club professionalised. By such means movements organised themselves. It was said in 1896 of the university movement that 'the founding of that institution had called forth. . .an amount of local patriotism and pride which was one of the things that had hitherto been lacking in many of their large towns'.[33] This was not just incidental to the movement. It was elevated into a principle in the early stages. Thus at a meeting in 1891 of those interested in extension work, the main speaker (E. Sadler) was in favour of development into a college and beyond, with the proviso that 'he believed the meeting would agree with him that any aid from the government which superseded local effort was to be deprecated'.[34] They might have been discussing welfare.

The aim was to take local students, especially students who were not 'those who could afford to pay for a good education', and to provide 'facilities not only for the professional instruction of many adult students. . .but in the widest sense for the education of citizens'. In the eight years up to 1900, of the 5,000 students who had 'received instruction' three-quarters were from Reading and its immediate neighbourhood.[35] An Industrial Classes Committee worked closely in the early years with the Academic Board. Free studentships were organised in evening classes, with the students selected from 'appropriate institutions in the town'. Some of the early lectures were held at one or other of these institutions rather than at the University College, 'a policy is thus being gradually shaped which aims at the affiliation of appropriate trade, friendly, philanthropic and other similar organisations to the college with the object of raising the standard of adult popular education in the town and of increasing our power of recruiting students'.[36] Institutes, Pleasant Sunday Afternoon gatherings, Friendly Societies and the like were seen as allies doing the same sort of job as the College, but inevitably with less resources. There were even courses for Sunday School teachers in 1909; the YMCA were granted special rates for evening classes beyond the free studentship schemes.[37]

To grasp what the University was trying to be, there is no substitute for paying close attention to the most important man in its history — W.M. Childs.[38] For Childs there was a tension between two sorts of education. There was 'useful knowledge'; there had been many developments in that area in the nineteenth century. Then there was another type,

Much less most unfortunately had been done in the last fifty years

during which educational institutions had made such progress, to
enable the workers to receive thorough, systematic and first-rate
teaching, in the great liberal subjects of knowledge, such as history,
economics, literature, philosophy, music and science, knowledge
not to sell again in a higher market, but for the sake of knowledge
. . .of what he might almost call spiritual instruction among the
working classes.[39]

In answer to the question 'why do not the universities do more of
this particular kind of work?' Childs put forward two reasons. Firstly,
that the demand for it had to be there independent of the supply,
'any university that went about offering this teaching whether it was
wanted or not would create failure upon failure and discredit the whole
business'. Secondly, that to do the things universities *had* to do, and
in increasing numbers – to 'train' the seventeen to twenty-four
age-group – was expensive and left less and less resources over for the
other type of education. Nonetheless he continually expressed the
aspiration that he 'hoped [of evening classes, in 1904] that in addition
to what had been called the teaching of instruction, they would be able
to add before long more of what he could call the teaching of power,
or liberal teaching, more literary and historical, what was sometimes
called civic teaching'.[40]

Education was for him social criticism. It ran sharply counter to
some of the tendencies of the age. Universities should, he thought,
interpret and identify with the labour unrest of the five years preceding
1914. The unrest and the College were symptoms of a common
striving.[41] 'The College would be a sordid and dismal affair indeed if
it were a mere thing of fees and classrooms, a kind of intellectual
exchange, and incorporated cram shop. Happily that kind of destiny
is not ours.'[42] To this end he became 'Reeve' and founder of a
medieval-type Guild – the Gild of the Red Rose – at the College in
1897 and gave it much of his energy and beliefs. In 1897 he said,

Half our blunders in education, half our failures in self-culture, half
the wrongs we do our own minds, are due to our refusal to take
into our lives once and for all, a clear and generous ideal of
intellectual life. If we do not even know what we would be at, how
can we apply ourselves to the pursuit with constancy? If we do not
even know where lies our goal, how can we tell what road to
follow? Never was there a time when the need for such a clear and
generous ideal was greater. Lost to us amid the hail of cram-books,

the bondage of examinations, the babel of tongues, the roar of business, the worship of fashion, the tyranny of conventionalism, the jargon of the philistine, the prig, the wrangle of interests, lost to us in its glory is that image of the perfect shining-in-use of all the human faculties dear to John Milton, as it was dear to the Greek of old. What matter the swollen resources of a Jubilee year, if the chamber of the mind be bare or choked with rubbish? Here then is the place for us; here is the *Gild work*. Under the shelter of a great college, hammering mightily upon its many anvils, tempering and sharpening industriously the weapons of the mind, do we bind ourselves together to treasure and pursue, not in the spirit of cram or dilettantism, but in all sincerity, the old and ever new ideal of mental being.[43]

He encouraged, and himself pursued, local history, for that would give students consciousness of the community in which they should become active participants.[44] He tried to make Reading into a civic university in the fullest sense, informed by values some of which come straight from Matthew Arnold, some from Ruskin, and some from Childs himself. It was to be a social movement rooted in Reading, springing from its inhabitants and expressing their highest possibilities of corporate morality and social behaviour. We needed 'a larger supply of trained capacity. . .to enable us to meet the competition of foreign countries'. That was one role for a university, legitimate in its subordinate place. We also needed similar capacity 'as a democracy'.[45] That was to be, for Childs, Reading's main emphasis; as he wrote in 1933, 'the University of Reading was the outcome of a movement which never in any of its stages owed its driving power to merely utilitarian motives. From first to last it drew its energy from ideas which, taken together, stood for a coherent university gospel'.[46]

This was the ideal and, in the early stages, part of the practice. But the question remained – how, in the conditions of the time, changing as they were – how to turn aspiration and embryo into a large organisation capable of survival and growth? This was as important a question for shaping its nature as it was for, say, the Football Club, or the Hospital.

George Palmer was a realist: down-to-earth, forthright, spare in his use of words, always revealing things beyond himself on the rare occasions when the historian can catch him talking. Education was one of his major concerns,[47] so that he was excited by the Extension movement. At its annual meeting in 1892 he was nostalgic for the days of the Mechanics' Institute (stopped in 1866) and expressed 'an absolute yearning and longing in the minds of many for another institution to take up the threads of the old one'.[48] But there were problems: 'the fact was people generally did not pay for their education.' He did not believe 'these intellectual movements could be made self-supporting. . .he knew that had never been and could not be'. His conclusion was that 'therefore it required that they should have the goodwill of the whole town. . .to support the movement in its best form'.

'The good will of the whole town', as in the case of the Town Hall, turned out over the succeeding twenty-five years to amount to the cash of very few members of it. These were mostly Palmers. Between 1896 and 1902 £19,000 was obtained for the movement. Half of that came from two individuals. Only £2,000 came from public bodies.[49] Both the Treasury and the Corporation played a minimal role. Without substantial sums given at critical moments by rich men in the town, and one woman (Lady Wantage) outside it, the University would have been quite unable to survive and grow. It was not a case of regular support by a middle class interested in extension work; in the long term it was a case of national funds paying for a primarily national organisation; in the medium term, certainly up until 1914 and a bit beyond, it was a case of massive sums from individuals, cleverly obtained by Childs, which at each point rescued a seemingly hopeless situation. So Alfred Palmer provided the site in 1903-4 when 'the college. . .seemed likely to be baffled'.[50] So George William Palmer 'at a critical moment in 1905 when hope and ambition seemed about to falter under the burden of financial difficulty, (by) his intervention (£50,000) changed the situation and re-established confidence'.[51] So it was above all that the £200,000 needed for an endowment fund in 1911 came from G.W. Palmer, Alfred Palmer and Lady Wantage. Whether or not he would get the money was an open question which makes Childs' own account of *Making a University* genuinely exciting reading. It would not have been possible to remain open with the continual deficit on annual working which characterised the years 1892-1903, let alone to develop. The recipe was not to rely on 'gate money', nor on the continually expressed interest of a whole segment or class of Reading society, nor on a limited liability company, but, in our period on last-minute 'millionaire endowments'.[52] The University was in a sense the last major product of an earlier phase of leadership and finance in Reading; but, so confined to two or three persons was the support, that it tends to confirm the notion that the late nineteenth century and early twentieth century was a period when such leadership and finance was, although not dead, at least in its death throes, to be replaced by the State.

When G.W. Palmer died in 1913 Childs wrote an appreciation of him in the *University College Review*. He had been, thought Childs, through his association with the College, 'a link between the spirit that is civic and local and the spirit that is academic and detached'. In the long term, in a twentieth-century perspective we can see that the connection broke. Whether or not 'academic and detached' is the correct way to describe mid-twentieth-century Reading University, neither it nor any other major university was to be informed significantly by a 'spirit that is civic and local'. Professor Max Muller saw it early, when he urged people in Reading in 1891, 'if you want something complete and systematic in Reading, a real university....you should bring pressure to bear on government, or rather on Parliament, not to allow this truly national movement to languish or die from want of funds'.[53] That was the direction in which change was going to go.

It would be a distortion to compress all the changes we are trying to describe in these chapters into a neat 1890-1914 time span. In the case of the university, it is signs of the times rather than completed developments which can be detected. By becoming a college and ultimately a full university a social movement was clearly on the way towards a particular type of institutionalisation.

The movement had always seen itself as *for* the working class, and for the education of citizens rather than experts. W.M. Childs and the Registrar assured the Committee of the Reading Industrial Co-operative Society in 1904 that they 'were specially and personally interested in affording the workers every possible opportunity to educate themselves'. There is no reason to doubt their sincerity. But the special interest, and the way in which the Co-op. began to regard the University as being *of* themselves, looks sad in the long perspective of twentieth-century university development. It was true that the success of the College movement in Reading was 'a success in which the working classes have had at least a substantial share'. But even the alteration of the relationship between leaders and led in cultural matters which Esrom was so pleased about in relation to the College, has not lasted. Leave aside the language used, could any voluntary, working-class, labour movement spokesman write about the University in 1976 as Esrom wrote in 1904:

Being gentlemen of education and refinement they do not presume

to patronise us and never (as the good book says) 'speak like one
having authority'. For this most distinguished consideration they
are entitled to our grateful thanks, in as much as many workers are
made to wince (and wink) at the arrogant assumption of those
'placed in authority over them'.[54]

In a number of ways the 'liberal studies', citizen-oriented, local version
of the University was already visibly under strain in our period. Popular
lectures, for example, were initially an integral part of the work of the
movement — even its main agency. By 1902 they were incidental.
Audiences had been and went on being large — at an average in 1898,
for example, of 1,000-1,400 attenders they were claimed as being the
largest in the UK. In 1905 for a series on electricity the audience was
'the largest which had attended lectures of that description in this
country or the USA'. But after about 1902 lectures were entertaining
frills seen as separate from the main business of extension work.[55]
Through them students might be encouraged to come to more regular
work, such work as Evening Classes provided. Classes were more
professionally oriented, and increasingly so.[56] There were complaints
in 1898 that classes were too expensive for the majority to attend, and
that since the College got more money from day classes they were
beginning to concentrate upon these, with an obvious effect on who
could come to them.[57]

Very early on in the life of the movement there were interesting
fears expressed. At a conference of extension centres in the South of
England in 1895 Herbert Sutton felt that Reading was at a critical
moment. 'When the University Extension movement was first started it
was started with the object of supplying a very definite want in modern
life.' That 'new ideal of education' was in danger of being swamped,
'perhaps the impression might get abroad that they were only a
technical college, and that the original work carried on by the Extension
Association was being overlooked and forgotten'.[58] Professional
training for groups such as teachers was coming to predominate over
the type of 'liberal' or 'power' studies Childs wished to stress. Efforts
were continually made within the College, via a Students' Association,
the magazine, the Gild of the Red Rose, to keep alive the idea of an
organic local organisation. The idea in the case of Reading probably
lasted longer than elsewhere. But in the long run, like other universities,
it was to serve a national, professional function for predominantly
non-manual workers and their children. George Palmer's aspirations
for it in terms of 'popularisation', and for 'the real working men and

women', and in terms of how 'they wanted the great bulk of the inhabitants of Reading to be brought within the circle of those who were seeking to improve on the education of the past, and come alongside in some degree with those who were given the advantages of a university education', expressed in 1892, stood as a criticism of what it had become by 1925, rather than an expression of its main role as a full university.[59] This was even more true of the Co-op.'s aspirations for the University.

Two moments in W.M. Childs' life in relation to the University may serve as final indices of change. In 1895, a year after he had arrived in Reading as a lecturer, he had urged the Students' Association to start 'grappling' at first hand with the study of local history. They should thoroughly study the local press from 1750 onwards as a major accent of their work. The theme as it then appeared to him would be 'the rise, the fall and resurrection of municipal patriotism'. The College was to aid and be part of this resurrection. In 1933, eight years after retiring as Principal, Childs' tone about universities in general and about Reading was less confident:

It would be strange indeed if, for example, the new speculations about the nature and origin of the universe, the questioning of religious assumptions, the disintegration of received morality, and the new ideals of domestic and world order, were to pass unheeded by intelligent youth. They do not so pass. But how far does the university itself heed such questions in their relation to thought, faith and conduct. What light is thrown – or can be thrown – upon these questions by official courses of instruction in preparation for professional careers? Where, exactly, in a modern university, can the student find, thanks to the action of the university, an opportunity to weigh views responsibly put forward, and to receive, if he is so minded, counsel, exhortation and warning? Yet in the make-up of a man or a woman, which matters most – technical or special proficiency in a branch of knowledge or practice, or a clear understanding of what makes for right living? Men may differ about values, but hardly about the importance of knowing that different values exist. The university does not fail to help students to find a livelihood, does it always do all it might to help them to live?[60]

10 LABOUR AND POLITICS

> Men fight and lose the battle, and the thing that they fought for
> comes about in spite of their defeat, and when it comes turns
> out not to be what they meant, and other men have to fight
> for what they meant under another name. (William Morris,
> *A Dream of John Ball*)

In 1891 the columns of the *Reading Observer,* a Liberal paper, were full
of nervous apprehension about a new force which had appeared in the
town — Socialism. From March onwards a correspondence went on
under the title 'Socialism in the Radical Club'.[1] A Fabian lecturer
(E.R. Pease) had been in the town and had excited much interest. 'I
cannot help tracing the present deplorable position of Liberalism in
Reading', wrote one correspondent in August, 'to the alienation of the
working classes. . .all sorts of red herrings (like Socialism) have been
traced across their scent'.[2] By March 1892 it was 'the late Radical club'
which was referred to in the same newspaper.[3] F. Critchley, its
ex-President, had become a member of the local branch of the Social
Democratic Federation.[4] The SDF was not the only section of the
labour movement present in Reading in these years. There had been a
local Co-operative Society since 1860, and a Trades Council had been
started in 1874, only to be re-started twenty years later. But the
presence and activities of the SDF excited more comment, and that
comment was more centred around the idea of Socialism, than other
parts of the movement.[5]

It is clear from the national SDF newspaper that soon after its
foundation Reading became one of the more 'active provincial
branches'.[6] Meeting every Monday evening at 7.30 and with at least
two public meetings a week on Sundays,[7] they ran a local supplement
to *Justice*, sold with the national paper, and maintained it for at least
three years. As with the local ILP paper, *The Reading Pioneer,* I have
only been able to trace references to these local papers. This has meant
that sources for labour movement ideology and organisation have been
primarily non-labour movement in type. For readers who might be
tempted to regard Reading as a 'Mugsborough', a backward town for
labour politics, however, it is interesting to note the labour press it
supported. There was a *Reading Co-operative Record* (1894 onwards),
a local *Justice,* a local *Pioneer* preceded by a *Labour Herald* (1904),

a *Reading Worker* (1915-18?) and a *Reading Citizen* (after 1918).

In terms of numbers the local SDF was not impressive. They had only reached about twenty in 1893.[8] But their presence in the town was considerable and can be measured in the reactions of others to them. 'Just now the Socialists are very much to the fore', observed the Conservative local newspaper in October 1894, 'if they do not regenerate mankind at all events they advertise themselves'.[9] The dismissal of one of their members from Huntley and Palmers 'caused dozens of members to come into the Reading branch'.[10] Persecution at this stage of SDF history only served to reinforce commitment.

They were a body which needed commitment in order to survive. One of the features of the history of socialist organisations in late nineteenth-century form in Reading was the victimisation to which its members were subject. Especially if members were involved in a labour dispute, or if they got elected on to local bodies like the Board of Guardians they experienced difficulty in keeping their job, and even greater difficulty in finding another job once dismissed.[11]

This fact is important, not only in establishing what type of body the SDF was in Reading in the early 1890s, but also in helping to understand the processes of change to which the SDF and other organisations on the left were subject in the years after 1891. One of the ways out of victimisation was to find a job within the movement. There were various alternatives; to become secretary of a trade union branch and then go on to be a full-time union official (like Ben Russell in Reading), or to act as an itinerant socialist 'missionary' organiser/election agent (like Lorenzo Quelch). Regardless of the political philosophy originally held by the sacked member, such situations were bound to affect both the individuals concerned and their organisations.

As a small body working in what was a difficult and hostile town to penetrate, the SDF assumed an appropriate separate form.[12] They were sure in belief, aware of the ramifications of the social system they were up against and determined not to be tainted or seduced by it, and critical of the means others of their class had chosen to 'help themselves' within capitalism. They included trade unionism in this criticism. Thus, it was not only the manner in which money was raised for an organisation like the Royal Berkshire Hospital which seemed to be wrong,through Hospital Sunday parades and the like, but the whole idea of the Hospital itself. Capitalist economic depression was for them endemic. It could not be met by local action; only by a total change of the system.[13] Until 1894 the Reading SDF deliberately avoided localising their propaganda in speeches and writings about capitalism.

The system was the same wherever you looked. Huntley and Palmers was a factory like other factories. They would not attack it specifically, preferring to take their illustrations about capitalism from the national press. It was only after a member had been dismissed that they diverted, or localised their aims. The *Reading Observer*'s part in the switch of emphasis to direct attacks on the biscuit factory was described by the SDF as 'despicable'. 'Right from the inception of the movement in Reading it had been recognised that this factory is no better and no worse than most others', yet in the columns of the *Reading Observer* 'the firm was practically invited by insinuation. . .to smash down its Socialist employees'. It is quite clear that the sacking of G.H. Wilson was the trigger for the change rather than any deliberate policy decision by the local SDF.[14]

The branch had a test for intending members, a catechism which had to be grasped before joining,

> Because of the difficult times it was considered unwise to take into membership persons whose hearts only were stirred by the socialist appeal and a system was set up under which each applicant had to submit to an interview and a series of questions, and his admission to the branch was dependent on the replies he gave. If he failed in the interview he was given literature to study and told to apply again.[15]

One who first became interested at one of the regular Sunday street meetings later recalled how 'at that time I was. . .a member of a church nearby (Cumberland Road Primitive Methodists) and time after time class leaders used to speak with admiration of the zeal manifested by the SDF members who in season and out of season held meetings and distributed free literature from door to door. . .we were urged to go and do the same'. After a period of thought he joined. Membership meant more than just another gain on an agent's list, or another subscription in a treasurer's book. 'I applied for admission to the SDF wondering if a novice so crude as myself would be admitted. I was duly interviewed and to my great joy was admitted as a member of the local branch.'

Once a member, missionary zeal grew with intellectual conviction. 'A dictionary was of course indispensable and persistent plodding study led to the acquirement of the meaning of economic terms. There was a famous article in the ninth edition of the Encyclopedia Britannica and several comrades visited the students room at the Central Free Library and copied the whole article, and when the meaning was mastered the student found the average Liberal or Tory working man easy to tackle in argument'.[16]

A vivid example of SDF attitudes to their socialism was later recalled by Lorenzo Quelch. In his draft autobiography he described an encounter between himself and Herbert Samuel:

> a few days after the Liberal meeting. . .I called at Hines' place and found Herbert Samuel there. After being introduced Samuel and I sat down to chat. He told me he was a Socialist. I expressed doubt and asked him to tell me what Socialism was, after a pause he said he was not sure that he could. I said it was strange that a man should call himself a Socialist and yet be unable to explain his idea of Socialism. He replied if it was so easy perhaps I would explain it. This I did briefly, whereupon he said if that is Socialism I certainly am not a Socialist. I said that I quite agreed.

The first annual report of the Reading SDF in *Justice* in October, 1892, gave a further indication of the atmosphere of the branch: 'we are embarked confident that we shall win in the end, when the hydra-headed dragon of capitalism will be crushed under the heel of social democracy and when a genuine peace and good will to all men will reign on earth.' The branch was a small, active, convinced organisation of socialists who anticipated success, partly through an increase in their own number and power, and partly through the internal crisis through which capitalism appeared to them to be passing. Such success meant change of a total kind, at a national level, and soon.

What was happening in relation to labour and politics in our period was also endowed by others outside the SDF with tremendous significance, even with a kind of finality. In the longer term, from a mid-twentieth-century perspective 'the real problem' may be 'why the coming of mass politics and a mass political labour movement has not led to greater changes',[17] but at the time it looked different to people on the left and on the right. It looked to some observers as though the subject of this chapter was *the* major strand of contemporary history. Politics, especially labour politics, appeared to be 'taking over' where other things were draining away. The change was sometimes presented as if it had already occurred. M.J. Sutton, the seed manufacturer, referred in 1892 to 'the working classes of this country who now have the power'.[18] More often the tone was tentative.[19] That a 'social revolution' was happening was not doubted. That its carrier was politics, especially working-class politics, was assumed.[20] The question for a contextual understanding of organisations in society thus becomes: what, in fact, happened?

In a number of ways the activities of the SDF had a self-defeating logic imposed by developments in the system they wished to destroy. 'Success' in a sense implied 'failure'. They wished, as we have seen, to preserve ideological unity and discipline, to attack the system rather than get involved with particular expressions at the local level of the horrors of that system. To do the latter would be to compromise, to settle for reform in a capitalism whose nature implied that reformist demands were utopian, impossibilist goals.[21] Coherence implied a certain separateness, which could be called by its political enemies 'sectarianism', and which did involve organising as a sect. And yet dynamism generated an organisation deeply involved in the locality. The better they did, in terms of activities designed to establish their presence in Reading, the less they came to look like what they wanted to be. This was partly forced by the actions of others. When Huntley and Palmers refused to give Barnes time off for his work on the Board of Guardians, the branch had to open a store with Barnes as manager. For some months both he and G.H. Wilson had to be paid out of a branch wages fund.[22] Running a store and raising money for wages were not lines of action likely to produce an ideal SDF branch. They took much effort. So did more deliberately chosen activities, in response to conditions in the town. The branch ran a Labour Bureau, opened in 1892 for the unemployed.[23] They did a social survey of housing in the town in 1894.[24] They pressed on the Board of Guardians for the same food to be given to officers and inmates; they lobbied for work for the unemployed at 4½ d. an hour.[25]

Above all they sought positions on elected bodies – the Guardians, the School Board, the Council and, in 1898, Parliament. There was no contradiction in theory here. They had, in common with most other socialists in the Second International period in Europe, a foreshortened time perspective. The SDF thought it would be possible not only to get represented on the legislative bodies of the state and the municipality quickly, but to capture them completely. In practice the nature of the representational quest changed through the 1890s; it had a logic of its own. It was not a question of selling out, or of deliberate compromise; what you did in a particular context, changing as it was, was bound to shape what you were. The better you did it, the more this was the case, whether you were a church or a political group.

Thus the initial presence of the two SDF representatives on the

School Board was clearly more in the nature of a demonstration,
drawing out differences, fomenting conflict, emphasising an end to
deference. In their report on their early work on the Board, Wilson and
Hodgson wrote, 'at the preliminary meeting of the Board the Chairman
lectured to us on our duties, etc. and unexpectedly received a back
answer (*vide* the capitalist press)'. They then described the issues they
had raised: raising the age of half-timers, evening meetings, getting the
half-yearly financial report inserted in *Justice* as well as in the local
capitalist papers, higher minimum wage for office boys, caretakers'
wages, better warming of schools in poorer districts, equalisation of
pay between men and women teachers. Between them they sat on
every possible sub-committee.

> We opposed the recording in the minutes the eulogy of the late
> vice-chairman, which was moved for by the Progressives, as he was
> of that Party. The man in question was undoubtedly the most
> genuine educationalist of the whole lot of them, but was defeated
> at the polls. We called them canting hypocrites, telling them they
> were only shedding crocodile tears. . .The Church Party who hated
> the late member voted out of spite with the Progressives, although
> they had previously declared against it. . .we are to move that
> religious instruction be discontinued. We have succeeded in bringing
> down upon us the hatred of the hypocritical kept parsons and we
> have not got a friend on the Board. That ought to do.

Justice commended them: 'it is indeed a record of thorough good work
done.'[26] Such a presence was a logical extension of the kind of
organisation they were trying to be. But others, and then they
themselves, came to give different definitions to their presence.

E.P. Collier, a Baptist businessman and Progressive member of the
Board, by 1902 liked having them there. He wanted to move the times
of the meetings to suit them better. They had become 'useful' as an
interest group on a certain range of issues: 'they had been there at
times past at great inconvenience to themselves but at very great
advantage to the Board on many points.'[27] They had never meant to be
a 'great advantage to the Board on many points', nor to be seen as
useful on some matters affecting their 'interests'. They had got on to
the School Board in order to raise issues which did not end with
education; educational ills and deprivations were symptoms of a larger
galloping disease. But being a zealous and effective member of the
Board turned Hodgson, for example, into an expert on education. He

came to see difficulties socialist strategy encountered in terms of educational deprivation of the working class, instead of seeing that deprivation in terms of the necessity for wider socialist struggle. After their 1898 parliamentary election defeat, the SDF held a post-mortem. The remaining SDF member on the Board (Hodgson) argued for a wider coalition of workers beyond the SDF 'in order to get rid of this state of things'. This coalition was to seek representation to achieve three main aims: the State maintenance of scholars, a raising of the school leaving age to sixteen, and a legal eight-hour day. They had to break out of working-class apathy which he had noticed while he was on the Board. These reforms would 'alter the materials which the socialist had to work on', i.e. the working class.[28]

Having members and chief activists on town Boards, committees and councils was bound to alter both the SDF and its members. Individual biographies can reveal much about the effect of being a representative, or for that matter a trade union leader, on what job the individual could get or was, more usually, unable to get, on what else he would have time to do politically, where he would have to live and what the content of his political advocacy would have to become. They also show that the churches were not alone in living with the results of constantly moving membership.

G.H. Wilson, for example, was dismissed from Huntley and Palmers in 1894; in 1896 he was on the Board of Guardians; in 1899 he left Reading unable to find a job. Lorenzo Quelch was first active politically in 1881; in 1892 he was organising secretary of the Berkshire Agricultural and General Workers' Union; in 1893 he worked for the English Land Restoration League and lived at their headquarters in Reading; in 1896 he contested a seat for the Council and lost; he also contested a seat on the Board of Guardians and lost. About 1896 he had to leave Reading and worked in a foundry in Wandsworth until about 1901; he then became a canvasser for Singer's Sewing Machines in Deptford until 'the whole thing became disgusting'. In 1902 he was in the North as an SDF propagandist organiser. From 1902 to 1904 he had work in Reading, which he lost until he had another spell of work up to 1907 at a foundry in Reading. He was sacked from there and went to Newbury for three years looking for foundry work. He lost a job in about 1910 and was intermittently employed in Guildford, Newbury and Reading. In 1914 he was back, as Secretary of the Reading Trades and Labour Council. Being a socialist and a foundry worker together in Reading over a continuous period of time was clearly impossible.

Ben Russell, for a time secretary of the Reading SDF and on the Board of Guardians for Katesgrove Ward, found his solution in self-employment and, latterly, in being employed by a trade union. He had been unemployed in London and came to Reading in 1896. He worked in the Warehouse and Despatch Department of a local firm, did well, and was promoted, until 1908 when he resigned after instigating a three-day strike. He became a tobacconist and confectioner. While doing this he worked for the establishment of the first local branch of the General and Municipal Workers. In 1911 he became the secretary of the branch. By 1914 he was full-time and had given up his shop; his politics had become defined by the many administrative jobs which came to him: 'during the war the branch struggled on. Personally I was very busy on the Prince of Wales Committee for the Distressed.' In 1911 he became the first working-class Borough Auditor; by 1920 he was a JP. A leading Labour Councillor – S.G. Jones – emigrated after only a few years as a representative.

There are many other examples of local biography which could be pieced together to demonstrate the constraints within which organisations like the SDF had to operate. The number of bodies upon which it was possible to sit, the contradictory situations in which it was possible for an activist to find himself, increased enormously in this 'age of administration'. The nature of the issues discussed on those bodies, in terms of their complexity, their definition in prior reforming legislation, and their relationship to established State apparatus also developed in ways likely to increase the contradictions which individuals and organisations had to deal with.

The SDF had success in getting representatives on to the Guardians and School Board until 1895. But during the years immediately following, the initial perspective of capturing for socialism the councils of the land receded rapidly. In 1892 they had topped the poll for the School Board. In 1893 they won two more seats. In 1894 they contested four seats for the Guardians and won two. 1896 saw a turning of the tide; although they contested more seats than ever before they lost heavily. For the *Berkshire Chronicle* in April 1896, the Guardians' elections of that year 'provided satisfactory evidence of the decline of Socialism in Reading', and the Council elections in November proved that 'the Socialists, notwithstanding their continual propaganda are in a state of evanescence'. Even before the parliamentary by-election, alongside their high hopes, *Justice* (16 July 1898) was regretting that 'Reading has not been so active a socialist centre recently as it was. . . our comrades having had very bad luck in more than one way'.

The climax both of trust in the perspective and traumatic disillusion at its failure was the candidature of Harry Quelch in a by-election in 1898. Hopes were very high. Good meetings were held. The line-up was favourable; the Liberal candidate being G.W. Palmer, the best possible symbol of the injustices of capitalism for Reading, 'the man who discharges and tries to starve workmen who do not share his political opinions, the man who has built up a fortune by sweating the workers of Reading, the man who of all others the independent workers of Reading ought to reject with contempt'. 'If "Radical" democracy is worth anything at all it must support our comrade H. Quelch against the capitalist Liberal G.W. Palmer.' Reports in *Justice* were optimistic, 'the contest could have come at no better moment'. To Hyndman the result was immensely important. The candidate 'voices the discontent and gives expression to the aspirations of millions of his fellow men', and 'I for one as a man of the class economically and socially opposed. . .to the wage earners can scarcely comprehend how any voter among the workers of Reading can fail to cast his vote into the ballot box for Quelch on Monday next'.[29]

The following week it was 'Reading and after' in *Justice*. The language of disappointment when the Liberals achieved their largest majority in Reading since 1878 and Quelch only collected 270 votes as against 4,700 for the Liberals was as heightened as that of any Christian minister complaining about working-class indifference to his church or chapel. The candidate deplored how, 'as at other places where the opportunity has been presented them of striking a blow for their own class, the majority of the workers have deliberately turned their backs upon that opportunity and have cordially hugged their chains. . .it is amazing, and would be ludicrous, were it not so sad'. Hyndman's fears about 'apathy' expressed at a meeting in 1897 in the town seemed amply confirmed.[30] Introspective post-mortems were held, new ways out of seemingly blocked avenues were debated. No longer did 'the capture by the workers of the legislative and local councils as the best means of obtaining what they want' appear so possible.[31] The SDF began to explore alternative strategies with the Co-op., and with other groups looked at the possibility of united action towards labour representation rather than working-class power.[32]

The terms upon which a body like the early SDF in Reading could succeed or fail, what they had to become in order to survive and grow, the way in which what they did came to shape what they were, were as deeply set in changing late nineteenth-century capitalism as was the experience already described of the Reading Football Club, the WEA,

Hospital Sunday, or of churches and chapels. Analogies between the SDF in its early form and religious organisations are more direct in one sense, since in both cases it is the social history of organisations designed in a total sense to relate men to their fate, or their history, which is being studied. A felt sense of failure, of being out of touch and unable to embrace the majority of the working class was common to both. Both underwent processes of institutionalisation, processes whereby what they did in society and for themselves came to limit what they could be, and in time came to exist in some disharmony with what they had set out to achieve. Such common pressures already described in other areas of social life in Reading, along with some unique to the political area, are the main interest of the story of socialist and labour organisation for this chapter.

That story does not end with the SDF. Nor was it exclusively a story of failure. One of the most striking changes in this period, caused by and reflected in political organisation, was an alteration taking place in the relationship between leaders and led. This took quite explicit, argumentative forms in politics.

An older relationship was under strain certainly, but none the less was expressed from time to time. William Isaac Palmer's reaction to Mr William of the SDF contesting Church ward in a council by-election in 1892 was a beautiful example of it. There had been a compact agreed by Conservatives and Liberals. 'Mr William had brought forward questions which at the present moment were engaging the thought and attention of wise men. . .he did not think they should send people to the Council to discuss these questions.' Sympathy — but reserved, and felt from within a still partly deferential view of the world — came not only from Palmers like William Isaac, but to Palmers like George William. At an annual tea of the Co-op. in 1900, with 1,500 attending, a presentation was made to the latter. He was spoken of benevolently, as a great 'captain of industry'. A speech was made by a Co-op. official who said that capital and labour did have conflicting interests, but 'they in Reading were particularly fortunate in that respect. He believed that the conditions of capital and labour in Reading were on most friendly terms. In walking through the town he was struck by the various indications of kindly consideration and sympathy which the employers had for the people and he hoped these conditions would long remain'. It was a delicate occasion this, a moment of interaction between two quite different, but related, versions of voluntary action. The full Co-op. position (which we shall see later) was put; G.W. Palmer spoke of his father, as if it was he who really should have been there; and he also chose as the main theme of his speech 'local self-government', moving towards his hosts as far as they moved towards their guest.[33]

Signs of strain and of the development of a new independence on the part of labour were more frequent during these years than plain reassertions of older styles. Working-class, but explicitly non-socialist , councillors, such as the bricklayer S.G. Jones, frequently shocked others by their independence and lack of deference. After a dispute with G.W. Palmer on unemployment in 1908 a local paper felt obliged to take Palmer's side — for 'the really genuine and deserving unemployed as a rule is a modest and unassuming person, he is not always pushing himself forward and desiring to hear his own voice in public'.[34] The best register of change was a labour dispute at Huntley and Palmers in 1912, after the firm had sacked a number of workers at Christmas. The reasons for choosing who to sack, the manner of appeal from the directors to their workpeople, their indignation at 'leading' local citizens who took the workers' part, the language of the militancy of the workers, all showed how a whole local way of relating to the led was under strain. In an article called 'The Rajahs of Reading' the national ILP newspaper concentrated on how 'the firm have publicly stated that doubts as to the "loyalty" of certain workpeople was one of the reasons for dismissal'.[35] When Hart Davis, an Anglican minister, started to lead the public argument on behalf of efforts to establish a trade union, the directors were 'deeply grieved that a man of education, a minister of religion, and a magistrate, should have so misdemeaned himself on a public platform'.[36]

Slowly and with difficulty the changed relationship between leaders and led was being embodied in new organisations — trade unions. The new attitudes and new national organisational bases were data with which all subject-areas of voluntary organisation would from then on have to work. In 1899 although twelve out of the fifteen trades in the town were represented on the trades council, one estimate was that there were only 500 trade unionists in Reading.[37] In the previous forty years 'masters and men' societies, locally based, such as the Reading Printers' Relief and Provident Association (1877) or the Reading Society of Railway Servants, which had annual dinners at which leading local citizens and 'honorary members' spoke, and whose main ideology was harmony, mutual protection, relief and mutual insurance, were the typical forms of labour organisation in the town. Such strikes as took place were locally arbitrated through *ad hoc* conciliation boards, but 'trade disputes and labour troubles are happily almost unknown'.[38]

A new and more national pattern was, albeit slowly, replacing the older one in the years before 1914. Branches of London-based unions or national unions established themselves trade by trade.[39] In 1909 there were thirteen unions affiliated to the trades council with 830 members, in 1913 twenty-two unions with 2,000 members. A trade union consciousness was developing, and with it a nationalisation or centralisation of labour disputes, and confidence that organised labour had or would gain a recognised place in the sun, as an interest group. When in 1914 the organising secretary of the Gasworkers and General Labourers Union bemoaned the slowness of trade union growth in Reading, a speaker at the May Day rally put him right: 'Mr Switzer did not understand the workers' position in Reading, or he would not have deplored the position of the local branch. In the circumstances as they knew them it was most remarkable that they had been enabled not only to manage a gas workers' branch but also to establish a banner. . .five years ago they could not have had a demonstration like that in Reading.'[40] By the time of the Huntley and Palmers dispute of 1912 it was felt that 'it is really too late in the day for a firm to try to break down the power of organised labour, if they persist in their present course the issue must be taken up on national lines'.[41] It was to take world war to put industrial relations in the biscuit factory on a less local, less discreet, and trade union basis; but the change had begun before.

The mere growth of trade unions, with their national links and class confidence, was an important change in Reading. But, as in the case of the major political parties, there is a key dimension to their existence which could only be traced at the local level and yet which, at least in Reading, cannot easily be traced even there. What was happening to them at branch level, how much attendance there was, what kind of meetings were held, and in what ways they were changing as organisations from the members' point of view – all this would be of similar interest to supporters' relations with the Football Club or the Hospital. Records unfortunately are inadequate.[42] Some observations can be made on the meaning of the social history of trade unionism in these years in Reading, but the great gap there is in even the most modern national studies of trade unionism when the individual member's or the branch perspective is sought has been too little acknowledged. What it was like to be a member, at different dates, of either a trade union or a political party, or of many other organisations whose formal history is well known, is a question as yet insufficiently asked.

Before getting back to the significance of trade union development, one other positive achievement of labour politics should be signalled. The SDF may have had difficulties after the mid-1890s in achieving representation on elected bodies, but, sometimes with SDF co-operation and sometimes against it, labour representation was achieved on a significant scale.

Until 1898 the 'labourist' tendency was slightly less successful than SDF candidates. Thereafter candidates of the labourist type did significantly better. They established themselves as a recognised presence on the Town Council and on the Board of Guardians. An important year in this process was 1900, a bad year for socialists, but one in which S.G. Jones the bricklayer won a seat on the Council. The *Berkshire Chronicle* called him 'conservative in politics'; he called himself 'the labour candidate' and the first working-man's representative to win a seat on the Council.[43]

Thereafter progress was quite rapid and representatives quite 'effective', ironically enough from a socialist perspective, especially on the Board of Guardians where considerable reformist gains were made in terms of humanising the workhouse.[44] In 1902, for the local Tory newspaper, 'the strength of the Labour vote (was) astonishing'; 'the Labour Party is doing very well'; and 'we hope that the Labour Party choose good men, they are clearly going to have an increasing say'.[45] Alliances of a Labour Representation Committee type in order to achieve electoral gains were not just a matter of one meeting with a resulting concordat which then lasted for years; they had to be continually formed and re-formed in the years before 1914. But they were effective.[46]

Again, such a development implied the achievement of a measure of independence for working-class politics, a separation from earlier middle-class local business leadership and from earlier agencies of change such as the local Liberal party. But what else was involved? On what terms was the labour movement growing in this period in Reading? Was it 'taking over' from religion? In what forms was it developing, and in what relationship to people's aspirations? The changes involved in new national ways of conducting industrial relations in the town, and in new ways of conducting council business with the working class included, were important changes, clearly related to changes described in the three preceding chapters, but their extent and nature should not be misunderstood.

'The Tories had made a sad mess of everything, but where was the Liberal Party? It had fulfilled its historic mission, and was now a moribund body. It had emancipated the great commercial class and the new issue was the emancipation of the working classes. The Liberals would not do that because they were members of the commercial class itself. . .'[47] So said a socialist spokesman in Reading in 1902, with a confidence typical of the time that 'history' would deliver the instrument to deal with 'the new issue' just as the Liberals had dealt with the old. Social change, he felt, was going his way. But social change, as we can observe it in Reading, did not in fact produce a dynamic, deeply-rooted, widely-based, participatory organisation for 'the emancipation of the working classes'. Just as late nineteenth-century and early twentieth-century capitalism was altering the context within which chapels, football clubs, dispensaries or universities could develop, so too it imposed severe constraints upon what type of labour movement came into being. The society described in Chapter Two was not going to have the working class peacefully added to it through a broadening of the base of existing organisations and the addition of new ones. Contradictions were not to be so peacefully resolved in the twentieth century. Socialist groupings, like religious organisations, have tended to internalise the blame. Where they have felt themselves to be failing, they have argued that they must have been using the wrong tactics or strategy, or that the workers were not yet ready. To some extent such re-appraisal is desirable and necessary in difficult twentieth-century circumstances, but only in the context of an understanding of developments outside their own organisations affecting them and others — an understanding of what was happening to them.

The terms upon which the new-found independence and delocalisation of labour politics developed are fairly clear, at least up until about 1912. Labour spokesmen wanted to stress, like S.G. Jones after his election to the Council in 1901, 'the importance of the working classes taking more interest in municipal matters than in the past', or, like a speaker at a meeting to discuss labour representation in 1899, 'the object of arousing a healthy and active public interest in municipal affairs'.[48] But the task was recognised to be difficult. There was 'the terrible indifference shown by the mass of the workers to these vital questions'. In response to 'indifference' the same spokesmen limited their perspective, away from organisations of the early SDF type towards more frankly interest-based, particular, limited politics. The 'indifference' was deplored, but a speaker at a conference in Reading in 1902 'was even more concerned to see the tremendous power of the two great organisations — the trade-union movement and

the co-operative movement – being frittered away and wasted instead
of being used to get to the root of the evil and change the character of
the legislative machine'.[49] They should use their resources to get a
share in government. In fact the object of 'arousing interest' was 'in
order to secure for the working classes *a proper share* (my italics) of
representation on local bodies'.

This indeed was what happened. Not an organisation attracting active
mass support and altering the actual relationship between the people
and their social fate, not something which in any sense 'took over'
loyalties, leisure time and energies of the working class from, for
example, 'religion', but very particular and identifiable alterations in
who did what and how in Reading. A successful interest group,
an organised working-class lobby, came into being. 'It is evident that
labour is a force in Reading which cannot be ignored', wrote a local
paper in 1914. And it was – both in the factory and in the town. So
when the Corporation was demanding in January 1914 that new
dustbins should be compulsory for the convenience of refuse collection,
at first the committee recommendation had been that the tenant should
pay. J. Rabson and Hodgson managed to get this decision reversed, 'so
strong a line was taken by the Labour Party against the dustbins clause
...that it would have been surprising if it had got through'. Landlords
had to pay.[50] On issues like wages paid by council contractors, or the
provision of a TB clinic through the local Insurance Committee under
the 1911 Act, or a minimum wage for council employees, labour was
consulted and increasingly often its advice was taken.[51]

Labour was an interest group which often came to put its demands,
for instance on unemployment relief, without any analysis of the
system which produced unemployment. Demands on this and other
issues were made in a different situation from that of the early 1890s.
Fifteen years after 1890 it began to be a question of seeking to amend
existing inadequate measures, rather than demanding comprehensive
new legislation. That was a different type of politics. Moreover, new
legislation, and later world war, produced many new official bodies
from which such demands could come. So W.G. Ayres, secretary of the
Reading ILP and a militant on the Board of Guardians, found himself
with another Labour member on the Distress Committee set up under
the Unemployed Workmen Act of 1905 administering charity to the
unemployed in 1906. So four Labour members found themselves on
the Prince of Wales Relief Committee in 1914. Lorenzo Quelch was
one of them: 'our Joint Committee members took an active part,
frequently coming into conflict with other members of the main

committee because of the niggardly amount given and the low scale
adopted by the London Committee. So much was this scale resented
that we were threatened with dissolution of the main local committee
and the appointment of a new one if we persisted in our demands for
a new scale. However, our protesting resulted in an increase of the
payments made to the distressed.' However effective in terms of the
improvements they could win, theirs was an utterly different type of
politics from that, for example, of the first two SDF representatives
on the School Board. The emphasis had shifted towards demands for
rights within a system, for a place within an ongoing society. The tone
of voice was important. It is possible to hear Councillor Rabson talking
in November 1912, after he had been Beating the Bounds of a new area
of the borough with all the other councillors, and to visualise the bricks
and mortar which have resulted from such twentieth-century labour
perspectives, when he said that 'he had been struck during the
perambulation by the amount of non-urban land. There was enough
land for building purposes and he hoped the time was not far distant
when they would pull down the slums and put up good residences for
working people'.[52]

Such development within labour politics could be embraced by
'friends of the working man', and spoken of by them in terms which
do not fundamentally distort the reality. So Hart Davis, previously
often present at 'masters and men' predecessors of trade unions in
Reading, and a champion of the Friendly Societies, by 1912 called
himself a 'labour' man. Working people had 'proper claims' on the
government of the day; government had 'duties' to perform in meeting
those claims. The government must 'give to every man, woman and
child those absolute necessities of life without which they have no
chance of self-development', i.e. education, housing, water, sanitation.
'It is the want of them that turns men into slaves.'[53] Two years later he
returned to the theme:

the working man is looking forward to better enforcement of those
laws (laws about sanitation, healthy homes, fair wages, short hours,
etc.) under councils on which he himself will be represented. . .the
spirit of social reform was abroad. Indeed whereas not very long ago
every hand was raised against him, now, if they had a danger, it was
in praises so universally bestowed ... but who that knew him could
doubt that with the conscious possession of new powers would
come to him a growing sense of responsibility.

In 1913 he wrote to the *Reading Observer* that the increase in the
Labour vote at the election of that year was fully justified, for 'until
Liberalism in Reading realises that the true prosperity of the town lies
not in the wealth of the few, not in the success of the trader and of the
professional man, but in the well-being of the worker, in his ability to
earn a living wage, and to pass his days unharassed by the dread of
poverty, it deserves and must expect defeat'. Those were the terms
upon which he welcomed and observed changes in labour and politics.

Trade unionism, too, was acceptable — even necessary. For Hart
Davis trade unions were the means through which a man 'kept his
independence and self-respect'. They had 'prevented revolution in
England'.[54] For Rufus Isaacs, the Liberal MP for Reading, they were
'the mainstays of peace in the industrial world'.[55] For the Rev. R.H.
Sewell, who objected to the manners and methods of much of
independent socialist politics, they were bodies which should not be
attacked. They were in the 'highest interests of the Nation'.[56] The SDF
had perhaps been correct in the early 1890s in rejecting trade unionism
as an agency for their type of political action, even if their chosen
alternative had not turned out in the short term to be more productive.
Incorporation into an existing and continuing system, the finding of a
place within an administrative hierarchy, the making of an 'interest'
had been the terms upon which changing capitalism had allowed labour
politics to succeed.

This was certainly the case until the beginning of the second decade of
the twentieth century. Thereafter new organisations (new in Reading)
began to dominate, new tendencies to emerge. The Reading branch of
the ILP was re-started in 1906 after an earlier fleeting existence in the
mid-1890s. A Fabian Society, a 'Sunday Social Conference', a Marxian
Club, a group for the implementation of the Minority Report of the
Poor Law Commission, a Reading Anti-Betting and Gambling League,
a Reading Social Democratic Party all existed intermittently during the
next decade. In August 1912 the British Socialist Party (BSP) held a
two day 'mission' in the town and the SDF developed into a branch of
that organisation.[57]

Intensive activity on particular issues and around particular events
was sometimes co-operative between different branches of such
organisations and sometimes exclusive to one of them. On issues like
supporting the Royal Berkshire Hospital out of taxation rather than
out of the pennies of Working Men's Hospital Associations, or on
unemployment, alliances were forged.[58] On local government

candidatures, division of labour was arranged and wards allotted to each
tendency. Some parliamentary candidatures, both actual and intended
ones, were exclusive to a group. Others, notably that of J.G. Butler in
1913, seem to have been representative of the whole movement.[59] It
was not until after the outbreak of war in 1914 that divisions of a type
which were to be institutionalised in political party machines appeared.
They were to last through the first three-quarters of the twentieth century
in the Labour and Communist Parties. In the years immediately before 1914
there had been a move to the left by the growing trade union element
in Reading, in tandem with the BSP and the Reading Trades and Labour
Council, leaving a section of the ILP in a centre position. But two-thirds
of the local BSP membership together with the Trades Council, which
set up a recruiting committee, came out in favour of active aid for the
war effort later on. Opposition, such as it was, was left to surviving ILP
elements.[60] Contradictions between aims and performance became
increasingly sharp through the war years.

The context of pre-1914 labour politics needs establishing before
more precise local details. Speculative perspectives are involved, for
here more than in most historical moments, what is seen depends on
the vantage point, what is thought to have happened at one moment
depends on what is assumed to have happened afterwards.

Political indifference, 'apathy', grass roots separation from issues as
articulated in the centre of professional politics, lack of mass enthusiasm
for parties either as political or as social agencies – all these are axioms,
even clichés, for students of mid-twentieth-century society, and
depressing daily obstacles encouraging many types of evasion for
activists. That such phenomena exist is hardly doubted; their real
meaning in terms of actual attitudes and behaviour, how they came to
exist, whether there was a time when they did not exist, or what their
concomitants are in other areas of social life, are matters less frequently
explored. Already in the period of this study there was no lack of
witnesses who can be summoned to testify that something like these
phenomena was getting worse. Beatrice Webb wrote in late January
1900:

> to us public affairs seem gloomy; the middle classes are materialistic,
> and the working class stupid, and in large sections sottish, with no
> interest except in racing odds. . .pleasure and ease are desired by all
> men and women; science, literature and art, even social ambition
> and party politics, have given way to the love of mental excitement
> and physical enjoyment.[61]

In 1945
labour govt!

C.F.G. Masterman in his anxious way identified gaps between labour leaders and the working class,

> figures like Mr Snowden, with his passionate hunger for reform, like Mr Henderson with his preaching of religion and ethical ideals in Wesleyan chapels, like Mr G. Barnes or Mr Jowett with their almost pathetic appeals to rational argument in the belief that reason directs the affairs of the world, are figures in whose disinterested service and devotion to the work of improvement any class might be proud. But in their excellences as in their defects they stand sharply distinct from the excellences and defects of the average English artisan. They care for things he cares nothing for; he cares for things which seem to them trivial and childish.[62]

Such statements about the working class have been common for almost two hundred years. Less common is an expression of the positive outlook behind this withdrawal, what is meant not just by way of supposed 'affluence' but also in shrewd, perceptive, accurate political attitudes. Because somebody does not listen or does not applaud what they hear, it does not follow that his mind is empty and his mouth drooling vacantly open. Given what is being offered, but even more, given the social context in which it is being offered, the deaf ear may be a most appropriate and sophisticated response.[63] The context was altering in large ways in the early twentieth century, and with it the relationship between people's views of actions/inactions in regard to their social fate, and formal politics.

> States of mind, changes and trends of opinion, among large masses of people are notoriously difficult to ascertain — to catch on the wing, as it were, and to fasten down in plain statements — additionally so among working people whose only form of publicity is talk. The whole of the evidence can never be gathered together, and against that which can be brought, contrary examples are nearly always obtainable. Opinion is fluid. Feeling is mostly unconscious. To try and arrest either is like scooping up water in a net.

Stephen Reynolds and Frank Woolley warned of the difficulty in 1911 but bravely attempted to chart some at least of what was happening. They noticed 'the rapid growth among working people of a political opinion that is separate from, and almost independent of, party opinions',

Between master and man, ruler and ruled, top-dog and under-dog;
the man who has something to start on and something to fall back
on, and the man who has neither; the man who looks forward to a
competency at the end of his working days, and the man who can
only look forward to a bare subsistence at best; the man to whom
failure means bankruptcy and diminished ease, and the man to
whom it means starvation for himself and his wife, and children;
between the man of one tradition and of another, of one education
and another, of one domestic habit and of another, the line of
cleavage runs through town and country alike. *Compared with that
wide cleavage, the political cleft is narrow and artificial* (my italics).
It serves to obscure the issue, and is used for that purpose.

Political feeling, they observed, was not absent, 'for among working
men there is no subject more often discussed than the relation between
"they there starch-collar articles" and "the likes o' us", between that is,
capital and labour in the wider sense; no subject on which they are more
agreed (when they are not aware they are talking politics)'.[64] But it was
not dependent upon, or in any permanent sense organised by, the
machinery and hierarchy of politics and parties, about which it had no
illusions.

The machinery at the top included such developments as the
formation of the Labour Party, finally constituted in Reading in
1918.[65] By looking closely at what preceded it we can see that it was
not so much the climax of a widespread social movement involving
masses taking active decisions about their collective fate in the present
and in the future, although there were still people attempting to do so,
in the SDF as much as in Zoar Chapel. It was an event among other
similar events in a changing political stratosphere. Beneath it there was,
as the main context of labour organisation in its specific local situations,
a sophisticated alienation, an accurate, perceptive and appropriate
apathy. In various ways politics *was* becoming less amenable to local
control by organisations or individuals. Recognition of the fact
constituted intelligence not slothfulness. In various ways the context
of BSP or ILP actions and aspirations *was* different in 1910 or 1918
from what it had been in the early 1890s. Political rhetoric, legislation,
the links between international events and domestic events, the ease
with which organisations of certain kinds could be sustained, were all
being altered in fundamental ways. There was a confinement of
'politics' to a small fragment of people's aspirations, rather than an
investment of mass enthusiasm in, say, the formation of the Reading

Labour Party, or the later creation of a local Communist Party.[66] To
say this is not to romanticise any previous state of things, not to
postulate any time when things were utterly different, but to observe
a process which was at work, beyond the incorporation already
described, and partly as a result of it.[67]

That there was a kind of apathy few would deny from a 1975
vantage point, even if the reality behind the apathy should not be seen
in the terms chosen by those who identified and deplored it at the
time. Positive attitudes there were, even if not the attitudes the
observers wanted there to be. The holders of these attitudes, already
emancipated from ties of deference to a local civic leadership, did not
turn in new loyalty towards the organised structures of formal national
politics. Rather did they turn away from what is usually called politics
altogether, towards realistic cynicism about 'them' up there in politics,
combined either with settling for satisfactions which could be had
without involving 'them', or with deliberate attempts at by-passing
politics via different forms of intermittent 'syndicalism'. What is called
'apathy' is often another name for positive, in certain circumstances
militant, rejections of current structures and ideologies in politics.
Organisations and 'leading' individuals are admittedly uncertain guides
to what was happening beyond them in the minds of the majority.
They are nevertheless the sources which have to be used, but used in a
certain way. Looking at the small size of the presence of early
twentieth-century labour political organisations in Reading in relation
to the rest of the society, only an observer who identified totally with
one particular organisation, seeing in it, however small, the inevitably
growing seed of a future social order, could deny that the proper
context for studying these organisations is one of withdrawal, albeit
sometimes positive, justified withdrawal. Most people were not in these
organisations.

Such generalities need locating in Reading. To resume the local
story: after the 1898 election defeat of Harry Quelch, and in response
to the national defeat of the Engineers in their struggle of the previous
year, there had already been a Co-op./SDF conference in Reading
which showed a turning to one version of by-passing politics.
Co-operative distribution backed by co-operative production seemed a
possible way forward. 'Co-operation affords a more excellent way out
of the difficulty than any yet devised.' The strategy was to build
within, in order to break, existing bonds, by 'bringing the forces of the
commonwealth under the control of a democracy co-operatively
organised'. In that way 'profits might fight profits, not profits fighting

wages'; 'distributive co-operation carried to its logical conclusion. . .goes far to solve the whole industrial trouble'.[68]

Problems encountered by the Co-op. as a social movement rather than as a simple retailing organisation will be mentioned below; for the moment it is the type of strategy advocated at this conference which matters. Fourteen years later, early SDF supporters and trade unionists like Ben Russell were part of a similar by-passing, but this time through a syndicalist strategy, when they took part in the British Socialist Party mission of 1912. 'A bitter spirit of hostility to the government was manifested at the meetings.' It found expression in the advocacy of 'a complete industrial organisation in all workshops and factories with the object of demonstrating that the interests of every working man were identical. When that was done, out of the present system or society would evolve a system in which all the wants of the people would be attended to'.[69] Two years later, after a speech at a May Day rally by the 'Socialist and Labour Candidate' J.G. Butler, a resolution was passed saying, 'we the workers of Reading are of the opinion that the time has arrived when all organised workers should instruct their executive committee to bring about a fusion of all forces into one industrial union, preventing lock-outs and giving labour the power to frustrate any more employers who may set upon the community with their organised capital'.[70]

Such militancy was a direct response to what had happened to labour politics in the previous twenty-five years. As Ben Russell stated in 1912, 'the policy of the socialists was now advocated in many respects by the newspapers that in other days opposed them, this being especially the case in the feeding of school children'.[71] Militancy was, in one sense, anti-political – the other side of a coin stamped 'apathy' or 'withdrawal'. Its leadership and main spokesmen in Reading were to change when war broke out and altered alignments, but it was part of a set of attitudes which would be there and would intermittently surface through the twentieth century. It was difficult to inject any other versions of politics into working-class organisations in Reading in the early years of the twentieth century. The SDF tried, both in the Co-op. and in the WEA. J.F. Hodgson resigned his Presidency of the WEA in 1909 in case 'sectarianism and political flavour is keeping people away'. With the Co-op. the SDF was continually pressing through the *Record* (June – August 1905) for more 'politics' and less chat in the magazine. Esrom, compared to whom few in Reading in this period were more active and, in the widest sense, political, replied rudely in August:

> Personally as regards politics I say with Shakespeare 'write me down
> an ass'. . .Bee (Ben Russell) and his brigade have been preaching their
> own opinions to the proletariat for a number of years and their
> success is shown by the number of their converts. . .as to the
> methods of Bee and Co. they once had a sort of co-operative shop
> of their own. But it did not come off. They sold 'bread and lard'
> there too I am told.

This was a cruel reference to the shop the SDF had opened after their
members had been sacked from Huntley and Palmers. Moreover, the
earlier SDF leadership, particularly Lorenzo Quelch, became steadily
more involved in existing administrative arrangements, in such a way
that fighting the injustices of those arrangements meant fighting, at
least temporarily, a generation of labour and socialist leadership. The
few who had not already rejected that leadership became even fewer
when it was found defending food shortage or labour discipline during
the war.[72]

When Ben Russell noticed how the newspapers had taken up socialist
demands of a few years before, he referred to a crucial way in which
'success' for labour politics involved 'failure' and difficulty. This was a
further dimension of incorporation to add to the biographical
incorporation already explored.[73] An ideological incorporation, or at
least an ideological elision, was taking place by the time Russell took
part in the BSP mission in 1912. The role and situation of particular
organisations in this process was often ambiguous and contradictory.
But there is no doubt about the ideological and organisational strains
and pressures to which a working-class version of democratic
voluntarism and egalitarian brotherhood was subject before 1914.
   Organisations with a different class base and a different ideology
came to insist upon their own definitions of socialist demands like
those made by the Reading SDF during the early 1890s. It was almost
as if society, like medical science a little earlier, and against similar
working-class resistance, had discovered the use of vaccination. Small
doses in expert benevolent hands could prevent large eruptions in
ignorant bodies. So a type of 'social politics' moved into territory
previously occupied only by more dangerous progressives.[74]
Organisations like the Christian Social Union (flourishing in Reading
especially 1906-9), the Reading Citizens' Association, the Reading
Health Society (with the Medical Officer of Health as its President and
supported by leading ILP members), began to press at election times on

the same issues that socialists raised. Edith Sutton, daughter of the
leading local manufacturer, M.J. Sutton, was co-opted on to the
Education Committee in 1902, and elected unopposed to the Council
in 1907. She was active in the Christian Social Union and was to join
the Labour Party by the early 1920s.[75] Such organisations and
individuals gave their own 'from above' meanings to the politics of
social problems – children, wage boards, unemployment, State
insurance, pensions, or sweating. What had been 'stepping stones' for
socialists became buffers for social reformers and men of goodwill,
closely tied to the state. When J. Rabson died in 1936 his career could
be interpreted in the non-labour press as that of a kindly welfare worker,
particularly fond of children.[76] His ideas before 1914, embodied as
they were in throbbing organisations such as the PSA or the Co-op., had
contained elements of a more substantial challenge than that.

A rhetoric of brotherhood and mutual concern came to inform
politics at all levels in the first fifteen years of the twentieth century.
Churches and chapels (notably Anglican churches), professional
politicians of all parties, and many organisations learned the rhetoric
well and used it often. So,

> The Unionist Party wished to live at peace with all men, to injure
> none, but to improve the conditions of all classes, especially of the
> poorest of the poor. In that connection they, as Tariff Reformers,
> wanted to do to their neighbours as their neighbours did unto
> them. . .[77]

So too,

> It is significant, though not surprising, that the great tendency in the
> world of commerce and industry towards combination and
> co-operation finds a counterpart in the religious world. This tendency
> is not confined to adherents of any one church or creed, but is
> common to them all. In the Church of England it began with the
> Oxford Movement, which laid emphasis on the organic and corporate
> side of Christianity, the teaching of St. Paul that we are all members
> one of another. One of the most concrete results of this movement is
> the rapid growth of the CEMS, a form of Christian Brotherhood that
> has extended itself throughout the length and breadth of the land. . .[78]

Outside Reading, but quoted in the local press, there was the case of
one hundred clergymen and ministers of various denominations whose

social politics were so distrusted by more directly political socialists that they had to make a declaration that the socialism they believed in was, after all, the same as the socialism of 'recognised socialist organisations'.[79] It would be a mistake to claim that this rhetoric of brotherhood was universally used. But it was certainly more widely present than twenty years before, and even where it was not shared, a tone of mocking diffidence signalled its presence.[80] Whether because of fears of national survival after the shock of the revelations of the physical condition of recruits to the Boer War, or because of desire for social stability threatened by domestic discontents, or because of education in the facts of poverty by statistical and journalistic investigators, or because of genuine attachment to ideas of corporate concern and mutuality, or because of rediscovery of the roots of social concern in Liberalism, the fact was that much of what socialists had fought for was being talked about from within utterly different theoretical perspectives, particularly in the years of Liberal government from 1906 onwards.

Some sectors of Labour politics self-consciously and willingly accepted this ideological incorporation. They could be proud that such had been the result of committed street agitation away from cosy centres of national politics. Aware of the trends described in this chapter, and realistic about the gap in consciousness between themselves and their followers noticed by Masterman in 1909, they were prepared to settle, at least for the time being, for the benefits which social politics could deliver to their class. If you could not have everything, then to get something from a reforming period of national politics was a beginning. This was especially true of parliamentary Labour representatives.

ILP circles in Reading also defined their own position against that of the BSP in terms of the gains to be won from social politics.[81] ILP language in Reading in these years was noticeably like the rhetoric of brotherhood coming from other quarters. An ILP lecture by A. Broadley in 1912 provides a classic example.[82] Reforms like pensions, workmen's compensation, medical inspection of school children were for him 'acknowledgements of valuable principles of collective responsibility'. They were better than increased wages, for 'a man with increased wages was more likely to remain individualistic, and was not likely to see so clearly that all were members of the body politic, and socially dependent on each other'. Socialism meant 'bearing one another's burdens'. He mocked the old SDF and the new impossibilists,

They brought the Red Flag out into the open in the summer and

denounced society as it passed by or paused to listen to their
antiquated phrases. . .to men, women, and children who were dying
of starvation, and suffering privations, these impossibilists would
say, 'Read this tract on surplus value, you are a wage slave, a
proletarian, you must be class conscious, then you will get the new
Jerusalem'.

By contrast, his own organisation 'was now a great power'. It had caused

an intellectual revolution. Instead of a feeling against State
interference we now had the two orthodox parties tumbling over
one another in their efforts to remould the present industrial system.
More striking still was the change in the minds of the people;
unemployment and poverty were no longer to be looked upon as
laws of nature. The ILP had 850 or 900 branches, with 60,000
members, 1,019 members of local government bodies, 23 members
of Parliament.

Not surprisingly the Liberal *Reading Observer* liked these sentiments.
They made the statistics of organisational size, which the ILP was fond
of producing nationally, tolerable, even welcome.

Similar ideas were expressed elsewhere in working-class political or
social organisations. Aspirations towards fraternity, the diminishing of
conflict, celebration of harmony and mutuality were expressed in many
organisations, including the Reading Co-op., the PSA movement,
Friendly Societies, Ye Ancient Cogers, or the Reading Temperance
Band. They seemed to be a central element in the segment of
working-class consciousness for which such organisations may be used
as a guide. Brotherhood and a 'fair' society, with a place in it for many
social groups and social functions, was being called for by working-class,
as well as other, quarters in Reading. The language is important. 'The
community should not be a mass of warfare, but should be joined
together by good feeling and brotherly love. . .they had been taught to
love their neighbours as themselves and the co-operators were carrying it
out practically, for all employed by them were employed under fair
conditions.'[83] 'The true relationship between capital and labour was
that the employer should get the rewards for the capital expended and
that the employee should receive the reward for the labour which was
his capital.'[84] 'The Oddfellows are undoubtedly doing good work in
propagating the principles of good fellowship. . .and it behoves every
young fellow to join one of the lodges without delay.'[85]

How rhetorical was such language? Was it just an ache in the social arm, signifying no more than the safe after-effects of vaccination, shortly to turn into a pleasantly nostalgic itch? Or was it part of a working-class version of the ideology and organisation described in Chapter Two which, just because it did not come through into actualisation later in the twentieth century, should not be overlooked altogether and which, just because it might have come through into actualisation, had to be actively contained in the interests of those for whom such an outcome constituted a threat? There is no simple answer, partly because the question remains an active one even in the 1970s, let alone before 1914. It is difficult to draw sharp lines, for example between working-class and middle-class groupings in this period because there was increasing ambiguity within the working-class movement. Nevertheless, the emphasis on equality, democratic control, self-production and dynamic development did distinguish working-class voluntarism from the ideology and organisations dominant earlier in Reading. The stress on collective, participatory control as the ultimate objective and participatory activity as the strategy of advance was, however, closer to the first-generation Palmer version of voluntarism than the variety of social politics (statised and commercialised) which relied on legislation administered by experts for the good of the workers which overtook them both.

In the last few paragraphs an uneasy course has been steered between the words 'language' and 'rhetoric'. This uneasy course reflects a similar course in the experience of organisations. There *was* both a language and a rhetoric of brotherhood, social concern, mutual obligation, shame at the poverty in which so many passed their lives, help which did not spill over into demeaning charity. The language and the rhetoric competed in early twentieth-century social life and politics, with the language a survivor from earlier times.[86] The language came mostly from those with a committed interest in the development of a different social order, and the rhetoric was expressed *for* them by those with deep investment in the continuance of the existing social order, modified as it would have to be in order to flourish. The language was expressed from within organisations which depended upon the leisure energy of their primarily working-class membership; the rhetoric came mostly from individuals in possession of formal political or social power or from organisations into which went, by then, only residual amounts of money and leisure energy of their middle-class or professional sponsors. The two overlapped, and speakers of the language obtained formal power over aspects of local government. But that the rhetoric should have come to replace most of the language; that many of those who had talked the language came into positions and did things which clearly signalled that it had become rhetoric; that the language survived only as the dialect of 'extremist' groups or sects far from the seats of political and social power – these developments were not inevitable. To see that they took place at all requires an understanding of the earlier aspirations of some of the organisations within which the language was spoken. To see the process taking place requires an understanding of what was happening to those organisations.

Of all the working-class organisations which could be used to answer our questions the most political in the conventional sense – the ILP – may well have been the most rhetorical and the most immediately incorporated. For this reason some, including Broadley, later left it for more left-wing politics. Although there had been a branch earlier on, the Statist SDF left insufficient space for it in Reading until it was re-founded in 1906. ILP politics in Reading eased the passage of ethical and professional concern (especially that of ministers and doctors) into Labourism. Until the War it was frankly ameliorative, and prepared to modify and extend existing and proposed state legislation.[87] In the long perspective of forty years later, however, even that presence was greatly missed. W.L.R. Crosswell, an ILP and Reading General Railway Workers' Union man, felt that 'nowadays (1950) the workers' movement is too much like a business'. He missed 'the idealism, the evangelistic spirit, and the warm comradeship' of the old ILP.[88]

More interesting here were two rather more dynamic organisations – the Pleasant Sunday Afternoon movement or Brotherhood,[89] and the Reading Industrial Co-operative Society, or Co-op. The PSA started (in Reading) in 1892 at Broad Street Congregational Chapel. It spread quickly, like many other supra-chapel, interdenominational agencies.[90] It was distinguished by its activism, width of concern, internal democracy, ambition, willingness to relate to other working-class initiatives (such as the WEA or the Buffaloes Soup Kitchen), and, perhaps most interesting from our point of view, by the pattern of problems it faced early in the twentieth century. At Broad Street the boast was that the Brotherhood was working-class and male; the regret was that in some of the suburban and later foundations white collars prevailed and meetings were open to the family. There were in fact important connections between later Labour politics and the PSA; several leading Labour activists received much of their organisational initiation at Broad Street.[91] On each occasion when working-men delegates came together to discuss a common objective, such as

furthering the WEA branch, the PSA formed a strong constituency of
its own.

The perspective was one of 'a movement destined to revolutionise
society by the dissemination of the principles of Brotherhood'.[92]
Attendances at Broad Street Sunday meetings, and at others too,
sometimes exceeded 500. It was one of the most successful membership
organisations in Reading. At Broad Street they demanded 'not charity
but the fulfillment of a duty man to man, a duty fully and freely
recognised by the members of a society which urges Brotherhood as
one of its cardinal virtues'. They did not want 'priestism', 'but a healthy
belief in something higher than themselves'. The Secretary urged that
'we are a working-man's society which advocates a universal
brotherhood, and I maintain that there are pressing questions today
which will not be ignored. There are social conditions entailing
suffering on thousands of men. . .to which the PSA dares no longer
turn a deaf ear'. They passed resolutions of sympathy with strike
victims, petitioned on behalf of the unemployed, protested against the
injustices of national politics.[93] There was a constant tension between
the immediate needs of their own members for relief collections during
periods of exceptional poverty and the needs of their peers in the town,
but the latter were not forgotten.

Constant voluntary participation either in agitation, or in building
up mutual insurance and relief against the accidents of life in capitalist
society, or in providing meetings for mutual support and recreation, or
in demonstrating models of alternative modes of conducting business,
worship and social life, was integral to such organisations. Such activity
made the aspiration towards brotherhood not just an aspiration, but
also a comprehensible political/social strategy. More of it, much more
if it, sustained over a period of time and acquiring a momentum of its
own, might have delivered the goods. Or so it appeared. Such activity
amounted to a culture within which the language was understood, and
from whose growth that language might have become the language
expressed in the institutions of the surrounding social order.

So far as Broad Street PSA was concerned the base was to be a
religious movement with a high degree of internal solidarity. After
committee elections in 1905 (with sixteen nominations for twelve
vice-presidents and sixty nominations for a committee of twenty) they
discussed how the Visiting Committee was to 'prepare a plan whereby
the town shall be divided into districts for the purpose of visitation of
every member of the society at the beginning of each session'. Visitors
should 'seek all information without unduly interfering with private or

domestic affairs with a view to assistance being given, or a deeper interest and sympathy obtained by a closer and more real spirit of brotherhood being assured'. Activity was vital 'for the moment any organisation stands still it begins to recede. That is why our watchword is Advance!' Closed meetings, and meetings confined to men, were thought by Rabson to be vital, and at least in the early days he persuaded his brothers. They generated more moral force and energy. 'Should not our almost unique powers of combination be used as a lever to uproot some of the crying evils of the day?', was the question he kept on posing to his fellow members. Atmosphere mattered, the 'real PSA feeling', 'charged in an unusual degree with the spirit of gladness and unity and hopefulness'. In 1898 Rabson was pleased with 'a regularity of attendance and a heart-whole enthusiasm which overshadows all previous records'. He was determined to keep it that way: 'I doubt if any of us leave an open meeting so strengthened for the coming week as we feel at the close of one of our own meetings. I think we are getting to value more and more the freedom, equality, and whole-heartedness which makes our Brotherhood so eminently a personal necessity to each of us.' The meetings had a sect-like strength about them. 'The coming week' when things were going well must have been incredibly full for Rabson and others in the organisation.

Unfortunately the ideal versions of these organisations, struggled for by leading activists like Esrom or Rabson, were losing ground in the years before 1914. It was difficult to keep them alive in ways which would continue to challenge outside society, rather than just serving its need for routinised, Hebraic recreation. If the activity was not of the kind which could be taken over by the State (as could labour politics, the WEA, the Hospital, or Friendly Societies), and if it did not have a viable base in a pay-at-the-gate, distribution-of-goods, or commercial mode (as with football or co-operative retailing), the only major alternative in the twentieth century for a working-class organisation like the Brotherhood would have been a more thorough-going sectarianism than was compatible with denominational affiliation. As it was, leading members (such as Rabson after 1905) were pulled in other directions, (in his case Labour council work). And there was the recurrent bewilderment: 'why is not Broad Street and every other meeting or movement full, or, and this is a lesser concern, why are they not fuller than they used to be?'[94]

The problem was undoubtedly there, and growing. Because the records are so intimate, its dimensions can best be seen in the Brotherhood at Broad Street. There were three main tendencies at work. First, a problem of declining membership and declining participation after about 1907, for which they did not blame economic depression. By October 1910 there were 444 members (the highest figure had been 600). This 'represents a decided decrease on the figures of three or four years ago. The disquieting fact is that the decrease has been gradual but persistent'. Even before that, it was not unusual to talk of the old days of the Brotherhood in Reading, when it was at its zenith. It could get back, they thought in November 1911, 'if there were that activity or interest which is so essential to a live institution'. The second tendency was towards a looser, less socially concerned, more entertainment-oriented, less cohesive type of movement. Rabson had to work harder and harder to keep his version of the organisation central to its nature. Excursions, Bands, open meetings, mixed meetings, the non-political social club-and-institute side of the PSA at Broad Street began to increase. Such aspects of the organisation had always been more prominent in other PSAs in the town, especially the ones founded in the first ten years of the twentieth century rather than in the early 1890s. Each time a mixed Brotherhood was founded Broad Street only gave it a qualified welcome. By March 1911 they were 'taking narrower views of (their) role than the founders did'. A year before they had had to re-christen themselves 'the Reading (Broad Street) PSA Brotherhood', in order to make clear where they stood in relation to other PSAs: 'the object of this change is that we shall not be confused with the many PSAs which have sprung up of late years with a mixed membership, and in some cases with a hazy idea of the principles upon which PSAs were founded.' The third tendency was a weakening of their earlier instinct against centralisation. They resisted national and county federations for a time in the interests of local adaptability and liveliness, only to yield when it appeared that in a weakening context wider affiliation might have a rationale.

Similar pressures, sometimes explicitly described, sometimes only to be detected in their results, can be traced elsewhere. There was a gap, for example, between what the Co-op. could achieve as a set of retail shops, and what it could achieve as the kind of organisation it aspired to be. Sales shot up (1897 – £48,000; 1911 – £159,814). So did membership (1894 – 3,304; 1911 – 9,644). But the familiar complaint was made: 'the interests of our members in the Co-operative movement was small. There was a great difference between a Co-operative member and a Co-operator.' The tone of activists speaking of their fellow members was not that of men successfully part of a dynamic movement. Instead, there was talk of 'sleeping sickness', 'there appeared to be the same lack of enthusiasm not only with regard to politics, but also religion and everything else'.[95] A tone of resignation crept in: 'people want everything done for them now. . .I bewail the torpor and apathy of the workers. . .but. . .you cannot get away from it.'[96]

The detail of the aspiration, the experience, and the reaction to the experience can, in this case, be traced through surviving volumes of the *Reading Co-operative Record* for the period 1899 to 1905. The *Record* was brilliantly edited from its beginning to 1894 by Esrom. A contemporary referred to it in 1900 as 'really the smartest little monthly of the movement, and quite a miniature *Clarion, Pick-Me-Up* and *Tit-Bits* rolled into one'. The Co-op. in Reading (founded in 1860) was trying to be a mass working-class membership organisation, appealing not just to the upper strata of the class, and aiming at nothing less than total 'social salvation'. Capital, they thought, was combining in cartels and limited companies. The working class, which produced the wealth of the nation, should therefore combine in co-operative societies. These should distribute goods, preferably the whole range of goods needed by members (including houses). But they should also buy goods supplied by the national Co-operative Wholesale Society which, in turn, should preferably manufacture the whole range of goods needed by stores and members. The perspective in its most developed form envisaged co-operation employing and supplying the whole working class and spreading its modes through the rest of society. Meanwhile the agency towards such a dream (which was, of course, more powerfully present in the pages of the *Record* than in every shopper's head) should be local, federated to other societies, and as missionary to outlying regions as any church or chapel, but proudly and deliberately local. It should also be democratic, not dependent upon the patronage of any outside 'vice-presidential' stratum, and a centre for a wide range of inter-connected and participatory agencies, each serving the overall purpose rather than distracting from it.

From a 1976 standpoint the extent to which the aspiration was embodied in organisation is perhaps more remarkable than the extent to which it was not. The overall enterprise was growing, and therefore seemed to have no finite limits. There was a remarkable penumbra around the main business of the Society — the shops and the governing meetings of members. This included reading groups, a cricket club, a regular prize essay competition on aspects of co-operation (for employees), children's classes, a Womens' Guild, sick requisites for members, legal advice, a savings club (along the lines of an enlarged Christmas Club at a corner-shop), a choir, the *Record* itself, propaganda

and missionary meetings with accompanying self-produced
entertainment (songs, comic recitals, etc.), rambles, tea meetings and
soirées. The parts of the penumbra were related to each other, and the
whole operation was related to other working-class initiatives, with the
activities of the WEA, the Hospital's financial problems, the Buffaloes
Soup Kitchen, and Friendly Societies receiving attention in the *Record*
alongside the Co-op. itself. Rambles to the new reservoir at Tilehurst,
to the Gas Works, the Sewage Plant, as well as into the country, were
'actuated by a desire to increase the knowledge and information of
their members and friends regarding local institutions'. According to its
chief advocate, the Choir was designed to be of the 'kind which shall
have an ennobling influence on men's characters, which shall
demonstrate to them "the harmony of Co-operative effort", and prepare
them for the ideal of substituting a Co-operative commonwealth for the
present competitive commercialism'. When a 'Hobbies and Pastimes'
exhibition was suggested in 1905, it was not just for passing the time.
'The object would be the encouragement of art and industry at home
amongst the members, as most people are better off for having some
inclination to art and industry for their own sakes, rather than for
mere monetary rewards.'[97] Elections for a quarter of the Committee
took place every quarter, with contests in almost every case and with
voting (until the early twentieth century) taking place through
attendance at a meeting rather than in the decentralised points of
distribution, i.e. casually, whilst shopping. The effort was to get
everyone to join and participate in a range of activities. In this way
local social leaders, commercial and passive forms of entertainment,
competitive forms of manufacture and distribution, and State control
over social life would be made redundant. They would learn to do for
themselves what others had previously done for them, or were
threatening to take over.

The aspiration, and the activity achieved, make a modern reader
stretch tiredly towards his weekend or annual holiday. Esrom himself
wrote all about it in the *Record*, did much of it himself (serving on the
Committee, speaking, singing and entertaining at meetings), was active
elsewhere – in the Athletic Club, Ye Ancient Cogers, the Foresters, as
well as finding time to go on long walks, bicycle, and know a lot about
flowers.

But the leading participants were not satisfied. For one thing, they
knew about the constraints on organisations seeking to appeal to the
working class and to become *of* the class. They knew, for example, that
overtime stopped people coming to meetings. They knew how 'the

barest necessities of life absorb all that a working man can earn'. They
knew the penalties of what they were trying to do in society as then
constituted. They wanted to include everyone. They also did not want
to exploit the poorest classes, which meant not buying (in order to
re-sell cheaply) the cheapest goods. But the poor could not afford to
buy more than the cheapest goods. So at different times during this
period lower dividends, less elaborate buildings, lower prices, better
Club schemes (letting members spread their payments for more
expensive items over weeks when they wanted less), were suggested.[98]
'The great majority of women among the working-class when they go
a-shopping are ruled by *prices. Just quantity,* and *honest quality* are of
very secondary importance; they *know* they can get a pound or a yard
of this at a *lower price* at "Cutem, Litewate, Dultrate & Co's" than
they can at the Stores. That's enough for them, because they've got to
make eighteen bob or a pound do the purchasing of thirty bob or £2
in most cases...'[99]

In April 1904 the Education Secretary wrote a paper deploring the
fact that only the better-paid artisans could play a full part in their
Society. There was no easy way out, although he thought better display
in the stores might help. 'No tampering with entrance fees and
inauguration of easy methods of joining the Societies would augment
the wages of such as could not afford many of the high prices charged
for articles of food.' The only way, he thought, to reduce prices was
for the Divi. to go down, and for the Co-op. nationally to make capital
available for their stores at four per cent rather than the existing five
per cent loans.[100] This might enable new strata to participate.

The Society was also experiencing a process as well as a situation of
strain as time went on. In the longer, twentieth-century term it
survived, as did the WEA. But as what? It survived as a mass, even
expanding, organisation but with many of its functions and aspirations
atrophied, statised or commercialised. From a mid-twentieth-century
perspective the membership mode of relating to the organisation has
almost wholly given way to the pay-at-the-gate mode following the
introduction of trading stamps. There is intense pressure towards
rationalisation, centralisation and merger from Beeching-style national
bosses. That the organisation has survived at all as an organisation with
faculties other than a memory, has largely to do with the fact that it
has a viable base, now become the whole, in the distribution of
commodities.

The spreading of this base was noticed and deplored during the late
nineteenth and early twentieth centuries. The Committee of the Society

exercised a watchful eye on Esrom, in case his lively pen strayed into territory (like religion or politics) considered likely to lose customers. After one issue, sub-edited in Esrom's absence by 'Observer' (probably J. Rabson), went too far in a socialist direction, all subsequent copy had to be vetted by a Committee censor. Esrom had already been stopped from writing the advertisements, by the Trade sub-committee, which made them less distinctly Co-operative and ideological in flavour. Esrom was ground between two millstones; to his left were the SDF state socialists trying to penetrate the Co-op. (Ben Russel, J.F. Hodgson *et al.*). They attacked the *Record* in such a way as to push Esrom further to the right, into the hands of his increasingly business-oriented Committee. In July 1906 Ben Russell complained that 'the trade "puffs" had encroached on the eight pages given over to literary matter'. There had, he thought, been a decreasing amount of political education in the paper. 'This constant trying to say only what will pass without any comment, i.e. trying to please everybody, has reduced the writers to say nothing in particular.' The number of advertisements increased considerably after April 1903.

This process was not just a matter of free choice. Even more than Huntley and Palmers, they were victim as well as villain. The Co-op. felt itself to be under active pressure from the competitive, capitalist manufacturing and retailing world. The low wages, willingness to compromise on quality, deceitful advertising, and concentration on packaging which characterised this commercial world forced a competitive situation on to the Co-op. which became more intense the more they tried to appeal to a wider section of the working class. The Co-operative Wholesale Society faced a boycott from suppliers in 1902 which was identified in the *Record* as part of a more general counter-attack on working-class organisation in the political, economic, as well as in the retailing, sector.[101] The trouble was that the more the Co-op. was tempted to adapt to this context the more it risked losing the distinctive features which would have enabled it to stick to a separate path. This was why ideologues in the movement worried about what seemed to them to be insufficient attendance at meetings, lack of support for educational efforts, and low polls in Committee elections.[102] There seemed to be penalties inherent in size and success, in society as then constituted. 'It is strange', wrote 'Observer' in August 1901, 'that from a commercial point of view alone, co-operators, many of them at least, cannot see the necessity of definite and strenuous efforts to counteract the influence of the millions of pounds spent yearly by the private traders in advertising, and surely no better way of doing it can be found than by spreading a knowledge of the Co-operative principles of justice and fair dealing, and the advantage to be derived from mutual effort, directed by common consent toward the improvement in the position, not of individuals, but of a whole class'.

Esrom and 'Observer' understood some of the key features in the changing context within which the Co-op. and other organisations had to work. They felt, and could articulate, the intensity of pressure from private traders and chain stores, and tried to rally the small shopkeeper to their side against big multiples. They, and others in the Society, felt that a whole context of discouragement of voluntarism was taking shape. 'People want everything done for them now.' This they understood to be partly the result of new styles in the leisure industry creating a 'spectatorate', new styles in the 'new press' leading to a centralised manufacturing of opinions, gambling, and 'glaring gas-lights, flaunting banners, mammoth boards with giant letters, floods of puffing circulars, extraordinary presents, unlimited credit, every artifice that the cunning of devil or man can devise....'[103] Co-operators also distrusted the increasing presence of the State, and of mechanically devised change from above as the correct way forward. At a meeting in June 1901 a speaker 'on education...strongly urged the workers to stand up for themselves enthusiastically as it was an undoubted fact that the Government intended to strike at the people's own schools managed by themselves'.

Much that was good had happened. The improved position of the working class in Reading as an interest group in relation to local government, national government, employers and retailers was undeniable. The official formation of the Reading Labour Party in 1918, with all its officers trade unionists and many of them Brotherhood, Friendly Society or Co-op. men, was to be a major milestone in this improvement.[104] There need be no nostalgia for earlier versions of the proper relationship between leaders and led. But that the end product in wider terms was the capturing of a language of brotherhood by organisations resembling businesses or agencies of the State, and its incorporation into the rhetoric of formal politics and commercial populism, leaving organisations which knew the language surviving only as shadows of their former selves and in different (often sect-like) forms, cannot easily be denied. Without the possibility of active, growing, committed 'from below' participatory organisations, the ideologic incorporation which worried Ben Russell in 1912 would go on taking place. In the conditions of late nineteenth and early twentieth-century capitalism, some sorts of organised activity found circumstances favourable, others did not. This was as true in political life as in other subject areas for organisation. An understanding of a context beyond Broad Street and beyond the Brotherhood movement was necessary to service the disquiet felt at the twenty-first anniversary of the PSA in Reading in November 1912. 'For over twenty years to hundreds of men Sunday afternoon at Broad Street has been an oasis in the desert of life's worryings.' But 'why have the suspicion, the ridicule and the abuse that greeted the advocacy of practical brotherhood changed to tolerance, indifference, and eulogy? Is there much more of brotherly love in the outer world than there was twenty years ago?'

An understanding of a context beyond Esrom's own activism, and beyond the Co-op. was also necessary to relate helpfully to his, ultimately evasive, article on 'Good Old Reading' in the *Record* in January 1899. 'Great strides (had been) made by our society during recent years.' But why not more?

> Probably because of the apathy of the inhabitants, and their selfishness. Thousands of our neighbours will talk football almost incessantly, many others go in for gambling, others too waste a lot of time in party politics, some of the latter have been at this particular game for many years, yet are not a little bit the better for it. Others have their own particular fads, hobbies, sports, pleasures or public houses, and the numbers of the latter are in no wise insignificant, or to be sneered at. But overhanging them all, in most cases, is the cloud of apathy and indifference to the collective good. So many of our fellows pass away their time in dreaminess as though they were mentally chloroformed. Often when there is a vacancy on the local parliament a self-seeking somebody comes out, and goes in. Nobody offers to contest his right, or to question his ability. Possibly the political parties have squared matters to their own satisfaction. A man in Reading may have brains, capacity, education, enthusiasm, or many other good qualities, natural or acquired, but unless he has 'oof', or a suave and 'kidding' tongue, his services are not, as a rule, sought for by the Burgesses of this borough.

11 CONCLUSIONS AND DIRECTIONS FOR FURTHER WORK

As minister of Trinity Congregational Chapel, the Rev. Ambrose Shepherd was one of the most active religious spokesmen in Reading in the early 1890s. He ran a chapel which flourished. Trinity grew to be an organisation with many sub-agencies and a £2,000 a year budget.[1] Shepherd started life as a 'common factory worker in one of the large industrial towns co-terminous with the city of Manchester'. He was deeply concerned for 'the political interests of the people'. 'I am from the workers', he wrote, 'and their hurt is my hurt'.[2]

By 1902, a few years after he left Reading, he had become bitterly disappointed. He had been keenly aware of how poverty and snobbishness restricted the class composition of his congregation at Trinity. Later, he returned to remind Park Institute Congregational Chapel that they should try to be for the working class as well as for other social groups. By the time he wrote *The Gospel and Social Questions* (1902) there had been, he thought, 'a huge breakdown of the hopes and efforts of genuine reformers'. Collapse stemmed from 'the failure of the masses to rise to their opportunities'. His language was bitter, echoing that of others in the culture less high-minded than he:

the truth is. . .that the overwhelming majority of the masses of the people no more want the economic ideals of the 'Labour Programme' than either the classes or the masses want the distinctive message of the Church. Find them a religion that can make them sober without giving up the drink, that can give them clean lives without self-struggle, that can make them do well without ceasing to do evil, and they will accept it with acclamation. . .The class that Karl Marx defined as a nation do not, to any large extent, want a land of promise that can be entered only through aspiration, struggle and self-sacrifice; give them the means to drink and bet, and they have no serious quarrel with what their labour leaders describe as the bondage of Egypt.

Addressing those who attacked the churches for not being alive to the labour movement he asked, 'in what sense indeed has the Labour Propaganda, which Mr Hall Caine characterises as "profoundly religious" in its nature, been more effective with the workers than the efforts of

the despised Churches?' There was no sense here of a political
band wagon taking over from religion; all worthwhile wagons were
bogged down in the 'sodden apathy' of the workers.

Shepherd held 'no brief for the churches'. He did not want to shield
them from rebuke. But he was desperately sure, 'with no bated breath
and with no whispered humbleness', that the root cause of the situation
lay with the workers themselves. 'Surely we have a right to look for
some evidence of character, some assertion of will, some display of
self-respect. They are men and not children.' Shepherd resented the
way in which workers were 'encouraged to put the blame of their own
self-defeat either upon the Churches or upon social conditions'. 'There
are thousands of ministers like myself who find our daily heartbreak in
the sodden apathy and crass indifference of the people as a whole about
their political interests and social uplifting.' Then, in a chapter called
'Hindrances to Realisations', Shepherd made it sound simple, 'If the
Churches do not help them [the workers], then let them forswear the
Churches or establish new and better ones. If the God whom the
conventional churches worship be but a reflection of the class spirit,
such worship is only the concern of those who care to indulge it'.

Does the material in this study allow of such simplistic diagnosis?
Was there such freedom of manoeuvre for demand 'from below' to
express itself in new or transformed organisations, religious or otherwise?
Did changes in organisation over the period 1890 to 1914 happen
because 'the masses' wanted it that way? Did changes reflect what 'the
masses' were 'really like'? Can 'social conditions' be specified in such a
way as to make them an appropriate place, as elements in a whole
context, to 'put the blame'? Were the churches also to blame? Do the
expectations and disappointments of a man like Shepherd become more
intelligible when located, along with their corresponding organisations,
in a particular society changing in specific ways? Why the language of
'sodden apathy', 'crass indifference' and the snarling imputation of
collective stupidity? Such language seems more strange coming from a
genuinely committed man like Shepherd, than from others in the same
culture who were using it, namely mass-market salesmen such as
newspaper proprietors as well as minority culture enthusiasts and
socio-political élitists.[3] Was such language functioning to displace
blame? Was the language shrill precisely because it was whipping the
wrong horse and whipping it alongside others who were profiting from
the horse's passivity?

Shepherd and others like him must, of course, be listened to with
some care. As labourers in the vineyard, they were serious witnesses as

to the condition of the grapes. Indeed, Nonconformist spokesmen in Reading are invaluable guides to critical points in the changing context in which they had to work, even if their understanding had important limitations. The prophetic role, when it was undertaken, produced rhetoric rather than analysis; the signs of the times being catalogued rather than explained. But it was played with an intensity which grew as one of its principal media, the pulpit, declined in relative importance in the culture.[4]

Shepherd and similar witnesses testified to a whole change taking place in the nature of society which was felt to affect their own organisations as well as others. This change was visible locally, and was often experienced in Reading as crisis. 'These are stirring times. . .in every direction they are so, political, social, scientific, certainly not less ecclesiastically. All round us we can hear the mutterings of a rising storm.'[5] 'At the present moment society was undergoing changes the nature and trend of which none of them could quite understand.' It was uncertain 'whether the social revolutions which were coming were going to end in chaos, or whether they would emerge from the darkness to the joy of light'.[6]

As transmitters of wider culture to their chapels (a function which was being taken over by agencies like the non-denominational national press, libraries and schools), ministers tried to break down what was happening into components.[7] They took their congregations on fascinating tours (for the historian!) through social history. 'Sober history', it was thought at the London Street Primitive Methodist anniversary service in 1900, 'has outdone fairy stories'. The preacher tried to react to the bicycle, the camera and new means of transport ('Abraham could travel as fast as my great-grandfather'). Achievements there had been in staggering quantity, but, for the preacher, they had been perverted by an inadequate social system and had benefited the people hardly at all. 'He was convinced that a magnificent material civilisation requires an equivalent moral condition.'[8]

Trams, telephones, letters and newspapers multiplied, affecting both organisations and consciousness. When Edward VII succeeded to the throne in 1901 the Rev. H.H. Snell preached a sermon in front of the Mayor and Corporation trying to understand how 'we are being fed day by day with the extraordinary',

the last reign has been one of unparalleled social change. Never before in the history of the world has there been compressed into a similar period of time such advance in knowledge, in wealth, in invention, in convenience. The strides that have been made in locomotion, in illumination, in the multiplication and communication of ideas have been so vast that we may almost say the panting mind of man toils after them in vain. Civilisation cannot yet be said to have accommodated itself to the swelling proportions of its powers. Lines and wires and pipes, in entangling complexity cover the face and subcutaneous tissues of the land, throbbing and pulsating every moment of the day with the conveyance of living people and living speech. At every telegraph post, and every telegraph receiver, it was possible to tap an overhead or underground Babel of talking. Papers, magazines, and books pour forth from the heated presses hot with the latest news of an excited and progressive world. No one has time to read his paper through before the next edition treads upon its heels with other matters of importance. The physical powers of active and responsible men are strained to their utmost to keep their places in the van of life when it is being run at such a headlong pace. All our senses seem occupied to their fullest capacity with momentous incidents of the outer world. But the most momentous incident after all is the evolution of the inner world of civilisation. And the greatest question — how fares the soul of man in all this? What kind of manhood is being evolved therefrom?[9]

Such spokesmen were disturbed, especially about some of the springboards of twentieth-century capitalism, which they called 'Mammon', 'Commercialism', or 'Materialism', and their effect upon the individual. It was, perhaps, a small minority who felt deeply on these matters. Most ministers were either broadly satisfied with what was going on in the wider society, or were too encased within the formidable weight of affairs in their church to have time to raise their eyes. But the minority had sensitive antennae, signalling developments in the urban environment bearing upon much else besides religion. 'The gravity of the new economic temper which is growing in volume and intensity every day' seemed to them to have particular, obnoxious and novel bases. One was in commercially directed leisure — the connection between 'the modern craze for amusement' and 'increased indifference about the moral and social questions that so vitally affect. . .welfare'. Gambling, 'whether it be gambling on a horse, on the Stock Exchange, or in a raffle', 'the multiplication and sale of sporting papers subservient to betting transactions', was an evil, acquiring major organisational outlets and coming to dominate new areas of previously more 'pure' activity. It requires an imaginative leap to understand the depth of feeling generated in the mind of a man like Ambrose Shepherd, whom we noticed earlier warning about 'Athleticism', when Lord Rosebery's horse Ladas won the Derby in 1894. It provoked him to consider leaving the Liberal Party altogether. It triggered despair, '[I have given] twenty years of service to the Radical cause with no other reward than the hope of a brighter future for the people. . .when I see how indifference, born out of hopelessness and poverty is eating out the heart of all aspirations in our democracy. . .'[10]

The threat of all this lay in the attack upon the individual's capacity to associate in order to control himself, and in order to extend that control over the society in which he lived. The basic conviction, in Shepherd's words, was that 'thought is greater than things'; yet things seemed to be getting bigger than thought. Power seemed to be becoming centralised and yet diffused, and not amenable to moral influence; indeed, the very structures of power seemed to be prohibiting the entry of such influences. A localism, an anti-centrism was asserted against these trends. But there was a detectable feeling that such assertions would not win. The enemy was getting too strong. A reading of Shepherd's letters in the Trinity Chapel Magazine, and an appreciation of the cripplingly manifold town activities which he undertook while in Reading, suggest that he was talking to himself as well as to his congregation when he wrote at the beginning of the *Annual Report* for 1894,

> let us, more and more, make Trinity the centre of our prayers, and toil and love. It may seem at times a very narrow thing to belong to a single church and love it with all our heart. Yet for all that, it is the only means I know of getting into such vital connexion with the church universal as shall really make the church any more than an idea, or our relation to it anything more than a theory.

He was feeling the tensions himself and resolving them by reasserting one direction of the pull. The Rev. Albert Swift argued in 1908 that 'power has become centralised in a measure never before known'.[11] R.H. Sewell (of Broad Street Congregational Chapel), like Shepherd, tried to assert a countering localism. One of Sewell's arguments against the SDF was that they had nationalised all political issues. When he was challenged to produce working men who would stand for the School Board with the same self-sacrificing dedication as the SDF members, he said that 'he knew plenty of working men who were too independent to join a body which was controlled by London wire-pullers'.[12] But, all the same, he felt in his own chapel at Broad Street that 'our Free Churches are tired of their isolation, (they) feel the need of a larger life than any one of them can supply within its borders'.[13]

With the advantage of a longer perspective than contemporary activists had, the social historian can itemise six major contextual forces bearing upon the experience of religious and other organisations in Reading in the late nineteenth and early twentieth centuries. These were: the withdrawal of the local middle-class 'Vice Presidential' stratum from its active, local commitment of time and money; poverty, both absolute and relative in the form of inequality; the increasing expression and containment of an undeferential working-class consciousness; the actions or inactions of religious and other organisations themselves; the growing and altering presence of capitalist ideology and organisational modes, particularly in such areas as leisure.

These forces overlapped; data already used to establish one could, in many instances, also illustrate another. Although they had a particular impact in Reading, they have much wider reference. Although they had a particular collective impact in the hard times of the early twentieth century, they had continuing consequences in later, 'affluent' circumstances as well. Of the six, the last two were overarching factors subsuming others and were decisive in creating a situation less favourable to the realisation of middle-class or working-class visions of mass voluntary action. They will therefore be considered at some length on their own.

The altering presence of the State and the altering presence of capitalist modes in subject-areas such as leisure did not, of course, have all the effects on organisations before 1914 which they were to have later in the twentieth century. Nonetheless their importance is clear in early twentieth-century Reading to the historian, even if it was not clear enough to most social activists, religious or otherwise, to enable them to formulate conscious ideological and organisational responses.

First, the State. Miliband's judgment in 1969 that 'more than ever before men now live in the shadow of the State. What they want to achieve, individually or in groups, now mainly depends on the State's action and support' would have been less true sixty years before, but similar judgments were already being made at that time.[14] The experience of what men were wanting to achieve in groups in Reading in the late nineteenth and early twentieth centuries suggests four main headings under which 'the shadow of the State' may be considered.

First, there were conscious and deliberate demands from a number of quarters for positive State action, or at least for actions which were bound to have the consequence of enlarging the State. Secondly, there were, either as a result of these demands or for wider reasons, legislative and other developments which qualitatively altered the State/citizen and the State/voluntary organisation relationship. An enlarged, and in some ways more accessible State, encouraged into being certain organisational types and styles as ways of relating men to it. It may be possible to speak of the hegemony of these organisational types and styles during the twentieth century, or at least their growing dominance in the ecology of organisations in Reading in this period. Thirdly, this hegemony produced dialectically opposite responses, which included alienation from organisations as such, and a 'sectarian' or exclusive response. Fourth, international, inter-state competition was of growing importance for organisations in some subject-areas. The effect of this competition upon religious organisations was especially striking.

Deliberate demands for positive State action were made in the late nineteenth-century context of the breakdown of negative or 'freedom from' notions of individualism. This ideological change in late nineteenth-century liberalism has been well described in a number of studies.[15] It has recently been shown by Stedman Jones to have had a distinctly illiberal face stemming from a felt need for social control rather than from a benevolent and progressive welfarism.[16] In Reading, groups of Anglican clergy like the Christian Social Union pressing especially upon consumer matters, groups of Nonconformists including the Free Church Federation (1897 onwards) pressing especially on educational matters, groups of socialists like the Social Democratic Federation or the Independent Labour Party (1891 onwards) pressing on a wide front, groups of educationalists like the Association for the Advancement of the Higher Education of the Working Classes (1904 onwards) pressing on educational and other labour matters, groups of poor law reformers pressing on the Local Government Board, groups of trade unionists turning to 'legislative enactment' as a mode of advance alongside collective bargaining — all these, whether they ultimately wanted it or not, were working towards a larger State. Theoretical anti-Statism, in the form of syndicalism and anti-parliamentary socialism, did not penetrate the organised political left in Reading, as elsewhere in Britain, until the second decade of the twentieth century. Such a new direction in left politics may itself be seen as a consequence of a bigger State as well as of independent decisions on the left. Everything that the SDF said or did in the 1890s, in their concentration

upon the representational quest and in their advocacy of State action
on problems like education or unemployment, was working in a Statist
direction.

As administrative historians have noted, 'the nineteenth-century
revolution in government' acquired autonomous momentum. An
enlarging State requires enlarging actions which go against the beliefs of
those who take them, but which need to be taken in self-defence. So in
1877 the first joint action of the biscuit trade was taken, when there
was a delegation to the Home Secretary on the Factories Bill. Thereafter
it was a slow, and on the part of Huntley and Palmers, a reluctant
process which transformed a local factory into part of a national,
possibly eventually an international amalgamation. The nature of the
factory as an organisation in the locality was as transformed by this
process as was the Reading Football Club by professionalisation. A
further example of the unintended consequences of purposeful social
action was the way in which denominational rivalry in the educational
field in the years 1870-1906, especially in Reading in the years 1902-6,
inevitably led to both major denominational interests losing control to
the State, whose actions they tried so hard to influence in their own
directions.

The second heading – legislative and wider cultural changes which
qualitatively altered the State/citizen and the State/voluntary
organisation relationship – to some extent followed from the first. But
it also had causes in, for example, inter-state competition. The main
Acts were products of the 1906 Liberal government, like Pensions
(1908), Labour Exchanges (1909), and National Insurance (1911).[17]
New State organisations such as the Board of Trade Labour Exchange
arrived in Reading (1910), to join other State organisations which were
also to displace older, locally controlled and voluntary organisations.
Since the 1870s the Post Office Savings Bank had become heir to some
of the business of local Trustee Savings Banks. The National Insurance
Act was to be a particularly important agency. The propaganda
connected with it was of a new type, announcing the presence of an
aggressive publicity-conscious State long before any benefits under the
Act were paid in 1913.

The effects of legislation upon local organisations across a wide
spectrum have already been noted. They were sharply felt by the
Reading Dispensary, the biscuit factory, and the Friendly Societies.
They were also felt by churches and chapels, but not because of
anything which had happened to 'religion', in the form of belief. As in
the case of the State advance after 1870 in education, or the advance

in public libraries, so too in welfare legislation, an activity which had been carried on in small groups attached to clusters of other small groups themselves attached to churches/chapels (aided by local middle-class money and bound together by the most local of all professional leadership cadres, priests), was now slowly being transferred elsewhere. An estimate for 1908-9 in Reading calculated that 'official' bodies already spent £27,523 on 'Relief' whereas voluntary organisations spent £8,349.[18]

Cultural changes were also taking place, with implications for local relationships. These were often the result of voluntary initiative but were soon to replace it by public authority at the national or local level. When the 'Stranger' observed Reading in 1810 he could say confidently that *Moore's Almanac* 'may be found not only in every house in the town but also in every one in the neighbourhood and partakes nearly of the same degree of belief in its prognostications as the Bible itself. . .as to works of science, history and general information few trouble themselves about them; and as to religious books, they consult none but what are written by their own sect, or in support of their own religious opinions.'[19] Before 1883, the first year of the Public Library, such a description would already have to be drastically modified. But between 1883 and 1912 the statistics indicate that nothing like the Stranger's opinion could any longer be true. In the first year of opening of the Library there were about 550 readers daily. By 1898 there were 2,000. In 1883 there were 9,000 books stocked and 118,000 loans made; in 1912 there were 59,560 books stocked and 207,674 loans made.[20] Trinity might have been the 'centre of. . .prayers, toil and love', but its library in the vestry would no longer have been the centre of information and reading for its members. Nor would its minister have been a main source for opinions and books of the day.

The consequences were not confined to 'religious' or to 'welfare' organisations. The organised labour movement also had to face the fact that, in the words of a local trade union militant quoted earlier, 'the policy of the socialists was now advocated in many respects by the newspapers that in other days opposed them, this being especially the case in the feeding of school children'. The problem of the capture of a language and its transmutation into State or local authority or voluntary association rhetoric has been discussed above. If total incorporation was to be avoided, adjustment of both ideology and organisation, possibly towards anti-Statist or sect-like forms of the kind embodied in some towns in groups like the Socialist Labour Party (1903 onwards) would

have to be made.[21] Action by public authority presented as great a
problem of adjustment to the labour movement in the early twentieth
century as it did to any church or chapel.

An early twentieth-century historian, R.H. Gretton, called this
period 'the age of administration'. Administration was expensive. The
nationalising of the upper stratum of the local bourgeoisie was partly
caused by the increased incidence of national taxes following increased
State expenditure. Income tax was certainly one subsidiary cause of
the change which Beatrice Webb once singled out as the greatest in her
life-time, the decline of personal alms-giving.[22] Almsgiving amongst the
first generation of Palmers, whose reign at the factory ended in the
mid-1890s, involved time as well as money. Until the late nineteenth
century there was a whole stratum of local businessmen in Reading
who played an active role in voluntary organisations. The increasing
difficulty of getting the support of such men, both for cash and
attendance at meetings, was a fact observed in a wide spectrum of
organisations between 1890 and 1914. Organisations like the WEA
which did not want to be of the 'Vice-Presidential' type, with an active
list of local middle-class supporters, and which could not develop in a
more strictly capitalist/company direction like the Football Club,
showed, by the difficulties they met in the early twentieth century,
how crucial local middle-class support was for *any* organisation without
a dominant national centre, or a numerous enough working-class base.
Even where middle-class money was available and welcome, as in the
case of the University Extension movement, it was not sufficient for
the job in hand.[23] The replacement of local donors for church/chapel
building by national denominational enterprises like the Wesleyan
Twentieth Century Fund was part of a much wider phenomenon, going
far beyond religion.[24] Studies of nineteenth-century cities have shown,
moreover, that the less 'nationalised' second tier of local businessmen
and shopkeepers (the kind who got on to the Board of the Reading
Football Club, as opposed to the sponsors of the Amateur Club) were
liable to be less widely active as local social entrepreneurs and more
cheese-paring than their richer counterparts. In late nineteenth-century
Reading, major local manufacturers were decreasingly to be found on
the Town Council. Town Councillors also had a decreasing width of
commitment to a range of local voluntary organisations.[25]

The age of administration also meant that new social groups became
important, or older social groups became important in new, less local
ways. Reading University, which grew out of a local Extension
movement from 1885 onwards, and saw itself as an heir to Mechanics'

Institute or Literary and Scientific Society work, was first incorporated by the State, via the Board of Trade, as an Extension college in 1896. There was resistance to the domination of the organisation by 'professional students who went there for the purpose of taking a degree', but the resisters were fighting a losing battle. In the first two decades of the twentieth century, an organisation which was to be part of a national system of higher education, financed out of national taxation, was rapidly replacing one which 'had no more vital function than that of persistently striving to be a rallying point [for] all thinking people who were within the radius of its influence'.[26] A similar resistance to professionalisation, this time in social work, was conducted by local agencies like the Guild of Help (1908 onwards). This also was a losing battle against experts, professionals and the State, as replacements for neighbours. Doctors had long been important in the life of the town (as in other nineteenth-century cities), but not in the exclusively professional and medical role which was leading them early in the twentieth century to wrest governing control over such organisations as the Royal Berkshire Hospital or the Reading Dispensary from local lay social leaders. They too were decreasingly to be found on the Town Council. Dr J.H. Walters was defeated in a Council election by a Labour candidate in 1904, after ten years on the Council. The depth of the change was registered in his subsequent speech at the annual dinner of the Reading Rowing Club. There had, he thought, been a distinct deterioration in the composition of the Council of late. There should be 'some machinery by which only men with the very best business capacity should be chosen to contest the various wards'.[27]

The age of administration entailed multiplication of opportunities for activists in local organisations, whether in the Social Democratic Federation, local chapels, the WEA, or Friendly Societies, to become incorporated into municipal or State agencies with particular specialised administrative tasks rather than continuing as part of organisations with more total goals. The 1914-18 War was to multiply these opportunities still further. The Reading WEA registered one of the changes vividly in 1914 by having a fierce debate about the relative priority of taking the opportunity of getting a few workers into University, as compared with being an organisation concerned with the emancipation of the class as a whole.

A larger State meant, in ideology and to some extent in fact, a more accessible and benevolent State. New agencies of social administration sprang up, and impediments like financial qualifications, preventing working-class election to older bodies like Boards of Guardians, were removed (1894). Working men were elected to local Councils as working men rather than socialists, in Reading from 1900 onwards. Parties competed with each other as agencies of 'social politics', and especially in the case of the Liberal Party absorbed many smaller local and national organisations. By 1902 the revolutionary SDF members had been such 'a very great advantage to the Board on many points' that there were moves to get School Board meeting times altered to suit them better.

But what was the overall effect on organisations of this apparently greater openness? A firm answer to this question cannot be given until more work is done on the chronology of social movements studied nationally and comparatively, of the kind exemplified in Brian Harrison's *Drink and the Victorians* (1971). But three types of organisation clearly became much more important in the late nineteenth and early twentieth century. They were: *a)* specialised agencies of municipal or State administration of the kind already referred to; *b)* pressure groups concentrating upon specific interests and issues, but without the mass 'from below' regional base or the total, almost millenial, perspectives which characterised the great 'moral crusades' of the first half of the nineteenth century; and *c)* political parties which mainly functioned as 'machines' (they were commonly so called from the 1870s onwards) for winning elections and transmitting national policies from above downwards, rather than as social movements allowing masses of men actively to decide upon their social fate from below.[28] There was one other type — the organisation concentrating upon pure leisure provision or entertainment — which had some affinity with the political parties.[29] These types of organisation did not merely become more important in this period. They established a hegemony which meant that unless deliberate and self-conscious steps were taken by other organisations (including churches) to resist their dominance both in ideology and in organisation (say by adopting sect-like forms), they would come to resemble these hegemonic types in important respects. To argue and illustrate this point fully is a matter for twentieth-century research rather than for argument based on the years 1890 to 1914. But if it is at all true that the whole organisational landscape within which organisations (of whatever type and in whatever subject-area) had to operate was changing in these leading directions in the late nineteenth and early twentieth centuries, this would be of enormous importance for understanding (even changing) the situation of religious organisations.

The nationalising process in the late nineteenth century was also mediated through different types of issue dominating the socio-political agenda, and through technological advance. The two were connected in the 'nationalisation of news and opinions' in the new cheap national press, involving the eventual weakening and parochialising of the provincial press. The *Berkshire Chronicle* in mid-1901 became less full as a means of communication between local organisations. Both imperialism and socialism were powerful nationalising issues in the politics of the 1880s and 1890s, both involving an enlargement of the state in obvious ways.[30] Both in cause and in remedy, social problems like unemployment, poverty in old age, and sickness were increasingly products of a national, even an international, situation. Early in the twentieth century it was becoming more orthodox to see them as such. No longer could local activists of whatever persuasion see a Mayor's meeting or a charitable fund as the only, or even the main, solution for cyclical 'distress' or unemployment. Organisations like the local Distress Committee set up under the Unemployed Workmen Act of 1905 were interesting transitional types. Brought into being by national legislation, they relied for the most part on voluntary finance and local membership made up of activists from a cluster of organisations like the ILP or the churches, with wider voluntaristic perspectives. Their short life was an index to the growing presence of specialised agencies of municipal or State administration already described.[31]

Characteristic late nineteenth-century diagnoses of the signs of the times outside as well as inside Reading pointed to this nationalising process with trepidation — fearful of its effects upon the human will and 'the essential quality of manhood — the godlike power of modifying and controlling conditions'.[32] Technological advance did not help either, in spite of a technological romanticism in some quarters that it would.[33] The early Palmers had invented their own machines, and had them made wherever possible in their own workshops. They were fond of them, and kept them going for an economically irrational length of time. Such attitudes were criticised early in the twentieth century; no longer could the factory be that kind of organisation and still flourish. Elsewhere too technology, alongside other factors, was de-localising organisations which had had a leading place in the ecology of organisations earlier on. The Royal Berkshire Hospital, for which many voluntary organisations had worked particularly after the starting of the Hospital Saturday Fund in 1886, was a good case in point. The cost per bed was escalating through a greater sophistication in treatment.[34] Beyond Reading, but eventually to involve the town as everywhere else, the technological advance in the means of communication heralded in Britain in 1896

by Marconi arriving in London to sell his wireless inventions to the
Post Office, was to be a major factor in home-orientation later in the
twentieth century. Wireless eventually became a powerful nationalising
and domesticating agent to which all organisations, whether they liked
it or not, had to adjust. By the 1930s, according to one historian 'the
world was now in men's homes instead of being outside them'. 'The
Englishman still belonged to a community, though shut up in a box,
listening to a tinier box.' There had been by then a clear decline in 'the
old social centres, churches, chapels, clubs and literary societies'.[35] An
interesting portent of domestication in Reading was a paper called the
Reading Record distributed free for a few months in 1912-13. Although
purporting to be full of 'local social views and sound articles of general
and domestic interest', and to be concerned with 'religious, social and
domestic and trading activities', there was a heavy stress on the
'domestic' and the 'trading elements'. It was dominated by
advertisements and home-oriented chit-chat and was much more like
the local advertising 'newspapers' of the 1970s than like the civic
minute-book local press of the 1870s.

Either explicitly against the hegemony of types of organisation
dominant in this context, or functionally related to that hegemony,
opposite or complementary responses were noticeable in Reading
before 1914. The main opposite response may be described as the
sectarian or exclusivist response. The main complementary response
may be described as the home-oriented response, frequently although
not always correctly, confused with 'apathy'. Both responses have
become more central later on in the twentieth century than they were
before 1914.[36] The problem lies not so much in showing that they
were significant minor features in the organisational landscape in
Reading before 1914, as in showing their precise relationships to the
hegemonic types of organisation listed above. These relationships will
be left as hypotheses for research. All that can be done here is to make
concrete the two responses in Reading, and to suggest that the
hypothesis about their connection with the growing hegemony of the
four types of organisation described above is at least worth investigating.

The adjective sectarian rather than the noun sect is used to describe
the 'exclusivist' response because that response was not confined to the
classical subject-areas for sects — religion and politics — nor was it
confined to the classical sect form. Accounts of the experience of a
variety of organisations in Reading between 1890 and 1914 show a
common 'sectarian' response to the magnet of one of the four
hegemonic directions for organisations, especially to the leisure-provision

or entertainment direction. Against the possibility, or in some cases the actual beginning of development in one of those four directions, the following imperatives were stressed in a variety of organisations: *a)* localness of control; *b)* strictness of criteria for membership; *c)* relative smallness of size; *d)* diffusion of participation in the main activity of the organisation amongst all its members rather than having an 'honorary member' stratum above the participators and a 'spectator' stratum below them; *e)* concentration upon the real goals of the organisation rather than upon 'institutional sideshows'; and *f)* intensity in the style and format of meetings of the group.

The organisations in Reading which struggled for these 'sectarian' imperatives, often with initial success but ultimate failure, and sometimes against other branches of the same organisation who had already given way, included the Pleasant Sunday Afternoon or Brotherhood movement (especially the Broad Street Congregational branch), Christian Endeavour Societies, Church of England Men's Societies, the Reading Literary and Scientific Society, the Reading Athletic Club, the Workers' Educational Association and the Social Democratic Federation.[37] On a national level in the late nineteenth and early twentieth centuries, among organisations which had branches in Reading but which could not by any means be called classical sects, there was a fascinating degree of 'sectarian' self-consciousness about organisational matters, such as the best size of unit to achieve maximum collective input, avoiding irrelevant diversions which might achieve temporary success at the cost of real failure, and so on.[38] Such awareness paralleled the much better-known organisational self-consciousness amongst socialists early in the twentieth century, epitomised for example in Lenin's *What is to be Done?* (1902) and in the Socialist Labour Party in Britain. It is relatively easy to show that the 'sectarian' response was significantly widespread, and relatively easy to show that it was an explicit reaction to the hegemonic types of organisation described above. It is less easy to point to the functional connections between sect-like organisations and the development of impersonal structures and complex states which some sociologists have postulated.[39]

Orientation toward the 'home' may be seen, in part, as a deliberate step, by large numbers of individuals and families, to vote with their feet against the growing hegemony of the organisations described above. The development of industries making consumer goods and changes in the techniques of marketing, like advertising in the 'new press', meant that concentration upon the family and home as an increasingly

age-differentiated nest of consumer markets became characteristic of
capitalism. But domesticity was also partly a matter of choice, aided by
inventions like the telephone, the gramophone, and later the wireless.
For the poor in our period it was also a necessity. Ministers anxious
to attract them into religious buildings and agencies forgot that on the
whole they did not even go into shops, let alone other public buildings.
'The poor in cities', according to a recent history of shopping, 'did
most of their shopping of every kind in the street'. Hence the opposition
of the Reading Trades Council in 1900 to a proposed bye-law forbidding
street cries. Such a law would be 'against the interests of the poorer
classes who had to buy at their doors'.[40] The judgment of a
mid-twentieth-century student of leisure in Reading already quoted that
'the majority of the people of Reading spend the greater part of their leisure
time in individual home and unorganised group activity rather than in
provided amusements and commercially directed individual activities
or organised group activities (cultural and religious)' may already have
been applicable before 1914.[41] Certainly, organisations were at that
time adapting their styles to meet the tendency. So the annual
Hospital Sunday Parades in Reading, which consisted of marches,
meetings and public events put on by a whole cluster of voluntary
organisations led by 'the Friendly and Trade Societies', turned in 1896
to house-to-house collections to supplement their revenue. So the new
Halls or Chapels built in the Methodist extension scheme in Reading
were designed to make a public Hall in the image of a private home,
for those whose homes were not quite adequate.

The final heading under which the impact of the changing presence
of the State on organisations may be considered was international or
inter-state competition. This was not, of course, a new phenomenon in
the late nineteenth century. It was novel in Britain during 'the
imperialist phase of the historical evolution of the bourgeois class' only
in three senses. First, in that international economic competition
from other industrial states was ending the advantages and beginning
the disadvantages of early industrialisation in Britain, leading to an
obsession with international competition and an aggressiveness which
came from awareness of outside threats. Secondly, in that this led to a
great preoccupation with 'the fitness of the race' and the strength of
the State or people in relation to other peoples. This preoccupation
was both organised from above on an extensive scale (in organisations
like the Imperial Federation League 1884-93) and registered in
movements, like the Volunteers (1859 onwards), which flourished
on enthusiasm 'from below'. Thirdly, inter-state competition reached

a novel and devastatingly violent climax in 1914, with four years of
world war.

The width of preoccupation with international competition was
manifest in the way so many activities were related to it by those who
wished them well. These included education, welfare legislation, and
athletics. In education, Britain needed 'a larger supply of trained
capacity. . .to enable us to meet the competition of foreign countries.'[42]
In welfare legislation, the examples of foreign legislators, and the
weakness of the physical state of the British population revealed by
shocks like the state of recruits to the Boer War, were crucial spurs to
action. The state of the poor became a matter of national life and
death rather than a matter for individual conscience. Hence the
welfare aspect of the 1897 Jubilee celebrations, registered in Reading
in the Queen Victoria Institute for Nursing of the Sick Poor (1897). In
athletics, the way in which those besieged in Mafeking had turned to
sport was singled out in Reading as an element in their success, and it
was claimed in the Reading Athletic Club in 1903 that, 'if there had
been an athletic club half so successful and so prosperous as the RAC
in every town in the land, there would have been no need for the public
discussion on the state of physique and public feeding of school
children which had taken place in politics in that year'.[43] This
widespread preoccupation with the strength of 'the heart of the empire'
was the context within which sport and some aspects of the behaviour
of both religious and political organisations can best be understood. A
major feature of church and chapel life from the 1880s onwards was
the way in which they adopted branches of national organisations with
a distinctly military flavour as agencies for doing certain tasks, such as
disciplining and keeping within the churches' orbit the post-Sunday
School age-group.[44] Elm Park Methodists debated whether to accept
aid from 'the military authorities' in 1911. A whole denomination, the
Salvation Army, the principal religious invention of the period, was cast
in a symbolically militaristic mould from 1880 onwards, leading to an
Anglican imitation, the Church Army in 1882.[45] Important sections of
the labour movement, from the Blatchford/Clarion wing of the ILP, to
the nationalist elements in the SDF, were also increasingly identified
with the same nationalist and patriotic culture during the early years
of the twentieth century. There had, in fact, been long preparation
before two-and-a-quarter million men volunteered for war before
conscription in 1916. The Bishop of Oxford's letter to Reading branches
of the CEMS, cited earlier, encouraging them to render a great deal
under Caesar in 1914, was not just an example of the supineness of the

Anglican Church. Such a letter could have been equally well received in
a wide range of organisations in Reading in 1914. It was a register of
the active presence of the State in organisational life over the preceding
half-century made sharper by competition with other states.

The second overarching contextual factor bearing upon the experience
of voluntary action in Reading was the growing and altering presence
of business modes of ideology and organisation from the late nineteenth
century onwards, particularly, but not exclusively, in subject-areas
such as leisure.[46] Reading Dispensary became a limited company as
well as Reading Football Club; Reading Council issued bonds after
1881 as well as the Primitive Methodists.

In earlier chapters, dominant forms of religious organisation in
Reading have been seen supplying a range of activities and agencies,
which might be called their range of products. These products were
designed, for the most part, to be consumed in leisure time.[47]

The dominant means of production in Reading, the biscuit factory,
has been used to help define the society dominated by its first
generation of entrepreneurs and has also been watched as it changed
under pressure. Competitive pressures were moving the factory in the
following directions: away from the earlier departmentalised factory
community, away from aspirations for local self-sufficiency, towards
amalgamation in national or international combines, towards centralised
management, towards automation, towards marketing innovations in
packaging and advertising and a change in the nature of retail outlets.
The most important pressure for the argument here, however, had to
do with the product itself — the biscuit. W.I. Palmer, like Ambrose
Shepherd, thought he was making a range of products for the 'great
mass of the people'. In his life-time and for fifty years afterwards, the
vast majority could not afford the products, any more than they could
afford characteristic religious products in the same period. Already in
1905, visiting valuers were recommending a rationalisation of
production in order to respond to new competitive circumstances and
new potential demand. For a time Huntley and Palmers did what,
mutatis mutandis, religious organisations have sometimes done in order
to relate to a wider market. They broke up good biscuits and sold them
cheap as broken biscuits. Eventually, however, the firm adapted in ways
which would be dangerous for religious organisations, but which were
appropriate for those who wished to obey the modern 'laws by which
the business game should be played': they changed the product. The
number of lines was drastically slashed; the quality of ingredients and

durability of the biscuits were emphasised less. They sacrificed quality
for quantity. Associated Biscuit Manufacturers Limited (1921-69)
remained dominant in the 'quality trade', but with products more
geared to the mass market through mass retailers.[48]

There is no doubt that the first generation of Palmer manufacturers
would have preferred it another way. They would have preferred the
late nineteenth- and twentieth-century story to have been one of how
gradually more and more of 'the great mass of the people', as producers
as well as consumers, became part of *their* modes of manufacture and
consumption and embodied *their* aspirations. They would have disliked
twentieth-century laws of the business game. But no one in the first or
any other generation of Palmers, or anywhere else for that matter, has
been tempted towards a moral explanation of what in fact happened,
analogous to Ambrose Shepherd's moral explanation of the alienation
of the 'overwhelming majority of the masses of the people' from
Labour programmes or from churches. No one has suggested that it was
because of sodden apathy or crass indifference, or lack of will,
character and self-respect that people could not consume Huntley and
Palmers' biscuits in the way they became able to consume those made
by cheaper competitors. No one has even suggested that it was a matter
of taste, in other words that 'the great mass' preferred cheaper biscuits
to the four hundred varieties so carefully produced by Huntley and
Palmers. Not even Henry Ford, among his extravagant claims for mass
production, claimed that people in general preferred Model-T Fords to
Rolls Royces. It was a simple matter of economic fact, reflecting what
you could sell given systematic inequality in the distribution of
resources, and reflecting the fact on the supply side that no one was
supplying Rolls Royces at the price of Model-T Fords.[49]

Shepherd was not borrowing his language from manufacturing
industry, although important areas of religious ideology and
organisation later in the twentieth century have adapted in ways
analogous to those described for manufacturing industry. He was,
however, borrowing from — perhaps even anticipating — another crucial
sector of the late nineteenth- and early twentieth-century economy, the
leisure and communications industries. Leisure, distribution and
communications, amounting to a whole 'service economy', were
becoming much more important in the total economic landscape
during this period. Indeed it could be argued that this new sector
administered a kiss of life to British capitalism. Taking into account
developments in this area, analogous to those in Huntley and Palmers,
Shepherd's diagnosis of the 'failure of the masses' comes to look like a

tragic misdirection of ire. He was blaming demand for a whole change
in the structure of supply.

From the mid-nineteenth century onwards, a mass leisure industry
was coming into being in Britain.[50] Its products ultimately included
such items as cheap daily newspapers, the cinema, football, broadcasting
and the car. As a way of 'spending' 'unmortgaged time', shopping
should also be included in its post-1880s manifestations; indeed the
whole leisure industry was ultimately connected with the distribution
of commodities.[51] With the anomalous exception of broadcasting, until
commercial television brought it into line in 1955,[52] this industry had
certain characteristics. It was frankly commercial and often closely tied
to advertising; it was not attached to a nexus of local organisations with
ambitious aims; it was specialised, having a long-term tendency to
conglomerate with other specialists for financial advantage; it was
largely based on a technological revolution as significant for ways of
life as the first industrial revolution; it was subject to the normal laws
of the business game — where individual enterprises flourished they
exploded into very large concerns thereby setting the context for
others, where they did not flourish they tended, as the phrase became,
to go to the wall. With the exception of expensive consumer durables,
the industry relied upon the intermittent expenditure of small sums of
money by large numbers of consumers, rather than on larger
subscriptions by a smaller and more regular number of people — in
other words, it relied on payment at the gate (a spectator mode) rather
than on membership; it encouraged an occasional, 'spectator' and often
home-based relationship to the activity concerned, rather than an
active, participatory organisational relationship. 'To an economic
historian. . .surveying the vast field [of "Mass Entertainment"]' wrote
Asa Briggs, 'the main conclusion must be that the chief theme of the
story is the way in which massive market interests have come to
dominate an area of life which until recently was dominated by
individuals themselves'. Innumerable efforts have been made to
comprehend the results of this phase as a whole, mainly under the
label 'mass society'. Passive 'audiences' have been contrasted
unfavourably with active 'publics'. The growth of the former has been
seen as being accompanied by 'the decline of the organised group',
increasing 'segmentalisation' of individual lives, the growth of
'specialised institutions where one works, plays, goes to school and so
on', and a pervasive 'anomie' which provides a fertile ground for odd
sects and which 'is likely to run to extreme panaceas — to orgiastic
religious movements on the one hand, and to all-explaining,

all-dominating dictatorships on the other hand'.[53]

The mass leisure industry represented economic and social constraint on demand 'from above' rather than reflecting taste 'from below'. Later the industry itself became a constraint. Organisations, commercial or otherwise, aiming to rely on or to profit from mass working-class support have had problems throughout most of the nineteenth and twentieth centuries. Either they have had to confine themselves to the limited stratum of workers who could afford them, or they have needed other class or public patronage, or they have had to provide a low-cost product, sometimes of limited range and quality, or they have had to rely, like businesses, upon the intermittent moneys of large numbers of alternating consumers who drop in and out as finances allow – or some combination of these options. These constraints have applied to shops or pubs as much as to religious and voluntary organisations.[54] An alternative for the working class has been small, independent, face-to-face, low (financial) cost, sectarian forms of association. Such constraints continued to apply long after economic circumstances improved from their low state described in the Bowley survey of Reading. As real wages improved later in the twentieth century, partly because of massive overtime working, dominant leisure commodities like the car or television were so financially demanding that leisure hours were foregone in the interests of wage to pay for such items.[55] Leisure became the new work discipline.

More important than reflecting the constraints upon the expression of any mass demand in a situation of inequality and absolute poverty, this area of capitalist development has tended to ratify its creations in terms of ideology about 'what the masses are really like'. This ideology then suggests odious ways of relating those 'masses' to a whole range of organisations. Suppliers and the context are not responsible for what is produced and consumed on a mass scale; unlike cheaper biscuits, new products and styles of leisure consumption and voluntary organisations are, so the argument runs, a matter of majority taste. What develops is 'what the people want'; thus populism becomes the daily ratifying rhetoric of commercialism. Language like that of Shepherd has not only been produced by high-minded, disappointed religious and political activists. Its paradigms have come from the mouths of powerful context-shapers, against whom the activists' anger should have been directed in the first place – the new types of leisure capitalist, as influential upon twentieth-century life styles as manufacturing capitalists were upon nineteenth. The politer forms of their language are such familiar props on the twentieth-century ideological stage that it is difficult to think without them.

Examples from the newspaper industry, however, may make the point. A writer who had worked for Lord Northcliffe, proprietor of the *Evening News* (1894), the *Daily Mail* (1896), the *Daily Mirror* (1903), *The Times* (1908), and the most significant herald of the new advertiser-dominated cheap daily press, described his attitude to 'the public' thus:

> A creature that slobbered over its bib and cooed with contentment over the results of races which it didn't bet on, and pictures of the underclothes of actresses in another continent, and details of the weddings of royalties it had never seen. . .He felt that the public was like a great ape begging you to scratch it, and he was willing to scratch it; after all, perhaps the poor thing itched.

> A personal revelation had told him that mankind did not really care for politics, but for politicians; not about religion but about comic curates. . .Sometimes when he walked north of Regent's Park, towards Highgate, he looked at the rows of villas that were just running up, and told himself that all those houses were alike, all those gardens alike; thus they must be let to people whose tastes were alike. If one could discover that taste one would be able to sell the same newspaper, all along the row, just as one sold the same quality of tea.[56]

Such a view was a characterisation rather than a caricature of Northcliffe and his descendants, and of many other powerful figures in the history of the late nineteenth- and twentieth-century worlds of 'mass production', 'mass consumption', and the 'mass market'. An inheritor of the *Daily Mirror* (Cecil King) who, of course, boasted that he never read his own paper, dared to say that 'it is only the people who conduct newspapers and similar organisations who have any idea quite how indifferent, quite how stupid, quite how uninterested in education of any kind the great bulk of the British public are'.[57] Such men could not have had a more inappropriate, but nevertheless close, echo than in Ambrose Shepherd when he complained about what the workers did and did not want, their sodden apathy and crass indifference. Shepherd has to be understood as a tragic Fool to the Kings who were partly responsible both for his disappointment and for the whole context in which his type of organisation found itself trapped in the twentieth century.

Before the impact of the mass entertainment industry the context for religious and other voluntary organisations of the kind studied in Reading was more favourable.[58] It was not, however, a matter of a leisure band wagon taking over from voluntary organisation in the twentieth century, in any simple sense.

There were certainly efforts by religious organisations to imitate modes current in other areas. Such efforts caused great distress to those who foresaw the consequences. 'Let us carefully avoid', wrote 'A Methodist Layman' discussing 'Meetings for the Masses' in 1888, 'making any of our religious services mere entertainments, and not cease to emulate, both in conduct and belief, the purity and simplicity of the immediate followers of our Lord. The cause of true religion is God's and we must not dishonour him by a conformity to the usages of the world'.[59] Another Methodist, the Rev. Henry T. Hooper, wrote an important article in 1906 attacking those who wished to make churches feel small compared to political meetings, theatres, University Extension classes and football. He was not convinced that such models were any more 'successful' anyway. They were spasmodic and intermittent, and 'public preaching is held. . .in almost every street and not merely at one central building' many times per week. Besides, he had recently walked past a variety theatre where 'a loud-voiced man was emphasising the attractions catalogued in the loud-coloured play-bill of a variety entertainment'. 'The show was attracting only solitary individuals.' And even if they *were* more popular from time to time,

> what preacher, in the calm possession of his senses, ever does want to compete with the theatre any more than he wants to kick a ball about his church by way of competing with the football field? The pulpit and the stage can no more be in competition with each other than a baker's shop can be in competition with a wild beast show . . .The question is not how to fill a chapel most speedily, but how to preach the Gospel most effectually and faithfully. To argue that the preacher must remember that he is in competition with the theatre which youths in the congregation may have been attending on Saturday night, is just as silly as to argue that the preacher must remember that he is in competition with the grocer's shop in which the young people vere selling sugar on Saturday morning.[60]

It is not even as though the absolute quantity of leisure-time, as it were at the disposal of chapels or their competitors was increasing across the

board. It is doubtful whether actual hours worked have decreased for
most British workers since the 1920s: *la semaine Anglaise* was so named
for its shortness in the late nineteenth century. Now it stands out
because of its comparative length. The period in recent British history
when there was the highest preference for free time as against money
wages was probably the third quarter of the nineteenth century.[61]
Besides, as has already been argued, religious organisation was itself
part of the leisure market. 'The cure of needless perturbation', therefore,
as pointed out by Henry T. Hooper, 'would be found in seeing the
matter steadily and seeing it whole' — in other words directing attention
to the whole change of context within which both religious and other
leisure providers were working during the late nineteenth and early
twentieth centuries. Partly because of the sheer scale of their internal
organisational commitments, the attention of 'organisers' rather than
'prophets' tended to focus on secondary symptoms like Sunday
observance or secondary producers like bookmakers rather than on
changes in the dominant styles and organisation of capitalist leisure
itself or, for that matter, capitalist manufacturing industry, as dominant
elements in the changing context within which they had to work.[62]

Commercial leisure providers (even perhaps the pub) in many of the
forms they took during the second half of the nineteenth century,
religious organisations, other voluntary organisations, retailers and
manufacturers were part of a common ecology or context in which they
had some features in common.[63] These features included: a pride in
local autonomy and maximising self-sufficiency; a suspicion of centrism
even where there had to be a central organisation; and an ambition to
provide a wide range of goods — even to be a little totality federated to
other little totalities, a feeling that their main function (e.g. making
biscuits, selling groceries, providing services for worship, doing sport,
etc.) was set in a wider context of organisation and aspiration, a
resistance to specialisation and twentieth-century meanings of
'professionalism', and a high regard for activity, continuity, and the
quality of the experience of participation. Within that context, there
were dominant directions of economic and social change, becoming
particularly powerful from the 1880s onwards. These directions should
by this stage be familiar. They were towards delocalisation; alteration
or standardisation and specialisation of the product in the interests of
faster turnover and a mass market; an increase in the size, commercialism
and remoteness of the local units or outlets; amalgamation; a diminishing
of ambition so that the experience of consumption became no more
demanding and had no wider implications than consuming a cheap

biscuit; constraints on active participation; and so on.

Out of the public houses grew, for example, the music halls, from the 1850s onwards. In its longer-term trajectory the music hall depended upon a growing distinction between spectator and performer; it attracted large audience-type crowds, and it took off at a time when the commercial star-system was also developing.[64] To that extent, it foreshadowed (and was to be killed by) later types of leisure product such as the cinema, hegemonic during three decades of the twentieth century. But in its earlier period the music hall was more importantly part of, and can help to define, our period. Like other leisure products in that phase, it was associated with a local organisation (the pub) which was also the nexus for a range of other activities. Initially payment was indeed for drink rather than for the entertainment, and in some sense the experience of consumers of the product was, anyway, compared to later products, an intimate and participatory one, having 'a warmth, immediacy and conviviality which mass entertainment can never provide'.[65] Then, during the 1890s, came heavy capitalisation of the music halls, the twice-nightly system, seats for 2-3,000 in one building, chains with as many as thirty halls, and so on.[66] Dominant forms in the music hall industry resembled dominant forms in the later cinema industry long before one succeeded the other.

Interpretation of this particular story, or, for that matter, the facts, remain to be established by research on a national scale. On the local level, it did not prove possible to get evidence on what was happening to the Reading Theatre or early cinemas in our period. But the details of any individual story matter less here than the point that a whole range of organisations was affected by similar changes. Clearly, the experience of some (e.g. manufacturing organisations like Huntley and Palmers) was more determining than determined, at least on the local level. The experience of others (e.g. religious organisations) was conversely but not inevitably, more determined than determining, and, seen in relation to their central goals, more disastrous. There were recurring themes of concerned self-criticism within religious organisations: about selling out to 'the big hall, with its electric lighting, its band of music, its absence of pew rents and its freedom from conventionalities', at the expense of the small chapel; about concentration on means leading to a displacement of ends — means including penumbral agencies as loss leaders, and business modes of raising money; about a centralisation of organisation and initiative, tending 'to repress personal effort, to create in the recipients an undue reliance on others and too little reliance on themselves'; about a false inclusiveness which sacrificed all criteria of quality for superficially calculated quantity; and about a connected increase in the spectator mode of relating to services rather than the membership mode (the Primitives' national calculation in 1890 was that they had 194,000 members but 581,000 hearers). Such criticisms registered dominant directions of development and, with the special self-consciousness of religious organisations, even registered the necessary opposites of these dominant directions 'small Bethsedas worked on unsectarian principles'.[67] It would be as perverse to attribute this whole history to the demand, needs, or moral attributes of 'the masses', as it would to offer a similar interpretation of industrial changes. It is as much of an ideological evasion, and as convenient a smokescreen for the forces of supply, to suggest that the public gets the voluntary organisations it deserves as to suggest that the public gets the industry or the politicians that it deserves. The story has been more complicated than that: the context, including patterns of industrial and political development on the supply side, more powerful.

Voluntary organisations in general, and religious organisations in particular, loomed large on the leisure landscape during the second half of the nineteenth century. The church or chapel, the pub and reforming social movements, which had been the chief alternatives in the early nineteenth century, became even more fertile seed-beds for new enterprise in this area[68] and were joined by a proliferation of new voluntary organisations. By 1908 in Reading 'the question seems to be not so much what there is as what there is not'.[69] Non-commercial buildings resulted on a large scale, most notably and most locally, but not exclusively, churches and chapels. In Reading, the Temperance Society, Athenaeum, YMCA and Foresters all had their own premises. Public houses – in the sense of buildings which anyone might enter, other than state and commercial structures or private dwellings – were a larger feature on the urban landscape during this period than before or since. Indeed the destruction of such buildings in the twentieth century, accompanied by the parallel destruction of many independent pubs and corner-shops, has provided this generation with continual reminders that the phase has passed.[70] Like old teeth, public buildings are being torn out of the urban landscape by speculative dentists eager for the profits on gold fillings.

The public audiences assembled for recreation during the second half of the nineteenth century were probably not so large as they had been for occasional events in the first half of the nineteenth century like fairs; nor were they so large as the aggregate of 'the greatest public audience ever collected' in the heyday of the cinema during the twentieth century.[71] But there were, as has been seen in Reading, large audiences of a recreational type in the second half of the nineteenth century. They were, however, mostly subsumed under the organisational and ideological/moral umbrella of a parent voluntary organisation which regarded them as means to a higher end. Entertainment was, up to a point, acceptable, but only as a means of attracting attention to higher things involving the active and hopefully sustained participation of the audience in something more 'worthwhile'. In this setting, religious organisations had an obvious place. The view of nineteenth-century voluntary organisations as recreational bodies, and the glib analogy between, say, temperance orators and modern pop-singers, only has plausibility from a strictly functional point of view. It should not be allowed to conceal the far more significant differences in the intentions and the experiences involved in these 'recreations' in different historical periods.

Pressures on organisations to allow the means to become the end, to allow the agency to become the main work, or to allow the agency to escape altogether from the confines of the organisation and to become a specialised organisation in its own right on a pan-town or national level, was a major part of the experience of voluntary organisation in Reading between 1890 and 1914. Resistances to these pressures were described above with the adjective 'sectarian'. In this context they were, however, wider than that adjective implies. A loss of spontaneity, a displacement of goals, a diminution of local initiative and local control, a decrease in active participation, a loss of that 'integration' where 'no part of its service was wholly distinct from the rest', which Reith tried to make the new medium of broadcasting embody, were all being felt by organisations which self-consciously resisted, or at least deplored, the pressures of the time, like the YMCA or the Saturday Evening Entertainments of the Reading Temperance Society.

Above all, the notion that professionalism, commercialism or profit were to be the determinants of leisure provision was occasionally seen by some organisations as heralding a social order which threatened both their principles and their organisations. It was the business model of organisation invading leisure which disturbed many activists (including Shepherd on some occasions) at this time of transition, more than the actual activities involved. Not only, for example, did the cinema even further remove spectators from spectator sport, not only did it desecrate Sunday — but it did those things for profit.[72] Such

developments were part of the 'growing materialism of the day'.[73]
Worse than the major entrepreneurs and owners of the new leisure
products were the new middlemen or parasites upon the industry —
the promoters, bookmakers, agents, or 'secondary producers' as recent
sociology has called them.[74] It was these people who made horse-racing,
still more the involvement of Lord Rosebery in horse-racing, so utterly
distasteful to a man like Shepherd. They were acquiring considerable
power not only in frankly commercial organisations such as the music
hall, particularly when massive 'chains' were formed in the 1890s, but
also in voluntary organisations such as working-men's clubs attached to
the Working Men's Club and Institute Union.[75] There was direct conflict
both of ideology and interest between voluntary organisations as leisure
entrepreneurs and the increasingly concentrated 'market interests' of
the late nineteenth and twentieth centuries. There was great pressure
on voluntary organisations to adapt or to sink. The conflict was made
worse for Nonconformity by the fact that precisely the 'same sort of
self-made businessman, who was with lessening frequency to be found
in Nonconformist congregations, and who once would have given
lip-service at least to the general moral attitudes which the Free
Churches commended',[76] was often involved directly in these market
interests.

Voluntary organisations did not immediately assimilate the models
of conduct provided by the 'massive market interests', as some were to
do by the mid-twentieth century. But such models represented an
ever-present magnet of attraction. The reliance on market research and
public relations, together with the willingness to adapt the product and
the relation between consumers and the organisation, which have
become typical of large voluntary organisations recently, would have
been incomprehensible to most organisational entrepreneurs and
activists during our period. But there were already signs of pressures in
that direction, and they were not always resisted. 'In older times',
wrote a Reading Baptist already quoted, 'the church and the world
were in antagonism, today they are merely in competition. So far the
church has come off second best. She has not provided so full a choice
of amusements, but she is gradually widening her selection and at the
present rate of progress should soon overtake her rival'.[77] A better
packaging of the product, better advertising, a sufficiently 'attractive'
programme or building (not yet 'image'), a dilution of the product
itself, were seen by many organisations in Reading between 1890 and
1914 as the best response to their difficulties. The Edwardian period
in Britain was one in which 'public relations' were, for the first time,

coming to mean something other than relationships with individuals and aggregates of individuals. This occurred at the same time as the main manufacturing organisation in Reading, Huntley and Palmers, was also turning, against previous policy, to such resorts. Later there were to be signs of increasingly analogous patterns of activity between rival professional organisers of leisure-time activities within the voluntary organisations sector and within the market-interest sector, such as religious ministers and sporting promotors. This has been suggested as the best perspective for analysing 'the new mass, professionally organised religious revival campaigns' of the late nineteenth and twentieth centuries.[78]

The connections in our period are difficult to make and need much more exploration. For activists in the 1970s they are crucial to unravel, from the point of view of a stage in the process where it no longer excites comment that a double-decker bus should become an integrated, multi-coloured graffitos advertising a supermarket chain, or that a church site on a main thoroughfare should be surrounded (for the profit of the church) by huge advertising hoardings, or that a sport (soccer) should be so clearly allied to the distribution of consumer goods. During the late nineteenth and early twentieth centuries some religious activists clearly had some sense of opposition between their own organisational imperatives and business modes of organisation or modern ways of distributing goods. A sense of dissonance was there in their own minds, even if, perhaps because of other commitments, it was confused and off-centre. The Primitive Methodists may have adopted a business form for their Chapel Aid Association, but they obviously thought there was something wrong with 'a church in which livings are sold like shares in a gas company'.[79] There may have been a reliance in many quarters on bazaars, but, as we have seen, there was some sensitivity about what forms of money-raising were appropriate for what forms of religious activity, and means like raffles were commonly ruled out.[80]

In Reading, business company modes were becoming more prominent in the culture during the late nineteenth century. Distributors as opposed to producers of goods were also becoming more powerful in the early years of the twentieth century. The Corporation itself began to issue Bonds as a way of raising money for the first time in 1881. For a few years after 1900, earlier generalisation about the local business élite ceasing to be so active in local affairs has to be qualified by the prominence on the Council of the largest local retailers. The most notable was A.H. Bull, who came to Reading in

1886, built up a large store (taken over by Selfridges – as Heelas was
by John Lewis – during the 1920s), and who was Mayor for a uniquely
long term, from 1900 to 1904.[81] And there was indeed a connection
between retailing modes and, for example, the Wesleyan extension
scheme, climaxing in the week-long bazaar with an 'Abbeys and Castles'
theme in 1908. 'Originality and ingenuity of setting are at a premium
in bazaars today. It is difficult to achieve something which will cater to
the public's desire for something new.'[82] Other organisations also got
involved with the distribution of goods as a means of survival, including
the SDF with their co-operative store and Ben Russell's confectionery
shop. Distributing non-alcoholic drinks under their own brand name
has been the Reading Temperance Society's life-line into the second
half of the twentieth century. In spite of the reservations of a man like
J.J. Cooper, however, no paradigm case of elision between business and
religious modes and no protest like the classic one in the *British Weekly* of
1891 has been found locally. 'A Constant Reader' wrote to the *British
Weekly* in September of 1891, under the heading 'Pulpit Notices or The
Latest Advertising Medium':

> Dear Sir,
>   I take the liberty of addressing you on the matter of 'pulpit
> notices', and to ask if something cannot be done to reform our
> present practice in the matter. I am sure many of my fellow
> worshippers would rejoice if some other means were found of
> making known matters in connection with modern church work
> but which savour so much of the theatre and shop, that, whatever
> their aim, do most certainly succeed in interrupting that quiet
> sabbath peace which ought to pervade our time of worship. I have
> heard notices from the pulpit concerning bazaars, concerts, living
> waxworks, gymnasium performances, etc., but I think last Sunday's
> experience capped all previous. In a suburban church, under the
> supervision of a young and promising pastor, after some ordinary
> notices as to a coming bazaar, the following appeal was made: 'In
> connection with this bazaar a well-known firm of coal merchants
> have promised us that if all our friends here will combine to buy all
> their coal off them, they will then, in proportion to the quantity of
> coals purchased, do so and so for us. Now, this is a well-known firm
> and I am sure you will get as good coals off them as anyone else, so
> if our friends will kindly take this up and get their coals in this way,
> we shall get the benefit according to the quantity, but to do this
> you must order all coals off our friend Mr – whose address is – .'

Need I say more? What a fine scope it opens up for Pear's soap and Coleman's mustard, but is it not time we drew the line somewhere?[83]

The growing and altering presence of the State and of capitalist modes in leisure and elsewhere were powerful contextual factors by any standards. Powerful prophecy, in the sense of correct analysis of the signs of the times, and dynamic unencumbered activism across a wide front would have been needed to contain or divert such factors. In the particular place and period of this study, their impact was made more formidable by the coincidence of two further factors: absolute deprivation for large numbers of inhabitants of Reading, and the tendency of leading middle-class activists to withdraw from active personal and financial presence in non-business matters in local society. This greatly reduced the freedom of manoeuvre for religious organisations — freedom which had already been reduced by what they had decided to try to be.

The central fact which religious and many other organisations should have faced during the period 1890 to 1914 in Reading was that twentieth-century development was not going to be the fulfilment and embodiment of the local and voluntarist aspirations described in Chapter Two. For one thing, Reading itself was no longer to be so important in Reading affairs.[84] 'Up to the 1890s', said J.J. Cooper in 1913, 'Reading's tradesmen were all natives, but today the natives are in a minority, and many have been superseded by the local branches of vast firms with shops all over the country'.[85] Development of Reading society, or of British society for that matter, was not going to be smooth and continuous, in spite of mythology to that effect. It was not going to be a matter of successfully 'adding the masses' to the aspirations and organisations of the liberal phase of the evolution of British capitalism, of which Reading in the second half of the nineteenth century was such a prime example. History would have been less disappointing for men like Shepherd if this had been the general direction of development. Trinity could then have gone on being 'the centre of our prayers and toil and love', but 'our' would have successfully reached the inclusive level to which Shepherd aspired; Huntley and Palmers could then have developed into the kind of factory it aspired to be (many varieties, departmental, self-sufficient, characterised by long service and promotion from the ranks, a centre for social life and mutual insurance, a local focus and presence, not the victim of national forces and organisations, emphasising quality and durability), but successfully reaching 'the great mass of the people' for whom W.I. Palmer thought he was making biscuits; Reading Football Club could then have remained a club not a business, but also have done the job (not yet done) of making football accessible to the skills and participatory control of the working class; the Royal Berkshire Hospital, Reading Dispensary, Reading University and the WEA branch, could then have remained as local social movements, at the same time as providing medical care and education for those whom J.F. Hodgson cared about; Broad Street PSA, Reading Athletic Club, Reading Athenaeum, the Reading Literary and Scientific Society, Reading Temperance Society, Reading YMCA could then have turned, alongside parallel organisations, into contours on a map of general social development instead of threatened islands for particular strata.

Instead there were, of course, pressures on these various organisations. Some of these pressures already traced were 'from above', encouraging them in directions in which they did not initially want to go. Others were 'from below' — pressures of demand asking them to provide different things for a wider clientele. The experience of the Biscuit Factory Recreation Club suggests that even exceptionally well-placed 'Vice-Presidential' clubs were not satisfactory from the point of view of providing access to sport for wide sections of the working class. However deformed by its professional and limited liability company mode, it is clear that the Reading Football Club was a limited advance in this respect. Esrom and Rabson had other visions of what football might be. Rabson in particular was prepared to try to modify the Reading Club's development, rather than simply to oppose it, by bringing it into close touch with its supporters. They both had reservations about modern capitalist modes in sport. Similarly, the national working-class newspaper most interested in these matters — Robert Blatchford's *Clarion* — had a firm line on professionalism in sport through the 1890s. *Clarion* too had reservations about capitalist modes. But they were better than shamateur hypocrisy and were, at that time, the most possible modes if the working class was to enjoy sport on any scale as players or spectators.[86] There was demand, and it was met or contained, albeit in an increasingly deformed way. So too there were obvious pressures of demand from below on the Saturday Evening Entertainments of the Reading Temperance Society, the premises of the YMCA and the meets of the Reading Athletic Club. These pressures were towards 'entertainment', and away from styles of close moral, physical and ideological dependence upon figures like W.I. Palmer.

A whole alteration of relationship between leaders and led in local affairs was a clear achievement of labour politics during these years, with the non-socialist strands of labour representation (S.G. Jones onwards) playing at least as important a role as the socialists. Activists like Rabson and Esrom were strongly asserting a working-class version of voluntary action which was democratic and egalitarian both in multi-class organisations like the hospital or football club and in wholly working-class organisations. The Co-op. still aspired ultimately to put production, wholesaling and retailing under the control of working-class citizens in a movement which also provided a centre for brotherly social life. What the WEA aspired to be was a clear advance, from a working-class point of view, on the previous efforts at locally provided self-education and literary and scientific culture. Some of the difficulties and directions of containment faced by such advances before 1914 have been noticed in previous chapters. The way ahead was not to be easy, and at times in the twentieth century it has looked like being permanently blocked. Proper understanding of the dialogue between aspiration and containment in the new context obviously requires work on twentieth-century phases of Reading's development. The story is a complicated one, with necessary agents of rescue for mass advance in subject-areas such as medicine, education, welfare or work – such as the State – also being potential gaolers.

What happened in our period, in the interests of the survival of the capitalist system, was a whole change in context for organisations in every subject-area. This change was then ratified wholly in terms of demand, leaving out the contextual forces of supply, in language like that of Shepherd. The change in context involved the destruction, or emasculation, of many of the aspirations and organisations of the liberal phase, and the consequent sour flavour pervading books like *The Gospel and Social Questions* (1902). Capitalism does not develop in straight lines; nor can it realise the best of itself. It generates aspirations and organisations at all levels of society whose full development it cannot contain without being transformed into another kind of system. The tragedy was that 'seeing it steadily and seeing it whole' was not done in this period of great change by potential prophets such as Shepherd, whose organisations were to suffer in the change. There were limits beyond which a society which placed such central weight on local voluntary organisation, on the locality as a focus, on organised will, and on the interconnections between subsequently specialised subject-areas for organisation, could go – if it was to remain 'economically competitive'. There were also economic and social limits on the extent to which most people could ever 'join' such a society. Other settings for the continuing dialogue between the expression and containment of working-class aspiration in subject-areas such as leisure had to be found.

Such a heavy way of articulating the context for religious organisation could, however, be misleading. It could suggest that the role of the powerless victim was the only one available to them, and that they were bound to become mere consequences of consequences.

One obvious way in which such a perspective should be qualified is that the overarching factors singled out above themselves offered religious and other voluntary organisations new possibilities for adaptation, as well as for resistance. Whether the adaptations were ultimately compatible with deeper goals is another question. But there was room for freedom of manoeuvre within the new parameters. For example, in the case of business modes of ideology and organisation in the leisure/entertainment area, churches could and did appropriate these, or even become part of them.[87] The possibilities for 'succeeding' through adopting bingo; or through becoming organisations which serve as pure 'hobbies' or 'pastimes' in the interstices of society rather than as embryos of a different social order and instruments for 'the instruction and building up of saints and the conversion of sinners'; or through taking the advice of public relations experts, management consultants, or advertising agencies; or through asset-stripping in urban areas ...have been considerable throughout the twentieth century. One of the ways of stopping the devil having all the best tunes is simply to act as if all the devil's tunes are now holy.

But, more fundamental than this, one of the six contextual forces singled out earlier was what religious organisations themselves did, or failed to do. What organisations in other subject-areas did was also of course critical. Several ministers in Reading were fascinated by the commitment generated by the Social Democratic Federation, as much as by opposite developments in the Football Club. Directions of development of organisations in other subject-areas, as part of the context within which religious organisations had to work, have already been collected under the large headings above. Hegemonic directions for change in organisations became so not just because of an abstract, system-derived context. The context was itself composed of, and the hegemony derived from, the actions and semi-deliberate adaptations of many organisations in different subject-areas.

What religious organisations themselves did or failed to do was important because it regulated and mediated the extent to which they were the mere results and the ratifiers of the wider context. As Ralph Miliband has put it in a different context, 'facts only become compelling as one allows them to be so'. Religious organisations have a special obligation to disentangle their central, enduring goals from non-essential, cumbersome, and incapacitating historical baggage. They have a companion task, made more difficult by longevity, widespreadedness and earlier 'success', to search for appropriate organisational expression of fundamental goals in particular historical periods. Both tasks depend upon a sensitive awareness of context, and of the type of capitalist society from which the most recent part of their legacy of aspirations and organisations come, and of the changed type of capitalist society and directions of change within which they have to work. Their inbuilt ambition as voluntary organisations makes adaptation all the more problematical, but all the more necessary.

Religious organisations clearly represented some of the best of the society which waxed in Reading *c.*1850-90 and which has been waning since. They were deeply part of a local system of associations; they had crucial roles to play in it (providing plant, hosting groups in their early stages, servicing activists in their early stages, and so on); they put its aspirations in some of their most extreme forms (for example, in the notion of 'something for all and a place for everyone' at a very local level); they contained its most local and most universal of cadres. And yet they were also especially confined by its informing constraints to an unnecessary degree. Elaborate buildings, expensive numbers of professionals, cripplingly large penumbras – from schools to cricket clubs to Lads' Brigades, etc. – meant that (in a society where spare economic and cultural resources were a minority possession) whether they liked it or not they were bound to have affinities with the church as J.N. Figgis saw it in 1910. They were bound to be 'the church of the upper and middle classes, dispensing bounty to the others, treated as a sort of preserve into which the poor come now and then, like working men to look round our well-swept cathedrals with all the "nice" people living in the precincts.'[88] They were bound to suffer an in-turning of perspectives, leading to concentration upon institution-building rather than on external social development. That was what it took, in that society, to run that kind of operation.

They were also likely, given the nature of the surrounding society, and given the choices they made within it, to come to accept subordinate, specialised, particular functions even where they had previously had more inclusive, more ambitious goals. The function of such organisations, in such a society, would be likely to veer more towards particular goods for its members (social mobility, status differentiation, etc.) rather than towards any wider effect upon the world at large. The sheer scale and nature of the operation would also mean that, when its local props weakened, it would have to remove itself still further from any organic 'from below' base by being incorporated into elaborate denominational, and latterly super-denominational machinery.

Even given the commitment to elaborate institution-building, religious organisations also made further choices which aided and abetted developments which were to cause severe problems for their own ideologies and organisations later. For example, they fragmented their clientele into innumerable specialised sub-groupings — divided by age, sex, status and class — and tended to see each sub-group as a separate target or market, demanding separate agencies, meetings, and even worship. This process began with the separation of Sunday Schools from the main chapel communities early in the nineteenth century — 'when the welfare of the poor was no longer a concern of the rich, the instruction of the young was no longer of interest to the old'.[89] By such sub-divisions they not only vitiated any notion of community or common humanity which inhered in their creed, they also anticipated or reflected the way in which subsequent competitors in the mass leisure market would behave, thereby weakening any reasoned oppositional role they might have developed in relation to those competitors and to the system of which they were only the most modern manifestation. They thereby made more likely the Northcliffe-like moralisations of Ambrose Shepherd, as a replacement for critical analysis.

It was not as though there was no opposition in Reading to the general directions of development described here. Those who wish to see post industrial revolution history as the steady satisfaction of progressive demand, and as the story of how more and more hungry sheep looked up and were fed, forget the rams that got caught in the thicket. They equate the survivors with 'humanity', and thereby encourage all to jump aboard the band wagon. Even in this one case, in Reading in the late nineteenth and early twentieth centuries, there were many who worked for a different way. Some (the resisters of professional football, for example, or the advocates of organised local working-class finance for hospitals) resisted in the name of forms which were not the same as dominant earlier forms (although they were related) and not the same as forms which were later to become dominant, as though the working class *could* be peacefully added to older forms and thereby fulfil them by transforming them. Others (the SDF) resisted with an

organisational type, the sect, of enormous potential – a type which will
be likely to play a crucial part in any successful long-term resistance.
'Sectarianism', more loosely used, has been seen as one of the choices
made in the face of pressures towards adaptation by a range of
organisations in Reading. The presence of such a response, together
with its organisational correlates, has been noticed in preceding
chapters. It was probably more widely present in Reading than this
study suggests, because of problems of sources in studying religious
sects across a gap of more than half a century. Zoar Strict Baptist
Chapel was the only sect whose minute books, for example, were
available for inspection. But, among the agencies surrounding churches
and chapels, the Christian Endeavour movement, Broad Street
Brotherhood, some guilds, and to a limited extent the Church of
England Men's Society, have been shown to have had an element of
this exclusive stance. Outside churches and chapels, the Reading
Literary and Scientific Society was another organisation which was
seen deliberately deciding on a 'better fewer but better' strategy. It has
already been suggested that, at times when the business response
outlined above flourishes, this 'sectarian' response is also likely to
flourish as a functional alternative, forced upon organisations by the
counter-pressure of adaptation.[90] J.N. Figgis advocated this response
eloquently in 1910. 'Our first thought', he wrote, 'should be one of
gratitude that so many have left us. People often seem to be regretting
the number of the lapsed; but I always feel more inclined to regret that
the Church is so big, than to be sorry that so many have frankly given
up a profession which is at variance with the whole structure of their
lives. . .In the future we shall be few, but intense. Christians are to be
the salt of the earth, the leaven, and the sooner they give up trying to
be the whole lump the better'.[91]

There are a number of possible responses when a 'sectarian' strategy
does not produce 'success'. The limitation can be inflated into a virtue.
That very few, only the elect, can appreciate what an organisation
provides confirms its significance and deepens its meaning for the few.
While there are undoubtedly organisational gains from this response –
'better fewer but better' might mean that the fewer will in fact be
better – it tends to go with Shepherd-like strictures on the masses, and
the inherent incompatibility between quantity and quality.

Or, more hopefully, the limitation can be regretted, and seen to be
temporary and removable. Apathy can be recognised as existing, but
more as the result of the particular patterns of supply and the particular
structures of power prevailing, rather than the result of the innate

328 *Religion and Voluntary Organisations in Crisis*

moral, intellectual or spiritual qualities of individuals or collectivities within those structures. If the message is adhered to in a committed way, rather than another one being substituted for it in the manner of the business mode, these are perhaps the only two major routes forward available.

The question for Christians is: what kind of a route should their creed and the type of organisations which they want to create lead them to take? Should they blame individuals and 'masses' — preach at them, hector them, approach them in ever more flanking movements through myriads of agencies, loss leaders and the ultimate in systematic visitation — or only dare to do this when they have identified key elements of the social context which encourage or constrain those individuals or collectivities to be what they are? To put the question as it appeared to a writer in the late nineteenth century (since artists were such a powerful source for the idea of apathy connected with the tendency to blame 'the public'), should not Christians identify with Grant Allen, when he could not help 'remarking how much nobler and happier the life of the artist of every sort would be in a free and equal community, where, instead of having to produce work which is often distasteful to him in order to please the low and vulgarised tastes of a wealthy public, he would be able to deliver direct to a sympathetic world the message which his genius and his conscience impose upon him'.[92] Did not the absence of 'a free and equal community' have more to do with 'apathy' than any supposed tendencies of crowds to like simple entertainments? Perhaps the most hopeful response was also the most arduous, to hold firm to the essentials of the message which 'genius and conscience' imposed, to express it whenever possible in aspiration and organisation, but to concentrate on removing the systematic obstacles without which it had no hope of wide realisation.

For Christians, there is no doubt that continual and renewed debate about, and efforts to arrive at, a specifically Christian understanding of the whole nature of the changing society within which 'religion' has to operate is a prime necessity. At the end of his study of *Churches and the Working Classes in Victorian England,* K.S. Inglis suggested that 'the estrangement of the industrial working classes from formal Christianity awaits its Weber'.[93] This is not so. Such a plea implies a misunderstanding of Weber in the first place. It assumes that somehow he has 'done' the 'origins of capitalism' period, and that somebody now has to 'do' the nineteenth and twentieth centuries in the same way. Weber's work is, however, more relevant as it stands, or at least as relevant, to the modern period as it is to the seventeenth century. It will have to be used as data for any Christian understanding of modern 'rational' capitalism and its implications for organisations. How correct is his view that 'religious ethics are confronted by a world of depersonalised relationships which for fundamental reasons *cannot* submit to even the primary norms of religious ethics'? How right was he to follow on from this with the conclusion that 'the more a religion is aware of its opposition in principle to economic rationalisation as such, the more apt are the religious *virtuosi* to reject the world, especially its economic activities'? The result then becomes that asceticism of a withdrawn, passive variety helps to support the intractable situation with which it is faced. Certainly he was right that numbers of 'factors have tended to work against any consistent religious opposition to worldly economic activities'. As the rules of rationalising capitalism acquire their own momentum, routinisation sets in and in the last resort 'every organisation and particularly every institutional religion requires sources of economic power'.[94] How right was Ernst Troeltsch that there is an inherent incompatibility between modern societies and Christianity?[95]

The answers to such questions depend upon an understanding of the nature and chronology of the type or types of society which succeeded Reading society *c.*1890. This is beyond the scope of a study of this type. But such an understanding is urgently necessary for people in religious as well as other types of organisation. The consequences of 'an age which had taken for its aim the accumulation of economic power', of a time when property rights 'swell into something which is in effect sovereignty over persons',[96] are bound to be sharp for such organisations, whether they object to such trends or not.

Prophetic understandings of twentieth-century society, when achieved, lead to situations in which religious organisations have either to ignore them or make choices based upon them.[97] Even the social history covered by preceding chapters might perhaps encourage a more self-conscious facing up to choices. This is slowly happening anyway, as religious organisations are forced to follow the advice given by J.N. Figgis. One choice, put in a deliberately simplistic form is: how much do you blame yourself and how much do you blame the context for the situation in which you find yourself? Once large qualitative changes in the nature of society are recognised, organisations deeply embedded in a particular phase have several choices. If they do not like either the old society or the emerging new one, then they surely have to work for revolutionary change. If they wish to keep to the forms, beliefs and assumptions of the earlier time, then they surely must devote a major part of their energy to attacking and endeavouring to reverse the social, political and economic changes which are leading to the succeeding phase. If they wish to adapt — to choose new organisational forms, new beliefs more likely to 'succeed' in the emerging phase — then they should self-consciously do so. They might wish to resist. They might, for example, deliberately have chosen a 'better fewer but better' option during our period. They might have tried to cut down the range and number of their surrounding agencies, to stop trying to get large numbers of people participating at a minimal level of commitment in some area of their penumbra, in order to concentrate on the worshipping centre of their organisational life, without elaborate buildings. Paradoxically, this might have released energy to grapple with wider contextual factors such as gross social inequality.

There is a way of getting the worst of all possible worlds, and it is a way frequently not chosen, but drifted into. Organisations can stick to the forms and assumptions of the earlier phase (and, of course, human organisations being what they are it is extremely difficult not to), find that they are not experiencing the success which they desire except on unacceptable terms, and proceed to blame themselves for this situation rather than surrounding circumstances. Nothing is more demoralising for activists in any type of organisation than this. The longer such an attitude lasts the more powerfully it begins to act as an independent cause of weakness and apathy.

Even if the particular overarching factors singled out here are challenged on the basis of other studies of organisations over time in other places, it is hoped that the general point about the importance of such contextual factors for understanding the changing situation of religion (and much else) in society stands. Further studies which look at other organisations in specifically defined places and periods of time alongside 'religion' would be helpful. R.H. Tawney's *Religion and the Rise of Capitalism* is not in fact, although it is sometimes taken to be, a study of the role of religion in the rise of capitalism. It fits uneasily into the controversy on the subject dominated by Max Weber, being far more preoccupied with the devastating and unresisted consequences for religion of a defined social change — 'the rise of capitalism' — with clearly identifiable features. Work in Tawney's tradition is still needed, and for the same radical purposes as those for which his work was originally undertaken. But in order to do that work in later periods it will be necessary to find specific equivalents of 'the rise of capitalism' as the major contextual factor. It may be impossible to be as confident as Tawney could be in his definition of the context, but it is necessary to ask, in different periods, 'Religion and. . .what?'

NOTES

The place of publication of books is London unless otherwise indicated.

CHAPTER 1

1. K.S. Inglis, *Churches and the Working Classes in Victorian England* (1963) documents this attempt nationally, without seeing that the attempt itself needs explanation as much as the means chosen or the 'failures' involved.
2. For clear exposition of this double optic, with reference to literature, see Raymond Williams ed., *The Pelican Book of English Prose,* 2 (1969) 24-5, and 'Base and Superstructure in Marxist cultural theory' in *New Left Review,* 82 (1973): for a 'sociohistorical', context-sensitive view of religion see V. Lanternari, *The Religions of the Oppressed* (1963) VI, 301 *et seq.* For discussion of how 'a theory that maintains a continuous and systematic interest in the *interaction* of religion and society seems to be difficult to develop', see J. Milton Yinger, *Religion, Society and the Individual* (New York, 1957) 59-60. For an historian who operates with a sensitive notion of that interaction, see J.F.C. Harrison, *Learning and Living 1760-1960, a study in the History of the English Adult Education Movement* (1961) 155, 172. See also H.P. Douglass, *How to Study the City Church* (New York, 1928) and H.P. Douglass and E. de S. Brunner, *The Protestant Church as a Social Institution* (New York, 1935); David O. Moberg, *The Church as a Social Institution: The Sociology of American Religion* (New Jersey, 1962) 349; G. Brenan, *The Spanish Labyrinth: An Account of the Social & Political Background of the Spanish Civil War,* second edit. (Cambridge, 1969) vii.
3. 'The function of the priest', in *The Sociological Review,* IX (Autumn, 1916) 27.
4. For pretentiously-titled reflections on this experience see Stephen Yeo, 'How Socialists Need to See Themselves', in *The Spokesman,* 21 (1972) 49-61.
5. For which see David Hugh McLeod, 'Membership and Influence of the Churches in Metropolitan London, 1885-1914', unpublished D.Phil. (Cambridge, 1971) and James Obelkevich, 'Religion and Rural Society in South Lindsay, 1825-1875', unpublished D. Phil. (Columbia, 1971). McLeod has 'two points of reference in explaining collective relationships to the churches: the status system and the cultural group'.
6. For a useful survey of specificities of religious behaviour see M. Argyle, *Religious Behaviour* (1958) *passim,* and summary p.140-2: for attempted definitions, J. Milton Yinger, *Religion, Society and the Individual* (New York, 1957) 3, 8-16, 58-9: for a survey of many interpretations, R. Robertson, *The Sociological Interpretation of Religion* (Oxford, 1969). For the status of religion among 'other social variables' see, for example, David O. Moberg, *The Church as a Social Institution: the Sociology of American Religion* (New Jersey, 1962) 349; Joan Brothers, *Religious Institutions* (London, 1971) 84; T. Brennan, E.W. Cooney, H. Pollins, *Social Change in South-West Wales* (London, 1954) 111. For religion and passivity or activity in relation to socio-political conditions, see, for example, E.P. Thompson, *The Making of the English Working Class* (1963) 350-400; E.J. Hobsbawm, 'Methodism and the threat of revolution in Britain' and 'Economic Fluctuations and some Social Movements', in *Labouring Men* (1964); E.J. Hobsbawm, *Primitive Rebels* (Manchester,1959), chapters 4-6,8; Liston Pope, *Millhands and Preachers: a Study of Gastonia* (Yale, 1942); Peter Worsley, *The Trumpet*

Shall Sound: a study of Cargo Cults in Melanesia (1957); V. Lanternari, *The Religions of the Oppressed: a study of modern messianic cults* (1963).
7. Victor Branford, *Interpretations and Forecasts* (1914) 71-2, a section devoted to criticising Charles Booth. By looking at magic and non-Christian beliefs and practices, one recent piece of local research has attempted to tackle this problem, see James Obelkevich, 'Religion and Rural Society in South Lindsay, 1825-1875', unpublished D.Phil. (Columbia, 1971); for an earlier period Keith Thomas, *Religion and the Decline of Magic* (1971).
8. In 'Towards eliminating the concept of secularization', in the *Penguin Survey of the Social Sciences* (1965) 176, David Martin suggested that 'the contemporary decline in religious institutions may be part of the general malaise which is affecting every kind of social institution in a time of rapid social change'. The aim of this book is to be more specific about 'general malaise' and 'rapid social change'.
9. For data on many voluntary organisations put together see W.H. Beveridge, *The Evidence for Voluntary Action* (1949): for a model biography of a single voluntary organisation 'based primarily on the author's own experience from 1947', see J.F.C. Harrison, *Learning and Living (1790-1960)* (1961) 'Leeds: the Story of a W.E.A. branch', 275-89.
10. See the works of Bryan Wilson, including: *Sects and Society* (1961), *Patterns of Sectarianism* (1967), *Religious Sects: a Sociological Study* (1970). In his 'An Analysis of Sect Development', in *American Sociological Review,* 24 (Feb. 1959) 3-15, Wilson includes as one of his three components of analysis of sect emergence 'external social conditions prevailing', 7-9. *Patterns of Sectarianism* is especially useful for building up a contextual view of sect development.
11. For which see R. Currie, *Methodism Divided* (1968) 141-172; J.H.S. Kent, 'The Role of Religion in the Cultural Structure of the Later Victorian City', *Transactions of the Royal Historical Society,* 23 (1973) 158. In an American context, for denominational convergence 1890-1925 see R.S. Lynd and H.M. Lynd, *Middletown: a Study in Contemporary American Culture* (New York, 1929) 315-412.
12. D.O. Wagner, *The Church of England and Social Reform since 1854* (New York, 1930) 98. See also *Industrial Tyneside: a Survey* (1928); Paul A. Welsby, 'Church and People in Victorian Ipswich', in *Church Quarterly Review* (April-June, 1963); A.I. Abell, *The Urban Impact on American Protestantism 1865-1900* (Harvard, 1943); the works by Wickham and Inglis cited in n.13; K.A. Busia, *Urban Churches in Britain: a Question of Relevance* (1966).
13. For example, K.S. Inglis, *Churches and the Working Classes in Victorian England* (1963) or E.R. Wickham, *Church and People in an Industrial City* (1957) or Stephen Mayor, *The Churches and the Labour Movement* (1967). For more successful integration in works on nineteenth-century religion, see Elizabeth Isichei, *Victorian Quakers* (Oxford, 1970); E.T. Davies, *Religion in the Industrial Revolution in S. Wales* (Cardiff, 1965); R. Currie, *Methodism Divided* (1968).
14. Instead of religion being seen as part of the 'cognitive and normative apparatus by which a socially constituted universe (that is "knowledge" about it) is legitimated', or part of 'the fundamental categories through which men apprehend and organise their experience' and how these categories 'originate, survive and are transformed', P. Berger and T. Luckmann, 'Sociology of Religion and Sociology of Knowledge', *Sociology and Social Research,* 47 (1963) 424, Alasdair MacIntyre, 'Gods and Sociologists', in *Encounter* (March, 1974) 68-74. J. Obelkevich, 'Religion and Rural Society in South Lindsay, 1825-1875', 432-3, asserts that 'not only is every society religious, every individual is too. On this assumption, the question is not whether an

individual is religious, but how he is religious'. For a Christian plea for not separating church and world see L. Bright and S. Clements, *The Committed Church* (1966) xii-xvi.

15. For critical discussion of 'secularisation', see David Martin, 'Towards Eliminating the Concept of Secularization', in *Penguin Survey of the Social Sciences* (1965) 169-83: and for other essays on the theme, David Martin, *The Religious and the Secular* (1969). 'To talk in terms of men "coming of age" as if this were a sociological generalisation accounting for institutional decay is as absurd as the rationalist explanation in terms of intellectual development' (Penguin, 181). See also D. Martin, 'The problem of secularisation', in *Encounter* (April, 1971) 72-9. For confident uses of the term see B.R. Wilson, *Religion in Secular Society* (1966); and A. MacIntyre, *Secularization and Moral Change* (1967).

16. For the sweeping judgments to which historians and others have been tempted in this area, see, for example, R.C.K. Ensor, *England 1870-1914* (Oxford, 1936) 527; A.J.P. Taylor, *English History 1914-1945* (Oxford, 1965) 168; C.F. Garbett, *In an Age of Revolution* (1952) 245; D.H. McLeod, 'Membership and Influence of the Churches in Metropolitan London, 1885-1915', 254; E.J. Hobsbawm, *The Age of Revolution, 1789-1848* (1962) 217, 220. For conceptual problems on what is meant by 'Religion', see A. MacIntyre, 'Gods and Sociologists' in *Encounter* (March, 1970) 68-74, and 'A Confusion of Sects' in *New Society,* 9.2.1967. For empirical caution about wide sweeps, see K. Thomas, *Religion and the Decline of Magic* (1971) 173, 'We do not know enough about the religious beliefs and practices of our remote ancestors to be certain of the extent to which religious faith and practice have actually declined. . .Not enough justice has been done to the volume of apathy, heterodoxy and agnosticism which existed long before the onset of industrialism'; for caution in relation to the late nineteenth century, see T.H.S. Escott, *England, Her People, Polity and Pursuits* (1885 edit.) 160.

17. See S. Yeo, 'Religion in Society', D.Phil thesis (University of Sussex, 1971) Appendix, a-h for a first list of indices. Since then more have been collected and are available on request. They will be published in a separate paper.

18. G.L. Prestige, *The Life of Charles Gore* (1935) 274; R.A. Bray, *Labour and the Churches* (1912) 10-11, 64; Beatrice Webb, *My Apprenticeship* (1926) 140; H. Pelling, *The Origins of the Labour Party,* 2nd edition (Oxford, 1965) 131-2; for a thoughtful analysis of the labour band wagon see W. Muir, *Christianity and Labour* (1910).

19. Max Weber, *The Sociology of Religion* (1965) 100-101. See also H. Richard Niebuhr, *The Social Sources of Denominationalism* (1929) Meridian Books edit. (1957) 72; Ernst Troeltsch, *The Social Teaching of the Christian Churches* (1931) 24, 991.

20. F. Engels, *The Condition of The Working Class in England* (1845) ed. W.O. Henderson & W.H. Chaloner (1958) 270; by 1892 Engels was less sure, see his 1892 introduction to *Socialism Utopian and Scientific* in Marx and Engels, *Selected Works,* II (Moscow, 1962) 110.

21. E.J. Hobsbawm, *The Age of Revolution* (1962) 224; see also T. Brennan, E.W. Cooney, H. Pollins, *Social Change in South-West Wales* (1954) 141-3, where reference is made to 'a mainly working-class population recently converted to socialism'.

22. For an identification and critique of this view see Asa Briggs, 'The Welfare State in Historical Perspective', in *European Journal of Sociology,* II (1961) 221-58.

23. Rev. L. Harman, *The Parish of St. Giles in Reading* (Reading, 1946) 89; see also Rev. J.C. Carlile, 'Church Organisation', in *Baptist Times and Freeman,*

28.8.1903 for a classic band wagon perspective.

24. Rev. Albert Swift, *The Institute Department* (1910) 19-20.

25. Stuart Mews, 'Puritanicalism, Sport and Race: A Symbolic Crusade of 1911', in *Studies in Church History* (Cambridge, 1971) 311, 320. The medium was often thought to be inherently blasphemous, Thomas A. Newall, 'Contemporary Comment and Controversy Surrounding the Rise of the Cinema in Brighton between 1908 and 1914', unpublished M.A. thesis (University of Sussex, 1968) 31.

26. 'Reply to the Critics', *Bioscope*, 30.9.1909, p.3. See also 'Sunday Evening', in *The Times*, 5.9.1910, quoted in Thomas A. Newall, *op.cit.*, 9.n.3, 'of all the new forms of Sunday observance that Londoners have learnt to profess in the last 20 years, none is more striking, or less known in more critical circles, than the cult of the evening "show" among the younger representatives of the People. Whereas a few years ago the "sacred concert" was almost the only Sunday entertainment, pride of place in popular favour now goes to the "cinematograph theatres"'.

27. 'It would be possible to write the history of the decline of sabbatarianism in terms of the invention of the bicycle', Elizabeth Isichei, *Victorian Quakers* (Oxford, 1970) 91; David Hugh McLeod, 'Membership and Influence of the Churches in Metropolitan London', unpublished Ph.D. (Cambridge, 1971) 289. For a discussion, with excellent first-hand quotation, of the effect of the car on religious habits see Robert S. Lynd and Helen Merrell Lynd, *Middletown: a Study in Contemporary American Culture* (New York, 1929) 259.

28. G.S. Spinks, *Religion in Britain Since 1900* (1952) 11.

29. Ed. H. Gerth and C. Wright Mills, *From Max Weber: Essays in Sociology* (1948) 21. In 1908 Weber founded a Sociological Society which 'stimulated collective research enterprises such as an investigation of voluntary associations ranging from athletic leagues to religious sects and political parties'.

30. For the *Clarion*'s position on these matters see *Clarion*, 16.6.1894, 11.8.1894, 18.8.1894, 8.9.1894, 5.1.1895, 19.1.1895, 4.5.1895, 22.6.1895, 13.7.1895, 5.10.1895, 18.1.1896, 14.3.1896, 28.3.1896, 2.5.1896, etc.

31. For a brilliant outline of how to study a political party in this context, see ed. Q. Hoare and G. Nowell-Smith, *Selections from the Prison Note-Books of Antonio Gramsci* (1971) 150-1; for treatment of non-consumption of an organisation as evidence on working-class culture see J.F.C. Harrison, *Learning and Living* (1961) on Mechanics' Institutes, 53, 65-71, 80, 127-30; E.T. Davies, *Religion in the Industrial Revolution in S. Wales* (Cardiff, 1965) 92, points out how Nonconformist chapels 'in their own way. . .affected the outlook and conduct of thousands who never entered them'.

32. For examples back to 1818, and for fuller treatment of the ideology of apathy see Stephen Yeo, 'On the Uses of "Apathy"', in *Archives Européenes de Sociologie*, XV (1974) 279-311.

33. *Reading Co-operative Record* (Feb.-March, 1903 and June, 1904).

34. *Evening Argus* (Brighton), 19.1.1973.

35. See G.N. Ostergaard and A.H. Halsey, *Power in Cooperatives, a Study in the Internal Politics of British Retail Societies* (Oxford, 1965) chapter III, 'The Problem of Apathy', 67-102; J.A. Banks and G.N. Ostergaard, 'Cooperative Democracy', in *Cooperative College Papers*, 2 (March, 1955).

36. For inspection of this line of argument see Stephen Yeo, 'On the Uses of "Apathy"'; and Graeme Duncan and Steven Lukes, 'The New Democracy', in C.A. McCoy and J. Playford, *A-Political Politics: a Critique of Behaviouralism* (New York, 1967).

37. *The Recorder* quoted in R. Currie, *Methodism Divided* (1968) 195-6; for another example of advocacy of actions by religious organisations in language

likely to lead to justified non-cooperation see Horace Mann 'The Masses not Inaccessible', in *Census of Great Britain 1851, Religious Worship ... Report and Tables* (1853) clxii.

38. R. Michels, *Political Parties*, Collier edit. (New York, 1962) 86-7.

39. See, for example, 'Centralisation in Congregationalism', in *Congregational Review*, 4 (1890) 151 and 'The New Movement in Congregationalism' in *Wesleyan Methodist Magazine*, CXXXII (1909) 600; for denominationalisation of informal popular evangelicalism in the 1830s see W.R. Ward, *Religion and Society in England, 1790-1850* (1972) 5-6, 'its (the 'new denominationalism's') work in separating the churches from the characteristic religion and characteristic politics of a broad public now became extremely costly. The ecumenical end-product of this process, a single denomination with impeccable Catholic order and no popular appeal at all, is now in sight'. For Beveridge's view that 'the decline in the intensity of inner life is a natural consequence of the growth in size', see *Voluntary Action* (1948) 294.

40. R.H. Tawney, *Religion and the Rise of Capitalism* (1922) Pelican edit. (1938) 17.

41. R.H. Tawney, *ibid.*, 166.

42. I do not mean to suggest that no previous attempts to evaluate religion in this period in a contextual way have been made. For example: E. Halévy, *A History of the English People in the 19th Century*, V, (Paperback edit. 1961) 163-85, 'The Religious Problem', sets out 'the spirit of the age' and tries to measure religion against it. More interesting is Helen Lynd, *England in the 1880's* (Oxford, 1945) especially Chapter VIII, 299-348, 'Religion'. The scheme of the book is in Part I to describe the changes in the period and in Part II to evaluate the role of institutions in those changes. 'Religion' is a section of Part II. Her opening assertion (299) is, 'the change in social philosophy which took place in late nineteenth century England involved questions of the deepest human values which are the special concern of religion'. The questions she was interested in were: 'How free is man to determine his own destiny? What can be the range of his hopes? For what acts is he morally responsible? In what can he put his trust? Are the underlying powers of the universe friendly to him, hostile, or indifferent? Should he rely upon reason, faith, or authority? Upon spiritual or material values? Between self-development and sacrifice? Between body and spirit?'

43. 'History as a discipline does invite grubbing for detail, but it also encourages a widening of one's view to embrace epochal pivotal events in the development of social structures', C. Wright Mills, *The Sociological Imagination* (New York, 1959) 143-4; 'One of the difficulties of an attempt to write the social as distinct from the political history of a nation is the absence of determining events and positive dates by which the course of things can be charted', G.M. Trevelyan, *English Social History* (1944) 551.

44. For example, the results of trade union bargaining following the hegemony of 'open' over 'closed' unions since the 1920s; or the non-necessity of joining the WEA to consume its classes after 1924; or the replacement of the 'divi', for which you had to join, by stamps in the Co-op. during the 1960s.

45. When J.M. Baernreither, *English Associations of Working Men* (1893 edition) 72, 67, thought that voluntary associations had 'succeeded in becoming, so to speak, a new life-blood for the age, permeating all the arteries of the nation and shaping all its thoughts and energies anew'. 'Taken collectively (they) represent a new conception of society in the popular mind destined to initiate a new stage of civilisation in England'; see also M. Fothergill Robinson *The Spirit of Association* (1913).

46. For a religious example, 'A managerial theology applying critiques derived from administrative theory is in being on both sides of the Atlantic',

338 *Religion and Voluntary Organisations in Crisis*

W.R. Ward, *Religion and Society in England* (1972) 8. He refers to P.F. Rudge, *Ministry and Management* (1968), and *Conversations between the Church of England and the Methodist Church: an interim statement* (1958) 19.
47. R. Currie, *Methodism Divided* (1968) 189-90.
48. Arnold M. Rose, 'The Problem of a Mass Society', in *Theory and Method in the Social Sciences* (Minneapolis, 1954) 40; R. Poblete and T.F. O'Dea, 'Sectarianism as a Response to Anomie' in R. Lees ed., *Cities and Churches: Readings on the Urban Church* (Philadelphia, 1962) 195-206.

CHAPTER 2

1. C.A. Moser & W. Scott, *British Towns: A Statistical Study of their Social and Economic Differences* (1961) arranged 157 towns in a typology using 60 variables. Of all the towns, Reading and Worcester were least often in the 'extremes' section of the classification.
2. C.F.G. Masterman ed., *The Heart of the Empire* (1901) 7.
3. E.J. Hobsbawm, *The Age of Revolution (1789-1848)* (1962) 'The World in the 1780's'. The actual figure used there is 100,000. Between 1801 and 1891 the population of cities of 20,000-plus multiplied by 10, while the rest of the population multiplied by slightly less than 2; see A.F. Weber, *The Growth of Cities in the Nineteenth Century: a Study in Statistics* (Cornell U.P. edit., New York, 1963) 43 – originally published in 1899. See also W. Ashworth, *The Genesis of Modern British Town Planning* (1954) Chapter 1, 'The Growth of Urban Population'; R. Price Williams, in *Journal of the Royal Statistical Society,* XLIII (1880) 462-96; J.A. Banks, 'The Contagion of Numbers', in H.J. Dyos & M. Wolff ed., *The Victorian City: Images and Realities,* I (1973) 105-22. There were 22 towns in the U.K. with a population of between 50 and 100,000 in 1841; 49 in 1901.
4. See, for example, D.V. Glass, *The Town and a Changing Civilization* (1935) 2-6, 96, or Ruth Glass, 'Urban Sociology, Research in Great Britain', in *Current Sociology,* XIV, 4 (1955) 5.
5. It might be as well to remember when making assertions of this type that the public buildings of Silchester, the nearest Roman town of importance to Reading, now under ploughed fields, covered nearly twice the space occupied by Reading Town Hall, Municipal Buildings, the Library, the Corn Exchange and the Market, all put together. W.T. Pike (publisher), *In and Around Reading* (c.1910).
6. *The Clarion,* 23.11.1895, 'At Reading'; *All The Year Round* 9.6.1888, 536-41. By 1908 W.M. Childs was comparing 'the individuality of long ago' with the 'dull uniformity of the institutions of today', *The Teaching of Local History,* Historical Association Leaflet, 11 (March, 1908) 8; modern journalism on Reading tends to be disdainful, 'For politicians and journalists Reading is a difficult place to pin down. Like so many other towns in Britain, in the last generation it seems to have been stripped of personality, to have dissolved into an ill-defined sprawl of new office blocks and old pubs, private housing estates and council flats. There are few big institutions to inspire loyalty or hostility', Max Hastings in *Evening Standard,* 14.2.1972. For a lively recent portrait see Alan Wykes, *Reading: A Biography* (1971); see also supplement to *The Times,* 7.6.1972; Q.F. Adams, 'Reading, England – Our English Parent Towns', in *New England Historical and Genealogical Register,* 60 (Boston, 1906) 57.
7. Tosland, *Extracts from the Reading Mercury, the Berkshire Chronicle and the Reading Observer,* no.2, 146; W.M. Childs, *The Story of the Town of Reading* (Reading, 1905); Tosland, *Extracts,* no.2, 143 (Feb. 1895); see also Reading

Literary and Scientific Society, Proceedings (1899-1900) 23-4, A.H. Leaver, 'Vanishing Reading', and *Reading Observer*, 26.12.1891.

8. *Reading Observer*, 27.6.1891. The population figures are as follows, with the nearest estimate of nos. in the factory adjacent in brackets:

1556	c.	3,500*		
1600	c.	4,700*		
1801		9,421		
1841		19,074	(1844 ... 17)	
1851		21,456	(1851 ... 143)	
1861		25,876	(1861 ... 535)	
1871		32,323	(1873 ... 2,500)	
1881		42,056	(1878 ... 3,000)	
1891		60,054	(1889 ... 4,053)	(borough extension 1887)
1901		72,217	(1900 ... 5,409)	
			(1905 ... 6,000)	
1911		88,603	(1910 ... 4,857)	(borough extension 1911)
			(1914 ... 4,966)	
1921		92,278		

*Estimates in E.W. Gilbert, 'Reading its position and growth', in *Transactions of the S.E. Union of Scientific Societies'*, 13.7.1934 and M. Hinton, *A History of the Town of Reading* (1954) 132.

9. P.L. Payne, 'The Emergence of the Large-Scale Company in Great Britain, 1870-1914', in *Economic History Review*, XX (New Series) 1967, table I.

10. For 'the age of cloth' in Reading see W.M. Childs, *The Town of Reading During the Early Part of the Nineteenth Century* (Reading, 1910) 21; J.M. Guilding ed. *Reading Records: Diary of the Corporation*, 4 vols. (1892-6) covering 1431 to mid-seventeenth century; Harman and Brymer, *The History of Christianity* (Reading, 1952) 50, suggests that in 1536 Berkshire was the 6th richest county in England, but by 1649 had declined to being the 21st.

11. W. Fletcher, *Reading Past and Present*, 2nd edition (Reading, 1839) 89.

12. See also Rev. A.G. L'Estrange, *Life of Mary Russell Mitford*, 3 vols. (1870), and for visual aids W.H. Timms, *Twelve Coloured Views of Reading* (1823).

13. The generational transition took place in stages: George Palmer's sons George William and Alfred were admitted into partnership in 1874. Then in 1879 and 1880 Ernest Palmer (Samuel's son) and George's third son Walter were admitted. They were followed by Samuel's other sons Charles (1885), Howard (1887) and Albert (1892). William Isaac never married.

14. *Daily Mail* 20.8.1897, in Huntley and Palmers, *Scrapbooks*.

15. A. Gramsci, *Soviets in Italy*, IWC pamphlet series no. 11, p.7.

16. *Reading Observer*, 7.11.1891.

17. William Mavor, *General View of the Agriculture of Berkshire* (1809) 80-88; see also N. Gash, *Politics in the Age of Peel: a study in the techniques of Parliamentary Representation 1830-1850* (1953) 270; Mary Russell Mitford, *Belford Regis* (1942 edition) 95, 340; when he was elected Mayor in 1847 Councillor Weedon was proud that Reading was 'beyond the influence of aristocratic domination in castle, cathedral or barracks', *Reading Mercury* 13.11.1847.

18. *Reading Mercury*, 30.9.1865.

19. *Berkshire Chronicle*, 29.5.1897 (Y.M.C.A.). See also *Reading Observer*, 13.11.1897 (Football), *Reading Observer*, 4.11.1897 (Town Hall); for the W.I. Palmer testimonial, *Reading Mercury*, 16.2.1884, 21.3.1885.

20. *Reading Observer*, 1.11.1890.

21. W.M. Childs, *The Future of the Town of Reading* (n.d.)

22. *Berkshire Chronicle*, 19.12.1891.

23. For national concern about participation in sport see Stuart Mews,

'Puritanicalism, Sport and Race, a symbolic crusade of 1911' in Canon
G.J. Cuming and Derek Baker eds., *Studies in Church History 8* (Cambridge,
1971) 303-31, and W.T. Stead, *The Revival in the West* (1905). It was a
common theme particularly amongst Nonconformists at this time.
24. The 'great change' was so called by the best existing work on Reading,
W.M. Childs, *The Town of Reading During the Early Part of the Nineteenth
Century* (Reading, 1910). The four features Childs singled out defining this
'great change', other than the obvious industrial/demographic changes, were:
an increase in the humaneness of the population, a better understanding of
the laws of health, wider interests, and more reading. The book was based
upon extensive local newspaper research, which Childs wanted to extend
through collective work in the early days of Reading University, as a means of
developing local self-consciousness. For the Reading May Day Fair which
began the fair season in the region during the 1830s see 'Lord' George Sanger,
Seventy Years a Showman, 1st edition 1910, (London, 1952) 43-4.
25. See: *Reminiscences of Reading by an Octogenarian* (Reading, 1888). The
author was Alderman W. Dart. He had been a member of St. Giles church, an
active Liberal, Chief Constable, and Mayor. He was 'one who made his
appearance in Reading two years before Nelson fell'; *The Stranger in Reading*
(1810); P.H. Ditchfield, *Reading Seventy Years Ago: a record of events from
1813-1819* (Reading, 1887); Childs, *The Town of Reading ...,* 219.
26. Tosland, *Extracts* ... no.2, 160, also *ibid.,* 122 for another memory; also
Octogenarian ... 6-7 for the celebrations at the end of the Napoleonic wars,
involving large processions including 'a diminutive journeyman tailor of the
name of Hilton ... dressed in the costume of Napoleon who rode through the
streets accompanied by a miscellaneous throng'.
27. L. Oldershaw, ed. *England: A Nation, being papers of the Patriots' Club*
(1904) 89-90.
28. T. Brennan, E.W. Cooney, H. Pollins, *Social Change in South-West Wales*
(1954) 92. Anne Cook (see n.43 below) 9, 53, built up a list of 150-2– overlapping
'economic and social notables' in the 1830s-1840s and 350-400 in 1901, by
adding the names of individuals elected to representative bodies to those in
governing positions on charities and utilities, judicial, educational,
philanthropic, intellectual, political, religious and temperance organisations.
29. References for this paragraph are: Elihu Burritt, *A Walk from London to
Land's End and Back with Notes by the Way* (1868) 64-72; *Telegraph,*
23.8.1897, in Huntley and Palmers, *Scrapbooks;* J.B. Jones, *Sketches of
Reading, Historical Archaeological and Descriptive* (Reading, 1870) 8; *United
Magazine* (Oct. 1896); W.M. Childs, *The Future of the Town of Reading;*
W. Fletcher, *Reading Past and Present* (Reading, 1839) 83, 'While a
compulsory system is insufficient to promote the comfort of the helpless
poor, it will rather tend to foster than to deaden in the minds of the pious
and benevolent those kindly feelings and sympathy between individuals and
classes'. This last is an interesting survey of institutions and movements, from
within a particular ideological framework.
30. *Berkshire Chronicle,* 2.1.1892, 1.2.1890.
31. *United Magazine* (March, 1898).
32. *Official Programme of the Celebration ... 20th to 27th June 1897 in honour
of the 60 years reign of Queen Victoria,* twelve page pamphlet (Reading,
1897).
33. *Reading Mercury,* 25.4.1885.
34. *Berkshire Chronicle,* 11.8.1894. The festival was not the only kind of social
activity which took place under the umbrella of temperance organisation
during this period. There was a Temperance and General Philanthropic Society
(1878), a Social Centre (the 'British Workman' in Coley) in 1876, and a

Temperance Hotel (1878).

35. *Berkshire Chronicle,* 1.10.1898; for national statistics on University Extension see J.F.C. Harrison, *Learning and Living 1790-1960* (1961) 243.

36. See P.H.J.H. Gosden, *The Friendly Societies in England, 1815-1875* (Manchester, 1961).

37. The Annual Reports of the Chief Registrar of Friendly Societies are important sources for social historians but not every secretary sent in returns every year.

38. Information from Reading and District Office of Ancient Order of Foresters.

39. Big-name election meetings were not frequent in Reading. When they happened, as in the 1910 elections, they were attended by large numbers (in buildings like the tram sheds) but probably not much larger than can be contrived occasionally by modern political equivalents when they organise carefully. Tom Mann, George Lansbury and local socialist speakers attracted about 2,000 to an open-air meeting in 1898, but a more typical meeting expressing local grievances 'from below' was about 500 strong; *Berkshire Chronicle,* 23.7.1898, 14.1.1893. For political crowds during 'the golden age of the platform' see P.F. Clarke, *Lancashire and the New Liberalism* (Cambridge, 1971) 134-7.

40. *The Temperance Record,* 13.5.1880.

41. Some recent attacks upon 1950-60s behaviouralist political science, by going back to mid-nineteenth-century theorists of democracy for their critiques, have expounded mid-nineteenth-century aspirations in terms which help in the understanding of aspirations central to Reading in this period. For example, Lane Davis, 'The Cost of Realism. Contemporary Restatements of Democracy', *A-Political Politics: A Critique of Behaviouralism,* ed. Charles A. McCoy and John Playford (New York, 1967) 189,

> The immediate objective of classical democracy has always been to extend the opportunity for individuals to take an equal and an effective part in the management of public affairs. Through this opportunity, it was believed, the horizons of the participating individual would be widened, his knowledge extended, his sympathies made less parochial, his practical intelligence developed. Participation in the management of public affairs would serve as a vital means of intellectual, emotional. and moral education leading towards the full development of the capacities of individual human beings. Participation in politics would provide men with opportunities to take part in making significant decisions and to transcend the narrow bounds of their private affairs. It would build and consolidate a sense of genuine community that would serve as a solid foundation for government. It would provide a strenuous and rewarding field of endeavour by extending opportunities for free activity and self-government beyond the frequently petty sphere of private life into the realm of the public domain which had hitherto been largely beyond the control, or the hope of control, of ordinary men. This opportunity for education in public responsibility is the peculiar and distinguishing contribution which classical democracy makes to the ideal of human dignity and development.

42. Beatrice Webb, *My Apprenticeship* (1929) 194-5, n.1.

43. *Reading Observer,* 2.4.1892; for other examples see Anne Cook, 'Reading 1835-1930; a Community Power Study', unpub. Ph.D. thesis (Reading, 1970) 56, 86-7, 92, 107, 112, 114-7.

44. *Reading Observer,* 4.11.1879.

45. Council Minutes, 9.11.1864, quoted in Anne Cook, 'Reading', 151.

46. The Freemasons in late nineteenth-century Reading would be an important object of study, bearing upon many arguments in this book. They had a Hall or Temple, into which I went but was not allowed to consult records. A

Congregationalist minister in the 1960s, showing me the photographs of
Deacons, etc. on the wall of the vestry of his chapel, told me that I could not
really understand late nineteenth-century chapel life without knowing about
the Masons. He pointed to a number of Deacons and leading chapel laymen
who were Masons. The Vicars of St. Mary's and of St. Giles at different dates
before 1914 were both high in the local masonic hierarchy.

47. *Reading Mercury*, 2.1.1864, quoted in Anne Cook, 'Reading', 97.
48. *Reading Observer*, 4.11.1879, 7.1.1893; *The Christian World*, 17.1.1889, in
    Huntley and Palmers, *Scrapbooks*. The building was completed in May, 1882.
49. *Reading Observer*, 21.3.1885.
50. *Reading Observer*, 7.11.1891.
51. *The Nature and Progress of the Reading or Ninth Lodge of the Western
    Philanthropic Institution for the Relief of the Necessitous and Deserving
    Poor* (Reading, 1843).
52. The ideology of organised voluntarism in the third quarter of the nineteenth
    century, and the contradictions that ideology got into when it produced
    unintended results, such as State action or professionalism, has been well
    expounded in Melvin Richter, *The Politics of Conscience: T.H. Green and his
    Age*, (1964) 288-95, 324-36, 374-5.
53. K. Marx, *Wage Labour and Capital*, in Marx/Engels, *Selected Works in one
    Volume*, (1960) 74.
54. Through such works as Donald Read, *The English Provinces c.1760-1960: A
    Study in Influence* (1964).
55. In 1785 there were 5 or 6 daily coaches to London, as well as regular coaches
    to places like Oxford and Brighton, Tosland, *Extracts* ... (1884-5) no.2, 41;
    London was influential in the early nineteenth-century Reading economy,
    W. Mavor, *General View* ... (1808) 507; the dates of the main canal
    developments were: 1723 Reading-Newbury, 1772 improvement London-
    Oxford route, 1790 access to Birmingham and the Midlands via Oxford, 1810
    access to Bristol, 1840 to Shropshire and Wales. J. Man, *The History and
    Antiquities of the Borough of Reading* (1815) 65, was of the opinion that
    canal trade played the critical role in capital formation and the entrepreneurial
    base of Reading's early growth. In 1835 of the annual import/export trade
    50,000 tons were water-born and only 100 tons road-born, W.M. Childs, *The
    Town of Reading* ... (1910) 15.
56. See, *Reading Seventy Years Ago, a review of events from 1813-1819*,
    (Reading, 1887).
57. See Chapter Nine below.
58. Printed by James Golder (Bookseller), *Reading Handbook* (Reading, 1872) 31.
59. K.G. Burton, *The Early Newspaper Press in Berkshire 1723-1855* (Reading,
    1956). Cheap photo-lithography may be removing the technical and economic
    barriers to such a burst in the 1970s. But it will be in the shadow of a
    transformed national press and against tendencies to monopolise the supply
    and increase the price of paper.
60. For the post see *Reading Mercury*, 6.2.1841; for the telephones see *Reading
    Observer*, 2.1.1892, and the *Proceedings* of the Reading Literary and Scientific
    Society (1894). Reading Tramways were municipalised in 1901 and electrified
    in 1903. In the mid-twentieth century they were abolished.
61. E.J. Hobsbawm, *Industry and Empire* (1968) 89. Other places for the
    discussion of the effects of railways upon cities are: John Betjeman, *English
    Cities and Small Towns* (1943) 37; A.F. Weber, *The Growth of Cities in the
    Nineteenth Century* (1963 edit., New York) first published in 1899, 200-01
    D.V. Glass, *The Town and a Changing Civilisation* (1935). For Abingdon's
    lack of enthusiasm about becoming a railway town, see R.C. Baily, 'The
    Parliamentary History of Reading between 1750 and 1850', unpublished

M.A. thesis (University of Reading, 1944) 9. The best recent book is John R.
Kellett, *The Impact of Railways on Victorian Cities* (1969).

62. Daltry, *Public Health,* 172; relevant chronology for Reading in this area is:
1785 Paving Commissioners set up, the first authority for general improvement
in the town; *1820-1* two residents of Reading who had become the principal
share-holders of the Reading Waterworks Company (granted a monopoly in
1694) determined to improve the waterworks and called in Mr Cubbitt of
London to advise them; *1826* an Act of Incorporation for the Waterworks
Company; *1826* a new Act sought by the Paving Commissioners to get more
power for 'better paving, lighting, cleansing, watching and otherwise improving
the Borough of Reading' – led to great opposition called by the *Reading
Mercury* the 'All Perfection Act'; *1850* Local Board of Health; *1834* Board of
Guardians – a period of overlapping responsibilities since the Guardians had
MOs for the parishes in the Union; *1846* an unusually unhealthy year in the
town; *1847-8* minor cholera outbreak; *1846* Corporation applied for increase
in powers under the Municipal Corporations Act 1835, but abandoned the
attempt following the Public Health Act 1848, specifically charging bodies
such as the Local Board with responsibilities for public health; *1847* an Inquiry
into the sanitary state of Reading, drainage and water, etc; *1848-9* the *Reading
Mercury* went over to the sewage cause; *1850* an Inspector sent to report on
the needs of Reading as to drainage, water-supply, etc.; *1852* new Waterworks
at Southcot, the Local Board of Health having taken over the powers of the
Paving Commissioners in 1850; *1853* Reading Corporation Market Act; *1854*
drainage scheme defeated; *1855-60* Forbury Gardens laid out; *1858* another
drainage/sewage scheme failed; *1866* Thames Purification Bill forbad the
discharge of sewage into the Kennet; *1868* Waterworks municipalised; *1869*
Scarlatina and Diarrhoea outbreak led to shock reports on the state of the
town; *1870* Reading Improvement Act, led in the end to a new system of
drainage; *1872* MOH appointed; *1872* Public Health Act made the town
councils the urban sanitary authorities; *1874* corporation bought Whitley
Manor Farm for sewage, total cost of whole scheme £228,000, first house
connection November, 1875; *1878* more waterworks built at Fobney Lane;
1881 compulsory notification of infectious diseases. Main source, R.H. James,
'The development of the Public Health Movement in Reading', 1785-1872
unpublished dissertation (University of Durham, 1954); R.W. Daltry, 'A
History of the Public Health of the borough of Reading up to 1872',
unpublished M.A. thesis (University of Reading, 1933); H.T. Walker, 'The
Water Supply of Reading, Past and Present', in *Proceedings,* Reading Literary
and Scientific Society, (1890-91); Dr H. Gilford, 'The Sanitary History of
Reading', *ibid.* (1889-90); Anne Cook, 'Reading', 79-162; for Birmingham and
Leeds and a national and international setting see E.P. Hennock, *Fit and
Proper Persons* (1972).

63. For the doctors in Reading see James, *Public Health, passim;* Tosland, no.2,
53; Ernest W. Dormer, *The Story of the Royal Berkshire Hospital 1837-1937*
(Reading, 1937); J.B. Hurry, *A History of the Reading Pathological Society*
(1909).

64. The boundaries between politics and other forms of activity were differently
drawn in this period, and less firmly drawn than they have become later in the
twentieth century; see Elizabeth Isichei, *Victorian Quakers,* (Oxford, 1970)
xx, and John Vincent *The Formation of the Liberal Party 1857-68,* (London,
1966); for G.W. Palmer on local self-government see *Reading Co-operative
Record* (March, 1900) 7, a speech at a Co-op. meeting.

CHAPTER 3

1. James Obelkevich, 'Religion and Rural Society in South Lindsay 1825-1875', unpublished Ph.D. thesis (Columbia, 1971) 432-3; for a contemporary view of the non-coincidence of churches, church-going and religion see M. Loane, 'The Religion of the Respectable Poor', in *The Contemporary Review*, LXXXVI (Nov. 1904) 722.
2. George Eliot, *The Mill on the Floss* (1860) Everyman edit. (1908) 255 and Book IV, Chapter I, 'A Variety of Protestantism Unknown to Bossuet' *passim.*
3. P.T. Forsyth, *Socialism, the Church and the Poor* (1908) 50.
4. E.T. Davies, *Religion in the Industrial Revolution in South Wales* (Cardiff, 1965) 141.
5. Tosland, *Extracts from the Reading Mercury* ... (1884-5) vol. 2; *Reading Observer*, 1.11.1890; *Mate's Guide to Reading* (1904); Canon Garry, St. Mary's parish, *Annual Report* (1894-5).
6. For this 'index of attendance' see K.S. Inglis, 'Patterns of Religious Worship in 1851', in *Journal of Ecclesiastical History*, XI (April, 1960), 74-86.
7. As follows: Church of England, 3969 out of 5457; Independents, 1497 out of 1715; Particular Baptists, 640 out of 700; Baptists, 130 out of 120; Friends, 80 out of 414; Wesleyans, 348 out of 689; Primitives, 590 out of 420; 'isolated congregations', 35 out of 100; Roman Catholics, 220 out of 262; Latter Day Saints, 31 out of 100.
8. For Membership Population Ratios, 'the crucial index of strength of a religious organisation', see R. Currie, *Methodism Divided, a study in the sociology of ecumenicalism* (1968) 89-93.
9. Already in the introduction to the tables in the 1851 census Horace Mann pointed out that buildings were not, or soon would not be, the problem, *Census of Great Britain 1851, Religious Worship, England and Wales, Report and Tables, (1853) lxi.* He thought that methods of mission would soon need more attention than plant. K.S. Inglis, *Churches and the Working Classes in Victorian England* (1963) 165, judged that explanations of irreligion in mid-century were normally given in terms of facilities, but by 1880 in terms of social habit. For arguments against the notion of a national 'religious boom' between 1850 and 1900, a notion put forward by E.R. Wickham, *Church and People in an Industrial City* (1957) and J.E. Orr, *The Second Evangelical Awakening in Britain* (1949), see R. Currie, *Methodism Divided* (1968) 85-103.
10. Smiths, *Directory* (1894).
11. Max Weber, *The Sociology of Religion* (1965) 64.
12. Smiths, *Directory* (1902).
13. *The Methodist Times*, 23.2.1905. A meeting of Congregational ministers in 1900, *Berkshire Chronicle* (27.10.1900) felt that they were losing out in relation to the Baptists, Primitives and Wesleyans in the percentage of the population for whom they had seats in 1900 compared to 1870. They felt that they needed a dynamic building programme. Denominational merger and decrease of competition leads, conversely, to concentration on over-supply of churches, see R. Currie, *Methodism Divided* (1968) 192. In Trinity Congregational Church Pamphlets, vol.9, there are *Some Facts and Figures Concerning Reading Congregationalism* (Reading, 1902) of a comparative, retrospective kind:

	1861	1871	1881	1891	1901
Population	25,045	32,324	42,050	60,054	72,214
All Evangelical Free Churches, seats per 100 population	24	24	25	16	18
Congregationalists	9.1	9.7	7.8	4.4	3.7
Baptists	3.8	4.5	4.2	2.9	4.2
Particular Baptists	3.4	2.6	2.0	1.4	1.2
Wesleyans	2.4	1.9	3.5	2.4	3.0
Primitives	2.4	2.7	3.9	2.7	3.2
Presbyterians	-	-	1.5	1.0	1.2

14. The Hospital phrase for older women who continue to have children.
15. Figures extracted from the annual Smith's *Directories,* where each year the names of priests and ministers were listed.
16. *Church of England Temperance Chronicle,* 2.4.1887; for examples from Yorkshire of church provision, in the mid-nineteenth century, of an array of 'associated movements' see J.F.C. Harrison, *Learning and Living* (1961) 184-5, 196.
17. For pubs in this context see Brian Harrison, *Drink and the Victorians, The Temperance Question in England 1815-1872* (1971) General Index, Drinking places: meetings at, and recreation at, p. 483; and Harrison, 'Pubs' in H. Dyos and M. Wolff, *The Victorian City, Images & Realities,* I (1975).
18. 'It can no longer be alleged with even an appearance of truth that the Christian Churches are indifferent to the social conditions of the people', editorial in the *Reading Observer,* 16.10.1909, on 'the churches and social betterment'.
19. *Reading Observer,* 15.6.1907.
20. For the personnel of the Reading Guild of Help which included men like W.M. Childs of Reading University and A.L. Bowley the statistician, as well as the ministers mentioned, see Reading Guild of Help, Executive Committee, *Minute Books,* 24.1.1910-24.2.1911 and 1911-1917.
21. St. Giles, *Parish Magazine* (Oct. 1914).
22. St. Giles, *Parish Magazine* (Jan. 1902).
23. Sport had a long history in connection with Anglican parishes in Reading: see Rev. Charles Kerry, *A History of the Municipal Church of St. Lawrence, Reading* (Reading and Derby, 1883) 226-40, 'Sports, Pastimes, Mysteries'.
24. An example of the latter is St. Saviour's Football Club. It had started off in the parish as Garfield FC in 1892, and became St. Saviour's FC in 1901, see *Berkshire Chronicle,* 25.3.1905. Parish football clubs, and Sunday School clubs were often the basis for professional clubs in the 1880s – e.g. Aston Villa. For a Wesleyan Cricket Club in Reading which lasted until the 1930s and claimed to be the oldest in town, see A.H. Lowe, *Sunlit Fields* (London, 1929).
25. The first Board in 1871 had 5 church and 4 Nonconformist members. In 1874, 1877, 1880 and 1883 there were no contested elections, even though the personnel of the Board changed completely through 'natural wastage'. In 1895 there were 7 Moderates, 4 Progressives, 2 Socialists. For full details see the *Berkshire Chronicle,* 16.2.1901, 23.2.1901; *Reading Mercury,* 24.2.1883, 12.3.1892; Anne Cook, 'Reading', 305.
26. *Berkshire Chronicle,* 6.9.1902.
27. Kings Road Baptist Chapel, *Minutes of Church Meeting* (Nov. 1903). In vol. III of the *Scrapbooks* in the vestry library at Trinity Congregational Chapel there are many cuttings relating to passive resistance in Reading in 1903-4; see also T.A.B. Corley, *Quaker Enterprise in Biscuits* (1972) 5, for Palmer resistance to Church Rates in the mid-nineteenth century.

346 Religion and Voluntary Organisations in Crisis

28. *Broad Street Independent Church Magazine* (May, 1905). The month before the magazine had asked 'where are the many other Nonconformists who ought to be standing side by side with our friends? It is quite clear that when an alteration in the law takes place under a Liberal government, and come it certainly will ... it will be owing to the passive resisters'.

29. 'Those who know intimately what is passing in the Free Churches are agreed that this Education trouble has stirred them to increased activity and has helped them to greater prosperity in manifold ways. Never were they more united, more earnest and hopeful ...', *Reading Observer*, 29.12.1906.

30. St. Giles, *Parish Magazine* (May, 1906).

31. St. Giles, *Parish Magazine* (July, 1906).

32. *Reading Observer*, 20.3.1892, 2.4.1892; *Reading Mercury*, 12.3.1892. Burness left the SDF in November 1893 but stayed for a time on the Board.

33. Before that there had been Juvenile Total Abstinence branches in the town set up under the plan of Dr Grindrod and Mrs Carlile – going back to 1846 at the British School, *Berkshire Chronicle*, 23.4.1904; *Reading Observer*, 7.3.1894; for early Primitive Methodist temperance work see *Primitive Methodist Magazine* (1887) 397.

34. Hosier St., *Chapel Minutes*, 27.7.1896, 25.9.1899 and many other references.

35. *Reading Mercury*, 10.8.1878. See also P.H. Ditchfield ed., *An Ecclesiastical History of Reading* (Reading, 1883) 108.

36. Reading Temperance Society, *Annual Report* (1872-3).

37. For the outstanding recent study of temperance see Brian Harrison, *Drink and the Victorians* (1971); pp.169-71 deal with the functions of temperance organisation amid the rest of the Nonconformist 'host of voluntary activities taking place on the chapel premises during week nights'. See also Lilian L. Shiman, 'The Church of England Temperance Society in the Nineteenth Century', in *The Historical Magazine of the Protestant Episcopal Church*, XLI, 2; 'The Band of Hope Movement', in *Victorian Studies*, 17 (Sept. 1973); 'The Birstall Temperance Society', to be published in the *Yorkshire Archaeological Journal*. I am most grateful to the author for giving me copies of these articles.

38. Reading Temperance Society, *Annual Report* (1887-8).

39. Reading Temperance Society, 1932 Centenary Celebration, *Letters; Annual Report 1838* (reprinted in *Annual Report*, 1886-7); *Annual Report* (1896-7); Rev. G.E. Diggle, 'The Story of the Reading Temperance Society', in *Gospel Temperance Monthly* (May, 1885); *Reading Observer*, 7.1.1893; cutting on a public meeting in honour of W.I. Palmer held 19.3.1885; W.I. Palmer, *Temperance Testimonies* (National Temperance League); *Reading Mercury*, cutting Dec. 1877, in Huntley and Palmers, *Scrapbooks;* pamphlet at Trinity Congregational Church, *Report of the Evidence of Sixteen Witnesses who Testified in Favour of the Practice of Entire Abstinence from Intoxicating Drinks at a Public Meeting held in West Street Hall, March 2nd 1868.*

40. *Berkshire Chronicle*, 13.5.1905; RTS, *Annual Reports* (1887-8 and 1904-5); *Reading Observer*, 18.4.1891. And for a typical meeting 'to reaffirm their vital and solemn allegiance to the great principle of total abstinence', *Berkshire Chronicle*, 25.2.1893. Other occasions: *Berkshire Chronicle*, 2.1.1892, 2.5.1896, 7.5.1898.

41. *Reading Observer*, 2.10.1909. Other examples of agencies which themselves acquired agencies were: Broad Street PSA, Kings Road Young Men's Guild, Cumberland Road Primitive Methodist Sunday School, the Fireside Club and Mission started in Silver Street (for which see *Berkshire Chronicle*, 24.4.1900 23.9.1905 and 16.6.1906). The Band of Hope started in Reading as an agency of a Primitive Methodist Sunday School.

42. *Berkshire Chronicle*, 16.6.1906.

43. Rev. Forbes Jackson, *The United Magazine* (Feb. 1898).
44. Rev. L. Harman, *The Parish of St. Giles in Reading* (Reading, 1946) 89; for the ambition fulfilled at Elm Park Methodist Hall, see *Methodist Recorder*, 1.10.1908, p.10.
45. This was stated diagrammatically by the Rev. Albert Swift, minister of Trinity Congregational Chapel, in his *First Principles of Christian Citizenship* (1908) 129. For further systematic exposition of the ambition see his *The Institute Department* (1910). The fate of this minister's reorganisation of Trinity is described in the Welfare chapter. According to Swift's chronology, the first Institute Department in his sense was in 1874, see *ibid*, xxiv. There is an interesting treatment of the same phenomenon in the USA in Chapter IV of A.I. Abell, *The Urban Impact on American Protestantism 1865-1900* (Harvard & Oxford, 1943) 137. He describes how 'the adjective "institutional" (was) employed to describe the numerous church missions which were expanding their functions to cover the entire life of man'. An example was St. Bartholomew's in Manhattan which went over to the new style in 1888. A parish house paid for by the Vanderbilts was built on East 42nd Street in 1891 at a cost of $400,000. It had a floor space of three and a half acres and was allegedly the most elaborate of its kind in the world. Between 1891 and 1901, $11,000,000 was spent. Each year the church *Year Book* ran to 150 pages.
46. W.T. Stead, *If Christ Came to Chicago* (London edit. 1894) 258-9, 'the various churches (in Chicago) are wealthy, comfortable, served by able and zealous ministers and sung to by choirs of ecclesiastical nightingales. Very few are as fruitful in good works in the shape of institutional sideshows as we are accustomed to in England ... I do not know of any Church in Chicago which utilises the whole of its ecclesiastical plant as vigorously as do some of the leading churches of England'.
47. The classic reorganisation was that of Albert Swift at Trinity Congregational, between 1908 and 1913. Although it was the most complete and self-conscious, it was not the only one. Farrow's work at Broad Street Congregational in 1906, leading up to the organisation of the Young People's Union into 5 sections in 1911, was analogous. The new Pastor at Park Chapel in 1911, the School Buildings at the back of Tilehurst Congregational chapel put up in 1907-8 at a cost of £700, the Young Men's Guild of 1897 and the Young Men's Institute of 1908 at Kings Road Baptists, the Christian Effort Committee of May 1893 at Caversham Free, the Quaker Institute, the London Street Primitive Methodist Institute for which, in March 1894 'without more accommodation it is simply impossible, and we shall be losing ground', the St. Luke's Boys' Institute going in 1891, the St. Mary's Club and Church' Institute (folded in 1909), St. Mark's Mens' Institute, All Saints Institute, St. Luke's Institute, Christ Church Institute 'almost indispensable to the effective carrying out of parish work', 'to promote the social and moral well-being of the parish' — all these were in the same territory. No sooner was the debt on St. Mark's within sight of being cleared in 1906, the parish was anticipating that it would be 'a real joy to aim at securing the necessary funds for a Men's Institute which is much needed in this district'.
48. St. Giles, *Parish Magazine* (March, 1911, and May, 1912). At St. Peter's Caversham they had initially a Parish Room which, reported a departing Vicar in 1893, had been very useful 'while the parochial machinery and church organisation were in the course of formation'. By May 1901 they wanted a more elaborate Hall. Money, as for St. Giles, All Saints, and Christ Church Institute, came very slowly. By October 1901 they had a mere £153. In October 1902 a rescue familiar in church building during the previous 50 years in Reading took place: Miss Radcliffe gave them 'Balmore Hall' free

49. Broad Street, *Magazine* (April, 1893).
50. Albert Swift of Trinity Chapel wrote often on this theme; see his *The Institute Department* (1910) 19-20.
51. Similar ideas were expressed at the opening of the West Memorial Institute attached to the Caversham Baptist Free Church in February 1911.
52. One of the problems is that the ones which did resemble our description necessarily left more records and are easier to research into than the ones which did not. The size of the sample (not selected, but conditioned by presence or absence of materials) from which I am working is as follows: of the 29 Anglican churches 21 have been studied, in varying detail: 5/7 Wesleyan, 3/6 Primitive (2 only very scanty, one in much detail), 1/4 Salvation Army (with scattered references elsewhere), 6/9 Baptist chapels, 1/2 Strict Baptist, 1/2 Brethren, 4/7 Congregationalist, scattered information on both the 2 Presbyterian churches, full records of the one Congregational Methodist, equally full on the Friends, rather less on the Unitarians, a small amount on the Railway Mission and the Synagogue, very little indeed on the three Roman Catholic Churches, scattered references to the Agapemonites.
53. J. Piper and J. Betjeman eds., *Murray's Architectural Guide to Berkshire* (1949) 138, the reference to the Smyth-Piggott follower, architect Frank Morris, was the first clue to the existence of Agapemonites in Reading; see also 'The Agapemonites; the present position of the movement', in *British Weekly*, 18.8.1892, p. 261. London, Reading and Norwich were the centre of activity 'the cause at Reading is said to be in a flourishing condition'.
54. E. Franklin Frazier, in *The Negro Church in America* (Liverpool, 1964) 52, discusses this question of size in relation to type of church organisation and members' needs. The average membership of Southern Negro churches was less than 400. In the new Northern immigrant city context the average size of churches created went up to *c.*800. This meant a change in the nature of the religion provided so great that a reaction towards small intimate 'storefront' churches took place in cities like Chicago and New York. There is also an interesting discussion of size and the function of smallness in very different types of religious and political groupings in E.J. Hobsbawm, *Primitive Rebels* (Manchester, 1959) 18-19.
55. *Berkshire Chronicle*, 14.4.1906.
56. St. John's, *Annual Address to the Parishioners with reports* (1896).
57. *Reading Mercury*, 20.10.1894, discussed the changes within Primitive Methodism locally since 1866 – with the introduction first of music and choirs into the services, and then, as at London Street, much else besides.
58. Within the Baptist denomination, for example, using the figure at which the books were balanced as an index, the scale of their operations varied thus: King's Road, £2,000 p.a. plus (1887-1891 they raised £9,000), Carey (1893-4) £550, Grovelands (1892) £136 (1905) £377, Wycliffe (1891) £534, Anderson (1904-5) £129. Other denominations varied across the same range, usually with one chapel at the Kings Road level, although in the case of the Church of England there were several.
59. Anglicans in Reading had few small buildings, just under half of the churches having 750 seats or more. 14 out of 27 Nonconformist chapels had less, in many cases far less, than 500 seats. Each of the major denominations had one building with 900-1,000 seats. The Primitive Methodists had one chapel with 900 seats, but the rest had 400, 300, 200 and 200. For denominational convergence see R.F. Horton, 'The Free Church in England' in *Fortnightly Review*, CCCLXI (1897) 597-607, and Rev. Enoch Salt, 'The New Movement in Congregationalism', in *Wesleyan Methodist Magazine* (1909) 600-1.
60. Carey Baptist Chapel, letter to Berkshire Baptist Association, 26.5.1892; St. Giles, *Parish Magazine* (Jan. 1903); for national doubts in a denomination obsessed by figures see *Primitive Methodist Magazine* (1896) 315.

61. *Free Methodist*, 26.4.1900, quoted in R. Currie, *Methodism Divided* (1968)
    97.
62. Rev. G.P. Crawford, *Recollections of St. Mary's Reading 50 years ago*
    (Reading, 1932) 33; for the function of Mission Halls preventing rich and
    poor worshipping together, see *Primitive Methodist Magazine* (1896) 158.
63. For the Athenaeum see Chapter 7.
64. Christine Dinnis of the University of Sussex is working on the Salvation Army
    from this point of view; but see in particular William Booth, 'What is the
    Salvation Army?', in *Contemporary Review* XLII (1882) 175-82 and
    B. Watson, *Soldier Saint: George Railton* (1970). Railton is a fascinating index
    of pressures on a dynamic sect such as the Salvation Army, since 'his
    Franciscan spirit revolted against those commercial involvements with the
    world which, for better, for worse, became necessary to a movement which
    aimed to save the world'.
65. For the biscuit factory in this regard see Chapter 4. The Reading Working
    Men's Regatta had races between the various sub-units of the factory,
    themselves called 'Factories'; Huntley and Palmers did not move to take over
    Serpells in Reading, nor did they merge with Huntley, Boorne and Stevens until
    1918. They did, however, vigorously pursue those companies which pretended
    to be Huntley and Palmers, see T.A.B. Corley, *Quaker Enterprise in Biscuits*
    (1972) 43-4.
66. *Berkshire Chronicle*, 13.9.1902; St. Giles' *Parish Magazine*, (Aug. 1902).
67. R.R. Suffield, later a Minister in Reading, defined his new faith in a letter of
    22nd August 1870 as follows (he had been a Catholic): 'a communion of
    Christian worshippers bound loosely together, and yet by the force of great
    principles enabled quietly to maintain their position, to exercise an influence
    elevating and not unimportant and to present religion under an aspect which
    thoughtful men can accept without latent scepticism and earnest men
    without the aberrations of superstition, or the abjectness of mental
    servitude to another – such approved itself to my judgment and commended
    itself to my sympathy'. For Suffield see M.O. Suffield, *The Life of R.R.
    Suffield* (London, 1893).
68. *Berkshire Chronicle*, 10.6.1893; *Reading Standard*, 5.10.1907.
69. Park Institute: 'for the better rendering of service to God by public preaching
    of His work, by the provision of suitable opportunities of social fellowship,
    and by the adoption of any means, educational and otherwise which the
    church may deem for God's honour and the welfare of men'. This was the
    purpose. To help fulfill it every member entered into a covenant, 'I agree to
    belong to the Church of Christ meeting at Park Institute ... and I will work
    with that fellowship to the utmost of my power for the benefit of our fellow
    men. I agree that the common ground of our belief is the Headship of Christ
    as the spiritual foundation of our whole life, and the value of the Bible as a
    record of the Grace of God. Having promised my life and service to Christ I
    will make it my aim to carry that promise out in actual deeds through this
    church'.
        Caversham Hill: 'At a meeting of members of the Congregation worshipping
    in the Independent Chapel Caversham Hill ... divine guidance and direction
    having been devoutly sought in earnest prayer to the Great Head of the Church
    it was unitedly resolved.
        That we whose names are hereto subscribed having been wont to meet
    for the worship of God in the Independent Chapel Caversham Hill, feeling our
    responsibility to the Great Searcher of hearts do solemnly record the deep
    conviction of our souls that as sinners in the sight of God, born in sin, we
    were altogether the children of wrath, even as others. That in us dwelt no
    good thing, and that if we are saved from the power of sin here and its

consequences in the world to come it must be by salvation freely given to us
of God.

Believing that God because of his infinite and eternal love has been
pleased to give His Well Beloved Son Jesus Christ to make full atonement for
our guilt, and to open a way that God may be just and the justifier of all them
that believe in Him in order that whosoever believeth in Him might not perish
but have everlasting life, and that in answer to His intercessory prayer the
Holy Spirit may be granted to sanctify and sweeten us for Glory by the
instrumentality of His revealed truth wholly contained in the Sacred Volume
of inspiration our precious Bible, and rejoicing that there is no other name
given under heaven whereby we may be saved, we have humbly fled for refuge
to Jesus as the one only and all sufficient hope set before us in the gospel and
resolve in the strength of the Lord to continue looking for the mercy of
Jesus Christ and Eternal Life.

Humbly adoring Him who loved the Church and gave himself for it and
has made us to be no more strangers and foreigners but fellow citizens with
the saints and of the household of God and feeling that it is alike our duty and
privilege to present to Him our bodies, souls and spirits a living sacrifice, we
desire to testify our gratitude together as members of the one body of which
He is the head and ruler for the observance of His graciously appointed
ordinances and worship. We do therefore in humble dependence upon His
promised blessing unite ourselves together as a Christian Church for the
worship of God and observance of religious ordinances agreeable to the
principles and usages of the Congregational churches, devoutly praying for
grace and wisdom to love one another, bear one another's burdens, maintain a
consistent profession, honour the Lord Christ, and serve our generation
according to His will, to whom be glory now and ever, Amen'.

70. *Reading Observer*, 4.4.1891.
71. As Davies wrote of South Wales Nonconformity earlier in the nineteenth
century, 'the chapels made life bearable and meaningful to thousands of
people both through their means of grace and their character as social and
cultural centres,' E.T. Davies, *Religion in the Industrial Revolution in South
Wales* (Cardiff, 1965) 92.
72. St. John's Church of England Temperance Society, a bound volume of *Annual
Reports* (1898-1913) 1903-4.
73. *Sunday School Record*, 24.4.1890, in the *Minute Book* of the chapel; there
were many such stories in the national denominational press; cp. Miss Loane,
'The Religion of the Respectable Poor', in *The Contemporary Review*,
LXXXVI (Nov. 1904) 726.
74. Hosier St. *Minutes*, 11.1.1901.
75. Kindly lent to me by Rabbi Sichel. These *Rules* are not dated, but precede
1914.
76. *Trustees' Minutes* (1909-1934) and a volume called *Caversham Society,
Minutes of Leaders' Meetings*, 25.4.1888-23.9.1910.
77. *Church Minutes* (1903-1929). By September 1910 the seats had been
numbered.
78. *Reading Standard*, 19.10.1901; *Primitive Methodist Magazine* (1890)
532-6.
79. *Parish Magazine* quoted in *Berkshire Chronicle*, 6.3.1914; *Statistical Return
of Parochial Work* (1891-2); Broad Street *Magazine* (Feb. 1905).
80. References for the preceding three paragraphs in order are: *Methodist Times*,
5.1.1905, pp. 1 & 7; *Wesleyan Methodist Magazine* (1889) 715-8 – for
reference to 203 Prize Essays on the Class Meeting; *ibid.* (1896) 535, (1897)
783-4; *Methodist Times*, 1.2.1900; *Primitive Methodist Magazine* (1909) 301;
Methodist Times, 5.1.1905; *Wesleyan Methodist Magazine* (1888) 812.

81. For two case studies of the different meaning of membership in Quaker Meetings (Norwich and Manchester) based upon Visitors' Reports, see Elizabeth Isichei, *Victorian Quakers* (1970) 118-43.

82. Rev. J. Wilding, *Broad Street Congregational Church News* (1962): C.A. Davis, *History of the Baptist Church, Reading* (Reading, 1891) suggests that throughout the nineteenth century membership obligations and ties were diminishing. R. Currie, *Methodism Divided* (1968) suggests the same for Methodist denominations nationally in the second half of the nineteenth century.

83. The ones I have found are: at Caversham Methodist Church the expulsion in 1888 of two young people for six months, amidst great congregational shock, for a moral offence, *Caversham Society, Minutes of Leaders' Meetings:* a split at Zoar leading to resignation, on the Articles of Faith, 27.9.1905; E.T. Davies, *Religion in the Industrial Revolution in South Wales* (Cardiff, 1965) 53-54, reveals an opposite situation in the first half of the nineteenth century in South Wales. Discipline was strict and 'Baptist *Circular Letters* reveal that occasionally the number of excommunicated exceeded that of the Baptised'.

84. Carey Baptist Chapel, *Minute Book* (1866-April, 1901), and *Rules and Obligations,* 14.2.1877.

85. Caversham Free Church, Church Meeting, *Minute Books,* vol. covering 1885-1904, 16.2.1893.

86. *A Description of the Town of Reading Including its Origin* (Reading, 1841); J.B. Jones, *Sketches of Reading ...* (Reading, 1870). Or George Hillier, *The Stranger's Guide to the Town of Reading* (Reading, 1859).

87. 'Religion', announced a speaker at the celebrations to mark the construction of the new Reading Town Hall in 1879, 'is a matter of paramount importance to each one of us as individuals, and as a nation. It will be found to exercise its benevolent and all-pervading influence upon our character and institutions without distinctions. It binds man to man, it unites all classes and all degrees of men. It gives us the sound principles for our legislation; it is the main security for social order, it is the sole foundation for good government', *Reading Observer,* 4.11.1879.

88. Broad Street, *Magazine* (Dec. 1894).

89. *Berkshire Chronicle,* 2.2.1901.

90. *Reading Observer,* 12.5.1910, 27.4.1912, 1.6.1912.

91. I have been unable to estimate the relative use of pubs and church/chapel plant for voluntary organisations' meetings in this period. Arthur Sherwell, a temperance reformer, studied 2393 local branches of the engineers', carpenters', railway workers', boilermakers', shipwrights', cotton spinners', iron founders', plasterers' and boot and shoe operatives' unions in 1903, and found that 72% met in pubs, see A. Fox, *A History of the National Union of Boot and Shoe Operatives* (Oxford, 1958) 361; for pubs and meetings during the nineteenth century see Brian Harrison 'Pubs', in H.J. Dyos and M. Wolff eds., *The Victorian City: Images and Realities* I (1973) 175-6. For non-religious halls in Reading see *Reading Mercury,* 22.4.1876 (Victoria Hall Co.); *ibid.,* 25.9.1880 (Abbey Institute).

92. At five-yearly intervals 1890-1914 the figures were as follows: Anglicans, 21,21,22,29,30,34. All others, 20,19,20,26,26,29. From Smith's *Directories.*

93. *Reading Standard,* 11.1.1908.

94. Examples were: Rev. P.H. Ditchfield as Hon. Sec. of the Berkshire Archaeological and Architectural Society (1890), Rev. J.M. Guilding as Worshipful Master of the Greyfriars Lodge of Freemasons (1895) and Canon Garry active in Freemasonry too 'because he perceived that religion was the foundation of it', *Berkshire Chronicle,* 21.1.1893, Rev. J.J. Goadby for the last five years of his life very active in the Reading Literary and Scientific

Society, *Berkshire Chronicle,* 26.3.1898.

95. *Berkshire Chronicle,* 8.6.1901, 22.6.1901; for a sketch of a week in the life of a minister, see Rev. J. Watson, 'A Plea for the Spirituality of the Church', in *British Weekly,* 30.5.1895; and for a typical day, *Methodist Recorder,* 1.10.1908, p.10.

96. St. Giles, *Parish Magazine* (July, 1904).

97. David Owen, *English Philanthropy, 1660-1960* (1965) noticed this phenomenon in his own field. Examples in Reading were: Rev. R.H. Hart Davis who retired to Reading in the early twentieth century after being vicar of Dunsden for twenty-eight years. He was one of the agencies through which discussion of Pensions got into the town, *Reading Observer,* 14.7.1906, 20.6.1908. He also played a key initiating role in the strike of 1912, see *Reading Observer,* 27.12.1911, and 6.1.1912. Also Rev. W. Butler in the University Extension Movement, *Reading Observer,* 25.1.1890. A Roman Catholic priest was instrumental in starting the movement which led to the Royal Berkshire Hospital early on in the century. Bishop Gore was prime mover of the Bowley survey, used later in this study, see G.L. Prestige, *The Life of Charles Gore* (1935) 335. In view of the facts of their employment and education, this role is not surprising, but it needs systematic documentation alongside the role of other professional groups outside their professional spheres in the nineteenth century. See also A.J. Russell, 'A Sociological Analysis of the clergyman's role, with special reference to the early-nineteenth century', unpub. D.Phil. (Oxford, 1970). *Much in his late book.*

CHAPTER 4

1. The chronology of my indebtedness for material in this chapter is as follows: first to Mr Paxton of Huntley and Palmers who obtained for me a number of family scrapbooks and other documents and who allowed me to look around the then disarranged archives; secondly to T.A.B. Corley of Reading University who was generous with his time and knowledge while he was writing the official history of the firm; thirdly to that excellent history, published in 1972 as *Quaker Enterprise in Biscuits: Huntley and Palmers of Reading 1822-1972.* Mr Paxton also kindly provided a desk in the reception room for visitors to the factory, where I could study the records. Interpretations put on the material are of course my own.

2. A cutting from the mid-1880s in the Reading Temperance Society records; for similar comments see Huntley and Palmers, *Scrapbook, passim; The Christian Messenger,* I (1865) 161-5; *The Working Man, a Weekly Review of Social and Industrial Progress,* 2.6.1866; *The Leeds Mercury,* 16.7.1881; *All The Year Round,* 9.6.1888, 536-41; *Daily Mail,* 7.8.1913, 21.2.1914; E. Burritt, *A Walk from London to Land's End and Back with Notes by the Way* (1868) 64-74.

3. Joseph Hatton, 'Biscuit Town', with illustrations by W.H. Margetson, in *The English Illustrated Magazine,* I (1891-2) 855-64. This article gives a vivid feel of the factory at that date; for earlier modes of biscuit making see 'The Manufacture of Biscuits', in *Penny Magazine,* 9 (1840) 130.

4. 1857/8-1873/4:12.4%; 1874/5-1889/90: 13.6%; 1889/90-1897/8: 14.5%. The absolute figures are set out in T.A.B. Corley, Appendix III, 306-8.

5. For a rare voice from below see *Reading Standard,* 8.3.1913: 'My occupation? I was in the manufacturing department. Had to drive the horizontal machine, which cuts the dough to the required size before it drops into tins and runs along to the ovens to be baked. That was my daily task for well nigh fifty years. Monotonous? Rather ...'

6. Joseph Hatton, 'Biscuit Town', 857-60; see also *The Pictorial World,* Sept. 1877, where it was said that Sutton's seed firm 'like that of Messrs. Huntley and Palmers is a perfect town on a small scale, and exhibits the same degree of order and system'.

7. The 'Plan of Fire Service Mains' (1903) in the factory archives is a perfect coloured visual aid for understanding the nature and variety of departments in the factory. There was a tin department, a carpenters' department, a building department, an engineering department. 'Out in the yards and on the Kennet wharves one might be inspecting the premises of some great railway company with its workshops. Here are hundreds of tons of timber layer upon layer, cut and uncut. Close by a saw-mill is buzzing and humming. On one hand is an engineering shop where the mysteries of rapid and perfect biscuit-making by machinery are worked out; on the other, tin-men are at work with ingenious contrivances for making boxes while the joiner is constructing giant packing cases for ocean voyages.' Joseph Hatton, 'Biscuit Town', 864.

8. Joseph Hatton, 'Biscuit Town', 862.

9. *Reading Standard,* 7.3.1908.

10. *Reading Examiner,* 25.5.1872; cuttings in Huntley and Palmers, *Scrapbooks.*

11. *Reading Observer,* 5.2.1881.

12. *Reading Standard,* 16.6.1923, 'I can see him at his machine near the mixing plant of the factory, his locker close at hand, filled with necessities for an emergency or accident, with probably a bunch of grapes or some delicacy to be left at some sick person's house during the dinner hour, or as he left in the evening'.

13. *The Temperance Record,* 6.9.1883.

14. Huntley and Palmers, *Scrapbooks,* cutting from *Reading Standard;* see also *Berkshire Chronicle,* 22.2.1896.

15. *Reading Observer,* 7.11.1891.

16. T.A.B. Corley, *Quaker Enterprise* ... 120-1. The information comes from a letter sent to Lord Salisbury in 1885 by W. Dorchester, a Reading butcher. He was pressing William Isaac's claim to an Honour because he thought that such a gesture to a Liberal might help Unionist prospects in Reading.

17. *Reading Observer,* 7.1.1893.

18. Good sources for the first generation of Palmers are: *Berkshire Chronicle,* 30.3.1894; *Reading Observer,* 28.6.1892, 14.1.1893, 21.8.1897; *The Daily News,* 20.8.1897; *The Hampstead and Highgate Express,* 18.4.1902; *The Christian World,* 26.8.1897; Huntley and Palmers, *Scrapbooks;* T.A.B. Corley, *Quaker Enterprise* ... 111-124. A rare piece of hostile writing is in the *Daily Mail,* 20.8.1897. One of the grounds for attack was the personal nature of their charity, 'hence Reading has been for decades the Mecca of vagabondage'.

19. The Programme, beautifully printed, survives in the Factory. The report is in *Reading Observer,* 22.11.1873. For the institution of 'factory suppers', annual until 1850 and succeeded by excursions every other year in the 1850s and 1860s see T.A.B. Corley, *Quaker Enterprise* ... 65, 102.

20. *Morning Star,* 26.9.1860. The Palmers were not strict, no out-relief, back-to-the-principles-of-1834 men, see *Berkshire Chronicle,* 6.2.1892. T.A.B. Corley, *Quaker Enterprise* ... Chapter 8 *passim.*

21. The Rules again recall similarly printed Public School Rules. They may be compared over time: 'Rules and Regulations in force at the Reading Biscuit Factory for the purpose of preserving good order', pasted into the *Wages Book* of the Manufacturing Department (1841-50), the 'Rules and Regulations at the Reading Biscuit Factory', 24.5.1893, and, with the significant change of language 'Conditions of Work at the Reading Biscuit Factory' (March, 1923).

22. *Household Words,* 28.6.1884; *Evening Times,* 2.9.1884; *Grocers Chronicle,* 11.10.1884.

23. T.A.B. Corley, *Quaker Enterprise* ... 77. A phrase of George Palmer's, used in 1849-50 with reference to those who were trying to undercut prices.
24. T.A.B. Corley, *Quaker Enterprise* ... 59.
25. F. Dolman, 'The Man and the Town, Mr. George Palmer J.P. and Reading', in *English Illustrated Magazine,* XIII (April-Sept. 1895) 418-25; Weldon and Company, *Brave Boys Who Have Become Illustrious Men of our Time Forming Bright Examples for Emulation by the Youth of Britain,* chapter on 'M.H. Sutton, a model man of business and philanthropist'; Alexander H. Japp, *Successful Business Men* (1892); *Agricultural Gazette,* 4.7.1897; *Leisure Hour* (May, 1897).
26. R. Currie, *Methodism Divided: A Study in the Sociology of Ecumenicalism* (1968) 190-1.
27. *Reading Observer,* 7.11.1891.
28. T.A.B. Corley, *Quaker Enterprise* ... 136; for Reading's insulation until 1886, see *Reading Mercury,* 11.1.1879, 20.2.1886; Anne Cook, 'Reading', 165.
29. T.A.B. Corley, *Quaker Enterprise* ... 256; J. Burnett, *Plenty and Want, A Social History of Diet in England from 1815 to the Present Day* (1968) 96.
30. Between 1897 and 1914 home sales of Huntley and Palmers actually decreased – by 12%. Peak Freans started to outstrip Huntley and Palmers using advertising techniques, phasing out slower sellers, etc. T.A.B. Corley, *Quaker Enterprise* ... 135, 161.
31. Percy Redfern, *The Story of the C.W.S.: The Jubilee History of the Co-operative Wholesale Society Limited* (Manchester, n.d.) 75-6, 169-70, 209.
32. T.A.B. Corley, *Quaker Enterprise* ... 221, 231, 137.
33. At a time when, according to Dorothy Davis, *A History of Shopping* (1966) 263, 'the poor did most of their shopping of every kind in the street'.
34. J. Sainsbury, David Greig and Thomas Lipton all opened their first shops between 1869 and 1871, Lipton's later established their own biscuit factory; during the 1880s the Home and Colonial and the Maypole Dairy arranged their own biscuit supplies, T.A.B. Corley, *Quaker Enterprise* ... 136.
35. For the report of the valuers, Wheatley, Kirk Price and Co. see T.A.B. Corley, *Quaker Enterprise* ... 158. The information in the following five paragraphs is taken from Corley, although he is of course not responsible for the interpretation put upon it.
36. In 1902 there were proposals to set up an Association of Biscuit Manufacturers. In 1903 it had thirty-five members. Huntley and Palmers refused to meet a deputation from the Association. In 1910 a firm of brokers put forward a proposal to amalgamate the various biscuit makers and turn them into a public company. Huntley and Palmers rejected it, and it was stillborn. In 1911 there was a proposal for the big five firms to amalgamate along the lines of the Imperial Tobacco Company. Huntley and Palmers made no active move to encourage this. It was not until 1921 that Associated Biscuit Manufacturers Limited subsumed Huntley and Palmers. Complete integration into Associated Biscuits Ltd. was not brought about until the 1960s.
37. Huntley and Palmers' *Scrapbooks,* cutting. He mentioned the electric telegraph, the typewriter and the bicycle.
38. *Reading Mercury,* 25.6.1926. The Golden Jubilee of the partnership was not marked by festivities in the factory, *Berkshire Chronicle,* 27.6.1891. The dinners given to Assistant Directors, travellers and heads of department, for which records survive in the factory from 1906-1912 seem not to have had the flavour of earlier occasions.
39. In 1904-5 advertising expenditure excluding samples rose from a mere £3,500 to £12,500. It doubled again before 1910.
40. Amongst biscuit firms: Jacobs changed their status in 1883, Carrs in 1894, Meredith and Drew in 1891, Middlemass in 1896, Mackenzie and Mackenzie in

1898; Peak Frean in 1901, and Macfarlane Lang in 1904.

41. This language comes from 'A Programme of Change' (June, 1962) circulated by Rupert Carr within the company in order to create a 'climate of ideas for efficient modern operation', quoted by T.A.B. Corley, *Quaker Enterprise ...* 272-3.

42. *Berkshire Chronicle,* 8.2.1890, 9.2.1895. The 1890 annual meeting of the Reading YMCA was the first for 40 years which M.H. Sutton had missed. Mr Preston spoke of the importance of his commitment to the branches of their work in 1895.

43. For example Alderman Colebrook, *Reading Observer,* 29.3.1890 (1856, came to Reading; 1871, on Council; 1880, first teetotal Mayor; 1871, stood for School Board, later its chairman; active in University Extension; 'a liberal of the most robust type'; a member of Trinity Congregational Church for thirty years; President of the Sunday School Union 1882-3; active in Sunday School work in the poor district of Silver Street; started an Allotments scheme in Redlands Estate. From 1885 lived in his country house at Peppard for six months of every year). Other cases: Attwells, *Reading Observer,* 27.8.1892; Esdell, 31.5.1890; Collier, 28.6.1890; Messer, *Berkshire Chronicle,* 7.7.1900; Fidler, 2.1.1904. Further documentation of the withdrawal of the local bourgeoisie is in Anne Cook, 'Reading', 33, 97, 106, 182, 234-40, 255, 352-3, 369.

44. Joseph Hatton, 'Biscuit Town', in *English Illustrated Magazine* IX, (1891-2) 857.

45. *Reading Observer,* 10.11.1888.

46. *Reading Standard,* 3.12.1902; for another occasion when G.W. Palmer clearly felt his father ought to be there not him, see *Reading Cooperative Record* (March, 1900) 7.

47. *Berkshire Chronicle,* 19.7.1902.

48. Although 'the most serious row that ever erupted in the Board room' was provoked by one of the junior directors who, without consulting his colleagues had become joint master of the S. Berks Hunt, an office which demanded much time, T.A.B. Corley, *Quaker Enterprise ...* 181.

49. For the Palmers and the University, see W.M. Childs, *Making a University* (1933) and T.A.B. Corley, 'The Palmer Family and the University of Reading', in University of Reading, *Staff Journal,* 6 (Nov. 1968).

50. For the official historian's delicate steering between recognising that, at the turn of the century, 'their worst fault (the Palmers) was to mortgage the future by drawing all the profits', and yet exonerating them from 'consciously milking the company in order to keep up their status as country gentlemen', see T.A.B. Corley, *Quaker Enterprise ...* 163-4. For the family see also 131, 146, 149.

51. For assessment of increases in real wages of Huntley and Palmers' employees during 'the Great Depression' 1873-96, see T.A.B. Corley, *Quaker Enterprise ...* 127-8, 136. For subsequent pressure on real wages, leading to decline, see Corley, 175 and *Report of an Enquiry by the Board of Trade into Working Class Rents, Housing and Retail Prices,* Cmd. 3864 (1908) 385-91 and *ibid.,* Cmd. 6955 (1913) 226-7. Prices and rents went up in Reading by seven per cent between 1905 and 1912, but wages did not. See also *Reading Mercury,* 2.2.1907, 9.2.1907; Anne Cook, 'Reading', 230.

52. *Self-Help* (1859) 234. The other books were: Shakespeare, Gulliver's Travels, Robinson Crusoe, Pickwick Papers, Burns, Pilgrim's Progress and a History of England.

53. T.A.B. Corley, *Quaker Enterprise ...* 78, 99, 101, 127, 129.

54. *The 'Borough' Pocket Guide to Reading* (1907) 79 'Reading as a Commercial Centre'.

55. B.S. Rowntree, *Poverty, a Study of Town Life* (1901) 133-4. This description
was designed to show what 'merely physical efficiency' means. The 'wages
paid for unskilled labour in York are insufficient to provide food, shelter and
clothing adequate to maintain a family of moderate size in a state of bare
physical efficiency'.

56. *Berkshire Chronicle*, 10.5.1902.

57. The material here was extracted from the fourteen volumes of 'Record
Papers' of the Reading Distress Committee (set up following the Unemployed
Workmen Act, 1905) which were in the offices of the Council for Social
Service, Wellington Street, Reading. Using the index to the 1913 volume, and
Section 18 of each Record Paper ('previous record, if any, of applicants') it is
possible to trace back a single applicant through all his applications. Each
Record Paper has twenty questions answered on it, and it is from these that I
have constructed the details of this family. These papers are an invaluable and
dynamic source which could be used more extensively, especially in towns
where less material on economic conditions exists than is the case in Reading.
The total applications year by year were as follows:

13 November	1905	–	20 March	1906	569
3 April	1906	–	9 April	1907	723
5 April	1907	–	1 April	1908	1058
3 April	1908	–	3 March	1909	990
2 April	1909	–	31 March	1910	847
5 April	1910	–	31 March	1911	508
5 April	1911	–	22 March	1912	401
1 May	1912	–	31 March	1913	131
15 April	1913	–	30 March	1914	84
10 April	1914	–	8 March	1915	327

Another quantitative source is in *Accounts and Papers*, XCII, 355 (1908)
where breakdowns of the 2,768 persons relieved under the Poor Law in
Reading between 1.10.1906 and 30.9.1907 were made. Two of the analyses
are interesting:
a) Periods of Relief: not exceeding one week, 227; 1 week – not exceeding 4
weeks, 682; 4 weeks – not exceeding 13 weeks, 419; 13 weeks – not
exceeding 26 weeks, 255; 26 weeks – 1 year, 315; whole year, 870.
b) No. of times a person relieved: once, 2315; twice, 315; three times, 90;
four times, 22; five times or more, 26.

58. R.H. Tawney, 'The Theory of Pauperism', in *The Sociological Review,* III
(October, 1909) 369.

59. W.H. Beveridge, *Unemployment, A Problem of Industry* (1909) 146.

60. See *Berkshire Chronicle*, 20.8.1892 – a report of an inquest on a death by
starvation headed 'Poverty in Reading'. See also *Berkshire Chronicle*, 2.1.1904
– a letter from a church worker in Coley, 'Here are a whole lot of people
starving for want of fuel and bread'. See also An Octogenarian, *Reminiscences
of Reading* (Reading, 1888) where he pleaded for action in distress, 'so that our
feelings may not be outraged by hearing of a fellow creature dying from
starvation here'; and *Reading Mercury*, 25.11.1893, an appeal by a Reading
inhabitant to the Local Government Board to remedy a situation in which
'820 good workmen in a small town like Reading ... are going about in an
actual state of starvation'; and *ibid.*, 3.8.1907, quoted in Anne Cook,
'Reading', 229; for starvation see also *Reading Co-operative Record,* (Jan. 1903)
5; (Feb. 1903) 10; (Feb. 1905) 4.

61. *Berkshire Chronicle*, 17.6.1893.

62. *Reading Co-operative Record* (January, 1905).

63. Lady Bell, *At the Works: a Study of a Manufacturing Town,* 2nd edition
(1911) 81.

64. A.L. Bowley and A.R. Burnett-Hurst, *Livelihood and Poverty* (1915). Bowley
    was a Professor at University College, Reading. Earlier publication of some of
    the Reading results was in an article 'Working-class Households in Reading' in
    Journal of the Royal Statistical Society (June, 1913) 672-701. The book
    contained work on Northampton, Warrington, and Stanley as well as Reading.
    There was a sequel by A.L. Bowley and M.H. Hogg, *Has Poverty Diminished?*
    (1925). The method as well as the substance of the 1912 work was important.
    It was the first survey to borrow the sampling technique from the biological
    sciences, see D. Caradog-Jones, *Social Surveys* (Hutchinson's University
    Library) 66. Bowley wrote a companion volume to his surveys called *The
    Measurement of Social Phenomena.* As Bowley himself stated in a speech to
    the Reading Trades and Labour Council in 1914 (*Reading Observer*, 16.1.1914)
    'the particular value of the inquiry was that it showed the position of
    working-class households in a way such as was not known in any other town'.
65. Overcrowding indices, as Charles Booth admitted, having tried in his *Industry*
    series to use them, were not a good index of poverty. T.S. and M. Simey,
    Charles Booth, Social Scientist (1960) 166, 204.
66. For this see *Livelihood and Poverty*, 79-83.
67. *Livelihood and Poverty*, 41.
68. *Livelihood and Poverty*, 16. Wages at Huntley and Palmers in the nineteenth
    century represented less than 10% of costs, see T.A.B. Corley, *Quaker
    Enterprise ...* 59, 303-4.
69. *Reading Co-operative Record* (October, 1905).
70. *Berkshire Chronicle*, 10.7.1914. There was a comparative survey of builders'
    wages in *The Builder* in 1914. Reading was about half-way down the towns
    surveyed. Labourers' wages in the trade were 6d. per hour in Reading (lowest
    was 4d. in Bridgwater, highest was 8d. in London).
71. This twelve per cent is made up of: brick, plain tile, terra cotta makers; boot,
    shoe, slipper, patten, clog-makers; domestic outdoor service; messengers,
    porters, watchmen (not railway or government); general labourers, factory
    labourers (undefined); agriculture on farms, woods and gardens.
72. In this category I have included: Commercial or business clerks; professional
    occupations and their subordinate services; merchants; agents, accountants,
    banking, insurance; national and local government.
73. This category has been deliberately widened to its maximum extent in order
    to avoid any exaggeration of economic constraints. It includes occupational
    groupings which would themselves have included many very poorly paid
    workers as well as better paid workers. It is made up of: conveyance of men,
    goods and messages on railways and on road; general engineering and machine
    making; iron, steel, etc., manufacture, tools, dies, etc., arms, misc. metal
    trades; printers and lithographers; wood, furniture, fittings and decorators;
    cycles, coaches and other vehicles; tailors; electrical apparatus; precious metals,
    jewels, watches, instruments and games.
74. For an excellent comparison with the London area and further useful insights
    into the 'Condition of Reading' see *Report of an Enquiry by the Board of
    Trade into Working Class Rents, Housing, Retail Prices and Standard Rates of
    Wages in the U.K.* Cmd. 3864, 1908. Two sentences were important – one on
    wages, the other on prices:

    > Wages in London being taken as 100, the wages index numbers for Reading
    > are, for skilled men in the building trades 68; for labourers in the building
    > trade 87; for skilled men in the engineering trades 80, for labourers in the
    > engineering trade 84; for skilled men in the printing trade 74.
    >   The level of predominant prices in Reading approaches very closely to
    > the level of prices in London ... London predominant prices being in each
    > case taken as 100, the following are the Reading index numbers: all

commodities (i.e. groceries, coal, and meat), 101; groceries (i.e. excluding coal), 105; coal 85; meat 99.

See also a surveyor giving evidence to the Royal Commission on London Traffic in 1904, 'the employers of Trade Union labour, have already in many instances withdrawn from London where the highest rates of wages obtain', quoted in E.H. Phelps Brown, *The Growth of British Industrial Relations (1959)* 10. Hence the Reading printing trade, for which see also A.H. Anderson, *The Town of Reading, residential, educational, industrial* (1911) 63.

CHAPTER 5

1. Guy Rogers, *A Rebel at Heart* (1956) 75-92.
2. *Reading Observer,* 24.8.1912; for the CWS jam factory see Percy Redfern, *The Story of the C.W.S. 1863-1913* (n.d.) 209.
3. *Reading Observer,* 15.7.1893.
4. Such as the Rev. C.W.H. Kenrick's sharp fights with socialists on the School Board, *Reading Observer,* 12.3.1892, 17.10.1892, 17.12.1892; or the forbidding of the band of Spring Gardens Methodist church to play for the Trades Council when it came of age in 1912, *Reading Observer,* 4.5.1912. For a study of subservient religious organisations see Liston Pope, *Millhands and Preachers* (New Haven, 1942). Broad Street Chapel (Congregationalist) evidently ejected a demonstration of the unemployed in 1908, *The Reading Pioneer,* 48 (December, 1908) quoted in Broad Street, *Magazine* (July, 1962) in a series of historical articles by the Rev. J. Wilding. Such demonstrations were on other occasions embraced and preached to, see *Reading Standard.* 1.2.1908 (Trinity Congregational) and *Berkshire Chronicle,* 28.1.1893 (St. Lawrence's Anglican church).
5. For a plea for this kind of self-consciousness in religious organisations see T. Brennan, E.W. Cooney, H. Pollins, *Social Change in South West Wales* (1954) 142. Also K. Mannheim, *Freedom, Power and Democratic Planning* (1951) 312; World Council of Churches, *The Church and the Disorder of Society* (1948).
6. 'It was surely a great credit to the town that they had not the amount of poverty in Reading that there was in other parts of the country'; 'And the work people. These are bright, happy men and women and girls and boys ... you cannot help thinking "what a healthy, happy, lot of people"'; 'the town is altogether free from the worst evils of manufacturing cities', *Reading Observer,* 17.3.1906; *Answers,* 11.1.1908; A.H. Anderson, *Homeland Handbooks* 48 (1906-7) 122. Among other instances of such comment are: *Reading Illustrated,* 1904; *Reading Observer,* 24.12.1892, 14.5.1892; *Reading University College Review* (March, 1910) vol. 1, no. 5; *Berkshire Chronicle,* 15.5.1914. Such comment in relation to known conditions makes it difficult to use 'optimists' in the late nineteenth-century 'standard of living' controversy (like Sir Robert Giffen) as reliable guides to the real social effects of economic change in this period.
7. C. Gore, ed., *Lux Mundi* (1889), Campion's essay, 'Disestablishment and The People', 458; see also G. Gissing, *Demos* (1886) vol. I, 180.
8. *Labour Prophet,* Sept. 1893.
9. Broad Street, *Magazine* (Feb. 1905).
10. See Albert Paul, *Poverty, Hardship But Happiness* (QueenSpark Books, Brighton, 1974) 38-9; Dot Starn, *When I Was a Child* (Hackney WEA, 1973) 14; C. Violet Butler, *Social Conditions in Oxford* (1912) 170, E. Hiscock, *Last Boat to Folly Bridge* (1970) 4; J. Springhall, 'The Boy Scouts, Class and Militarism in Relation to British Youth Movements, 1908-1930', in

International Review of Social History, XVI (1972) 140-1; A.A. MacLaren,
'Presbyterianism and the Working Class in a Mid-Nineteenth-Century City', in
Scottish Historical Review, XLVI (1967); I owe the Butler and Hiscock
references to John Gillis of Rutgers University — Violet Butler claimed that
some children were sent to church three times a day just for the prizes given
for regular attenders. On the other hand, R. Hoggart, *The Uses of Literacy*
(1957) 39, saw expense as a barrier to attendance at organisations like the Boy
Scouts; in Fred Kitchen, *Brother to the Ox: The Autobiography of a Farm
Labourer* (1940) 237, there is an extract from his diary (*c.*1927) which
stressed the cost of attendance rather than the benefits: 'Have just returned
from a do at the church institute. It was in aid of the heathen Chinee, and as
our children were in a sketch the Sunday School got up, our Lizzie took me
to see them. My, but they do slate you at these church and chapel do's. I gave
our Joyce sixpence to get me a cup of tea. She brought me the the tea all right,
and good tea it was, whether Hindoo or Chinee, but she brought me no change.
I thought sixpence pretty strong, even for the best tea, and went to investigate;
but the brassy-faced wench at the buffet just grinned at me, and said; "It's for
the heathen Chinee, and the vicar wants us to take all we can".'; see also
R. Tressell, *The Ragged Trousered Philanthropists* (1914) Panther edition
(1965) 165, 169, 173, 250; and for the prohibitive cost of the Scouts, and the
relative cheapness of the Church Lads Brigade, see R. Roberts, *The Classic
Slum* (Pelican, 1973) 161n.4.
11. Joseph J. Beecroft, *A Handy Guide to Reading* (Reading, 1882); St. John's
Annual Address (1893); *ibid.* (1900); see also St. Peter's Caversham, *Parish
Magazine* (Jan. 1891). For costs of membership see also *Primitive Methodist
Magazine* (1890) 534, (1907) 701.
12. Hosier Street, *Chapel Minutes,* vol. 2, 1859-68 and vol. 5, 1886-96.
13. *Berkshire Chronicle,* 30.1.1904.
14. Greyfriars Church, *Annual Report* (1908) and Iron Mission Room, *Preachers
Book* (1887-1929); among other instances of such comment are: *Reading
Standard,* 27.6.1906, on Hosier Street Chapel; St. Giles, *Parish Magazine*
(April, 1912); and on St. Mark's district in 1889, *Parish Magazine* (1890).
After their burst of twentieth-century building, Reading Methodists were
proud of an average attendance of 2,500-3,000 a week, see *Methodist
Recorder,* 20.4.1911.
15. *Broad Street Independent Church Magazine* (Sept. 1905).
16. Caversham Heights Methodist church located their social aspirations rather
precisely in the *Trustees Minutes* (May, 1909): 'A number of gentlemen are
now living upon the Heights whose interest and help it is most desirable should
be secured'. They had three 'gentlemen' listed as such among their Trustees.
The rest were: three builders; three commercial travellers; two clerks; and one
each of the following — ironmonger, furniture dealer, silversmith, merchant,
outfitter, dairyman, laundry manager, insurance agent, farmer, tutor and
manufacturing joiner.
17. The Registers are separate but cover, in the first two instances, more than one
chapel: London Street, used 1837-80; Cumberland Road (in circuit safe of
Queens Road Wesleyan chapel); Friar Street, 1880-1914.
18. See also James Obelkevich, 'Primitive Methodism in South Lindsay,
1825-1875', paper to Davis Center seminar, Princeton University, 12th April
1974, 20-21; he, and R. Currie, *Methodism Divided* (1968) 130, suggest that
baptism was of declining significance amongst Primitive Methodists through
the nineteenth century, at least as seen from below. Precise information on
who did what, in occupational terms, has been hard to come by in Reading
between 1890 and 1914. It may, therefore, be worth citing 'the various
occupations of the borrowers from the lending department' of the Reading

Public Library between 1896-8. The figures are given in *Free Public Library and Museum and Art Gallery, Report 1889-1898*, 37-8. There were 4,186 borrowers in the two years analysed. Of these the major categories were: Ladies or Gentlemen of no occupation, 38% (Ladies, 1,327; Gentlemen 280); Clerks and Warehousemen, 9%; Scholars, students and teachers, 9%; Labourers or factory operatives, 8%; Drapers, dress and mantle makers, and milliners, 3%; Shopkeepers' assistants, 3%; Domestic servants, 3%.

19. W. Rauschenbusch, 'The Stake of the Church in the Social Movement', in *The American Journal of Sociology*, III (1897-8) 29-30; see also Keir Hardie, *Can a Man be a Christian on a Pound a Week?* 3rd edition (1905) 11.

20. For example, C.F.G. Masterman, *In Peril of Change: Essays Written in time of Tranquillity* (1905) 214, 'I think we may safely affirm that this creation of a city race is in no small degree responsible for the present manifest failure of appeal of our spiritual creeds'. Or a description of the 'moral change' involved in being a proletarian in G.B. Shaw, 'The Economic Basis of Socialism', in *Fabian Essays* (1889) 1962 edition, 44. Or, for a later view, Helen Lynd, *England in the 1880s* (1945) 328-9 for an interpretation of urbanism and the market system in terms of their isolation of the individual. Or Beatrice Webb, *Our Partnership* (1948) 208 'the town workman ... is simply indifferent to the whole question of religion or metaphysic'. Compare Booth's judgment, *Life and Labour of the People of London*, III (1902-3 edition) 87, 'the London working man is great in all forms of discussion ... religious subjects are the most popular'; for the best modern treatment see H. McLeod, 'Class, Community and Religion: the religious geography of nineteenth-century England' in ed. M. Hill, *A Sociological Year Book of Religion in Britain*, 6 (1973) 29-72.

21. Max Weber, *The Sociology of Religion* (1965) 100-01; see also H. Richard Niebuhr, *The Social Sources of Denominationalism* (1929) Meridian books edition (1957) 72; Ernst Troeltsch, *The Social Teaching of the Christian Churches* (1931) 24, 991.

22. A. Morrison, *Tales of Mean Streets* (1894) 175.

23. R. Hoggart, *The Uses of Literacy* (1957), 52, 55, 59; in relation to trade unionism, H.A. Turner, *Trade Union Growth Structure and Policy* (1962) argues that the hegemony of mid-nineteenth-century exclusive unionism led later on to prejudice amongst other sections of the working class against trade unions as such.

24. T.A. Welton, *England's Recent Progress* (1911) 13. The pace of population movement was quickening in this period nationally. In 1901 the men who were found by the census in some part of England and Wales other than their native county made up 28% of the whole; ten years later it was 36%, E.H. Phelps Brown, *The Growth of British Industrial Relations: a study from the standpoint of 1906-14*, paperback edition (1965) 12.

25. St. Bartholomew's, *Parish Magazine* (Jan. 1899); in 1884 Chamberlain estimated in Birmingham that 'probably one-fifth of our votes move from one ward to another during the year', J. Vincent, *The Formation of the Liberal Party* (1966) 252, 16; for turnover in a Baptist chapel in Bristol 1868-94 see J.H.S. Kent, 'The Role of Religion in the Cultural Structure of the Later Victorian City', in *T.R.H.S.* (1973) 156.

26. Rev. J. Consterdine, *Early History of St. Mary's, Castle Street, Reading* (pamphlet).

27. St. Peter's Caversham (included St. Andrew's, St. John the Baptist, St. Barnabas) *Parish Magazine* (Oct. 1912).

28. *Reading Standard*, 13.10.1899. See also *Baptist United Magazine* (June, 1897).

29. G.P. Crawford, *Recollections of St. Mary's 50 years ago* (Reading, 1932) 16, 40.

30. *Reading Observer*, 29.3.1890.
31. W. Ashworth, *The Genesis of Modern British Town Planning* (1954) 23.
32. For an article by W.R. Nicholas, an Estate Agent and Reading Councillor, on 'The Property Market in Berkshire in 1892' which brought out the dynamics of house building in Reading and resulting 'over-building' see *The Reading Observer*, 7.1.1893. For suggestive writing on the connections between types of urban and suburban districts and 'human purposes and the development of being and relationship', see W. Ashworth, 'Types of Social and Economic Development in Suburban Essex', in Centre for Urban Studies, *London: Aspects of Change* (1964) 72; R. Williams, *Culture and Society, 1780-1950*, Pelican edition (1961) 211; M. Simey, *Charitable Effort in Liverpool in the Nineteenth Century* (Liverpool, 1951); E.J. Hobsbawm, *Primitive Rebels* (Manchester, 1959) Chapter VII, 'The City Mob', 108-26.
33. *Berkshire Chronicle*, 15.3.1902; for means of transport in relation to types of urban decentralisation see Centre for Urban Studies, *London: Aspects of Change* (1964) 41ff. Tramways in some areas (e.g. Woodford) were actively resisted by inhabitants who thought they would lead to working-class immigration. R. Hoggart, *The Uses of Literacy* (Pelican, 1958) 116, romantically refers to trams as 'representative working-class vehicles, the gondolas of the people'; see also R. Roberts, *The Classic Slum* (Pelican, 1973) 146-7.
34. M.B. Simey quoted an 1883 report which blamed religious organisations for 'constantly trailing like a skirt behind prosperity, following it step by step away from where its comforts ... are most sorely needed', see *Charitable Effort in Liverpool in the Nineteenth Century* (Liverpool, 1951) 16; Hosier Street Congregational Methodists blamed their predecessors in the building they leased, see below; for interpretation of the sorting out of the Edinburgh population, in terms of demand for social differentiation among the working class, see R.Q. Gray, 'Styles of Life, the "Labour Aristocracy" and Class relations in later-nineteenth-century Edinburgh', in *International Review of Social History*, XVIII (1973) Pt.3, 434-5.
35. Thus St. Peter's Caversham, *Parish Magazine* (July, 1884) referred to 'the growing importance of a parish which must now be regarded rather as a suburb than a village'.
36. R. Williams, *Culture and Society 1780-1950*, Pelican edition (1961) 211.
37. For descriptions of working-class houses in Reading, see *Report of an Enquiry by the Board of Trade into Working-Class Rents, Housing, Retail Prices and Standard Rates of Wages in the United Kingdom* (1908) Cmd. 3864, in *Accounts and Papers* (1908) cvii, 763-4.
38. For corner-shops see J.A. Hobson, *The Evolution of Modern Capitalism* (1894) 2nd edition (1954) 164, where he described how in the 1890s 'the wealthier classes are beginning to buy all their goods at the big stores in the centre of towns or by post ... so that the small dispersed retail businesses are becoming more and more dependent upon the supply of the needs of the working classes'; and R. Hoggart, *The Uses of Literacy* (1957) 70; for an Edinburgh cricket club which needed to appeal to the Trades Council in 1891 to help preserve their ground, see R.Q. Gray, *op. cit.,* 444.
39. For such churches in London, see D.H. McLeod, 'Membership and Influence of the Churches in Metropolitan London', unpublished D.Phil. (Cambridge, 1971) 33, 145.
40. The buildings were: London Street (1866), Cumberland Road (1871), Friar Street (1872), Oxford Road (1878). Later a chapel in Wokingham Road was also built. See 'On the Work of God in Reading Circuit', in *Primitive Methodist Magazine* (1840) 131; 'Protracted Meeting at Reading', *ibid.* (1841) 267; 'Missionary Services at Reading', *ibid.* (1844) 299; 'Primitive Methodism

in Reading', *ibid.* (1887) 262, 395; 'Primitive Methodism in the Conference Town', *ibid.* (1915) 518.

41. R.H. Tawney, *Equality* (1964 edition) 34; for a useful study here see C.M. Elliott, 'The Social and Economic History of the Principal Protestant Denominations in Leeds, 1760-1844', unpublished D.Phil. thesis (Oxford, 1963). This has 'three basic themes': 'The first centres on the reactions of the five principal Protestant denominations ... to the economic problems posed by the rapid urbanisation of a large parish. The second concerns the extent to which certain social groups were given power within the denomination by the various denominational financial systems. The third is an examination of the effects of that power on the social teaching of the denominations concerned '

42. Wycliffe Chapel, *Minute Books*, vol. I, 1881. The information on Wycliffe is taken either from vols. I and II of the *Minute Books,* or from the *Jubilee Brief History,* or from Messrs. Woodham, Osted Smith and Gill in Reading, and Caversham, all of whom supplied information.

43. Information on Anderson Memorial Chapel is taken from a pamphlet by one of the founders, *The Beginnings of Anderson Baptist Church* (1932); *Handbook of the Baptist Cause at Earley Rise Reading, afterwards known as the Anderson Baptist Church* (Early days, pioneers, progress, buildings, statistics, etc.); *Church Minutes,* volume covering 1903-29.

44. Information in St. Bartholomew's *Parish Magazine,* 1890-1914; *A Chronicle of events connected with the Parish of St. Bartholomew's Reading from the Beginnings of its history to the present day* (1929).

45. The main source for this narrative is Caversham Baptist Free Church, *Church Minutes,* vol. I, 'a narrative of the origin of the Free Church in Caversham'.

46. The full figures are in the *Reading Mercury,* 21.4.1866 and details of the opening in the *Berkshire Chronicle,* 21.4.1866.

47. Rev. Charles Hole, *The Life of William Whitmarsh Phelps, M.A.* (London and Reading, 1871) 189. See also *The Methodist Recorder,* 1.10.1908, p.10, for the effect of Elm Park Hall on its neighbourhood.

48. M. Hinton, *A History of the Town of Reading* (1954) 141. It was said that 300 people professed conversion under his ministry.

49. W.M. Childs, *The Town of Reading during the early part of the Nineteenth Century* (Reading, 1910) 49; Rev. L. Harman and Rev. K.R. Brymer, *The History of Christianity in Reading* (Reading, 1952) 65; for undenominational evangelical missionary work leading to four new congregations in early nineteenth-century Reading see W.R. Ward, *Religion and Society in England 1790-1850* (1972) 49.

50. Information on St. Mary's is in Rev. J. Consterdine, *The Early History of St. Mary's Castle St. Reading,* derived from the Chapel Committee, *Minutes, Transactions of the Trustees, 1836-1895. Reminiscences of Reading by an Octogenarian* (Reading, 1888) 11-12 gives a good account of the atmosphere of the preacher-and-doctrine-oriented, schismatic Anglicanism/Congregationalism of this time. The elders of the church in 1821 included a brewer, the leading doctor in Reading, a bookseller, Mr. French 'a refined and well educated man', an attorney, and the clerk of St. Giles.

51. There is very full and interesting documentation of this chapel at the minister's house in Caversham. For this paragraph the source is a section in the *Church Records* volume called 'Historical Account of this Church', and *Caversham Hill Church Book* (1855-c.93).

52. *Berkshire Chronicle,* 13.9.1902; G.P. Crawford, *Recollections of St. Mary's Reading 50 years ago* (Reading, 1932) 40. The building of St. Mark's and St. Saviour's was a crippling strain on the resources of time and money of St. Mary's, and realised to be so, 'I much regret that my remarks', said the vicar in 1904, 'should be almost entirely about money, but you will, I know,

forgive me ... (there was) great anxiety in his mind about the machinery of the parish'.

53. They were: the three major parish churches of St. Giles, St. Mary's and St. Lawrence's; Grey Friars, the Caversham church of St. Peter's and St. Michael's Tilehurst.

54. Kings Road Baptists started as the Church Lane Baptists.

55. St. Mary's Episcopal Chapel, Holy Trinity Oxford Road and St. John's Watlington Street were the only legacy of these years, and the last two were transformed later on.

56. Wesley's first visit to Reading was in 1739. Thereafter he came in 1740 (twice), 1777 and 1781. In his journal (10.3.1777) he thought Reading was full of 'a people stupid as oxen'. There was a 'preaching house' in 1777 at London Street, rented. Visitors conducted preaching services until 1804. The shoemaker who paid the rent left in 1804, so the room went to the Particular Baptists. Another room was hired until 1815, until two cottages were bought in Cross Street because the Rev. J. Waterhouse was attracting large crowds. In 1816 Church Street was considered a better site and the first foundation stone was laid. The debt on Church Street lasted until 1867. Wesley Church, School Rooms and Class Rooms were built in 1872-3 at a cost of £7500, of which £3,500 was promised at building. Oxford Road Society was the first missionary offshoot, growing out of the requisitioning of West Street Hall for Sunday services and a Sunday School. For early Wesleyanism see J.J. Beecroft, 'Reading and its Methodism', in *The Methodist Recorder*, 2.4.1905, and Wesley Methodist Church, Reading, *Centenary Souvenir Brochure: 1873-1973*. The Berkshire Mission of the Primitive Methodists reached Reading in 1835, the circuit was constituted in 1837, they rented a London Street chapel between 1835 and 1839, when they bought a chapel, Salem Chapel in Minster Street. This was headquarters until 1866, when the London Street Chapel was bought. For early Primitive Methodism see 'Primitive Methodism in Reading', in *Primitive Methodist Magazine* (1887) 262 and 395.

57. The Unitarians tried to get going in 1814, and the Presbyterians' first effort ended in 1780.

58. Restoration in the three major churches (St. Mary's 1864, 1865, 1872; St. Lawrence's 1870s-1880s, mainly 1882; St. Giles 1873) amounted almost to total rebuilding. More was spent than on many new churches. Greyfriars was re-opened, after disuse since the sixteenth century, in 1863. At least ten new churches were built in this phase. Caversham parish church was restored in 1878, Tilehurst in 1855. St. John's, although only recently erected, was entirely rebuilt in 1873. Four new churches were built 1890-1914.

59. Joseph J. Beecroft, *A Handy Guide to Reading* (Reading, 1882). Asa Briggs, *Victorian Cities* (1963) 260, on Middlesbrough, judged that in that town 'chapel building was the biggest single corporate enterprise; the "propensity to give" expressed itself most notably in this form'.

60. Reading Salvation Army Corps I and II were founded without a permanent home before 1890. The army acquired its main-street citadel, and Corps III (1907) and the Caversham Corps (1904) during the years 1890-1914: see a note on the Army below. The Wesleyan Methodists had a great burst of buildings as a result of their Twentieth-Century Fund — Tilehurst (1904) Elm Park Hall (1905) Whitley Hall (1906) Caversham Heights (1909). Earlier they had built Lower Caversham (1892). Another congregation beginning in this period was the Agapemonites, see *Berkshire Chronicle*, 13.9.1902. They had a congregation of about forty, meeting first in Victoria Hall, Fatherson Road then at a private house in Craven Road. They were followers of Brother Prince (d.1899) and Rev. J.H. Smyth-Piggott of the Church of the Ark of the Covenant at Clapton. They sustained a good following in Reading 'for many years'.

61. Mr Wiltshire of 2 Woodcote Road, Caversham kindly let me read the Zoar *Church Meetings, Minutes* 1881-1965, and *Church Register* 1881-1965. They are kept in his house; for parallel cases see E.T. Davies, *Religion in the Industrial Revolution in South Wales* (Cardiff, 1965) 17.

62. Caversham Methodist Church (as opposed to Caversham Heights Methodist Church) started from an Evangelistic venture by members of Oxford Road Chapel, Reading. Weekly prayer meetings in cottages at the junction of Gosbrook Road and Star Road, then open-air meetings, then, in August 1881, an Iron Church costing £360, then a full church ten years later. The full church started as a 'school chapel' costing £1,090 in Oct. 1891, and was not extended into its present form until 1899 at a cost of £1,600. There is no record of hostility from the parent church as there was in the case of the analogous Anderson Baptist Chapel. E.R. Mills, Caversham Methodist Church Diamond Jubilee 1899-1959, *Souvenir Programme;* 'Caversham Society' *Minutes of Leaders' Meetings,* volume covering 25.4.1888 – 23.9.1910.

63. For a chronology and typology of 'offshoots' and 'secessions' from Wesleyan Methodism in the nineteenth century, see R. Currie, *Methodism Divided: A Study in the Sociology of Ecumenicalism* (1968) 54-76. They were characteristic of Methodism up to the mid-nineteenth century.

64. These include the Presbyterians in Sun Lane, a secession from Broad Street; the first arrival of the Unitarians in the town (1811-14) formed partly by schism; a body of Congregationalists in Salem Chapel who seceded from St. Mary's Episcopal in 1808 and also from Broad Street and Hosier Lane Baptists; of the ones which survived, Broad Street Congregational, Kings Road Baptists, St. Mary's Episcopal, Zoar Strict Baptist, Providence Strict Baptist were pre-1840. Castle Street, St. Augustine's and Trinity Congregational chapels, and Hosier Street and Caversham Hill chapel (in its post-1902 form) were post-1840. Major elements of many other congregations must also have come from secessionist or schismatic impulses.

65. *Reading Observer,* 21.9.1910; St. Giles, *Parish Magazine,* (Dec. 1902).

66. There is fascinating material on this nationally, in the denominational press. For example, Rev. H.T. Hooper, 'Preachers and Competition', in *The Methodist Times,* 25.1.1906, 52, where there is a deeply-felt argument against chapels adapting to the modes of organisation suitable for political meetings, theatres, and football; or Rev. T.B. Stephenson, 'Methodism and the New Century' part IV, in *Wesleyan Methodist Magazine* (1901) 272-5, where there is doubt cast on the model of the new Hall, 'with its electric lighting, its band of music, its absence of pew rents, and its freedom from conventionalities'. The penalty of such 'appliances', however 'successful', is to introduce 'the speculative element' into religious building, i.e. letting-off sections of the buildings, which 'could not be adopted as a general method in the erection of buildings for worship'. Also they forced centralisation of finance, since 'every such Mission, when its members have done most generously, must still draw largely upon the liberality of the church at large'.

67. *Berkshire Chronicle,* 14.8.1897.

68. Other examples of this type of large local donor playing a critical role in the bringing into being of a church or chapel between 1840 and 1890 are: Holy Trinity Church, Oxford Road; St. John's second church; St. Agnes, Silver Street; Christ Church Whiteley; St. Luke's; St. Bartholomew's. Sometimes it was the original donation of the land which set the whole process in motion, as at St. Mark's; Greyfriars Mission Room, Great Knollys Street; St. Andrew's, Caversham; St. George's, Tilehurst; Caversham Heights Chapel; Oxford Road Wesleyan Church (£1,500 out of £4,500 given by Mr Minty); Queen's Road (large donations, from Palmers and others, were important but not quite predominant here); Cumberland Road schoolrooms; Caversham Free Church; Wycliffe

(again large donations of critical importance but not quite predominant);
Grovelands Baptist first chapel.

69. Sources for this scheme are: *The Methodist Times*, 23.2.1905; *The Methodist
Recorder*, 2.4.1905, 1.10.1908, 20.4.1911, 21.11.1912, Wesley Methodist
Church, *Centenary Souvenir Brochure 1873-1973* (Reading, 1973). The two
Halls built were Elm Park and Whitley (£6,890 and £6,500 respectively). Other
buildings were Tilehurst Chapel and Caversham Heights School Room (£1,600
and £2,450). A third Hall at Cholmeley Road (£4,500) was also planned. For
the launching meeting of the scheme, see *Reading Observer*, 30.5.1903; for
opening of Elm Park, *Reading Observer*, 4.2.1905.

70. Mainly on: Oxford Road Chapel, which grew out of using the West Street Hall
for Sunday services and a Sunday School; Wesley Church Queens Road and
school-rooms (1872-3, £7,250; see *Berkshire Chronicle*, 7.12.1872); Spring
Gardens Chapel — the predecessor of Whitley Hall; Wesley Manse (1899 —
they still had £800 to raise for this in 1901).

71. See n.69 above; the Salvation Army makes an interesting case in the context
of the argument here. They were very self-conscious about the manner of
bringing Corps into being. The General was insistent on local cadres being
forced to rely on the support of their locality for everything except the most
minimum of wages for Officers sent from Headquarters. In that way he hoped
to build a genuine participatory (although undemocratic) movement, see
William Booth, 'What is the Salvation Army?', in *The Contemporary Review*
(Aug. 1882) 178-81. Reading I started in 1881, II in 1882, III in 1897 (East
Corps) and Caversham in 1904. A common feature of the Corps in their early
days was their having to make shift with a variety of buildings, never being
able, or never perhaps thinking it appropriate until much later, to acquire
permanent homes with all that that implied (Reading East 1927, West 1932).
As a Salvationist recorded, 'apart from Caversham there is a common feature
in the history of the Reading Salvation Army Corps, all have had a number of
homes', *Berkshire Chronicle*, 9.7.1965. But intervention by one local rich
man moved the main Corps into a permanent and main-street site in the early
years of the century. J.C. Fidler was converted in 1896 and then ten years
later built a Citadel for £5,000 and sold it to the Army for £3,000. They
raised the money locally partly by large gifts and partly by small subscriptions.
This move may well have been a critical one in dividing the early attack on
Reading via the old boat house on Canal Wharf, and the premises in Willow
Street, from the Salvation Army as a denomination more like other
denominations. But it has not been possible, in the absence of surviving Corps
Books, to trace through the effects of the intervention by Fidler on the life
and nature of the Central Corps.

72. Reading was expected to be a contributor rather than a withdrawer from the
Twentieth Century Fund, but it did not turn out to be possible. Reading had
been asked to supply £1,000, but the building scheme was vastly more
expensive than that. The number of contributions can be seen in the *List of
Subscribers to the Twentieth Century Fund* in the safe at Oxford Road
Chapel — there were 250 at Wesley Chapel, 212 at Oxford Road, 23 at Spring
Gardens, 34 at Caversham and 9 at Tilehurst. Other examples of 1890-1914
creations which did not rely on large donors or on local pennies were:
St. Michael's; St. Paul's, Lower Whitley; St. Mark's; St. Andrew's, Caversham
Heights; St. Barnabas, Emmer Green; Oxford Road, Primitives; Grovelands
second church; Anderson Memorial; Tilehurst Mission Hall; St. Paul's,
Presbyterian. There were, of course, exceptions, as in the case of Park Institute
Congregational Church, where Owen Ridley played a vital role, but although
exceptional between 1890 and 1914 in that it was a large donor who enabled
it to happen, it was not exceptional in that it was a different type of church

from others — more like the Wesleyan Halls.
73. *The Methodist Recorder*, 21.11.1912, pp.9-10.
74. St. George's, *Diary*, 1885.
75. For the decay of the Class meeting in the second half of the nineteenth century, see R. Currie, *Methodism Divided* (1968) 125-9; and Chapter 3 above.
76. *Reading Observer*, 1.6.1907; *Berkshire Chronicle*, 25.6.1904, Rev. W.G. Dixon on 'Why Mission Halls?'.
77. *Primitive Methodist Magazine* (1890) 379, 533-4, 562; (1896) 395, 474.
78. The Amish are sometimes referred to as 'House Amish' among other Pennsylvania Dutch sects; they hold bi-weekly Sunday meetings at the homes of members on a rotating basis. There was a schism leading to the 'Church-Amish' in 1927. Amongst other Pennsylvania Dutch church organisations there is also self-consciousness about the burdens of buildings, many 'have proudly held mortgage-burning ceremonies at which they freed themselves from debt'; see Elmer L. Smith, *Meet the Mennonites* (Lebanon, Pa., 1961) 24-5, and Elmer L. Smith, *Pennsylvania Dutch Folklore* (Lebanon, Pa., 1960) 7. For early Puritan awareness of the dangers of buildings see Keith Thomas, *Religion and the Decline of Magic* (1971) 57-9.
79. Calculations on the basis of Smith's *Directories* for Reading shows that the average length of time a senior Anglican priest stayed in the town between 1890 and 1914 was eleven years, compared to four years for Curates. The average for all other churches combined was six years; but this conceals enormous variations from a Presbyterian church where one man stayed twenty-three years, to the Salvation Army where initially Captains and Adjutants stayed one year and, once the early assault on Reading was over, two to three years. The notional three-year rotation amongst Wesleyans and Primitives was adhered to if one takes the average; but in fact there were wide variations even in these denominations between seven- and one-year stays in Reading.
80. W.R. Ward, *Religion and Society in England, 1790-1850* (1972) 7, 42, etc., has good material from this period on the constraints imposed by finance and buildings; see also E.T. Davies, *Religion in the Industrial Revolution in South Wales* (Cardiff, 1965) 17, 55, 100. Wesley would not let a chapel be built unless two-thirds of the money was pre-subscribed, but such caution was soon abandoned, Ward, p. 98.
81. This analysis was made easier by an index of Primitive Methodist obituaries compiled by Mr William Leary, in the Methodist Archives in Epworth House. The index (also covering places and preachers) makes local analysis of this kind feasible, whereas before it would have taken months. Of the 35 Reading obituaries, 13 fall before 1860, 18 after, and 4 have been counted in both halves. The contrast is stark when the quality of individual mentions of specific features of the subjects' lives is set alongside the quantity. But figures can give an indication. There were three mentions in 17 pre-1860 obituaries compared to 28 mentions in 22 post-1860 obituaries of contribution to building works, work in the penumbra of chapel organisations, wordly success and gentle virtues. There were 28 mentions in 17 pre-1860 obituaries compared to 17 mentions in 22 post-1860 obituaries of qualities such as experience of conversion, manner of meeting death, strength under persecution, and aggression in evangelism. Many of these 17 out of 22 post-1860 mentions were in fact extremely perfunctory compared to the great length of earlier mentions. For changing emphasis on events in chapel life see *Primitive Methodist Magazine*, references in n. 40 above, plus *ibid.* (1846) 755, (1850) 56, (1851) 753, (1856) 750, (1858) 53, (1866) 116. For the Sunday Schools: (1844) 299-300, (1846) 228, (1852) 632, (1858) 627. The Primitive Methodist Sunday Schools started in Reading in 1838. The idea of obituary

analysis was suggested to me by James Obelkevich of Princeton University, who has used it in his forthcoming work on Lincolnshire.

82. For the effect of individual ministers, see David Hugh McLeod, 'Membership and Influence of the Churches in Metropolitan London, 1885-1914', unpublished Ph.D. thesis (Cambridge, 1971) 115-6. He endorses C.F.G. Masterman's judgment that 'You may by special effort of preaching, music or excitement, draw a large and active congregation, but you have done so by emptying the churches of your neighbours. The water is not increased in quantity, but merely decanted from bottle to bottle', *The Condition of England* (1909) 204. McLeod calls this 'only a very slight exaggeration'.

83. Fourteen months after the Rev. D. Annal took over in the Caversham Presbyterian Chapel the membership had increased from 40 to 140. At Broad Street Congregational Chapel the minister before Sewell had been in deepest despair; 5 years after Sewell's coming in 1893, only 86 of the 206 members on the church roll dated their membership before his arrival. C.A. Davis at Kings Road Baptists added 291 members to the roll at an average rate of 54 a year during the first five years of his ministry; the baptism figures at Friar Street Primitive Methodist Chapel moved steeply upwards after the arrival of a new minister. There are problems in analysing Anglican communion figures from this point of view since a complete change of staff in a single year was rare. Presbyterian annual reports between 1911 and 1914 show that the proportion of new members who were recruited from other denominations in those years was: 1911, 6 out of 20; 1912, 4 out of 31; 1913, 8 out of 20; 1914, 6 out of 12. This is the only case I have found where such a calculation was made.

84. Although admittedly the previous minister had left after a scandal; he had been convicted of travelling on the railway without a ticket. In the first half of the nineteenth century itinerant and part-time ministers were characteristic of Nonconformity in its dynamic South Wales setting, E.T. Davies, *Religion in the Industrial Revolution in South Wales* (Cardiff, 1965) 65.

85. *Berkshire Chronicle*, 12.6.1914.

86. St. Giles, *Parish Magazine* (April, 1906). This Magazine between 1902 and 1914 is an excellent source for seeing the overwhelming size of this issue in parish affairs. It makes depressing reading for the historian, and must have had a similar effect on a contemporary parishioner.

87. For example, St. Giles, *Parish Magazine* (May-June, 1907) — an argument between the chairman of the Education Committee (Mr Collier) and the Vicar of St. Giles (Carew Hunt) over the merging of St. Giles with George Palmer School.

88. *Berkshire Chronicle*, 16.2.1901, the Chairman's review of the work of the school board 1871-1901. Other complete lists of schools with their population and average attendances can be found in *Smith's Directory* for Reading (1896) and other years.

89. St. Mary's parish, for example, devoted time and money raising to foreign missions on a large scale — up to £500 in a single year. There were, in 1900, twenty-four missionaries in the field owing some or all of their livelihood to St. Mary's.

90. *Berkshire Chronicle*, 2.1.1904.

91. St. John's Church of England Temperance Society, *Annual Reports 1898-1913; The Temperance Chronicle*, 14.1.1910.

92. Friends Meeting House, *Monthly Meeting Minutes* (March, 1909) part of the 1906-9 *Triennial Report*.

93. *Handbook of the Baptist cause at Earley Rise Reading, afterwards known as the Anderson Baptist Church*, the date of the quotation is Feb. 1892. See also *The Beginnings of Anderson Baptist Church* (Reading, 1932) a pamphlet

written by one of the original Mission Band. The information for the rest of the paragraph is taken from Anderson Baptist Church, *Church Minutes* (1903-29).

94. Ideology was also of course a cause of introversion, as for example the view of the Vicar of Greyfriars in 1908 that few should be helped amongst the poor or unemployed because 'there is a large class of people living in our midst whose poverty is of their own seeking', and because the opposite category broadly coincided with those 'attending in most cases our places of worship', Greyfriars, *Annual Report* (1908); for basic information on this church see F. Gordon Spriggs, *History of the Church of Greyfriars Reading* (Reading, 1963).

95. Sharply observed by 'Athos' in the *Reading Observer*, 4.5.1907; for criticisms of Nonconformity in terms of the introversion of its preoccupations in an earlier setting see E.T. Davies, *Religion in the Industrial Revolution in South Wales* (Cardiff, 1965) viii, 86.

96. This was partly because the SDF was militantly secularist at this stage, and the Hosier Street Trust Deed (1872) had stipulated that the building was not to be used 'for any purpose at variance with or calculated to bring into disrepute the principles of religion set forth in the Holy Scriptures, but the same may be used, under proper regulations, and with the consent of two-thirds of the members of the church in general meeting assembled for promoting the arts and science, the diffusion of general knowledge and the cause of Temperance and Peace'.

97. The 1890-1914 records show the following concerns: the persecuted Salvationists in Eastbourne (Dec. 1891); international arbitration not war (Feb. 1892); the Miners' Relief Fund (1893); Turkish atrocities in Armenia (Dec. 1894) – calling on the government to invoke the Treaty of Berlin; the Czar's projected Peace Conference (Sept. 1898); against seven-day newspapers (May, 1899); Indian Famine Relief Fund (May, 1900); Concentration camps in South Africa (Dec. 1901); the 1902 Education Bill (Sept. 1902); Turkish Atrocities in Macedonia (Sept. 1903); against the proposed introduction of Chinese indentured labour into the Transvaal (Feb. 1904); against the government Licensing Bill (May, 1904); arbitration not war (March, 1911).

CHAPTER 6

1. Wycliffe, *Minute Book* (April, 1907); see also Trinity Congregational Chapel, *Yearbook* (1890).

2. St. Giles, *Parish Magazine* (Oct. 1911); see also *Baptist Times and Freeman*, 29.5.1903, p.377. *British Weekly*, 31.12.1891, 'the best men in the Church are already overtaxed by the multifarious character of their duties. They are bustled out of their spirituality'.

3. *Berkshire Chronicle*, 2.6.1900.

4. (New York, 1907) 186. The conflict between institutional and spiritual success was also observed by T.H.S. Escott, *England Her People, Polity and Pursuits* (1885 edition first published in 1879) Chapter XXIV, 'Religious England', 'there is hurrying to and fro, much parade of the machinery of faith, much insistence upon its routine business, and its spectacular effects ... excessive organisation is an omen of decay as well as a sign of growth ... an age in which all religions are highly-organised but not on that account generally and profoundly believed in'; see also the rise of the 'Conversazione' at the Methodist New Connexion Conference replacing the 'Tea Meeting' after 1881, Currie, *Methodism Divided*, p.134, 'evidently popular support for the

organisation *had* been secured, but the organisation to which loyalty was demanded had itself changed'.

5. *The Occasional Magazine,* vol.II (1900).
6. Rev. R.H. Sewell, *Farewell Sermon,* 27.9.1903 (printed as a pamphlet).
7. This was the question put at the 1901 annual meeting, *Berkshire Chronicle,* 8.6.1901.
8. Whitley Hall, *Management Committee Minutes and Executive of M.C. Minutes* (1907-12) and Spring Gardens Society, *Leaders' Meeting Minute Book* (1892-1912).
9. For how the Evening School Code of the Education Department could be used to finance the entire Institute penumbra of chapels see F.B. Meyer in *Wesleyan Methodist Magazine* (1898) 830-2.
10. *Methodist Recorder,* 7.5.1896, quoted in Currie, *Methodism Divided,* 94.
11. *Baptist Times and Freeman,* 24.7.1903, interview with Dr E. Judson of Judson Memorial Church New York on 'The Institutional Church'; for the Reading Wesley Cricket Club acting as a recruiting aid to the Queen's Wesleyan Brotherhood, see A.H. Lowe, *Sunlit Fields: Cricket and the Greater Game* (1929) 69.
12. For a study of some of the national movements of the type described in this paragraph, especially those inspired by Lord Meath (1841-1929) see John Springhall, 'Youth and Empire' unpublished D.Phil. (University of Sussex, 1968). The movements attached to churches and chapels were only a part of a wider flourishing of such movements in Edwardian Britain, e.g. Empire Day, National Service League, Navy League, Imperial Maritime League League of the Empire, Frontiersmen, Lads' Drill Association (1899), National Service League (1906), Duty and Discipline Movement (1911); for a view of the CLB in Manchester from a member see R. Roberts, *The Classic Slum* (Pelican, 1973) 161 n4.
13. St. Giles, *Parish Magazine* (June, 1905).
14. Boys' Brigades of which there is evidence were: Trinity (1901), Park Institute (1908), Broad Street (1900) and the Methodist ones noted above. But there were many more in the town. Church Lads' Brigades: St. Luke's (1902), St. Bartholomew's (1909), St. George's, St. Michael's, St. Giles, Christ Church, St. John's Caversham. St. John's in Reading also had a Boys' Brigade attached to its Albert Road Mission Room. Other agencies were of the same type, like the St. Alban's Guild at St. Peter's Caversham 'to foster in our boys the spirit of Christian brotherhood, patriotism, and Holy Religion' (1902). At St. Saviour's a Cadet Corps was started in 1905, but 'they had not been able to touch the lads in Coley in the way they so much desired', *Berkshire Chronicle,* 13.5.1905. Baden-Powell Scouts and the rival British Boy Scouts (founded 1910 by Sir Francis Vane an ex-BP Commissioner in London) both existed in the town. For instance Greyfriars started BP-Scouts in 1909 because 'one sad feature of our work among the young ... (is) our inability to keep in touch with the young lads of the age of fifteen and upwards ... we are to try the Boy Scouts as a means of keeping them there'.
15. *Reading Standard,* 13, 20, 27.5.1911, 30.9.1911. I owe these references to John Springhall.
16. *Berkshire Chronicle,* 18.9.1914, 18.12.1914; for the aspiration to please 'local authorities' by the penumbra of Wesleyan organisation in Reading, see *Methodist Recorder,* 20.4.1911.
17. Christine Dinnis of the University of Sussex is currently studying the Salvation Army's attitudes to organisation, as well as actual developments in its own organisation. For suspicion of Boy Scout ideology and organisation see C.B. Booth, *Bramwell Booth,* (1933) 340 and R. Sandall *et al. The History of the Salvation Army,* (1947-) V, 271.

18. For the Young Men's Society, see the Trinity *Year Book* (1895). For the difficulties of the Broad Street Working Men's Evening College, see the Broad Street *Magazine* (April, 1898, July, 1898, August, 1898, December, 1898, June, 1899, November, 1899, June, 1900). Further examples of the trend described in this paragraph were the taking over by the Reading Temperance Society of the temperance activities previously led by Hosier Street Congregational Methodist Chapel, or the demise of the Greyfriars YMCA because of the growth of the Reading YMCA.

19. Information about it is in *Trinity Congregational Church Magazine* (Sept. 1905) where there is a full history of it by O. Ridley — an ex-member.

20. St. John's, *Annual Address* (1901).

21. This story is reconstructed from the records both of Park Institute itself and its parent — Trinity Chapel. Another case of the same tensions is that of East Reading Adult School in relation to Church Street Quakers between 1905 and 1915. Initially a Quaker meeting was growing out of Adult School work, but tensions between the two led to a foundering in January 1915. In the case of the Unitarians in Reading an agency did become the church, and brought the latter into being. In 1876 the services were clearly more reverend forms of the lectures which had preceded them, *The Inquirer*, 25.3.1876, and E.C. Towne's sermon, *ibid.*, 21.7.1877.

22. The first CE Society which took firm root in Britain (the movement came from New England where it was started in 1881) was in Crewe in 1887. It 'caught on' from *c.*1891 onwards. See W. Knight Chaplin and M.J. Street, *Sixty-Five Years of Christian Endeavour*, souvenir of Jubilees of 1931 and 1946; W. Knight Chaplin, *Francis E. Clark* (n.d.); W. Knight Chaplin and M.J. Street, *Souvenir Report of the World's Convention 1900*. For denominational competitiveness on Christian Endeavour, and for the importance it assumed, see 'Notes and Queries for Christian Endeavours' in the *Baptist Times and Freeman* 1903 *passim*.

23. For the years 1904-14 when the CEMS 'became rapidly a movement rather than a society', and when 20,000 members enrolled in 600 branches see, J.G. Lockhart, *Cosmo Gordon Lang* (1949). Lang was preoccupied with 'the danger of quantity as compared with the need for quality'.

24. St. Giles, *Parish Magazine* (April, 1906). The CEMS was founded in 1906. For a mass meeting of its Reading membership see *Reading Observer*, 15.9.1906. Other reports of its work are in *ibid*, 19.6.1906, 2.11.1907, 28.12.1907, 9.1.1908, 23.3.1912. Nationally in 1906 there were already 350 branches.

25. Such organisations as Communicants' Guilds, or the Baptist Golden Chord Society, *United Magazine* (Oct. 1896).

26. For example, Trinity Christian Endeavour Society (started 1894) and Young People's Society for Christian Endeavour (started 1897) dissolved in 1903, 'having had a longer life than any other similar society in connection with the church', *Trinity Congregational Church Magazine*, vol. I, no. 1 (1904). Statistics collected by the Reading and District Christian Endeavour Union show considerable fluctuations in the history of individual societies even in the short period 1898-1904.

27. E. Margrett, Ms. 'History of Trinity Book Club', in *Pamphlets*, vol.6, in Minister's Library at Trinity Chapel, Queens Road.

28. Reading Monthly Meeting Institute Committee, *Minutes*, 1904-38.

29. St. John's CETS, *Annual Reports 1898-1913*. Their performance was worse than the 20 out of 70 members who attended meetings of the Reading Pathological Society (founded 1841) in 1886, and a lot worse than the 471 out of 689 and 431 out of 601 possible attendances achieved by two WEA tutorial classes in 1914.

30. There are exceptions: a Football Club started at St. Giles in 1913, and at Wycliffe Baptist Chapel in 1907, and one was prospering under the St. John's CETS, in 1911-12. But even in football they prove the rule, see the lament about football at this level in *Berkshire Chronicle, 6.9.1902.*

31. The places where this chronology can be substantiated, usually from qualitative statements from within the records rather than by tables of statistics are: Trinity YPSCE (dissolved 1903), Trinity Guild started in 1904, with very similar aims to the Literary and Social Union of 1894, and complete reorganisation on local lines after 1908; reorganisation of Broad Street young people's work under Farrow after 1911 into five local sections; Tilehurst CE started in 1906 with an attendance of about 40 but folded in 1913 in favour of an ordinary chapel-centred Bible Class; no mention of CE work after 1909 at Kings Road Baptists, even though active before that; at Carey, where 'we have never known an Institution before so decidedly helpful to young people' (1894) there is less mention of it through 1897-1900; at Wycliffe youth work was reorganised *c.* 1908-10, as it was at Caversham Free in 1911. There is similar evidence for a halt in the growth of the CEMS, but much less for the military and para-military movements before 1914.

32. a) Membership compared to congregation: Park Institute (1908) 29:30 (morning, 29:70 (evening); London Street Primitives (1893) 300:7-800; all Primitive Methodist chapels in Reading (1904) 618:1,500; London Street Primitives (1898) 275:650; Broad Street Chapel (1901-3) 350:240 (morning), 350:378 (evening). b) Auxiliary agencies, membership compared to attendance; Trinity Guild (1906) 46:40; St. Giles CEMS (1907) 73:30; Carey Baptists Sunday School (1893) 234:103 (morning), 234:162 (evening), Band of Hope (1893) 130:80; St. Bartholomew's CEMS (1911) 86:42; Boys' Brigade Reading 8th Coy (1913-14) 23:10; Elm Park Hall Sunday School (1905) 250:150; Hosier Street Band of Hope (1904) 179:81; Cumberland Road Sunday School (1904) 353:193 (morning), 353:229 (evening). For Adult School evidence see Adult Schools, *Year Book and Directories* (1912). There is one interesting case where a change over time can be observed as the Greyfriars Men's Services alter from being of the membership: congregation ratio to the auxiliary agencies:membership ratio as they develop more and more into an auxiliary agency:

Date	Numbers on Register	Average Congregation
April 1906	28	69
July 1906	60	130
Dec. 1907	300	111
1908	266	135
1909	276	129

see also R. Currie, *Methodism Divided* (1968) 198, n.3.

33. Cuttings from *Daily News* and *Telegraph* (June, 1894) at YMCA headquarters in Reading.

34. W.R. Ward, *Religion and Society in England 1790-1850* (1972) 8. He adds, 'Yet every machine retained its symbolic apologists, and the worst horrors were perpetrated by those who gave symbolic status to ecclesiastical arrangements which were no more than devices'.

35. The quotes are from the London Street Primitive Methodists in 1902-3, Greyfriars in 1908, and Grovelands in 1903. Many similar expressions recur in the records of the churches and chapels of the day. For national utterances on advertising see 'The Art of Advertising', in *The Methodist Times*, 8.2.1900; 'Hints on Organisation', *ibid*, 19.2.1900.

36. For the quotations on Methodism in the preceding two paragraphs see R. Currie, *Methodism Divided* (1968) 129-38; for a first-hand account of the Band of Hope as entertainment in Salford in the early-twentieth century, see

R. Roberts, *The Classic Slum* (Pelican, 1973) 152; for attacks on such adaptation in the national denominational press see, 'Meetings for the Masses' in *Wesleyan Methodist Magazine* (1888) 812-5; Rev. J. Watson, 'A Plea for the Spirituality of the Church' in *British Weekly*, 30.5.1895, p.89., *Primitive Methodist Magazine* (1909) 202.

37. I am indebted to John Gillis of Rutgers University for discussions on this: see his 'Youth in History: Progress and Prospects', in *Journal of Social History*, vol.7, no.2. (Winter, 1974) 201-7; 'The Emergence of Modern Juvenile Delinquency in England, 1890-1914', unpublished paper; *Youth in History*, (New York, 1974) 94-131. In 1891 in Reading the proportion of the population under the age of 15 was 1:2.7, in 1901 1:3.0 in 1911 1:3.5. The numbers in the 15-20 age group increased from 5,972 in 1891 to 7,463 in 1901 to 8,219 in 1911. The proportion of adults between the ages of 20 and 55 remained constant at about half of the population.

38. For an example from Reading see a Trinity Congregational minister, Rev. William Guest, *A Young Man's Safeguard in the Perils of the Age* (1878); see also C.B. Penny, 'The Religion of the Errand Boy', in *Contemporary Review*, lxxxvi (Sept. 1904) 405-8.

39. *Baptist Times and Freeman*, 28.8.1903, Rev. J.C. Carlile, 'Church Organisation'. C.E. Schorske, *German Social Democracy, 1905-1917, the development of the great schism* (New York, 1955) 274, discusses the response of the SPD to declining membership in 1913 in an interesting way. The rate of increase of membership had been checked for the first time since 1881. What was to be done? Party organisers thought immediately in terms of more divided and aimed forms of propaganda and organisation. An illustrated newspaper, a family journal, a fashion periodical for women, a special paper for deaf-mutes, were proposed. There was the feeling that the press should be less high-brow, the party should acquire trained youth specialists etc. 'These and similar proposals, all in the well grooved tradition of mass manipulation were presented to the Jena party congress of 1913.'

40. The most notable being S.A. Barnett, see *Canon Barnett, his Life, Work and Friends*, by his wife (1918) and his *Practicable Socialism* (1888, 1894, and later series). For a lesser but interesting figure see also Stephen Yeo, 'Thomas Hancock, 1832-1903, the Banner of Christ in the Hands of the Socialists', in Maurice B. Reckitt, ed. *For Christ and the People, studies of four socialist priests and prophets of the Church of England between 1870 and 1930* (1968).

41. Quarterly meeting of the Parochial Church Council, St. Giles, *Parish Magazine* (November, 1917).

42. St. Bartholomew's, *Parish Magazine* (Dec. 1895).

43. See also Christ Church, *Parish Magazine* (Jan. 1897) where a new vicar insisted on the need for 'bright' and 'attractive' evening services to reach 'our poorer brethren'.

44. For 'humble mission halls' accompanying the 'smart and imposing Central Halls' which were added to Wesleyan Circuits after 1885 see R. Currie, *Methodism Divided* (1968) 211; for the social segregation resulting, see *Primitive Methodist Magazine* (1896) 158.

45. For class differences between Quaker Meetings and Adult Schools, see Elizabeth Isichei, *Victorian Quakers* (Oxford, 1970) 174.

46. Caversham Society, Leaders' Meetings, *Minutes* (Feb. 1904).

47. St. Giles, *Parish Magazine* (Jan. 1911).

48. St. Giles, *Parish Magazine* (1895).

49. *Reading Co-operative Record* (Feb. 1902) p. 10.

50. There are many illustrations of this trap: St. Luke's Cricket Club on its formation in 1893 discussed the matter in these terms, St. Giles, *Parish Magazine* (1893); Christ Church Cricket Club was forced to hope that 'all

who are alive to the importance of healthy recreation will encourage the club by subscriptions' even after having fixed the membership dues at 2/- p.a., Christ Church, *Parish Magazine* (April, 1895); St. Saviour's Popular Entertainments were similarly trapped, *Berkshire Chronicle*, 13.5.1905, 8.10.1909.

51. Information taken from Society of Friends, *Monthly Meeting, Minutes* at the Meeting House, Church Street. The national scene is described in J.F.C. Harrison, *Learning and Living* (1961) 301-11. National membership was 100,000 in 1910, 80,000 in 1914.

52. For these groups see the annual *Reports of the Parochial Charities and Associations*. In some years these contained a useful Vicar's Letter. Two volumes of St. Mary's *Parish Magazine*, for the years 1890 and 1894 also help. The language of the 'respectable' as opposed to other poor did not get into these Reports until 1901, and the word 'deserving' until 1909. They seemed to be operating with pre-'moral' attitudes to poverty, or else to reject such attitudes. They relied on much personal work and visiting as well as cash.

53. Rev. W.L. Watkinson, 'The Preacher and the Organiser', in *Wesleyan Methodist Magazine* (1895) 556; Rev. John Watson, 'A Plea for the Spirituality of the Church', in *British Weekly*, 30.5.1895, p.89. Watson's was a 'warning regarding the danger of burdensome machinery'. 'What kind of man flourishes best in this commercial atmosphere? Not the prophet, he withers and dies in the dust of figures, but ... the organiser ... he is a good business man and a capital manager ... but I grow suspicious and hesitate to have this man for my minister. Let us make him an electoral agent ... or the manager of a working-class insurance company that collects by street ... Don't hand over a number of poor souls to his preaching.'

CHAPTER 7

1. A contemporary discussion of this is in T.H.S. Escott, *England, Her People, Polity and Pursuits*, 2nd edition (1885) 536-53. See also F. Gale, *Modern English Sports: their use and abuse* (1885).

2. For a description of the atmosphere of part of that world, see G.N. Ostergaard and A.H. Halsey, *Power in Co- operatives, a Study of the Internal Politics of British Retail Societies* (Oxford, 1965) ix.

3. A. Briggs, *Mass Entertainment: the Origins of a Modern Industry* (Adelaide, 1960) 28: 'To an economic historian pausing briefly after surveying the vast field described in this lecture, the main conclusion must be that the chief theme of this story is the way in which massive market interests have come to dominate an area of life which until recently was dominated by individuals themselves ...' There is also discussion of the same theme in the chapter on Melbourne in A. Briggs, *Victorian Cities* (1963) 309-10.

4. For which see 'The Recreations of the People', in *Wesleyan Methodist Magazine* (1890) 664-8, 'there is a workhouse in every town, and there is a prison; why should there not be a Palace of Delight which should serve as the people's drawing room'. The article was a discussion of how much in the way of 'choral, literary and orchestral societies, and cycling, cricket, rambles and short-hand clubs, and technical schools and swimming baths and gymnasia ...' the church should provide. In 1894 F.B. Meyer began such a People's Drawing Room at Christ Church, Westminster Bridge Road, for working women, 'I have a number of palms for decoration, and shall try to procure one or two canaries to make the surroundings as comfortable and homelike as possible. Babies will have to be given up at the door and for them we have our creche ... and our kind amateur nurses will set the mothers free for an hour of quiet self-culture and social intercourse. I hope to read them selections from Tennyson and

Longfellow ...', 'The People's Drawing Room', in *Bristol Christian Leader*
(1894) 132, quoted in J.H.S. Kent, 'The Role of Religion in the Cultural
Structure of the Later Victorian City', in *TRHS* 23 (1973) 161.
5. Before 1872 basic hours at the biscuit factory were probably *c.*58½ a week. In
1872 they were reduced to 54, and remained so until in 1910 they became 48.
An employee who joined in 1850 recalled how he worked 6.30a.m. – 6.30p.m.
with 40 minutes for breakfast and 1 hour for dinner, and finished on Saturdays
at 2p.m., *Reading Standard,* 8.3.1913 and T.A.B. Corley, *Quaker Enterprise in
Biscuits* (1972) 99.
6. Broad Street Independent Chapel, *Magazine* (May, 1897); for the first Industrial
Exhibition in Reading see *Reading Mercury,* 11.2.1865, 30.9.1865.
7. *Reading Standard,* 13.11.1897.
8. C.H. Chandler, 'Workers at Play', in *The British Workman and Home Monthly*
(August, 1908); *Berkshire Chronicle,* 21.1.1899.
9. Reading Athletic Club, *Annual Report* (1898-9).
10. E.R.T. Morse (known as Esrom), 1858-1923. He lived in the North-East when
Blatchford was 'all the talk' there, as a writer on 'The Tissue'. A 'commercial
clerk' when he died, for (?) Huntley and Palmers; had worked as a seed worker
in Suttons for a time. After a three-month illness in *c.*1881 he took up
Dr Allinson's theories of whole food and lived by them thereafter. He thought
he owed his life to discovering Dr Allinson through the *Weekly Times and
Echo;* as he had been looking vainly in the public library for medical help before
that. He became interested in Co-operation while lodging in Dan Godsell's
house (a Reading founder-co-operator). Editor (unpaid) of *Reading Co-operative
Record,* 1894-(at least)1905. On the Board of the Co-op., 1895 until his death.
First speech at a Co-op. propaganda meeting 1903. Joined Reading Athletic
Club 1883. Hon. Sec. 1888-1892, thereafter Hon. Treas. until 1905. Active in:
Clerks Union; Ancient Order of Foresters; Volunteers; Reading and Caversham
Veterans' Association; Reading Philanthropic Institution; rambling; sport
(football, walking, boating); flower growing; singing/entertaining; Ye Ancient
Cogers. Wrote for *Berkshire Chronicle.* For expressions of his ideology (classic
examples of the *language,* as opposed to the *rhetoric* of brotherhood) see
Reading Co-operative Record, (March, 1904) 8; (Aug., 1904) 10; (Dec., 1904)
3; (Jan., 1905) 4-5; (Aug., 1905) 4. His life can be pieced together from
chance references in the *Record,* and from an obituary in *Berkshire Chronicle,*
30.3.1923. As with Rabson, the obituaries were part of the processes of
incorporation described in Chapter 10. The *Chronicle* chose to stress
athletics much more than the Co-op.
11. Reading Athletic Club, *Annual Report* (1899-1900). The Annual Reports of
this club throughout the 1890s are marvellously full and atmospheric
documents for the social historian. It was clearly a centre for social
commitment of an exceptionally zealous variety.
12. Reading Football Club, *Prospectus* (1891).
13. *Berkshire Chronicle,* 3.12.1898.
14. *Reading Observer,* 9.5.1891. Between 1,500 and 2,000 people visited the
Library each day at that date and one-ninth of the population were borrowers.
For further Reading statistics and for the voluntarism surrounding the public
library movement, see T. Greenwood, *Public Libraries: a History of the
Movement and a Manual for the Organisation and Management of Rate
Supported Libraries,* 4th edition (1894) inscription, and pp. 216-7.
15. *Reading Observer,* 2.5.1890; for the professionalising period in Edinburgh,
see R.Q. Gray, 'Styles of Life, the "Labour Aristocracy" and Class Relations
in later nineteenth-century Edinburgh', in *International Review of Social
History,* XVIII (1973) Pt. 3, 440-1; for Brighton, see D.G. Wilkinson,
'Association Football in Brighton before 1920', unpublished M.A. thesis

(University of Sussex, 1971). For recent national surveys see E. Dunning, 'The Development of Modern Football' in *The Sociology of Sport* (1971); I.R. Taylor, 'Soccer Consciousness and Soccer Hooliganism' in S. Cohen ed., *Images of Deviance* (1971); J. Walvin, *The People's Game: A Social History of British Football* (1975) 50-91.

16. *Berkshire Chronicle*, 5.5.1892, 3.5.1893.
17. Reading Football Club, *Minute Book* (1876-1890) entry for 7.3.1885.
18. *Berkshire Chronicle*, 8.9.1894.
19. *Ibid.*, 1.6.1895.
20. *Ibid.*, 15.6.1895.
21. *Reading Co-operative Record*, (May, 1905) p. 11; (March, 1904) p.7; (Nov., 1900) pp. 7-8. The last was an article on 'The Football Mania'.
22. *Berkshire Chronicle*, 1.6.1895.
23. *Ibid.*, 31.8.1895.
24. *Ibid.*, 8.6.1895.
25. *Ibid.*, 15.6.1895.
26. *Ibid.*, 4.4.1896.
27. *Ibid.*, 5.9.1896; for an Edinburgh Cricket Club which appealed to the Trades Council in 1891 to help preserve its ground, see R.Q. Gray, 'Styles of Life, the "Labour Aristocracy" and Class Relations in later nineteenth-century Edinburgh', in *International Review of Social History*, XVIII (1973) Pt. 3, p.444, n.4.
28. *Berkshire Chronicle*, 16.5.1896.
29. *Ibid.*, 29.5.1897.
30. *Ibid.*, 25.9.1897. The directors were mostly smaller tradesmen, only A.H. Bull and J.C. Fidler were representatives of the largest businesses in the town. The others included Cr. F.A. Cox, J. Higgs, Cr. F.R. Jackson, H. Lewis, J.B. Messer, A. Ridout, E. Bird, J. Warburton, W. Frame, E. Knowland, E. Farrer.
31. *Reading Observer*, 13.11.1897. This dispute can be followed through press cuttings at the Reading YMCA.
32. Figures were: 1896-7 – receipts £1,830, of which £293 came from subscriptions and donations and £1,647 from the gate; 1909 – accounts balanced at £5,918 of which £42 came from donations, £2,900 from gate and ground receipts, £450 from transfer fees and £115 from a special appeal fund.
33. *Berkshire Chronicle*, 21.10.1899.
34. *Ibid.*, 17.5.1902; for contemporary attacks on professionalism from two different class view-points outside Reading, see A. Player, 'Football, the game as a business', in *The World's Work*, I (Dec. 1902 – May 1903) and C.W. Alcock, 'Association Football', in *The English Illustrated Magazine* (1890-91) pp. 282-8.
35. *Ibid.*, 14.4.1906, 28.7.1906.
36. *Ibid.*, 27.1.1900.
37. *Ibid.*, 14.4.1900.
38. *Ibid.*, 3.2.1900.
39. *Ibid.*, 2.4.1904.
40. Rabson, J. (1864-1936). Came to Reading *c.*1886. Founded Broad Street PSA (with Rev. R.H. Sewell); Secretary of it from 1891-1912. Post Office Worker. Councillor (Minster Ward 1905-?). Active in: Buffaloes Soup Kitchen; Childrens' Holiday camps; Reading and District Cricket League; Reading Wednesday Football Club; Central Girls' Club; St. George's Lads' Club; Rambling; Co-op.; classes for Post Office workers, and many other initiatives. Retired from Post Office Oct. 1926. Resigned from Council 1936. Appointed JP 1915; first Labour Alderman, 1924; defeated for Mayor, May 1926; Mayor 1927-9. On Board of Guardians 1912-1919. On countless

Committees including: Education; Juvenile Employment; Schools Medical
Services; Insurance. Governor of Schools. 'It would be difficult, in fact, to
state with which committees and sub-committees of the Council he had not
been connected. He was at one time credited with the remark that if he had
the time he would belong to them all, and he certainly filled the whole of his
leisure time with public work.' Wrote for local press under pen-name
'Observer'. Obituaries: *Reading Standard,* 2.10.1936; *Reading Mercury,*
3.10.1936.

41. The 'Special Effort Committee' may be followed in *Berkshire Chronicle,*
    2.4.1904; 16.4.1904; 23.4.1904; 30.4.1904; 21.5.1904.

42. *Berkshire Chronicle,* 2.4.1904; for the difficulty the working class in nearby
    Swindon had in affording football, see A. Williams, *Life in a Railway Factory,*
    (1915), 287. The long-term fate of efforts like Rabson's in Reading may be
    gauged from a recent article on Supporters' Clubs in the official journal of the
    Football League, *Football League Review,* (Season 1970-71). The point of the
    article was to prevent Supporters' Clubs interfering with the affairs of their
    Football Club. One club secretary boasted to the *Review,* 'certainly there has
    never been any interference in football club matters from our supporters'
    club'. Another one complained, 'sometimes the tail tries hard to wag the dog.
    They hand over money but then start laying down how it must be spent'.
    Another said 'Supporters' clubs can be useful as long as they do not try to gain
    too much power.' The language used about modern football is of course
    utterly foreign to anything which could be quoted from Reading before 1914,
    see for example a modern manager referring to buying players: 'a great deal of
    money is involved. This is, after all, a commercial venture. The investment of
    large sums can only be justified after exhaustive feasibility tests. It is standard
    practice in commerce and industry. Why not football? I think this will
    become the trend'. Pat Saward (Brighton), *Evening Argus,* 12.1.1972.

43. Reading Athletic Club, *Annual Report* (1908-9) and (1903-4).

44. Reading Temperance Society, *Annual Report* (1903-4). For further evidence
    of the difficulties this situation was causing to the RTS see *Berkshire
    Chronicle,* 7.5.1898, 15.12.1900, 27.4.1901, 13.5.1905; and *Annual Reports*
    1906-7, 1909-10, 1911-12, 1913-14.

45. *Berkshire Chronicle,* 18.8.1900. I could find no minute-book records of the
    RWMR – only programmes and occasional newspaper reports.

46. For the BFRC see J. Oster, 'The History of the Recreation Club', *First Name
    News,* vol.4, no.3 (March, 1961) 21-5; the Club also has good archival material
    which they kindly allowed me to consult.

47. Reading Literary and Scientific Society, *Committee Minute Book* (Sept.
    1904).

48. Reading Literary and Scientific Society, *Historical Retrospect, 1880-1905.*

49. *Berkshire Chronicle,* 28.1.1899.

50. Unfavourable comment started in the *Annual Report* of 1897-8, thereafter,
    compared to the élan and optimism of earlier years, the reports make sad
    reading.

51. For the financial difficulties see YMCA *Executive Committee Minutes* (May,
    1890) and a *Circular* of May, 1899. For the 1910 crisis see *Executive
    Committee Minutes,* 31.1.1910 and 21.3.1910, 'a special report of the
    sub-committee appointed to consider statistics about membership and report'.
    For its national dimensions see *EC Minutes* (May, 1909) 'Report of a special
    Committee about the causes operating to weaken and imperil Association
    work', dated 29.3.1909.

52. The Reading Biscuit Factory Recreation Club could be cited as a similar case
    to the RAC, although they were less self-conscious about what was happening
    to them and how to adapt to it. Having tried (1905-6) to encourage members

by giving special prizes to successful collectors of weekly subscriptions in the factory, they introduced new 'attractions' instead – Whist Drives (1910), Entertainments (1910). They had already (1902-3) introduced 'side-shows' at their Sports, and Whippet Races at their Annual Show. The sources for the RBFRC are *Annual Reports and Balance Sheets* from 1898 to 1914; Reading Biscuit Factory Cricket Club, *Rules* (January, 1896); *Soccer Star,* 4.8.1962,) 19, article on the 'The Real Biscuitmen'; *The Club Secretary* (May, 1956) 12, article on 'Three Men in a Club'; *Reading Standard,* 11.11.1955, article on 'Huntley and Palmers Soccer Story'. The Cycling Clubs were another Sporting group subject to these pressures. In response to the decline of the 'Club Run' they became increasingly organised as Clubs for running races for enthusiasts, the sport failing to develop as it did in Italy into a major spectator sport.
53. For the quotations in this paragraph see the Reading Literary and Scientific Society, *Report and Proceedings* (1901-4) Foreword.
54. The sources for this story are *Annual Reports* (1898-9, 1905-14); *Minute Books* (1842-1899) (1899-1910) (1910 onwards); *Rules* (January, 1853).
55. For accounts of the YMCA which give essential facts but are not very useful for the periodisation of its history see: C.P. Shedd and others, *History of the World Alliance of YMCAs* (1955) and J.E. Hodder Williams, *The Life of Sir George Williams* (1906).
56. There is no doubt about the nature of its original aims. Sir George Williams the founder and prophet of the YMCA expressed them at the Jubilee celebrations at the Albert Hall in June 1894. It was 'an organisation managed by Christian men on a Christian basis and as an adjunct to the churches. Its aim was to rescue, to protect, to educate, to redeem young men ... It was a rendezvous for every manly fellow who though willing to help himself could not do so without some friendly hand to swing him on to the rock of security. It was the centre for the development of strong, healthy, religious tone, where cant was held at a discount and where an honest confession to have any weight must be backed by honest living'. The original name of the Association was to have been 'The Society for Improving the Spiritual Condition of Young Men Engaged in Trade'. See *Daily News,* 6.6.1894, and cuttings from the *Daily News* and *Telegraph* for June 1894 at the Reading YMCA.
57. *Berkshire Chronicle,* 29.5.1897.
58. *Minutes of General Meetings* (1892-1918).
59. *Executive Committee Minutes* (1899) and for the divisions of the work *Reading Standard,* 20.11.1895.
60. *Berkshire Chronicle,* 29.5.1897.
61. *Ibid.,* 20.5.1893.
62. *Reading Standard,* 20.11.1895; *Reading Observer,* 20.11.1895.
63. *Reading Mercury,* 13.11.1897.
64. *Executive Committee Minutes* (May, 1909). The *Report* of the Special Committee dated 29.3.1909 was stuck into the Minutes of the Reading YMCA.
65. *Executive Committee Minutes,* 11.10.1909.
66. *Ibid.,* 30.8.1909.
67. *The Temperance Record,* 13.5.1880.
68. *Berkshire Chronicle,* 19.4.1890, 7.6.1890.
69. Reading Temperance Society, *Annual Report* (1889-90).
70. *Reading Observer,* 26.4.1902.
71. *Berkshire Chronicle,* 13.5.1905.
72. Reading Temperance Society, *Annual Report* (1908-9) described a change in the character of the Saturday night entertainments to 'Free and Easy Harmonic Meetings', 'with the object of providing a counter-attraction to the public house'.
73. Athenaeum Club, *Annual Report* (1907-8).

74. Reading Athletic Club, *Annual Report* (1909-10).
75. Reading YMCA *Executive Committee Minutes,* 21.3.1910.
76. Reading Athletic Club, *Annual Report* (1910-11); I have not been able to study the music-hall, the cinema, or the pub locally, but these three are obviously crucial to the periodisation of leisure in capitalism and to understanding the changing context in which religious organisations had to work – see Chapter Eleven below. Before 1919 *c.* 30% of cinema audiences were allegedly under eighteen years of age, see Asa Briggs, *Mass Entertainment,* 18; PEP, *The British Film Industry* (1952) xiii; and 'Sunday Evening', in *The Times,* 5.9.1910.
77. *Berkshire Chronicle,* 13.9.1902.

CHAPTER 8

1. *Reading Observer,* 13.1.1912.
2. The most useful examples of which are Bentley B. Gilbert, *The Evolution of National Insurance in Great Britain: the origins of the welfare state* (1968); and Gareth Stedman Jones, *Outcast London* (Oxford, 1971).
3. B. Seebohm Rowntree, *Poverty: a study of town life,* 2nd edition (Nelson) 147.
4. On Hospital Sunday in 1894 the SDF ran a rival meeting to the 'Friendly and Trade Societies' meeting in support of the Hospital, see *Berkshire Chronicle,* 12.5.1894. In the national SDF newspaper *Justice,* 26.5.1895, Harry Quelch called on the workers of Reading 'not to support by their pence the Hospitals which were at present so many slaughterhouses and training grounds for the younger of the medical profession'.
5. *Reading Observer,* 28.2.1891; *Reading Co-operative Record* (May, 1899) 6.
6. *Berkshire Chronicle,* 9.5.1891.
7. *Ibid.,* 8.4.1899.
8. *Ibid.,* 2.3.1901, 25.1.1904, 3.3.1906.
9. *Ibid.,* 4.3.1899.
10. For the origins nationally of the Hospital Sunday and Saturday Funds see David Owen, *English Philanthropy 1660-1960* (1965) 485-6. Birmingham was the first in the field for co-operative money raising efforts of this type with a church collection for Hospitals in 1859; London, under Sir Sydney Waterlow's leadership, started in 1873. For difficulties experienced in Birmingham from 1871-2 onwards in voluntary finance for Hospitals see Asa Briggs, *The History of Birmingham* (1952) 264.
11. *Berkshire Chronicle,* 2.3.1895.
12. B. Kirkman Gray, in his *Philanthropy and the State, or Social Politics* (1908) 232-3, treats these strains in their national context, 'in some provincial towns the pressure is already extreme. The changing habits of the people render it more and more difficult to keep the Sunday collections up to standard, and this is accentuated by the fact that many more people are beginning to question the policy of eleemosynary payment for what is coming to be regarded as a public responsibility. In some towns it has become necessary to resort to a house-to-house collection, when there is an underlying expectation that the annual donation will be in proportion to the size of the house ... In working-class centres also where the workshop collection is in force, the opinion so we are told is gaining ground that since the proletariat finds the funds its representatives should call the tune, and we are warned that if we would avoid rate-supported hospitals the well-to-do classes must bear a larger share of the burden. There is in short that general anticipating of coming change which goes so far as to bring the change about'. The whole book, a neglected study, is the best national reading for the themes of this chapter.

13. *Berkshire Chronicle*, 4.3.1899, 3.3.1900.
14. *Ibid.*, 9.5.1891.
15. This line and the story of how it was argued for by W.J. Braithwaite against the Doctors and the Insurance Companies during the National Insurance Bill preparations, and how it was eventually weakened by Lloyd George during the passage of the Bill in 1911 is well documented in H.M. Bunbury ed. *Lloyd George's Ambulance Wagon, being the Memoirs of W.J. Braithwaite 1911-12* (1957).
16. *Berkshire Chronicle*, 7.5.1892.
17. By 1955 the process signalled here had of course gone much further: 'the majority of the people of Reading spend the greater part of their leisure time in individual home and unorganised group activity rather than provided amusements and commercially directed individual activities, or organised group activities (cultural and religious)', Francine M. Taylor, 'An Inquiry into the leisure interests of the people of Reading', unpublished Ph.D. Thesis (University of Reading, 1955) 3; for the growth of home consumption of drink, see Brian Harrison, 'Pubs' in H.J. Dyos & M. Wolff eds., *The Victorian City: Images and Realities* I (1973) 166-7, 178. By 1896 off-licences of all kinds accounted for one-sixth of drink-retailing licences in England and Wales. The same process was to affect corner-shops, which used to be used as extra-domestic gathering places on mid-week nights by men who could not afford the pub until the end of the week. See Elsie Whife's ms. 'Memories of a Brighton Newsagent/Confectioner' in my possession.
18. For two 1851 Primitive Methodist processions, in connection with the 'annual camp-meeting' in Reading, one at 8a.m. and one preceding an evening love-feast, see *Primitive Methodist Magazine* (1851) 625, 'The singing in these processions appeared to produce a happy effect. Nearly all the windows were thrown open as the procession passed along, and a pleasing interest in the proceedings was displayed by the householders'. The Salvation Army used processions to great effect in the 1880s. For the first grand procession in the Reading Co-op.'s history, see *Reading Co-operative Record* (July, 1901) 4.
19. *Berkshire Chronicle*, 11.5.1901.
20. *Ibid.*, 12.5.1894.
21. *Ibid.*, 25.5.1895.
22. *Ibid.*, 11.5.1901, 10.5.1902.
23. For increasing costs, caused by developments such as X-rays after 1895 and Radium treatment, see Ernest W. Dormer ed. *The History of the Royal Berkshire Hospital 1837-1937* (Reading, 1937) 142.
24. *Berkshire Chronicle*, 8.4.1899, 26.4.1899.
25. *Ibid.*, 8.4.1899, 26.4.1899.
26. *Ibid.*, 29.2.1896.
27. *Reading Co-operative Record* (May, 1899) 6; (Aug., 1900) 9; (March, 1902) 6; (Aug., 1902) 4.
28. *Berkshire Chronicle*, 26.4.1902, 18.10.1902 and Ernest W. Dormer ed. *The Story of the Royal Berkshire Hospital 1837-1937* (Reading, 1937) 79.
29. *Reading Co-operative Record* (March, 1904) 5; (Feb., 1905) 4; (March, 1905) 4, 13; *Berkshire Chronicle*, 27.1.1906; 3.2.1906.
30. Figures reported in the local press were: 1902, £400; 1903, £850; 1904, £900; 1905, £900; 1906, £910.
31. *Berkshire Chronicle*, 3.5.1902, 17.5.1902; *Reading Mercury*, 3.5.1902.
32. *Berkshire Chronicle*, 18.10.1902.
33. For a convenient list in 1899 see Mate's Illustrated Guides, *Reading Illustrated A Concise Guide* (1899). For a proud speech about them, see *Berkshire Chronicle*, 13.2.1897.
34. *Berkshire Chronicle*, 5.11.1898. F.B. Bourdillon, 'A creative social policy', in

Reading University College Review (March, 1910) estimated that in 1908-9 there were fifty-two official and voluntary relief-giving bodies in Reading. The balance between official and voluntary he estimated thus:

	Official	Voluntary	Total
Medical	£ 4,738	£12,000	£16,738
Relief	£27,523	£ 8,349	£35,872

35. *Reading Observer,* 16.1.1909.
36. For example, Mayor Attwells in 1891, *Reading Observer,* 12.12.1891; Mayor Ridley in 1896, *Berkshire Chronicle,* 17.10.1896; a Central Aid Association, *Reading Mercury,* 17.4.1897.
37. C.L. Mowat, *The Charity Organisation Society 1869-1913* (1961) 80-81, 'if I were asked why I joined the Society I should answer that through its work and growth I hoped that some day there would be formed a large association of persons drawn from all churches and all classes who disagreeing in much, would find in charity a common purpose and a new unity. That it seemed to me was "worth anything". Such an organisation, I thought, could do more than Parliament, or preaching, or books, or pamphleteering ... Such an organisation might bring to bear on the removal and prevention of evils a combined force that would far exceed in weight and influence any yet existing. It could make legislation effective, could see that it was enforced. Apart from all legislative interference and with the use of means and influences more far-reaching it could renew and discipline the life of the people, by a nobler, more devoted, more scientific religious charity. It could turn to account all that newer knowledge would bring to the help of charity. It could eventually provide out of all classes and sects a great army of friendly and by degrees well-trained workers. It could help us to realise in society the religion of charity, without the sectarianism of charity. It would open to many a new path for the exercise of personal influence – influence with the churches, the Guardians, the Friendly Societies, the residents of a district, and "the common people". Differing in much, many might agree in this.

    This, this hope that there might be what I have sometimes called a church of charity, undeclared it might be and invisible, but in a very real sense actual – a peace-making unifying body – has been constantly in my mind'.
38. *Reading Standard,* 22.2.1908; for the foundation date of the COS see *Reading Mercury,* 18.5.1878.
39. *Berkshire Chronicle,* 17.10.1896.
40. The annual reports of the COS in Reading can be traced through the *Berkshire Chronicle* in late January – early February of each year from 1891-1909. Thereafter they disappeared for two years and then became intermittent. Only two references to Reading appear in *The Charity Organisation Society Review:* in one of these (July, 1885) 331, already 'at Reading the work is falling off'.
41. R.A. Bray, *Labour and the Churches* (1912) 47.
42. *Reading Observer,* 7.12.1907.
43. In the *Reading Mercury.* Exact reference not known. The cutting is with the RPI records at the house of the Hon. Sec. H.F. Weait, 138 Amity Road, Reading.
44. *The Nature and Progress of the Reading or Ninth Lodge of the Western Philanthropic Institution for the Relief of the Necessitous and Deserving Poor: instituted 6th June 1822 and holden at the Peacock Inn, Broad Street* (Reading, 1843).
45. Founded 1802, see *An Account of the Reading Dispensary, Instituted 1802, for Administering Advice and Medicine to the Industrious Poor at the Dispensary or, in some cases, their own Habitations* (Reading, 1802). A later *Account* (Reading, 1806) tells how the idea was first suggested 'several years ago' by a Rev. Edward Barry MD who did a trial experiment of a small

dispensary which preceded the larger one. See *Reading Mercury*, 31.10.1796, 20.3.1797. For the change to the Provident principle see *Annual Report* (1870). An almost complete set of *Annual Reports* survive for 1870 to 1920 with 1910 and 1914 missing.

46. *Berkshire Chronicle*, 27.1.1900.
47. The controversy was in the *Berkshire and Oxon Advertiser* during December 1878. Cuttings in the headquarters of the Reading Temperance Society.
48. *Report of Conference of Representatives of Working Men's Clubs at Birkbeck December 1885, to consider the question of total abstinence in relation to the progress and prosperity of the working classes.* W.I. Palmer and W. Caine convened this conference to ask the representatives, in Palmer's words, 'can you come outside your clubs and help us?'.
49. *Berkshire Chronicle*, 26.11.1904.
50. *Reading Observer*, 30.1.1892.
51. For example; in the Reports of the District Committees, 18.4.1912, in the *Minute Book* of the Executive Committee of the Guild of Help (1911-1917), also the *Annual Report* (1914) of the Guild containing a 'Report on the progress of the Guild up to Dec. 1914 made at the request of the EC'.
52. *Reading Observer*, 16.1.1909.
53. *Berkshire Chronicle*, 19.2.1897; J.B. Hurry, *A History of the Reading Pathological Society* (1909) 106.
54. For the COS see the annual meetings of 1894 and 1895, *Berkshire Chronicle*, 20.1.1894 and 26.1.1895.
55. It circulated a reprint of Bowley's article on 'working-class households in Reading' with one issue in 1912. Bowley was actively involved with the Guild of Help, chairing a meeting of the Advisory Committee in March, 1912. He was as much convinced as the rest of the Guild of the importance, even within the problem of unemployment, of doing nothing which might interfere with the independence and capacity to help themselves of the unemployed. He thought within the categories of 'character' as a vital motor to harness in the solution of any social problem – even the appalling one he had so clinically analysed in his study of Reading. Executive Committee, *Minute Book* (1911-17) 18.3.1912.
56. Reading Guild of Help, *Annual Report* (1913).
57. See Reading Council of Social Welfare, *Report and Statement of Accounts for the Year 1927*, 'day-to-day service of our fellows ... occupies a much larger share of our time and attention than the more spectacular task of delivering a frontal attack on particular social problems'. By then there was complacency about this description of their work, no longer was there the impulse even to try to create something different – the same impulse which had led to the Guild of Help, many preceding efforts, and the Council itself.
58. J.B. Hurry was a local doctor, botanist, historian and social activist who wrote about the social problem in terms of a 'vicious circle' of causation which had somehow to be broken. The three headings under which he analysed possible strategies in 1917 were Legislation, Voluntary Organisations, and Personal Effort, see his *Poverty and its Vicious Circles* (1917) 135. For earlier self-conscious discussion of the themes being raised at the end of this Chapter see his 'Social Problems and Vicious Circles', in *The Charity Organisation Review* (July, 1913) 34-7, and his *The Ideals and Organisation of a Medical Society* (1913).
59. Executive Committee, *Minutes*, 28.6.1910. These Minutes show how Guild of Help ideology and organisation could not deal with the problems they identified:

382   *Religion and Voluntary Organisations in Crisis*

	Total No. of Cases	Cases due to unemployment	Unemployment cases for causes other than Age, Health, Drink or Incapacity	Help obtained
1912	504	366	173	142
1913	560	192	92	120
1914	750	547	331	153

60. *Reading Mercury*, 12.11.1904, quoted in Anne Cook *op. cit.*, 280. Miss Cook documents another carrier of Statisation – education, via the Provision of Meals (1906), Play Centres, School Camps, Medical Inspections (1907), Medical Treatment (1909), Advice on Employment for School Leavers (1910), administration of Mental Deficiency Act (1913). Other carriers were Small Holdings and Allotments Act, with corresponding local committees (1908), Shop Hours Act, with corresponding Council-appointed Inspectors (1912).
61. A letter from A.L. Bowley to the *Berkshire Chronicle*, 31.12.1904.
62. *Proceedings of Distress Committee* (1907-8), and W.H. Beveridge, *Unemployment, A Problem of Industry* (1909 and 1930) (1931) 183, n.1. For the beginnings of the Distress Committee in Reading see *Berkshire Chronicle*, 7.10.1905.
63. *Reading Standard*, 6.1.1912.
64. 1905 was an important year for this pressure, although it was continuous throughout our period. Examples in that year were: *Berkshire Chronicle*, 2.12.1905, a Conference of Distress Committee and Boards of Guardians; *ibid.*, 23.12.1905 the SDF; *ibid.*, 4.11.1905, Reading Town Council; *ibid.*, 25.11.1905, Rufus Isaacs the Liberal MP for Reading; *ibid.*, 11.11.1905, editorial in the newspaper on unemployment. In each of these cases some form of central government action was urged.
65. For a long Guild discussion of the issue, with an attempted breakdown of the causes of the unemployment of those who applied to the Board of Guardians, see the Annual meeting of the Guild, 29.1.1913, in the Executive Committee, *Minutes*. See n. 59 above.
66. *Reading Standard*, 3.2.1913.
67. *Reading Standard*, 20.7.1912, editorial, 'Historians will make striking comparisons with regard to sickness and death prior to and during the days of State Insurance, but they will only vaguely realise what the change from one to the other meant to millions of workers, their wives and little ones'. Earlier the *Reading Observer* had dramatised the situation, 29.6.1912, 'as the great important day approaches the air seems charged with the electricity of preparation'. Lloyd George was a sophisticated publicist.
68. For example there was a meeting for the Reading Chamber of Commerce to hear the Act expounded, a series of articles on 'the Great Insurance Act' by MPs for local papers, a series of outdoor meetings for a week, a question-and-answer service in the *Reading Standard* on the Act, and lectures by government appointed lecturers: See the *Reading Standard*, 17.2.1912, 2.3.1912, 6.4.1912, 8.6.1912, 29.6.1912, *Reading Observer*, 23.3.1912.
69. *Berkshire Chronicle*, 9.1.1914.
70. One of the most striking things about the best contemporary source for the National Insurance Bill as it went into final form, H.N. Bunbury ed. *Lloyd George's Ambulance Waggon, being the memoirs of W.J. Braithwaite, 1911-1912* (1957) is the picture it gives of Friendly Society representatives and Labour MPs being drawn into a struggle with insurance company representatives and the organised medical profession in which they had not got the resources factually or administratively to compete. There is a tragic inevitability about the defeat of the Braithwaite/Friendly Society voluntaristic mode of operating the Bill. It was not just Lloyd George's manipulative

ability but the direction of twentieth-century social history which left Braithwaite a forlorn loser. A little known portrait of the new type of bureaucrat reformer in action is provided by E.T. ed. *Keeling Letters and Recollections* (1918). Keeling was involved with the administration of the new Labour Exchanges and was a convinced Webbian. Webb wrote a typical letter to the *Berkshire Chronicle,* 16.1.1914, calling for detailed statistical information on the availability of hospital beds, in order to make the Act work better. For the contradictions involved in professionalisation and the growing power of the State for Liberals see M. Richter, *The Politics of Conscience: T.H. Green and His Age* (1964) 374-5.

71. *Reading Observer,* 28.12.1912.
72. For the setting up of the Provisional Committee in Reading with its forty members see the *Reading Standard,* 15.6.1912, 29.6.1912. For an instance of J. Rabson pressing on the treatment of TB through the Insurance Committee see the *Berkshire Chronicle,* 3.7.1914.
73. The information is taken from the *Annual Reports* of the Dispensary.
74. Huntley and Palmers, *Scrapbooks,* an interview with the General Manager, H. Pretty in 1913 or 1914, 'since we had so many long-service men we were in just a temporary difficulty when the Insurance Act came into force. During the six months before the benefits began our employees found themselves in a dilemma, for our Sick Fund was suspended. Since then things have sorted themselves out satisfactorily. We have retained the services of our doctor and kept on our dispensary for the sake of all in our employ who are over sixty-five'.
75. *Berkshire Chronicle,* 4.2.1905, 29.7.1905. Affiliated to the Council were six lodges of Oddfellows ,six Foresters, two Hearts of Oak, three Sons of Temperance; see also the *Berkshire Chronicle,* 15.2.1902, 22.2.1902. The *Reading Co-operative Record* asked in August, 1905: 'where would the workers be if it were not for the Friendly Societies?'
76. *Reading Standard,* 17.2.1912.
77. *Ibid.,* 25.5.1912 'hitherto Friendly Societies had trod a well-known path, now by the passing of the Insurance Act there appeared another path running parallel with the old, destroying somewhat their ancient traditions but which they now had to tread'.
78. *Reading Observer,* 30.1.1909.
79. For a report of it by a Liberal newspaper see *Reading Standard,* 9.1.1909.
80. For the procedure involved in setting up this committee see the *Reading Standard,* 22.8.1908.
81. Friendly Societies were in most cases suspicious of State pensions. For one example see a Hearts of Oak meeting, *Berkshire Chronicle,* 9.4.1898. They came on to the local Pensions Committee and helped to administer the Act once passed. The measure had affected their work before it got on to the statute book for 'with a national scheme in the air no great development in this direction could be expected', *Reading Observer,* 5.1.1907. But no long-term alleviation of the plight of the old was possible in terms of Friendly Society finance. The biscuit factory had for a long time given 'allowances' (the word Alec Douglas-Home used in the 1964 election with such, for him, unfortunate political consequences) to their retired workers, see *The Lady of the House,* 15.12.1908 in Huntley and Palmers, *Scrapbooks.* The total spent was estimated to be two-thirds of the total spent on outdoor relief by the Board of Guardians. There was a conference on pensions convened by the Reading Amalgamated Friendly Society in 1892, *Reading Observer,* 13.2.1892. Hart Davis and G. Palmer both made well-reported speeches. G. Palmer was in favour of a scheme. 'His friend, Canon Blackley, had discussed it with him ... he had never thought that the Poor Law ... or the

Poor Law system had carried out the intention of its originators in respect of this very question of disabled old age.' Hart Davis 'had always been a stout opponent of going to the State for help. He saw nothing even now to move him from that position and so far, he presumed, they would all be in agreement'.

82. *Berkshire Chronicle,* 20.2.1897.
83. His visit was sometime before 1890. It is referred to in the *Reading Observer,* 30.1.1892.
84. The whole correspondence and Lloyd George's use of it is referred to in the *Reading Standard,* 4.7.1908.

CHAPTER 9

1. The first *Minute Book* (1904-15) of the Association is the main source for its early history. It is very full and detailed. *Minute Book,* Council Meeting, 11.1.1911. The four earliest branches, started between Oct. 1904 and March 1905, were Reading, Derby, Rochdale and Ilford, R.C.K. Ensor, *England 1870-1914* (Oxford, 1936) 538.
2. *Berkshire Chronicle,* 8.10.1904; for the founding meeting see *Reading Co-operative Record* (Dec., 1904) 11; for other references see *ibid.,* (Sept., 1903) 3; (Nov., 1903) 4; (June, 1904) 12; (Feb. 1905) 5; (Oct., 1905) 13.
3. *Reading Co-operative Record* (Jan. 1905).
4. For W.M. Childs I have used the local press, cuttings in the University archives, and his published works. In his 'The Palmer Family and the University of Reading', in *Staff Journal* 6 (Univ. of Reading) Nov. 1968, 6-12, T.A.B. Corley used 'some fragments of Childs' unpublished journal'. Childs wrote the DNB piece on George Palmer, and a tribute to G.W. Palmer in *The Times,* 10.10.1913. He was a considerable local historian, as well as an educational activist, becoming first Vice-Chancellor of Reading University.
5. *Berkshire Chronicle,* 8.10.1904, 3.12.1904.
6. *Reading Co-operative Record* (Feb. 1905) 5; (Oct. 1905) 13.
7. A letter to the *Reading Observer,* 5.9.1891, answering people who were surprised that the working class did not attend in large numbers the Schools of Science and Art or the University Extension lectures.
8. Including: the Mechanics' Institute (1840) which became the Literary, Scientific and Mechanics' Institution (1843), because its members were respectable tradesmen rather than the mechanics originally intended, of whom by then only fifteen had joined; the Athenaeum (1841); 'Public Rooms', for lectures, etc. (1842).
9. *Berkshire Chronicle,* 1.4.1905; the particular situation of the WEA, the detailed experience of the Leeds branch, and the wider context of other adult educational organisations have been well explored in JFC Harrison, *Learning and Living 1790-1960* (1961).
10. *Minute Book,* Council Meeting, 4.9.1912.
11. *Berkshire Chronicle,* 1.4.1905; for the sect-like quality of the tutorial class and the smaller study, or reading circles see *Learning and Living ...,* 269, 281.
12. Delegates to the original meeting were from: the Bricklayers, Carpenters, Railway Servants, Shop Assistants, Iron Founders, Lithographers, Postmen's Federation, Amalgamated Society of Engineers, Plasterers, Amalgamated Society of Tailors, Painters, National Union of Teachers, SDF, Trades and Labour Council, Plumbers, Masons, Postal Telegraph Clerks, Typographical Association, Postal Clerks ,Labourers Union (Builders) — plus ten local Co-operative Societies, *Minute Book.*
13. The Annual Report (1914) in the *Minute Book* gives details of

Professor F.M. Stenton's class that year, and that of Professor Edith Morley. The former (for men) was made up of: one labourer, one electrical machinist, two gardeners, one train inspector, one railway clerk, two bank clerks, two Co-op. assistants, one dancing master, one paper hanger, one motor body trimmer, two motor body makers, eight factory labourers, two teachers, one joiner, one draper, one assistant school attendance officer, one compositor, one wholesale tobacconist. The latter (for women) consisted of: five housekeepers, six dressmakers, one clerk, some tailoresses, some chemist's assistants, three teachers. Attendance for Stenton's class was 471 out of a possible 689, for Edith Morley's 431 out of 601.

14. *Minute Book,* Council Meeting, 11.1.1911.
15. *Berkshire Chronicle,* 1.4.1905; *ibid.,* 31.3.1906.
16. *Minute Book,* Council meetings, 4.9.1912, 7.1.1914.
17. *Reading Observer,* 7.10.1909.
18. For J. Rabson on the apathy problem in relation to previous efforts, see *Broad Street Independent Church Magazine* (Dec., 1904) PSA Notes; For 1909 difficulties see *Reading Observer,* 20.3.1909.
19. *Berkshire Chronicle,* 8.10.1904.
20. *Minute Book,* annual meeting, 18.3.1914.
21. *Ibid.,* 7.1.1914, 21.1.1914. *Berkshire Chronicle,* 2.1.1914, 9.1.1914, 23.1.1914.
22. *Reading Observer,* 7.10.1909.
23. *Berkshire Chronicle,* 30.1.1897.
24. *Reading Standard,* 12.10.1912.
25. The best printed source for this is W.M. Childs, *Making a University: an Account of the University Movement at Reading* (1933). For Childs see also A. Mansbridge, *Fellow Men, a Gallery of England 1876-1946* (1948) 20, 21, 38. The University has excellent archives, including press-cutting books, in the Registrar's Office, Whiteknight's Park.
26. *Reading Observer,* 28.5.1892.
27. *Berkshire Chronicle,* 11.6.1898.
28. *Ibid.,* 14.3.1896.
29. *Reading Standard,* 12.10.1912, 'the Literary and Scientific Society not only indirectly, but in a very real sense, contributed to the influences and forces which some twenty years ago brought the college into being'.
30. The Schools had grown out of Science and Art Classes in connection with the Boys' School in Queens Road in 1877. Their committees were entirely local, and manned by, for instance, Palmers and Suttons. For complete details of their personnel and of the courses they taught immediately before the 1892 amalgamation, the most convenient sources are the Smith's *Directories* (1890, 1891, 1892) in the Reading Reference Library. For their financial dependence on Palmer money see *Reading Observer,* 12.6.1891, where a grant from the Council was discussed. Art classes started in 1860, Science classes in 1870.
31. Reading Literary and Scientific Society, *Annual Reports* (1880-1905). The volume contains a quarter-centenary pamphlet by Dr J.B. Hurry and P.H. Turner, *Historical Retrospect, 1880-1905.*
32. *Berkshire Chronicle,* 11.6.1898.
33. *Ibid.,* 14.3.1896.
34. *Reading Observer,* 9.5.1891.
35. A meeting of the Court of Governors, *Berkshire Chronicle,* 8.12.1900.
36. *Ibid.,* 13.11.1897.
37. St. John's, *Annual Report and Balance Sheet* (1909).
38. In addition to *Making a University* (1933) there is much else of interest: W.M. Childs, *The New University of Reading, some ideas for which it stands* (Reading, 1926); W.M. Childs, *A Note on the University of Reading* (n.d.);

Reading College: plans and views (Reading, 1898); *Journal of the University Extension College, Reading,* vols. I-VI, Dec. 1894 − April 1900, mostly written and edited by Childs; volumes of press cuttings in Registrar's Office at the University.

39. *Reading Mercury,* 24.1.1914.
40. *Berkshire Chronicle,* 1.10.1904.
41. *Reading Mercury,* 24.1.1914, address on 'The Universities and the Workers'.
42. *Journal of the University Extension College, Reading,* III, no. 3 (Feb., 1897) 54.
43. *Journal,* III, no. 5 (May, 1897) 128-9 ; for comparable figures in adult education, such as M.E. Sadler, see J.F.C. Harrison, *Learning and Living* (1961) Chapter VI.
44. See W.M. Childs, *The Teaching of Local History,* Historical Association leaflet no. II (March, 1908); *The Story of the Town of Reading: a first sketch for Children* (Reading, 1905); *The Town of Reading During the Early Part of the 19th Century* (Reading, 1910). The latter is the best thing yet written on the town, it is informed by detailed use of the local press and does not seek merely to illustrate at the local level a known national story.
45. *Reading Observer, Reading Standard,* 13.2.1909. Reports of a lecture by Childs on 'the Universities in relation to national and local life'.
46. W.M. Childs, *Making a University* (1933) 294.
47. He had been on the Committee of the London Street Mechanics' Institute, 1843-48; was initially the Treasurer of the Reading YMCA and at its inauguration 31.1.1856; was intimately connected with the Schools of Science and Art, on the Committee at least 1881-91, President 1889-91; on the Committee of the Reading School Board 1871-6, Vice-Chairman 1874-6; on the Committee of the Extension Association in 1887, Vice-President, 1891-2.
48. *Reading Observer,* 4.6.1892.
49. *Berkshire Chronicle,* 12.7.1902.
50. *The Times,* 20.5.1936.
51. *Berkshire Chronicle,* 2.1.1914.
52. There is an interesting analysis of these and attack upon them, using the phrase, by J.A. Hobson, *The Crisis of Liberalism: New Issues of Democracy* (1909) 218-32, part III, Chapter IV.
53. *Reading Observer,* 24.10.1891.
54. *Reading Co-operative Record,* (April, 1904) 5; (Jan., 1905) 12; (Oct., 1904) 6.
55. *Berkshire Chronicle,* 12.7.1902, referring to the new title of Reading College, 'the change in title corresponds to a real change in the character of the work done. Extension lectures as a separate department have practically ceased, though popular evening courses are still given'.
56. *Berkshire Chronicle,* 1.10.1904. In 1900 there were 500 students at these classes, in 1903, 698. *Ibid.,* 4.2.1905.
57. See a correspondence between Mackinder and a member of the public in *Berkshire Chronicle,* 8.10.1898, 15.10.1898.
58. The second Annual Conference of the Southern Counties Federation of Oxford University Extension Centres, *Berkshire Chronicle,* 18.5.1895.
59. *Berkshire Chronicle,* 20.2.1892.
60. W.M. Childs, *Making a University* (1933) 287.

CHAPTER 10

1. *Reading Observer,* 14.3.1891; in E.D. Mackerness ed., *The Journals of George Sturt 1890-1927,* I (Cambridge, 1967) 146, there is reference to 'Some letters

on Socialism for the Reading Observer' by Sturt, in his journal for 15.3.1891. These 'have not been traced' (Mackerness). The earliest reference to Reading socialists I have found is in *Primitive Methodist Magazine* (1841) 267. They were in the Reading ironworks, which was also the matrix of the Co-op. twenty years later.

2. *Reading Observer*, 28.8.1891.

3. *Ibid.*, 12.3.1892.

4. For the foundation of the SDF in 1891 see *The Reading Citizen* (Feb. 1931).

5. There is now a lot written on the labour movement nationally in the late nineteenth and early twentieth centuries. The best starting point is still H. Pelling, *The Origins of the Labour Party, 1880-1900*, 2nd edition (1965) and Walter Kendall, *The Revolutionary Movement in Britain 1900-1921* (1969). There is a shortage of local studies without which the story will never be properly understood. Two good ones are: D. Cox, 'The Labour Party in Leicester: a study in branch development', in *The International Review of Social History*, VI (1961), and E.P. Thompson, 'Homage to Tom Maguire', in Asa Briggs and John Saville eds. *Essays in Labour History* (1960). I am currently working on a full study of Reading labour/socialist politics up to the mid-1920s.

6. *Justice*, 13.1.1894, 20.1.1894, 6.10.1894.

7. *Smith's Directory* for Reading (1895).

8. Lorenzo Quelch papers in my possession. Lorenzo was a brother of the better known Harry Quelch. His papers consist of parts of an uncompleted autobiography kindly lent to me by a relation.

9. *Berkshire Chronicle*, 27.10.1894.

10. *Justice*, 20.10.1894.

11. See *Justice*, 19.1.1895 for dismissal of F.S. Barnes; for this victimisation, which has been understressed nationally, especially with reference to membership figures, see Goddard H. Orpen, 'Socialism in England', in *Socialism of Today*, Emile de Laveleye (1884) 287-331. He quotes a letter from an SDF member saying, 'it is not possible to give any approximate estimate of our numbers, for the reason that thousands who would join us are kept back by the fear of losing employment, as too many have done already'.

12. For examples of branches elsewhere which highlight the Reading branch see, among many, Bow and Bromley in George Lansbury, *My Life* (1928) 78-9, Coventry in Percy Redfern, *Journey to Understanding* (1946) 31, Bristol in G. Elton, *The Life of James Ramsey Macdonald 1866-1919* (1939) 43-5. Redfern, who joined in 1894-5, is worth quoting: 'we few of the Coventry branch formed a happy band of brothers. We sang Morris's "No Master" and "All for the Cause". We talked of the Revolution – now overdue. Reduced to three or four under a gas lamp on a foggy winter night, publicly we continued to argue and declaim. *That the rest of the city took no notice of us whatever was a fact that only increased our zeal'* (my italics). See also E.J. Hobsbawm, *Labouring Men* (1964) 235, 'like the traditional Dissenters (but unlike the emotionally soggy Methodists) like the Owenites and secularists who were their ancestors, the men in the SDF wanted to read, study and discuss and to work out a general theory of the workers' lot and the world in general by systematic thought ... to study and report upon a great working-class thinker was as natural to Scots tailors like James Macdonald, or the SDF's atheist Northamptonshire shoemakers, as it had been for their fathers and grandfathers to study and reflect upon Robert Owen, Paine and Spence, and for their great grandfathers to discuss the Lord's design in the light of Calvin's Institutes'.

13. See SDF statement on 'the depression' sent to the Mayor and Corporation in 1892, *Berkshire Chronicle*, 10.12.1892.

14. *Justice,* 6.10.1894, 13.10.1894.
15. See article on 'The Pioneers' by L. Quelch in *The Reading Citizen* (Feb. 1931).
16. Jim Harris's two articles in *The Reading Citizen,* 15.8.1926, 15.9.1926. For Adult Classes in economics with the SDF see also *The Reading Citizen* (Aug. 1941).
17. E.J. Hobsbawm, 'Twentieth-Century British Politics', in *Past and Present,* 11 (1957) 100. This is also the basic question behind W.G. Runciman, *Relative Deprivation and Social Justice* (1966).
18. *The Times,* 20.8.1892.
19. Rev. Ambrose Shepherd, *Reading Standard,* 5.10.1907.
20. Political parties beyond the labour movement would of course be helpful for this chapter. Unfortunately records of them are, in Reading, slight. Owing to the local party ceasing to exist for a while there are no records, so far as I can discover, of the Liberal Party. If they turned up they would be fascinating sources. Conservative records exist, but almost all of them refer to the inter-war period. Local studies of the two major parties of the kind done for Rochdale by J. Vincent for his *The Formation of the Liberal Party* (1966) are much needed. J. Blondel, 'The Conservative Association and the Labour Party in Reading', in *Political Studies,* VI, no.2 (1958) is interesting for the post-1918 period. The chronology of party political organisation in Reading from scattered references in the local press was: Reading Liberal Electors Association (1850); Reading Constitutional Club (1850) following an earlier Reading Conservative Association; Conservative Working Men's Association (1867); Liberal Association (1874); Liberal Working Men's Association (1874); Liberal Association and Working Men's Association merged (1880); Reading Conservative Association (1879).
21. They were not the only people who imagined a revolution involving Reading. For a lurid account of a revolution starting in the town and following the route of the Aldermaston marches of CND see Charles Gleig, *When All Men Starve: Showing how England hazarded her naval supremacy, and the horrors which followed the interruption of her food supply* (1898).
22. Quelch papers.
23. *Berkshire Chronicle,* 24.12.1894.
24. *Justice,* 13.1.1894. In 160 tenements varying in rent from 2/- to 5/- a week there were 31 water taps and 96 water closets. In them 78 people were out of work. 'In one square our comrades found only one tap to the entire water supply for 20 houses.'
25. *Justice,* 6.7.1895. They had already formed an 'Unemployed Organisation Committee' in 1893 to press for work, and for free school meals for children, *Reading Observer,* 14.1.1893.
26. *Justice,* 8.6.1895.
27. *Berkshire Chronicle,* 29.3.1902.
28. *Ibid.,* 12.11.1898. George Lansbury and Harry Quelch came down to this meeting.
29. *Justice,* 16.7.1898, 23.7.1898, 30.7.1898; one of the contradictions was that 'the workers of Reading' did not all have the vote. In 1904 it was estimated that 1,500 of Huntley and Palmers employees could vote, T.A.B. Corley, *Quaker Enterprise* ... 169.
30. *Berkshire Chronicle,* 23.1.1897.
31. *Ibid.,* 15.10.1898.
32. A joint conference with the Co-op. was called. Pressure for action towards joint labour representation came through *The Reading Co-operative Record* by means of letters from SDF leaders – Feb. 1899 and July 1899.
33. *Reading Observer,* 19.11.1892; *Reading Co-operative Record* (March, 1900) 6-9. That deference to employers had been an obstacle to organisation in

Reading was noted by William Morris in 1887. He had tried to start a Socialist League branch but, 'it was a dead failure, a good many had given their names to attend, but when it came to the scratch with one consent they all began to make excuses; I note this because it is characteristic of the present stage of the movement; for as aforesaid there was plenty of agreement at the meetings we have held there, this hanging back is partly fear of being boycotted by the masters but chiefly from dislike to organisation ... also fear of anything like revolt or revolution'. Entry in Morris's *Diary,* 23.2.1887, pp.21-2, B.M. Add. Mss. 45335.

34. *Reading Standard,* 1.2.1908; for some excellent examples of the explicit defeat of earlier patterns of deference by working-class electoral victories in 1901, 1903 and 1905, see Anne Cook ..., 240, 247, 250.

35. *The Labour Leader,* 29.11.1911.

36. *The Labour Leader,* 2.2.1912. The language of this labour dispute makes it clear that leader-led relations were part of what was at stake. This can be seen in statements such as that of 9th January 1912, *From the Directors of Huntley and Palmers Limited to their workpeople,* or the *Verbatim Report of Mass Meeting of Employees of Messrs. Huntley and Palmers Limited, To protest against the shameless and lying statements which are being circulated about the conditions of employment at the Biscuit Factory,* or the *Reply of the Workmens' Committee appointed at the Mass Meeting held 29th December 1911 to the Shameless and Lying statements Circulated in the Town,* or *The Victimisation at Huntley and Palmers, A Fight for Life and Liberty,* by the Reading Trades and Labour Council. All these were among the printed pamphlets during the troubles. Copies are in the author's possession. See also *Daily Telegraph,* 15.3.1912, *Berkshire Chronicle,* 7.2.1912.

37. *Berkshire Chronicle,* 25.2.1899. A guide book in 1899 considered the small numbers to be 'probably due to the fact that the greater part of labour is unskilled'.

38. *Reading Illustrated: A Concise Guide* (1899). Examples of local arbitration (often by one Councillor – C.G. Field) were: 1893 a strike at Wokingham Road Improvement scheme, 1894 a bricklayers' strike, 1898 a Carpenters' and Joiners' strike.

39. A chronology of Reading trade unionism can be built up from scattered mentions of unions as follows:

1892   Berkshire and Wiltshire Agricultural and General Workers Union established. (The Annual Report of the Chief Registrar of Friendly Societies included this union in 1893 and 1894. In 1893 there were 245 members, in 1894 120.)

1892   Already there: Stonemasons, Operative Bricklayers, Amalgamated Engineers, Iron Founders, Boiler Makers, Coachmakers and 'several other' unions.

1898   National Union of Shop Assistants, Warehousemen, and Clerks held a meeting.

1900   United Kingdom Builders Labourers Union started recruiting in Reading.

1904   Municipal Workers Association.

1905   Amalgamated Union of Co-operative Employees.

1907   London Society of Compositors established themselves in Reading against the older Typographical Association.

1907   Associated Society of Locomotive Engineers, Firemen and Cleaners met and attacked the Railway Servants.

1909   First branch of the General and Municipal Workers started. Christmas 1911 had 800 members. By 1917 claimed to be the largest branch in UK.

1909   Amalgamated Society of Lithographic Printers; Postmen's
             Federation also existed.
1911-12   Efforts to establish National Federation of Women Workers and
             Gas Workers and General Labourers Union.
1912   Branch of General Railway Workers Union started in Reading.
1914   National Union of Vehicle Workers and National Amalgamated
             Society of Operative House and Shop Painters and Decorators, both
             existed.
This is clearly incomplete, the names of unions vary in the local papers each
time they are mentioned. In reminiscence the later name is often attached to
the original body. See also list of Unions represented at original meeting of
WEA branch in 1904, Chapter Nine.
40. *Berkshire Chronicle,* 8.5.1914.
41. *The Labour Leader,* 29.12.1911.
42. Local newspapers reveal interesting working-class groups which probably
occupied a larger slice of activists' time and energies as social movements than
did trade unions. For instance there was a group active in Reading in the early-
twentieth century called 'Ye Ancient Cogers'. It was a philanthropic,
entertainment-giving, social evening, politically involved grouping which, in
1905, had 135 members and a committee of twelve. The committee met
sixteen times in the season 1904-5 and the society or 'order', whose motto
was *concordia et comitas,* much more often. The names who figure in reports
of its meetings are many of the same names as are active in trade-union and
labour politics. One 'Brother' argued at a meeting in 1905 that 'societies such
as theirs must have a reason for their existence, and possess something
tangible, such as they had in the debating and philanthropic part of their own
society'. For examples of them at work see the *Berkshire Chronicle,* 7.10.1905,
25.11.1905.
43. *Ibid.,* 27.10.1900.
44. The most effective representative on the Guardians was W.G. Ayres (ILP)
who made a lot of running in 1905 and 1906. The *Reading Observer,*
30.3.1907, was moved to observe, when he was seeking re-election, 'there are
Socialists and Socialists, but a reformer of Mr Ayres' type should not be
elected on a public body'. Soon after this (*Reading Observer,* 24.11.1909)
George Lansbury visited Reading workhouse and was impressed by the reforms
achieved. Workhouse reform in Poplar was one of the SDF's best achievements
on elected bodies.
45. *Berkshire Chronicle,* 8.9.1902: the paper referred to 'the growing strength of
the labour party in Reading'.
46. The first (?) such alliance was the Co-op./SDF conference in 1899. In
October 1901 the Reading Workers' Electoral League met to plan Council
election co-operation. By 1904 it was the Labour Electoral League doing the
same work, but it by no means controlled the entire labour slate at the
elections – they alloted only one contest exclusively to the LEL, one to the
Municipal Workers Association, two for the Trades and Labour Council, one
or two to 'the Socialists' – see *Berkshire Chronicle,* 6.2.1904. In 1909 Keir
Hardie presided over the formation of a Labour Representation Committee in
Reading, but in 1914 it was formed again owing to the initiative of the Trades
Council; *Reading Observer,* 8.4.1909, 15.5.1909, 1.1.1910; *Berkshire
Chronicle,* 29.5.1914.
There is no point here in detailing each electoral gain; perhaps the most
important single individual was J. Rabson, elected to the Council in 1905 and
to become the first Labour Mayor in 1927. He has already been encountered
at several points in earlier chapters.
47. *Berkshire Chronicle,* 29.3.1902.

48. *Berkshire Chronicle*, 4.5.1901. *The Reading Co-operative Record*, (Dec. 1899).
49. *The Reading Co-operative Record*, (April, 1902).
50. *Berkshire Chronicle*, 23.1.1914.
51. For a typical labour programme in local affairs in the early twentieth century that of the Reading Trades and Labour Council for the 1904 municipal elections will serve: free secondary schooling, free meals for school children, secular education in council schools, free use of schools for meetings, eight-hour day for municipal employees, immediate adoption of Workmen's Dwelling Act, rating of unoccupied houses, insertion of trade-union clause in all municipal contracts, no sub-contracting, public works to relieve unemployment, municipal hospitals, municipal savings bank, municipal cemeteries, municipal baths and wash houses, municipalisation of all monopolies, evening meetings of the council. These were the demands they sent to all candidates, *Berkshire Chronicle*, 29.10.1904.
52. Newspaper cutting in local collection, Nov. 1912; for a campaign by a Fabian/CSU/WEA activist (F.B. Mason) to get the Council to use its housing powers see *Reading Mercury*, April-May 1912.
53. *Berkshire Chronicle*, 7.5.1892. In answer to the item 'chief hindrance to Pastoral labour', in the 1890 Episcopal Visitation Returns Hart Davies, as vicar of Dunsden near Reading, had put 'the serfdom of the labouring man'. The Returns covering Reading are in the Bodleian Library, Oxford.
54. *Berkshire Chronicle*, 25.2.1899.
55. *Reading Observer*, 13.1.1906.
56. *Berkshire Chronicle*, 25.2.1899.
57. *Reading Standard*, 17.8.1912.
58. *Berkshire Chronicle*, 10.5.1902, 6.2.1904, 23.12.1905. The last reference is to a meeting on unemployment at which J.F. Hodgson, L. Quelch, J. Harris, W.G. Ayres, S.G. Jones and J. Rabson all spoke. It was the most widely representative labour political meeting, not in numbers attending but in shades of ideology represented, that I have come across in Reading.
59. In 1906 the SDF were thinking of running their own parliamentary candidate, *Reading Observer*, 3.2.1906. In 1909 the LRC were 'contemplating' putting a Labour candidate in the field, having secured a prospective candidate in the person of Mr John I. Fox of Queen's College Oxford, 'who is no stranger to Reading audiences', *Reading Observer*, 2.1.1909, and, for his withdrawal, 1.1.1910. In 1911 J.G. Butler emerged as a 'Socialist and Labour candidate', *Reading Observer*, 6.5.1911. For his candidature 'on a straight socialist ticket' see also Quelch papers.
60. Quelch papers. Quelch incurred great odium by agreeing to serve on military tribunals, 'these things altogether had caused a split in the local BSP and the same thing happened all over the country more or less'.
61. Beatrice Webb, *Our Partnership* (1948) 195.
62. C.F.G. Masterman, *The Condition of England* (1909) 143.
63. For a contemporary study to which this paragraph is much indebted see S. Reynolds and B. and F. Woolley, *Seems So! A Working Class View of Politics* (1911). H. Pelling in his *Popular Politics and Society* (1968) makes use of this extremely interesting book.
64. The quotations are from *Seems So!*, 167, 166, xx, and 181; for similar insights in Reading, see *Reading Co-operative Record* (May, 1900) 7; (Oct., 1900) 4; (Jan., 1903) 3.
65. *Berkshire Chronicle*, 19.4.1918.
66. For a classic twentieth-century definition of politics as one 'hobby' or leisure-pursuit among others, all right for those who like it, but of no more significance – a definition from within the Working Men's Club and Institute Union, where such views had not been characteristic twenty years before –

see *Club Life,* 9.9.1905, p.21. I owe this reference to T.G. Ashplant.

67. The social history of popular attitudes and relationships to politics is a very difficult area to document. Helen Lynd in her *England in the 1880s* (1945) draws attention to the mass of local Parliamentary Debating Societies which existed in the third quarter of the nineteenth century in many towns, including Reading. Interestingly enough they had passed their peak as a movement by the early twentieth century. For a later period A.J.P. Taylor in his *English History 1914-1945* (1965) 315-6 speculated about the effects of the cinema in a way which needs testing: 'the real effect of the cinema went deeper: it provided a substitute for real life and helped people to become watchers instead of doers. The unemployed man could forget, for a few pence, his harsh surroundings and could move into a world of palatial halls, obsequious servants, and marble baths (though no lavatories). Why should he bother with demonstrations? Real life was itself turned into a spectacle ... Politics seemed more passionate, international events were more widely discussed than ever before. Yet with it all was a feeling that these great happenings had no more connexion with real life than those seen every night in the cinema palaces.'

68. *Berkshire Chronicle,* 15.10.1898.

69. *Reading Observer,* 17.8.1912. I am indebted to R.J. Holton for references to earlier syndicalism in Reading. The British Advocates of Industrial Unionism had a branch in Reading in 1908, see *Industrial Unionist,* no.4, p.8. By 1909 the BAIU had become the Industrial Workers of Great Britain, *Industrial Unionist,* no.10, p.8 had an article called 'What Reading Industrial Unionists have to say about organising the IWW'. The IWGB had a branch in Reading in March, 1909, see *Industrial Unionist,* no.11, p.8.

70. *Berkshire Chronicle,* 8.5.1914. J.G. Butler's adoption had been in 1911, *Reading Observer,* 6.5.1911.

71. *Reading Observer,* 17.8.1912.

72. Lorenzo Quelch did this: *Berkshire Chronicle,* 18.1.1918, 25.1.1918, 8.2.1918, 1.3.1918, 2.8.1918. When Arthur Henderson went to the Board of Education in 1915 his conception of at least part of his duty was publicised in the Reading press, *Reading Observer,* 5.6.1915: 'if industry is to be thoroughly organised, there will be a rash of disturbances, and I shall do everything my experience will assist me in doing to prevent those risks being realised by actual stoppage'.

73. A Coventry socialist, Percy Redfern, in his *Journey to Understanding* (1946) 143-4, linked the two. He was disappointed with the way politics went after the mid-1890s but 'it was not all a cheat. The South African settlement, the Old Age Pensions, the feeding and care of school children, the Employment Exchanges, the instalment of unemployment insurance, the equalising trend of the next budgets, the political democracy of the Parliament Act, seemed to be transforming the State into that servant of the people for which we at the street corners had cried out in wind and rain ... nevertheless, having taken part in contests for democratic power, I could not do other than wonder whether those old comrades would not be themselves absorbed' (he meant Snowden, Macdonald, Jowett, Parker of Halifax, *et al.*).

74. It is rare to get statements as explicit as that of Balfour at Manchester on 16th January 1895: 'social legislation as I conceive it is not merely to be distinguished from socialist legislation, but is its most direct opposite, and its most effective antidote. Socialism will never get possession of the great body of public opinion ... among the working class if those who rule the collective forces of the community show themselves desirous ... to ameliorate every legitimate grievance and to put society upon a proper and more solid basis', quoted in E. Halévy, *History of the English People in the Nineteenth Century,*

vol. 5. (1961 edition) 201.

75. For the CSU see *Reading Observer*, 12.5.1906, 14.7.1906. F.G. Bettany in
his life of *Stewart Headlam* (1926) 95, thought that 'what was said about it —
"here's a social evil, let's read a paper on it" — was not so very unfair'. For the
Reading Citizens' Association see *Reading Standard*, 1.5.1909, for an account
of a meeting on the municipal care of consumptives. For the Reading Health
Society, founded in 1907, see their *Annual Report* (1912-13). The family of
Dr. Gilford kindly gave me what was left of his personal collection of press
cuttings shortly before he died.

76. *Reading Standard*, 2.10.1936; *Reading Mercury*, 3.10.1936.

77. Reading Women's Conservative Association, *Minute Book of the Central
Council* (Dec. 1905 onwards). A speech by Major Leslie Wilson, the
prospective candidate, 12.11.1909.

78. The *Reading Observer*, 10.4.1909.

79. Quoted in *Reading Standard*, 25.1.1908. It was the Liverpool Clarion Club
which made the challenge to the ministers. They replied: 'We the undersigned
ministers of Christian churches of various denominations ... desire to make
this declaration in view of the widely circulated suggestion which has been
made in the press and elsewhere that the Socialism we believe in differs
fundamentally from the Socialism advocated by the recognised Socialist
organisations. We declare that the Socialism we believe in ... is ... essentially
the same as that which is held by Socialists throughout the world.' Much
earlier the SDF had made their position on this type of elision clear, 'although
we should be ready to accept the whole bench of bishops as members of the
SDF if they chose to come along, there is little doubt that nowadays the
friendship of the church is more harmful than its enmity', *Justice*, 28.9.1895.
C.A. Bradford, a Socialist in the Co-op. in Reading wrote in 1900, 'I should
like to see a better appreciation on the part of the clergy of the men who are
endeavouring to uplift the working classes. The leaders of the working classes
deserve the confidence of the clergy because to a very great extent their aims
are similar to those of the clergy', *The Reading Co-operative Record* (Dec.
1900); for churches embracing unemployed demonstrations and giving their
own meaning to them, see *Reading Standard*, 1.2.1908 and *Berkshire
Chronicle*, 28.1.1893. (Trinity Congregational and St. Lawrence's). For a
more hostile reception, see Broad Street *Magazine*, (July, 1962) referring to
The Reading Pioneer, no.48 (Dec. 1908).

80. For example Birrell wrote an article on 'The State and the Child' for *Reading
Observer*, 9.8.1906, 'there had been a time when a public elementary school
was a place where children were taught reading, writing and arithmetic. But
now they lived in another world, and ever since he had been at the Board of
Education he had been pursued by deputations of learned and zealous men
and women, who looked upon the schools as places where they were to
consider the health, future happiness and what he might call the breed of the
English speaking race'.

81. In 1906-7 there was intense discussion on Liberal/Labour-ILP relationships
emanating from the Parliamentary situation and percolating into Reading
political discussion. Snowden was writing a syndicated column for the *Reading
Observer* at the time. When that paper and the Liberal Whip, the Master of
Elibank, were worried about the ILP being too socialistic for it to be possible
to co-operate on the politics of liberal social reform, Snowden reassured them
that 'the Labour Party in the British Parliament is not a Socialist party',
although he thought it would evolve into one, the *Reading Observer*, 8.9.1906.
Keir Hardie made a similar point in a speech reported in the *Reading Mercury*,
2.2.1907. For a local ILP speech by W.C. Anderson which was in no respect to
the 'left' of current liberal social politics see the *Reading Observer*, 13.1.1912.

82. *Reading Observer*, 20.3.1912.
83. *The Reading Co-operative Record* (Jan., 1899).
84. A speech by the secretary of the Building Labourers' Union, *Berkshire Chronicle*, 4.5.1901.
85. *The Reading Co-operative Record* (Sept. 1903).
86. J.F.C. Harrison's treatment of the Adult Schools in *Learning and Living 1790-1960* (1961) 300-12, with reference to their ideal of Fellowship, is relevant to this distinction between language and rhetoric. At their best the Adult Schools were examples of the use of the language referred to, at their worst, rhetoricians.
87. Meetings were attended by such men as Rev. H.J. Basden, and to a meeting on 'the State's duty to children' the Rev. Carew Hunt sent his apologies in May 1909. He had previously made clear his reservations about other versions of socialism, see St. Giles, *Parish Magazine* (Feb. 1908). For the ILP at work see *Reading Observer*, 15.11.1912 on the Insurance Act, or their 'war against poverty', *Reading Observer*, 19.10.1912. It was not only the context in which they were putting forward their demands which had changed utterly since the meetings of the SDF in the 1890s, but also the type of class mixture which attended, and the language used. There was loud applause when Canon Fowler spoke on the evolution of the idea of temperance at an ILP meeting in 1907, *Reading Mercury*, 11.11.1907. F.B. Mason tried to persuade the CSU to initiate the Elberfield system of poor relief in Reading at a meeting in May 1907. This system 'involved the subdivision of the city into small districts presided over by unpaid visitors, serving in rotation. The service was compulsory for the citizens, although the individual was consulted about his willingness to act. The districting was carried to such a point that on average the total population from which a visitor might draw his cases was only about 200', see K. de Schweinitz, *England's Road to Social Security*, paperback edit. (1961) 148-9.
88. Reminiscences of W.L.R. Crosswell in *The Reading Citizen* (Oct. 1950).
89. For the background to this movement elsewhere see K.S. Inglis, *Churches and the Working Classes in Victorian England* (1963) 79-85. It was invented in 1875 by an Independent deacon in West Bromwich but did not start spreading until 1885.
90. Wycliffe Baptists started in 1894, Oxford Road Wesleyans in 1894-5; Elm Park Hall, Whitley Hall, Grovelands, Oxford Road Primitives, Queen's Road Wesleyans and Pangbourne all had active PSAs within the next fifteen years.
91. J. Rabson was the leading figure at Broad Street for fifteen years until he became a Labour Councillor in 1905. J.W. Burness, Jim Harris, Coppuck and many other Labour cadres were active in the Brotherhood movement. The Labour Representation Committee candidate for West Ward in the Guardians elections in 1909 was an ILP activist described as being 'well known in PSA circles'.
92. Quotations and facts about the Broad Street PSA are taken from the Broad Street Congregational Chapel, *Magazine*. The PSA notes were very full, and most of them were clearly written by J. Rabson.
93. For their support of the Engineers in the 1897 Lock-out, see *Berkshire Chronicle*, 4.12.1897; for their support of the South Wales Miners, see *ibid.*, 18.8.1898.
94. Broad Street, *Magazine* (Nov. 1911).
95. *The Reading Co-operative Record* (June, 1904; March, 1903). At a conference in 1899 Councillor S.G. Jones 'regretted that the intelligence of so many of the workers was spent in following horse racing and football', *ibid.*, (Jan. 1899); for other organisations worried about keeping alive or about keeping to their main purpose see the Sunday Social Conference, *Reading Observer*,

4.3.1909; the Reading Debating Society, *Berkshire Chronicle* 14.10.1905; the Reading WEA, *Reading Observer,* 20.3.1909. Even the promoters of frankly social clubs like the Conservative Beaconsfield or Salisbury Clubs were worried, for 'the object ... of these is not merely the amusement of and promotion of social intercourse among the members, but also the dissemination of political principles'. For a survey of these clubs, see *Berkshire Chronicle,* 18.2.1899.

96. *The Reading Co-operative Record* (Feb., 1903).
97. For Rambles, see *ibid.,* (Nov. 1901) 7; for the Choir (Nov. 1904) 12; for hobbies (May, 1905) 11.
98. *Ibid.,* (Jan. 1899) 4; (Dec. 1899) 8; (Feb. 1902) 9; (April, 1904) 3. etc.
99. *Ibid.,* (Jan. 1899) 9.
100. *Ibid.,* (April, 1904) 8.
101. For Reading Co-op.'s awareness of competitive pressures from capitalist concerns, see *ibid.,* (June, 1899; April, Dec., 1900; March, August, 1901; April, August, Sept., 1902; Jan. 1903; March, 1904).
102. *Ibid.,* (Feb., Dec. 1900; Sept., Oct., Nov. 1901; May, Sept. 1904; May 1905).
103. *Ibid.,* (April 1899; Oct. 1900; March 1901).
104. *Berkshire Chronicle,* 19.4.1918; see also *The Reading Citizen* (Feb. 1931) for earlier moves towards this in mid-1917.

CHAPTER 11

1. The scale of individual church/chapel budgets at this time gains some perspective from comparison with one of the most famous and fertile of religious organisations of the day, Toynbee Hall in E. London. The initial capital costs of Toynbee Hall were about £7,000, and its annual operating budget no bigger than that of many chapels – c.£1,200.
2. All the following quotations are from Ambrose Shepherd, *The Gospel and Social Questions* (1902), mostly from a chapter called 'Hindrances to Realisations', pp.3-22. The book was provoked by Hall Caine's article in the *British Weekly,* 12.12.1901; for a sermon by Shepherd on Municipal Responsibility, to the Mayor and Corporation, *ibid.,* 15.11.1894.
3. For further examples of such language, and an attempt to make sense of them, see Stephen Yeo, 'On the Uses of "Apathy"', in *Archives Européennes de Sociologie,* XV (1974) 279-311. See also *idem.,* 'Religion in Society ...', unpublished D.Phil. thesis (University of Sussex, 1971) Chapter XIII, 452-488.
4. For work on 'the Nonconformist conscience', see John F. Glasier, 'English Nonconformity and the Decline of Liberalism', in *American Historical Review,* lxii, 2 (January, 1958); John Kent, 'Hugh Price Hughes and the Nonconformist Conscience', in G.V. Bennett and J.D. Walsh, eds., *Essays in Modern Church History* (London, 1966); I. Sellers, 'Nonconformist Attitudes in later 19th century Liverpool', in *Transactions of the Historical Society of Lancs. and Cheshire,* CXIV (1962).
5. Broad Street's *Magazine* (Dec. 1908); for another Sewell description see an interesting comparison of 'the life of Reading of 1903' with that of 1888 when he arrived in the town, in *Magazine* (April, 1903). See also *Reading Observer,* 20.10.1900.
6. *Reading Standard,* 5.10.1907; there was a millenial quality to the language of socially concerned Nonconformist spokesmen at this time. Rev. F.B. Meyer told the London Federation of PSA Brotherhoods in January 1911 that, 'the time is ripe for our testimony ... the year 1911 ... is likely to be the most fateful year of a new era – one in which democracy shall be able to take its

untramelled course', *British Weekly,* 26.1.1911. Later in the same year he said, 'we are at one of the crises of our national life. Two ages were meeting like sundown and sunrise in the Arctic sky. The rule of the few was being superseded by the rule of the many', *Manchester Guardian,* 18.9.1911, quoted in Stuart Mews, 'Puritanicalism, Sport and Race: A Symbolic Crusade of 1911', in Canon G.J. Cuming and Derek Baker, eds., *Studies in Church History* (Cambridge, 1971).

7. F. Rogers, *Labour, Life and Literature* (1913) 61, described this function of cultural transmitter well, from the point of view of one who sat in the pew. See also E.T. Davies, *Religion in the Industrial Revolution in South Wales* (Cardiff, 1965) 120.

8. *Reading Observer,* 20.10.1900. The preacher was the Rev. A.T. Guttery.

9. Trinity Congregational Church, *Pamphlets,* vol. 5; for effects of penny post, telephones, etc. on local consciousness, see also W.M. Childs, *The Story of the Town of Reading* (1921) 230.

10. Sources for this paragraph, in order: Ambrose Shepherd, *op.cit.,* 43, 184; *Reading Standard,* 30.6.1898 or 1901 (cutting in YMCA *Minute Book*); *Reading Observer,* 6.3.1909; *The United Magazine* (Aug. 1896); *Berkshire Chronicle,* 9.6.1894, 16.6.1894. Other places for similar diagnoses are: *Berkshire Chronicle,* 29.5.1914 – a sermon by Guy Rogers on Empire Day; Albert Swift, *The First Principles of Christian Citizenship* (1908); Broad Street, *Magazine* (May, 1898) – a sermon by Sewell; the activities of the Reading Anti-Betting and Gambling Committee, *Berkshire Chronicle,* 4.11.1905 – this contained a report of a big public meeting which promoted the movement, at which Will Crooks and Labour men like S.G. Jones and J. Harris were there together with many other strands of Reading opinion taking a significantly united stand; *Reading Observer,* 22.11.1890 – a revisit to Reading after a thirty-year gap by a New Zealander.

11. Albert Swift, *The First Principles of Christian Citizenship* (1908) 144.

12. *Justice,* 8.6.1895.

13. Broad Street, *Magazine* (Dec. 1897).

14. Ralph Miliband, *The State in Capitalist Society* (1969) I; for an influential contemporary statement see Hilaire Belloc, *The Servile State* (1912); or A.V. Dicey, *Law and Public Opinion in England,* 2nd edition (1914), Introduction, xxiii-xciv. See also Asa Briggs, 'The Human Aggregate', in ed. H.J. Dyos and M. Wolff, *The Victorian City,* I, p. 97, 'it is not strange that studies which begin with the Victorian city end with the twentieth-century State'; Emil Davies, *The Collectivist State in the Making* (1914).

15. Helen Lynd, *England in the Eighteen-Eighties: Towards a Basis for Freedom* (Oxford, 1945); Melvin Richter, *The Politics of Conscience: T.H. Green and His Age* (1964); D.A. Hamer, *John Morley. Liberal Intellectual in Politics* (Oxford, 1968); Brian Harrison, *Drink and the Victorians. The Temperance Question in England, 1815-1872* (1971) chapter 9.

16. Gareth Stedman Jones, *Outcast London: A study in the relationship between classes in Victorian society* (Oxford, 1971) 313-4.

17. The best treatment of this legislation is in Bentley B. Gilbert, *The Evolution of National Insurance in Great Britain: the origins of the welfare state* (1966) 9. He takes the six measures which began with the Education (Provision of Meals) Act (1906) as marking a qualitative change in the nature of State action in this field. See also for an excellent contemporary interpretation, B.L. Kirkman Gray, *Philanthropy and the State, or Social Politics* (1908).

18. F.B. Bourdillon, 'A Creative Social Policy', in *Reading University College Review* (March, 1910). The ratio in medical relief was still in favour of voluntary organisations (offical, £4,738; voluntary, £12,000).

19. The Stranger, *The Stranger in Reading* (Reading, 1810) 117. For pre-1850

culture described in much the same way, see E.T. Davies, *Religion in the
Industrial Revolution in South Wales* (Cardiff, 1965) 121.
20. W.H. Greenhough, *The Public Libraries, a retrospect of thirty years 1882-1912*,
a pamphlet in the local collection.
21. Incorporation was the main result in Reading, but there was some syndicalism
and industrial unionism (1908-14) as its antidote, see *Industrial Unionist,* IV
(1908) 8, X (1909) 8, Xi (1909) 8.
22. Beatrice Webb, *My Apprenticeship* (London, 1926) 194-5, n.I; for critical
income-tax developments in this period see B.E.V. Sabine, *A History of the
Income Tax* (London, 1966) 125-56, F. Shehab, *Progressive Taxation*
(Oxford, 1953) 189-259.
23. For financial problems in relation to University Extension elsewhere, see
J.F.C. Harrison, *Learning and Living* (1961) 240-3.
24. Preceded by such explicit observations as that of a New Connexion minister
in 1889 that 'Modern conditions make advancement more and more difficult
for the smaller denominations. It must be remembered ... how the power of
propagation has relatively declined, or has come to be more and more
dependent on large material resources ... The social forces are against small
Denominations, and their struggles will be greater', in *Methodist New
Connexion Magazine* (May, 1889) quoted, with other examples, in Robert
Currie, *Methodism Divided: a study in the Sociology of Ecumenicalism* (1968)
88.
25. E.P. Hennock, 'Finance and politics in Urban Local Government in England,
1835-1900' in *Historical Journal* VI, 2 (1962) 212-225; for Reading
Councillors, occupations and associational links, see Anne Cook ..., 33 53,
106, 170, 182, 234-40, 252, 352, 367; for similar trends elsewhere, see
A.H. Birch, *Small Town Politics* (Oxford, 1959) 39, F. Bealey, *Constituency
Politics* (1965) 387-99.
26. *Reading Standard*, 12.10.1912.
27. *Reading Mercury*, 4.11.1905.
28. The process by which the 'from below' social movement leading to the
formation of the first modern British political party, described by John
Vincent, *The Formation of the Liberal Party, 1857-1869* (1966), became the
political machines analysed as 'agencies of legitimation' by Ralph Miliband,
The State in Capitalist Society (1969) chapter 7, is a long, complicated and
politically controversial one. To describe it would involve analysing the
'Brummagem' caucus system and the development of the Liberal machine,
followed by parallel developments in the Conservative party. It would also
involve showing that the origins of the Labour Party, in its Labour
Representation Committee form, lay not in a natural development out of the
socialist social movement of the 1880s and 1890s, but in trade-union/
pressure-group politics. See M. Ostrogorski, *Democracy and the Organisation of
Political Parties, I, England* (1902) for a contemporary analysis of these themes.
29. Conservative clubs seemed to be flourishing more than Liberal ones in
Reading in the late nineteenth century, partly because of their greater stress
on recreation. But even clubs like the Beaconsfield or the Salisbury clubs
became worried and had to remind members that 'the object ... of these clubs
is not merely the amusement of, and promotion of social intercourse among
the members, but also the dissemination of political principles'. There was a
survey of such clubs in *Berkshire Chronicle*, 18.2.1899. D. Cox has shown the
developing recreational function of the ILP in 'The Labour Party in Leicester:
a study in branch development', in *The International Review of Social History*, VI
(1961); it is interesting that the movement around Robert Blatchford and *The
Clarion,* having lost the battle against the machine-party as the appropriate
form of organisation for democratic socialists took on more and more of a

leisure-provision or entertainment function, *c.*1896-1914, see Keir Hardie's observation of this in *Labour Leader,* 21.10.1899.

30. Asa Briggs, *Victorian Cities* (1963) 370.

31. For the beginnings of the Reading Distress Committee, *Berkshire Chronicle,* 7.10.1905; and for Distress Committees and unemployment, W.H. Beveridge, *Unemployment: a Problem of Industry* (1909).

32. Henry George, *Progress and Poverty* (1879) William Reeves ed. (n.d.) 219-20. George was worried that 'the very power of exerting his (the worker's) labour for the satisfaction of his wants passes from his own control, and may be taken away or restored by the actions of others, or by general causes over which he has no more influence than he has over the solar system'; see also William Clarke's essay in, *Fabian Essays* (1889) 6th edition (1962) 94, 100: 'there had been and is proceeding an economic evolution, practically independent of our individual desires or prejudices; an evolution which has changed for us the whole social problem by changing the conditions of material production, and which *ipso facto* effects a revolution in our modern life'. 'It is well to witness all these processes going on in one large factory in order to grasp fully the idea that the old individual industry of the last century is almost as extinct as the mastodon — that the worker in a shoe factory today is, so to speak, a machine in a vast complex system.'

33. By 'technological romanticism' is meant the widespread late nineteenth-century belief that technology would solve all problems, particularly the belief in such thinkers as William Morris, that electricity plus small machines (like the typewriter or sewing machine) would lead to decentralisation, over against the centralising process of the previous hundred years.

34. For increasing costs, caused by developments such as X-rays after 1895 and Radium treatment, see Ernest Dormer, ed. *The Story of the Royal Berkshire Hospital, 1837-1937* (Reading, 1937) 142.

35. A.J.P. Taylor, *English History 1914-1945* (1965) 307.

36. For advocacy of 'the domestic hearth', even against voluntary organisations such as reading rooms, as early as 1866, see J. Symington, 'The Working Man's Home', prize essay in J. Begg, DD, *Happy Homes for Working Men and How to Get Them* (1866), quoted in R.Q. Gray, 'Styles of Life, the "Labour Aristocracy" and Class Relations in later nineteenth-century Edinburgh', in *International Review of Social History,* XVIII (1973) pt.3 p.436.

37. For national sources on the PSA (founded 1875, in West Bromwich), see K.S. Inglis, *Churches and the Working Classes in Victorian England* (1963) 79-85; for Christian Endeavour (founded in New England in 1881, took root in Britain in Crewe in 1887), see W. Knight Chaplin and M.J. Street, *Sixty-Five Years of Christian Endeavour* (1946); for CEMS, (founded in 1904), see J.G. Lockhart, *Cosmo Gordon Lang* (1949) 161-4; for the WEA, see J.F.C. Harrison, *Learning and Living* (1961).

38. The Boy Scouts adopted the patrol system of six boys under a leader, and the troop system of a maximum of forty boys, quite deliberately as the best size units for encouraging independence and initiative under the example and firm guidance of a leader, see *Encyclopedia Britannica,* 12th edition (1922) new vols. (30). For organisational self-consciousness in the Salvation Army about different cadres of leadership, see General Booth's address to officers of the London divisions in 'Councils of War', in ten instalments, in *The War Cry,* 2.1.1883, etc., and about success being achieved in diversionary branches of work but only at the cost of failure in the real purpose of the Army, see a 'General Order' from Booth in *The War Cry,* 13.1.1883 repeated 17.1.1883, 'The attention of the General has been called to the programme of some meetings recently held, generally under the name of "Hosanna Meetings" or

"Fruit Banquets", much after the style of entertainments which used to be
provided in connection with Christian Mission Temperance meetings and
which were put a stop to years ago. There is no doubt that these
entertainments have been devised with the best intentions, but even if all the
songs used were our own it is clear that the songs, singings and recitations
carried on after the manner of a performance designed to please the hearers
must be quite contrary to the spirit of the Army, improper in our buildings
and calculated to do great injury to our work. No recitations or performance
upon musical instruments, whether by grown-up persons or children can be
consistent with real spiritual service and nothing of the kind can be permitted
in connection with any of our Corps. We cannot too carefully guard against
the coming in amongst us of anything which would prevent our saying truly
that we meet together always and only for Salvation purposes'; see also
General Booth's didactic novel, *Sergeant-Major Do-Your-Best of Darkington
No. 1* (n.d.).

39. Renato Poblete, S.J., and Thomas F. O'Dea, 'Sectarianism as a Response to
Anomie', in ed. Robert Lees, *Cities and Churches: Readings on the Urban
Church* (Philadelphia, 1962) 195-206; same authors, 'Anomie and the Quest
for Community: The Formation of Sects among Puerto Ricans of New York',
in *American Catholic Sociological Review,* 21 (Spring 1960) 18-36; Arnold M.
Rose, 'The Problem of a Mass Society', in *Theory and Method in the Social
Sciences* (Minneapolis, 1954) 40. For a social historian who has seen sect
development as a means of adjustment to the breakdown of community see
J.F.C. Harrison, *Robert Owen and Owenites in Britain and America* (1969).

40. D. Davis, *A History of Shopping* (1966) 263; *Reading Mercury,* 13.1.1900,
quoted in Anne Cook ..., 326.

41. Francine M. Taylor, 'An inquiry into the leisure interests of the people of
Reading', unpublished D.Phil. thesis (University of Reading, 1955) 3.

42. 'The universities in relation to national and local life', a lecture by W.M. Childs,
Reading Observer, 13.2.1909; see also, *The 'Borough' Pocket Guide to Reading*
(1907?) 82, for educational competition with Germany.

43. Reading Athletic Club, *Annual Report* (1899-1900) (1903-4). The modern
Olympic games, launched in Athens in 1896, were a sign of growing
inter-state competition in sport.

44. The Boys' Brigade (1883), the Church Lads' Brigade (1891), the Boy Scouts
(1907). The Salvation Army had doubts about the Boy Scouts, and started
their own Life Saving Scouts in 1913, see Catherine Booth, *Bramwell Booth*
(1933) 340.

45. The Salvation Army started as a Christian Mission in 1865, but was not
uniformed until 1880.

46. 'This form (that of the capitalistic industrial enterprise SY) is one of the
institutional *genera* that dominate our (the American SY) modern political,
military, religious and educational life as well as the contemporary economic
world', Alfred D. Chandler, *Strategy and Structure: Chapters in the History
of the Industrial Enterprise* (Cambridge, Mass., 1962) 400, n.5; for
organisational change in the Church of England seen in this setting,
Kenneth A. Thompson, *Bureaucracy and Church Reform: The organisational
response of the Church of England to Social Change 1800-1965* (Oxford,
1970) esp. pp.xiv-xvi, see also K.F. Boulding, *The Organisational Revolution*
(New York, 1953); for a good framework for mass communications and the
leisure industries, see G. Murdock and P. Golding, 'For a Political Economy of
Mass Communications', in R. Miliband and J. Saville eds., *The Socialist
Register 1973* (1974) 205-34, esp. 207-23: one of their conclusions is that the
'increasing interpenetration of the media and general leisure industries is
accompanied by increasing rationalisation leading to the deletion of small

units of relatively low profitability and the application of common
management techniques and marketing strategies in the overall interests of
corporate growth. The cumulative result of this is increasingly to restrict the
variety of entertainment and leisure options on offer to the majority of
people, and to standardise the content'.

47. 'For the most part', because Suttons had daily services for their employees
before work available in their Abbey Hall, and the Reading Gas Company
during the 1890s employed missionaries to preach at their works 'between
draws'. There were also many occupational missions during the nineteenth
century, such as the Railway Mission, the Navvy Mission and so on. Primitive
Methodists also preached during work at the Reading Ironworks, see
Primitive Methodist Magazine (1841) 267.

48. For how 'quality biscuits' became 'within the range of most family incomes',
see T.A.B. Corley, *Quaker Enterprise in Biscuits,* 278.

49. Corley, p.278, refers to demand 'being held down artificially by a lack of
purchasing power'.

50. For the best introductory treatment of many of the themes here see
Asa Briggs, *Mass Entertainment: the Origins of a Modern Industry* (Adelaide,
1960). John Myerscough of the University of Sussex is working on a general
study of the economic history of leisure, with special reference to the seaside
holiday industry.

51. The Sunday Press was one of the first major products in this industry. See
R. Hoggart ed., *Your Sunday Newspaper* (1967) 14-15. There was a total sale
of 275,000 Sundays in 1850 (against 60,000 weekday papers), and almost two
million in 1900, see R. Williams, *Communications,* Penguin edition (1962)
22-34. For how time 'characteristically in a pecuniary society is "spent"',
see R.S. and H.M. Lynd, *Middletown* (New York, 1929) 225; for the language
of 'unmortgaged time', see P.F. Lazarsfeld and R.K. Merton, 'Mass
Communication, Popular Taste and Organised Social Action', in B. Rosenberg
and D.M. White eds., *Mass Culture, The Popular Arts in America* (New York,
1957) 460. For the 'retail revolution' of the late nineteenth century see
Asa Briggs, *Friends of the People* (1956), J.B. Jeffreys, *Retail Trading in
Great Britain, 1850-1950* (1954), Dorothy Davis, *A History of Shopping*
(1966).

52. The language Reith used about broadcasting was not unlike that of many
a Congregational or Baptist minister about his chapel *c.*1890, see J.C.W. Reith,
Into the Wind (1949) 116, 135-6. The means by which private capital got into
television broadcasting were as specific to the period as was the fact of
commercial television itself, see H.H. Wilson, *Pressure Group: the Campaign
for Commercial Television* (1961).

53. Arnold M. Rose, 'The Problem of a Mass Society', in *Theory and Method in
the Social Sciences* (Minneapolis, 1954) 40. For the concept of 'the public' as
distinct from the 'mass' or 'audience', see Rose, and also Herbert Blumer,
'Collective Behaviour', in Alfred M. Lee, ed. *New Outline of the Principles of
Sociology* (New York, 1922); A.L. Lowell, *Public Opinion and Popular
Government* (New York, 1913).

54. For pubs in this regard, and the change from being 'nothing more than an
enlarged home' to being 'a large shop with specialised equipment and a bar' in
the nineteenth-century city, in the interests of the 'casual urban drinker', see
Brian Harrison, 'Pubs', in H.J. Dyos and M. Wolff, eds., *The Victorian City:
Images and Realities,* I (1973) 170.

55. See S.B. Linder, *The Harried Leisure Class* (1970). I owe this reference to
John Myerscough. Myerscough pointed out, in an unpublished paper on 'The
Transformation of Popular Recreation' (1973), that the relative preference
for leisure against income has fallen during the last hundred years, 'the hours

worked each week have been more or less the same for the last fifty years'.
56. W.L. George, *Caliban* (London, 1920) quoted by Paul Ferris, in *The Observer,*
    16.5.1971. This novel is an excellent document from the inside, of the
    commercial side of 'New Grub Street'. Richard Bulmer represents Alfred
    Harmsworth. G. Gissing's *New Grub Street* (London, 1891) is a vivid
    interweaving of these and other themes.
57. Raymond Williams, *Communications,* Penguin edition (1968) 91.
58. For reference to the effect of the transition to mass entertainment in other
    contexts see, R.Q. Gray, 'Styles of Life, the "Labour Aristocracy" and Class
    Relations in later nineteenth-century Edinburgh', in *International Review of
    Social History,* XVIII (1973) pt.3, 440-1; and I.R. Taylor, 'Soccer
    Consciousness and Soccer Hooliganism', in S. Cohen ed., *Images of Deviance*
    (Harmondsworth, 1971).
59. *Wesleyan Methodist Magazine* (1888) 812-15; see also *Primitive Methodist
    Magazine* (1890) 702, article on the Congregational Union address by
    Rev. T. Green, 'The Secular Element in our Church Life'.
60. Rev. Henry T. Hooper, 'Preachers and Competition', in *The Methodist Times,*
    25.1.1906, p.52.
61. I owe this suggestion to John Myerscough of the University of Sussex, n.55 above.
62. There was intense preoccupation amongst progressive Nonconformists with
    symptoms like gambling, even down to bolting the empty stable door with
    suggested measures like blacking-out racing odds in public reading room
    newspapers. See, for just one year, *The British Weekly: a Journal of Social and
    Christian Progress,* 7.3.1890, 10.6.1890, 5.9.1890, 11.12.1890; for
    preoccupation with Sunday, see J.H.S. Kent, 'The Role of Religion in the
    Cultural Structure of the Later Victorian City', in *Transactions of the Royal
    Historical Society* 23 (1973) 167-8.
63. For an example of 'ties and relations that they know not of' between
    opposites, in this case nineteenth-century pubs and temperance societies see
    Brian Harrison, *Pubs* 185.
64. For example, 'In 1853 three Manchester beerhouse music-saloons were
    attracting 25,000 customers a week, to what was virtually the sole public
    entertainment of local working people', Brian Harrison, *Drink and the
    Victorians,* 324; for the 'star system' in the late 1840s with P.T. Barnum
    (1810-91), and Jenny Lind 'the Swedish Nightingale' being paid $1,000 a
    time for 150 appearances plus one-fifth of the net profits, see Asa Briggs,
    Mass Entertainment: The Origins of a Modern Industry, 10.
65. Brian Harrison, *Drink and the Victorians,* 325; pubs' other activities even
    included running museums, *ibid.,* 339; for an analogy between late
    nineteenth-century Methodism and the music halls see R. Currie, *Methodism
    Divided* (1968) 138, where he describes 'the metamorphosis of religious act
    into entertainment' but a very specific type of entertainment.
66. For these developments see G.J. Mellor, *The Northern Music Hall*
    (Newcastle, 1970): for concentration in the brewing industry and tied houses,
    see B. Harrison, *Drink and the Victorians* (1971) 292, 312.
67. *Wesleyan Methodist Magazine* (1901) 272-5, (1895) 556; *Primitive Methodist
    Magazine* (1890) 187, 562; *British Weekly,* 28.6.1894, p.153; *PMM* (1887)
    396, (1890) 379, (1907) 414; *WMM* (1909) 600; *PMM* (1909) 302; *BW*
    22.1.1901, 205; *BW* 30.5.1895 and 6.6.1895, J. Watson's 'Plea for the
    Spirituality of the Church', and letter following.
68. E.T. Davies, *Religion in the Industrial Revolution in South Wales* (Cardiff,
    1965) 143, *et. seq.,* charts the changes in one region, with Literary and
    Scientific Institutes, Libraries, Miners' Institutes, etc.; see also Brian Harrison,
    Drink and the Victorians, 339, 'an incidental consequence of extending State
    activity since the 1820s has been the proliferation of so many types of

"public house" that the original public house has acquired a specialised
meaning and a hyphen ... Town halls, museums, picture galleries, public
lavatories, cinemas, public assembly-halls and trading centres have all become
accessible to the general public since the 1820s.'

69. C.H. Chandler, 'Workers at Play', in *The British Workman and Home Monthly*
(August, 1908); G.W. Palmer in a speech to the Reading Biscuit Factory
Recreation Club in 1899 was staggered by the facilities available at that date
compared to those of his youth when there was only 'a certain amount of
recreation associated with the everyday business of life', *Berkshire Chronicle*,
21.1.1899; see also, W.E. Adams, *Memoirs of a Social Atom* (1903) II, 468.

70. Activists worried about church density in working-class areas since the
mid-nineteenth century should perhaps be aware that there has also been a
steady decrease in pub density in England and Wales since the 1860s: the
more crowded the area the larger the number of persons per pub — although
pub *size* was also increasing. Similarly activists worried about the takeover of
functions once performed by churches/chapels by specialised pan-town
or national organisations should be aware of a similar experience by publicans
who 'had the initiative to provide the community with a new service, then
specialized in it, then lost control of it altogether', Brian Harrison, *Pubs,* 171,
175.

71. Cinema audiences reached nineteen million a week in 1939, and a peak of
thirty-one million a week in 1946, see P.E.P. *The British Film Industry* (1952),
Asa Briggs, *Mass Entertainment: The Origins of a Modern Industry,* 18.
Already by 1912, there was concern about the consequences: 'Is this to be the
theatre of the future? We have almost abolished thinking from our theatre; are
we also to abolish hearing and seeing in any except one dimension? ... These
things really narrow the life and experience of men, and it will soon be
possible for people to have all the adventurous experience they want within
half a mile of their own house ... All of which is bad and means loss of life in
its fullest and most serious sense', Filson Young, 'Kinema', in *Saturday
Review*, 27.1.1912, p.108.

72. *The Times*, 26.10.1912, 'Cinematographs on the Life and Death of Christ';
Brighton Gazette, 26.4.1911, 'Sunday Amusements'.

73. Raymond Blathwayt on F.B. Meyer in *Great Thoughts* (January, 1904),
quoted in W.Y. Fullerson, *F.B. Meyer, A Biography* (n.d.) 173; see also
J.N. Figgis, *Religion and English Society* (1910).

74. John W. Loy and Gerald S. Kenyon, *Sport, Culture and Society: A Reader
on the Sociology of Sport* (1969) 69; and Stuart Mews, 'Puritanicalism, Sport
and Race, A Symbolic Crusade of 1911', in *Studies in Church History,* 8
(Cambridge, 1971) 308. Literary agents were also new middlemen of the
1880s, see Kay Daniels, 'New Grub Street, 1890-1896', unpublished D.Phil.
thesis (University of Sussex, 1966) 145-6.

75. T.G. Ashplant of the University of Sussex is tracing the increasing hegemony
of entertainment and 'payment at the gate' (i.e. for beer) in Club life,
compared to the earlier interconnected nexus of membership-type activities,
during the late nineteenth and early twentieth century. He is also interested
in similar constraints and pressures at work in the experience of a range of
other working-class organisations, including the ILP.

76. Stuart Mews, 'Puritanicalism, Sport and Race: A Symbolic Crusade of 1911',
319.

77. J.J. Cooper, in *The Occasional Magazine,* II (1900).

78. Stuart Mews, 'Puritanicalism, Sport and Race: A Symbolic Crusade of 1911',
311, no.2, draws this interesting analogy quoting religious revival campaigns
like those of Charles Finney, Dwight Moody, and Billy Sunday. R.S. Lynd and
H.M. Lynd, *Middletown* 378-81, described this kind of managed revival

campaign at a later stage of its development in one town. For complaints about 'too much dependence upon imported evangelism, and too little upon local life and church work', see *Primitive Methodist Magazine* (1890) 379.

79. *Primitive Methodist Magazine* (1890) 703.

80. *British Weekly,* 8.12.1892.

81. Corporation Bonds were pioneered by Nottingham and Liverpool in 1880, and first suggested in Reading by Arthur Hill, a manufacturer of rubber goods, see Anne Cook ..., 171; see also J. Watson Grice *National and Local Finance* (1910) 328-5. For retailers on the Council see Anne Cook ..., 242. Other examples were: W.M. Colebrook, W.J.D. Venner, W. McIlroy, Edward Jackson.

82. *Reading Standard,* 24.10.1908. Two immediately preceding bazaars had already raised £1,500.

83. *British Weekly,* 24.9.1891.

84. A.H. Anderson, *The Town of Reading* (1911) 10; W.M. Childs, *The Story of the Town of Reading* (1921) 230-1. T.H.S. Escott, *England Her People, Polity and Pursuits,* 2nd edition (1885) 56, described similar towns thus, 'the place which thirty years ago was only the medium of distribution for local products in the locality itself, is now a kind of petty emporium of the empire, the headquarters of whose business no longer lie within the boundaries of the borough, but are in London ... consequently many even most, of the chief representatives of local business are immediately identified with London'.

85. *Reading Mercury,* 14.6.1913, quoted in Anne Cook ..., 234.

86. Early in the life of the *Clarion* there was more suspicion; later more 'realism' about professionalism. At one stage the paper suggested the distribution of gate receipts as a way of counter-acting professionalism. For examples of the paper's preoccupation with the subject, see *Clarion,* 14.10.1893, p.7; 16.6.1894, p.7; 30.6.1894, p.7; 5.8.1894, p.8.

87. R. Currie, *Methodism Divided* (1968) traces these adaptations in late nineteenth- and early twentieth-century Methodism.

88. J.N. Figgis, *Religion and English Society* (1910) 30.

89. J. Obelkevich, 'Religion and Rural Society ...' Unpublished Ph.D. (Columbia, 1971) 221.

90. Arnold M. Rose, *Theory and Method in the Social Sciences* (Minneapolis, 1954) 40.

91. *Religion and English Society,* 29.

92. Grant Allen, 'The Wrongfulness of Riches', in Andrew Reid ed., *Vox Clamantium* (1894) 144-5.

93. K.S. Inglis, *Churches and the Working Class in Victorian England* (1963) 325.

94. Max Weber, *The Sociology of Religion* (1965) 216-19.

95. E. Troeltsch, *The Social Teaching of the Christian Churches* (1931) 86, 'it is clear that Christianity has a distinct leaning towards comparatively simple conditions of living in which immediate contact with God's gifts in Nature determines the way of earning a living and thus the possibility of maintaining life, and keeps vivid the feelings of dependence and gratitude towards the gifts of God in Nature. It also has a leaning towards little groups and corporations which are closely bound together in personal relationships, in which the formal, legal and economic tendency of a dehumanised and abstract organisation of the common life has not yet forced the purely personal relationships and decisions into the sphere of isolated instances'.

96. J.L. & B. Hammond, *The Town Labourer 1760-1832, The New Civilisation* (1917) vii-viii; R.H. Tawney, *The Acquisitive Society* (1921) Fontana edition (1961) 77.

97. R.H. Tawney set out the alternatives in his usual lucid manner, in *Religion and the Rise of Capitalism,* Penguin edition (1938) 30, 'there are, perhaps four main attitudes which religious opinion may adopt towards the world of

social institutions and economic relations. It may stand on one side in ascetic aloofness and regard them as in their very nature the sphere of unrighteousness, from which men *may* escape – from which, if they consider their souls, they *will* escape – but which they can conquer only by flight. It may take them for granted and ignore them, as matters of indifference belonging to a world with which religion has no concern; in all ages the prudence of looking problems boldly in the face and passing on has seemed too self-evident to require justification. It may throw itself into an agitation for some particular reform, for the removal of some crying scandal, for the promotion of some final revolution, which will inaugurate the reign of righteousness on earth. It may at once accept and criticise, tolerate and amend, welcome the gross world of human appetites, as the squalid scaffolding from amid which the life of the spirit must rise, and insist that this also is the material of the Kingdom of God. To such a temper, all activities divorced from religion are brutal or dead, but none are too mean to be beneath or too great to be above it, since all, in their different degrees, are touched with the spirit which permeates the whole. It finds its most sublime expression in the words of Piccarda: "Paradise is everywhere, though the grace of the highest good is not shed everywhere in the same degree"'.

INDEX

The reference note in which full bibliographical details of a work are given is cited under the author's name; in cases where the author is substantively indexed, the note is cited under the sub-heading 'work(s) by'.

Reading is abbreviated as R.

Government departments, Acts of Parliament, and Bills, are grouped under the heading *Government and Legislation*.

Local government institutions and officers are grouped under the heading *Reading: local government*.

All voluntary organisations in Reading, except churches and chapels, and local branches of nationally-based friendly societies and trade unions, are grouped under the heading *Reading: organisations*.

The major conceptual themes of the book are indexed under the following headings:

Activists	*Ideology*	*Religious organisations*
Apathy	*Leisure*	*Sources*
Buildings	*Localness*	*State*
Capitalism	*Organisations*	*Statistics*
Class	*Politics*	*Sub-agencies*
Context	*Reading: 1850-90*	*Voluntarism*
Finance	*Reading: 1890-1914*	*Welfare*

n29, 322
Blathwayt, Reymond & Meyer, F.B. 402 n73
Blondel, Joan 388 n20
Bolam, T. 25
Booth, Charles 357 n65, 360 n20; work by, 360 n20
Booth, C.B. 369 n17
Booth, William 365 n71, 155, 169, 173, 398 n38; works by 349 n64, 398 n38
Boulding, K.F. 399 n46
Bourdillon, F.B. 379 n34
Bowley, A.L. 352 n97, 113, 357 n64, 118, 230; on R. Guild of Help, 345 n20, 381 n55; works by 357 n64
Boy Scouts 167, 369 n14, 169, 398 n38
Boys' Brigades 165-6, 167, 369 n14, 371 n32
Bradford, C.A. 393 n79
Braithwaite, W.J. 379 n15, 382 n70
Branford, Victor 334 n7
Bray, R.A. 13; work by, 335 n18
Brenan, G. 333 n2
Brennan, T., Cooney, E.W., Pollins, H. 333 n7
bricks-and-mortar *see* buildings
Briggs, Asa 310; works by, 335 n22, 363 n59, 373 n3, 378 n76, 378 n10, 387 n5, 396 n14, 400 n51
Bright, L. & Clements, S. 335 n14
Brighton Co-operative Society ratifies apathy, 18
British Medical Association 232
British Socialist Party *see* Social-Democratic Federation
'The British Workman' Coffee House 149
Broad Street Congregational Chapel 128, 144, 364 n64, 295-6; amusement resisted, 176; attendances, 371 n32; Boys' Brigade, 167, 369 n14; C.E., 172; collections, 119; congregations, 120; increase in membership, 156, 367 n83; Industrial Exhibitions, 185-6; meaning of membership, 84; PSA 20, 60, 168-9, 176-7, 195, 375 n40, 237, 280-3, 394 nn91-3, 289; reorganisation, 347 n48, 371 n31; secession from, 143, 364 n64; unemployed

demonstration at, 358 n4, 393 n79; Working Men's College, 59, 169
Broadley, Arthur 277-8, 280
Brooke, J.R. 228
Brother Prince 363 n60
Brothers, Joan 333 n6
Brown, Charles 93
Buffaloes *see* Royal Antediluvian Order of Buffaloes
builders 127-30
buildings: 86-7, 128, 132, 146; chronology of, 144-5; consequences of, 154-5; finance for, 147-51; Halls, 153-4; as legacy, 133-43; preceding/following congregations, 151-3; rejected, 161; strengthen context, 154-5; time taken over, 154
Building Labourers' Union 278, 394 n84
Bull, A.H. 127, 375 n30, 193-4, 217, 319-20
Bunbury, H.M. 379 n15
Burghfield 98
Burness, J.W. 62, 346 n32 394 n91
Burnett, J. 354 n29
Burritt, Elihu 340 n29
Burton, K.G. 342 n59
Busia, K.A. 334 n12
Butler, C. Violet 358 n10
Butler, J.G. 270, 391 n59, 274, 392 n70
Butler, Rev. W. 352 n97, 243

Caine, Hall 395 n2, 291
Campion, W. 358 n7
capitalism: 126-7, 149; changing forms of, 91, 95; Co-op. awareness of, 287-8, 395 n101; effect on organisations, 108; ideals of, 34, 108-9; and leisure, 399 n46; SDF critique of, 254-6; twentieth-century form of, 104, 308-9
Caradog-Jones, D. 357 n64
Carew-Hunt, Rev. R.W. 57, 367 n87, 222-3, 394 n87
Carey Street Baptist Chapel 348 n58, 87, 117, 152; CE, 171, 371 n31; membership criteria, 82, 84-5; Sunday School attendances, 371 n32
Carlile, Rev. J.C. 372 n39